"No other guide[...] a pleasure to re[...]

". . . Excellently organized for the casual traveler who is looking for a mix of recreation and cultural insight."
Washington Post

★ ★ ★ ★ ★ (5-star rating) "Crisply written and remarkably personable. Cleverly organized so you can pluck out the minutest fact in a moment. Satisfyingly thorough."
Réalités

"The information they offer is up-to-date, crisply presented but far from exhaustive, the judgments knowledgeable but not opinionated." *New York Times*

"The individual volumes are compact, the prose succinct, and the coverage up-to-date and knowledgeable . . . The format is portable and the index admirably detailed."
John Barkham Syndicate

". . . An abundance of excellent directions, diversions, and facts, including perspectives and getting-ready-to-go advice — succinct, detailed, and well organized in an easy-to-follow style." *Los Angeles Times*

"They contain an amount of information that is truly staggering, besides being surprisingly current."
Detroit News

"These guides address themselves to the needs of the modern traveler demanding precise, qualitative information . . . Upbeat, slick, and well put together."
Dallas Morning News

". . . Attractive to look at, refreshingly easy to read, and generously packed with information." *Miami Herald*

"These guides are as good as any published, and much better than most." *Louisville* (Kentucky) *Times*

Stephen Birnbaum Travel Guides

Canada
Caribbean, Bermuda, and the Bahamas
Disneyland
Europe
Europe for Business Travelers
Florida for Free
France
Great Britain
Hawaii
Ireland
Italy
Mexico
South America
Spain and Portugal
United States
USA for Business Travelers
Walt Disney World

ADVISORY EDITOR

Claire Hardiman

CONTRIBUTING EDITORS

Cathy Beason
Janet Bennett
Jeri Bostwick
Lois Brett
Mary Ann Castronovo Fusco
Ben Harte
Brian McCallen
Richard John Pietschmann
Dee Prather

COVER   Robert Anthony

MAPS   Etta Jacobs

SYMBOLS   Gloria McKeown

A Stephen Birnbaum Travel Guide

Birnbaum's
HAWAII
1990

Stephen Birnbaum
Alexandra Mayes Birnbaum
EDITORS

Lois Spritzer
EXECUTIVE EDITOR

Allan Seiden
AREA EDITOR

Laura Brengelman
Managing Editor

Kristin Moehlmann
John Storch
Senior Editors

Cathy Langevin
Julie Quick
Associate Editors

Stephen Coleman
Assistant Editor

HOUGHTON MIFFLIN COMPANY / BOSTON   1989

This book is published by special arrangement
with Eric Lasher and Maureen Lasher.

ISSN: 0749-2561 (Stephen Birnbaum Travel Guides)
ISSN: 0883-2471 (Hawaii)
ISBN: 0-395-51150-X

Printed in the United States of America

WP 10 9 8 7 6 5 4 3 2 1

Contents

GETTING READY TO GO

A compendium of all the practical travel data you need to plan your vacation down to the final detail.

When and How to Go

Preparing

In the Islands

PERSPECTIVES

A cultural and historical survey of Hawaii's past and present, its people, politics, and heritage.

ISLAND-BY-ISLAND HOPPING

Thorough, qualitative guides to the islands. Designed to be used on the spot, each section offers a comprehensive report on the island's most compelling attractions and amenities. Directions and recommendations are immediately accessible because each report is presented in consistent form.

DIVERSIONS

A selective guide to over 20 active and cerebral vacations, including the places to pursue them where the quality of experience is likely to be highest.

For the Body

For the Mind

For the Experience

A Word from the Editor

My wife is not a major fan of islands. Instead, her travel trail usually leads from Los Angeles and San Francisco to New York, and then through London, Paris, Rome, and Hong Kong, with a fair number of other urban rest stops in between. The constant in her journeying seems to be a surfeit of asphalt and concrete, which she evidently finds as relaxing as most people do hammocks and palm trees.

So it takes some substantial effort to get her motivated to meander around any atoll, no matter how attractive. She shares a not uncommon view that one island is pretty much like any other and that when you've seen one pristine strand of sand, you've pretty much experienced what beaches in general have to offer. That was, until she saw Hawaii.

I won't bore you with a long description of the Hawaiian experiences that left this otherwise worldly woman traveler wide-eyed and a bit slack-jawed, but on island after island, she found herself entranced and enchanted by natural wonders and extraordinary vistas that a first-time visitor to Hawaii just doesn't believe possible. I knew how she felt. I had gone through precisely the same open-mouthed wonder years before.

Still, all is not swaying palms and shimmering sands even in this idyllic Pacific paradise. As with world news reporting in general, headlines about Hawaii have described some troubles in Eden, and there's no denying that these exist. On the whole, however, Hawaii's remarkably multi-ethnic and polyglot population has confronted most of the malaise of civilization as intelligently as it is possible to in a world that sometimes seems to defy sense and sanity.

Among these problems are tourists by the jumbo-jetful, and the islands' economy has come more and more to rely on a sizable, constant influx of tourist currency. Inevitably, the sheer numbers of these visitors have affected island life — and not always for the better. For example, certain segments of Waikiki Beach in Honolulu on Oahu and parts of the Kaanapali coast on Maui bear the scars of overzealous development. But these are really the only two areas that can be cited as being significantly marred. Other areas — like Hana (on Maui) and Hanalei (on Kauai) and Hilo (on the Big Island) — remain just about as immune from contemporary commercial crassness as ever.

In recent years, the nature of travel to and through the Hawaiian archipelago has altered somewhat to reflect changing travel tastes. More and more visitors are leaving Honolulu in their jet trail to spend more time on other, less crowded islands. The newly updated guide to Hawaii which you hold in your hand hopes to expand this trend by directing prospective Hawaii visitors to those special corners of the islands that are not necessarily part of the most publicized package tours. A burgeoning number of discount and excursion air fares, plus subsidized inter-island air fares, make travel among the islands inexpensive and extremely easy, so there's no excuse for any visitor to remain anchored in some less than desirable high-rise hotel. The real wonders of Hawaii glisten along the cliffs of the Na Pali coast on Kauai, among the steaming craters of Hawaii Volcanoes National Park on the Big Island, and in dozens of other similarly magical places. The pages that follow contain as many leads to Hawaii's enduring magic as can be found anywhere.

Obviously, any guidebook to Hawaii must keep pace with and answer the real needs of today's travelers. That's why we've tried to create a guide that's specifically organized, written, and edited for the more demanding modern traveler, one for whom qualitative information is infinitely more desirable than mere quantities of unappraised data. We think that this book, and the other guides in our series, represent a new generation of travel guides, one that is especially responsive to modern needs and interests.

For years, dating back as far as Herr Baedeker, travel guides have tended to be encyclopedic, seemingly much more concerned with demonstrating expertise in geography and history than in any analysis of the sorts of things that genuinely concern a typical tourist. But today, when it is hardly necessary to tell a traveler where Honolulu is located, it is difficult to justify devoting endless pages to historical perspectives. Since it's not impossible that the guidebook reader may have been to Hawaii nearly as often as the guidebook editor, it becomes the responsibility of that editor to provide new perceptions and to suggest new directions to make a guide genuinely valuable.

That's exactly what we've tried to do in our series. I think you'll notice a different, more contemporary tone to the text, as well as an organization and focus that are distinctive and more functional. And even a random reading of what follows will demonstrate a substantial departure from the standard guidebook orientation, because we not only have attempted to provide information of a different sort but also have tried to present it in a context that makes it particularly accessible.

Needless to say, it's difficult to decide precisely what to include in a guidebook of this size — and what to omit. Early on, we realized that giving up the encyclopedic approach precluded the inclusion of every single route and restaurant, a realization that helped define our overall editorial focus. Similarly, when we discussed the possibility of presenting certain information in other than strict geographical order, we found that the new format enabled us to arrange data in a way that we feel best answers the questions travelers typically ask.

Large numbers of specific questions have provided the real editorial skeleton for this book. The large volume of mail I regularly receive seems to emphasize that modern travelers want very precise information, so we've tried to organize our material in the most responsive way possible. Readers who want to know the best restaurants in Poipu or the best golf courses on the Big Island will have no trouble whatever finding that data in this guide.

Travel guides are, above all, reflections of personal taste, and putting one's name on a title page obviously puts one's preferences on the line. But I think I ought to amplify just what "personal" means. I don't believe in the sort of personal guidebook that's a palpable misrepresentation on its face. It is, for example, hardly possible for any single travel writer to visit thousands of restaurants (and nearly as many hotels) in any given year and provide accurate appraisals of each one. And even if it *were* possible for one human being to survive such an itinerary, it would of necessity have to be done at a dead sprint and the perceptions derived therefrom would probably be less valid than those of any other intelligent individual visiting the same establishments. It is, therefore, impossible (especially in an annually revised and updated guidebook *series* such as we offer) to have only one person provide all the data on the entire world.

I also happen to think that such individual orientation is of substantially less value to readers. Visiting a single hotel for just one night or eating one hasty meal in a random restaurant hardly equips anyone to provide appraisals that are of more than passing interest. No amount of doggedly alliterative or oppressively onomatopoeic text can camouflage a technique that is essentially specious. We have, therefore, chosen what I like to describe as the "thee and me" approach to restaurant and hotel evaluation and, to a somewhat more limited degree, to the sites and sights we have included in the other sections of our text. What this really reflects is personal sampling tempered by intelligent counsel from informed local sources, and these additional friends-of-the-editor are almost always residents of the city and/or area about which they have been consulted.

Despite the presence of several editors, writers, researchers, and local correspondents, very precise editing and tailoring keep our text fiercely subjective. So what follows is the gospel according to Birnbaum, and it represents as much of my own taste and insight as I can manage. It is probable, therefore, that if you like your beaches largely unpopulated and your mountainsides mostly uncrowded, prefer small hotels with personality to huge high-rise anonymities, and can't tolerate fresh fish that's been relentlessly overcooked, we're likely to have a long and meaningful relationship. Readers with dissimilar tastes may be less enraptured.

I should also point out something about the person to whom this guidebook is directed. Above all, he or she is a visitor. This means that such elements as restaurants have been specifically picked to provide the visitor with a representative, enlightening, stimulating, and above all pleasant experience. Since so many extraneous considerations can affect the reception and service accorded a regular restaurant patron, our choices can in no way be construed as an exhaustive guide to island dining. We think we've listed all the best places in various price ranges, but they were chosen with a visitor's pleasure in mind.

Other evidence of how we've tried to tailor our text to reflect modern travel habits is most apparent in the section we call DIVERSIONS. Where once it was common for travelers to spend an island visit nailed to a single spot, the emphasis today is more likely to be directed toward pursuing some sport or special interest while seeing the surrounding countryside. So we've selected every activity we could reasonably evaluate and organized the material in such a way that it is especially accessible to activists of either an athletic or cerebral bent. It is no longer necessary, therefore, to wade through a pound or two of superfluous prose just to find the very best surfing spot or the supreme scenic vista within a reasonable distance from your hotel.

If there is a single thing that best characterizes the revolution in and evolution of current holiday habits, it is that most travelers now consider travel a right rather than a privilege. Travel today translates as the enthusiastic desire to sample all of the world's opportunities, to find that elusive quality of experience that is not only enriching but comfortable. For that reason, we've tried to make what follows not only helpful and enlightening but the sort of welcome companion of which every traveler dreams.

Finally, I should point out that every good travel guide is a living enterprise; that is, no part of this text is carved in stone. In our annual revisions, we refine, expand, and further hone all our material to serve your travel needs even better. To this end, no contribution is of greater value to us than your own personal reaction to what we have written, as well as information reflecting your own experiences while using the book. We earnestly and enthusiastically solicit your comments about this book *and* your opinions and perceptions about places you have recently visited. In this way, we will be able to provide the most current information — including the actual experiences of the travel public — and to make those experiences more readily available to others. So please write to us at 60 E. 42nd St., New York, NY 10165.

We sincerely hope to hear from you.

STEPHEN BIRNBAUM

How to Use This Guide

A great deal of care has gone into the organization of this guide-book, and we believe it represents a real breakthrough in the presentation of travel material. Our aim has been to create a new, more modern generation of travel books, and to make this guide the most useful and practical travel tool available today.

Our text is divided into four basic sections in order to present information in the best way on every possible aspect of a Hawaii vacation. This organization itself should alert you to the vast and varied opportunities available in these islands — as well as indicating all the specific data necessary to plan a Hawaiian trip. You won't find much of the conventional "swaying palms and shimmering sands" text here; we've chosen instead to deliver more useful and purposeful information. Prospective Hawaiian itineraries tend to speak for themselves, and with so many diverse travel opportunities, we feel our main job is to explain them and to provide the basic information — how, when, where, how much, and what's best — to let you make the most intelligent choices possible.

Here is a brief summary of our four basic sections — what you can expect to find in each one. We believe that you will find both your travel planning and on-island enjoyment enhanced by having this book at your side.

GETTING READY TO GO

This mini-encyclopedia of practical travel facts is meant to be a sort of a know-it-all companion, with all the precise information necessary to create a Hawaiian holiday. There are more than two dozen separate entries, including how to travel, what preparations to make before you leave, how to deal with possible emergencies while traveling, what to expect on the different islands, what your trip is likely to cost, and how to avoid prospective problems. The individual entries are specific, realistic, and, where appropriate, cost-oriented.

We expect you to use this section most in the course of planning your trip, for its ideas and suggestions are intended to simplify this often confusing period. Entries are intentionally concise, in an effort to get to the meat of the matter with the least extraneous prose. These entries are augmented by extensive lists of specific sources from which to obtain even more specialized information, plus some suggestions for obtaining travel information on your own.

PERSPECTIVES

Any visit to an unfamiliar destination is enhanced and enriched by an understanding of the cultural and historical heritage of that area. We have, therefore, provided just such an introduction to Hawaii — its history, people, food and drink, music and dance, folklore and myths, and language.

ISLAND-BY-ISLAND HOPPING

Individual reports on the eight major islands have been prepared with the aid of researchers, contributors, professional journalists, and other experts on the spot. Useful at the planning stage, ISLAND-BY-ISLAND HOPPING is really designed to be used during your trip. Each report offers a short-stay guide to its island within a consistent format: An essay introduces the island as a historic entity and a functioning contemporary place to live and work; *Sources and Resources* is a concise, islandwide listing of pertinent tourist information meant to answer myriad potentially pressing questions as they arise, such as where to find the tourist office, how to get around, which sightseeing tours to take, when the island's special events and holidays occur, and where the best golf, tennis, fishing, and swimming are to be found. *Around the Island* is an area-by-area analysis of each island, with emphasis on the most important sights to see and things to do, the best places to eat and sleep, the savviest places to shop, and the liveliest nightspots to try.

DIVERSIONS

This very selective guide is designed to help travelers find the very best places in which to pursue a wide range of physical and cerebral activities, without having to wade through endless pages of unrelated text. With a list of more than 20 activity and theme vacations, DIVERSIONS provides a guide to the special places where the quality of experience is highest. Whether you want to surf, swim, or sail, dine elegantly, or shop wisely, each entry is the equivalent of a comprehensive checklist of the absolute best in Hawaii.

Although each of the book's sections has a distinct format and a special function, they have been designed to be used together to provide a complete package of travel information. To use this book to full advantage, take a few minutes to read the table of contents and random entries in each section to get a first-hand feel of how it all fits together.

Pick and choose needed information from different sections. Assume, for example, that you have always wanted to explore Hawaii's volcanoes, but you never really knew how to organize such a trip. Turn first to the hiking section of GETTING READY TO GO, as well as the chapters on planning a trip, accommodations, and climate and clothes. These short entries provide plenty of practical information. But where to go? Turn next to ISLAND-BY-ISLAND HOPPING. Perhaps you choose to watch the famous sunrise at Haleakala on Maui or examine the fissures in the crater of still-steaming Kilauea on the Big Island. Your trip will probably include a stopover in Waikiki, and for a complete rundown on that complex area, read the Waikiki section of the Oahu chapter. Finally, turn to DIVERSIONS to peruse the chapters on sports, hotels, restaurants, museums, historic sites, and other topics that interest you to make sure you don't miss anything in the neighborhood.

In other words, the sections of this book are building blocks intended to help you put together the best possible trip. Use them selectively as a tool, a source of ideas and options, a reference work for accurate facts, and a guide to the best buys, the most exciting sights, the most pleasant accommodations, the tastiest food — *the best travel experience* — that you can have.

KAUAI

OAHU

NIIHAU

THE
HAWAIIAN
ISLANDS

N

PACIFIC OCEAN

MOLOKAI

LANAI

MAUI

KAHOOLAWE

THE
BIG ISLAND

GETTING READY
TO GO

When and How to Go

What's Where

Hawaii's geographic isolation is awesome. Lying in the central Pacific, its nearest neighbor is the minuscule Christmas Island chain, some 2,000 miles to the south. North America, the nearest continent, is 2,400 miles to the east, and it's necessary to travel almost 3,000 miles to the west before hitting any land larger than a big rock in the ocean. Given Hawaii's remoteness, it's not surprising that human beings didn't stumble upon this string of perfect isles until around the 6th century, or that it would be another millennium before the rest of the world discovered what are now among the best known and most visited 6,424 square miles on earth.

What we think of as the Hawaiian islands — eight major islands lying at about the same latitude as Mexico City — are in fact only the youngest of a chain of 132 islands, reefs, and atolls that stretch 1,600 miles to the northwest. The first of these, Kure Atoll, now a semicircle of coral reef, was pushed up from the sea floor about 25 million years ago. As the earth's plates shifted slightly to the northwest, the stationary volcanic vent broke through other weak spots in the earth's crust, thrusting up a succession of lava mountains. The latest of these to break the surface of the sea is the Big Island, whose continuing growing pains fascinate geologists and laypeople alike.

The oldest of the major islands is Kauai. Over the eons, the smooth-sloped volcano that formed this roughly circular island has been transformed by wind, rain, and the sea into craggy peaks creased with steep and narrow valleys and brimming with rich tropical life. At the heart of the island is 5,148-foot-high Mt. Waialeale, which catches an average of 500 inches of rain a year and feeds the many rivers, streams, and waterfalls that bejewel the island. To the northwest, along the Na Pali Coast, Kauai meets the sea with towering cliffs and vertical valleys of heart-stopping beauty. To the west is Waimea Canyon, a long, deep gorge of pale greens and pinks. To the east, south, and southwest, the island levels out into gentle slopes of sugarcane fields and ends in a chain of beaches about as perfect as one could imagine.

Seventeen miles southwest of Kauai is Niihau, a small, dry island whose central plateau of gently rolling grasslands supports sheep and cattle ranching. As on most of the islands, the windward side ends in black lava cliffs and the leeward side in a long strand of sandy beaches. Lying just off the north coast of Niihau, like a diacritical mark, is Lehua, a crescent of shiny black rock left from an ancient volcanic explosion.

Shaped a bit like an old-fashioned boot, Oahu, about 80 miles southeast of Kauai, is made up of two parallel mountain ranges — the Koolau and the Waianae — with a saddle of pineapple fields suspended between them. Honolulu and its environs occupy most of the southeast, from Pearl City at the instep to Koko Head at the tip of the boot. As the city outgrew the coastal plain, it spread up into the Koolau Mountains behind it, and at night, the lights scattered in the upper reaches of the black valleys blink like low-slung stars. Along the south coast are all the familiar landmarks — Waikiki, Diamond Head, and the Punchbowl. The southeast coast is rocky, with lava cliffs sculpted in multileveled terraces that conceal caves and blowholes, lava tubes and rock pools. Farther up the east side, the coast tempers down into swimmable beaches, while the famed surfing beaches — Sunset Point, the Banzai Pipeline, Pupukea — line the North Shore.

The geographic center of the Hawaiian chain is Molokai, about 25 miles southeast of Oahu. A long, narrow island about the size of Manhattan, Molokai breaks into two distinct regions: the upland plateau of grazing and pineapple land in the west and the deep gorges of rain forest in the east. Molokai's most spectacular feature is its northeast coast, where sea cliffs 2,000 feet high jut out into the blue Pacific like so many flying buttresses of kelly green. Isolated at the foot of these cliffs is the beautiful lava plain of Makanalua Peninsula, where Kalaupapa, the much-discussed leper colony, has existed since the 19th century.

It's a little less than 10 miles from the eastern tip of Molokai to Maui, an island created by two separate volcanoes whose lava flows ran together to create a low-lying plain of remarkable fertility. The central core of West Maui, the older and smaller of the two sections, is carved into steep, nearly inaccessible, and wildly beautiful valleys. But as the slopes smooth out near the coast, sugarcane and tourism take over. West Maui's beaches are long, lovely, and world famous. Dominating East Maui is Haleakala, the 10,023-foot volcano whose 7½-mile-long and 2½-mile-wide crater is a national park. Its gentle west slope is covered with vegetable and flower farms, while the south face is dry and cut by numerous deep ravines. Along the north coast as far as the eastern tip of the island is scenery so lush that the name of the district, Hana, is almost always (and accurately) preceded by the adjective "heavenly."

Due west of Maui and tucked south of Molokai is Lanai, a small tear-shaped island devoted mostly to pineapple growing. Deeply etched valleys are drawn along the eastern side, but past the central plateau, the land slopes easily to the sea. Slightly southwest of Maui is Kahoolawe, an arid, desolate island that swelters in the shadow of Haleakala, which blocks the rain and cooling trade winds. Heavily populated by wild goats, Kahoolawe has not had a human resident since the navy began using the island for artillery and bombing target practice in 1941.

Dropping like a heavy pendant from a delicate chain is Hawaii, the Big Island. Unlike the older islands, the Big Island doesn't have an abundance of spectacular cliffs and hidden valleys, and little of its shore has been pulverized into sandy beaches. But with two active volcanoes, the Big Island boasts scenery that delights and amazes. The east central coast is hot and humid, a perfect climate for the wild orchids that carpet its meadows and hillsides. Farther up the east coast, sugarcane fields cover the lower slopes of Mauna Kea, the 13,796-foot dormant volcano of the north, which is capped with snow in the winter. Between Mauna Kea and the northwest-facing peninsula of the Kohala Mountains is the high grassy plateau of the Parker cattle ranch, which is as close to mainland country-style as any ranch in Texas.

As Mauna Kea dominates the north, so active Mauna Loa, called the long mountain, curves to embrace the southeast part of the island. Kilauea, the Big Island's other, intensely active volcano, sits in the shadow of Mauna Loa and is the center of Volcanoes National Park. Covering 230,000 acres, the park encompasses scenery of startling variety — sterile landscapes of shiny black lava newly laid down; a barren and blasted desert where not even the sturdy kiawe tree grows; black sand beaches lined with majestic coco palms; and thick jungle where giant ferns grow in greens of incandescent intensity. The entire west coast exhibits signs of the volcanic process, too. Between patches of land denuded by lava flows is the lush greenery of resort cultivation. What resort-style beaches exist on the Big Island are here, but the sand on some is so shallow that it often gets carried away with the tide, leaving the rock shelf as exposed as a new layer of lava from Mauna Loa, which looms in the background.

Although these islands constitute the Hawaii currently available to visitors, the Hawaiian islands are not "finished." Even as you stand on the shore just south of

Hawaii Volcanoes National Park, with Kilauea crackling and sputtering at your back, another Hawaiian island is being formed under the Pacific, only about 30 miles south of the spot on which you are standing. It's called Loihi, and as recently as 1980 this volcanic cone, rising almost 16,000 feet from the ocean floor, exploded as it added to its own size. Scientists say that it won't be too many centuries before another Hawaiian island begins to take shape *above* the surface, and who knows how many visitors will then have the opportunity to enjoy this as-yet-invisible isle.

When to Go

 Although readings as low as 30F have been recorded in Hawaii's mountainous regions, pleasant temperatures in the 80s and balmy trade wind breezes are more typical. The four seasons are virtually indistinguishable, with good weather persisting throughout much of the year. Only the winter season (November to March) sees frequent, but passing, showers and temperatures that may drop into the 70s — and possibly the 60s. At any time of year an uncomfortable kona wind may blow in from the south or west, bringing with it high humidity and clammy air, but, like the rain, it passes quickly. And unlike the Caribbean islands, Hawaii has no hurricane season. (Hurricane Iwa, which struck in November 1982, was an aberration.) Due to this near-perfect weather year-round, more vacationers have begun to visit Hawaii during the so-called off-season; that is, in the spring, summer, and fall, when air fares and hotel and car rental rates are slightly lower than they are in winter.

Hawaii's benevolent climate also ensures a full calendar of events that will enhance any vacation. In addition to the usual national holidays observed in the rest of the United States, Hawaiians enjoy many athletic competitions, music festivals, parades, ethnic fairs, and horticultural exhibits. Listed below are some of the most important festivities; more specific information can be found in the chapters on the individual islands, and a comprehensive list is also available from the Hawaii Visitors Bureau. For a list of the mainland offices of the Visitors Bureau, see *Tourist Information Offices.*

January
> *Narcissus Festival:* Lion dances, fireworks, beauty contest, and coronation ball in Honolulu's Chinatown; celebrates the Chinese New Year.
>
> *Cherry Blossom Festival:* A 6-week Japanese cultural celebration in Honolulu with tea ceremonies, flower arranging and cooking demonstrations, a fashion show, beauty contest, and coronation ball.
>
> *Hula Bowl Game:* College football classic at *Aloha Stadium,* Honolulu.
>
> *Opening of the State Legislature:* Legislative sessions begin with speeches, hula demonstrations, leis, and Hawaiian music.

February
> *Hawaiian Open International Golf Tournament:* Part of the PGA tour, at *Waialae Golf and Country Club,* Honolulu.
>
> *Pro Bowl:* Annual football game featuring National Football League all-stars at *Aloha Stadium.*
>
> *Great Waikoloa Horse Races and Rodeo:* Major rodeo events with matched horse races in Waikoloa on the Big Island.

March
> *Maui Marathon:* Annual marathon from Maui Mall to Kaanapali Whalers Village, in Kahului, Maui.
>
> *St. Patrick's Day:* A parade and Irish-flavored activities in Waikiki.

Prince Kuhio Day: State holiday commemorating Prince Jonah Kuhio Kalania-naole (1871–1922), Hawaii's first representative to Congress, with music and dance dating from his time.

Merrie Monarch Festival: Competition between Hawaii's best hula schools, held in honor of Hawaii's last King, David Kalakaua, in Hilo.

April

Buddha Day: Various festivals at island temples celebrate the birth of Buddha.

Easter Sunrise Service: At the Punchbowl National Memorial Cemetery of the Pacific, in Honolulu.

Hawaiian Festival of Music: In Honolulu, a competition drawing entrants from the mainland as well as the islands, performing music from many genres — jazz, swing, symphonic, rock.

May

Lei Day: Everyone sports a lei on this holiday (May Day on the mainland) and visits lei-making contests and exhibits. Honolulu.

50th State Fair: Commercial exhibits, produce, food stalls, entertainment. Honolulu.

Pacific Handcrafters Guild Spring Fair: Crafts displays from Hawaii's finest artists. Ala Moana Park, Honolulu.

June

King Kamehameha Celebration: State holiday honoring Kamehameha, who conquered and consolidated the Hawaiian islands and reigned as King at the turn of the 19th century; events include parades, arts and crafts exhibits, and hula and chant demonstrations. All islands.

Festival of the Pacific: A celebration of Pacific culture, including music, song, dance, and athletic competitions.

Mission Houses Museum Fancy Fair: An open crafts market in Honolulu, featuring entertainment and authentic island foods.

July

Makawao, Naalehu, and Parker Ranch Rodeos: Hawaiian cowboys — *paniolos* — do their stuff at these competitions on Maui and the Big Island.

Tin Man Triathlon: Triathletes gather at Ala Moana Park (Honolulu) to swim 800 meters, bike 25 miles, and complete a 6.2-mile run around Diamond Head to Queen Kapiolani Park.

August

Establishment Day: Big Island festival celebrating native Hawaiian culture with hula, artifact shows, and workshops in lei-making and other crafts.

Hawaiian International Billfish Tournament: Marlin fishing competition held at Kailua-Kona on the Big Island.

September

Waikiki Annual Rough Water Swim: A 2-mile swim meet from Oahu's Sans Souci Beach to Duke Kahanamoku Beach, open to all ages and levels of skill.

Aloha Week Festival: Successive festivals on each island add up to a full month of activities and events, including luaus, parades, crafts shows, a royal ball, and the famous 27½-mile canoe race from Molokai to Oahu.

October

Ironman World Triathlon Championship: One of two triathlons (the other is in Nice, in the south of France) that claim to be the "world" championship, this grueling competition — a 2.4-mile swim, a 112-mile bike ride, and a 26.2-mile run — is centered at Kailua-Kona on the Big Island.

Annual Orchid Plant & Flower Show: Largest orchid exhibition in the islands, in *Blaisdell Center,* Honolulu.

November

Na Mele O Maui: Hawaiiana festival in Lahaina and Kaanapali with arts and crafts shows, luaus, and music and dance demonstrations.

Christmas Fair: At the Mission Houses Museum in Honolulu, crafts including Christmas items are sold in an open market.

December

Hawaiian Pro Surfing Championships: The islands' most important surfing competition, at the Banzai Pipeline on Oahu's north shore.

Bodhi Day: Ceremonies at Buddhist temples commemorate the "Day of Enlightenment."

Annual Honolulu Marathon: A 26-mile race beginning at Aloha Tower and ending at Kapiolani Park.

Pearl Harbor Day: A service is held at the USS *Arizona* memorial to honor those killed on December 7, 1941.

Aloha Bowl Game: Collegiate football at *Aloha Stadium,* Oahu.

Travel by Plane

For the tourist who lacks a rich uncle willing to lend his private yacht, it's probable that flying will be the mode of transportation used to get to the 50th state. Furthermore, if you intend to visit more than one island, an airplane, not a boat, is the most expedient way to island hop. The following are some basic facts about air travel, the kinds of flights available, and the rules governing them.

SCHEDULED FLIGHTS: Airlines offering regularly scheduled flights from the mainland to Hawaii, most on a daily basis, are: Air America, American, Continental, Delta, Hawaiian Airlines, Northwest, Pan Am, TWA, United, and Ward Air. In addition, new discount carriers frequently enter the market for a brief period, then disappear.

As of this writing, direct flights — with no change of plane between the originating and terminating cities, though the flight probably won't be nonstop — depart from Anchorage, Atlanta, Baltimore, Boston, Chicago, Dallas/Fort Worth, Denver, Detroit, Houston, Kansas City, Las Vegas, Los Angeles, Minneapolis/St. Paul, New York/Newark, Philadelphia/Wilmington, Portland (Oregon), St. Louis, Salt Lake City, San Diego, San Francisco/Oakland, Seattle/Tacoma, and Washington, DC. This lineup is, however, subject to frequent change, so check current schedules carefully before making final arrangements. (Occasionally, an airline may include a change of aircraft — from a 727 to a 747, for instance — but as long as the flight number is the same, the flight is still considered a direct one.) Nonstop flights depart from all of the West Coast cities noted above, except Portland. Elsewhere, only Anchorage, Atlanta, Chicago, Dallas/Fort Worth, Denver, Las Vegas, New York, and St. Louis have nonstop service.

Most flights land at Honolulu International Airport on Oahu, though service directly from the mainland to the neighbor islands, especially Maui, has been increasing steadily. For example, United flies to the four major islands with nonstop or connecting service via Honolulu. At press time, it flew nonstop service to Kahului on Maui from Chicago, Los Angeles, and San Francisco, and to Kailua-Kona on the Big Island from San Francisco.

The flying time from Los Angeles to Honolulu is about 5½ hours, nonstop from Chicago about 9 hours. Nonstop service from New York to Honolulu takes approximately 10 hours, while a one-stop flight from New York usually spends approximately 11 hours in the air, to which about 1½ hours on the ground at an intermediate stop should be added. Nonstop flights from Dallas/Fort Worth will be in the air a little under 8½ hours; from Denver, 7½ hours. Return flights (west to east) are slightly shorter.

A number of foreign airlines stop in Honolulu on their way from the mainland US to foreign cities, but they are prohibited by law (the Jones Act of 1896, which originally was intended to be applied only to ships) from carrying passengers solely between two points in the US. You are permitted to fly to Hawaii aboard a foreign carrier if your visit there is a stop en route to a foreign destination, however, and you may use a foreign carrier to fly to Hawaii from a foreign city. If you live closer to Vancouver than to any American gateway, there's no reason not to fly CP Air's nonstop service to Honolulu. As of this writing, CP Air also flies direct from Toronto to Honolulu.

Fares – Air fares are changing so rapidly that even the experts find it difficult to keep up with them. This volatile situation is due to a number of factors, including airline deregulation, high labor costs, and vastly increased competition. Before the Airline Deregulation Act of 1978, airlines had no choice but to set their rates and routes within the guidelines of the Civil Aeronautics Board (CAB), and they could compete for passengers only by offering better service than their competitors. With the loosening of controls (and the dissolution of the CAB), airlines are now engaged in a far more intense competition relating to price and schedule, which has opened the door to a wide range of discount fares and promotional offers. Intensifying the competitive atmosphere has been the creation of several new carriers offering fewer frills and far lower prices. These carriers seem to appear and disappear with dismaying regularity. They have, however, served to drive down fares and make the older, more entrenched carriers aware that they are in a genuine competition for travelers' dollars.

As a result, virtually anyone contemplating a trip to Hawaii can save some money if he or she can comply with the operative restrictions and regulations. A discussion of the various types of fares available follows, but remember that at any moment, the lowest fare of all may be a short-term promotional tariff or one bought as part of a package tour.

In general, the great variety of domestic air fares can be reduced to three basic categories: first class, coach (sometimes called economy or tourist class), and excursion or discount fares. (Business class, an intermediate class between first and coach that many airlines have added in recent years, generally is not offered on flights to Hawaii.) A first class ticket is your admission to the section of the aircraft with larger seats, more leg room, and better food than in coach, along with free drinks and free headsets for the movie and music. This service can cost almost twice as much as a full-fare coach ticket.

Coach passengers sit more snugly, as many as 10 in a single row, behind the first class section and receive standard meal service. Alcoholic drinks are not free, nor are the headsets. Like first class passengers, however, passengers paying the full coach fare are subject to none of the restrictions that are usually attached to less expensive discount fares. There are no advance booking requirements, no minimum stay requirements, and no cancellation penalties. Tickets are sold on an open reservation system: They can be bought for a flight up to the minute of takeoff if seats are available, and if the ticket is round-trip, the return reservation can be made any time you wish — months before you leave or the day before you return. Both first class and coach tickets are generally good for a year, after which they can be renewed if not used, and if you ultimately decide not to fly at all, your money will be refunded. Stopover privileges on both tickets are unlimited or extremely generous.

Excursion and other discount fares are the airlines' equivalent of a special sale, and usually apply only to round-trip bookings. Because it costs almost as much to run a half-empty plane as it does to run a full one, the airlines may, in an effort to fill seats, offer lower prices to a limited number of people in the hope of attracting some who might not otherwise take the trip. They may cut down the number of reduced fares available per flight when they expect business to be good and add more when they expect it to be poor. Needless to say, these reduced-rate seats are most limited at busy times such as holidays, when full-fare coach seats sell more quickly than usual. Passengers fortunate enough to get a discount ticket sit with the full-fare coach passengers and for all intents and purposes are indistinguishable from them. They receive the same basic services, even though they have paid anywhere between 30% and 55% less for the trip. Obviously, it's wise to make plans early enough to qualify for the least expensive transportation.

These discount or excursion fares may masquerade under a variety of names, they may vary from city to city (from the East Coast to the West Coast, especially), but they invariably have strings attached. A common requirement is that the ticket be purchased a certain number of days — usually no fewer than 7 or 14 days — in advance of departure, though it may be booked weeks or months in advance (it has to be "ticketed," or paid for, shortly after booking, however). The return reservation usually has to be made at the time of the original ticketing and cannot be changed later than a certain number of days (again, usually 7 or 14 days) before the return flight. If events force a passenger to change the return reservation after the date allowed, the difference between the round-trip excursion rate and the round-trip coach rate will probably have to be paid, though most airlines allow passengers to use their discounted fares by standing by for an empty seat, even if they don't otherwise have standby fares. Another common condition is a minimum and maximum stay requirement; for example, 6 to 14 days, or 1 to 6 days but including at least a Saturday night. Last, cancellation penalties of up to 50% of the full price of the ticket are currently being assessed — check the specific penalty in effect when you purchase your discount/excursion ticket — so careful planning is imperative. Of even greater risk — and bearing the lowest price of all the current discount fares — is the ticket where no change at all in departure and/or return flights is permitted, and where the ticket price is totally nonrefundable. And even if none of the above conditions apply, prospective passengers can be fairly sure that the number of discount seats per flight at this price is strictly limited or that the fare offering includes a set expiration date, which means it's absolutely necessary to move fast to enjoy the lowest possible prices.

Most major airlines have traditionally offered their most attractive special fares to encourage travel in slow seasons and to inaugurate and publicize new routes. But increasingly in today's economic climate, the stimulus for special fares is the appearance of airlines consistently associated with bargain rates on the same routes. These tend to be smaller carriers that can offer more for less because of lower overhead, uncomplicated route networks, and other limitations in their service. On these airlines, all seats on any given flight generally sell for the same price, which is somewhat below the lowest discount fare offered by the larger, more established airlines, even after these cut their fares in response. This gap, too, may disappear in the future, but it is important to note that tickets offered by the smaller airlines specializing in low-cost travel frequently· are not subject to the same restrictions as the lowest-priced ticket offered by the more established carriers. They may not require advance purchase or minimum and maximum stays, may involve no cancellation penalties, may be available one way or round trip, and may, for all intents and purposes, resemble the competition's high-priced full-fare coach. But never assume this until you know it's so.

Given the frequency with which the air fare picture changes, it is more than possible that by the time you are ready to fly, the foregoing discussion may be out of date. That's why it is always wise to comparison shop, and to do a good job of it, it's necessary to read the business and travel sections of your local newspaper regularly and call all the airlines that serve your destination from your most convenient gateway. The potential savings are well worth the effort.

Ask about discount or promotional fares and about any conditions that might restrict booking, payment, cancellation, and changes in plans. Check the prices from other cities. A special rate may be offered in a nearby city but not in yours, and it may be enough of a bargain to warrant your leaving from that city. If you are extremely flexible, investigate standby fares. But remember that, depending on your departure point, these may not work out to be the rock-bottom price. (And Easterners should beware of having to stand by a second time at the West Coast stop.) Also be sure to investigate package deals, which are offered by virtually every airline. These may include car rental, accommodations, and dining or sightseeing features in addition to the air fare, and the combined cost of packaged elements usually is considerably less than the cost of all of them purchased separately.

When you're satisfied that you've received the lowest possible price (it may be necessary to call each airline desk several times, because different clerks have been known to quote different prices), make your booking. Then, to protect yourself against fare increases, purchase your ticket as soon as possible after you've received a confirmed reservation. Airlines generally will honor their tickets, even if the operative price is higher by the time you fly; if fares go up between the time you reserve a flight and the time you pay for it, you will be out of luck. Finally, with excursion or discount fares, it is important to remember that when a reservation clerk says that you must purchase a ticket by a specific date, this is an absolute deadline. Miss the deadline, and the airline may automatically cancel your reservation without telling you.

If you don't have the time and patience to investigate personally all possible air departures and connections for a proposed trip, remember that a travel agent can be of inestimable help. A good agent should have all the information on which flights go where and when, and which categories of tickets are available on each. Most have computerized reservation links with a major carrier, so that a seat can be reserved and confirmed in minutes. An increasing number of agents also possess fare-comparison computer programs, so they are often very reliable sources of detailed competitive price data. (For more information, see *How to Use a Travel Agent.*)

Reservations – When making plane reservations through a travel agent, ask the agent to give the airline your home phone number as well as a daytime business number. All too often the agent uses the travel agency number as the official contact for changes in flight plans. During the winter especially, weather conditions hundreds or even thousands of miles away can wreak havoc with flight schedules. The airlines are fairly reliable about getting this sort of information to passengers if they can reach them, but often they can't if the agency is closed for the night or the weekend. Remind your travel agent that you want a home phone contact given to the airline; if you have any doubts, call the airline and do it yourself.

Most return reservations from international destinations are automatically canceled unless you reconfirm at least 72 hours before your return flight. Reconfirmation is not required on domestic flights, but it is still a good idea, allowing you to make sure in plenty of time that the airline did not slip up in entering your original reservation or in registering any changes you may have made since. If you plan not to take a reserved flight, by all means inform the airline of your cancellation. Because the problem of "no-shows" is a consistently annoying one for airlines, they are allowed to overbook flights, a practice that often contributes to the threat of denied boarding for a certain number of passengers (see *Getting Bumped,* below). Let the airline know you're not coming and you'll spare everyone some confusion. Bear in mind that only certain kinds of tickets allow the luxury of last-minute changes in flight plans — those sold on an open reservation system (first class and full-fare coach) do, while excursions and other discount fares are often restricted in some way. Even first class and coach passengers should remember that if they do not show up for a flight that is the first of several connecting ones, the airline will cancel all of their ongoing reservations unless informed *not* to do so.

Seating – Airline seats are usually assigned on a first-come, first-served basis at check-in, though some airlines make it possible to reserve a seat at the time of ticket purchase. You must decide if you want to sit in the smoking or non-smoking section; in a seat where your view of the movie is unobstructed; in a window, aisle, or middle seat; or in one of the few non-reclining seats.

Just reserving an airline seat in advance, however, may actually guarantee very little. Most airlines require that passengers arrive at the departure gate at least 30 minutes (sometimes more) before departure to hold a seat reservation. A far better strategy is to visit an airline ticket office (or one of a select group of travel agents) to secure an actual boarding pass for your specific flight. Once this boarding pass has been issued, airline computers show you as "checked in," and you effectively own the seat you have selected. This is good insurance against getting bumped from an overbooked flight and is, therefore, an especially valuable tactic for air travel undertaken at peak holiday times.

Some airlines furnish a seating chart, which makes choosing a spot much easier, but, in general, there are a few basics to consider. Airline representatives claim that most craft are more stable toward the front and midsection; seats toward the front of the aircraft are also the quietest. Passengers with long legs should request a seat directly behind an emergency exit (because seats next to the exits are often removed). Be aware, too, that the first row of a section (called a "bulkhead" seat) does *not* offer extra leg room since the fixed partition will not permit passengers to slide their feet under it, and that watching a movie from the first row is difficult and uncomfortable. A window seat protects a passenger from aisle traffic and clumsy serving carts, and also affords a view, while an aisle seat enables you to get up and stretch your legs without disturbing your companions. Middle seats are less desirable, and seats in the last row are the most undesirable of all, since they seldom recline fully. If you want peace and quiet, it is probably a good idea to request a seat in the first section of coach. Some airlines have designated this area as the "quiet" or "business" zone. Not all airlines have special quiet sections on domestic routes, however. Once in the air, if you find that you are sitting in an especially noisy section, you are usually free to move to any unoccupied seat — if there is one. If you wish to avoid children on your flight, remember that families generally do not sit in the smoking areas.

Smoking – The government has adopted minimum standards to ensure that non-smokers will not be "unreasonably burdened" by passengers who smoke. For a wallet-size guide, which notes in detail the rights of non-smokers according to these regulations, send a stamped, self-addressed envelope to *ASH (Action on Smoking and Health)*, Airline Card, 2013 H St. NW, Washington, DC 20006 (phone: 202-659-4310). The US Department of Transportation has determined that non-smoking sections must be enlarged to accommodate all passengers who wish to sit in a non-smoking section. According to a recently added proviso, however, the airline does not have to shift seating to accommodate non-smokers who arrive late for the flight or travelers flying standby. Cigar and pipe smoking are prohibited on all US flights, even in the smoking sections. If you plan to fly Northwest, which is noted for its smoke-free flights, remember that although smoking is prohibited during flights within the continental US, smoking is allowed on flights to Hawaii and abroad.

Flying with Children – On longer flights, the bulkhead seats are usually reserved for families traveling with small children. Infants under 2 years of age travel free on most domestic flights, provided they do not occupy a seat (a second infant without a second adult would pay the fare applicable to children ages 2 through 11, generally 75% of the adult fare). Most airlines make complimentary bassinets available. Ask about obtaining one when you make your reservation, and when checking in, request a bulkhead or other seat that has enough room in front to use it. Even if you do use a bassinet, babies must be held during takeoff and landing.

Meals – It is possible to order many kinds of special meals for your flight if you give the airline at least 24 hours notice. The available cuisines and diets include high protein, vegetarian, kosher, Muslim, low calorie, and low sodium.

Getting Bumped – A special air travel problem is overbooking: An airline might accept more reservations than there are seats on a given flight. This is entirely legal and is done to compensate the airlines for "no-shows," passengers who don't show up for a flight for which they have reservations. If the airline has oversold the flight and everyone does show up, there simply aren't enough seats. When this happens, the airline is subject to stringent rules designed to protect travelers.

In such cases, the airline first seeks ticketholders willing to give up their seats voluntarily in return for a negotiable sum of money or some other inducement, such as an offer of upgraded seating on the next flight or a voucher for a free trip at some other time. If there are not enough volunteers, the airline may bump passengers against their wishes. Anyone inconvenienced in this way is entitled to an explanation of the criteria used to determine who does or does not get on the flight as well as to compensation if the resulting delay exceeds certain limits. If the airline can put a bumped passenger on an alternate flight that will get him or her to the original destination within 1 hour of the originally scheduled arrival time, no compensation is owed. If the delay is more than an hour — but less than 2 hours on a domestic flight and less than 4 hours on an international flight — the bumped passengers must be paid denied-boarding compensation equivalent to the one-way fare to the destination (subject to a maximum of $200). If the delay is more than 2 hours beyond the original arrival time on a domestic flight or more than 4 hours on an international flight, the compensation must be doubled (but not more than $400). Compensation is paid by check at the airport, but if you feel that being bumped cost you more than the airline is willing to pay, you can refuse the check and try to negotiate a higher settlement through the airline's customer service department. Airlines are also allowed to offer bumped travelers a voucher for a free flight instead of the denied-boarding compensation. The passenger can choose either the money or the voucher, the dollar value of which may be no less than the monetary compensation to which the passenger is entitled. The voucher is not a substitute for the ticket the bumped passenger may have been unable to use; the airline continues to honor that as well.

To protect yourself as best you can against getting bumped, arrive at the airport early, allowing plenty of time to check in and get to the gate. If the flight is oversold, ask immediately for the written statement explaining the airline's policy on denied-boarding compensation and its boarding priorities. If the airline refuses to give you this information, or if you feel they have not handled the situation properly, file a complaint with both the airline and the appropriate government agency (see *Consumer Protection,* below).

Delays and Cancellations – Each airline has its own policy for assisting passengers whose flights are delayed or canceled or who must wait for another flight because their original one was overbooked. Most airline personnel will make new travel arrangements if necessary. If the delay is longer than 4 hours, the airline may pay for a phone call or telegram, a meal, and in some cases a hotel room and transportation to it.

Baggage – Though domestic airline baggage allowances vary slightly, in general all passengers are allowed to carry on board, without charge, one piece of luggage that will fit easily under a seat of the plane and whose combined dimensions (length, width, and depth) do not exceed 45 inches. A reasonable amount of reading material, camera equipment, and a handbag are also allowed. In addition, all passengers are allowed to check two bags in the cargo hold: one usually not to exceed 62 inches when length, width, and depth are combined, the other not to exceed 55 inches in combined dimensions. No single bag may weigh more than 70 pounds. Most airlines will allow you to check the 45-inch bag in the hold if you prefer not to carry it with you, but a few require that it be stowed in the cabin under a seat. Charges for additional, oversize, or overweight bags are usually made at a flat rate on domestic flights, the actual dollar amount varying from carrier to carrier. If you plan to travel with a bike, surfboard, scuba diving equipment, or other sports gear, be sure to check with the airline beforehand. Most have procedures for handling such baggage, but you will probably have to pay for transport regardless of how much other baggage you have checked.

To reduce the chances of your luggage going astray, remove all airline tags from previous trips, label each bag inside and out, and lock them. Double-check the tag that the airline attaches to make sure that it is coded for your destination: HNL for Honolulu, for instance, or ITO for Hilo. If your bags are not in the baggage claim area after your flight, or if they're damaged, report the problem to airline personnel immediately. Keep in mind that policies regarding the specific time limit in which you have to make your claim vary from carrier to carrier. Fill out a report form on your lost or damaged luggage and hold on to a copy of it and your claim check. If you must surrender the check to claim a damaged bag, get a receipt for it to prove that you did, indeed, check your baggage on the flight. Most airlines have emergency funds for passengers stranded away from home without their luggage, but if it turns out your bags are truly lost and not simply delayed, do not then and there sign any paper indicating you'll accept an offered settlement. Since the airline is responsible for the value of your bags within certain statutory limits, you should take time to assess the extent of your loss (see *Insurance*). It's a good idea to keep records indicating the price you paid for the bags and their contents; these help to eliminate arguments in establishing the amount of either loss or damage. An alternative suggestion is to take a Polaroid picture of the most valuable of your packed items just after putting them in your suitcase.

Airline Clubs – US carriers often have clubs for frequent travelers who pay for membership. These are not clubs for first class passengers. Membership (which by law now requires a fee) entitles the traveler to use the private lounges along their routings, to refreshments served in those lounges, and to check-cashing privileges at most of their counters. Extras include special telephone numbers for individual reservations, embossed luggage tags, and a membership card for identification. Airline club membership is the key to never getting bumped. Two that offer membership in such clubs are: TWA — the *Ambassador Club,* single yearly membership $150, spouse an additional $25, lifetime memberships also available — and Pan American — the *Clipper Club,* single yearly membership $150, spouse an additional $45, 3-year and lifetime memberships also available. However, these companies do not have club facilities in all airports. Lounge privileges are also offered to first class passengers, and other airlines also offer a variety of special club and lounge facilities in many airports.

CHARTER FLIGHTS: By actually renting an entire plane or at least booking a block of seats on a specially arranged flight, charter operators have long been able to offer travelers air transportation — often coupled with a hotel room, meals, and other arrangements — for less money than most economy fares on scheduled flights. Charters were once the only air fare bargains available, but this is no longer the case. Various promotional fares on scheduled airlines are often just as low, especially on the most competitive routes, and they are usually more flexible. As a result, charter flights have been discontinued in many areas, but to some popular vacation spots, including Hawaii, they can still be a good buy. They are especially attractive to people living in smaller cities or out-of-the-way places, because they frequently take off from nearby airports, saving travelers the inconvenience and expense of getting to a major gateway to begin a Hawaiian trip. Where demand persists, charter operators will continue to rent planes or seats from scheduled airlines (or from special charter airlines) and offer flights to the public directly through advertisements or travel agents. You buy the ticket from the operator or the agent, not from the airline owning the plane.

Charter travel once required that an individual be a member of a club or other "affinity" group whose main purpose was not travel. But since the approval of "public charters" years ago, operators have had some of the flexibility of scheduled airlines, making charters more competitive. Public charters are open to anyone, whether belonging to a group or not, and have no advance booking requirements or minimum stay requirements. One-way arrangements are permitted, though charters are almost always round-trip, and it is unlikely that you would be sold a one-way seat on a round-trip flight. Operators can offer air-only charters, selling transportation alone, or they can offer charter packages — the flight plus a combination of land arrangements such as accommodations, meals, tours, or car rental. Some things to keep in mind about the charter game are:

1. It cannot be repeated often enough that if you are forced to cancel your trip, you can lose much (and possibly all) of your money unless you have cancellation insurance, which is a *must* (see *Insurance*). Frequently, if the cancellation is well in advance (often 6 weeks or more), you may forfeit only a $25 or $50 penalty. If you cancel only 2 or 3 weeks before the flight, there may be no refund at all unless you or the operator can supply a substitute passenger.
2. Charter flights may be canceled by the operator up to 10 days before departure for any reason, usually underbooking. Your money is returned in this event, but there may be too little time to make new arrangements.
3. Most charters have little of the flexibility of regularly scheduled flights regarding refunds and the changing of flight dates; if you book a return flight, you must be on it or lose your money.
4. Charter operators are permitted to assess a surcharge, if fuel or other costs warrant it, of up to 10% of the air fare up to 10 days before departure.
5. Because of the economics of charter flights, your plane almost always will be full, so you will be crowded, though not necessarily uncomfortable.

Bookings – If you do take a charter, read the contract carefully and note:

1. Instructions concerning the payment of the deposit and the balance, and to whom the check is to be made payable. Ordinarily, checks are made out to an escrow account, which means the charter company can't spend your money until your flight has been completed. The charter company should be bonded (usually by an insurance company), and you should know the name of the bonding agent. If you want to file a claim against the charter company, the claim should be sent to the bonding agent.
2. Stipulations regarding cancellation by the consumer. You may forfeit much or all of your payment if you cancel closer to the departure date than allowed.
3. Stipulations regarding cancellation and major changes made by the charterer. Flights may not be canceled within 10 days of departure except when circumstances — such as natural disasters or political upheavals — make it physically impossible to fly. Charterers may make "major changes," however, such as in the date or place of departure or return, but you are entitled to cancel and receive a refund if you don't accept these changes. A price increase of more than 10% up to 10 days before departure is considered a major change; no price increase is allowed during the last 10 days prior to departure.

DISCOUNT TRAVEL SOURCES: An excellent source of information on economical travel opportunities is the *Consumer Reports Travel Letter,* published monthly by Consumers Union. It keeps abreast of the travel scene on a variety of fronts, including package tours, rental cars, insurance, and more, but it is especially helpful for its coverage of air fares, offering guidance on all the options from scheduled flights on major and low-fare airlines to charters and discount sources. For a year's subscription, send $37 to Consumer Reports Travel Letter, Subscription Dept., Box 5248, Boulder, CO 80322 (phone: 303-447-9330).

Still another way to take advantage of bargain air fares is open to those who have a flexible schedule. A number of organizations, usually set up as last-minute travel clubs and functioning on a membership basis, routinely keep in touch with travel suppliers to help them dispose of unsold inventory at discounts of between 15% and 60%. A great deal of the inventory consists of complete tour packages and cruises, but some clubs offer air-only charter seats and, occasionally, seats on scheduled flights. Members pay an annual fee and receive the toll-free number of a telephone hot line to call for information on imminent trips. In some cases, they also receive periodic mailings with information on upcoming trips for which there is more advance notice. Despite their suggestive names, last-minute travel does not necessarily mean that you cannot make plans until literally the last minute. Trips can be announced as little as a few days or as much as 2 months in advance of departure, but the average is from 1 to 4 weeks' notice. It does mean that your choice at any given time is limited to what is offered, so you might not find what you want, no matter how attractive the bargains. Among these organizations are:

Discount Club of America, 61-33 Woodhaven Blvd., Rego Park, NY 11374 (phone: 718-335-9612, 800-321-9587). Annual fee: $39.

Discount Travel International, Ives Building, 114 Forrest Ave., Suite 205, Narberth, PA 19072 (phone: 215-668-2182). Annual fee: $45.

Encore Short Notice, 4501 Forbes Blvd., Lanham, MD 20706 (phone: 301-459-8020) Annual fee: $48 per household.

Last-Minute Travel Club, 132 Brookline Ave., Boston, MA 02215 (phone: 617-267-9800 or 800-LAST-MIN). Annual fee: $30 per person, $35 per couple or family.

Moments Notice, 40 E. 49th St., New York, NY 10017 (phone: 212-486-0503). Annual fee: $45 per family.

On Call to Travel, 14335 S.W. Allen Blvd., Suite 209, Beaverton, OR 97005 (phone: 503-643-7212, members may call collect). Annual fee: $39 per family.

Spur-of-the-Moment Tours and Cruises, 10780 Jefferson Blvd., Culver City, CA 90230 (phone: 213-839-2418 in California; 800-343-1991 elsewhere). No fee.

Stand Buys Ltd., 3033 South Parker Rd., Suite 900, Aurora, CO 80014 (phone: 800-255-1487). Annual fee: $45 per family.

Worldwide Discount Travel Club, 1674 Meridian Ave., Miami Beach, FL 33139 (phone: 305-534-2082). Annual fee: $50 family; $40 individual.

NET FARE SOURCES: The newest notion for reducing the costs of travel services comes from travel agents who offer individual travelers "net" fares. Defined simply, a net fare is the bare minimum amount at which an airline or tour operator will carry a prospective traveler. It doesn't include the amount that would normally be paid to the travel agent as commission. Traditionally, such travel agent commissions amount to about 10% on domestic fares and from 8% to 20% on international tickets — not counting significant additions to these commission levels that are payable retroactively when agents sell more than a specific volume of tickets or trips for a single supplier. Instead of making their income from individual commissions, such agencies assess a fixed fee that may or may not provide a bargain for travelers; it requires a little arithmetic to determine whether to use the services of a net travel agent or those of one who accepts conventional commissions.

McTravel Travel Services (130 S. Jefferson, Chicago, IL 60606-3691; phone: 312-876-1116 in Illinois; 800-333-3335 elsewhere) is a formula fee–based agency that rebates its ordinary agency commission to the customer. For domestic flights, an agent will find the lowest retail ticket price, then rebate 8% of that price minus an $8 ticket-writing charge. The rebate percentage for international flights varies from 8% to 20%, depending on the airline selected, and the ticket-writing fee is $20. *McTravel* will rebate on all tickets including max-savers, super savers, and senior citizen passes. Available 7 days a week, reservations should be made far enough in advance to allow the tickets to be sent by first class mail, as extra charges accrue for special handling. There may also be charges for reservations that require a considerable amount of research. It's possible to economize further by making your own airline reservation, then asking *McTravel* only to write/ issue your ticket. For travelers who live outside the Chicago area, business may be transacted by phone, and purchases may be charged to a credit card.

One of the potential drawbacks of buying from agencies selling travel services at net fares is that your options may be limited. *McTravel Travel Services* recently engaged in a court battle with American Airlines, which refused to do business with the discounter on the grounds that travel agencies are only agents and not independent businesses. A US District Court in Chicago ruled in the airline's favor, and other carriers are expected to follow suit.

BARTERED TRAVEL SOURCES: Say a company buys advertising space in a news-paper for a hotel. As payment, the hotel gives the company a number of hotel rooms in lieu of cash. This is barter, a common means of exchange among hotels, airlines, car rental companies, cruise lines, tour operators, restaurants, and other service companies. When a bartering company finds itself with excess hotel rooms (or empty airline seats or cruise ship cabin space, and so on) and offers them to the public, considerable savings can be had.

Bartered-travel clubs can often offer discounts of up to 50% to members, who pay an annual fee (approximately $50 at press time) that entitles them to select from the flights, cruises, hotels, that the company obtained by barter. Members usually present a voucher, club credit card, or scrip (a dollar-denomination currency negotiable only for the bartered product) to the hotel, which in turn subtracts the dollar amount from the bartering company's account.

Selling bartered travel is a perfectly legitimate means of retailing. One advantage to club members is that they don't have to wait until the last minute to obtain room or flight reservations. However, hotel rooms and airline seats are usually offered to mem-bers on a space-available basis. Ticket vouchers are good only for a particular hotel and cannot be used at other hotels. The same goes for car rentals, cruises, package tours, and restaurants. The following clubs offer bartered travel at a discount to members.

> *IGT (In Good Taste) Services,* 22 E. 29th St., New York, NY 10016 (phone: 212-725-9600 or 800-444-8872). Annual membership fee of $48 includes $25 credit toward future charges.
>
> *The Travel Guild,* 18210 Redmond Way, Redmond, WA 98052 (phone: 206-885-1213). Annual membership fee: $48.
>
> *Travel World Leisure Club,* 225 W. 34th St., Suite 2203, New York, NY 10122 (phone: 212-239-4855 or 800-444-TWLC). Annual membership fee: $50 per family.

CONSUMER PROTECTION: Consumers who feel that they have not been dealt with fairly by an airline should make their complaints known. Begin with the customer service representative at the airport where the problem occurs. If he or she cannot resolve your complaint to your satisfaction, write to the airline's consumer office. In a businesslike, typed letter, explain what reservations you held, what happened, the names of the employees who were involved, and what you expect the airline to do to remedy the situation. Send copies (never the originals) of the tickets, receipts, and other documents that back up your claims. Ideally, all correspondence should be sent via certified mail, return receipt requested. This provides proof that your complaint was received.

If you still receive no satisfaction, the US Department of Transportation can also help. Passengers with consumer complaints — lost baggage, compensation for getting bumped, smoking or non-smoking rules, deceptive practices by an airline, charter regulations — should write to the Consumer Affairs Division, Room 10405, US Department of Transportation, 400 Seventh St. SW, Washington, DC 20590, or call the office at 202-366-2220. DOT personnel stress, however, that consumers should initially direct their complaints to the airline that provoked them.

To avoid more serious problems, *always* choose charter flights and tour packages with care. When you consider a charter, ask your travel agent who runs it and carefully check out the company. The Better Business Bureau in the company's home city can report on how many complaints, if any, have been lodged against it in the past. As emphasized above, protect yourself with trip cancellation and interruption insurance, which can help safeguard your investment in the event that you or a traveling companion is unable to make the trip and must cancel too late to receive a full refund from the company providing your travel services. (This is advisable whether you're buying a charter flight alone or a tour package for which the air fare is provided by charter or scheduled flight.) Some travel insurance policies have an additional feature, covering the possibility of default or bankruptcy on the part of the tour operator or airline, charter or scheduled.

Should this type of coverage not be available to you (state insurance regulations vary, there is a wide difference in price, and so on), your best bet is to pay for airline tickets and tour packages with a credit card. The federal Fair Credit Billing Act permits purchasers to refuse payment for credit card charges where services have not been delivered, so the onus of dealing with the receiver for a bankrupt airline falls on the credit card company. Do not rely on another airline to honor the ticket you're holding, since the days when virtually all major carriers subscribed to a default protection program that bound them to do so are long gone. Some airlines may voluntarily step forward to accommodate the stranded passengers of a fellow carrier, but this is now an entirely altruistic act.

INTER-ISLAND AIR TRAVEL: The airplane is just about the only means of island-hopping in Hawaii. Two inter-island carriers — Hawaiian Airlines and Aloha Airlines — connect major island airports with numerous flights daily, and smaller commuter lines serve both the large and small airports with frequent flights.

There's not a lot of variation in the fares charged by the various inter-island carriers. A regular one-way coach ticket between any of the larger islands — from Honolulu to the Big Island or from Kauai to Maui, for instance — costs, at the time of writing, between $30 and $50. On shorter hops, say between Honolulu and Molokai or Lanai, the fare runs between $30 and $45 each way. (Aloha Airlines offers first class service for about $20 more than the coach fare.) Fares on the smaller lines, which used to be among the best bargains in the islands, are generally in line with the major airlines' fares, though they may be a few dollars lower.

If you plan to do a lot of traveling between islands, it would pay to look into various discounts offered by inter-island carriers. Aloha and Hawaiian both have discount fares that are about 10% to 30% less expensive than full fares. These low fares are usually available for a limited number of seats on selected flights — often the first or last flight of the day. Discounts for children are available on most airlines, while discounts for senior citizens are less common and less generous. Another discount, long in existence, is the joint fare, available to any passenger holding a round-trip ticket on a scheduled flight between Hawaii and the continental US or Canada. The joint fare used to be something of a bargain, but nowadays it seldom knocks more than a few dollars off the regular fare.

A roundup of the airlines operating within Hawaii, and the routes they fly, follows. Keep in mind that the smaller lines probably won't get you to your destination as quickly as the big carriers, but the lower altitudes will provide a more scenic view en route, which is why some passengers prefer the small carriers. Also, be aware that baggage allowance on small aircraft may not be as generous as it is on larger planes. However, a baggage limit of 70 pounds per piece of luggage (with a check-in limit of two pieces plus one carry-on that will fit under an airline seat) is common on some of the commuter lines listed below.

Air Molokai–Tropic Airlines flies 9-passenger Cessna 402s to Honolulu, Molokai, Maui, and Lanai (phone: 800-262-6055).

Aloha Airlines, one of the three largest inter-island carriers, has extensive service to all the islands except Molokai and Lanai aboard 737s (phone: 800-367-5250). It does offer service to Molokai and Lanai through its sister carrier, *Aloha IslandAir* (formerly Princeville Airways) (phone: 800-323-3345).

Hawaiian Airlines, the oldest of the major inter-island carriers, flies to more island airports than its competitors, using mainly DC-9s. Its service to and from Molokai and Lanai and on some flights to Maui and Kauai uses 50-passenger De Havilland Dash-7 turboprops (phone: 800-367-5320).

Panorama Air links Honolulu and Kapalua–West Maui with 9-passenger Piper Chieftains (phone: 800-367-2671).

Travel by Ship

 As of late 1985, the SS *Constitution* and the SS *Independence,* two American-flag passenger liners that still sail around the islands, had discontinued their transpacific crossings. That fact, coupled with the existence of the Jones Act, explains why it's virtually impossible to journey to Hawaii from the US mainland aboard a cruise ship. According to the Jones Act, in effect since 1896, foreign ships (and now foreign airlines) are prohibited from carrying passengers between two US ports unless they carry them on to an ultimate foreign destination (or vice versa) or from one US port to another with an intervening foreign stop. Thus, if you've the time, the money, and the inclination to treat yourself to the luxury of an ocean voyage, and you wish to see something of Hawaii as well, your choices are somewhat limited. You can reserve a stateroom on one of the several foreign cruise ships that frequently include Hawaii as a port of call on their long Pacific or around-the-world cruises. Or you can go along as a passenger on a freighter plying the same routes. Both alternatives have drawbacks: They are expensive; they require a fair hunk of time, anywhere from 16 to 90 days; and the time spent in Hawaii is very brief, as little as 12 hours, never more than 2 days. Furthermore, it is virtually impossible to book a cruise on a foreign passenger ship or a freighter (US or otherwise) that begins or ends in Hawaii, an alternative that would at least allow the passenger to tack a tour of the islands to the beginning or end of a voyage. A third alternative is to fly to Honolulu and from there embark on one of the oceangoing passenger liners presently cruising Hawaiian waters. What you cannot usually do is book passage from the US directly to Hawaii and disembark, because for the moment there is no ship flying the US flag that offers regularly scheduled cruises to the islands from the mainland.

AROUND-THE-WORLD AND PACIFIC CRUISES: At least five foreign steamship lines continue to call at Hawaiian ports as part of Pacific or around-the-world itineraries: *Cunard, Princess Cruises, Royal Cruise Lines, Royal Viking Lines, and Sitmar.* The cost of a 3-month world cruise starts at around $20,000 and climbs to as high as $70,000 per person, double occupancy.

Although there are less expensive ways to see the islands, the romance of a sea voyage is irresistible for some, so a few points should be considered by such sojourners before they sign on for a seagoing vacation. (After all, it's hard to get off in mid-ocean.)

The single most important factor in determining the price of any cruise is the location of a given cabin or stateroom. Size has become a less important consideration, since many cruise ships now offer rows of very similar cubicles that would hardly dazzle even the most inexperienced traveler.

Cabins located amidships are believed to be subject to the least motion from the rolling sea and thus have been deemed the most desirable. Of these, center cabins on the highest decks are the most expensive, especially if their portholes open directly onto the sea. However, many experienced cruise passengers eschew expensive accommodations, for they know that they will spend very few waking hours in their cabin. They tend to opt for interior cabins of similar size, which offer the same accommodations for considerably less money.

One of the major attractions of cruises is the fixed price for the entire trip. That means there are no hidden extras or surprises en route. The price paid up front includes accommodations, transportation, and all meals, which may amount to as many as eight a day on some ships.

What it doesn't include is gratuities and shore excursions. Tipping may be the single most disconcerting experience on board ship, though usually more in anticipation than in fact. Service on a cruise vessel is normally a level or two above that found in even the most deluxe hotels, and the price you pay for all this pampering is the occasional feeling that you're sailing on a sea of upturned palms.

The general rule of thumb (or palm) is to expect to pay from 5% to 25% of your total cruise budget for gratuities — the lower figure on a long cruise, the higher on a short one. This includes tips to the cabin stewards, dining room stewards, busboys, deck stewards, bartenders, wine stewards, masseurs and masseuses, hairdressers, and anyone else who may at some point provide a special service for you. The questions are how much to whom and when should it be paid?

As a rule, tips are usually handed out on the last night of a short cruise and once a week on a longer one. The only person it makes sense to tip in advance is the maître d' of the dining room. He can adjust where you sit for meals, so it's wise to make friends with him at about the time the ship pulls away from the dock. Tip the cabin steward as well — you'll get better service.

The cabin steward usually gets from $2 to $5 a day per person, as does the dining room steward, while the busboy should be given at least $1 a day per person. The wine steward traditionally receives 15% of the cost of each bottle he serves. Deck stewards provide more services on some ships than on others. On many ships, a tip of $5 to $7 a week should be sufficient, but on others, between $3 and $5 a day is more appropriate. Other members of the crew should be compensated only when they perform a specific service.

Unfortunately, this tipping treadmill is one of the sins of the seas and, while it rarely becomes oppressive, it is a fact of cruise life. Furthermore, even the cruise lines that have tried to decree a no-tipping policy haven't really managed to get the message across to their crews in great numbers. Crew members on their ships still seem to expect at least a token gratuity.

Shore excursions are almost always optional and available at extra cost. Before you leave, do at least a little basic research about the ports you'll be visiting and decide just what sights will interest you. If several of the most compelling of these are some distance from the pier where your ship docks, the chances are that paying for a shore excursion will be worth the money.

Shore excursions usually can be booked through your travel agent at the same time you make your cruise booking, but this is worthwhile only if you can get complete details on the nature of each excursion being offered. If you can't get these details, better opt to purchase your shore arrangements after you're on board. The fact is, your enthusiasm for an excursion may be higher once you are on board because you will have met other passengers with whom to share the excitement of "shore leave." And depending on your time in port, you may decide to eschew the guided tour and venture out on your own.

FREIGHTERS: An alternative to cruise ships is travel by freighters, cargo-carrying ships that also take a limited number of passengers (usually about 12) in reasonably comfortable accommodations. The idea has romantic appeal, but there are a number of things to keep in mind. Though freighters are usually less expensive than cruise ships, they are not as inexpensive as excursion or even economy air fares. Accommodations and recreational facilities vary, but freighters were not designed to amuse passengers, so it is important to enjoy the idea of freighter travel itself. Schedules are erratic, and the traveler must fit his or her timetable to that of the ship. Passengers have found themselves waiting as much as a month for a promised sailing, and because freighters follow their cargo commitments, it is possible that a scheduled port could be omitted at the last minute, or a new one added. The prerequisite to travel by freighter is flexibility.

Although at the present time there are no freighters regularly carrying passengers to Hawaiian ports, this situation may change. Anyone contemplating a freighter trip should be aware that there are specialists who deal only or largely in this type of travel. They provide information, schedules, and, when you're ready to sail, booking services for prospective passengers.

> *Freighter World Cruises, Inc.:* A freighter travel agency. Publishes the twice-monthly *Freighter Space Advisory,* listing space available on sailings out of US and foreign ports (yearly subscription $27). 180 S. Lake Ave., Suite 335, Pasadena, CA 91101 (phone: 818-449-3106).
>
> *Pearl's Freighter Tips:* Run by Pearl Hoffman, an experienced hand in freighter travel. Mrs. Hoffman finds sailings for her customers and sends them off with all kinds of background advice. 175 Great Neck Rd., Suite 306, Great Neck, NY 11021 (phone: 516-487-8351).
>
> *TravLtips Cruise and Freighter Travel Association:* A freighter travel agency and club ($15 a year) whose members receive the bimonthly *TravLtips* magazine. PO Box 188, Flushing, NY 11358 (phone: 718-939-2400; 800-872-8584 outside New York).

HAWAIIAN CRUISES: On any trip to Hawaii, all but the most resolute landlubber sooner or later gets out on the water. The excursion might be an hour-long glass-bottom boat ride, a half-day Pearl Harbor sightseeing cruise, an evening dinner cruise, or a full-day sail from Maui to Lanai. All of these possibilities are described in the *Sightseeing Tours* sections of the chapters on the individual islands. Visitors to the islands can choose between two cruise operators that operate luxury liner tours of the Hawaiian islands:

American Hawaii Cruises' SS *Constitution* leaves Honolulu on Saturday nights year-round, cruises by Molokai, Lanai, and Kahoolawe, and docks at Kahului on Maui; at Hilo and Kailua-Kona on the Big Island; at Nawiliwili on Kauai; and arrives at Honolulu again on Saturday morning. Its sister ship, the SS *Independence,* sails on Saturday nights in the opposite direction, docking first at Kauai, then at Kailua-Kona and Hilo, then Maui, before cruising by Molokai on its way home to Honolulu. Optional shore excursions by bus — sightseeing, shopping — are offered in each port of call or you can rent a car if you prefer to travel at your own pace rather than with a large group. A car rental desk is set up on board in every port, and cars are parked at the bottom of the gangway. Unless you're traveling alone, renting a car is also less expensive than some of the ship's shore excursions. Back aboard, there's dining, danc-

ing, and Hawaiian-style entertainment. Prices for these 7-night packages in 1989 ranged
from $1,025 to $3,595. There are also 3- and 4-day cruises coupled with 4- and 3-day
resort stays from $699 to $1,599. Air/sea supplements are available that provide the
round-trip air fare from a city near your home for about half the regular rate. Contact
American Hawaii Cruises, 550 Kearney St., San Francisco, CA 94108 (phone: 800-227-
3666).

Aloha Pacific Cruises offers a 50-week schedule of Saturday-to-Saturday cruises on
the 600-passenger SS *Monterey,* departing Honolulu with stops at Kauai, Maui, and
the Big Island. Pre- and post-cruise hotel stays, as well as separate golf and tennis
packages, are also available through *Aloha Pacific,* and air/sea supplements can be
arranged with American Airlines. In 1989, cruise prices ranged from $1,195 to $3,595.
Contact Aloha Pacific Cruises, 1350 Old Bayshore Hwy., Suite 400, Burlingame, CA
94010 (phone: 800-544-6442).

■ **A final note on picking a cruise:** A "cruise-only" travel agency can better help
   you choose a cruise ship and itinerary than a travel agency that does not specialize
   in cruises. Cruise-only agents are best equipped to tell you about a particular ship's
   "personality," the kind of person with whom you'll likely travel on a particular
   ship, what dress is acceptable (it varies from ship to ship), and much more. At
   press time, there were over 275 agencies across the country that belonged to the
   National Association of Cruise Only Agencies (NACOA). For a listing of the cruise-
   only agencies in a particular state (requests are limited to three states), send a
   self-addressed, stamped envelope to NACOA, c/o Ship Shop, 18675 E. 39 St.,
   Suite P, Independence MO 64057; or call 816-795-7372.

Touring by Car

The automobile is the most popular means of transportation in Hawaii, as
it is in the rest of the US. While you may be able to get around Honolulu
and the island of Oahu easily enough on "TheBus," the island's one-fare
public transportation system, or see Hilo and travel to some other spots on
the Big Island of Hawaii via the Hele-On Bus, the same is not true of the remaining
islands, where public transportation is limited or nonexistent. A car is a necessity there
if you plan to venture any distance from your hotel or see more than the sights included
on an organized sightseeing excursion. And even where a car is not essential, driving
is still a highly desirable way to explore the state. It will allow you to take the scenic
stretches at your own pace, satisfy your curiosity about some out-of-the-way corner,
and stop for a snack, a swim, or a photograph at will.

RENTING A CAR: Because of aggressive competition, renting a car can be less
expensive in Hawaii than on the mainland. Let your fingers do the walking through
the island phone books and you'll find more than 80 car rental firms on Oahu alone
(give or take a few as they appear or disappear with the ebb and flow of the commercial
tide), about 40 or more on Maui, more than 30 on Hawaii and nearly as many on Kauai,
several on Molokai, and even one or two on Lanai. They can be divided into three basic
categories: large national or international companies such as *Avis, Budget, Dollar,
Hertz,* and *National;* statewide or regional companies such as *Tropical Rent-A-Car
Systems of Hawaii* or *Robert's Hawaii Rent-A-Car;* and single-island locals, some of
them with catchy names such as Maui's *El Cheapo Rent-a-Car* and *Word of Mouth.*
In addition, there are agencies specializing in convertible rentals, camper rentals, and
Jeep rentals.

Given all the competition, the price to be paid for a rental car changes continuously, rising and falling according to the level of tourist traffic. The rate your friend paid last December may have been higher than the one you'll pay in May, and a super-bargain rate may be withdrawn as soon as the advertiser moves some cars off the lot and onto the road again. Nevertheless, there are some constants governing pricing in the U-drive business, as it's called in Hawaii. For one thing, most companies offer flat per-day rates with unlimited free mileage rather than per-day, per-mile rates. Make sure that the low, flat daily rate that catches your eye, however, is indeed a per-day rate: Often the lowest price advertised by a company turns out to be available only with a minimum 3-day rental — fine if you want the car that long, but not the bargain it appears if you really intend to use it no more than 24 hours.

Most companies offer flat weekly rates, and some, flat monthly rates that represent a further saving over the daily rate. If the company does business on several islands, it may offer a multiple- or all-island weekly rate that can be applied to shorter rentals on a combination of those islands, say 4 days on Maui, followed by 3 days on Kauai. Some companies charge even less for this weekly "touring" rate than they do for a week-long single-island rental, but it can also cost the same or more.

Other factors influencing cost naturally include the type of car you rent. Charges may increase by only a few dollars a day through several classes of subcompact and compact cars — where most of the competition is — then increase by great leaps through the remaining classes of full-size and luxury cars and passenger vans. Note also that in Hawaii, the lowest price quoted is usually for a car with standard shift; one with an automatic transmission will usually add a dollar or two to the cost of renting. If you plan to turn the car in at a location other than the one from which it was rented, there are often, but not always, drop-off charges (or one-way service fees) which must be considered as well. These can range from $10 to $15 on the island of Maui and from $20 to $30 for a one-way rental from Hilo to Kailua-Kona on the Big Island of Hawaii (or vice versa).

The increasingly high cost of optional collision damage waiver protection must also be added to the price tag. The renter may be responsible for the full value of the vehicle being rented, but you can dispense with any obligation to pay even this amount by buying the offered waiver at a cost of about $10 a day. If your own personal auto insurance policy covers rented vehicles, you probably won't need to pay for the waiver. That's why it's very important to check your existing coverage with your own insurance broker before making any decision about optional rental car waivers. In addition, certain credit cards (among them, American Express) cover the collision damage waiver automatically, and at no charge, when the car rental is charged to the bank card in question.

Finally, don't forget that car rentals are subject to the 4.16% state sales tax, or that the price of gas, on the whole, is higher in Hawaii than on the mainland. At the time of writing, the average price per gallon of premium unleaded ranged from $1.70 to $2.20. If you're staying in Waikiki, you might want to add parking costs to your calculations. Some of the large hotels and condominiums have free parking for guests, but just as many charge for it — from about $2 to $5 a day. Parking isn't a problem in the rest of the state. Hawaii is essentially suburbia, with free and convenient parking a given. Outside Honolulu, the most you might have to shell out for parking is the tip you give the attendant at places with valet parking.

Finding the most economical car rental will require some telephone shopping on your part. As a *general* rule, expect to hear lower prices quoted by the smaller, strictly local companies than by the well-known international names, with those of the statewide companies falling somewhere between the two. (A recent survey of rental companies across Hawaii turned up flat rates from $16 a day to $30 a day for each company's least expensive subcompact or compact car. Charges by the one-island locals hovered toward the lower end of that range; those of the international chains tended toward the upper end. Weekly rates ranged from $70 to $148, and even better prices were available on temporary specials.) Given this situation, it's tempting to wait until arriving to consult the yellow pages and scout out the lowest rental from the company located the farthest from the airport high-rent district and offering no pick-up service; but if your arrival coincides with a peak period — Christmas to Easter and during the summer — you may be disappointed to find that the least expensive car in town was spoken for months ago. It is best at all times to reserve in advance, anywhere from a few days in slack periods to a month or more during the busy winter season.

Listed below are the major national rental companies represented in Hawaii along with some of the statewide ones that have toll-free information and reservations numbers that can be dialed from the mainland. The Hawaii Visitors Bureau *Accommodation Guide* contains a partial list of car rental firms with their 808 (area code for all Hawaii) numbers, and many, many more companies are listed in the various island phone books. Remember, too, that if you balk at the thought of ferreting out the most advantageous rental deal yourself, a rental car is part of many attractively priced package tours to Hawaii.

> *Alamo Rent-a-Car:* Rentals on Oahu, Hawaii, Maui, and Kauai. 800-327-9633.
>
> *Avis Rent-A-Car:* Rentals on Oahu, Hawaii, Maui, Kauai, and Molokai. 800-331-1212.
>
> *Budget Rent-A-Car:* Rentals on Oahu, Hawaii, Maui, Kauai, and Molokai. 800-527-0707.
>
> *Dollar Rent-A-Car:* Rentals on Oahu, Hawaii, Maui, Kauai, and Molokai. 800-367-7006.
>
> *Hertz:* Rentals on Oahu, Hawaii, Maui, and Kauai. Continental US, except Oklahoma, 800-654-3001; Oklahoma, 800-654-3131.
>
> *National Car Rental:* Rentals on Oahu, Hawaii, Maui, and Kauai. 800-CAR-RENT.
>
> *Thrifty Rent-A-Car:* Rentals on Oahu, Maui, and Kauai. 800-367-2277.
>
> *Tropical Rent-A-Car:* Rentals on Oahu, Hawaii, Maui, Kauai, and Molokai. 800-367-5140.

To rent a car, you must have a valid driver's license, and it usually helps to have a credit card as well. Without one, you will have to leave a hefty deposit when you pick up the car — generally between $200 and $400 for a weekly rental. Some companies insist on running a credit check on anyone who wants to rent a car and does not use a major credit card; this check can be time consuming, so you should try to have it done before you leave home. (Each company has a different policy; look around for the best deal.) Some companies will rent to no one under the age of 25; for others, the minimum age is 21 or even 18, provided the would-be renter has a credit card to prove responsibility and personal creditworthiness.

RENTING A JEEP: The main roads on almost all the islands are in good condition and most travelers will not need anything sturdier than the ordinary rental car. Four-wheel-drive vehicles, though not plentiful, can be rented on all the islands, but they are a necessity only if you intend to explore Lanai. You can rent one for about $75 per day plus gas from the island's gas station–cum–car rental agency: *Oshiro Service and U-Drive,* 850 Fraser Ave., Lanai City, HI 96763 (phone: 808-565-6952). Note that *Oshiro* also rents cars, which are of little use to sightseers on this island of largely unpaved roads.

The southern route on East Maui and the northern route on West Maui plus parts of West Molokai are other areas where a four-wheel-drive vehicle will be of service to the adventuresome. Of the car rental companies with toll-free numbers listed above, *Dollar* rents Jeeps on Oahu, Hawaii, Maui, and Kauai. In addition to these islands,

Avis rents Jeeps on Molokai as well. Other companies renting Jeeps, including special-ists such as *Rent-A-Jeep* (phone: 808-877-6626 for Maui; 808-245-9622 for Kauai), are listed in the yellow pages of the respective island phone books. Jeep rentals range from about $40 to $60 a day; even at these prices, you'll have to reserve well in advance to get one.

Package Tours

 If the mere thought of buying a travel package conjures up visions of a trip spent marching in lockstep with a horde of frazzled fellow travelers, remem-ber that packages have come a long way. For one thing, not all packages are necessarily escorted tours, and the one you buy does not have to include any organized touring at all — nor will it necessarily include traveling companions. If it does, however, you'll find that people of all sorts — many just like yourself — are taking advantage of packages today because they are economical and convenient, save the purchaser an immense amount of planning time, and exist in such variety that it's virtually impossible not to find one that suits at least the majority of any traveler's preferences. Given the high cost of travel these days, packages have emerged as a good buy.

In essence, a package is a combination of travel services that can be purchased as a single booking. It may include any or all of the following: round-trip air transporta-tion, local transportation (and/or car rentals), accommodations, some or all meals, sightseeing, entertainment, transfers to and from the hotel at each destination, taxes, tips, escort service, and a variety of incidental features that might be offered as options at additional cost. In other words, a package can be any combination from a fully escorted tour offered at an all-inclusive price to a simple fly/drive booking allowing you to function totally on your own. Its principal advantage is that it saves money: The cost of the combined arrangements invariably is well below the price that would be paid if all the elements included were bought separately, and (particularly if transportation is provided by charter or discount flight) it could even be less than a round-trip economy airline ticket on a regularly scheduled flight. An important additional advantage is that because the traveler purchases all of the elements at the same time, the burdensome details are taken care of quickly.

The lower prices are possible through package travel as a result of high-volume commerce. The tour packager negotiates for services in wholesale quantities — blocks of airline seats or hotel rooms, group meals, dozens of rental cars, busloads of ground transportation, and so on — and they are made available at a lower per-person price because of the large quantities purchased for use during a given time period. Most packages, however, are subject to restrictions governing the duration of the trip and require total payment by a given time before departure.

Dozens and dozens of packages to Hawaii are available, put together by wholesale tour operators, some retail travel agencies, airlines, hotels, charter companies, and special interest organizations. They can run the gamut from deluxe everything to simple budget amenities or even bare-bones necessities. Though usually designed to appeal to the broadest possible public, they can also aim to indulge a select few in a sport, hobby, or a cultural or scientific interest. A travel agent is the best guide to help sort through this abundance, and a good one will even provide information on specialized tours and be able to book them.

To determine whether a package — or more specifically, which package — fits your travel plans, start by evaluating your interests and needs, deciding how much and what you want to spend, see, and do. Gather whatever package tour information is available for your time schedule and read the brochure carefully to determine what is included. Tour brochures almost always highlight the lowest price at which a tour is offered. This price, however, may be available off-season only, at the lowest-priced hotel among several in the program (which nonetheless may be quite satisfactory), or in such limited numbers that it is available only on a waitlist. Note, too, that prices quoted in brochures are almost always based on double occupancy. The rate listed is for each of two people sharing a double room, and if you travel alone, the supplement for single accommodations can raise the price considerably (see *Hints for Single Travelers*).

Increasingly, in this age of rapidly rising air fares, the brochure will *not* include the price of the airline ticket in the price of the package, though sample applicable fares from various gateway cities will usually be listed separately as extras to be added to the price of the ground arrangements. Before doing this, get the latest fares from the airline, because the samples will invariably be out of date by the time you read them. If the brochure gives more than one category of sample fares per gateway city — such as an individual tour-basing fare, an excursion or other discount fare, or a group fare — your travel agent or airline tour desk will be able to tell you which one applies to the package you choose depending on when you travel, how far in advance you book, and other factors. (An individual tour-basing fare is a fare computed as part of a package that includes land arrangements, thereby entitling a carrier to reduce the air portion almost to the absolute minimum. Though it always represents a saving over full-fare coach or economy, lately it has not been as inexpensive as the excursion and other discount fares to Hawaii that are also available to individuals. The group fare is usually the least expensive fare, and it is the tour operator, not you, who makes up the group.) When the brochure does include round-trip transportation in the package price, don't forget to add the round-trip transportation cost from your home city to the departure city to come up with the total cost of the package.

Finally, read the responsibility clause (usually in fine print at the end of the descriptive literature) to determine the precise elements for which the tour operator is — and is not — liable. In reading, ask the following questions:

1. Does the tour include air fare or other transportation, sightseeing, meals, transfers, taxes, baggage handling, tips, or any other services? Do you want all these services?
2. If the brochure indicates that "some meals" are included, does this mean a welcoming and farewell dinner, two breakfasts, or every evening meal?
3. What classes of hotels are offered? If you will be traveling alone, how much is the single supplement?
4. Does the tour itinerary or price vary according to the season?
5. Are the prices guaranteed; that is, if costs increase between the time you book and the time you depart, can surcharges unilaterally be added?
6. Do you get a full refund if you cancel? (If not, be sure to obtain cancellation insurance.)
7. Can the operator cancel if too few people join?

The responsibility clause should be read very carefully, because it is there that the tour operator frequently expresses the right to change services or schedules as long as equivalent arrangements are offered. This clause also absolves the operator of responsibility if circumstances beyond human control affect the operation of the tour.

One of the consumer's biggest problems is finding enough information to judge the reliability of a tour packager, since individuals seldom have direct contact with the firm putting the package together. Usually, a retail travel agent is involved between customer and tour operator, and much depends on his or her candor and cooperation. So ask a number of questions about the tour you are considering. For example: Has the agent ever used the package provided by this tour operator? How long has the tour operator been in business? Is the tour operator a member of the *United States Tour*

Operators Association (USTOA)? (The *USTOA* will provide a list of its members upon request and also offers a useful brochure, *How to Select a Package Tour;* contact the USTOA, 211 E. 51st St., Suite 12B, New York, NY 10022; phone: 212-944-5727). Which and how many companies are involved in the package? If air travel is by charter flight, is there an escrow account in which deposits will be held, and, if so, what is the name of the bank?

This last question is very important. The law requires that tour operators deposit every charter passenger's deposit and subsequent payment in a proper escrow account. Money paid into such an account cannot legally be used except to pay for the costs of a particular package or as a refund if the trip is canceled. To ensure the safe handling of your money, make your check payable to the escrow account — by law, the name of the depository bank appears in the operator-participant contract; it's usually found in that mass of minuscule type on the back of the brochure. Write the details of the charter, including the destination and dates, on the face of the check; on the back, print "For Deposit Only." Your travel agent may prefer that you make your check out to the agency, saying that it will then pay the tour operator the fee minus commission. But it is perfectly legal to write your check as we suggest, and if your agent objects too vociferously (the agent should have sufficient faith in the tour operator to trust him to send the proper commission), consider taking your business elsewhere. If you don't make your check out to the escrow account, you lose the protection of escrow should the trip be canceled or the tour operator or travel agent fail. Furthermore, recent bankruptcies in the travel industry have served to point out that even the protection of escrow may not be enough to safeguard a traveler's investment. Increasingly, insurance is becoming a necessity (see *Insurance*), and payment by credit card has become popular since it offers some additional safeguards if the tour operator defaults.

It is doubtful whether anyone has ever seen a "packaged" traveler emerge from Honolulu International Airport without a string of plumeria, orchids, hibiscus, or other blossoms around his or her neck, because the traditional lei greeting is the first thing a tour operator figures into any package to Hawaii. Beyond that fixed feature, however, you can get nearly anything you want in a Hawaiian package and for as long as you want it: The keynote is flexibility. Perhaps the most common arrangement — especially for the first-time visitor — is a week-long stay at a Waikiki hotel including transfers between the airport and the hotel, baggage handling, taxes and tips, a limited amount of Honolulu sightseeing, and very few, if any, meals. Nearly every tour operator offers such a basic package, which usually can be prolonged by the addition of extra days or even extra weeks at the same place. Those who have already been to Honolulu, or who wish to get beyond the hustle and bustle of a city straightaway, will find the same sort of week-long, stay-put package available at resort areas on other islands — Kailua-Kona on Hawaii, or the Kaanapali Beach area on Maui, for instance.

There is a do-it-yourself quality to Hawaiian tour offerings, and the basic package is immediately subject to variation. The week in Waikiki becomes a 10-day, 2-island holiday with the addition of a 3-day neighbor island "extension," or it becomes a 2-week, 3-island holiday with the addition of a second neighbor island extension. In fact, most packagers offer a series of 2-, 3-, or 4-day mini-packages at various islands that travelers may string together at will, adding them to a block of time spent in one place or island-hopping for the entire length of their stay. You will rarely see Lanai listed among the extensions or mini-packages available, but all the other major islands, including Molokai, can be seen this way.

Another common variation is the marketing of any one package in two versions — a sightseeing version and a U-drive version. In the latter instance, a rental car will be waiting at the airport, and transfers to and from the hotel will be eliminated from the package ingredients, along with any organized sightseeing that might have been included. An operator with a hefty catalogue of tours may offer both options on all of the islands it packages, providing the opportunity to drive on some islands and be driven on others. When selections are more limited, it's most likely that the Honolulu portions of tours will be the ones set up for organized sightseeing, while visits to the neighboring islands will tend to include a rental car. Because driving yourself is such a popular way of seeing Hawaii, and because rental cars are relatively inexpensive, nearly every company that offers tours to Hawaii has a certain number of wholly U-drive plans available. Even in the most basic stay-in-one-place package, a "car for a day" may be a feature.

A rental car is also part of most condominium packages, a type of vacation that is becoming more and more important in the overall Hawaiian tourism picture. The package usually includes nothing more than daily car rental and accommodations, which are in privately owned condominiums whose rates for a couple compare very favorably with double-occupancy hotel rates, and they become even more attractive when two couples or a family travel together. In addition, fully equipped kitchens or kitchenettes allow travelers to save money by preparing many meals themselves, breakfast in particular. Some condominium developments have all the amenities and services of a hotel, whereas others stress simplicity and seclusion (see *Accommodations* for a full discussion of what's included); in either case, the spaciousness and frequent luxury of the premises, together with the prime locations of the properties, prevent their being considered as mere cost-cutting alternatives to hotel rooms. The condominium vacations packaged by specialists such as *Condo Resorts International; Condominiums Unlimited,* and *Creative Leisure* can be booked through travel agents, as can those of tour operators and others who offer condominium holidays among their regular tour programs.

All of the foregoing packages could be described as independent tours or, at the most, hosted tours. Having gotten you to your destination and having provided a place to stay, they leave you by yourself, free to do as you want. A representative of the tour company may be available at a local office to answer questions, or a company host may be stationed at a desk in the hotel or condominium development, again to answer questions, handle problems, or assist in arranging activities or optional excursions.

Not everyone prefers lack of structure, however. While fully escorted, all-inclusive group sightseeing tours to and through Hawaii are not as common as they are to Europe, they do exist.

For example, *Tauck Tours* (PO Box 5027, Westport, CT 06881; phone: 203-226-6911) has a 13-day Complete Tour of Hawaii that visits Oahu, Molokai, Maui, the island of Hawaii, and Kauai. Except for five lunches, all meals (many with dinner shows) are covered by the package price, with a sightseeing trip — by motorcoach, boat, or helicopter — featured nearly every day in addition to free time for the beach, pool, or shopping. All transfers, baggage handling for two bags per person, local transportation (including inter-island air fare), tips to maids and waiters, and entertainment accompanying dinner are included for the 1989 price of $2,275 per person, double occupancy. Besides round-trip air fare between your home and Hawaii, the only thing not included is gratuities to sightseeing guides and drivers and to the tour escort, who remains with the group from beginning to end. *Cartan Tours* (phone: 800-422-7826) and *Maupintour* (phone: 800-255-4266) have similar 13-day, 4- and 5-island escorted tours with many meals included. Other companies also offer a range of escorted tours, most of them with a choice of hotel categories to vary the price, most including very few meals, and some escorted only in the neighbor island portions and hosted in Honolulu.

There is also a wide variety of packages designed to appeal to particular groups of people. One operator specializing in packages for the over-50 traveler is *Grand Circle Travel.* Among its offerings is an air/sea package featuring *American Hawaii* cruises with 2 nights at a Honolulu hotel included (see *Hints for Single Travelers*). Because Hawaii presents fewer obstacles to mobility than most other destinations, it is a favorite among travel agencies and tour operators who specialize in organizing tours for the handicapped. For their names and addresses, see *Hints for Handicapped Travelers.*

Prominent among the special-interest packages are vacations built around sports or those designed to bring nature lovers as close as possible to the beauty of the Hawaiian landscape. *Mountain Travel,* which specializes in wilderness expeditions, has three 7-day hiking trips, each centering on one island: Hawaii, Maui, or Kauai. Offered in March, July, and October, the trips can be booked back to back. Overnights are spent in cabins or tents. Contact Mountain Travel, 6420 Fairmount Ave., El Cerrito, CA 94530 (phone: 415-527-8100; 800-227-2384 except in Alaska). The *Sierra Club* also sponsors hiking and biking trips to Hawaii each year. For more information, write to the Sierra Club Outing Dept., 730 Polk St., San Francisco, CA 94109 (phone: 415-776-2211).

A subset of the wilderness specialty tours is offered by Carole Latimer, founder of the *Outdoor Woman's School* in Berkeley, California, whose hiking and camping trip to the Na Pali coast of Kauai is open to women only. A 9-day tour includes 6 days of camping on isolated Na Pali beaches, and a 7-day tour combines 2 nights' camping at Miloli on Hawaii with a condo stay on the Kona coast. Both tours are limited to 14 people. To book, contact the Outdoor Woman's School/Call of the Wild, 2519 Cedar St., Berkeley, CA 94708 (phone: 415-849-9292).

It is not unusual for Hawaii to be packaged in concert with other domestic destinations to be visited en route to or from the islands. These "stopover" packages are especially appealing to Easterners and Midwesterners who can thus visit one or more Western city, such as Los Angeles, San Francisco, San Diego, or Las Vegas, usually for no additional air fare. *Gogo Tours,* a wholesaler whose packages are available through *Liberty Travel,* its retail operation, and other agents around the country, offers a 2-week package that combines 3 days in San Francisco and 7 in Honolulu with a choice of 3 days in either Las Vegas or Los Angeles on the return trip. *Liberty Travel* has about 120 retail outlets; for the one nearest you, contact Liberty Travel, 69 Spring St., Ramsey, NJ 07446 (phone: 201-934-3500).

Hawaii itself, finally, may be offered as a stopover or extension on packages to more distant destinations in the Far East or the South Pacific. If you are booking such a package, ask your travel agent whether the applicable air fare allows a stopover. For instance, *Globus-Gateway Cosmos Tours,* 95-25 Queens Blvd., Rego Park NY 11374 (phone: 718-268-1700 in New York State; 800-221-0090 elsewhere) has designed a short, 4-day Hawaiian extension, visiting Honolulu only, which can be added to any of its escorted tours to Australia, New Zealand, the South Pacific Islands, and the Orient.

Camping and Hiking, Biking, and RVs

CAMPING AND HIKING: Hawaii's balmy climate and splendid scenery can make for delightful adventures. The islands boast numerous parks that are open year-round and offer camping facilities, hiking trails, fishing, swimming, and other amenities. Reservations and permits are often required, and campers are usually limited to between 3 and 7 nights' stay. Brief descriptions of the individual parks and campgrounds may be found in *Woodall's Campground Directory, Western Edition* (Woodall; $8.95) or *RV Park and Campground Directory* (Prentice-Hall; $13.95; $9.95 for the Western Edition). For a more thorough discussion of Hawaiian campgrounds as well as advice on a number of related topics, consult *Hawaiian Camping* by Shirley Rizzuto (Wilderness Press). Though out of print, this handy little book may be available in your library. For permits and further information, contact the appropriate authority, as listed below:

National
   Superintendent, Hawaii Volcanoes National Park, PO Box 52, HI 96718
   Superintendent, Haleakala National Park, PO Box 369, Makawao, HI 96768

State
   Oahu: Division of State Parks, PO Box 621, Honolulu, HI 96809
   Hawaii: Division of State Parks, PO Box 936, Hilo, HI 96721
   Kauai: Division of State Parks, PO Box 1671, Lihue, HI 96766
   Maui and Molokai: Division of State Parks, PO Box 1049, Wailuku, HI 96793

County
   Oahu: Department of Parks and Recreation, 650 S. King St., Honolulu, HI 96813
   Hawaii: Department of Parks and Recreation, 25 Aupuni St., Hilo, HI 96720
   Kauai: Department of Recreation, County of Kauai, 4191 Hardy St., Lihue, HI 96766
   Maui: Department of Recreation, War Memorial Gym, Wailuku, HI 96793
   Molokai: County Parks Department, Kaunakakai, HI 96748

Necessities – For outdoor camping, necessities include a nylon tent, a lightweight sleeping bag, foam pad, ground cloth, first-aid kit (including mosquito repellent and sunscreen), backpack stove (building fires is illegal), nested cooking pots, canteen, jackknife, and flashlight. Keep food simple; unless backpacking deep into the wilderness, you will probably be close enough to a store to stock up on perishables.

If you want to take to the outdoors unencumbered, just park the car and go off for a day's hike. There are fabulous trails all over Hawaii. The series *Hiking Kauai, Maui, Oahu,* and *Hawaii,* by Robert Smith, discusses each island's trails in terms of difficulty, scenery, hiking distance and time, and lists which permits are required (Wilderness Press; $7.95 each). Although the Kauai and Maui editions are out of print, you still may be able to find them on bookstore and library shelves. Smith's *Hawaii's Best Hiking Trails* combines highlights of the four books on the individual islands and gives additional information on Molokai and Lanai (Wilderness Press; $11.95). *Hawaiian Hiking Trails* (Fernglen Press; $9.95), by Craig Chisholm, features 49 trails on the five major islands, along with useful information about relative difficulty, time, altitude, and average calories expended on each hike. State Forest Reserve trail information and maps are available from each island's Department of Land and Natural Resources, Division of Forestry and Wildlife, at the following addresses:

   Oahu: 1151 Punchbowl St., Honolulu, HI 96813
   Hawaii: PO Box 4849, Hilo, HI 96720
   Kauai: PO Box 1671, Lihue, HI 96766
   Maui: PO Box 1015, Wailuku, HI 96793

To make outings safe and pleasant, find out about the trails you plan to hike and be realistic about your own physical limitations. Choose an easy route if you are out of shape. Stick to the trails unless you are an experienced hiker or know the area well. If it is at all wild, let someone at the beginning of the trail know where you are going, or at least leave a note on your car.

All you need to set out are a pair of sturdy shoes and socks, jeans or long pants to protect your legs, a waterproof poncho for rain showers, a canteen of water, a hat to protect you from the sun, and, if you like, a picnic lunch. It is a good idea to dress in layers, so that you can add or remove clothing according to the elevation and weather. Make sure, too, to wear clothes with pockets, or bring a pack to keep your hands free. Some useful and important pocket or pack stuffers include a jackknife, a first-aid kit, a map, and sunglasses.

Organized Trips – Camping trips on which you can go far afield with an experienced guide and other campers are available through these organizations:

Mountain Travel, 6420 Fairmont Ave., El Cerrito, CA 94530
Outdoor Woman's School/Call of the Wild, 2519 Cedar St., Berkeley, CA 94708

BIKING: Biking in Hawaii can be challenging, as the roads are sometimes winding, steep, and poorly surfaced. However, the distances between points of interest are generally not great, so you'll be sure to enjoy any trip taken at your own pace. The book *American Biking Atlas & Touring Guide* by Sue Browder (Workman) describes three tour routes in Hawaii; *Bicycling in Hawaii* by Robert Immler (Wilderness Press) outlines 20 tours around all the islands and rates them according to distance, difficulty, and traffic. Both of these books are out of print, but are worth looking for in your library. For general biking information, consult the *The Complete Book of Bicycling* by Eugene A. Sloane (Simon & Schuster; $24.95) and *Anybody's Bike Book* by Tom Cuthberson (Ten Speed Press; $7.95).

Road Safety – While the car may be the bane of cyclists, cyclists who do not follow the rules of the road strike terror in the hearts of automobile drivers. Follow the same rules and regulations as motor vehicle drivers. Stay to the right side of the road. Ride no more than two abreast — single file where traffic is heavy. Keep three bike lengths behind the bike in front of you. Stay alert to sand, gravel, potholes, and wet surfaces; make sure to wear bright clothes and use lights at dusk or night.

Choosing and Renting a Bike – A bicycle is the correct size if you can straddle its center bar with feet flat on the ground and still have an inch or so between your crotch and the bar. (Nowadays, because women's old-fashioned barless bikes are not as strong as men's, most women use men's bicycles.) The seat height is right if your leg is just short of completely extended when you push the pedal to the bottom of its arc. Experienced cyclists keep the tires fully inflated (pressure requirements vary widely, but are always imprinted on the side of the tire) and pedal at an even pace. For roadside repairs, and especially on longer rides, carry a tool kit that contains a bike wrench, screwdriver, pliers, tire repair kit, cycle oil, and work gloves.

The few bike rental agencies on the islands are listed in the yellow pages of the phone directory. Bicycles must be picked up and dropped off at the same point and the rental fee for a 10-speed generally runs between $10 and $15 a day. For these reasons, it may be a better idea to bring along your own bike.

More than one organization offers cycling tours of Hawaii. An advantage of such a tour is that the organizer will take care of shipping your bike and the shipping fee is included in the total tour package. Otherwise, it is necessary to ship through an airline, and there are no standard procedures for this. Some carriers provide shipping cartons for bikes (you will have to disassemble it, but if you are contemplating a bicycle tour, you should be able to do this with ease) and charge as much as $30 each way for shipping, plus the cost of an airline box or bag to put it in. Another attraction of *some* organized tours is the existence of a "sag wagon" to carry extra luggage — or even you and your bike when you just can't pedal another mile. Accommodations on tours can vary from campgrounds to hotels, and as a result tour prices also vary. *Backroads Bicycle Touring* (PO Box 1626-Q414, San Leandro, CA 94577; phone: 415-895-1783) sponsors 10-day cycling tours of the Big Island of Hawaii from November to April. Accommodations tend toward the deluxe, and bicycle rental is available. For the more rugged cyclist, the *Sierra Club* sponsors hiking/biking/camping trips to Kauai and Hawaii as well as Maui; overnight stays are at campgrounds and other outdoor areas (see *Package Tours*).

RECREATIONAL VEHICLES: The term recreational vehicles — RVs — is applied to all manner of camping vehicles, whether towed or self-propelled. The level of comfort in an RV is limited only by the amount of money you choose to spend. At their simplest, they are fold-down campers, tents on wheels that unfold into sleeping spaces for several people when unhitched. The most luxurious RV is a fully equipped home on wheels, requiring electrical hook-ups at night to run the TV set and kitchen appliances.

An RV undoubtedly saves a traveler a great deal of money on accommodations and, if cooking appliances are part of the unit, on food as well. However, it is important to remember that buying or renting an RV is a major expense; also, any kind of RV increases gas consumption considerably. It is most expensive to tow a large trailer camper, which usually decreases auto mileage by about 50%. More economical, because it's smaller, is the fold-down tow camper, which will reduce normal car mileage by about 10% to 15%. Self-propelled RVs have no better mileage records — they usually average 7 to 12 miles per gallon of gas at best.

RVs will appeal most to the kind of person who enjoys camping with a little extra comfort. For information on how to operate, choose, and use a recreational vehicle, see Richard A. Wolters' *Living on Wheels* (Dutton; currently out of print; check your library or bookstore). You might also consider subscribing to *Trailer Life* (TL Enterprises, 29901 Agoura Rd., Agoura, CA 91301; phone: 818-991-4980). A 1-year subscription costs $11.98; $9 for for members of the Good Sam Club, which provides discounts on a variety of services for RV owners and which is also run by TL Enterprises.

Haleakala National Park on Maui, Hawaii Volcanoes National Park, and some of the state parks on these and other islands permit trailer camping. Rates vary depending on the size and complexity of the RV and the number of days rented; they also offer customer pick-up and drop-off services at the airport on Hilo.

Preparing

Calculating Costs

$ A realistic appraisal of your travel expenses is the most crucial bit of planning before any trip. It is also, unfortunately, one for which it is most difficult to give precise practical advice. Travel styles are intensely personal, and personal taste determines cost to a great extent. Will you stay in a conventional hotel for the duration of your trip? Will you eat every meal in a restaurant? Will you do some camping or picnicking? If published figures on the cost of travel were always taken as gospel, many trips would not be taken. But in reality, it's possible to economize. On the other hand, don't be lulled into feeling that it is not necessary to do some arithmetic before you go. No matter how generous your travel budget, you will discover that without careful planning beforehand — and strict accounting along the way — you will spend more than you anticipated.

Many variables affect the cost of a vacation, but the major expenses are transportation, accommodations, and food. A number of other expenses also must be considered: local transportation, sightseeing, shopping, sports activities, nightlife, drinks, and miscellaneous items such as laundry and tips.

TRANSPORTATION: Air fare is really the easiest cost to pin down precisely, though the range and variety of flights available may be confusing initially. The possibilities are outlined fully in *Travel by Plane*. Essentially the traveler can choose from various types of tickets on scheduled flights, ranging in expense from first class and excursion fares to discount tickets and charters. Travel among the Hawaiian islands is also accomplished mostly by plane, and detailed information about inter-island flights is provided in the same section.

The other important means of local transportation is car rental. Except on Oahu and the Big Island, public transportation is sparse in Hawaii, so most independent travelers will be renting a car even though distances on most of the islands are not very great. A list of car rental firms with toll-free numbers is provided under *Touring by Car* in this section, and by dialing a few of these, it's easy to arrive at an estimate of auto rental costs. Remember, however, that the smaller and more local the company (and the least likely to have a toll-free number), the less expensive its cars will tend to be. But if you're hoping to save money by waiting until after arrival to find a car, weigh the potential saving against the knowledge that these same cars are generally booked well in advance by repeat travelers. When calculating rental rates, don't forget to figure in the cost of gasoline.

ACCOMMODATIONS: Room rates run a very wide spectrum. At top resort hotels, a double room can cost $200 and up, though there is no sacred edict that says you must stay at a deluxe resort. If luxury is the goal, however, it is wise to investigate the very wide range of rates that sometimes exists under a single resort roof, even though the preponderance of accommodations may be in the expensive or very expensive categories. Also well worth looking into are the many luxury condominium resorts that dot the islands. By sharing a 2-bedroom apartment at one of these classy addresses, for example, two couples can get very deluxe and spacious accommodations at affordable prices, without giving up the amenities normally associated with hotels — daily maid service, restaurants, shops, and a full range of sports facilities.

The various types of lodgings available in Hawaii are discussed under *Accommodations* in this section. In the *Checking In* portions of the chapters devoted to the individual islands, specific hotels and condominiums are grouped in categories — expensive, moderate, and inexpensive — for which general price ranges are given. On the whole, the typical moderate accommodation for two people — either a hotel room or a 1-bedroom condominium — can be rented for an average $80 to $100 a night. Note that this is for a double room. As everywhere else, there are many more double rooms than single rooms, and those traveling alone should expect the price of a single to be no less than two-thirds that of a double. Note also that this is indeed an *average* (moderate, for instance, means anywhere from $40 to $105, depending on locale). Nevertheless, if you multiply those amounts by the number of days of your stay, you will come up with an estimate that will allow two people to stay in comfortable, pleasant surroundings and not feel they are missing any of the attractions Hawaii has to offer. The same estimate will often accommodate more than two people if they stay at a condominium, because it is quite common for the living room of a one-bedroom condominium to be furnished with a pull-out sofa bed where a child may sleep free, or an adult at not much additional cost. Condominium accommodations are plentiful in Hawaii, especially on Maui and Kauai, and they should be considered by all prospective visitors. They are eminently recommendable as dollar stretchers, and they have other merits that even those not interested in economy will appreciate. (See *Accommodations* for a fuller discussion of condominiums.)

FOOD: Meals are a more difficult expense to estimate. If you stay in a condominium, you will be able to prepare some meals yourself, and though groceries are probably more expensive in Hawaii than in most places on the mainland, they are certainly less expensive than eating out. Independent travelers eating all of their meals in restaurants should allow roughly $60 to $80 a day per couple for food. That includes breakfast (about $10 to $15 for two), lunch (about $15 to $20 for two), and an average dinner for two in a moderate, neither-scrimp-nor-splurge restaurant, not including alcoholic beverages or tips. You could easily add a beer and a glass of house wine to the dinner tab without wreaking havoc with these figures, but if you want the pick of the wine list or have a tendency to order lobster, expect the check, even in a moderate establishment, to run much higher. A steady diet of better restaurants will drive the average up higher still, but the figures can be revised downward, too, if you choose fruit for breakfast rather than bacon and eggs, put together your own picnic lunches for the beach, and frequently visit fast-food outlets. Our restaurant selections, chosen to give the best value for the money, are listed in the *Eating Out* sections of each island chapter. As with hotels, they are listed as expensive, moderate, or inexpensive; approximate price ranges for those labels are also supplied.

The expenses for certain types of recreational activities may figure heavily in your budgeting. Do you intend to rent a catamaran or take windsurfing lessons? Is daily tennis a part of your plan? Will your children be disappointed if they don't take a helicopter ride (a rather expensive but exciting way to see the sights in Hawaii) or a whale watching cruise? General guidelines on the costs of these activities can be found in our DIVERSIONS chapter as well as in the *Sources and Resources* sections of the chapters on the individual islands. Finally, don't forget that if haunting discos is an essential part of your vacation or you feel that one luau and/or Polynesian dinner show may not be enough, allow for the extra cost of nightlife. This one item alone can cost a great deal, whether in Honolulu or on the neighbor islands.

If at any point in the planning process it appears impossible to estimate expenses, consider this suggestion: The easiest way to put a ceiling on the price of some or all of the above is to buy a travel package. A totally planned and escorted one, with almost all transportation, rooms, meals, sightseeing, local travel, tips, and a dinner show or two included and prepaid, allows you to know beforehand almost exactly what the trip will cost, and the only surprise will be the one you spring on yourself by succumbing to some irresistible, expensive souvenir.

The various types of packages available are discussed under *Package Tours* in this section, but a few points bear repeating here. Not all packages are package *tours.* There are loosely organized arrangements including nothing more than a stay at a hotel, transfers between hotel and airport, baggage handling, taxes, and tips, which leave the entire matter of how you spend your time and where you eat your meals up to you. Equally common are the condominium-plus-car packages, which take care of your accommodations and local transportation. On such independent or hosted "tours," there may be a tour company representative available at a local office to answer questions, or a company host may be stationed at a desk in the hotel to arrange optional excursions, but you will never have to travel in a group unless you wish to. More and more, even experienced travelers are being won over to the idea of package travel, not only for the convenience and planning time saved, but above all for the money saved. Whatever elements you choose in your package, the organizer has gotten them for you wholesale, and they are prepaid, thus eliminating the dismal prospect of returning to your hotel room each night to subtract the day's disbursements from your remaining cash when you should be enjoying a mai tai on the lanai in peace.

Planning a Trip

123 For most travelers, a week-plus trip can be too expensive for an "I'll take my chances" type of vacation. Hence a little planning is crucial. This is not to suggest that you work out your itinerary in minute detail before you go, but by considering where you want to go, what you want to do, and how much you want to spend, you'll find it much easier to avoid delays, unexpected expenses, and the need to alter your plans because of unforeseen developments.

In thinking out your trip, start with the following basics:

1. How much time will you have to spend?
2. Do you want to visit one, a few, or several different places?
3. During what time of the year do you plan to travel? (It can make a difference in the cost and availability of transportation and accommodations.)
4. How much money do you have to spend on your trip?
5. Do you want an unstructured trip (in which you'll be on your own when you get to your destination) or would you prefer the company and schedule of an escorted tour?

With firm answers to these major questions, start reviewing the literature on the areas in which you're most interested. The mainland offices of the Hawaii Visitors Bureau (see *Tourist Information Offices* for a list of addresses) offer maps, brochures, and advice on the various islands. Other good sources of information are airlines, hotel representatives, and travel agents, who should be well supplied with literature from wholesalers and tour operators who organize packages and other travel arrangements to Hawaii. In other words, up-to-date travel information is plentiful, and you should be able to accumulate everything you want to know about the places you plan to visit and the tours and packages that are available for each (see *Package Tours*).

You can now make almost all of your own travel arrangements if you have the time to follow through with hotels, airlines, tour operators, and so on. But you'll probably save considerable time and energy if you have a travel agent make the reservations and arrangements for you. The agent also should be able to advise you of alternative arrangements of which you may not be aware. Only rarely will a travel agent's services cost a traveler any money, and they may even save you some (see *How to Use a Travel Agent*). Well before departure (depending on how far in advance you make your reservations), the agent will deliver a packet that includes all your tickets and hotel confirmations and often a day-by-day outline of where you'll be when, along with a detailed list of whatever flights you're taking.

Hawaii is said to have the ideal vacation climate: almost invariably warm and breezy. For details on the weather and on what clothes to pack, refer to *How to Pack*. To find out which special events may occur during your stay, consult *When to Go*. And if you are visiting Hawaii for the first time, you'll find it useful to read a bit about the islands' history, food specialties, people, and places of interest (see PERSPECTIVES).

While making vacation arrangements is fun and exciting, don't forget to prepare for your absence from home. Before you leave, attend to these household matters:

1. Arrange for your mail to be forwarded, held by the post office, or picked up at your house daily by a friend or relative. Someone should check your door occasionally to collect any unexpected deliveries. Piles of mail or packages are an announcement to prospective thieves that no one is home.
2. Cancel all deliveries (newspapers, for example).
3. Arrange for your lawn to be mowed at regular intervals.
4. Arrange for the care of pets.
5. Etch your social security number on all appliances (television sets, radios, cameras, kitchen appliances). This considerably reduces their appeal to thieves and facilitates identification.
6. Leave a house key and your itinerary with a friend or relative. Notify the police that you are leaving and tell them who has your key and itinerary.
7. Empty the refrigerator and lower the thermostat.
8. Immediately before leaving, check that all doors, windows, and garage doors are securely locked.

To further discourage thieves, set up several variable timers around the house so that lights (and perhaps even the television set or a radio) go on and off several times in different rooms of the house each night.

Make a list of any valuable items you are carrying with you, including credit card numbers and the serial numbers of your traveler's checks. Put copies in your luggage to facilitate identification in case of loss. Put your name and business address — *but never your home address* — on a label on the exterior of your luggage.

Review your travel documents. If you are traveling by air, check to see that your ticket has been filled in correctly. The left side of the ticket should have a list of each stop you will make even if you are stopping only to change planes, beginning with your departure point. Be sure that the list is correct, and count the number of carbons to see that you have one for each plane you will take. If you have confirmed reservations, be sure that the column marked "status" says "OK" beside each flight. Have in hand vouchers or proof of payment for any reservation for which you've paid in advance; this includes hotels, transfers to and from the airport, sightseeing tours, car rentals, and special events.

How to Pack

 The goal is to remain perfectly comfortable, neat, clean, and adequately fashionable wherever you go, but actually to pack as little as possible. The main obstacle to achieving this end is habit: Most of us wake each morning with an entire wardrobe hanging in our closets, and we assume that our suitcase should offer the same variety and selection. Not so — only our anxiety about being caught short makes us treat a suitcase like a mobile closet. This worry can be eliminated by learning to travel light and by following two firm packing principles:

1. Organize your travel wardrobe around a single color — blue or brown, for example — that allows you to mix and match clothes. Holding firm to one color scheme will make it easy to eliminate items of clothing that don't harmonize, and by picking clothes for their adaptability and compatibility with your basic color, you will put together the widest selection with the fewest pieces of clothing.
2. Use laundries to replenish your wardrobe. Never overpack to ensure a supply of fresh clothing — shirts, blouses, underwear — for each day of a long trip. Businesspeople routinely use hotel laundries to wash and clean clothes. If these are too expensive, opt for local dry cleaners and self-service laundries.

CLIMATE AND CLOTHES: Generally speaking, the weather in the islands is warm and dry from May to October and relatively cooler and wetter from November to March. Temperatures average in the low 80s in summer and the high 70s in winter, usually varying little from day to night. Hawaii is an informal place and calls for a casual style of dress. Clothes should be breezy, comfortable, and lightweight. Although drip-dry fabrics travel best, cotton and cotton blends are most practical in the heat. Prints look fresher longer than solids. If you will be on the move — in an airplane, car, bus, or boat — try to select clothes that do not wrinkle.

For daytime activities, women might pack jeans, shorts, T-shirts, at least two swimsuits, sandals, thongs, or espadrilles. Skirts are a cool choice for touring, as are Hawaiian muumuus, loose-fitting dresses in brightly flowered designs. Aloha shirts, similarly comfortable and brilliantly colored, are the Hawaiian counterpart for men.

For evenings, informal floor- or street-length summer dresses in pastels or prints with a pair of pretty sandals will make a woman feel appropriately attired. A shawl or other light wrap is also a good idea since the trade winds sometimes make nights a bit cool. Few establishments require a man to wear a jacket and tie, but it's best to take them along just in case. Light-colored slacks with a sport shirt usually suffice. If you're planning a number of more formal evenings during your vacation, add two or three changes of clothes.

Finally, prepare for changes in the weather or for atypical temperatures; for instance, if you're going on a day's outing in the mountains, where it is cooler, dress in layers so that as the weather changes you can add or remove clothes as required.

Sundries – Heading for a sunny climate means packing special items so you won't spend your entire vacation horizontal in a hotel room (or hospital) because of sunburn. Be sure to take a sun hat (to protect hair as well as skin), sunscreen, and tanning lotion, which is available in graduated degrees of sunblock corresponding to the level of your skin's sensitivity. (The quantity of sunscreen is indicated by number: the higher the number, the greater the protection.) A good moisturizer is necessary to help keep your skin from drying out and peeling. The best advice is to take the sun's rays in small doses — no more than 20 minutes at a stretch — increasing your sunbathing time as your vacation progresses.

PACKING: A recommended packing procedure is the so-called layer method, designed to get everything into the suitcase and out again with as few wrinkles as possible. Put heavy items on the bottom toward the hinges, so they do not wrinkle other clothes. Candidates for the bottom layer include shoes (stuff them with small items to save space), travel iron, books, toilet kit, handbags, alarm clock, and one or two skirt hangers (hotels usually don't provide them). Fill out this layer with things that will not wrinkle or will be fine if they do, such as socks, stockings, bathing suits, and underwear.

If you get this first, heavy layer as smooth as possible with the fill-ins, you will have a shelf for the next layer of more easily wrinkled items, like slacks, jackets, shirts, dresses, and skirts. These should be buttoned and zipped, then laid along the whole width of the suitcase, with as little folding as possible. When you do need to make a fold, do it on a crease (as with pants), along a seam in the fabric, or in a place where it will not show, such as a shirttail. Alternate each piece of clothing, packing on one side, then the other, to make the layers as flat as possible.

On the top layer, put the things you will need at once: nightclothes, an umbrella, a sweater. With men's two-suiter suitcases, follow the same procedure. Then place jackets on hangers, straighten them out, and leave them unbuttoned. If they are too wide for the suitcase, fold lengthwise down the middle, straighten the shoulders, and fold the sleeves in along the seam.

Some Packing Hints – Some travelers like to have at hand a small bag with the basics for an overnight stay, particularly if they are flying. Always keep necessary medicine, valuable jewelry, and travel or business documents in your purse, briefcase, or carry-on bag, not in the luggage you will check. Tuck a bathing suit into your handbag, too; in case of inter-island delays or lost baggage, it's frustrating to be without one. And whether carried in your overnight bag or checked luggage, cosmetics or other liquids should be packed in plastic bottles or at least wrapped in plastic bags and tied.

Golf clubs may be checked through as luggage (most airlines are accustomed to handling them), but tennis rackets should be carried onto the plane. Aqualung tanks, appropriately packed with padding and depressurized, and surfboards (minus the fin and also padded) may also go as baggage. Snorkeling gear should be packed in a suitcase. Check with the airline before departure to see if there is a specific regulation regarding any special equipment or sporting gear you plan to take.

It is always a good idea to add an empty, flattened airline bag or similar piece of luggage to your suitcase; you'll find it indispensable as a beach bag. Keep in mind, too, that you're likely to do some shopping, and save room for those items.

For more information on packing, ask for Samsonite's free booklet *Getting a Handle on Luggage.* Send a self-addressed, stamped envelope to Samsonite Luggage, 11200 E. 45th Ave., Denver, CO 80239.

How to Use a Travel Agent

 A reliable travel agent remains your best source of service and information for planning a trip, whether you have prepared a specific itinerary and require an agent only to make reservations, or need extensive help in sorting through the maze of air fares, tour offerings, hotel packages, and the score of other elements that may be involved in a trip to Hawaii.

You should know what you want from a travel agent so that you can evaluate what you are getting. It is perfectly reasonable to expect your travel agent to be a thoroughly knowledgeable travel specialist, with information about your destination and, even more crucial, a command of current air fares, ground arrangements, and other wrinkles in the travel scene. Most travel agents work through computer reservations systems (CRS) to assess the availability and rates of flights, hotels, and car rental firms, and can book reservations through the CRS. Despite reports of "computer bias," in which a computer may favor one airline over another, the CRS should provide agents with the entire spectrum of alternative flights to a destination and the complete range of fares in considerably less time than it takes to telephone the airlines individually — and at no charge to the client.

To make the most intelligent use of a travel agent's time and expertise, you should know something of the economics of the industry. As a client, you traditionally pay nothing for the agent's services; with few exceptions, it's all free, from advice on package tours to hotel bookings. Any money that the travel agent makes on the time spent arranging your itinerary — booking hotels, resorts, or flights, or suggesting activities — comes from commissions paid by the suppliers of these services — the airlines, hotels, and so on. These commissions generally run from 8% to 20% of the total cost of the service, although suppliers often reward agencies that sell their services in volume with an increased commission called an override.

Among the few exceptions to the general rule of free service by a travel agency are the agencies beginning to practice *net pricing*. In essence, travel agencies operating this way return all of their commissions and overrides to their customers and make their income instead by charging a flat fee per transaction (thus adding a charge after a reduction has been made). Sometimes, the rebate from the agent arrives later, in the form of a check. Net pricing, however, has become rather controversial since a major airline refused to do business with a leading proponent of net pricing and the courts supported this action (see *Net Fare Sources*).

Net fares and fees are a very recent and not very widespread practice, but even a conventional travel agent may sometimes charge you a fee for such special services as long-distance telephone or cable costs incurred in making a booking, for reserving a room in a place that does not pay a commission (such as a small, out-of-the-way hotel), or for special attention such as planning a highly personalized itinerary. A fee may also be assessed in instances of deeply discounted air fares. In most instances, however, you'll find that travel agents make their time and experience available to you at no charge, and you do not pay more for an airline ticket, package tour, or other product bought from a travel agent than you would for the same product bought directly from the supplier.

The commission system implies two things about your relationship with any travel agent.

1. You will get better service if you arrive at the agent's desk with your basic itinerary already planned. Know roughly where you want to go, what you want to do, and how much you want to spend. Use the agent to make bookings (which pay commissions) and to advise you on facilities, activities, and alternatives within the limits of your basic itinerary. You get the best service when you are requesting commissionable items. Since there are few commissions on camping or driving-camping tours, an agent is unlikely to be very enthusiastic about helping to plan one. The more vague your plans, the less direction you can expect from most agents. So do your homework.
2. Be wary. There is always the danger that an incompetent or unethical agent will send you to a place offering the best commissions rather than the best facilities for your purposes.

You should choose a travel agent with the same care with which you would choose a doctor or lawyer. You will be spending a good deal of money on the basis of the agent's judgment, so you have a right to expect that judgment to be mature, informed, and interested. At the moment, unfortunately, there aren't many standards within the travel agent industry to help you gauge competence, and the quality of individual agents varies enormously. At present, only seven states have registration, licensing, or other form of travel agent–related legislation on their books. Rhode Island licenses travel agents; Florida, Hawaii, and Ohio register them; and California, Illinois, and Washington have laws governing the sale of transportation or related services. While state licensing of agents cannot absolutely guarantee competence, it can at least ensure that an agent has met some minimum requirements. Perhaps the best-prepared agents are those who have completed the CTC Travel Management program offered by the *Institute of Certified Travel Agents* and carry the initials CTC (Certified Travel Counselor) after their names. This indicates a relatively high level of expertise. For a free listing of CTCs in your area, send a self-addressed, stamped, #10 envelope to ICTA,

148 Linden St., Box 82-56, Wellesley, MA 02181 (phone: 617-237-0280). An agent's membership in the *American Society of Travel Agents (ASTA)* can be a useful guideline in selecting a travel agent. But keep in mind that *ASTA* is an industry organization, requiring only that its members be licensed in those states where required; be accredited to represent the suppliers whose products they sell, including airline and cruise tickets; and be adherents to its Principles of Professional Conduct and Ethics code. *ASTA* does not guarantee the competence, ethics, or financial soundness of its members, but it does offer some recourse if you feel you have been dealt with unfairly. Complaints may be registered with *ASTA*, Consumer Affairs Department, PO Box 23992, Washington, DC 20026-3992 (phone: 703-739-2782). You should first try to resolve the complaint directly with the supplier. For a list of *ASTA* members in your area, send a self-addressed, stamped, #10 envelope to ASTA, Public Relations Dept., at the address above. There is also the *Association of Retail Travel Agents (ARTA),* a smaller but highly respected trade organization similar to *ASTA*. Its member agencies and agents similarly agree to abide by a Code of Ethics, and complaints about a member can be made to ARTA's Grievance Committee, 25 S. Riverside Ave., Croton-on-Hudson, NY 10520 (phone: 914-271-HELP). Agencies listed with the *National Association of Cruise Only Agencies (NACOA)* have demonstrated professionalism in the selling of cruises. For a listing of cruise-only agencies in your state (requests are limited to three states), send a self-addressed, stamped envelope to NACOA, PO Box 7209, Freeport, NY 11520. Agencies that belong to a travel consortium, such as *Associated Travel Nationwide* and *Travel Trust International,* have access to preferred rates, as do the huge networks of *American Express* and *Ask Mr. Foster* agencies.

Perhaps the best way to find a travel agent is by word of mouth. If the agent (or agency) has done a good job for your friends over a period of time, it probably indicates a certain level of commitment and concern. Always ask not only for the name of the company, but for the name of the specific agent with whom your friends dealt, for it is that individual who will serve you, and quality can vary widely within a single agency.

Once you've chosen an agent, be entirely candid. Budget considerations rank at the top of the candor list, and there's no sense in wasting the agent's (or your) time poring over itineraries that you know you can't afford. Similarly, if you like a fair degree of comfort, that fact should not be kept secret from your travel agent, who may assume that you wish to travel on a tight budget even when that's not the case.

Hints for Handicapped Travelers

From 35 to 50 million people in the US have some sort of disability, and at least half this number are physically handicapped. Like everyone else today, they — and the uncounted disabled millions around the world — are on the move. More than ever before, they are demanding facilities they can use comfortably, and they are being heard. The travel industry has dramatically improved services to the handicapped in the past few years, and though accessibility is far from universal, it is being brought up to more acceptable standards every day. Those who have chosen to visit Hawaii are in luck, because more and more disabled travelers are returning from this most luscious of destinations bearing tales of ramped Waikiki sidewalks, a style of warm-weather architecture that erects fewer barriers between the indoors and the outdoors, and of sightseeing tours designed especially for them. The island of Oahu, in particular, is rated among the most accessible of the popular vacation spots.

PLANNING A TRIP: Good planning is essential: Collect as much information as you can about your specific disability and about facilities for the disabled in Hawaii, make your travel arrangements well in advance, and specify to all services involved the exact nature of your condition or restricted mobility. The local chapter or national office of the organization that deals with your particular disability — for example, the American Foundation for the Blind or the American Heart Association — will give you the best, most up-to-date information on the subject. In addition, there are some excellent travel-oriented organizations for the disabled to help you plan your trip.

The *Information Center for Individuals with Disabilities, Inc. (ICID),* Fort Point Pl., 1st Floor, 27-43 Wormwood St., Boston, MA 02210-1606 (phone: 617-727-5540/1 or 800-462-5015 in Massachusetts only); both voice and TDD (telecommunications device for the deaf). *ICID* provides information and referral services on disability-related issues and will help you research your trip. The center publishes fact sheets on vacation planning, tour operators, travel agents, and travel resources.

Mobility International/USA (MIUSA), the US branch of *Mobility International,* a nonprofit British-based organization with affiliates in some 35 countries, offers advice and assistance to disabled travelers — including information on accommodations, access guides, and study tours. Among its publications are a quarterly newsletter and a comprehensive sourcebook, *World of Options: A Guide to International Educational Exchange, Community Service, and Travel for Persons with Disabilities.* Individual membership is $20 a year; newsletter subscription only is $10 annually. For more information, contact MIUSA, PO Box 3551, Eugene, OR 97403 (phone: 503-343-1284); voice and TDD (telecommunications device for the deaf).

The *Paralyzed Veterans of America (PVA)* is a national organization that offers information and advocacy services for veterans with spinal cord injuries. *PVA* also sponsors *Access to the Skies,* a program that coordinates the efforts of the national and international air travel industry in providing airport and airplane access for the handicapped. Members also receive several helpful publications as well as regular notification of conferences on subjects of interest to the handicapped traveler. For membership information, contact PVA/ATTS Program, 801 18th St. NW, Washington, DC 20006 (phone: 202-USA-1300).

The *Travel Information Service* at Moss Rehabilitation Hospital is a service designed to help handicapped people plan trips. It cannot make travel arrangements but, for a fee of $5 per package, it will supply information from its files on as many as three cities, countries, or special interests. Write to the Travel Information Service, Moss Rehabilitation Hospital, 12th St. and Tabor Rd., Philadelphia, PA 19141 (phone: 215-456-9600).

To keep abreast of developments in travel for the handicapped, you may want to join the *Society for the Advancement of Travel for the Handicapped (SATH),* a nonprofit organization whose members include travel agents, tour operators, and other travel suppliers as well as consumers. *SATH* publishes a periodic newsletter and can provide information on travel agents and tour operators in the US and overseas who have experience or an interest in travel for the handicapped. Annual membership is $40 ($25 for students and people over 65) and the fee is tax deductible. Send a self-addressed, stamped envelope to SATH, 26 Court St., Penthouse, Brooklyn, NY 11242 (phone: 718-858-5483).

Some excellent general travel guides have been written especially for the handicapped. Louise Weiss's *Access to the World: A Travel Guide for the Handicapped* (Facts on File; $16.95) provides extensive information on transportation and hotels and offers sound tips for the disabled traveler in the US and abroad. Information on Hawaii is scattered throughout various sections. *The Wheelchair Traveler* by Douglass R. Annand (Ball Hill Rd., Milford, NH 03055; phone: 603-673-4539) lists accessible hotels, motels, restaurants, and other sites by state, including the major islands of Hawaii. There is also a travel magazine — *The Itinerary* — for people with disabilities. Published every other month, it includes information on accessibility, listings of tours, and news of adaptive devices, travel aids, and special services as well as numerous general travel hints, and costs $10 a year. To subscribe, write The Itinerary, PO Box 1084, Bayonne, NJ 07002-1084 (phone: 201-858-3400). *SATH* makes available a free 48-page guide, *The United States Welcomes Handicapped Visitors,* that covers transportation, accommodations, insurance, and customs regulations. Send a self-addressed #10 envelope to SATH at the address above, and include $1 for postage.

Specific information on accessibility in Hawaii is contained in an indispensable series of four books, the *Traveler's Guide for the Physically Handicapped* for Oahu, Maui, Kauai, and the Big Island, prepared by the state's Commission on the Handicapped. Each book evaluates hotels, points of interest to tourists, shopping centers, and beach parks, and provides other relevant information for disabled visitors. To order the guides, write to the Commission on the Handicapped, Old Federal Bldg., 335 Merchant St., Room 353, Honolulu, HI 96813 (phone: 808-548-7606). Be sure to specify which book you want, and enclose a self-addressed, stamped envelope.

It should be noted that almost all of the material published with disabled travelers in mind deals with the chairbound traveler, for whom architectural barriers are of prime concern. For travelers with diabetes, a reprint of an article entitled *Your Turn to Fly* is available for 25¢ from the *NY Diabetes Foundation,* 505 8th Ave., New York, NY 10018 (phone: 212-947-9707). For breathing-disabled persons, the pamphlet *Travel for the Patient with Chronic Obstructive Pulmonary Disease* is available for $2 from Dr. Harold Silver, 1601 18th St. NW, Washington, DC 20009 (phone: 202-667-0134). Those who depend on Seeing Eye dogs should note the very strict enforcement of anti-rabies laws in Hawaii. *All* dogs and cats, except those arriving from Australia, New Zealand, or the British Isles, must spend 120 days in quarantine. Even dogs arriving from the mainland US must be quarantined, and Seeing Eye dogs are not exempt.

AIR TRAVEL: Disabled passengers should always make reservations well in advance and should give the airline all relevant details of their condition at that time. These details include information on mobility, toilets, special oxygen needs, and requirements for airline-supplied equipment such as a wheelchair or portable oxygen. Be sure that the person you speak to understands fully the degree of your disability: The more details provided, the more effective the help the airline can give you. On the day before the flight, call back to make sure that all arrangements have been taken care of, and on the day of the flight, arrive early so that you can board before the rest of the passengers. Carry a medical certificate with you, stating your specific disability or the need to carry a particular medicine. (Some airlines require the certificate, and you should find out the rules of the airline you'll be flying well beforehand.)

Because most airports have jetways (corridors connecting the terminal with the door of the plane), a disabled passenger can usually be taken as far as the plane, and sometimes right onto it, in a wheelchair. If not, a narrow boarding chair may be used to take you to your seat. Your own wheelchair, which will be folded and put in the baggage compartment, should be tagged as escort luggage to ensure that it's available at planeside upon landing rather than in the baggage claim area. Travel is not quite as simple if your wheelchair is battery-operated: Unless it has non-spillable batteries, it might not be accepted on board, and you will have to check with the airline ahead of time to find out how the batteries and the chair should be packaged for the flight.

Passengers who use oxygen may not use their personal supply in the cabin, though it may be carried on the plane as cargo when properly packed and labeled. If you will need oxygen during the flight, the airline will supply it to you (there is a charge) provided you have given advance notice — 24 hours to a few days, depending on the carrier.

Several airlines now have booklets describing procedures for accommodating the handicapped on their flights. Among the carriers to Hawaii, United Airlines has a list of travel tips for the handicapped; contact United Airlines, Consumer Affairs Department, PO Box 66100, Chicago, IL 60666. Useful information on every stage of air travel, from planning to arrival, is provided in the booklet *Incapacitated Passengers Air Travel Guide.* To receive a free copy, write to Senior Manager, Passenger Services, International Air Transport Association, 2000 Peel St., Montréal, Québec H3A 2R4 Canada (phone: 514-844-6311). For an access guide to 519 airports in 62 countries, write for *Access Travel,* from the Consumer Information Center, Dept. 570V, Pueblo, CO 81009. The free guide is published by the *Airport Operators Council International* and includes detailed information on the Honolulu, Hilo, Kailua-Kona, Kahului, Lihue, Lanai, and Molokai airports in Hawaii. *Air Transportation of Handicapped Persons* explains the general guidelines that govern air carrier policies. It is available free when requested in writing: Ask for Free Advisory Circular #120-32 from the Distribution Unit, US Department of Transportation, Utilization and Storage Section, M-443.2, Washington, DC 20590). For speedy service, enclose a self-addressed mailing label with your request.

The following airlines have TDD toll-free lines for the hearing-impaired: American (phone: 800-543-1586; in Ohio, 800-582-1573); Eastern (phone: 800-325-3553); Pan American (phone: 800-722-3323); Piedmont (phone: 800-334-5874); TWA (phone: 800-421-8480; in California, 800-252-0622); and United (phone: 800-323-0170; in Illinois, 800-942-8819).

GROUND TRANSPORTATION: Perhaps the simplest solution to getting around Hawaii is to travel with an able-bodied companion who can drive. Competition is fierce among rental car companies, and prices are as low as you'll find anywhere in the nation. If you are accustomed to driving your own hand-controlled car and want to rent one in the islands, you are in luck. Both *Avis* and *Hertz* will fit cars with hand controls. *Avis,* with offices on Oahu, Maui, Hawaii, Kauai, and Molokai, can convert a car to hand controls with as little as 24 hours notice, though it's a good idea to arrange for one earlier (phone: 800-331-1212). *Hertz*'s offices are on Oahu, Maui, Hawaii, and Kauai; they require a minimum of 5 days to install the controls, and make the additional stipulation that the car be returned to the office from which it was rented (phone: 800-654-3131). Neither company charges extra for hand controls, but both will fit them only on a full-size car, and both request that you bring your handicapped driver's permit with you.

Taking taxis or hiring a chauffeur-driven car are other solutions to the mobility problem. In addition, on Oahu there are the vans of Honolulu's *Handicabs of the Pacific, Inc.,* a unique taxi and tour company especially for people in wheelchairs. Handicabs provides transfers between the airport and hotels and performs all the usual services of a regular taxi company, except that in this case, you must call for the cab 24 hours in advance. The vans can be hired by the hour, too, for group charters of up to four passengers in wheelchairs and four ambulatory passengers per vehicle. The company also offers six sightseeing tours: a half-day city tour, an all-day or a half-day circle tour of the island including Sea Life Park, a full day at the Polynesian Cultural Center, a Pearl Harbor cruise, and a dinner cruise. For a flier describing services and prices, write to Handicabs of the Pacific, Inc., PO Box 22428, Honolulu, HI 96822 (phone: 808-524-3866).

Honolulu has another unusual institution, the city- and county-subsidized *Handi-Van,* which provides curb-to-curb service at $2 per round trip for those unable to use the regular bus (again, with 24 hours notice). It is not designed for the tourist, but you may use it if you have a Handi-Van pass. For particulars on how to obtain one, write MTL, Inc., Handicapped Bus Pass Program, 1133 Alapai St., Honolulu, HI 96813 (phone: 808-531-7066). The Handi-Van Pass is also good on regular city buses.

TOURS: The following travel agencies or tour operators specialize in making group or individual arrangements for travelers with physical or other disabilities, and all have either offered Hawaiian tours in the past or included the islands in trips to other destinations. Because of the requirements of handicapped travel, however, the same packages may not be offered regularly. Programs designed for the physically impaired are run by specialists who have researched hotels, restaurants, and places of interest to be sure they present no insurmountable obstacles.

Accessible Tours/Directions Unlimited, 720 N. Bedford Rd., Bedford Hills, NY 10507 (phone: 914-241-1700 in New York State; 800-533-5343 elsewhere). Arranges group or individual tours for disabled persons traveling in the company of able-bodied friends or family members. Accepts the unaccompanied traveler if completely self-sufficient.

Evergreen Travel Service, 19505 L, 44th Ave. W., Lynnwood, WA 98036 (phone: 206-776-1184; 800-562-9298 from Washington State; 800-435-2288 elsewhere). Handles cruises, group tours, sports programs, and individual arrangements for the physically disabled and the blind.

Flying Wheels Travel, 143 W. Bridge St., Box 382, Owatonna, MN 55060 (phone: 507-451-5005; 800-533-0363). Handles both tours and individual arrangements.

The Guided Tour, 555 Ashbourne Rd., Elkins Park, PA 19117 (phone: 215-782-1370). Arranges tours for persons with developmental and learning disabilities, and sponsors separate tours for members of the same population who are also physically disabled or who simply need a slower pace.

Handi-Travel, First National Travel Corporation, 300 John St., Thorn Hill, Ontario L3T 5W4, Canada (phone: 416-731-4714). Handles tours and individual arrangements.

InterpreTours, Ask Mr. Foster, 16660 Ventura Blvd., Encino, CA 91436 (phone: 818-788-4118; TTY: 818-788-4515). Arranges one group tour per year for the deaf, with an interpreter as tour guide.

Travel Horizons Unlimited, 11 E. 44th St., New York, NY 10017 (phone: 212-687-5121). Arranges cruises, tours, and independent travel for those who require hemodialysis.

Whole Person Tours, PO Box 1084, Bayonne, NJ 07002-1084 (phone: 201-858-3400). Publishers of *The Itinerary,* this agency also produces a brochure highlighting its various tours for the disabled. To get a copy, write to the address above and include first class return postage.

Hints for Single Travelers

Just about the last trip in human history in which the participants were neatly paired was the voyage of Noah's Ark. Ever since, passenger lists and tour groups have reflected the same kind of asymmetry that occurs in real life, as countless individuals set forth to see the world unaccompanied (or unencumbered, depending on your outlook) by spouse, lover, friend, or relative.

There are some things to be said for traveling alone. There is the pleasure of privacy, though a solitary traveler must be self-reliant, independent, and responsible. Unfortunately, traveling alone can also turn the traveler into a second class citizen.

The truth is that the travel industry is not very fair to people who vacation by themselves. Most travel bargains, including package tours, hotel accommodations, resort packages, and cruises, are based on *double-occupancy* rates. This means that the per-person price is offered on the basis of two people traveling together and sharing a double room. For exactly the same package, the single traveler will have to pay a surcharge, called the "single supplement," which can add 30% to 55% to the basic per-person rate.

If you prefer to have your accommodations taken care of for you, a number of tour operators cater solely to the single vacationer. Enterprising travel agents and other organizations have created travel clubs and tours, which charge minimal membership fees, for single people of every age. The basic service offered by all is the same: to match the unattached person with a compatible travel mate. The better established among these agencies are:

Grand Circle Travel: Arranges escorted Hawaii cruise/air packages for "mature" travelers, including singles. Membership, which is automatic when you book a trip through *Grand Circle,* includes a free subscription to its quarterly magazine, discount certificates on future trips, and other extras. 347 Congress St., Boston, MA 02210 (phone: in Boston, 617-350-7500; elsewhere, 800-221-2610).

Saga International Holidays, Ltd.: An organization for seniors over 60, including singles. 120 Boylston St., Boston, MA 02116 (phone: 800-343-0273).

Singleworld: About two-thirds of this agency's clientele are under 35, and about half this number are women, but *Singleworld* organizes tours and cruises with departures categorized by age group. There is a $20 annual membership fee. 401 Theodore Fremd Ave., Rye, NY 10580 (phone: 914-967-3334; 800-223-6490 in the continental US).

Travel Companion Exchange: Every 8 weeks this company publishes a directory of singles looking for traveling companions and provides members with full-page profiles of likely partners. Membership fees range from $3 to $11 per month (with a 6-month minimum enrollment) depending on the level of service needed. PO Box 833, Amityville, NY 11701 (phone: 516-454-0880).

Write to *Bed & Breakfast Hawaii* (PO Box 449, Kapaa, HI 96746; phone: 808-822-7771) for a directory listing bed-and-breakfast establishments on Oahu, Maui, Kauai, Molokai, Hawaii, and Lanai, together with information on how to reserve. The directory costs $8, including postage. Though a single person will likely pay more than half of the rate quoted for a couple even at a bed-and-breakfast home, the prices are still quite reasonable, and the cozy atmosphere will make you feel less conspicuously alone. (See *Accommodations* in this section.)

A special guidebook for solo travelers, prepared by Eleanor Adams Baxel, offers information on how to avoid paying supplementary charges, how to pick the right travel agent, how to calculate costs, and more. Called *A Guide for Solo Travelers Abroad,* it's out of print but may be available in your public library. The publisher was the Berkshire Traveller Press.

Two specific groups of single travelers deserve special mention: women and students. Countless women travel by themselves, and such an adventure need not be feared. You will generally find people very courteous and welcoming, but remember that, as elsewhere in the US, crime does exist in Hawaii and not just in Honolulu. Keep a careful eye on your belongings while on the beach; lock your car and hotel doors; deposit your valuables in the hotel's safe; and don't hitchhike.

One lingering inhibition many female travelers still harbor is that of eating alone in public places. The trick here is to relax and enjoy your meal and surroundings; while you may run across the occasional unenlightened waiter, solo diners are no longer an uncommon sight or scorned.

For students traveling to Hawaii on a strict budget, there are few accommodation options. In the whole state, there are two *American Youth Hostel Association (AYHA)* hostels: both in Honolulu. The main one will accommodate members of both *AYHA* and the International Youth Hostel Federation for a nightly fee of $7.50. They guarantee members a 3-night stay, which can be extended if there is room. But because it is in Honolulu and very popular, there often isn't a room available, so reservations are highly recommended (write-in reservations that include a deposit of one night's fee will be held until 11 PM). Contact the *Honolulu International Youth Hostel,* 2323A Seaview Ave., Honolulu, HI 96822 (phone: 808-946-0591). Non-members can stay here on a night-by-night basis for $11 per night, and it is also possible to obtain an *AYHA* membership card here. Recognized internationally at 5,000 hostels, these cards are also available at low cost from American Youth Hostels, Inc., PO Box 37613, Washington, DC 20013-7613 (phone: 202-783-6161). The cost of membership in *AYHA* varies, depending on the type of membership and age category, but generally annual fees are $10 for Youth memberships (17 and under), $20 for Adult (18-54), and $10 for Senior (55 and up). A $1 mailing charge should be added to each membership fee cited above.

The other *AYHA* hostel in Honolulu, the *Hale Aloha Hostel,* is open to *AYHA* members only. Here the nightly rate is $9.50, guests are guaranteed up to a 3-night stay, with extensions possible when space permits, and reservations are highly recommended. Contact the hostel at 2417 Prince Edward St., Honolulu, HI (phone: 808-926-8313). At the *Kona Lodge and Hotel* in Honalo on the Big Island, *AYHA* members are given a special nightly rate of $8. Contact them at PO Box 645, Kealakekau, HI 96750 (phone: 808-322-9056 or 808-322-8136). The *YMCA*-affiliated *Camp Keanae,* on Maui, has accommodations in cabins open to members and non-members for $5 and $6 a night, respectively. You can make reservations by writing to the Maui YMCA, PO Box 820, Wailuku, HI 96793 (phone: 808-248-8355).

Honolulu also has a *YWCA* and several *YMCA* residences. The *YWCA Fernhurst Residence* (1566 Wilder Ave., Honolulu, HI 96822; phone: 808-941-2231), for women only, is midway between downtown Honolulu and Waikiki, and has double rooms joined to one another by shared baths as well as a few singles, at daily and weekly rates. At the time of writing, the daily rate was $20 for a double room and $25 for a single for members, $23 and $28 for non-members, which included breakfast and dinner (except on Sundays and certain holidays). Note that *YWCA* membership is required for stays exceeding 3 nights. The residence has an outdoor swimming pool, and though the doors are locked at 11 PM for security reasons, the night watchman will let you in later. A reservation can be made at Fernhurst Residence by writing and enclosing a deposit equivalent to 1 day's fee in the form of a money order.

There are two *YMCA* residences for men only: the *Central Branch,* just outside Waikiki (401 Atkinson Dr., Honolulu, HI 96814; phone: 808-941-3344), and the *Nuuanu Branch,* in downtown Honolulu (1441 Pali Hwy., Honolulu, HI 96813; phone: 808-536-3556). Both have outdoor pools; only the Nuuanu Branch accepts reservations (with 1 night's lodging as deposit). The Central Branch has single rooms with private bath at $23 a night (or $33 when a cot is requested for a double), and singles and doubles using communal showers are available for less. The Nuuanu Branch has singles only at $27 a night with private bath (there are two) and at $22 a night with use of the communal showers.

The *Atherton Branch YMCA* (1810 University Ave., Honolulu, HI 96822; phone: 808-946-0253), generally open only to students at the nearby University of Hawaii at Manoa, will take non-student visitors during summer. Rates change frequently, so it's best to call for information.

Travelers who are (or have been) students of accredited colleges and universities elsewhere might consider taking some courses at the *University of Hawaii at Manoa.* The university gives two 6-week summer sessions, and anyone enrolled in a course carrying 3 or more credit hours qualifies for campus housing. Least expensive are the residence halls, where rooms are shared and meal plans mandatory (single rooms are also available). Double rooms in apartments on the university grounds cost more, but meal plans aren't required. Summer semester bulletins go out in February and, in addition to curriculum listings, the summer activities program for students is announced. For more information and application forms, write: Summer Session Office, University of Hawaii at Manoa, 2500 Dole St., Krauss Hall 101, Honolulu, HI 96822 (phone: 808-948-7221).

Considering Hawaii's year-round warm temperatures, one of the most inexpensive accommodations could be your own tent. Campsites are plentiful everywhere on the islands; see *Camping,* in this section.

Hints for Older Travelers

Special package deals and more free time are just two factors that have given Americans over age 65 a chance to see the world at affordable prices. Senior citizens make up an ever-growing segment of the travel population, and the trend among them is to travel more frequently and for longer periods of time. Retired travelers are also in a particularly good position to take advantage of off-season travel, thereby avoiding crowds and escaping higher prices. Although Hawaii — unlike most resort areas — has no distinct seasons, summer and the period between Christmas and Easter are very busy, with hotel rooms commanding higher prices than at other times of the year. Right before or right after these periods — during April, May, October, and November — there's still plenty of good weather and often lower rates.

An excellent book to read before embarking on any trip is Rosalind Massow's *Travel Easy: The Practical Guide for People Over 50,* available for $8.95 (plus $1.75 postage and handling per order, not per book) from AARP Books, c/o Scott, Foresman, 1865 Miner St., Des Plaines, IL 60016 (phone: 202-728-4313 or 800-238-2300). It discusses a host of travel-related subjects, from choosing a destination to getting set for departure, with chapters on transportation options, tours, cruises, avoiding health problems, and handling dental emergencies en route. Another book, *The International Health Guide for Senior Citizens,* covers such topics as trip preparations, food and water precautions, adjusting to weather and climate conditions, finding a doctor overseas, motion sickness, and jet lag. The book also discusses specific health and travel problems, and includes a list of resource organizations that can provide medical assistance for travelers. The book is available for $4.95 postpaid from Pilot Books, 103 Cooper St., Babylon, NY 11702 (phone: 516-422-2225).

HEALTH: Be sure to take along any prescription medication you need, enough to last *without a new prescription* for the duration of your trip; pack all medications separately in a carry-on bag in case your luggage is lost or detoured, along with a note from your doctor for the benefit of airport authorities. It is also wise to bring a few common nonprescription over-the-counter medications with you: aspirin and something for stomach upset may come in handy. Keep in mind that Medicare coverage operates nationwide, and will be honored by hospitals and doctors all over Hawaii. If you have specific medical problems, bring prescriptions and a "medical file" composed of:

1. A summary of medical history, current diagnosis.
2. A list of drugs to which you are allergic.
3. Your most recent electrocardiogram, if you have heart problems.
4. Your doctor's name, address, and telephone number.

A word of caution: Don't overdo it. Allow time for some relaxing each day to refresh yourself for the next scheduled sightseeing event. Traveling across time zones can be exhausting. Plan on spending at least one full day resting before you start touring. If you're part of a group tour, be sure to check the planned itinerary thoroughly. Some package deals sound wonderful because they include all the places you've ever dreamed of visiting. In fact, they can become so hectic and tiring that you'll be reaching for a pillow instead of your camera.

DISCOUNTS AND PACKAGES: Many hotel and motel chains, airlines, car rental companies, bus lines, and other travel suppliers offer discounts to older travelers. Some of these discounts, however, are extended only to bona fide members of certain senior citizens organizations. Because the same organizations offer package tours to both domestic and international destinations, the benefits of membership are twofold. Those who join can take advantage of discounts as individual travelers and also reap the savings that group travel affords. In addition, because the age requirements for some of these organizations are quite low (or nonexistent), the benefits can begin to accrue early. Among the organizations dedicated to helping you see the world are:

> *American Association of Retired Persons:* Travel programs designed exclusively for *AARP* members cover the globe and include a broad range of escorted tours, hosted tours, and cruises in Hawaii. Membership is open to anyone age 50 or older, whether retired or not. Dues are $5 a year, or $12.50 for 3 years, and include spouse. For membership information, contact the AARP at 1909 K St. NW, Washington, DC 20049 (phone: 202-347-8800); for travel information and reservations, contact the *AARP Travel Service,* PO Box 29233, Los Angeles, CA 90009 (phone: 800-227-7737).

> *Mature Outlook:* This organization has replaced the *National Association of Mature People.* Through its *Travel Alert,* last-minute tours, cruises, and other vacation packages are available to members at special savings. Hotel and car rental discounts and travel accident insurance are also available. Membership is open to anyone 50 years of age or older, and costs $9.95 a year for individuals or couples. Mature Outlook Customer Service Office, 6001 N. Clark St., Chicago, IL 60660-997 (phone: 800-336-6330).

> *National Council of Senior Citizens:* Here, too, the roster of tours is different each year, but the emphasis is always on keeping costs low. Although most members are over 50, membership is open to anyone, regardless of age, for an annual fee of $12 per person or $16 per couple. 925 15th St. NW, Washington, DC 20005 (phone: 202-347-8800).

Many tour operators specialize in group travel for older travelers. For example, *Gadabout Tours,* operated by Lois Anderson, runs monthly (except January, February, and March) 10-day, 4-island tours visiting parts of Hawaii, Maui, Kauai, and Oahu. For further information, write to Gadabout Tours, 700 E. Tahquitz Way, Palm Springs, CA 92262 (phone: 619-325-5556; 800-952-5068, except California; 800-521-7309 in California). *Grand Circle Travel* and *Saga International Holidays* are two other such operators that cater to the over-50 market (see *Hints for Single Travelers*).

Senior citizens get a small discount on *Aloha Airlines* and *Hawaiian Airlines* flights. On Oahu, *TheBus* is free for those over 65 who obtain a special pass from the *MTL, Inc.,* office (725 Kapiolani Blvd., Honolulu, HI 96813; phone: 808-531-7066). Application must be made in person, and you must present proof of age.

Hints for Traveling with Children

 What better way to be receptive to new experiences than to take along the young, wide-eyed members of your family? Their company does not have to be a burden or their presence an excessive expense. The current generation of discounts for children and family package deals can make a trip together quite reasonable.

A family trip will be an investment in your children's future, making geography and history come alive to them and leaving a sure memory that will be among the fondest you will share with them someday. Their insights will be refreshing to you; their impulses may take you to unexpected places with unexpected dividends. The experience will be invaluable to them at any age.

Here are several hints for making a trip with children easy and fun.

1. Using maps, travel magazines, and travel books, give children a clear idea of where you are going and how far away it is. Part of the excitement of the journey will be associating the tiny dots on the map with the very real places the children visit a few weeks later. You can show them pictures of streets and scenes in which they will stand within a month. Don't shirk history lessons, but don't burden them with dates. Make history light, anecdotal, pertinent, but most of all, fun. Children will also enjoy learning some Hawaiian phrases, and it's a good idea to familiarize them with the flora, fauna, and sea life they will encounter. Some plants — oleanders, for example — are poisonous if ingested, and your family should be aware of what they look like. If someone inadvertently swallows a dangerous substance, call the *Hawaii Poison Center* at the Kapiolani Children's Medical Center: 941-4411 in Honolulu or 800-362-3585 from all neighbor islands.

2. Children should help plan the itinerary, and where you go and what you do should reflect some of their ideas. If they know enough about Hawaiian sites beforehand, they will have the excitement of recognition when they arrive and the illumination of seeing how something is or is not the way they expected it to be.

3. Give children specific responsibilities. The job of carrying their own flight bags and looking after their personal things, along with some other light travel chores, will give them a stake in the journey.

Further helpful hints for parents are offered in the informative newsletter, *Family Travel Times,* published by *Travel With Your Children,* which focuses on the child traveler. Membership is $35 a year. For a sample copy of the newsletter, send $1 to Travel With Your Children, 80 Eighth Ave., New York, NY 10011 (phone: 212-206-0688).

HEALTH AND COMFORT: Choose your own and your children's clothes wisely to avoid excess baggage. Take only drip-dry, wrinkle-resistant items, comfortable shoes — sneakers or sandals — and a sweater for cool evenings. If you plan to visit one of the islands' volcanoes or to do some camping, a warmer wardrobe is necessary. (See *How to Pack* for more on the proper clothing.) Take along as many handy snacks as you can squeeze into the corners of your suitcase. These should include things like raisins, nuts, hard candies, and crackers. A thermos is also a helpful item if you anticipate day-long outings.

In addition, pack a special medical kit that's compact enough to take to the beach. Coral cuts and jellyfish stings are just a few of the hazards of swimming in tropical waters, and it's always wise to be prepared for minor emergencies. (Water safety is covered thoroughly in *Staying Healthy.*) Have your children choose a few favorite toys to accompany them. Pens, crayons, and paper take up the least amount of room. You might also encourage them to draw what they see around them or to keep a diary of their vacation. Anything you can do to help them assimilate their new surroundings will increase their enjoyment.

It's important to help your family adjust to the new time zone so that everyone stays healthy and in good spirits. During the first few days in Hawaii, plan early morning activities — watch the sun rise, go fishing, or take a swim before breakfast. Waking up and going to bed earlier at the beginning of the trip will quickly attune everyone's body clock.

ACCOMMODATIONS: Often a cot will be placed in a hotel room at little or no extra charge; some places do not charge for children under a certain age. Special rates are sometimes available for families in adjoining rooms.

The many resort condominium apartments available for rent in Hawaii provide excellent accommodations for families. The apartment becomes a "home away from home" and a considerable sum can be saved by preparing meals yourself rather than taking the entire crew out to restaurants three times a day. In addition, many complexes do not charge for children under 12 years old, and a few permit anyone under 18 to stay with their families for free. (Some condos don't allow children, so before you set your heart on a particular one, find out all the details of its rental policy.) Many of the condominium vacation packages include a rental car; these combination deals can be quite economical. If your family won't fit into the standard compact car offered, a few dollars more per day will usually buy a larger model. Hotels and condominium complexes can also recommend babysitters, and some, like the *Mauna Kea Beach* hotel on the Big Island, have activities programs especially for children. For more information, see *Accommodations.*

If you'd like a few moments to yourself, consider one of the many boarding or day camps in Hawaii that are open to nonresident children. Be sure to choose one accredited by the *American Camping Association,* which supervises children's camps throughout the country. *ACA* inspectors periodically visit camps to check on the overall maintenance of the property; the safety of the activities; the purity of the water supply; the cleanliness of the food preparation facilities; the quality of sleeping areas and infirmaries; and the professionalism of the camp's personnel. The *ACA* publishes *Guide to Accredited Camps,* which covers the whole country, including Hawaii. It can be ordered from the Publications Dept., American Camping Association, 5000 State Road 67 N, Bradford Woods, Martinsville, IN 46151 (phone: 317-342-8456; 800-428-CAMP). The 1989 edition costs $9.95. The association accepts telephone orders from people who wish to charge the book to their Visa or MasterCard accounts.

AIR TRAVEL: Generally, infants under 2 years of age travel with an adult for free if they don't occupy a seat. (A second infant without a second adult would pay the fare applicable to children 2 through 11, usually 75% of the adult fare.) Some of the inter-island carriers, including the small commuter lines, have reduced fares for children from 2 through 11, averaging about 20% to 30% off the regular fare.

Avoid night flights. Since you probably won't sleep nearly as well as your kids, you risk an impossible first day at your destination, groggily taking care of your rested, energetic children. Nap time is, however, a good time to travel, especially for babies, and try to travel during off-hours, when there are apt to be extra seats. When the plane lands and takes off, make sure your baby has a bottle, pacifier, or thumb in his or her mouth. This sucking will make the child swallow and clear stopped ears. For a small child, a piece of hard candy will do the same thing. Newborn babies, whose lungs may not be able to adjust to the altitude, should not be taken aboard an airplane.

Just as you would request a vegetarian or kosher meal, you are entitled to ask for a hot dog or hamburger in lieu of the airline's regular dinner if you give at least 24 hours' notice. Some, but not all, airlines have baby food aboard. While you should bring along toys from home, you can also ask about children's diversions. Some carriers, such as United, have terrific free packages of games, coloring books, and puzzles.

■ **Note:** Newborn babies, whose lungs may not be able to adjust to the altitude, should not be taken aboard an airplane. And some airlines may refuse to allow a pregnant woman in her 8th or 9th month aboard, for fear that something could go wrong with an in-flight birth. Check with the airline ahead of time and carry a letter from your doctor stating that you are fit to travel and indicating the estimated date of birth.

Hints for Traveling with Pets

You may wish to bring your pet along on your vacation in Hawaii. The rules vary, depending on the type of animal. Most stringent are those regarding the importation of dogs and cats from the mainland.

DOGS AND CATS: Hawaii strictly enforces its anti-rabies laws. Therefore, all dogs and cats (except those coming from Australia, New Zealand, and Great Britain) must be quarantined for 120 days. This includes dogs and cats from the mainland and even Seeing Eye dogs. The animals are kept at the Animal Quarantine Station, US Dept. of Agriculture, 99-770 Moanalua Rd., Aiea, HI 96701 (phone: 808-488-8462). There is also an Animal Quarantine Substation at Honolulu Airport (phone: 808-836-3228). Quarantine fees are $466 for dogs, $412 for cats. Also, you must bring a valid interstate health certificate from the pet's state of origin, signed by an accredited physician and dated no more than 10 days prior to shipping. You can obtain this form at your pet's veterinary office.

According to Hawaiian Dept. of Agriculture authorities, you won't require any special permits to bring your dog or cat — or even a dog or cat you purchased on the Hawaiian Islands — back to the mainland.

BIRDS: Many birds, including cockatiels, parakeets, and canaries, can be brought into Hawaii. But to do so, you need a special entry permit and a valid interstate health certificate signed by an accredited veterinarian and dated no more than 10 days prior to shipping. The latter form is available directly from your bird's veterinarian; the former, by contacting the Plant Quarantine Branch, US Dept. of Agriculture, 701 Ilalo St., Honolulu, HI 96804 (phone: 808-548-7175). There's also a Plant Quarantine Branch at the Honolulu Airport (phone: 808-836-3827). Some birds, such as lories, are prohibited from entering Hawaii. Call a Plant Quarantine Branch for details.

If you'd like to bring a bird back to the mainland from Hawaii, check with your home state's Dept. of Agriculture. Some states have rules against bringing in certain types of birds — usually those that may jeopardize the future of local crops.

OTHER ANIMALS: Turtles and guinea pigs may be brought into Hawaii, provided they are accompanied with the same papers required for importing birds (see above for details). Hamsters and gerbils, however, are prohibited, as are such harmful creatures as alligators, snapping turtles, and coyotes.

BY PLANE AND CAR: Many airlines require a health certificate for your pet. United, for example, requires that interstate health certificates be signed by an accredited veterinarian and dated no more than 30 days before travel. Check with your air carrier well in advance of your departure.

It's a good idea to buy a traveling kennel if your dog is being transported by plane or car. Most airlines sell them, as do pet stores. Any animal must be boxed for the plane trip; on a car trip a kennel is a good safety measure. The most important features of a kennel are size, comfort, and cleanliness. Your kennel should be large enough to permit room for your pet to walk around, turn around, and lie down; it should be constructed completely of non-chewable materials — metal or high-grade plastic. Chewable materials such as cardboard or fiberboard can be toxic. The kennel should have a sanitized pad on the bottom with a wire mesh floor that is raised at least 1 inch above the pad. The box should lock, be thoroughly ventilated, and be easy to handle and transport.

If your pet is traveling by plane, label the kennel with your name, address, destination, pet's name, and special handling instructions. Remove the animal's collar before putting it in the kennel. Dogs should not be muzzled. Put a few toys and familiar objects in the kennel to acquaint the animal with its box before the start of the trip.

Airlines will usually allow one kenneled pet to fly in the passenger compartment for a standard fee, if the kennel fits underneath the seat. This space should be reserved when you reserve your own seat. If there is no space in the passenger compartment, or the animal is too large to be brought in, it must fly as cargo, in a special area reserved for live cargo. Charges are established on the basis of weight and size of the animal.

Don't ship your pet during very hot or very cold weather; animals are sometimes left on the runway during the loading of the hold. Afternoon and evening flights are best in hot weather. Fly in off-peak times, when the cargo hold has less baggage and more ventilation and the personnel have more time to watch your pet. Pets should be the last cargo loaded, and the boxed pet should be given to the cargo officer, not to the ticket-counter person, who will place the kennel on a conveyor belt. Avoid flights with stopovers and transfers lest your pet be misplaced.

When you land, retrieve your pet as soon as possible. Return it to its normal feeding schedule slowly.

If you decide to drive with an animal, be aware that animals can suffer motion sickness. You can ascertain if your pet is susceptible by taking it for short trips before you undertake the real journey. Here are a few tips to make your trip with your pet as much fun as possible:

1. Bring along a kennel or sleeping box for dog or cat.
2. Make plenty of exercise and feeding stops. *You* may want to set a new record for the distance — your pet does not.
3. Take along some of your pet's toys or most adored objects.
4. Don't let your dog ride with its head out of the window. There are cinders, dirt, and rocks that can injure its eyes and head, and the wind can irritate its nasal and respiratory passages. Keep the windows almost closed, allowing enough ventilation for comfort.
5. If you have to leave your pet alone in the car, park in the shade and leave the windows down an inch or two for air. But don't leave the car unlocked. Hawaiians like dogs, too.

But it is best to leave your pet at home. That way you won't miss the thrill of finding out how glad it is to see you when you get back.

Insurance

 It is unfortunate that most decisions to buy travel insurance are impulsive and are usually made without any real consideration of the traveler's existing policies. Too often the result is the purchase of needlessly expensive short-term policies that duplicate existing coverage and reinforce the tendency to buy coverage on a trip-by-trip basis rather than to work out a total and continuing travel insurance package that might well be more effective and economical.

Therefore, the first person with whom you should discuss travel insurance is your own insurance broker, not a travel agent or the clerk behind the airport insurance counter. You may well discover that the insurance you already carry — homeowner's policies and/or accident, health, and life insurance — protects you adequately while you travel, and that your real needs are in the more mundane areas of excess value insurance for baggage or trip cancellation insurance.

To make insurance decisions intelligently, however, you should first understand the basic categories of travel insurance and what they are designed to cover. Then you can decide what you should have in the broader context of your personal insurance needs, and you can choose the most economical way of getting the desired protection: through riders on existing policies; with one-time short-term policies; through a special program put together for the frequent traveler; through coverage that's part of a travel club's benefits; or with a combination policy sold by insurance companies through brokers, tour operators, and travel agents.

There are six basic categories of travel insurance:

1. Baggage and personal effects insurance
2. Personal accident and sickness insurance
3. Trip cancellation and interruption insurance
4. Default and/or bankruptcy insurance
5. Flight insurance (to cover death or injury)
6. Automobile insurance (for driving your own or a rented car)
7. Combination policies

BAGGAGE AND PERSONAL EFFECTS INSURANCE: If baggage and personal effects are included in your current homeowner's policy, check with your broker about the necessity for a special floater to cover you for the duration of a trip. The object is to protect your bags and their contents in case of damage or theft anytime during your travels, not just while you're in flight and covered by the airline's policy. Furthermore, only limited protection is provided by the airline. Baggage liability varies from carrier to carrier, but generally speaking, for domestic air travel, luggage is insured to $1,250 — that's per *passenger,* not per *bag.* On international flights, the liability limit is $9.07 per pound of baggage (which comes to about $360 per 40-pound suitcase), and $400 per passenger on unchecked baggage. These limits should be specified on your airline ticket, but to be awarded even this amount, you'll have to provide an itemized list of lost property, and if you're including new and/or expensive items, be prepared for a request that you back up your claim with sales receipts or other proofs of purchase.

If you are carrying goods worth more than the maximum protection offered by the airline, you should consider excess value insurance, available from the airlines at an average, currently, of $1 per $100 worth of coverage. This insurance can be purchased at the airline counter when you check in, though you should arrive early to fill out the necessary forms and to avoid holding up other passengers checking in. Excess value insurance is also included in some of the combination travel insurance policies discussed below.

■ **A note of warning:** Be sure to read the fine print of any excess value insurance policy; there are often specific exclusions, such as cash, tickets, furs, gold and silver objects, art, and antiques. And remember that insurance companies ordinarily will pay only the depreciated value of the goods, not their replacement value. The best way to protect the items you're carrying in your luggage is to take photos of your valuables, and keep a record of the serial numbers of such items as cameras, typewriters, radios, and so on. This will establish that you do, indeed, own the objects. If your luggage disappears en route or is damaged, deal with the situation immediately, at the airport or bus station. If an airline loses your luggage, you will be asked to fill out a Property Irregularity Report before you leave the airport. If your property disappears elsewhere, report it to the police at once.

PERSONAL ACCIDENT AND SICKNESS INSURANCE: This covers you in case of illness on the road (hospital and doctor's expenses, lost income, and so on). In most cases it is a standard part of existing health insurance policies, though you should check with your broker to be sure that your policy will pay for any medical expenses incurred.

TRIP CANCELLATION AND INTERRUPTION INSURANCE: Most package tours, cruises, and charter flights require full payment a substantial period of time before departure. Although cancellation penalties vary (they are listed in the fine print in every tour brochure, and before you purchase a package tour you should know exactly what they are), rarely will a passenger get more than 50% of this money back if forced to cancel within a few weeks of leaving. Therefore, if you book a package tour or charter flight, you should have trip cancellation insurance to guarantee full reimbursement or refund should you, a traveling companion, or a member of your immediate family get sick, forcing you to cancel your trip or *return home early*. The key here is *not* to buy just enough insurance to guarantee full reimbursement for the cost of the package or charter in case of cancellation. The proper amount of coverage should be sufficient to reimburse you for the cost of having to catch up with a tour after its departure or having to travel home at the full economy air fare if you have to forgo the return flight of your charter. There is usually quite a discrepancy between a charter air fare and the amount necessary to travel the same distance on a regularly scheduled flight at full economy fare.

Cancellation insurance designed to cover a specific package is frequently offered by tour operators. Otherwise, it can be bought through travel agents or directly from insurance companies or their agents as part of a short-term, all-inclusive travel insurance policy. Read any policy carefully before you buy it, and again be sure the policy you choose provides enough money to get you home from the farthest point on your itinerary should you have to fly on a scheduled flight. Also, be sure to check the specific definition of "family members" and "preexisting medical conditions." Some policies will not pay if you become ill from a condition for which you have received treatment in the past.

DEFAULT AND/OR BANKRUPTCY INSURANCE: Trip cancellation insurance usually protects you in the event that you, the traveler, are unable to depart on — or complete — your trip. A fairly recent innovation is coverage in the event of default and/or bankruptcy on the part of the tour operator, airline, or other travel supplier. In some travel insurance packages this contingency is included in the trip cancellation portion of the coverage; in others, it is a separate feature. Either way, it is becoming increasingly important. Whereas sophisticated travelers have long known to beware of the possibility of default or bankruptcy when buying a charter flight or tour package, in recent years more than a few respected scheduled airlines have unexpectedly revealed their shaky financial condition, sometimes leaving hordes of stranded ticketholders in their wake. Moreover, the value of escrow protection of a charter passenger's funds has lately been unreliable. While default/bankruptcy insurance will not ordinarily result in reimbursement in time to pay for new arrangements, it can ensure that you will eventually get your money back, and even independent travelers buying no more than an airplane ticket may want to consider it.

Note, however, that because of differing state insurance regulations, default and/or bankruptcy insurance is not universally available. In addition, it can be expensive. In its absence, consider using credit cards to pay for travel arrangements whenever possible. The federal Fair Credit Billing Act states that credit card customers are not liable for charges assessed for services not rendered, and a plane ticket or package tour purchased from an airline that doesn't fly or a tour operator that doesn't operate are perfect examples of this contracted-for-but-not-delivered situation.

FLIGHT INSURANCE: Airlines have carefully established limits of liability for the death or injury of passengers. For international flights, they are printed right on the ticket: a maximum of $75,000 in case of death or injury. For domestic flights, the limitation is established by state law, with a few states setting unlimited liability. But remember, these limits of liability are not the same thing as insurance policies; they merely state the *maximum* an airline will pay in the case of death or injury, and every penny of that is usually subject to a legal battle.

This may make you feel that you are not adequately protected. But before you buy last-minute flight insurance from an airport vending machine, consider the purchase in light of your total existing insurance coverage. A careful review of your current policies may reveal that you are already amply covered for accidental death, sometimes up to three times the amount provided for by the flight insurance you're buying in the airport.

Be aware that airport insurance, the kind typically bought at a counter or from a vending machine, is among the most expensive forms of life insurance coverage available anywhere, and that even within a single airport, rates for approximately the same coverage can vary. Often the vending machines are more expensive than coverage sold over the counter, even when policies are with the same national company.

If you buy your plane ticket with an American Express, Carte Blanche, or Diners Club credit card, you are automatically issued life and accident insurance at no extra cost. American Express automatically provides $100,000 in insurance; Carte Blanche and Diners Club each provide $350,000 in insurance. Additional coverage can be obtained at extremely reasonable prices, but a cardholder must sign up for it in advance. With American Express, $4 per ticket buys an additional $250,000 worth of flight insurance; $6.50 buys $500,000 worth; and $13 provides an added $1 million worth of coverage. Carte Blanche and Diners Club each offer an additional $250,000 worth of insurance for $4; $500,000 for $6.50. Both also provide $1,250 free insurance — over and above what the airline will pay — for checked baggage that's lost or damaged. American Express provides $500 coverage for checked baggage; $1,250 for carry-ons.

AUTOMOBILE INSURANCE: Hawaii has "no fault" insurance, which means that if there's an accident, each party's insurance company pays his or her expenses. When you rent a car, the rental company is required to provide you with collision protection. In your car rental contract, you'll see that for about $10 to $12 a day, you may buy optional collision damage waiver (CDW) protection to relieve you of all responsibility for any damage to the rental car. If you do not accept the CDW coverage, you may be liable for as much as the full retail cost of the car you're renting. Before agreeing to this coverage, however, check your own personal auto insurance policy. It may very well cover your entire liability exposure without any additional cost, or you may be covered by the credit card company to which you are charging your rental.

COMBINATION POLICIES: Short-term insurance policies, which include personal accident and medical coverage, trip cancellation insurance, and baggage and personal effects insurance, are available through retail insurance agencies, automobile clubs, and many travel agents. These combination policies are designed to cover you for the duration of a single trip.

Staying Healthy

The surest way to return home in good health is to be prepared for medical problems that might occur in the islands. Below we've outlined everything you need to think about before you go.

FIRST AID: Put together a compact, personal medical kit including Band-Aids, antiseptic, nose drops, insect repellent, aspirin, an extra pair of prescription glasses or sunglasses, over-the-counter remedies for diarrhea, indigestion, and motion sickness, a thermometer, and a supply of those prescription medicines you take regularly. In a corner of your kit, keep a list of all the drugs you have brought and their purpose as well as duplicate copies of your doctor's prescriptions (or a note from your doctor). These copies could come in handy if you are ever questioned by police or airport authorities about any drugs you are carrying and also are necessary to refill any prescriptions in the event of loss. It is also a good idea to ask your doctor to prepare a medical identification card that includes such information as your blood type, your social security number, any allergies or chronic health problems you have, and your medical insurance number.

SUNBURN: The burning power of the sun in the tropics is phenomenal and can quickly cause severe sunburn or sunstroke. To protect yourself against these ills, wear sunglasses, take along a broad-brimmed hat and cover-up, and use a sunscreen lotion. When choosing a sunscreen, look for one that has a PABA (the para-amino-benzoic acid) base. PABA blocks out most of the harmful ultraviolet rays of the sun.

Some tips on tanning:

1. Allow only 15 minutes or so the first day; increase your exposure gradually.
2. You are most likely to get a painful burn when the sun is the strongest, between 10 AM and 2 PM.
3. When judging if you've had enough sun, remember that time in the water (in terms of exposure to ultraviolet rays) is the same as time lying on the beach.
4. A beach umbrella or other cover doesn't keep all the rays of the sun from reaching you. If you are sensitive to light, be especially careful.
5. As many ultraviolet rays reach you on cloudy days as on sunny days. Even if you don't feel hot, you are still exposed to rays.

If, despite these precautions, you find yourself with a painful sunburn, take a cooling bath, apply a first-aid spray or the liquid of an aloe plant, and stay out of the sun. If you develop a more serious burn and experience chills, fever, nausea, headaches, or dizziness, consult a doctor at once.

WATER SAFETY: Hawaiian beaches are so beautiful, with sands so caressing and waters so crystalline, that it's hard to remember they can also be treacherous. A few precautions are necessary. Beware of the undertow, that current of water running back down the beach after a wave has washed ashore; it can knock you off your feet and into the surf. Even more dangerous is the riptide, a strong current of water running against the tide, which can pull you out toward sea. If this happens, don't panic or try to fight the current, because it will only exhaust you; instead, ride it out while waiting for it to subside, which usually happens not too far from shore, or try swimming away parallel to the beach.

Sharks are sometimes sighted, but they usually don't come in close to shore, and they are well fed on Hawaiian fish. Should you meet up with one, just swim away as quietly and smoothly as you can, without shouting or splashing. The tentacled Portuguese man-of-war and other jellyfish drift in quiet waters for food and sting whatever they touch. If stung, do not wash the area because fresh water aggravates the stinging; instead, pour alcohol (rubbing alcohol, liquor, or perfume) over the stung area or apply meat tenderizer. Hot salt water is another effective treatment. Hawaii's coral reefs are extensive and razor sharp. Treat all coral cuts with an antiseptic and then watch carefully since coral is a living organism and may cause an infection. If you step on a sea urchin, you'll find that the spines are very sharp, pierce the skin, and break off easily. Like splinters, the tips left embedded in the skin are difficult to remove, but they will dissolve in a week or two; in the meantime, rinsing with vinegar is said to dissolve them more quickly.

If complications or allergic reactions such as vomiting, breathlessness, or cramps result from any of the above circumstances, *see a doctor.*

INSECTS AND OTHER PESTS: Although relatively free of insects, Hawaii does have its share of flies and mosquitoes; as we have said, be sure to pack a repellent. There are no snakes, although poisonous centipedes and scorpions are seen occasionally. Call a doctor if you are bitten by either one. Cockroaches and termites thrive in the warm climate, but pose no serious health threat. The gecko, a small lizard found everywhere, feeds upon insects and is quite harmless.

FOOD AND WATER: The tap water in Hawaii is considered among the purest to be found, so feel free to drink it; fruit, vegetables, and dairy products are likewise completely safe. However, you should avoid drinking water from streams or freshwater pools.

EMERGENCY MEDICAL HELP: If you have a medical condition that may require attention on your trip, have your doctor recommend a physician in the areas you plan to visit. If you need a doctor unexpectedly, ask your hotel to recommend one or call a hospital for a referral. In case of an accident or other emergency, you can get immediate help by dialing 911.

Emergency assistance is also available from the various medical programs designed for travelers who have chronic ailments or whose illness requires them to return home. The *Medic Alert Foundation* sells identification emblems that specify that the wearer has a health condition that may not be readily apparent to a casual observer. A heart condition, diabetes, epilepsy, or severe allergy are the sorts of things that these emblems were developed to communicate, conditions that can result in tragic errors if not recognized when emergency treatment is necessary and when you may be unable to speak for yourself. In addition to the identification emblems, the foundation maintains a computerized central file from which your complete medical history is available 24 hours a day by telephone call (the telephone number is clearly inscribed on the ID badge). The one-time membership fee of $25 to $45 depends on the type of emblem you select, stainless steel to 10K gold-filled. For information, contact: Medic Alert Foundation, Turlock, CA 95381-1009 (phone: 209-668-3333; 800-432-5378).

International SOS Assistance also offers a program to cover medical emergencies while traveling. Members are provided with telephone access — 24 hours a day, 365 days a year — to a worldwide, monitored, multilingual network of medical centers. A phone call brings assistance ranging from a telephone consultation to transportation home by ambulance or aircraft, and in some cases transportation of a family member to wherever you are hospitalized. The service can be purchased for a week ($15), a week plus additional days ($15, plus $2 for each additional day), a month ($45), or a year ($195). For information, contact: International SOS Assistance, Inc., PO Box 11568, Philadelphia, PA 19116 (phone: 215-244-1500; 800-523-8930).

Practically every phase of health care — before, during, and after a trip — is covered in *The New Traveler's Health Guide* by Drs. Patrick J. Doyle and James E. Banta. It is available for $4.95, plus $2 postage and handling, from Acropolis Books Ltd., 2400 17th St. NW, Washington, DC 20009-9964 (phone: 800-451-7771).

In the Islands

Credit Cards and Traveler's Checks

CREDIT CARDS: There are two different kinds of credit cards available to consumers in the United States, and travelers must decide which one best serves their interests. "Convenience" or "travel and entertainment" cards — American Express, Diners Club, and Carte Blanche are the most widely accepted — cost a basic annual membership fee but do not strictly limit the amount that the cardholder may charge in any month. However, the entire amount of monthly charges must be paid in full at the end of each billing period (usually a month), so the cardholder is not actually extended any long-term credit.

"Bank cards" are also rarely issued free these days, with the exception of Sears' Discover Card, and certain services they provide (check cashing, for example) can cost extra. But this category comprises real *credit* cards, in the sense that the cardholder has the privilege of paying a small amount of the total outstanding balance in each billing period. For the privilege, a high annual interest rate (currently three to four times the going bank passbook savings rate) is charged on the balance owed. Many banks now charge interest from the purchase date, not from the first billing date as they used to do; consider this when you are calculating the actual cost of a purchase. In addition, a maximum is set on the total amount the cardholder can charge, which represents the limit of credit the card company is willing to extend. The major bank cards are Visa and MasterCard with Discover growing rapidly.

Getting any credit card will involve a fairly rigorous credit check; to pass, you will need a job (at which you have worked for at least a year), a minimum salary, and a good credit rating.

Note that some establishments you encounter during the course of your travels may not honor any credit cards and some may not honor *all* cards, so there is a practical reason to travel with more than one. Following is a list of credit cards that have wide international use:

American Express: Emergency personal check cashing at American Express or representatives' offices (up to $200 cash in local currency, $800 in traveler's checks); emergency personal check cashing for guests at participating hotels (up to $250 in the US and Canada, $100 elsewhere) and, for holders of airline tickets, at participating airlines in the US (up to $50). Extended payment plan for cruises, tours, and air tickets. $100,000 free travel accident insurance on plane, train, bus, and ship if ticket was charged to card; up to $1 million additional flight insurance available at low-cost. Contact American Express Card, PO Box 39, Church St. Station, New York, NY 10008 (phone: 800-528-4800 except in NY; 212-477-5700 in NY).

Carte Blanche: Extended payment plan for airline tickets (up to $2,000). $150,000 free travel accident insurance on plane, train, and ship if ticket was charged to card, plus $1,250 checked baggage insurance, and $25,000 rental car insurance. Contact Carte Blanche, PO Box 17193, Denver, CO 80217 (phone: 800-525-9135).

Diners Club: Emergency personal check cashing for guests at participating hotels and motels (up to $250 per stay). Qualified card members are eligible for extended payment plan. $350,000 free travel accident insurance on plane, train, and ship if ticket was charged to card. Contact: Diners Club, PO Box 17193, Denver, CO 80217 (phone: 800-525-9135).

Discover Card: Launched in early 1986 by Sears, Roebuck and Co., it provides the holder with cash advance at more than 500 locations in the continental US (not on the islands, as of this writing) and offers a revolving credit line for purchases at a wide range of service establishments. Other deposit, lending, and investment services are also available. For information, call 800-858-5588.

MasterCard: Cash advance at participating banks worldwide and revolving credit line for purchases at a wide range of service establishments. Interest charge on unpaid balance and other details are set by issuing bank. Check with your bank for information.

Visa: Cash advance at participating banks worldwide and revolving credit line for purchases at a wide range of service establishments. Interest charge on unpaid balance and other details are set by issuing bank. Check with your bank for information.

TRAVELER'S CHECKS: Traveler's checks are as good as cash in most hotels, restaurants, retail stores, and banks. More and more establishments are, however, beginning to restrict the amount of traveler's checks they will cash, so it is wise to purchase at least some of your checks (if not all) in small — say, $20 — denominations. If you're traveling, traveler's checks are far better than cash because of their refundability if lost; in the US, travelers can usually receive partial or full replacement funds the same day if they have their receipt and proper identification. To avoid complications, keep your purchaser's receipt and an accurate list, by serial number, of your checks in a separate place from the checks themselves. You can buy traveler's checks at any bank. Some companies offer more extensive services, making provisions for refunds on weekends and after business hours. Here is a list of the major companies issuing traveler's checks and the numbers to call in the event that loss or theft makes replacement necessary:

American Express: To report lost or stolen checks in the US, including Hawaii and Alaska, call 800-221-7282.

Bank of America: To report lost or stolen checks in the US, including Hawaii and Alaska, call 800-227-3460 or 415-624-5400, collect.

Citicorp: To report lost or stolen checks in the US, including Hawaii and Alaska, call 800-645-6556, or collect 813-623-1709.

MasterCard: To report lost or stolen checks in the US, including Hawaii and Alaska, call 800-223-9920, or collect 212-974-5696.

Thomas Cook MasterCard: To report lost or stolen checks in the US, including Hawaii and Alaska, call 800-223-9920, or collect 212-974-5696.

Visa: To report lost or stolen checks in the US, including Hawaii and Alaska, call 800-227-6811.

Accommodations

 Deciding where to stay in Hawaii will not be easy, thanks to what some might call an embarrassment of riches. There are, first of all, a great many hotels, and standards of quality and service throughout the industry are quite high. Happily, too, the price of accommodations is quite reasonable compared to accommodations in a similar vacation area elsewhere. Travelers who want the finest in resort living — and can afford it — will not be disappointed, while others can be safe in assuming that they will find a clean and comfortable hotel in an acceptable price range. What's more, hotels are not the only lodgings available. About a third of the state's 66,000 rooms (or rental units) are in condominiums, a type of accommodation that provides the ordinary traveler with the extraordinary opportunity to live for a while in the kind of vacation home that only the very wealthy can afford to own. In addition, there are more choices — from bed-and-breakfast accommodations to the possibility of exchanging your own home for the home of a Hawaii family — that will appeal to those traveling on a shoestring, those in search of something a little bit different, or both.

HOTELS: The *Royal Hawaiian* — known affectionately as the Pink Palace or the Pink Lady because of the color of its Mediterranean stucco façade — was *the* Hawaiian hotel for a bygone generation, tourists who steamed graciously into Honolulu in the late 1920s and 1930s bearing enough baggage to settle in for a long, luxurious stay. The *Royal Hawaiian* still exists, but for the most part, the more than 5 million tourists who arrive in Hawaii each year stay at hotels that are only a few years old, the products of a building surge that has yet to subside. A fair number of these are high-rise towers that provide a view for their guests, but do not necessarily improve the general scene — as when strung wall to wall on and off the Waikiki beachfront. At the other extreme are low-slung, but equally modern, constructions scattered over the landscape in forms and finishes reminiscent of the indigenous architecture and in a manner that respects the integrity of the environment. Both types, as well as all the other structures in between, come in deluxe and more economical versions.

The larger, luxury hotels can be either independent or part of familiar national or international chains (as the *Royal Hawaiian* is now), leaving little doubt as to what to expect. They function as self-contained resorts, offering a wide range of sports, recreation, and entertainment facilities on the premises in addition to a large staff to run them. Rooms are comfortable (if not opulent), with conventional modern conveniences, air conditioning, TV sets, and, frequently, private ocean-view lanais (balconies or terraces). They feature a variety of restaurants, coffee shops, cocktail lounges, discotheques, and shops, and most have a small convention center or meeting rooms. Invariably, they have a swimming pool or two, even though most of these same hotels are either on the beach or not far from it. They usually have their own tennis courts, and a golf course is almost always nearby. Hotels of this kind can be found on all the major islands, and on the neighbor islands they often operate in conjunction with luxury condominiums (see below) and residences in the newer resort developments.

Moderately priced and inexpensive — but perfectly acceptable — hotels can also be found on all the islands, offering fewer amenities and located on less prized plots of real estate. Swimming pools are not unusual even in these hotels, though many of them are within easy walking distance of the beach (which is always public in Hawaii, with access almost always unobstructed). In Waikiki, a wide selection of these simpler, smaller establishments can be found on the side streets behind the major avenues that parallel the sea and along Ala Wai Boulevard. Some of them are apartment hotels, a once common feature of Waikiki that is now giving way to the condominium. What you get in an apartment hotel is a studio or a 1- or 2-bedroom unit with a money-saving kitchenette. The housekeeping facilities alone make the apartments a boon for any budget traveler, and because the modest rates tend to be the same whether the apartments are occupied by one, two, three, or four people, they are even more appealing to families or groups of friends traveling together. A few apartment hotels may be operated with a full range of hotel services, but usually they provide no more than regular (not necessarily daily) maid service, air conditioning, a parking space, the occasional TV set, and sometimes a pool. Room telephone service is not ordinarily available.

The most comprehensive listing of accommodations in Hawaii is the *Accommodation*

Guide, a booklet put out annually by the Hawaii Visitors Bureau. Although it includes only those hotels (and apartment hotels and condominiums) that belong to the bureau, and, therefore, not all the establishments in the state, it nevertheless includes most of them, from luxury to low-cost choices. Each entry gives room rates (not right up to the minute, but useful for comparison), a rundown of facilities, the address and location, and a phone number. Note that room rates in Hawaii are almost always European plan; that is, they do not include breakfast or any other meal. Note also that some hotels charge seasonal rates, with high season running approximately from mid-December to mid-April. Expect to pay an approximate additional $10 to $15 per day per room at this time. Finally, although room rates vary from island to island, it should be taken into account that, during the past year, prices tended to increase 10% to 15% on average.

CONDOMINIUMS: Condominiums are nothing new in the Aloha State. Because land has always been at a premium, Hawaii was a pioneer (in the late 1950s) in the development of the condominium as a solution to the problem of housing an expanding population. Not long after that, when the condo idea was applied to another of the state's primary concerns — tourism — Hawaii also pioneered the development of the resort condominium. What is new is the rapid growth in the number of luxury resort units — especially on Maui — in recent years, and the dramatic growth in their popularity as alternatives to traditional hotel rooms. This popularity is hardly surprising, however, because if the enthusiastic Hawaiian real estate boom of the last several years has caused prices to skyrocket and made ownership of a vacation condominium the province of the privileged alone, these same six-figure units, as short-term rentals, are well within the grasp of travelers with ordinary means.

The difference between a condominium complex and an apartment hotel is not always immediately apparent (and many apartment hotels are now being converted to condominiums). In either case, the vacationer is renting not a hotel room but a studio or 1- or 2-bedroom (or larger) apartment with a full kitchen or a kitchenette and private bath(s). The apartment hotel, however, is designed entirely for transient rental, whereas the condominium complex is designed to be sold unit by unit to private owners for whom, these days, it is usually not a permanent residence but an investment and a part-time vacation home; the rest of the year it can be rented to a series of transient occupants. Like apartment hotels, condominiums appeal to budget travelers because they provide the cost-saving feature of a kitchen. At their most modest, their appeal may go no farther, and in the past, travelers renting condominiums sight unseen could not always be sure they would get their money's worth. But recent trends — the development of ever more properties in prime locations and the tendency of professional management companies to take over the day-to-day operation of them — have imposed standards of quality and introduced a certain consistency in the equipment and services offered.

In appearance, top-notch resort condominium complexes vary from high-rise blocks to cottage clusters, just as resort hotels do. Some may provide all the facilities of a hotel — restaurants, lobbies, and lounges where you will bump into your fellow guests; and others may stress quiet or seclusion, with a definite lack of bustle. Some, with a view to easy maintenance, require that each unit be finished exactly like every other unit; others allow free rein to the individual owner's personal touches. (Most have at least a minimum standard of furnishings and equipment before any unit is accepted for inclusion in the transient rental pool.) First class condominiums of this sort, whatever the subtle differences in atmosphere, have spacious, tastefully furnished rooms and fully equipped kitchens (all dishes, pots and pans, and tableware are supplied, and many even have dishwashers). Linens are supplied, and a washer and dryer will be in your own unit or nearby. A TV set is almost always provided; air conditioning and room phones may or may not be. Most resorts have daily maid service, and there is usually some arrangement for babysitting services. Almost all apartment units have a private lanai, and if you're on the ground floor, you'll be able to walk directly from your quarters to the pool (one is de rigueur and there may be more) or to the beach if it is near (which it usually is). Tennis courts, saunas, outdoor barbecue grills, and on-premises grocery and liquor stores are added amenities at many such condo complexes.

The cost of all this for one traveler alone or even one couple is not inexpensive. But for a family, two or more couples, or a group of friends, the picture is different. A 1-bedroom condominium rented to two people at $65 per person a night, for instance, may rent to four people at $77 a night; that is, only $6 more per additional person (and if the extra two are children under 12, they would be accommodated free at quite a few resorts). At another resort, a 2-bedroom apartment may cost $124 per night, the same for four through six people, whether children or adults. (In either case, the two extra guests sleep in the living room on a sofabed, a standard furnishing.) Weekly and monthly rates are available to reduce costs still more. As with hotels, the rates at some condominium resorts are seasonal, rising from approximately mid-December to mid-April, while at others they remain the same year-round.

There are several ways of finding a suitable condominium. They are listed along with the other accommodations in the Hawaii Visitors Bureau *Accommodation Guide,* but perhaps the best course is to consult a travel agent. Many tour wholesalers regularly include a few condominium packages among their more conventional offerings. In addition, certain companies specialize in condominium vacations. Their plans typically include a rental car and rental of the condominium (at as many resorts on as many islands as you like, but usually for a minimum 2- or 3-day stay per resort), to which can be applied an excursion, individual tour-basing, or group air fare (whichever is least expensive when and from where you travel), just as it could be applied to any other package. If your travel agent doesn't have the brochures of these specialists, contact the companies listed below.

Condo Resorts International, PO Box 3008, Suite K8, Costa Mesa, CA 92628 (phone: 800-854-3823).

Condominiums Unlimited, PO Box 6085, Hayward, CA 94540 (phone: 800-227-1196 in the continental US except California; 415-785-5880 or 800-972-5900 in California).

Creative Leisure, 951 Transport Way, Petaluma, CA 94952 (phone: 800-4-CON-DOS in the US and Canada).

While perusing the brochures, look for answers to the following questions: How do you get from the airport to the condominium? How far is the nearest beach? Is it sandy or rocky and is it safe for swimming? What size and quantity of beds are provided? How far is the property from whatever else is important to you, such as a golf course or nightlife? If there is no grocery store on the premises (which may be comparatively expensive, anyway), how far is the nearest market? Are babysitters, cribs, bicycles, or anything else you may need for your children available? Is maid service provided daily? If you want air conditioning or a phone, does the apartment have them? Before deciding which resort is for you, make sure you have satisfactory answers to all your questions; ask your travel agent to find out or, if necessary, call the company involved directly.

BED-AND-BREAKFAST AND OTHER ACCOMMODATIONS: Bed-and-breakfast establishments are a relatively new phenomenon in the United States, so travelers who have become devotees of this type of accommodation through trips to Europe will be happy to hear that a bed-and-breakfast network exists in Hawaii and that it is growing. Bed-and-breakfast accommodations provide precisely what the name implies. The bed may be in an extra room in a family home, in an apartment with a separate entrance, or in a free-standing cottage elsewhere on the host's property, and a private bath often comes with it, as does, occasionally, a kitchenette. The breakfast will probably be a Hawaiian version of the continental breakfast: tropical fruit plus juice, toast or roll or homemade bread and marmalade, and coffee or tea. Or, if you're in a studio with a kitchen, you may be furnished with the makings of a breakfast you'll have to prepare for yourself.

Beyond these two fundamentals, nothing else is predictable about the bed-and-breakfast route. You may have a patio, garden, pool, and barbecue pit at your door, or only the bare necessities. You may not even have a bed, but a sleeping pad (futon) in a Japanese-style house. Some homes have only one room to let, whereas others may be large enough to have another party or two in residence at the same time. Some hosts enjoy helping guests with tips on what to see and do and even serve as informal tour guides, while in other places your privacy won't be disturbed. Whichever the case, the beauty of bed-and-breakfast establishments is that you'll always have a warm reception and the opportunity to meet many more Hawaiians than you otherwise would, which means you'll experience the hospitality of the 50th state in a special fashion.

Bed-and-breakfast accommodations range from $25 to $60 single; $30 to $250 double. They are found on all the islands, in beach, mountain, and town locations, but to stay in them, arrangements must be made through a reservations organization. The general procedure for making reservations through the three major bed-and-breakfast services requires that you contact them with specifications, they help find the right place, and upon receipt of a deposit, confirm your reservations. Any further information needed will be provided either by the service or by the owner of the bed-and-breakfast establishment. *Bed & Breakfast Hawaii* (Box 449, Kapaa, HI 96746; phone: 808-822-7771) offers a guidebook and directory that includes descriptions of host homes. As of this writing, the cost is $8, including postage. *Bed & Breakfast Honolulu Statewide* (3242 Kaohinani Dr., Honolulu, HI 96817; phone: 808-595-7533; 800-228-4666 from the mainland) requires a $5 booking charge and a deposit of at least 3 nights or 50% of the total lodging fee, whichever is greater, plus 4.16% state tax and 5.25% accommodations tax. *Pacific Hawaii Bed & Breakfast* (19 Kai Nani Pl., Kailua, Oahu, HI 96734; phone: 808-262-6026 or 263-4848) requires a deposit of 20% of the total lodging fee.

Besides bed-and-breakfast houses, there are other economical alternatives to hotels for travelers willing to accept a somewhat lower level of luxury. Honolulu's *YWCA* and *YMCA* residences are discussed at length under *Hints for Single Travelers,* in this section. The *YWCA* is for women only (most of its rooms are shared) and two of the *YMCA*s are for men only (single or double rooms). The main drawback to counting on the "Y" for accommodations is that they exist only in Honolulu. For information on *AYHA* youth hostels, refer to *Hints for Single Travelers.*

Hawaii's year-round warm climate and magnificent scenery make it a very popular place for camping. You could sleep in your own RV, your tent, or with nothing between you and the outdoors but your bedroll. In addition, several Hawaiian parks have cabins to rent. On the island of Hawaii, there are cabins in Hawaii Volcanoes National Park, Mauna Kea State Park, Kalopa State Recreation Area, and Kilauea State Recreation Area. On Maui, you can rent a cabin in Haleakala National Park, Polipoli Spring State Recreation Area, and Waianapanapa State Park; and on Kauai, in Kokee State Park and Kahili Mountain Park. Write to the national parks or the state parks divisions for information on renting a cabin. (For addresses, see *Camping,* this section.) You'll find discussions of these parks in DIVERSIONS and in the chapters on the individual islands.

HOME EXCHANGES: Another accommodations option may be of special interest to families. The home exchange is an exceptionally inexpensive way to ensure comfortable, reasonable living quarters with amenities that no hotel could possibly offer, often including a car. Moreover, it allows you to live in a new community in a way that few tourists ever do: For a little while, at least, you will become something of a *kamaaina* (native-born resident). Several companies publish directories of individuals and families willing to trade homes with others for a specific period of time. In some cases, you must be willing to list your own home in the directory; in others, you can subscribe without appearing in it. Arrangements for the actual exchange take place directly between you and the other homeowner. There is no guarantee that you will find a listing in the area in which you are interested, but each of the directories below has Hawaiian homes (mostly on Oahu, Hawaii's most populous island) among hundreds or even thousands of foreign and domestic properties.

> *International Home Exchange Service/Intervac US:* Part of the Intervac network of 22 countries, which publishes three books containing 7,000 listings per year. The $35 annual subscription entitles you to the three books and the opportunity to be listed. PO Box 3975, San Francisco, CA 94119 (call collect: 415-435-3497).
>
> *Vacation Exchange Club:* Subscriptions cost $24.70 a year for two directories. 12006 111th Ave., Youngtown, AZ 85363 (phone: 602-972-2186).
>
> *World Wide Exchange:* The $45 annual membership fee includes one free listing (for house, yacht, or motorhome) and three free guides. 1344 Pacific Ave., Suite 103, Santa Cruz, CA 95060 (phone: 408-425-0531).

RESERVATIONS: Advance hotel reservations are a must if you plan to visit Hawaii during the peak periods of December through April and June through August, and they are a good idea at any other time of the year, too. Never, *never* arrive during the Christmas season without a room at the inn; you'll find that everybody else staked a claim as long ago as the previous Christmas. (If you insist on just dropping by, do it in Hawaii's relatively unbusy months of May or October.) The simplest way to make reservations is to leave it all to a travel agent, who will provide this service at no charge if the hotel in question pays agents a commission (most of them do). Not much more difficult is reserving rooms yourself. The Hawaii Visitors Bureau *Accommodation Guide* lists the phone numbers of all hotels listed, and most of the larger ones have toll-free numbers, either to the hotel itself or, if it is part of a chain, to a central reservation system.

A word about overbooking: Although not unique to Hawaii, the international travel boom has brought with it some abuses that are pretty much standard operating procedure in any industry facing demand that outstrips supply. Assuming a certain percentage of no-shows, hotels overbook rooms. When cancellations don't occur and everybody with a reservation arrives as promised, you can find yourself with a valid reservation for which no room exists.

There's no sure way to avoid all the pitfalls of overbooking, but you can minimize the risks. Always carry evidence of your confirmed reservation. This should be a direct communication from the hotel to you or your travel agent and should specify the exact dates and duration of your accommodations and the price. The weakest form of confirmation is the voucher slip a travel agent routinely issues, since it carries no official indication that the hotel itself has verified your reservations.

Even better is the increasing opportunity to guarantee hotel reservations by giving the hotel (or its reservation system) your credit card number and agreeing that the hotel is authorized to charge you for that room no matter what. It's still possible to cancel if you do so before 6 PM of the day of your reservation (sometimes 5 PM in resort areas), but when you do cancel under this arrangement, make sure you get a cancellation number to protect you from being billed erroneously.

If all these precautions fail and you are left standing at the front desk with a reservation that the clerk won't honor, you have a last resort: Yell as long and as loud as necessary to get satisfaction. The person who makes the most noise usually gets the last room in the house.

Time Zones, Business Hours, and Holidays

 TIME ZONES: Hawaii operates on Hawaiian Standard Time; clocks in the islands read 2 hours earlier than those on the mainland's West Coast (Pacific Standard Time). This time lapse increases by 1 hour as you move eastward across the three other US time zones. Therefore, if it's 7 AM Hawaiian Standard Time, it's 9 AM Pacific, 10 AM Mountain, 11 AM Central, and noon Eastern time.

Since Hawaii never suffers from a lack of daylight hours at any time of year, it does not change to Daylight Saving Time in the spring. This means that from the last Sunday in April until the last Sunday in October, the above time differences increase by 1 hour (except in the few parts of the mainland US that don't turn their clocks ahead). Hence, if it is 7 AM in Honolulu, it's 10 AM in Los Angeles and 1 PM in New York City during those months.

BUSINESS HOURS: Most businesses in Hawaii are open from 8 AM to 5 PM, Mondays through Fridays. There are many exceptions to the blanket rule covering business hours, however, especially in the case of banks and retail stores. The traditional Hawaiian banker's hours are 8:30 AM to 3 or 3:30 PM. But, like the rest of the US, island banks are following the trend toward longer hours and most have later closings (about 6 PM) at week's end, usually on Fridays.

Shopping malls, also like those on the mainland, stay open late. For example, the Ala Moana Shopping Center in Honolulu (phone: 808-946-2811) is open Mondays through Fridays from 9:30 AM until 9 PM, Saturdays from 9 AM to 5:30 PM, and Sundays from 10 AM to 5 PM. There are several marketplaces in Honolulu that keep their doors unlatched even later into the night, but don't expect such late closings on the smaller islands.

HOLIDAYS: Most businesses and all banks and retail stores close on *New Year's Day* (January 1), *Easter Sunday, Thanksgiving Day* (fourth Thursday in November), and *Christmas Day* (December 25). Banks and a great many businesses, except for retail stores, are also closed on the following holidays: *Martin Luther King, Jr., Day* (third Monday in January); *Presidents' Day* (third Monday in February); *Prince Kuhio Day* (March 26); *Memorial Day* (last Monday in May); *King Kamehameha Day* (June 11); *Independence Day* (July 4); *Admission Day* (third Friday in August); *Labor Day* (first Monday in September); *Columbus Day* (second Monday in October); *Election Day* (first Tuesday in November); and *Veterans Day* (November 11).

■ **Note:** Be advised that Aloha Friday is not a holiday but a delightful local custom. It occurs any Friday when someone who might otherwise feel compelled to wear a business suit or mainland-style dress to work shows up in an aloha shirt or a muumuu, the ladies with flowers in their hair. This is also the day when any gentleman visitor who left his jacket at home, but nevertheless has his heart set on dining in a fancy restaurant where jackets are "suggested," is least likely to be embarrassed. The aloha spirit in aloha attire is irresistible.

Mail, Telephone, and Electricity

 MAIL: Post offices in Hawaii are generally open from 8 or 8:30 AM to 4:30 PM, Mondays through Fridays, with only morning hours on Saturdays. The General Delivery section of the Main Post Office at Honolulu International Airport (3600 Aolele St., Honolulu, HI 96820) is open from 8 AM to 7:30 PM on weekdays and from 8 AM to 2:30 PM on Saturdays.

Stamps are available at most hotel desks as well as at post offices; they are also dispensed from vending machines in drugstores, transportation terminals, and other public places. Stamps cost more from these machines than they do at the post office.

Before you leave home, fill in a hold request (available at the post office) to get the post office to hold your mail while you are away. If you are planning an extended stay in the islands, file a change of address card with the post office and they will send your first class mail to your vacation address. (Note that many post offices will need 2 to 3 weeks' notice to put this change of address into effect.) If you want to receive your mail but do not know what your address will be, have it sent to you in care of General Delivery. Hawaii's main post offices provide this service, among them the Honolulu post office mentioned above; the Lahaina (zip code: 96761) and Kahului (zip code: 96732) post offices on Maui; the Lihue (zip code: 96766) post office on Kauai; and the Hilo (zip code: 96720), Kailua-Kona (zip code: 96740), and Kamuela (zip code: 96743) post offices on Hawaii. Ask the sender to put "Hold for 10 Days" on the envelope and make sure that there is a return address so that it can be returned if you are unable to pick it up. The post office will keep it for only 10 days. To claim this mail, go to the post office, ask for General Delivery, and present identification (driver's license, credit cards, birth certificate, or passport). Mail must be collected in person. If you are planning to use this service, the Post Office recommends that you write in advance to the postmaster at the appropriate post office. Note that General Delivery service is available for 30 days only. After that, you're expected to have an address or a post office box.

American Express holds mail free of charge *for clients only* at its Honolulu Client's Mail office at the Hyatt Regency Waikiki, 2424 Kalakaua Ave., Honolulu, HI 96815 (phone: 808-922-4718). You must be able to show an American Express card or American Express traveler's checks. For a $3 fee, American Express will also forward your mail to any other American Express office.

TELEPHONE: The area code for the entire state is 808. Public telephones are available just about everywhere in a city or town — for example, in transportation terminals, hotel lobbies, restaurants, drugstores, sidewalk booths, and along the highways. On the islands, it costs 25¢ to make a local call, which is defined as a call placed to a number on the same island from which you are calling.

Inter-island phone calls, as well as those to the mainland, are considered long distance. The rates for long-distance calls are determined by when the call is placed. Daytime rates are highest; evening and holiday rates, next highest; and night rates, lowest. Operator-assisted long-distance calls — including person-to-person, collect, credit card, bill-to-a-third-number calls, and calls from pay phones and hotel guest rooms — are billed at a higher rate than calls not requiring an operator. Before phoning from your room, inquire about any surcharges the hotel may have, as they can be quite excessive. Guests are sometimes charged more than double the cost of the usual phone rate. Such extra fees are avoided either by calling collect or by using a telephone credit card (free from the phone company).

If you are planning to be away for more than a month, you may be able to save money by asking the telephone company to temporarily suspend your home telephone service. You can also arrange to have your calls transferred to another number.

In Hawaii, 911 is the number to dial in an emergency — no coins needed. Operators at this number will get you the help you need from the police, fire department, or ambulance service. It is, however, a number that should be reserved for real emergencies only.

ELECTRICITY: Hawaii has the same electrical current system as that on the mainland: 110 volts, 60 cycles, alternating current (AC). Appliances can be used throughout the islands without adapters or convertors.

Drinking and Drugs

DRINKING: In Hawaii, the legal drinking age is 21. The state has no dry towns, and in many areas you'll have no trouble finding a drink anytime of the day or night. However, the exact hours during which liquor is served depends on the type of establishment. Under Hawaii's liquor law, hotels may serve alcohol from 6 AM to 4 AM; discos, cabarets, and other places with dancing, from 10 AM to 4 AM; and bars where there is no dancing, from 6 AM to 2 AM. Unlicensed restaurants may also allow patrons to bring their own wine or other alcoholic beverage.

There are no state liquor stores in the Hawaiian islands. Beer, wine, and other spirits are available in numerous shops, delis, and markets, most of which keep usual store hours — 9 AM to 5 or 9 PM. On Oahu, and especially in Honolulu, many shops are open as late as 11 PM. Since restrictions on Sunday sales have been lifted, liquor may be purchased on any day on any island.

Almost every visitor to Hawaii tries at least one of its pretty rainbow-colored drinks served in tall glasses and decorated with skewered fruit chunks and tiny parasols. Don't be deceived by the innocuous appearance of these libations: They can be rather potent, sometimes laced with hefty amounts of rum or vodka or both. It's unwise to have more than a couple at one sitting. It's also unwise to drink and drive in the islands; the twisting roads are hard enough to negotiate when you're sober. If you have had too much to drink, take a cab home and retrieve your car the next day.

Last but not least, it is illegal to drink anything alcoholic on the beaches or in any other public place in Hawaii.

DRUGS: The Hawaiian word for marijuana is *pakalolo,* and our advice is "don't." Although grown in abundance throughout the islands — some well-informed wags contend that marijuana is Hawaii's largest cash crop — *pakalolo* is just as illegal in Hawaii as it is in any other part of the US, and penalties for selling, growing, and smoking it are just as stiff. Enforcement of drug laws is also becoming increasingly strict, and local narcotics officers are renowned for their absence of understanding and lack of a sense of humor. Furthermore, pot sold to gullible tourists often turns out to be something that wouldn't turn anyone on, and it all may be seized during an agricultural inspection of your luggage at the airport before departure for the mainland.

Shopping

Most people do more shopping in Hawaii than they originally intended, and not simply because shopping is an integral part of any holiday. It probably won't be long after you've stepped from the plane before you begin to feel constricted and lackluster in your mainland clothing, chic as it was at home.

Just as you conclude that absolutely everybody is wearing something loose and billowy, its surface rampant with splashy birds, flowers, and leaves, you'll notice that some commercially minded citizen has had the prescience to place, if not a shopping center, at least a shop, exactly where you happen to be. Before you know it, you will have outfitted yourself in a manner you never dreamed possible, in something you will probably never find occasion to wear again. Moreover, you will more than likely never regret your purchase and, once transformed, will look around to find what else is for sale. The only warning offered here is to plan for these purchases before you go. Take less sportswear rather than more — your Hawaiian wardrobe is going to include some pieces bought on the spot — and leave room in your suitcase for the souvenirs you'll inevitably acquire.

Except for a few local specialties, the merchandise for sale in Hawaii does not vary significantly from island to island. Hawaiian fashions are found everywhere. Almost everyone has heard of the muumuu, a cover-up for females introduced by missionaries in the early 19th century, but few visitors are prepared for the number of variations on the theme now sold, and the muumuu is only one item of the entire stock in trade known collectively as alohawear. The counterpart for men is the aloha shirt, which is equally colorful and worn loose outside one's trousers. In addition, alohawear includes sundresses and a number of garments of indefinite construction that stay in place by wrapping and tying; the qualifying factor is the comfortable fit and the bright print fabric, which can even be bought by the yard.

Swimwear is in equally abundant supply. Shops stock vast quantities of the bathing suits of well-known mainland manufacturers in addition to suits made in Hawaii, and the latter can be both in fabrics and styles that don't betray their origin or in unmistakably Hawaiian prints. T-shirts are also big business: Buy them with resort logos or sassy sayings, have them printed with your own immortal words, or choose hand-painted ones with abstract designs by a local artist. Other things to go with the casual clothing are hats woven of *lau hala* (pandanus leaves), coconut fronds, or other fibers, and locally made sandals.

Jewelry is another temptation. The many varieties of shells and seeds strung as necklaces are the simplest and least expensive examples available, but don't assume that every necklace of shells is a trifle, because the shell leis made on the island of Niihau are collectors' items and are priced accordingly. You'll find adornments made of puka shells (shells with natural holes), kukui nuts (candlenuts), and the leaves of the maile vine electroplated with gold. And above all, you'll find coral jewelry, from white through pink to red as well as black and a rarer gold (actually, yellow to beige). Hawaiian heirloom jewelry, in gold with black enamel, is an old form, modern copies of which can be inscribed with the Hawaiian version of your name.

Traditional crafts also are enjoying a renaissance. The ancient art of featherwork lives on in feather leis that can be used as hatbands or simply admired as the works of art they are; prices range from moderate to very expensive. A few master craftsmen know how to make tapa, or kapa, cloth, the bark cloth the early Hawaiians brought so close to perfection. But the real cloth for sale today is more likely to come from other Pacific islands, though the patterns typical of Hawaiian tapa decorate a number of items for the home, such as table linens and wall hangings. Similarly, though quilting — a craft learned from the missionaries — is very much alive today, you'll find quilts only rarely in stores, while distinctive Hawaiian motifs are common on small pillows and in do-it-yourself kits. *Lau hala* and coconut frond weavers produce placemats and baskets as well as hats, and wood carvers turn out everything from utilitarian bowls to statuettes (but be aware that a lot of wood carving is machine-made). Scrimshaw, the art of etching and carving on whale ivory, flourishes. Pieces of museum quality can be found, in addition to inexpensive trinkets that make very appropriate souvenirs, given Hawaii's whaling past. In addition, Hawaii has many native and transplanted artists and artisans — glassblowers, ceramists, painters in oil and watercolors, and sculptors — whose work reflects their island home. And because Hawaii is a halfway point between the East and the West, you'll also find Oriental imports such as jade jewelry and objets d'art, cloisonné vases, ivory figurines, linens, and embroidered clothing, not to mention the artifacts and handicrafts imported from other Pacific islands.

Irresistible, too, are the edibles. Macadamia nuts are the most popular and highly portable; pineapples can be bought at the airport, conveniently packaged for the trip home. Jams and jellies of papaya, mango, guava, and passion fruit, Maui potato chips, and Kona coffee are other treats. Airport shops also do a brisk trade in last-minute flower leis, and if you wish to try your hand at growing tropical specimens yourself, you'll find seeds or cuttings of plumeria, ginger, vanda orchids, ti plants, and many other varieties for sale at the same shops and elsewhere.

Finally, you may want to remember your visit by bringing back some Hawaiian records, a Hawaiian cookbook, or a book on the history, culture, or legends of the islands. Many bookstores have well-stocked Hawaiiana departments, and music stores can supply you not only with the traditional sounds as performed by others but also with sheet music and the ukulele with which to create your own rendition of "Lovely Hula Hands."

Sources and Resources

Books and Magazines

In the various sections of this guide that deal with particular topics or activities — such as hiking and whale watching — we have recommended informative and interesting books as additional reading. Travelers who wish to learn more about Hawaii before their trip also may find the following books helpful: *Shoal of Time,* by Gavan Daws (University of Hawaii; $8.95), relates the history of Hawaii from its discovery by Captain Cook in 1778 to statehood in 1959. *Holy Man* (Harper and Row; $8.95), Daws's book about Father Damien, the Belgian priest who ministered to the leper colony on Molokai until he himself died of leprosy, has interesting sidelights on how rapidly the Polynesian kingdom developed a Western bureaucracy. John Farrow's *Damien the Leper* includes, as an epilogue, a letter written by Robert Louis Stevenson to the Reverend George Hyde of Honolulu contrasting the comfortable life led by the New England missionaries of the late 19th century with the deprivations Damien accepted on Molokai. (Although out of print, it's worth looking for this title in bookstores with well-stocked travel sections.) *Six Months in the Sandwich Islands,* by Isabella Bird (University of Hawaii; $5.95), is an absorbing account of a prolonged stay in the islands in 1873 by a Scotswoman with an encyclopedic eye for detail. *A Hawaiian Anthology,* edited by Dr. Gerrit P. Judd (Macmillan; out of print — check your library), contains portraits of Hawaii by Mark Twain, Jack London, and Herman Melville, as well as some fascinating, if jaundiced, accounts by early missionaries of Hawaiian life in the first part of the 19th century. Highly personal and rich with unusual details, *Our Hawaii,* by longtime Honolulu residents John and Bobbye McDermott (ORAFA; $9.95), provides an intimate, insider's tour of the Islands. For an excellent introduction to Hawaiian lore, read Padraic Colum's *Legends of Hawaii* (Yale University Press; $30 cloth, $9.95 paperback), which was written more than 50 years ago and has recently been revised. The *Insight Guide to Hawaii* (APA Productions; $15.95), though short on practical travel data, is a colorful introduction to the culture of the islands. And for an unforgettable glimpse of the splendid Hawaiian landscape, there are Robert Wenkam's lavishly illustrated picture books, *Hawaii* and *Kauai, Hawaii's Garden Island* (Rand McNally; out of print).

These and other books are listed in the Hawaii State Library's catalogue of over 200 titles. For a copy of *What to Read About Hawaii: A Bibliography,* write to the Hawaii State Library, 478 S. King St., Honolulu, HI 96813. An even larger and more varied selection is available from the University of Hawaii Press; the catalogue, *Hawaii and the Pacific,* is available by writing University of Hawaii Press, 2840 Kolowalu St., Honolulu, HI 96822.

The books described above may be ordered directly from the publishers or found in the travel section of any good general bookshop or in any sizeable public library. The sources listed below specialize in travel literature; they offer (and will happily mail) books on Hawaii along with guides to the rest of the world.

Forsyth Travel Library, PO Box 2975, Shawnee Mission, KS 66201 (phone: 913-384-3440). Travel guides and maps, over the counter and by mail. Catalogue available.

Gourmet Guides, 1767 Stockton St., San Francisco, CA 94133 (phone: 415-391-5903). Travel guides and maps, along with cookbooks.

The Travel Suppliers, 727 N. Placentia Ave., Fullerton, CA 92631 (phone: 714-528-2502). Books and maps, plus travel paraphernalia, from luggage to small appliances. Catalogue.

The Traveller's Bookstore, 22 W. 52nd St., New York, NY 10019 (phone: 212-664-0995). Travel guides and maps, fiction and nonfiction, plus a valuable qualitative catalogue (send $2).

You may want to subscribe to magazines that specialize in information about Hawaii. *Aloha,* a bimonthly, spotlights places of interest in the islands and contains interviews of famous personalities, colorful photo essays, restaurant reviews, and a calendar of special events. Another bimonthly, *Hawaii–Gateway to the Pacific,* highlights customs, history, art, and sports; it also publishes events calendars, restaurant listings, and gallery dates. *Honolulu,* a monthly, focuses on life in the capital, with articles on home design, fashion, politics, restaurants, and the like. Subscriptions: *Aloha,* Subscription Department, PO Box 27810, San Diego, CA 92128-9972; *Hawaii–Gateway to the Pacific,* 3 Burroughs, Irvine, CA 92718; *Honolulu Magazine,* PO Box 80, Honolulu, HI 96810.

Tourist Information Offices

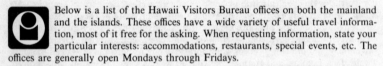

Below is a list of the Hawaii Visitors Bureau offices on both the mainland and the islands. These offices have a wide variety of useful travel information, most of it free for the asking. When requesting information, state your particular interests: accommodations, restaurants, special events, etc. The offices are generally open Mondays through Fridays.

Mainland Offices

Chicago: 180 N. Michigan Ave., Suite 1031, Chicago, IL 60601 (phone: 312-236-0632)

Los Angeles: 3440 Wilshire Blvd., Suite 502, Los Angeles, CA 90010 (phone: 213-385-5301)

New York: 441 Lexington Ave., Room 1407, New York, NY 10017 (phone: 212-986-9203)

San Francisco: 50 California St., Suite 450, San Francisco, CA 94111 (phone: 415-392-8173)

Washington, DC: 1511 K St. NW, Suite 519, Washington, DC 20005 (phone: 202-393-6752)

Island Offices

Hawaii: 180 Kinoole St., Suite 104, Hilo, HI 96720 (phone: 808-961-5797); 75-5719 W. Alii Dr., Kailua-Kona, HI 96740 (phone: 808-329-7787)

Kauai: 3016 Umi St., Suite 207, Lihue, HI 96766 (phone: 808-245-3971)

Maui: 380 Dairy Rd., PO Box 1738, Kahului, HI 96732 (phone: 808-871-8691)

Oahu: 2270 Kalakaua Ave., Room 801, Honolulu, HI 96815 (phone: 808-923-1811)

PERSPECTIVES

History

 As many as 25 million years ago, volcanic eruptions 19,000 feet below the surface of the Pacific began to build up mountains of lava that emerged from the water one by one and eventually presented themselves to the world as a chain of islands.

The isolated and slowly weathering mountain peaks we think of as Hawaii lie approximately 2,400 miles off the coast of North America, but the archipelago's eight major islands — Kauai, Niihau, Oahu, Molokai, Maui, Lanai, Kahoolawe, and Hawaii — are only the southernmost and youngest of a chain of 132 islands and atolls that stretch another 1,500 miles to the northwest. Kure Atoll, at the far end of the chain and now eroded to a semicircle of reef, is the oldest of the family. The approximately 2- to 3-million-year-old Big Island of Hawaii, with its active volcanoes, is, for the moment at least, the baby.

Geologists used to think that the islands were born when a fissure opened in a northwest-southeast direction across the floor of the ocean. According to this theory, volcanism progressed southeastward along the fissure so that volcanoes at the northwestern end ceased activity ages ago. A newer theory, however, propounds that the entire archipelago was created by a single "hot spot" that squeezed lava up, assembly-line fashion, through successive weak spots in the earth's crust as the sea floor slid north, then west, over the course of millions of years. The hot spot is presently under the Big Island, but this theory predicts that just as the other islands were carried away from their birthplace, the Big Island, too, will eventually move westward, its volcanic fires extinguished, and a new island will arise to take its place.

So much for geology. The Hawaiians have always basically understood this, because the correct geological sequence of events has long been pinpointed in Hawaiian myth and attributed to none other than that celebrated personage Pele, the explosive fire goddess who lives in the very heart of the Big Island, in the bubbling white heat of the constantly shifting molten lava of Kilauea volcano. Before taking up residence in Kilauea, Pele is credited with having created volcanoes first on Kauai, then on Oahu, then on the other islands, and finally on Maui, while continuously searching for the perfect home as well as the perfect lover. She brought the handsome high chief Lohiau with her to Kilauea, but when he fell in love with her younger sister, Hiiaka, and the pair tried to escape, the lovers were engulfed in molten lava sent after them by the jealous and angry fire goddess. With his last breath Lohiau called Pele's name, and the goddess, as the story goes, vowed, "Someday I will build for us a new island, a new land, where we will live in harmony."

Thus, both science and mythology have set the scene for Hawaii's latest volcanic island, and, indeed, 30 miles south of Kilauea, at 3,000 feet below the surface of the blue Pacific, is the cone of a volcano rising almost 16,000 feet from the ocean floor. It is called Loihi and has erupted as recently as 1980.

THE POLYNESIANS

Legend has it that Hawaii was named for the great Polynesian chief Hawaii Loa, who is believed by some to have been its discoverer. Today's consensus indicates that whoever led the initial expedition, the islands' first settlers came from the Marquesas Islands and from the Society Islands (Tahiti, Raiatea, and Bora Bora) as early as the 6th century AD (and possibly earlier), with another wave of migration in the 11th and 12th centuries directly from Tahiti.

Long before Christopher Columbus ventured out of sight of land and discovered that the world was not flat after all, Polynesians were freely sailing the Pacific without compass or sextant in double-hulled canoes (*waakauluas*) connected by a deck that could carry 50 passengers with their household goods, food, animals, plants, and their gods. These voyaging canoes, equipped with masts, sails, paddles, bailers, and stone anchors, were actually two canoes lashed together with connecting booms to support the deck, or *polu*. On this platform was a shelter, a firepit built of rocks on a base of sand, and an altar to the god Kane, whose aid was invoked by offerings during the long journey.

The Polynesians set their course by the stars, the prevailing winds, familiar cloud formations, and a sixth sense, logging 100 miles a day and voyaging thousands of miles from their home. In feats of navigation that are still fascinating and puzzling, these people sailed and settled the whole eastern Pacific just as they had probably sailed centuries earlier from the Malay Peninsula and Indonesia to settle the western Pacific.

The first great canoes to arrive in Hawaii landed on the island of Kauai. Many historians equate these first settlers, the Marquesans, with the mysterious race of people called Menehunes, who are depicted in Hawaiian legend as an ancient race of industrious elves, famous for undertaking and finishing large engineering projects overnight. If judged by the fish ponds, walls, and irrigation canals said to be their work, they were not only busy, they were brilliant. No one knows how they arrived or what became of them, but if they were indeed the Marquesans (Menehune legends are most persistent on Kauai), it seems probable that they were driven out or absorbed by the later Polynesians, who began to arrive in the 11th century from Tahiti.

.This second wave of immigration landed at South Point on the island of Hawaii, and many great canoes followed. There is also evidence in the Hawaiian tradition that for some time after their arrival, perhaps as late as the 15th or 16th century, the new settlers voyaged back and forth between their new and their old homelands, probably to pick up more relatives, animals, and plants — the Polynesians were responsible for bringing pigs, dogs, and chickens, plus breadfruit, yams, taro, bananas, sugarcane, coconuts, ti plants, and the paper mulberry, from which cloth was made, to Hawaii. Eventually, they seemed content to stay put in their ever more bountiful Hawaiian islands and sailed out the Kealaikahiki Channel (between Lanai and Kahoolawe; it means "the way to Tahiti") no more, isolated until the coming of the white man.

CAPTAIN COOK

There are indications that Spanish explorers sailed in and out of Hawaiian waters several times during the 16th century, loading provisions and water and leaving behind the pineapple, perhaps, and one or two shipwrecked sailors. They did not announce their discovery, if they considered it such, to the world, however, leaving that feat to the British explorer Captain James Cook. On his first two voyages, Cook had disproved the existence of a southern continent and explored or discovered several South Pacific lands. The object of his third voyage was to find a Northwest Passage from the Pacific to the Atlantic.

In December 1777, Cook and his two ships, HMS *Resolution* and HMS *Discovery,* headed north from the Society Islands to cross the equator and search the west coast of North America for the supposed passage to the Atlantic. On January 18, 1778, he sighted the island of Oahu and then Kauai, where he sailed into Waimea Bay and was ceremoniously welcomed by the natives, who believed him to be Lono, the god of agriculture and fertility, fulfilling a vow to return one day. Cook spent two weeks trading on Kauai and Niihau before sailing north on his original assignment, naming his discovery the Sandwich Islands in honor of the Earl of Sandwich, who had sponsored the expedition.

After a fruitless search for the Northwest Passage, Captain Cook returned to the Sandwich Islands in November of the same year. This time, his ships stood off the east coast of Maui, where the aged King of Hawaii, Kalaniopuu, who was waging war with the King of Maui, spent the night as a guest aboard the *Resolution,* along with his young warrior nephew, Kamehameha.

The British explorer then sailed south and discovered the island of Hawaii. Weeks of cruising for a safe anchorage followed, but when it was finally found at Kealakekua Bay in mid-January 1779, Cook was again welcomed as a god. Relations remained pleasant throughout the *makahiki* season (the 4-month fall festival, during which war was *kapu,* forbidden by law) while the British ships were repaired and provisioned.

On February 4, 1779, Cook resumed his journey, but from that moment, fate was against him. His ships ran into gale winds and the *Resolution* sprang her foremast, forcing a return to Kealakekua Bay for repairs. Strangely, there was no greeting for the ships on this occasion; in fact, the bay appeared deserted — the *makahiki* season was over and the natives no longer looked upon the captain as anything more than a mortal man. On February 14, 1779, a cutter from the *Discovery* was stolen and dismantled by Hawaiians eager for its highly prized iron nails. Cook and his men went after the boat, and in the pitched battle that ensued, he and 17 Hawaiians were killed. Cook's bones were claimed for burial by his sailing master, Captain Bligh, who later commanded the *Bounty.* A monument to Cook stands on the north side of the bay at Kaawaloa on the Big Island.

KAMEHAMEHA I AND UNIFICATION

At the time Captain Cook visited the islands, the Hawaiian populace was divided into a rigid class system made up of a hereditary group of nobles or chiefs called *alii;* of priests, *kahunas;* of the commoners, *makaainanas;* and of the outcasts or slaves, *kauwas.* At the top of the heap were the Kings, the highest-ranking chiefs, who held court, collected taxes, led the soldiery, consecrated the temples (*heiaus,*) oversaw religious rites, and upheld the *kapu* (taboo) system that was both religion and law, the foundation of society. Cook had not discovered a peaceful paradise by any means; life under the *kapus* was as difficult for the mass of commoners as the life of a European serf under feudalism, and warfare among chiefs and Kings was constant.

The night Kamehameha spent aboard Captain Cook's ship had been the young chief's introduction to Western civilization and to firearms. No doubt his imagination was stirred, reinforcing his resolve to rule more than a chief's section of Hawaii. When his uncle, Kalaniopuu, died in 1782, Kamehameha seized the opportunity to expand his domination of the Big Island. Though his cousin Kiwalao had been made heir to the throne, Kamehameha had become the keeper of the family war god, Kukailimoku. Kiwalao soon died in battle, but the struggle to defeat another cousin and rival, Keoua, went on for a full nine years. Finally, Kamehameha built a huge *heiau,* Puukohola, sacred to the war god, on a hill above Kawaihae in the North Kohala area. When it came time to dedicate Puukohola, Kamehameha enticed his cousin to the ceremony, slew him, and offered him as the ultimate sacrifice on the altar of the temple. Kamehameha's consecration was complete; he was now ruler of all the island of Hawaii, and he soon would rule over the entire chain.

The year before, Kamehameha had won an important battle over the King of Maui, Kahekili, who also controlled Molokai and Lanai. After the King's death in 1794, it was not long before Kamehameha disposed of his successor. Oahu fell in the Battle of the Pali in 1795, and with that decisive victory, no major island remained to be conquered except Kauai, which capitulated in 1810, won by diplomacy.

Kamehameha I is recorded in Hawaiian history as Kamehameha the Great, the creator of a united Hawaiian kingdom. A fierce and fearless fighter, he also proved a master statesman, maintaining power by appointing royal governors who had no ties of kinship with the islands they served. After so many years of devastation and impoverishment by war, he quickly restored the kingdom to peace and prosperity.

In his conquest, he had used foreign weapons and advisers — as did other island chiefs — and he kept these advisers with him, adopting their new ideas. Trade between Honolulu and Europe and America became increasingly important during this time, and the King took eagerly to it, establishing a royal monopoly. Though the sandalwood trade with China, which began in earnest around 1810 and continued for about 20 years, did not, in the end, prove beneficial to Hawaii (it depleted the forests), in other ways he encouraged agriculture and industry. Above all, he advocated hard work and a religious way of life.

Kamehameha had 21 wives, all high-born chiefs, but only two of them stand out in history. Queen Keopuolani, of Maui, was his "sacred" wife, so called because she was a *niaupio,* a child of a brother and sister union of great chiefs. Under the *kapu* system, such people represented an intensification of the power of their parents and were so sacred that all who came into their presence had to prostrate themselves. Keopuolani outranked Kamehameha and thus assured him of the noblest of offspring. She bore him two sons, Liholiho and Kauikeaouli, and a daughter, Nahienaena.

Queen Kaahumanu, a chief of high rank from Maui, was Kamehameha's "favorite" wife. A native 19th-century historian described her as a "handsome woman, six feet tall, straight and well-formed." Kaahumanu was intelligent, headstrong, and politically astute, and though she had no children, she became Hawaii's first *kuhina nui* (regent) for the two sons of Keopuolani who succeeded Kamehameha to the throne.

Kamehameha died in Kailua, on the Big Island of Hawaii, in May 1819, at about age 60. (His actual birth date is unknown.) He was accorded all of the *kapus* and funeral rituals of the ancient Hawaiian religion — the last Hawaiian King to be so honored. During a lengthy and complicated mourning, his body was prepared for burial, and at the end of the ten days needed to clean the bones, they were wrapped in black tapa cloth and placed in a basketwork container. After prayers and incantations spoken at his *heiau,* two close companions cached his bones in a safe spot where they could not be found (and have not to this day). It is said that "only the stars of the heavens know the resting place of Kamehameha."

KAMEHAMEHA II AND THE BREAKING OF THE KAPU

Kamehameha was succeeded by his son Liholiho, who became Kamehameha II at the age of 22 and had a brief but eventful rule. The powerful Queen Kaahumanu immediately named herself his regent — whether by command of the departed King or by her own initiative, it is not known — and at once urged him to abandon the ancient *kapu* system. The spirited Queen had already broken several *kapus* and escaped retribution from the gods, but there were *kapus* of greater importance that she wished to challenge. One of the strictest barred women from the *luakini heiaus,* where political and religious decisions were made. As a high female chief in her own right, a wife of one King and regent to another, Kaahumanu occupied a position of great rank, but her sex prevented her from exercising its authority to the fullest.

Kaahumanu enlisted the aid of Liholiho's mother, Queen Keopuolani, another chief who did not fear the retribution of the gods. Together they arranged a special public feast and insisted that the young King eat with them, thus breaking a most conspicuous *kapu* — the one preventing men and women from eating together no matter what their rank — and, symbolically, all of them.

Liholiho did not acquiesce without a great deal of thought, but acquiesce he did, and on the third or fourth day of October 1819, the eating *kapu* was broken. The following day, messengers were sent to all the islands informing the people that the *kapus* were no more and ordering the *heiaus* and the images of the gods destroyed. Surprisingly, few besides the King's cousin Kekuaokalani, protector of the war god, rebelled at these orders, but his and other uprisings were soon quieted.

The spectacle of a society in a few short weeks doing away with a system of religion and law that had served it for centuries was a strange one. In part, the arrival of foreigners was to blame: Not only did the chiefs see *haoles* (white men) violating *kapus* without punishment from the gods, but commoners also saw them go unpunished by the chiefs, whose duty it was to uphold the system. In this confusion, it seemed perhaps to all levels of society that the gods had lost their power or at least their interest in the Hawaiian people.

That it was two women who led the revolution does not surprise historians. From the beginning, Hawaiian women, who were condemned to an exceedingly subordinate role in their society, had had the closest and most frequent contacts with the *haoles* and consequently the greatest exposure to a liberated life, without *kapus*. But commoners of both sexes, who could be burned, strangled, or stoned to death for so much as allowing their shadow to fall upon the house of a high chief, had cause to rejoice in emancipation, even though the breaking of the *kapus* left a void at the heart of society.

Liholiho still ruled after the *kapus* were gone, though no longer by divine right. And in less than five years, both he and his favorite wife, Queen Kamamalu, would be dead as the result of an ill-fated trip to London. Since the days of the first Kamehameha, Hawaiian royalty had felt a particular affection for England. During the 1790s, Kamehameha the Great had been friends with the British explorer Captain George Vancouver, who had advised him on government and military matters and had presented him with sheep and cattle, thereby introducing them to the islands. Vancouver became so respected that the King accorded him the singular honor of "ceding" the island of Hawaii to Great Britain in 1794 and hoisting the British flag at Kealakekua Bay. (Recognition that the island was a British protectorate never came from London, however, and so the islands remained — for the time being — independent.)

Because England had a King and Queen, a court, and nobles, just as the Hawaiians did, Liholiho had a great desire to visit them. Once in London, he and his Queen were caught up in the social whirl, and their official presentation was imminent when both of them suddenly fell ill. The court physician diagnosed the illness as measles, a simple enough disease as far as Londoners were concerned, but not for the Hawaiians, who had never encountered it before. Kamamalu and Liholiho both died there in July 1824, and a small, sad, and weary party of Hawaiian *alii* returned to the islands to announce the news. Liholiho's younger brother, Kauikeaouli, not yet in his teens, became Kamehameha III, with Kaahumanu again as *kuhina nui.*

THE MISSIONARIES AND WHALERS

The breaking of the *kapus* set the stage for the arrival of the missionaries, who, at the very moment the gods were being thrown from their pedestals all over Hawaii, were sailing the high seas with the islands as their destination. They had been inspired by a particularly devout young Hawaiian convert,

Henry Obookiah (Opukahaia), who had worked his way aboard ship to New England during Kamehameha's reign and enrolled in a mission school. Stories of his home impressed two young students, Hiram Bingham and Asa Thurston, who, after Henry's death, volunteered to take Christianity to the Sandwich Islands.

They gathered a dedicated Calvinist group in Boston and on October 23, 1819, set sail aboard the brig *Thaddeus.* In the group were the two missionaries, a doctor, two teachers, a printer, and a farmer, along with their wives and children. Also aboard were four young Hawaiian boys who had been attending the mission school and who spent the five months at sea teaching the small band Hawaiian.

The impact of the missionaries on Hawaiian society began immediately. Within a few short years, they and subsequent missions had "clothed the naked," created an alphabet for Hawaiian and produced a written language, printed Bibles and hymnals in Hawaiian, established schools on all the islands, banned the hula, and become involved in commerce and politics. They introduced the seeds of their own foods along with the seeds of Christianity, and soon they replaced grass houses with clapboard saltboxes and built churches in the image of the ones left behind in New England.

Their progress was remarkable, considering their relatively small numbers, but the missionaries had several things in their favor: the mood of the islands, for instance, ripe for change, and the presence of the missionary wives and doctors. The wives labored as hard as their husbands and impressed the Hawaiian women with their skills in needlework and nursing. The physicians performed operations, fought epidemics, and established patterns of hygiene formerly unknown to the primitive Hawaiians.

Finally, the missionaries' desire to teach as well as preach stood them in good stead. The shrewd and powerful Kaahumanu, who had been wary of the missionaries at first, learned to read and write and immediately recognized the importance of education to her people. When she was won over by the content of her reading and converted to Christianity, she supported the American missions even more forcefully.

After Liholiho's departure for England, Kaahumanu ordered the strict observance of the Sabbath, and soon afterward, with the concurrence of the council of chiefs, she issued a code of laws against drunkenness, fighting, theft, and murder. Another law decreed that as schools were established, all Hawaiians should learn to read and write. These were the first laws to fill the vacuum left by the breaking of the *kapus,* and her subjects accepted the new code without protest.

The schools decreed by Kaahumanu grew rapidly. In 1824, there were 2,000 pupils. By 1831, 50,000 students filled 1,100 schools. At first, only adults were taught, but at about this time, adult attendance fell off and the children had their chance at *palapala* (writing). Lahainaluna School, the first high school west of the Rockies, was established in 1831 on Maui by the American Board of Commissioners for Foreign Missions (it is now the public high school for West Maui). Ten years later, the private Punahou School was opened in Honolulu for the children of missionaries and other foreigners. Such was the reputation of these schools that as the Gold Rush brought families to California, those who struck it rich sent their children to Hawaii to be educated.

A major thorn in the missionaries' side was the "drunken, roistering, iniquitous" behavior of the crews of the whaling ships. The first whalers had arrived in Hawaiian waters in 1819, the year before the arrival of the missionaries. Fishing grounds for the sperm whale had been discovered off Japan, and Hawaii was a convenient mid-Pacific station for refitting the whaleships and taking on stores. The number of ships increased rapidly. In 1822, more than 60 whaleships stopped in Hawaiian ports, and by 1830, an average of 150 a year, mostly American, were dropping anchor. In the 1840s and 1850s, they averaged several hundred — almost 600 in the peak year of 1846. Naturally, the crews of the ships raised hell in every port. They favored Honolulu in the beginning, but after the death in 1840 of Maui's native governor, Hoapili, a Christian convert who was an ally of the missionaries in banning brothels and grog shops, they found that Lahaina had all they needed.

The whaling crews and captains were in some ways the benefactors of the missions. They brought many of the missionaries to the islands and then brought mail from home as well as the famous "missionary barrels" of clothes and hand-me-downs. They brought supplies for schools, materials for housing, and even such luxuries as pianos. But mostly the whalers brought torment and anguish to the missionaries. For all their preaching, debauchery and prostitution still flourished, endangering not only the souls of the Hawaiians but their bodies, too. The first *haoles* aboard Captain Cook's ships had brought venereal disease to the islands; now it reached epidemic proportions. Other diseases entered the native bloodstream at Lahaina and Honolulu, and with the Hawaiians' limited resistance to infection, their population was shrinking.

The beginning of the end of whaling was signaled in 1859 by the discovery in Pennsylvania of the oil that would henceforth replace whale oil. Some whaling ships were lost in the Civil War, but the final blow was a major catastrophe in 1871, when a particularly good whaling season tempted the fleet to remain too long in the Arctic, which had supplanted the more southerly hunting grounds. The encroaching winter caused 33 ships to be abandoned and crushed in the ice floes; only 14 survived. In succeeding years, the few whaling ships still calling at Hawaiian ports were retired one by one.

KAMEHAMEHA III AND CONSTITUTIONAL GOVERNMENT

The King during the early half of the whaling era was Kauikeaouli, who had succeeded his brother in 1825 with Queen Kaahumanu again as regent. When Kaahumanu died in 1832, another high chief, Kinau (Kauikeaouli's half-sister), was named *kuhina nui,* but the King sensed her lack of power and assumed his duties and his title as Kamehameha III the following year.

At 20, the young King had yet to show any sign that he would make an impressive ruler. All the cultural confusion accompanying the transition of Hawaiian society from its old Polynesian ways to its new Western ways was apparent in the disarray of his private life. He drank to excess and was known as an inveterate womanizer. He was also known to have a strong attachment to his younger sister, Princess Nahienaena, whom he wanted to marry. In the old days, their marriage would have been expected of them and would have produced a child of the very highest — sacred — rank. In the new order, their relationship was merely incest.

Neither Kauikeaouli nor Nahienaena withstood well the thwarting of their desires and the mental strain of the cultural clash, and Kauikeaouli attempted suicide in 1834. Nahienaena, vacillating between a dissipated life and repeated returns to the missionaries' Christian fold, married a Big Island chief at their urging, then bore a child who many suspected was her brother's, not her husband's. The child lived only a few hours, and Nahienaena, ill and exhausted, lived only a few months longer, dying at the age of 20 in December 1836.

His sister's tragic death had a sobering effect on Kamehameha III. In 1838, he and his chiefs began to take instruction in "political economy" from the American missionary William Richards. A series of political innovations based on the Western model followed. In 1839, the King issued a declaration of rights and an edict of religious tolerance. In 1840, he gave his people a voice in the government by signing Hawaii's first written constitution, which provided for a bicameral legislature (with an upper house of hereditary chiefs and appointed nobles and a lower house of elected representatives) and a supreme court. In 1852, a revised constitution granted almost universal male suffrage.

Probably his most far-reaching move was the land reform of 1848, known as the Great Mahele (division). Previously, Hawaii's kings had owned the land, which was administered by their chiefs, who held it in fief, and worked by the commoners. The Great Mahele introduced the Western principle of private ownership of land, dividing it among the King (crown lands), the government (public lands), the chiefs, and the commoners. This division was welcomed as a great boon, especially to the common people, who were allowed a share of the land for the first time in their history. Shortly afterward, however, foreigners were also given the right to buy land, and they proved to be more experienced property owners than the natives. Many Hawaiian commoners lost their land by neglecting to perfect their titles to it; others realized that they could sell it, and did — mainly to the foreigners. In the end, the native Hawaiian holdings were insignificant compared to the *haole* holdings, and the way was paved for the great plantations that were to come.

The question of national sovereignty was another important issue during Kamehameha III's reign. In 1842, he dispatched a diplomatic mission (including his adviser William Richards) to the United States, Great Britain, and France, attempting to extract from them recognition of Hawaii's independence. President John Tyler, in an extension of the Monroe Doctrine to the Pacific, did recognize the islands as an independent kingdom, and Britain and France eventually did so, too, but not before Lord George Paulit, commanding the British frigate *Carysfort,* forced the King to cede the islands to Great Britain in February 1843. Paulit presumably acted to protect British interests, but without the approval of the British government. Nevertheless, it was five months before Admiral Sir Richard Thomas of the British navy arrived to repudiate his action.

Kamehameha III is credited with having spoken what is now the motto of the State of Hawaii — *Ua mau ke ea o ka aina i ka pono* ("The life of the land is perpetuated in righteousness") — in Honolulu's Kawaiahao Church at a thanksgiving service for the restoration of the island's independence after this incident.

The 29-year reign of Kamehameha III proved to be the longest of the Hawaiian monarchs. When he died in December 1854, at the age of 41, his nephew saluted him as a "great national benefactor" who had given Hawaiians a "constitution and fixed laws . . . title to their lands . . . a voice in his councils and in the making of laws by which they are governed." Because he died without an heir, that same nephew, Prince Alexander Liholiho, succeeded him.

THE LAST OF THE KAMEHAMEHAS

Kamehameha IV was a handsome, elegant, young man who had had all the advantages of an excellent education and a world tour. His Queen was the cultured and educated Emma Rooke, the granddaughter of the first Kamehameha's English adviser John Young. Their reign was aristocratic and ceremonial but pursued by calamity. In 1859, the King shot and severely wounded his friend and secretary, Henry Neilson, in a jealous rage over unfounded reports of Neilson's misconduct with the Queen. Kamehameha suffered agonizing remorse as Neilson slowly died, and his cabinet had difficulty restraining him from abdicating. Only three years later, his son, four-year-old Prince Albert, died of a fever several days after his father had held him in a cold shower to stop a childish tantrum. The following year, the 29-year-old King himself died of an asthmatic attack or, it was said, of a broken heart.

The overriding concern of Kamehameha IV's reign was the decimation of the Hawaiian population because of imported diseases: venereal disease, cholera, and smallpox, in particular, and the new scourge of leprosy from an unknown source. At the time that Captain Cook visited the islands, Hawaii is thought to have had from 250,000 to 300,000 inhabitants; by Kamehameha IV's time, the number of native Hawaiians had dwindled to a third or a quarter of that. Referring to the "wasting hand" that was destroying the people, the King pleaded with the legislature for funds for a public hospital; when the money was not forthcoming, he and Queen Emma personally raised it. By 1860, Queen's Hospital, Hawaii's first hospital for Hawaiians, was a reality.

Kamehameha IV was decidedly pro-British rather than pro-American, even to the point of naming his son after the consort of Queen Victoria, who was the child's godmother. Several reasons have been given for his stance, including a predilection for the life of the British and French courts, which he had visited as a teenager and where he had been treated as royalty, versus bitterness over an incident in Washington, DC, where he had been mistaken for a black and asked to leave a train. His stringent missionary upbringing had constrained him as a child, and as an adult he feared that the missionary influence on the Hawaiian government would lead to the loss of independence. He married his wife, an Anglican, in an elaborate Anglican ceremony, and later he brought the Church of England to Hawaii to upstage the missionaries' Congregationalism.

Kamehameha V was Lot Kamehameha, the older brother of Alexander Liholiho. He had accompanied his brother on their world tour as youths and shared his pro-British attitude; he exceeded his brother in antirepublicanism, and he was more of a nativist, believing that a strong monarchy was the only institution that could save Hawaii from the *haoles*.

His first act as King was to refuse to take the oath to uphold Hawaii's constitution of 1852 — the first of several royal revolts, actually protests against the loss of royal prerogatives, that would occur in the next 30 years. Instead, after abrogating the constitution, he enacted a new, less liberal, British-influenced document that gave more power to the crown than the previous one, which reflected its American influence. His constitution of 1864 remained in effect for 23 years, longer than any other Hawaiian constitution.

Kamehameha V was a stubborn, forceful ruler for nine pivotal years while whaling came to a halt and the sugar industry gradually became the islands' major source of revenue. When he died in 1872, he was a childless bachelor, the last of the Kamehameha line, and because he had named no successor, the next ruler was elected by the legislature from the ranks of the *alii*. The very popular "Prince Bill," described by Mark Twain as "affable, gentlemanly, open, frank . . . intelligent, shrewd, sensible . . . a man of first-rate abilities," became King William Lunalilo and ruled for 13 months before he died in 1874 of tuberculosis complicated by alcoholism. He, too, had been a bachelor.

KING SUGAR

Sugarcane had been grown in quantity in Hawaii from about the 1830s, but it was not until the Civil War, which cut the rest of the United States off from its Confederate sugar supply, that a demand for Hawaiian sugar was created in the American market. After the war, the price of sugar fell and Hawaii was threatened with the loss of this new market unless it could negotiate a favorable trade treaty, allowing its sugar to enter American ports without paying duty. In return, specified American goods entering Hawaiian ports would enjoy the same privilege. Reciprocity became a prime issue, but one fraught with political implications. Hawaii's *haole*-dominated (and largely American) sugar interests favored such a treaty, but Hawaiian natives, king and commoners alike, while admitting its economic necessity, were wary: It could either avert the dread possibility of annexation or hasten it.

Both Kamehameha IV and Kamehameha V tried to work out an acceptable agreement, but it wasn't until 1876, in the reign of David Kalakaua, that the reciprocity treaty was approved and passed. It came up for renewal in 1884 but was not ratified until 1887, when an amendment — granting US warships exclusive right of entrance to Pearl Harbor as a refueling and repair base — was the price of its extension.

Reciprocity caused such a boom in the sugar business that both the planters and the government were forced to come to terms with the islands' labor shortage: The native Hawaiian population had not been and would never be equal to the task of working the increasing number of plantations. As early as 1852, the first Chinese contract laborers had made their appearance in Hawaii, and thousands more followed them. A single shipload of Japanese had arrived in 1868. But after 1876, the need for immigrant labor became pressing. Arrangements were made to import Portuguese workers from the Azores and Madeira islands, with the first contingent of 180 arriving in 1878. Seven years later, nearly a thousand Japanese contract workers arrived, the spearhead of tens of thousands of their countrymen to come in the next quarter of a century.

Hawaii's social fabric was as changed by the influx of immigrant labor as it had been by the first wave of foreigners. Already, more and more control of the kingdom was passing into the hands of *haole* merchants and planters, among them the sons of missionaries, who had gone into commerce and would build themselves empires. Now, as the contracts of the plantation workers expired, most of them remained in their new home. Some married into Hawaiian families, thus acquiring their own tracts of land; some settled in the towns and went into their own businesses. The native population continued to decrease, so it was not difficult to make room for the newcomers.

THE END OF THE MONARCHY

In 1874, the Hawaiian legislature elected the high chief David Kalakaua to succeed Lunalilo. Kalakaua was not pro-American, but he was not against reciprocity, either: Before the year was out, he paid a visit to Washington to negotiate the terms of the treaty. Island businessmen were reassured by the trip, and when reciprocity became a fact in 1876, they were pleased.

Kalakaua was an educated and sociable gentleman, an accomplished poet and musician, and a scholar. He was conscious of the loss of Hawaii's traditional culture and tried to reclaim and revitalize it. He had the "Kumulipo," the Hawaiian creation chant, transcribed for the first time, and he collected the Hawaiian legends and myths into a book that is still a classic of the literature. Public performances of the hula, which had been suppressed by the missionaries, were reinstated during his reign. He wrote many new hula chants himself and is credited with having rescued at least 300 ancient ones from the brink of extinction. With the bandmaster of the Royal Hawaiian Band (an innovation of Kamehameha V), he co-wrote Hawaii's national anthem, "Hawaii Ponoi." He collected the feathered cloaks of former chiefs and helped to promote the nearly lost art of featherwork by encouraging the production of new ones. He formed a secret society, the Hale Naua, to revive the ancient sciences. As far as the *haole* community was concerned, all of this activity was nativism and tolerable. But his attempts to rally Hawaiians to vote as a bloc and to fill appointive positions with men of Hawaiian blood were, in their eyes, racism.

Kalakaua's extravagance also got him into trouble. He lived on a grand scale, signing his name "Kalakaua Rex." At great expense, he rebuilt the royal residence, Iolani, into the properly royal Iolani Palace, and while it was under construction, he became the first reigning monarch of any nation to travel around the world, calling on the royalty of Europe and Asia, the Pope, and the American president. When he returned, he invited his subjects to Hawaii's first — and last — coronation, a two-week celebration at which the feathered cloak of Kamehameha I was placed on his shoulders and a jeweled crown, fashioned for him in England, was placed on his head, matched by another for his Queen, Kapiolani. Among some of his subjects, such displays helped to earn him a reputation as "the Merry Monarch," but they did not endear him to the white men whose sugar lands were paying most of the kingdom's taxes.

Ironically, Kalakaua came to grief because of his relationship with two white men. One was his American adviser, Walter Murray Gibson, whose sentiments lay more with native Hawaiians than with foreigners and who was prone to encourage the King's grandiose schemes, including his dream of a federation of Pacific islands with himself as its head. The other was Claus Spreckels, a powerful California sugar magnate, who gained a foothold in the islands by lending the King money in return for favorable water rights to newly acquired sugar lands and who ended up with a stranglehold on the King's treasury.

By January 1887, *haole* planters and businessmen had had enough. Led by Lorrin Thurston, a grandson of one of the first missionaries, they formed a secret reform organization, the Hawaiian League, with a military wing in the form of a volunteer militia. By July 1887, using intimidation rather than actual firepower, they had forced the King to dismiss his cabinet and sign a new constitution — the so-called Bayonet Constitution — which severely curtailed his powers and denied the right to vote to most Hawaiians by basing the franchise on ownership of property.

Kalakaua lived out his last years as a figurehead. One of the first accomplishments of the new *haole*-dominated cabinet was the renegotiation of the reciprocity treaty, which had been renewed yearly since 1883, but now was extended by Congress only on the condition that the US be granted exclusive use of Pearl Harbor. Kalakaua, who had always been against the concession, was forced to ratify it nevertheless. An attempted counterrevolution in 1889, led by a part-Hawaiian, Robert Wilcox, failed miserably to overthrow the *haoles* and their Bayonet Constitution (it is not known whether the King played any part in the insurrection), and in 1890, an ailing Kalakaua left for San Francisco to nurse his health. He died there in January 1891, shortly before the US government replaced tariffs on foreign sugar with a bounty for domestic producers, thereby negating the advantages of reciprocity. The Hawaiian sugar industry faced collapse unless something could be done, and the Americans in Hawaii considered annexation the best solution.

Kalakaua's sister, Liliuokalani, was Hawaii's first reigning Queen and its last monarch. She was as musically talented as her brother and added many songs to the Hawaiian repertoire, including the beautiful and famous farewell song "Aloha-Oe." She was also as strong-willed as he and as much a believer in Hawaii for the Hawaiians. From the start, she resolved to restore power to the monarchy, but her efforts brought about its downfall a mere 2 years after her accession to the throne.

On January 14, 1893, the Queen dissolved the legislature and told her cabinet of her intention to proclaim a new constitution that would remove the checks to her power according to the Bayonet Constitution and that would allow only true Hawaiians to vote, whether property owners or not. Sheer political chaos ensued. A secret Annexation Club, which had been formed the year before with much the same *haole* membership as the old Hawaiian League, hastily set up a Committee of Safety to study the formation of a provisional government to replace the monarchy. The US Minister to Hawaii, John L. Stevens, and Captain G. C. Wiltse, the commander of the troops aboard the visiting USS *Boston,* were both approached by the committee to enlist their support and aid in "protecting American lives and property," should that become necessary. On January 16, 1893, the troops were posted at strategic locations around Honolulu, and on January 17, 1893, the provisional government declared itself in power, with Sanford B. Dole, another descendant of missionaries, as president. In order to avoid bloodshed, Queen Liliuokalani surrendered her royal authority, but under protest, certain that the US government would repudiate the actions of its representatives and reinstate her.

In fact, upon hearing of the events in Hawaii, President Grover Cleveland did send an investigator, who reported back that "a great wrong has been done to the Hawaiians." Cleveland sought congressional action but was ignored, just as a request to restore the Queen was ignored by the provisional government. Instead, it proclaimed a republican constitution on July 4, 1894, and Sanford Dole became the president of the new Republic of Hawaii.

Later that year, followers of the deposed Queen (led again by Robert Wilcox) staged one last abortive attempt to return her to the throne. Liliuokalani was linked to the plot and was put under house arrest in Iolani Palace on January 16, 1895. She was charged with treason, tried, and found guilty, but her sentence — 5 years at hard labor plus a $5,000 fine — was not enforced. She was paroled and, in late 1896, regained her complete freedom, which she used to go to Washington to plead the cause of the monarchy. By now, however, the US government was in an expansionist frame of mind, and the issue of Hawaii's annexation was caught up in the larger question of the country's Manifest Destiny.

Liliuokalani retired to her home to write music and poetry; she put aside her bitterness and led her people as loyal residents of the Republic and then the Territory of Hawaii until her death in 1917. Among her writings, her memoir, *Hawaii's Story by Hawaii's Queen,* was an exceptional farewell to the independent island kingdom.

FROM ANNEXATION TO STATEHOOD

As president of the republic, Sanford Dole negotiated for the annexation of the islands by the US, which became a fact by joint resolution of Congress in July 1898, during the administration of President William McKinley. Hawaii's flag flew over Iolani Palace for the last time on August 12, 1898, and its lowering, to the tune of "Hawaii Ponoi," played for the last time as the national anthem, was a solemn and dramatic occasion. Then the American flag was raised and the Royal Hawaiian Band struck up "The Star-Spangled Banner."

The islands officially became a US territory in 1900, when the passage of the Organic Act extended the US Constitution across the Pacific and automatically made American citizens of those who had been citizens of the Hawaiian republic. Sanford Dole was appointed governor of the territory, while the firebrand and revolutionary Robert Wilcox was elected its first delegate to Congress. Hawaii's next delegate to Congress was its greatest modern *alii,* Prince Jonah Kuhio Kalanianaole, a nephew of Queen Liliuokalani who had also taken part in the attempted coup of 1895 and been imprisoned for it.

Prince Kuhio was elected to Congress for the first of ten times in 1902, and though he was the candidate of the Republican party — the party of *haole* business interests, which dominated Hawaiian elections until World War II — he was a tireless fighter for the rights of the Hawaiian people. He introduced the first statehood bill to Congress in 1919 (it was submitted biennially for the next 40 years before meeting with success) and worked to restore dispossessed Hawaiians to their land by sponsoring the Hawaiian Homes Commission Act of 1920, which set aside 200,000 acres of government land to be leased as small plots by Hawaiians of more than half native blood. He founded the Hawaiian Civic Club to encourage his people to take an active role in public affairs and to preserve and promote Hawaiian culture. The "citizen prince" died in 1922, but because of his devotion to the cause of native Hawaiians, his birthday, March 26, was made a territorial, then a state, holiday. Only one other Hawaiian, Kamehameha I, is so honored.

The period between annexation and World War II saw the continued growth of the sugar industry and the emergence of the pineapple industry as a second income producer. (In 1922, James D. Dole — a distant cousin of Sanford Dole — bought the entire island of Lanai, on which to raise pineapples.) The same period also saw five major sugar companies — Castle & Cooke, Alexander & Baldwin, C. Brewer and Company, Theo H. Davies and Company, and American Factors — become Hawaii's Big Five, as they grew to control 95% of the sugar crop by the early thirties and simultaneously succeeded in monopolizing other sectors of the economy by expanding into refining, transportation and shipping, retail and wholesale merchandising, banking, insurance, and utilities. (Another company, Dillingham Corporation, not founded on sugar, made the Big Five the Big Six.)

Not surprisingly, the boards of these companies were sprinkled with men descended from the early missionaries and from businessmen who had been active in the annexation movement of the 19th century, and their power flowed into the politics of the 20th century. The *haole* plantation elite voted Republican, and they had enough money for campaign contributions to ensure that 80% of the candidates voted into the territorial legislature before World War II were also Republicans, and beholden to them.

The islands' population became increasingly multiracial as the influx of immigrants to work the vast plantations continued. Before annexation became official, the plantation owners, knowing they would be subject to US immigration laws, rushed to bring in as much labor as possible. Between 1896 and 1900, the Japanese population of the islands rose from 25,000 to 60,000, and 40,000 more arrived before an agreement with Japan in 1907 stopped the flow of workers, though women and children continued to come until Congress passed the Japanese Exclusion Act in 1924. By then, the Japanese had reached a peak of 42% of the population.

Still, more workers were needed. Labor recruited in Puerto Rico began to arrive in 1900, and from Korea in 1903, but the next massive influx came from the Philippines, which had been an American dependency since the Spanish-American War. Between 1906 and World War II, more than 100,000 Filipinos were brought to Hawaii. They eventually outnumbered the Japanese in Hawaii's fields and mills, though they never outnumbered them in the larger Hawaiian melting pot.

Another presence, the US military, was making itself felt. In 1908, Congress approved a bill for the establishment of a giant naval base at Pearl Harbor, to be the home of a great Pacific Fleet. In the mid-thirties, Hickam Field, adjacent to Pearl Harbor, became the largest American military airfield, and Schofield Barracks, in central Oahu, became the largest American army post. If the existence of these installations raised hopes that Hawaii would soon gain statehood (a movement that gathered momentum in the islands after 1934, when Congress passed a law detrimental to Hawaiian sugar interests), the existence of Hawaii's large Japanese population served to dampen them. The United States was on the brink of war with Japan, and as far as Congress was concerned, the Japanese in Hawaii were the enemy in the backyard, even though the majority of them were second- and third-generation Japanese Americans and already US citizens.

It took the attack on Pearl Harbor at 7:55 AM on December 7, 1941, to prove the loyalty of Hawaii's Japanese population. In the 2-hour surprise attack, the United States suffered 3,435 casualties, the loss of 188 planes, and the loss of or damage to 18 ships. Pearl Harbor was the greatest military and naval disaster in US history and the direct cause of America's entry into World War II.

Martial law was immediately declared against the threat of a possible Japanese invasion of Hawaii, an invasion that might be abetted by local Japanese. It never came, but a distrust of Japanese Americans continued, preventing them from enlisting in the armed services until mid-1942, when the 1,400-strong 100th Infantry Battalion was formed, and early 1943, when the call went out for 1,500 Japanese volunteers to become the 442nd Regimental Combat Team. More than 9,000 men answered the call; 3,000 were chosen. The 442nd absorbed the 100th, fought in Italy and France, and emerged from the war as the most highly decorated unit of the armed forces: The "Go for Broke" Japanese won seven presidential unit citations and nearly 6,000 individual awards.

The Japanese were not the only Hawaiians who fought in World War II. The islands' other ethnic groups — pure and part-Hawaiians, Chinese, Filipinos, Koreans, Portuguese — as well as the dominant *haoles,* largely of American and British descent, had all participated, and Hawaiian society was significantly changed by their experience. As long as Hawaii was a territory rather than a state, its residents were not first class US citizens, and their ancestry made some of them decidedly more second class than others. Yet they had all fought for the same principles of equality and democracy.

Even before the war, plantation workers had begun to question the paternalistic plantation system, and the militant International Longshoremen's and Warehousemen's Union (ILWU) had begun to organize the waterfront. After martial law was lifted, the labor movement developed rapidly. In 1946, the ILWU called a major strike against the sugar industry: 21,000 workers walked off the job for 79 days, winning, in the end, a wage increase and an end to the perquisite system by which they had received some of their pay in the form of company housing and vouchers to be used at the company store. The value of the perquisites would now be received in cash, granting greater freedom of decision to the formerly passive work force. In 1949, a 178-day strike of 2,000 longshoremen crippled the islands' economy and demonstrated once again the strength of organized workers.

Concomitant to the rise of labor was the rise of the Democratic party. Until the war, the party in power was the party of property, of planters and businessmen, of the Big Five. After so many years of staunch *haole* Republican rule, it was only natural that as more and more Orientals, particularly Japanese, took their university degrees under the GI Bill and became active in politics, they would join the ranks of the opposition, the Democrats. It was also only natural that the newly politicized and mainly Oriental working class should vote for them. In 1954, the Democratic party reversed a precedent of 50 years and swept both houses of the territorial legislature. Not incidentally, half of the legislative seats went to Japanese Americans.

By 1954, very little stood between Hawaii and statehood. The extreme tactics used by the ILWU, seen in the light of the Cold War of the early 1950s, had led to accusations that the Communists ran the territory, and these charges momentarily retarded progress. Then, too, Hawaii was still seen by some as too far away and too different to be a part of the Union, but when Alaska became the 49th state in January 1959, these objections were put to rest.

On January 7, 1959, the last of a long line of Hawaii statehood bills was announced. Appropriately numbered S-50, it went before the Senate on March 11 and passed overwhelmingly with no debate. The House passed it on March 12, and at 10:04 AM Hawaiian Standard Time, the church bells of Honolulu rang out; newspapers, already typeset, shouted STATEHOOD! in big, red headlines; and the Hawaiian population quit work for the day to dance and sing in the streets. An American flag with 50 stars flew over Hawaii, and that it was greeted with greater and more sincere enthusiasm than the one raised over Iolani Palace in 1898 was proved in June, when the people of Hawaii ratified the decision of Congress by a vote of 17 to 1. Only the island of Niihau rejected statehood.

In the same special election, the islanders celebrated their diversity by giving one Senate seat to Democrat Oren Long, a native Kansan and a former territorial governor, and the other to Republican Hiram Fong, a Harvard Law School graduate and the son of a Chinese plantation laborer. The state's seat in the House of Representatives went to Democrat Daniel Inouye, a territorial legislator of Japanese ancestry who had lost an arm fighting with the 442nd Regimental Combat Team in Italy. Hawaii's first elected governor was the appointed incumbent, Republican William Quinn, a former New

Yorker; its first elected lieutenant governor was Republican James Kealoha, a territorial senator of Hawaiian-Chinese ancestry. It remained only for President Dwight D. Eisenhower to proclaim Hawaii the 50th state on August 21, 1959.

THE ALOHA STATE

Statehood brought boom times. It coincided with the advent of regular jet service between the mainland and the islands, and gave tourism such a big boost that by the 1970s it became necessary to pose the question of how far development should go. The tourist industry, plus federal spending (mostly military), finally replaced sugar and pineapples as the state's principal money earners, though sugar and pineapples remain the state's major agricultural products. Statehood also brought a new influx of immigrants, this time a second migration of mainland *haoles*. Caucasians are now nearly evenly balanced with Japanese in the state's population, each with about 25% of the total; Filipinos make up about 10% and pure Hawaiians a mere 1%. But about 28% of the population are of mixed race, primarily part-Hawaiians, and this group has the highest birthrate. Combine that fact with the vitality of the present cultural renaissance — as more and more Hawaiians take up the study of their language and the customs of their ancestors — and there is hope that the Hawaiianness of Hawaii will increase rather than diminish in the future, and that the Aloha State will continue to be no place like home.

Music and Dance

She came dancing upon the waves
Her feet lightly tripping over the froth,
Her flesh glistening with the wild blowing sea spray.
She came with beauty shining in her eyes,
Wreathed in golden blossoms, her loins girdled with mountain vines.
And in her hair were ferns of the valley, fragile and fragrant.
She was Laka, child of music, goddess of the dance.
      — *Samuel Crowningburg Amalu*

 The origin of the hula is lost in Hawaiian legend. One story says that two gods named Laka — one male, one female — arrived from beyond the Great Western Sea in a canoe and danced for the people of Hawaii. After a time the male disappeared, but the female remained. The Hawaiians worshiped her, and she taught them the hula. It is said that the ruins of the *heiau* (temple) and dancing pavilion of Laka can be seen at Haena on the Na Pali coast of Kauai.

For whatever reasons now obscured by time, the hula was originally danced only by men and used only in religious rituals. Later, it evolved into a method of teaching, a form of entertainment, and the foundation for the art of *lua,* a style of hand-to-hand self-defense known only to Hawaiians. (*Lua* involved paralyzing nerves, breaking bones, leaping, quick thrusts with the spear, and swinging clubs, all of which was practiced with the *hula kui,* sham battle dance. Today's *hula kui* still incorporates steps of the war dance that were part of *lua.*) It is thought that as time went on and the island civilization became more complex, wars and governing and tax-collecting duties kept the men too busy to spare the years for the hula's rigid training. Women were then allowed to assume some of the chanting and dancing ritual.

Candidates for the supreme honor of hula training were required to enter the *halau* (house of hula instruction) to be supervised by a *kumu hula* (hula teacher), rather like a novice entering a convent. The selection of dancers was made at an early age on the basis of physical beauty, health, grace, agility, quickness of wit, and liveliness of imagination. Every aspect of the dancers' training was strictly regulated by *kapus* (taboos), and throughout their novitiate, generally from ages 3 to 16, they were seldom allowed beyond the school enclosure and no villager could speak with them. Only after the *uniki* (graduation) were they permitted to mingle with outsiders.

People with an oral tradition, such as the Hawaiians, often coupled chanted stories with dances. The hula movements and hand gestures reinforced for the audience the meaning and feeling of the story.

For example, graceful hand motions above the head of the dancer depict the sun, moon, stars, or creation. An abrupt arm thrust at shoulder level tells of a thrown spear or club; raised arms, bent at the elbow and with closed fists, show strength or bravery; a high, forceful kick may indicate battle. A knee bounce may mean billowing waves, a rough canoe ride, or riding a horse, or when combined with a hip-swiveling motion, it can be an allusion to sex. Foot movements can show ritual, coquetry, a journey, or boldness.

The stories narrated in the chants, the *meles,* were for commoners or for kings; they told of the origin of the islanders, the adventures of great island rulers, and about the gods and their exploits. There were name songs composed at the birth of kings and chiefs as well as prayer chants, nature chants, prophecies, war chants, love songs, funeral chants, and lullabies. In fact, from its start as a strictly religious expression, the hula gradually expanded into the opera of old Hawaii, with dancers and singers combining to tell its history and folk tales.

The chants were mostly accompanied by rhythm instruments, although "voice extenders," which had a short range of tones, were also used. The *ipu* was a drum made from a large gourd or two gourds fastened together; one played it by stamping it on a mat and then slapping it with the fingers of the right hand. The *pahu* is the largest of the Hawaiian drums; it's about 26 inches tall when used normally to accompany the hula and can be as tall as 46 inches when set on a carved base for use in temples. Made of a hollowed coconut or breadfruit tree log covered with a sharkskin membrane, it is played with one or both hands, and different parts of the drumhead are struck to produce varying depths of sound. The *punui,* half a coconut shell covered with a fish membrane, is struck with a flexible stick. Frequently played in counterpoint to the *ipu* for the hula, the *punui* is depicted in early sketches tied to the player's knee or thigh.

Uliuli are gourds or coconuts that have been filled with shells or pebbles and decorated along the handles with feathers, tapa, or woven disks. Hit against the dancer's hips or hand, *uliuli* produce a continuous rhythm and are now frequently used in *hapa haole* (half-foreign, meaning not traditional Hawaiian) songs.

Puili is a length of bamboo split into narrow strips at one end. The hula dancers hold two *puili* and hit them against their shoulders, hips, or each other, making a rattling, swishing sound.

Kaekeeke, the bamboo organ, is varying lengths of bamboo stamped on the ground to produce different tonal qualities.

Kupee niho ilio was the dog's-tooth rattle male dancers wore on their ankles in the old days. With the renaissance of traditional dances, men today often wear rattles made of seashells.

Ohe hano ihu, the nose flute, is a length of bamboo with a nosehole and several fingering holes on the upper side. Played by expelling breath from the right nostril, it functions as a "voice extension" to the chant.

The costume of the hula dancer was much the same for both sexes and hardly elaborate. Male dancers wore a simple, short wrap of tapa about their loins, large boar's-tusk bracelets on their arms, and rattles of dog's teeth around their ankles. Sketches by the traveler and novelist Jacques Arago in 1819 show female dancers in opulent wrapped skirts of colorful tapa and little else except, perhaps, a tattoo and a necklace. Garlands made of the plants and flowers sacred to Laka, the scarlet or white ohia lehua, maile, halapepe, and many fragrant ferns, were often worn around the head, wrists, and ankles.

This was the hula that so horrified the Protestant missionaries who arrived in Hawaii in 1819 and immediately began an intense campaign to suppress the ancient art form. First, they put the naked dancers into clothes — bulky middy blouses and long, voluminous skirts. Next, they introduced the Hawaiians to religious hymns and started classes to teach them the Western musical scale. It must have been a difficult task for the Hawaiians, who, after all, had their own quite different musical system, but curiosity and love of music bent them to the task, and they mastered scales fairly quickly. To the hymns they gave full and enthusiastic voice.

The first hymnal in Hawaiian, *Na Himeni Hawaii: He Me Ori Ia Iehova, Ke Akua Mau* (Hawaiian Hymns and Songs to Jehovah the Eternal God), was printed on the Honolulu mission press in 1823. It had words but no music; tunes were either memorized or interchangeable. The hymnal was an instant best-seller; 52,000 were printed and distributed to several hundred schools by 1853. Under the direction of the Reverends Hiram Bingham in Honolulu and Lorenzo Lyons in Waimea on the Big Island, whole congregations were soon singing day and night.

In the years that followed the missionary invasion, the Hawaiian islands saw the arrival of many other groups, each one with its own musical instruments. The *guitar* made its way to Hawaii on the New England whaling ships in the early 19th century. The *slack key guitar,* a style of playing devised by the Hawaiians, refers to the tuning of the instrument. The six strings are loosened (or slacked) to the lower registers and chord tuning is determined by the player's preference. The chant tradition is reflected in slack key play, with bass notes corresponding to *ipu* beats. Variations, including slapping strings, sliding into the next note, and beating the guitar body, all imitate *ipu* beats.

Hawaii is obviously the birthplace of the *steel guitar,* but exactly who invented it and when are open to argument. The nod is generally given to Joseph Kekuku, who as a schoolboy experimented with sliding a railroad bolt across the strings of his guitar. He later tried a penknife and a metal comb to produce the sweet sound; finally he designed and made a special steel bar. He then switched from gut to wire strings and raised the strings so the steel bar did not touch the neck frets. Later modifications in the bar, metal finger and thumb picks, and electric amplification produced the steel guitar as we know it today.

Hawaiians adapted the *ukulele* from the Portuguese *braguinha,* introduced to Hawaii in 1878 by immigrants who brought their favorite music from the island of Madeira, where it is still played today. During its early days in Honolulu, it was called the *pila liilii,* which means "little fiddle." Sometime in the late 19th century, the name became ukulele, which, freely translated, means "jumping flea." Queen Liliuokalani preferred a more romanticized translation: *uku* (gift) *lele* (that came). The little instrument was easy to tune and to play, with just four strings, and it was easier to carry and hold than the larger guitar. It was tremendously popular.

One of the very greatest influences on Hawaiian music appeared in the person of Henry Berger, who was brought to the islands from Germany in

1872 by King Kamehameha V to set up a Hawaiian brass band similar to Germany's. A great admirer of 19th-century Hawaiian music, "unique and of a type not known elsewhere in the world," Berger helped the Hawaiians make the transition to Western scales and instruments, organized the Royal Hawaiian Band and Orchestra, and wrote and arranged many popular songs. He later collaborated with King David Kalakaua and his sister, Queen Lili-uokalani, on much memorable music, including such songs as "Sweet Lei Lehua," "Koni Au I Ka Wai," "Kiss Me My Darling," "Hilo March," and — that most famous Hawaiian melody — "Aloha-Oe."

David Kalakaua, who reigned from 1874 to 1891, is fondly remembered for his interest in reviving traditional Hawaiian music and dance. He believed that "the hula is the language of the heart and therefore the heartbeat of the Hawaiian people." Under his patronage, more than 300 ancient hulas were saved from extinction, and he created a number of hula chants. Many new dances and songs were written to honor the King, whose spontaneous good spirits earned him the sobriquet of the Merry Monarch. The music and dance renaissance thus begun is still under way and is celebrated annually by the Merrie Monarch Festival, held each April in Hilo, at which the state's great-est hula troupes compete.

In this century, Hawaiian music was greatly popularized by the Panama-Pacific Exposition in San Francisco in 1915. Since the Hawaii Pavilion was one of its main attractions and hula shows were held several times a day, many of the 17 million visitors went away singing "On the Beach at Waikiki." And in 1916 there were more Hawaiian recordings sold on the mainland than any other popular music. Broadway's *Bird of Paradise,* starring Laurette Taylor, ran for a year in New York and toured for several years throughout the US and Canada.

Johnny Noble's Moana Hotel Orchestra played for tourists and naval personnel from 1917 to 1933 and started dancers singing his compositions, "My Little Grass Shack" and "Hawaiian War Chant." Next door at the "pink palace of the Pacific," the *Royal Hawaiian* hotel, Harry Owens and his Royal Hawaiian Orchestra kept visitors dancing under the stars to "Princess Poopooly Has Plenty Papaya" and his biggest hit, "Sweet Leilani," from 1934 through the start of World War II. This genre of Hawaiian music came to be known as *hapa haole* (half-foreign), or Hawaiian by way of Tin Pan Alley.

One of the country's best known and longest running radio shows, "Hawaii Calls," brought the music of the islands to an estimated 2 billion listeners during the 2,083 programs that were broadcast from 1935 to 1975. For four decades the popular show, featuring the best songs and best singers of each generation, was transmitted from the Banyan Court of the Moana Hotel. Each program began with the sound of the "waves at Waikiki," bringing a nostalgic tear to the eye of anyone who had visited Hawaii. At its peak, in 1952, "Hawaii Calls" was broadcast to 750 stations on the mainland, Canada, Japan, Korea, Europe, Latin America, New Zealand, and Australia. It can still be heard on the 28 "Hawaii Calls" records produced by the show's originator and director, Webley Edwards.

After World War II, Hilo Hattie and Ray Kinney took their special songs, "When Hilo Hattie Does the Hilo Hop" and "Song of the Islands," from the

Mural Room in San Francisco's St. Francis Hotel, to the Hawaiian Room of the Lexington Hotel in New York, and across the length and breadth of Canada and the United States. Until rock came in, everybody was singing their songs.

And that's because Hollywood was putting Hawaiian music and dance on the silver screen. There was *Waikiki Wedding* (1937), with Bing Crosby; *Moonlight in Hawaii* (1942); *Song of the Islands* (1941), with Betty Grable; *Bird of Paradise* (1951), with Jeff Chandler and Debra Paget; *From Here to Eternity* (1953); *The Revolt of Mamie Stover* (1956); *Gidget Goes Hawaiian* (1961); *Paradise Hawaiian Style* and *Hawaii* (1966); and the greatest, all-time most popular Hawaiian movie of them all — *Blue Hawaii* (1961), with Elvis Presley. Though a few Hawaiians, music and dance purists, were affronted by the cellophane skirts and the "wiggle" hulas of some of the early movies, most islanders laughed, enjoyed the movies, and felt that the public would remember the good and forget the bad.

The year 1959 ushered in the jet plane and statehood for the islands, followed closely by mainland hotel chains building luxurious resorts along the beach at Waikiki. This brought to Hawaii thousands of first-time visitors and introduced the era of the showroom star.

A holdover from the 1950s, with a magnificent baritone voice, Alfred Apaka kept female hearts beating to the old Hawaiian songs until his untimely death in 1961.

The stars of the 1960s were Ed Kenney, soprano Emma Veary, contralto Haunani Kahalewai, and Hawaiian crooner Don Ho. They sang Hawaiian songs, mainland songs, Japanese songs — ranging from the traditional "Ke Kali Nei Au," to the celebrated "Hawaiian Wedding Song," to the relatively recent "I'll Remember You."

In the 1970s, men began to dance the traditional hula in increasing numbers and from an increasing number of schools. Peter Moon and the Sunday Manoa played and sang their own compositions of new island songs in a new island style. Gabby Pahinui, with the Sons of Hawaii, put a fresh lilt in old "slack key" songs. Cecilio and Kapono were singing and playing up a storm of their own music.

As the 1980s continue, the Brothers Cazimero (Roland and Robert) and the Beamers (Keola and Kapono) best portray today's Hawaiian music. Interpreters of guitar music with a new sound, they compose, arrange, sing, and play their own songs; perform traditional hula and chants using traditional Hawaiian instruments; and are the leaders of the contemporary Hawaiian blending of the old and the new. Their performances are sellouts and popular with all generations.

Food and Drink

Eating with your fingers while sitting on the floor in your bare feet might sound unorthodox, but it isn't if you're doing it at a Hawaiian luau. Not simply a three-course meal but a major banquet that often lasted a whole day, this famed feast is a tradition as ancient as the islands themselves and an experience that has delighted practically every visitor to Hawaii since Captain Cook. All major occasions were celebrated with a luau, and the season of *makahiki,* a period of thanksgiving and rest in the fall, was virtually a 4-month luau.

In the old days, elaborate preparations were necessary for the luau, and villagers broke up into groups to share the tasks. Some gathered the *limu* or seaweed, a luau delicacy. Others combed the searocks for tiny shellfish called *opihi* and *pupu inu* (the latter of which gave its name to Hawaiian hors d'oeuvres). Still others caught fish, dug taro and pounded poi, and gathered coconuts, guava, and bananas. Finally, the *imu,* underground oven, was prepared.

Still used today, for no other cooking method is really better, the *imu* was a shallow, oblong hole dug in the ground that was flat on the bottom. It was lined with stones, upon which a fire of kiawe wood was built. When the stones were heated through, the wood and ashes were removed and a thick layer of ti or banana leaves laid over the stones to create steam. The food was placed on top of the leaves, and more leaves and banana stalks were spread over it. Often bunches of leaves were woven into a flat, circular lid, which was then covered with earth. All feasts included a pig *(puaa),* set in the center of the *imu,* where the heat was greatest. The other foods went around it — sweet potatoes, bananas, breadfruit, bundles of taro or sweet potato leaves wrapped in ti leaves, large fish, and perhaps a dog. The cooking time was from 2 to 8 hours, depending upon the amount of food. When the process was considered *pau* (finished), a careful uncovering took place and the meal was served.

The men tended the *imu* in ancient times and still do today, although the *kapu* (taboo) against women was lifted long ago. Since antiquity, however, women have done the serving.

At a traditional luau, mats of woven *lau hala* (pandanus leaves) covered the ground and the eating area was strewn with ti leaves. Large wooden calabashes (bowls) and gourds served as communal dishes. If there were individual plates at all, they were simply sturdy banana leaves. A place of honor was always left for the large koa wood tray, which held the pig when the *imu* was opened. Following the seating of the chief, guests were positioned around the eating area according to the strict rules of Hawaiian protocol. All sat cross-legged on the ground or partly reclined.

Poi was the Hawaiians' principal food. A paste made from the root of the taro plant, it is cooked, pounded into a powder, then mixed with water. One of the world's most nutritious foods, it has a rather insipid taste that is somewhat improved by allowing it to ferment for a day or two. To give it flavor, poi was always eaten with something else — the minced kernel of the oily kukui nut, fresh or dried fish, seaweed, or even salt crystals that were scraped from the shore rocks. Poi had to be made fresh daily since it was consumed in great quantities and there was no means of preserving it for more than a few days.

After taro, sweet potatoes were the major starch staple and were served often. Another starch, breadfruit, brought to Hawaii from south of the equator, did not do as well in the islands' cooler climate, and the fruit was seasonal. Eating or cooking bananas, wild or cultivated, were available year-round.

Coconut palms thrived in ancient Hawaii as they do today. The Hawaiians drank coconut milk and ate the flesh, but they did not grate and squeeze the meat to make coconut cream as did other Polynesians. The only sweets were sugarcane, cut into small sections for chewing, and baked ti root.

Chickens were brought into Hawaii from Tahiti and may have been eaten at certain times, but they were more prized for their feathers than for their meat. Dogs were not readily available and therefore were considered a delicacy for chiefs. They were carefully fed and fattened with poi and other starchy foods and cooked when very young. Fish was usually wrapped in ti leaves and broiled or steamed in the *imu,* but any that was left over could be salted and dried for future use.

Inu, liquid refreshments, were limited to water; the milk of young coconuts; a commoners' drink made from fermented ti roots, later known as *okolehao;* and *awa.* Basically a ceremonial drink, *awa* was supposed to be served to the gods as an offering. What the gods didn't drink, the priests did, and some chiefs and priests became addicted to it and drank it whenever and wherever they pleased. Commoners seldom had a chance even to taste it.

Prepared from the chewed root of a type of pepper plant and mixed with water, the effects of *awa* vary. A non-intoxicating drink, it is generally a benign narcotic that induces deep sleep and leaves no hangover — that is, in small amounts; overindulgence could present problems. A "safe" quantity for quaffing was gauged by the eye. When the light of a kukui nut candle seemed to be the light of two kukui nut candles, one had had enough. Excessive drinking caused arm and leg muscles to weaken, the eyes to become bloodshot, and the skin scaly. However, when the victim went on the wagon, the symptoms disappeared.

Bananas, guava, and sweet gourd or melon provided a "sorbet," a pause before the feasting began anew.

There are still luaus in Hawaii, great wonderful feasts for birthdays, anniversaries, church benefits, weddings, and other special occasions. However, just as Hawaii has changed in the centuries since Captain Cook, so too has the luau and for the same reason: The melange of races and peoples that came to the islands over the years brought along their own foods and added them to the traditional Hawaiian table.

The missionaries and whalers arrived in 1820 with molasses, popcorn, gingerbread, corn, carrots, cabbage, salt salmon, corned beef, and ship's bread. In 1852 the Chinese began to work on the sugar plantations; they contributed ginger root and spices, rice and soy sauce, bean sprouts and bok choy, duck and Mongolian barbecue, and new ways of cooking. With an 1868 shipload of Japanese workers came noodles, mochi, pickled cucumbers and turnips, rice tea, tempura and sushi, octopus and squid. The Portuguese, who settled here in 1878, shared their sweet breads and malasadas, spicy sausages and omelets, hearty fish stews and bean soups; and the Filipinos, who docked in Honolulu Harbor in 1906, offered sweet limes and sour oranges, lemon grass and fish sauces. Later waves of Koreans added kim chi and kal bi beef, and in the past 10 years exotic dishes from the cuisines of Indonesia and Vietnam have become part of the Hawaiian culinary scene. There's a dish for every taste in Hawaii.

Luaus are a special kind of party endemic to Hawaii, and most certainly all visitors should attend at least one, if only to be able to say that they tried poi and that once is enough. Luaus are relaxed and comfortable — wear a muumuu or aloha shirt — and are usually held in beautiful locations. The entertainment — Hawaiian melodies and hulas performed by young men and women — is rollicking and energetic, although sometimes romantic, and guests are often asked to participate.

Commercial luaus usually begin with a selection of Hawaiian specialty drinks aptly called exotic, which are a blend of various fruit juices and rum or other liquor. (Rum was the drink of the 19th-century whalers and seafaring men who came here from all climes and has remained a favorite in the islands.) Some of Hawaii's famous exotic drinks are the *blue Hawaii,* vodka and blue curaçao; *mai tai,* light and dark rum, orange curaçao, orgeat, and lemon juice; *planter's punch,* light rum, lemon juice, Angostura bitters, and grenadine; *Singapore sling,* gin, cherry brandy, and lemon juice; *tropical itch,* bourbon, rum, orange curaçao, Angostura bitters, and passion fruit juice; and *Waikiki chi chi,* vodka, pineapple juice, and coconut syrup.

When the pig comes out of the *imu* it is called kalua (roasted) pork. It is then shredded and served as the centerpiece of the luau buffet, which may have from 10 to 16 courses and will certainly include poi, laulau, chicken luau (see list below), and lomilomi salmon, and may also include such dishes as teriyaki steak, broiled chicken, mahimahi, various salads, tempura, pickled vegetables, sushi, homemade banana and coconut bread, fresh pineapple and papaya or bananas, several desserts, and Kona coffee. Even Mark Twain bragged about Hawaii's Kona coffee, the only coffee grown in the US, claiming, "It has a richer flavor than any other." And he was right; it's as habit forming as a Kona sunset.

The origin and ingredients of many of the dishes included in the luau and served by island restaurants are noted in the following glossary.

CONTEMPORARY HAWAIIAN FOODS

chicken luau: Chicken simmered slowly with taro leaves and coconut milk.
crackseed: Chinese preserved fruit, eaten like candy by island children (and adults).
haupia: Tender, sweet, white pudding made from coconut cream and arrowroot.
kim chi: Korean, *highly* spiced pickled vegetables.
laulau: Butterfish, pork, and taro leaves wrapped and steamed in fresh ti leaves.

lomilomi salmon: Salt salmon shredded and lomied (mixed) with chopped green onions, tomatoes, and crushed ice.

mahimahi: Everybody's favorite fish, delicately flavored. (It's dolphin *fish* — not related to the mammal.)

malasadas: Portuguese sugared doughnuts (with no hole) that are eaten hot.

manapua: Chinese, called *dim sum* everywhere but Hawaii, it's a steamed, yeast dough bun filled with *char siu* (sweet roasted) pork.

poi: Very Hawaiian, mashed taro root, it replaces potatoes as the local starch. Takes some getting used to; islanders like it a day or two old and slightly sour.

saimin: Noodles cooked in a chicken or shrimp broth; replaces the hot dog at baseball and football games. Garnished with fish cake and *char siu,* it's filling and inexpensive.

sashimi: Japanese, thinly sliced, very fresh, raw fish, served with a hot sauce of shoyu and Chinese mustard. Pick it up with chopsticks or a fork and dip into the sauce. Worth trying.

shave ice: An island confection. A large paper cone is generously mounded with finely shaved ice, which is flavored with delicious and wildly colored syrups — red, purple, orange, green — and eaten with a wooden or plastic spoon.

sushi: Japanese, for snacks or meals. Small patties of rice mixed with mirin vinegar and formed around bits of pickled vegetables or fish. Cone sushi is wrapped in a golden soybean skin.

tempura: Japanese, fish, shellfish, or vegetables dipped in delicious light batter and deep fried.

teriyaki: Could be a steak or strips of beef marinated in a local sauce of fresh ginger, sugar, and soy sauce.

Gods, Myths, and Legends

 Hawaiian *moolelo* (legend) often depicts the gods as great chiefs who dwell in the heavens or in distant lands but who occasionally visit particular places or groups of people in the islands. In the broad pantheon of the thousands worshiped by the ancient Hawaiians, four gods were considered the most powerful: Ku, Kane, Kanaloa, and Lono. Each one was noted for specific interests and talents, as illustrated in the following legend of creation:

> One day, Kane, often called the "leading god among the great gods," removed the cover of a great gourd calabash and, throwing it high into space, he formed the sky. He then plucked out the white seeds and, tossing them into the sky, made the clouds, the rain, and the wind. With more seeds, he produced the stars, the moon, and the sun. He then pulled the flesh from the gourd and molded it with his fingers to make mountains, valleys, and plains.
>
> After Kane had done this, Lono, the god of verdure, came and planted colorful flowers, tall trees, and swaying grasses to make the hills and valleys fragrant and beautiful.
>
> Next came the god Ku, who looked this way and that to see what more could be done and concluded that man was necessary; he therefore created him and the strife over right and wrong that is part of his existence.

Ku was the expression of the male generating power, the first parent by whom the race was made fertile and reproduced from a single stock. Hina, his wife, was the expression of female fecundity, the power of growth and reproduction. Together, they were invoked as ancestors of all mankind, past and future.

Ku's help was sought in producing bountiful crops, good fishing, a large family, long life, and national prosperity. There were at least 18 different manifestations of Ku, gods of taro, farming, mountains, and trees, but the two most feared and propitiated were the war gods Kukailimoku (Ku, the snatcher of land) and Kuwahailo (Ku of the mouthful of maggots). *Heiaus* (temples) were built in their honor and human sacrifices offered to win their assistance in battle. Their effigies were carried into war, sometimes in the form of great heads woven from sennit and covered with red or yellow feathers, with glaring mother-of-pearl eyes and fierce rows of dog's teeth, or sometimes represented by a simple ohia log, blessed and wrapped in yellow tapa cloth.

Kamehameha's battle effigy of Kukailimoku, which traveled with him at all times, was a small, roughly carved figure with a headdress of yellow feathers. It was said to cry out so fiercely in battle as to cause fear in the enemy and turn the tide in Kamehameha's favor.

Kane, who formed the three worlds — the upper heaven of the gods, the lower heaven above the earth, and the earth itself — was venerated as the great creator and patron of light and life. Thus, human sacrifices were not offered to him. Kane was usually coupled with the lesser god Kanaloa, about whom little is known. In some stories he seems cast as a Polynesian Poseidon, god of the sea, although Martha Beckwith, a scholar of Hawaiian chants and traditions, has said there is a tendency for Hawaiians to equate Kanaloa with the Christian devil, noting that there are several legends in which Kanaloa and his evil spirits rebelled against Kane and were sent to the nether regions.

Lono, worshiped as the god of clouds and rain, crops and agriculture, games and celebrations, was also never offered human sacrifices. Instead, each Hawaiian house had an *ipu,* gourd, of Lono hanging by the door, in which were kept bits of food, fish, and fruit; morning and evening the head of the household took down the gourd, placed it in the doorway, and prayed for the king, chiefs, commoners, and for his own family.

The fall *makahiki,* a harvest festival that lasted about 4 months, from October to February, was dedicated to Lono. It was a time when everyone ceased work, there were athletic games and feasting, all regular *kapu* (taboo) days were suspended, and rituals of thanksgiving were held. A royal procession moved through each district, collecting taxes out of the abundance provided by the god Lono in response to the prayers and offerings of the people. In these processions, Lono was represented by a straight wooden mast about a foot around and 10 to 15 feet tall. Close to the top, a crosspiece was tied to the mast from which were hung birds, feather leis, bundles of taro leaves, and, at each end, a long streamer of wide, white tapa cloth.

It was the legend of the *makahiki* that made the Hawaiians first mistake Captain Cook for Lono, and it was their discovery that he and his men were mortal that led to his ultimate death.

According to the legend, Lono sent two of his brothers from heaven to seek out a fair wife for him on earth. They traveled through each island and, finally, in the beautiful valley of Waipio on the Big Island beside the white-veiled falls of Hiilawe, they found the lovely Kaikilani, dwelling with colorful birds in a breadfruit forest.

Lono descended to her on a rainbow, made her his wife and a goddess, and took her to live at Kealakekua. One day Lono heard a mortal singing a wooing song to Kaikilani and, although she assured him that she loved him and had been faithful to him, beat her to death.

In remorse, Lono then instituted the Makahiki Games in her memory and traveled about the islands like a madman, challenging every human he met to a wrestling match. When he could no longer bear to live in Hawaii, he built a canoe, which was filled with great piles of provisions and required 40 men to carry it to the launching place. As Lono prepared to sail away, he said to his people, "I will return again to you, I promise. Not by canoe but on a floating island with tall trees and with many people and many birds and pigs."

Thus, when Cook sailed into Kealakekua Bay in January 1779 during the *makahiki* season, the Hawaiians naturally assumed he was Lono returned.

In addition to these four major gods — Ku, Kane, Kaniloa, and Lono — two other gods are of special interest — Maui and Pele.

Maui, a bit of a rogue and known as "the trickster," is celebrated throughout all Polynesia. Ethnologists have pointed out that one of the strongest pieces of evidence that Hawaiians, Tahitians, Samoans, and the Maoris of New Zealand sprang from a common ethnic root is the consistency with which stories of Maui's exploits are heard in the islands of all these people.

Maui's greatest deed was snaring the sun in Haleakala, the large crater that dominates the eastern part of the island of Maui (not, however, named after him). The legend goes that Hina, Maui's mother, complained that because the sun traveled so quickly through the heavens, the tapa cloth, which she produced from the paper mulberry, did not have time to dry.

Maui promptly fashioned a lasso from the fiber of coconut husks, journeyed to Haleakala, caught the sun by its rays (some versions say genitals), and extracted a promise that it would henceforth travel more slowly over the islands. The promise, it is said, has never been broken.

Another Maui legend — this one involving his mother's sister — tells how he tried to pull the Hawaiian islands together. Said the glib Maui (according to the story), "Oh beautiful Hinaopuhalakoa, I must have the strongest fishhook there ever was if I am to pull the islands together."

His aunt therefore changed herself into a long, hard, coral reef from which Maui broke a curved portion. Using a great rock from Kapalua to sharpen the point, he then fashioned a sturdy line from coconut palm fibers and, leaping over Molokai to the island of Oahu, he raced to Kaena Point.

With one mighty heave he threw the fishhook so far he caught the edge of Na Pali on Kauai. With all his human and godly strength he braced his feet and pulled and pulled. Suddenly the fishhook came springing back to shatter the rocks at Kaena. Kauai had not moved one hand's breadth, although some say that Waimea Canyon was created as the great hook dragged across the island. Somewhat sheepishly, Maui decided bringing the islands together couldn't be done and went on to other adventures, leaving the broken fishhook at Kaena Point.

Although Pele, goddess of volcanoes, is not one of the four major gods, she is perhaps the most popular Hawaiian god today. It is said that Pele was originally a human, who traveled to Hawaii with her brothers and sisters sometime in the 12th century. She became known on the islands of Oahu, Maui, and Hawaii as a beautiful and powerful sorceress who was killed by a cataclysmic outpouring of lava and returned as the very spirit of that white-hot lava. She is now said to reside in Kilauea Crater on the Big Island, and the various lava flows and eruptions that have taken place during recent years have been attributed to her wrath.

For example, when development of the Warm Springs resort area in the Puna District on the Big Island began, old-timers claimed that Pele was angered. They warned that the beautiful beach and *waiapele* (waters made warm by Pele) were given to the Hawaiians to enjoy without charge and forecast the destruction of the cottages and souvenir shops. Most people thought the possibility highly unlikely, for no eruption had disturbed the tranquillity of the beautiful district southeast of Hilo in hundreds of years. Early in 1955, however, before the area could become a real tourist destination, the peace of Puna was shattered by 88 days of volcanic fountaining.

When the eruption ended, enchanting Warm Springs was under 15 feet of lava.

Visitors to Volcanoes National Park who cart away "souvenir" rocks also risk incurring Pele's disfavor. When they return home, they may find themselves suffering a streak of bad luck, ranging from broken china to broken legs. Hawaiians say this is because each volcanic rock is a part of Pele — a finger, lock of hair, ankle, eyebrow, and so on — and the fiery goddess wants them returned. As a result, park rangers receive dozens of boxes of rocks each month sent back by repentant thieves.

To this tempestuous and irritable Pele, the early Hawaiians offered the young leaves of the taro plant and the sweet ohelo berries, which grow only on the summits of active volcanoes and are considered sacred to the goddess. Choice branches were tossed into Halemaumau firepit at Kilauea Crater before the rest of the berries were eaten. Today, believers still offer ohelo berries in respect, although of late it is rumored that Pele, a timely as well as timeless goddess, prefers a gift of gin.

Language

ALOHA
MAHALO
WAHINE
KANE

A visitor to the Hawaiian islands may hear as many as nine languages — Chinese, English, Filipino, Hawaiian, Japanese, Korean, Portuguese, Samoan, and a smattering of Spanish — spoken during even a brief stay. This diversity simply adds to the romance of the visit and does not cause problems, because English has been the spoken language of Hawaii since the 1850s and is the language taught in all island schools, even though certain conversations liberally laced with "pidgin" may belie this fact at times.

Unfortunately, a fluent speaker of Hawaiian is a rare bird, usually an elderly one. Hawaiian is a language that is gradually disappearing, scarcely spoken at home, taught in only a few schools and at the University of Hawaii, and transmitted to the new generation as a mother tongue only on the tiny, isolated, private island of Niihau (whose population is less than 250).

Visitors will, however, hear many Hawaiian words and phrases animating ordinary English sentences. In addition, because of the present cultural renaissance, many songs are sung in the Hawaiian language only, most major choirs sing in Hawaiian, and several churches, particularly Kawaiahao Church in Honolulu, present sermons in Hawaiian. All but a few street names and the names of most public buildings are in Hawaiian. Therefore, a traveler with some small knowledge of what Hawaiian is all about and able to pronounce the names of new native friends will be more comfortable in this paradise of the Pacific and, homeward bound, will have something to show off.

The Hawaiian language, as written today, has the shortest alphabet in the world, with only twelve letters. Five of them are vowels — *a, e, i, o,* and *u* — and seven are consonants — *h, k, l, m, n, p,* and *w.* All vowels are pronounced, there is a vowel at the end of each syllable, and a vowel always appears between consonants. Some words contain a glottal stop (') rather than a written consonant. The glottal stop, which could be considered the eighth consonant, is pronounced the way the breathy pause in "oh-oh" is pronounced.

Most words are stressed on the next to last syllable and some words have an even stress. Consonants are pronounced as in English except for *w.* When it is the first letter of a word, as in Waikiki, it is pronounced like a *w;* when it follows the vowels *e* or *i,* it is pronounced like a *v,* as in Ewa or Iwalani.

Anyone familiar with Spanish will have no trouble with Hawaiian vowels in general (and beginners shouldn't worry about exceptions). They are pronounced as follows:

a like *a* in far
e like *e* in bed

i like *ee* in see
o like *o* in sole
u like *oo* in moon

Spoken, Hawaiian is melodious and dramatic, with a lilting, romantic sound. Its vocabulary, as passed down through the written language, has only about 20,000 words, and considering how lately it became a written language — the early-19th-century missionary era — it has generated an overwhelming amount of books, manuscripts, and literature. The language is ingenious and sophisticated, often figurative in meaning, and tales and poems are filled with symbolism and plays on words. Given this complexity, it is sometimes difficult to read correctly unless glottal stops are stressed or accented vowels are marked in the text as they would be heard in speech; words otherwise pronounced the same way can have several different meanings: *ka'u* is mine, *'kau* is yours; *pua'a* is pig or pork and *pu'a'a* is confused or frightened. (These refinements in transcription do not appear in this guidebook because the only Hawaiian words included are those few, easily recognized words in almost universal use in Hawaii or the names of people or places. Glottal stops are not used on Hawaiian street signs, incidentally.)

Hawaiian differs from the Polynesian languages of other Pacific islands principally in the use of *k* for *t, l* for *r, n* for *nd* or *ng,* and *h* for *f* or *s,* and in its ambivalence about *w* for *v* (that is, using the written *w* and pronouncing it both ways).

Most Pacific sociologists and phylogenists believe that the languages of the Pacific islands derived from the root languages of Indonesia and Malaya. There are many similar words of everyday use and meaning. Coconut in Indonesian is *niur;* in Hawaiian, Samoan, and Tongan it is *niu.* Fire in Indonesian is *api,* in Hawaiian it is *ahi,* and in Samoan and Tongan it is *afi.* Sky in Indonesian is *langit,* in Samoan and Tongan it is *langi,* and in Hawaiian it is *lani.* If the missionaries who created the Hawaiian alphabet had not been so arbitrary in their choice of letters to represent the sounds they heard, these root words might even be closer in spelling and pronunciation.

Like many peoples of the Stone Age, the early Hawaiians carved their messages to posterity in the smooth lava rocks of their islands. Excellent petroglyph examples are on the Big Island of Hawaii at Puuloa near Kalapana Beach, at Kaupulehu near Kona Village, and at Puako near Kawaihae, South Kohala. Though each island has areas of petroglyphs, Hawaii seems to have more of them, probably because it is so much bigger.

Petroglyphs were once highly rated by romantic scholars and were considered transported derivatives of Egyptian hieroglyphics. In recent years they have been accepted for what they appear to be — stick pictures of people, animals, fish, canoes, battles, maps — depictions of virtually every aspect of ancient Hawaiian life. Some students say the pictures' deep and real meanings still have not been established, but most historians feel they are no more than what they seem, that they record a king's death, a good fish catch, the arrival of a great canoe from Tahiti, a family tree, or a war party.

This does not negate their importance as primitive art nor diminish the interest of the stories they tell. But it is obvious they are neither remnants of a forgotten written language nor the beginnings of one.

The Hawaiians did not have a written language until missionaries to the Sandwich Islands produced one so that the "pagans" could be taught to read the Bible. In January 1822, every *alii* (noble) in Honolulu was invited to watch the first book printed in Hawaiian, a little four-page primer, come off the small mission press. A number of the stalwart chiefs even gave printer Elisha Loomis a hand in turning the level of the old Ramage.

A full year and nine months' work had gone into the little book, all of it spent in creating an alphabet for the Hawaiian language. Each minister, doctor, carpenter, and missionary wife had given the project every available moment. Before a sentence could be written, speech variations had to be tabulated; before speech variations could be tabulated, sounds had to be distinguished. A spelling system had to be conceived, and before any of the problems could be solved, an alphabet had to be devised.

In the beginning, this diligent company identified 90 different sounds and for a few brief weeks was tempted to create an alphabet to match. But they thought it was hardly likely that the illiterate Hawaiians would be able to master an alphabet if they themselves couldn't, so they cut it as much as possible and wound up with just twelve letters, with "nine biblical consonants reserved for biblical names and Sunday school books."

Beginning with Captain James Cook, who was the first person known to have transliterated the Hawaiian spoken word, explorers and traders had given the language a confusing variety of spellings. But the phonetic decisions made by the missionaries were final. Hanarooru, Whyteetee, Owahoo, and Owhyhee became Honolulu, Waikiki, Oahu, and Hawaii forever, and *pule* (prayer) and *palapala* (writing) became the basis of the new kingdom.

Kaahumanu, a widow of Kamehameha I and the regent for the absent Liholiho (King Kamehameha II), quickly issued a decree that everyone in the kingdom was obliged to learn reading and writing. She herself ably demonstrated that the Hawaiians had the intellect to do so.

During this period only adults went to school. There wasn't room for the youngsters, whose turn, most Hawaiians felt, would come later. Besides, the alphabet was so simple that even the dullest citizen could master it. As fast as the students graduated, they were sent to organize other schools. Some classes were held under banyan trees, some under palm frond lean-tos, and some simply on the open plains, where students as often held their slates above their heads to ward off rain and sun as on their laps.

Twenty thousand copies of the Old Testament came off the presses in Honolulu and Lahaina in 1831 and 50,000 copies of the New Testament in 1832. By 1844, more than half of the adult Hawaiian population had been taught to read.

In their extreme simplification of the alphabet, the missionaries created difficulties for Hawaiians of the 20th century, for a major part of their cultural renaissance is the attempt to reclaim the rich linguistic expressiveness of their ancestors. The Hawaiian language was one of great descriptive beauty, with many nuances, but during these early "learning" years, much was lost, dual meanings were abandoned, and some words were irreparably forgotten. Today's Hawaiian scholars are making every effort to record the speech of their *kupunas* (elders) before these last few contacts with the past are gone.

This undertaking is described by Mary Kawena Pukui and Samuel H. Elbert in the introduction to the second edition of their definitive *Hawaiian Dictionary,* which begins with the saying *He loa ka'imina o ke ala o Hawai'i 'imi loa* ("Long is the search for the way of Hawaii's thinkers").

There's a tenth language spoken to a degree by everyone in Hawaii — pidgin. Pidgin is the catalyst of many Hawaiian conversations, and although it is now basically a language of fun and the peer language in all island schools, it also crops up in many a business dialogue, where it is the common medium of exchange. Hawaiian pidgin developed as a mixture of English and the various immigrant patois, to which schoolchildren have added the refinements of their own colloquial dialect. It varies not only from one island to another but from one school to another.

The ubiquitous pidgin expression is *da kine,* which can be used anywhere to describe anything. More expressive than whatchamacallit, *da kine* can cover weather, cars, lost articles, gadgets, and so on, and it can also be a flattering or a derogatory description depending upon the tone of voice. It is used when other people know what you mean and when you can't remember the name of something. Other expressions used in everyday conversations include:

> *an' den:* and then what? so what else? I'm bored!
> *brah:* friend, buddy, as in "Howzit, brah?"
> *cockaroach:* steal or sneak away with
> *geev um:* go for it, beat them, give it all you've got; similar to "go for broke," which is about the same exhortation
> *li' dat:* like that, and so; used to explain something one doesn't want to bother explaining
> *mo' bettah:* better, best, a good idea
> *shaka:* very good, right on, this is really OK; combined with a hand signal, with the thumb and little finger extended, is a "Howzit?" greeting
> *s'koshi:* a small thing or person, just a little bit
> *talk story:* gossip, shooting the breeze, bull session

The current dictionary of pidgin in Hawaii is *Pidgin to da Max,* by Peppo, found in most Hawaiian bookstores. It is lovingly done, interesting, amusing, and informative.

Pidgin is a very personal thing with the people of Hawaii, who use it every day. It's not an affectation and doesn't mix well with mainland English. Visitors can avoid embarrassing themselves and the Hawaiians by saving pidgin practice for friends and the tour escort and not including it in conversations with strangers. Using it does not make one an instant *kamaaina,* anyway. Mo' bettah to listen for it, sit back and enjoy it, but not try to get involved.

USEFUL, COMMON HAWAIIAN EXPRESSIONS

> *aikane* (eye-*kah*-nay): friend
> *akamai* (ah-kah-my): smart, clever
> *ala* (ah-lah): road or pathway
> *alii* (ah-*lee*-ee): chief, nobility

aloha (ah-*loh*-hah): welcome, love, greetings, sympathy, farewell

auwe (ow-way): too bad, oh damn

ewa (*eh*-vah): toward Ewa or westerly direction

haole (*hah*-oh-lay): Caucasian, foreigner

hapa (hah-pah): half

hapa haole (hah-pah *hah*-oh-lay): half-Caucasian

holoku (*ho*-loh-koo): long fitted dress with a train

hoomalimali (ho-oh-mah-lee-mah-lee): flattery, blarney

huhu (hoo-*hoo*): miffed, angry

kai (kah-ee): sea

kamaaina (kah-mah-*aye*-nah): native, local resident

kane (*kah*-ney): man, sign on men's room

kokua (koh-*koo*-ah): help, assistance, aid

lanai (lah-*nye*): balcony or patio

lei (lay): necklace or garland of flowers

lua (loo-ah): bathroom, not to be confused with luau

luau (loo-*ow*): party, feast, cooked taro leaves

mahalo (mah-*hah*-low): thank you

makai (mah-*kah*-ee): direction toward the sea

malihini (mah-lih-*hee*-nee): newcomer, visitor

mauka (*mau*-kah): direction toward the mountains

mele (*meh*-lay): chant, song

muumuu (moo-oo-moo-oo): very loose, long dress for all occasions

ohana (oh-*hah*-nah): family, extended family

okole (oh-koh-leh): butt, rear, bottom

okolemaluna (oh-koh-leh-mah-*loo*-nah): as in a toast "bottoms up"; literally "bottom to the moon" (luna)

ono (*oh*-noh): tastes good

opu (oh-*poo*): stomach

pali (*pah*-lee): cliff, escarpment

paniolo (pah-nee-*oh*-loh): cowboy

pau (pow): the end, finished

pehea oe (peh-hay-ah *oh-ee*): how are you?

pilikia (pee-lee-*key*-ah): trouble

poi (poy-ee): cooked taro corn pounded into paste

puka (*poo*-kah): doorway, entrance, hole, parking space

pupule (poo-*poo*-ley): crazy, pixilated

wahine (wah-*hee*-ney): girl, woman, sign on ladies' room

wai (wah-ee): water

wikiwiki (*wee*-kee-*wee*-kee): be quick, hurry, quickly

Hauoli la hanau (hah-oo-*oh*-lee lah hah-*nah*-oo): Happy Birthday

Mele Kalikimaka (meh-lay kah-lee-*kee*-mah-kah): Merry Christmas

Hauoli makahiki hou (hah-oo-*oh*-lee mah-kah-*hee*-kee ho-oo): Happy New Year

ISLAND-BY-ISLAND HOPPING

OAHU

What Oahu means to you probably depends on how old you are. If you are over fifty, chances are that it conjures up images of Japanese fighter planes strafing Schofield Barracks and Pearl Harbor. If you're younger, the island's iconography is more likely to consist of surfboards, blue seas, and the concrete exclamation marks along the Waikiki shoreline. Both images are valid, but they are recent motifs on a canvas that is much older and far more detailed.

Two million years ago, Oahu was two separate islands focused on the Koolau volcano in the east and the Waianae volcano in the west. Today, these once-turbulent volcanoes are relatively serene mountain ranges and for the most part little known except to forest rangers, a few hikers, and soldiers and airmen engaged in military exercises. Like the other Hawaiian islands, Oahu was first settled over 1,000 years ago by the Marquesans, who sailed the Pacific in huge catamarans with thatched roofs to ward off the glare of the sun. Tahitian immigrants followed, and as they mingled with the Marquesans, a distinct Hawaiian culture eventually developed, with its own language, traditions, and rituals. One is tempted to think of the islands as an earthly paradise, and in terms of beauty and climate, they probably were. Yet it was not entirely a simple life: There were such refinements as a complicated system of *kapus* (taboos), elegant feathered costumes and headdresses and tall *kahilis* (feather-decorated staffs carried by Hawaiian royalty), and intricate leis whose design symbolized the strict divisions in society. There was, too, a dark side to this life — one of internecine skirmishes and human sacrifice, as the chiefs of the various islands sought to extend their hegemony.

In the late 18th century, Kamehameha, a chief from the Big Island of Hawaii, began his ambitious campaign to conquer all of the Hawaiian islands. He took Oahu in 1795 in one of the last and bloodiest battles. All along, Kamehameha had been conducting a healthy business in firearms with Western ships arriving in Hawaii; and as the islands were consolidated, the traders discovered that Honolulu had the largest deepwater harbor in the islands. Ships began to sail here from all over the world, particularly Europe and America. In 1820, New England missionaries arrived, eager to convert and "civilize" the natives, and soon after came the great whaling ships, full of randy and hard-drinking seamen who made Honolulu their base. By the 1840s, at the decree of Kamehameha III, the nomadic Hawaiian royal court was permanently settled in Honolulu, and the island began to live up to its name, *O'a'hu,* or "the gathering place."

Most of the first Kamehameha's successors — including Kamehameha II (reigned 1819–24), Kamehameha IV (1855–63), Kamehameha V (1863–72), and King David Kalakaua (1874–91) — traveled to Europe, where they were notably impressed by the lifestyle of the court at Windsor Castle. Hawaiian women of fashion took to wearing bustles, and gentlemen donned epaulets.

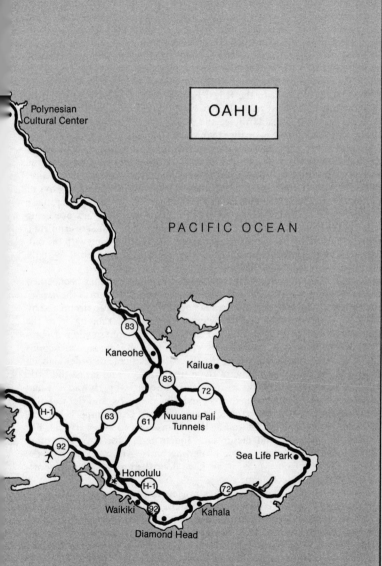

Palaces and summer retreats more suited to Surrey were built in the humid island capital. Kamehameha IV called his only son Albert, after the prince consort; played excellent cricket; and with his wife, Queen Emma, held musical soirées. David Kalakaua built a new Iolani Palace replete with sweeping staircases, stone balustrades, and Corinthian columns. To crown it all, he embellished the palace gardens with a bandstand, one of the most familiar symbols of life in provincial England.

Whatever the virtues of downtown Honolulu may be today — and they are many — they owe a debt to the Royal Family, who bequeathed to Oahu a capital as handsome as any in the Union. Now that the captains and the kings have departed, it is possible to see the comparatively simple buildings in perspective. Iolani Palace is smaller than some Newport, Rhode Island, mansions; Kawaiahao Church, "Honolulu's Westminster Abbey," looks like a prosperous village church; and St. Andrew's Cathedral could pass for the chapel of an English prep school. Washington Place, the governor's residence, and the Mission Houses are gracious reminders in their respective ways of how the rich and the bourgeois lived in New England. In scale, together, these buildings form the center of an area where other old buildings are being restored at the behest of wise members of both the city and state governments, and where new buildings are erected with an eye to harmonizing with the old. As a result, downtown Honolulu would be worth visiting even if Waikiki Beach were a million miles away.

Certainly this architectural legacy is more pleasant than that bequeathed by the early white men to the native Hawaiians. Within 20 years of the *haoles'* arrival in the islands, the native Hawaiian population had been decimated by illnesses to which they had never before been exposed, ranging from the common cold to venereal disease. And, as if Oahu were physically not paradise enough, plants, birds, and animals were brought in from similar regions to gild what was already — if we are to believe the insatiable recorder Isabella Bird — a considerable lily. Some of these tropical flora and fauna did little harm. The sugarcane (brought in from the Marquesas by Hawaiians) and pineapple provided produce for Europe and America, jobs, and (let it not be forgot) considerable private fortunes for a few people. Other imports had less value and have adapted to Hawaii at the expense of endemic varieties. For example, the charming and picturesque Indian mongoose is a pest, often destroying the eggs and the young of nesting birds. And trees such as the poinciana, brought from Madagascar, have flourished in the islands, sometimes displacing native specimens.

Some would say that the presence of strangers has been damaging, too, and that the muggings in the dark corners of Waikiki and the assaults and vandalism that have made news near the Waianae Coast resorts stem from the resentment *kamaainas* feel when *haoles* buy up property and fence it in. To the Hawaiian psyche, these compounds, especially when they are large or priced to suit only the budgets of wealthy mainlanders and equally rich locals, are chilling reminders of what are seen as historic abuses against the native Hawaiian at the hands of outsiders. Whatever the cause, crime is a problem on Oahu, though not nearly serious enough to deter the nearly 3 million visitors who annually swell Honolulu's 400,000 resident population.

But this is the debit side, and whether you put Waikiki here or on the credit side is purely a matter of taste. The area has been called colorful and exciting as well as crass and commercial, and some tourists never venture beyond its boundaries. Yet it is in the country, outside Honolulu, that the Oahu that is Hawaiian can most easily be found.

If the natural and spontaneous Hawaii fascinates you, go up to the Tantalus Drive and exult in the wonderland of a tropical rain forest; hike into the heart of Koko Crater and look at the weird and wonderful shrubs and plants that fight and survive in a wilderness of volcanic debris; walk around Kaena Point — it's hard on the feet — in the northwest of the island and look for whales spouting in the water; go to the North Shore on a rainy afternoon when the California beachboys are sleeping off six-packs and the young *kamaainas* ride the surf alone, recapturing the days when the island was theirs and theirs alone. At Kaaawa Beach, you may even spot a lone fisherman spearing squid for his family's table.

At Ewa Beach there are Hawaiian, Korean, and Japanese women scooping seaweed from the water and packing it in plastic bags to carry home for dinner, when it will be mixed with octopus or raw fish. At the *Sea View Inn* in Haleiwa, listen in as the island's old-timers make vocal sport with some lovely Hawaiian melodies. In the dry clefts way up in Makaha Valley, it's quite common to see a flurry of partridge and hear peacocks screeching. And be sure to ride TheBus, the surest way of coming into contact with *kamaainas,* all around the island, getting off when you want to savor fresh tropical fruits from run-down mom-and-pop stores. If you make even a few of these outings, you will have seen something of the real Oahu.

SOURCES AND RESOURCES

TOURIST INFORMATION: The Hawaii Visitors Bureau, 2270 Kalakaua Ave., Room 804, Honolulu, HI 96815 (phone: 923-1811), has a large number of illustrated guides, brochures, maps, and leaflets for all the islands, including materials distributed by hotels and tour guide operators. Visitor publications such as *Oahu Destinations, Here in Hawaii, Guide to Oahu, This Week, Spotlight Hawaii, Island News,* and the *Waikiki Beach Press* are available in hotel lobbies and at sidewalk stands. At car rental counters you can pick up the *Oahu Drive Guide,* designed for the motorist but with useful information for the tourist on foot as well. All the above are free and can point you in the direction of the more obvious tourist attractions and places to eat. In addition, they sometimes contain discount coupons.

Local Coverage – The *Honolulu Advertiser,* a morning daily, and the *Honolulu Star-Bulletin,* an afternoon paper, are major newspapers that cover world, national, and local events. They combine to produce a Sunday newspaper, which has a week-long review of events and a dining section containing restaurants, including some lesser-known "ethnic" places, and entertainment (editorial coverage is largely influenced by advertisers). Check the *Advertiser*'s Calendar or the *Star-Bulletin*'s Pulse of Paradise for listings of the city's often overlooked selection of movies, concerts, and shows. (Top name performers frequently include a Honolulu stopover on Asia or Australia tours.) The *Los Angeles Times* and *USA Today* are usually available in Honolulu by 9 AM on the day of publication; *The New York Times* generally arrives a day after publication. They are sold in the sundries stores of most large hotels. *Honolulu,* a monthly magazine, covers Oahu topics, people, and places, and also features a calendar of events. *Aloha* and *Hawaii* are bimonthly magazines. Both feature calendars of statewide events; *Aloha* features a restaurant directory and listing of gallery exhibits.

Telephone – The area code for Hawaii is 808.

 GETTING AROUND: Bus – TheBus: TheMarvel! A proofreader's and typographer's nightmare, TheBus is a dream come true for everyone else. It not only circulates through all the suburban veins of Honolulu but runs along most of the coastline and through central Oahu, too. Whether you go one stop or 80 miles around the island, it costs the same, 60¢ (at press time), which you must pay with exact change. TheBus is painted in shades of yellow, black, and gray. The main terminus on Oahu is at the Ala Moana Shopping Center on the Kona Street side of the ground-floor parking lot. The No. 8 bus is a shuttle between Kapiolani Park, near Diamond Head, and the Ala Moana Center, and passes through the main Waikiki hotel district en route. If you are coming from Waikiki, it will drop you on the *makai* (ocean) side of the shopping center. To reach the terminus, walk through the parking lot. Passengers proceeding by another bus can ask for a transfer upon boarding the first bus; this can be used only for a continuing journey in the same direction. If you are making several stops along a particular route, ask for a transfer each time you pay a fare.

A favorite trip on TheBus is the journey around the island: For 60¢ it's an extraordinary way to see a great deal of Oahu, besides being one of the best ways to meet local people. If you stay on the bus, the trip takes 4 hours. There are two ways to go: north across central Oahu, eastward along the North Shore, and south down the Windward Coast on bus No. 52, marked Wahiawa/Kaneohe or Wahiawa/Circle Island; or north along the Windward Coast, west along the North Shore, and south through central Oahu on bus No. 52, marked Kaneohe/Wahiawa or Kaneohe/Circle Island. Either way, the ride is splendid. Waimea Falls and the Polynesian Cultural Center are served by these routes; take the former for the falls and the latter for the center. To get to Pearl Harbor direct from Waikiki, take bus No. 20, marked Airport. You can also ride the No. 8 bus to Ala Moana and change to bus No. 50, 51, or 52, marked Wahiawa/Kaneohe or Wahiawa/Circle Island. Some buses that pass through Waikiki but do not require a trip to Ala Moana are the No. 58 Hawaii Kai bus, which can be boarded on Kuhio Avenue and makes stops at the entrance to Diamond Head Crater and Sea Life Park, and the No. 2 School Street bus, which passes the Bishop Museum. TheBus No. 19 Airport runs between Waikiki and Honolulu International Airport; however, there is no room for luggage on board, and what cannot be carried on your lap cannot be brought on. Telephone information lines provide route information at Ala Moana Center. Two publications that can be purchased for a couple of dollars are *TheBus Guide,* with details on 71 destinations and a great deal of other useful information, and *Honolulu and Oahu by TheBus,* which contains maps of Oahu, Greater Honolulu, and Waikiki showing every bus route as well as 35 small maps indicating the bus stops at some of the most frequently visited points of interest. For further information, contact the Honolulu Department of Transport, Mass Transit Lines (MTL), 725 Kapiolani Blvd. (phone: 531-1611).

A private enterprise, *Airport Motorcoach* (phone: 926-4747), provides hotel transfers for $5 and makes runs to the Arizona Memorial for $2.

Taxi – Technically, taxis are not allowed to cruise or pick up passengers on the street. However, most cabs will stop if they are not on radio call, and if the cabs are not creating a nuisance, the police usually turn a blind eye. Generally, to be sure of finding a cab, it is wise to call one yourself or through a hotel bell captain. *SIDA* (State Independent Drivers Association) taxis are owner-driven and have a good reputation for reliability (phone: 836-0011). Other major companies are *Aloha State Taxi* (phone: 847-3566), which serves the whole island and is especially popular with military personnel; and *Charley's* (phone: 955-2211), which will take you to any point on the island from the airport or drive you around the island in a Cadillac Fleetwood for a prearranged price. If you want to show up at your hotel in a Rolls-Royce, call *Silver Cloud Limousine Service* (phone: 524-7999). *Handicabs* (phone: 524-3866) specializes in transport for handicapped people and operates vehicles that will accommodate passengers in their wheelchairs. Best to call a day in advance.

Car Rental – This is a big business in Hawaii, with more firms coming up with different deals all the time. Generally speaking, the national and statewide firms are more expensive than the purely local agencies, many of which have been driven out of business in recent years by high insurance premiums. If you are traveling during July or August, over Christmas and New Year's, or in February, book your car ahead because auto rentals become very scarce in these periods. Prices decline in the late spring and the fall, but even then, it is never smart to listen to the auto rental shills who parade along Waikiki's main thoroughfares. *Alamo* (phone: 833-4585; 800-327-9633), *Avis* (phone: 834-5536; 800-831-8000), *Budget* (phone: 922-3600; 800-367-7006), *Dollar* (phone: 926-4200; 800-421-6888), *Hertz* (phone: 836-2511; 800-654-3011), *National* (phone: 836-2655; 800-227-7368), *Thrifty Rent-A-Car* (phone: 836-2388; 800-367-2277), and *Tropical Rent-A-Car* (phone: 836-1041; 800-367-5140) are the major national firms represented at the airport. *Budget's* coupon book features many free and two-for-one options. Some regional firms include *Robert's Hawaii* (phone: 947-3939); *Courtesy Car and Truck Rental* (phone: 522-7900); *Travelers Rent-A-Car* (phone: 833-3355); and *World* (phone: 833-1866), which offers the lowest rates for no-frills rentals. Whereas most of the Waikiki hotels have car rental desks that will deliver automobiles to the front door for their clients, an airport pickup will save the cost of airport-hotel transfers. *Nifty* (phone: 922-5600) has a fleet of vintage '50s and '60s convertibles for rent.

Bicycle Rental – Ideal for getting around town and along the coast, where there are no really intimidating hills, bikes are not good for the mountainside suburbs. *Aloha Funway Rentals,* 1984 Kalakaua Ave. (phone: 942-9696), is within easy reach of most Waikiki hotels. Rates range from $10 to $13 per day.

Moped and Motorcycle – They're a breezy way to see the island or just to cruise around Waikiki and the southeast. Be careful: Pickup truck drivers on the Waianae Coast tend to look askance at riders of these motorized "toys," and driving them on newly wet surfaces can be tricky if you're not completely accustomed to them. *Aloha Funway Rentals,* 1984 Kalakaua Ave. (phone: 942-9696), is the best-known motorcycle/moped rental outfit in Honolulu.

Trolley – *Waikiki Trolley* (phone: 599-2561) has launched a fleet of motorized, open-air reproductions of the horse-drawn trolleys that operated at the turn of the century. Today, they provide tour and point-to-point service both within Waikiki itself and between Waikiki and such shopping and cultural attractions as Kewalo Basin, Ala Moana Center, Chinatown, Aloha Tower, and the Waikiki Aquarium. Tours run between 8:45 AM and 6:30 PM; all-day passes cost $7.50. The trolley also shuttles between Waikiki and Restaurant Row, evenings from 5:30 to 10 PM; cost is 50¢.

 SIGHTSEEING TOURS: Boat – *Paradise Cruises* (phone: 536-3641) takes guests on a daily Pearl Harbor cruise that also includes offshore Waikiki aboard the *Pearl Kai.* Also offered by *Paradise* are daily sunset dinner cruises. *Hawaiian Cruises Ltd.* (phone: 947-9971) operates the *Adventure V* on dinner cruises along the Waikiki coast and the *Ani Ani,* from which you can ogle the Waikiki skyline or examine the coral and tropical fish on the ocean floor through the boat's glass bottom. A free bus carries *Ani Ani* passengers from and back to pickup points in Waikiki. *Aikane Catamarans* (phone: 522-1533) has twin-hulled boats with

"Polynesian" thatched roofs offering sunset dinner sails, "all you can drink," and live music and dancing. All of these cruises leave from the Kewalo Bay Boat Basin. *Windjammer Cruises* (phone: 521-0036) features sunset and dinner cruises aboard their thousand-passenger *Rella Mae,* which sets out from Honolulu Harbor. Waikiki pick-ups are provided. The slinky white catamaran with the three rainbow-colored sails that you see plying the Waikiki shoreline is the *Hilton Rainbow I.* The Twilight Buffet Dinner Sail ($39) on this boat, which is very popular and requires reservations a day in advance (phone: 955-3348), is based at the pier in front of the *Hilton Hawaiian Village* (2005 Kalia Rd., Honolulu). The *Mani Kai* departs daily at 5 PM from the beach fronting the *Hyatt Regency Waikiki* hotel (Hemmeter Center, 2424 Kalakaua Ave.) for a 1½-hour cocktail sail ($18). For individual trips by sea, hire one of the privately owned catamarans that depart from Waikiki beaches.

Bus or Van – Whether you choose one of the full-sized coaches or a minibus, the driver is going to introduce himself as "Uncle X" or "Cousin Y." It's an island tradition that all *kamaainas* are part of one big happy family, and on these tours they expect passengers to join in the spirit. If you're gregarious, it's fine; if you're misanthropic, you'll find it cloying. The information the drivers spout is generally — but not always — accurate. If you like traveling in large groups, *Robert's Tours of Hawaii* (phone: 947-3939) and *Gray Line* (phone: 834-1033) operate large buses accommodating 30 or more people. The minibus tours, carrying a maximum of 16 people, are more personal and more popular with most visitors traveling alone or in couples. *Akamai Tours* (phone: 922-6485) has a Polynesian Cultural Center package, which includes a guided tour, dinner, and an evening show. Its Circle Island Tour includes a peek inside Diamond Head Crater, Makapuu Point, the Nuuanu Pali Lookout, and Waimea Falls. The Arizona Memorial Tour offered by *Polynesian Adventure Tours* (phone: 922-0888) takes in not only Pearl Harbor but Punchbowl National Memorial Cemetery of the Pacific as well. On its Grand Circle Island Tour, admission to Waimea Falls Park and Byodo-In Buddhist Temple and a lunch stop at *Pat's at Punaluu,* a relaxing restaurant on a beach, is included; its Circle Island Beach & Picnic Tour has a beach picnic instead of the restaurant stop. *E Noa Tours* (phone: 599-2561) has a Circle Island Beach and Waterfall Tour that features Hanauma Bay, the Mormon Temple, North Shore surfing beaches, and a return to Waikiki over central Oahu's pineapple fields. For active people, *Action Hawaii Adventures* (phone: 732-4453) offers day trips led by Hawaii-born-and-raised guides; the agenda includes a fully narrated island tour by van, hiking through Manoa Valley's lush rain forest, Boogie boarding (using a small surfboard, or Boogie board) and snorkeling from Waimanalo's exquisite beach (accompanied by certified lifeguards), and Hawaiian-style fishing. Cost of $69 includes a picnic lunch. The *Moanalua Gardens Foundation* (phone: 839-5334) offers 4½-hour strolls through one of Oahu's most interesting valleys on the second Saturday and fourth Sunday of each month. Reservations required. *Charley's Sightseeing Tours* (phone: 941-2238) offers personalized limousine tours for $35 per hour, with a 2-hour-minimum required.

Plane and Helicopter – This is the only way, other than walking, to catch sight of many of Oahu's hidden mountainous slopes and crevices. Flying also provides a magnificent new perspective on favorite spots such as Hanauma Bay, Pearl Harbor, and Waimea Falls. *Hawaii Pacific Helicopters* (phone: 836-1566) conducts tours ranging from 6 to 60 minutes. The shortest tour covers Waikiki only; others fly over Honolulu and southeast Oahu; a longer excursion flies over Haleiwa and the surfing beaches of the North Shore. The Oahu Epic goes as far as Kaena Point, in the extreme northwest of the island, and goes past Kolekole Pass on the way back, duplicating the route the Japanese fighter planes took on their way to bomb Schofield Barracks and Pearl Harbor. (*Hawaii Pacific* operates tours from the *Turtle Bay Hilton* on the North Shore as well as out of Waikiki.) *Royal Helicopters* (phone: 836-2868) is another firm that offers tours of Oahu from Waikiki ranging from $28 to $150. *Helicopters Hawaii* (phone: 836-3315) and *Hawaii International Helicopters* (phone: 839-5509) both depart Honolulu International Airport on charters (1½-hour minimum) at $250 an hour for two. For a quite different and infinitely pleasing experience in aerodynamics, drive to Dillingham Field in Mokuleia on the North Shore and take a ride in a bubble-top glider under the auspices of the *Honolulu Soaring Club* (phone: 677-3404). *Hawaiian Airlines* (phone: 537-5100) also has a multi-island day tour called Islands in the Sky; land tours are included on Maui and Kauai. *Island Getaways* (phone: 922-4400), *Oceans Travel Services* (phone: 922-6481), and *Robert's* (phone: 947-3939) also feature overnight room and car excursions to the neighbor islands.

SPECIAL EVENTS: The *Hula Bowl,* played when you thought you could finally forget all about college football, takes place on the first or second Saturday in January at *Aloha Stadium,* Halawa Heights, and features all-stars from mainland college teams. The *Chinese New Year,* in mid-January to late February, is celebrated with traditional lion dances, drums, and firecrackers in Chinatown, downtown Honolulu. The Irish and would-be Irish celebrate with a lot of green and the traditional (and not so traditional) varieties of good cheer along Kalakaua Avenue, Waikiki, on *St. Patrick's Day,* March.17. A sunrise service is held each year at the Punchbowl National Memorial Cemetery of the Pacific on *Easter* morning. On May 1, a *Lei Day* queen is crowned at the Waikiki Band Shell in Kapiolani Park, where there is also a lei-making contest and, at sunset, a hula show. The most spectacular annual parade in the islands is seen each June 11 on *Kamehameha the Great Day,* when King Kamehameha I's statue, opposite the Judiciary Building in downtown Honolulu, is festooned with 40-foot leis. The *50th State Fair* also takes place on weekends from late May to mid-June; it features foods, crafts, livestock shows, and entertainment and takes place in the *Aloha Stadium.* July's *State Farm Fair,* held on McKinley High School grounds near the *Neal S. Blaisdell Center* downtown, provides a similar round of activities and a chance to mingle with locals. During the last 2 weeks of July (of even-numbered years), competitors in the *Transpacific Yacht Race,* who set off from San Pedro, California, on July 4, can be seen crossing the finish line off Diamond Head. The *Honolulu Symphony* begins its season at the *Blaisdell Concert Hall* in mid-September, with performances running through late April. Internationally renowned soloists are a highlight of the season, which also includes a December performance of Handel's *Messiah. Aloha Week,* the famous statewide celebration that on Oahu occupies the third or fourth week of September, sees a flower parade march from downtown to Waikiki as well as balls and luaus across the island. The *Honolulu Orchid Society Show,* held in October at the *Blaisdell Center,* offers lei-making and flower-arranging demonstrations as well as stunning floral displays. If you're in town during the last week of November or the first week of December, check out the free films offered as part of the impressive, annual *Hawaii International Film Festival.* Sometime during December is the *Honolulu Marathon,* with competitors running a 26-mile course from the Aloha Tower to the band shell in Kapiolani Park. December 7, *Pearl Harbor Day,* is commemorated with a service at the Arizona Memorial. It is especially moving to see veterans of the attack who still make the pilgrimage here each December, some from as far away as New England and Florida. It is ironic, too, to see the numbers of curious Japanese tourists who visit Pearl Harbor that day. For a very special Christmas experience, go to the *Christmas Eve Midnight Service* at Kawaiahao Church (957 Punchbowl St.), where you can hear carols sung in Hawaiian.

SPORTS: The conventional sports and games enjoyed across America have their adherents here, too, and whether you come to watch or participate, you will find plenty to do.

FOR THE SPECTATOR

Oahu and surfing are synonymous, but if you think that surfing is the major spectator sport on the island, try again. Here, as elsewhere across America, football draws the largest crowds and stirs the strongest passions. Hearts are frequently broken, and small fortunes lost, on the results of the University of Hawaii *Rainbows'* games, whose home turf is the *Aloha Stadium* at Halawa Heights (phone: 488-7731). The classic *Rainbows'* confrontation is the Western Collegiate Conference game against Brigham Young University (the Utah division, not the small Oahu branch at Laie). *Aloha Stadium* is the site of the *Hula Bowl,* which features top players from US colleges. The *Pro Bowl,* featuring the all-stars from the National Football League, is often held here as well. Local prep school and high school games also draw fanatical support. To observe island residents in action, it's worth going to a game between, for instance, St. Louis High and one of the tougher Western Oahu high schools, when the colorful behavior in the stands often outshines that on the field.

The *Rainbow Warriors,* the University of Hawaii's basketball team, also has its supporters, whose loyalty sometimes excels that of the football team's in quality if not in quantity. The *Warriors* play at the *Neal S. Blaisdell Center,* 777 Ward Ave., Honolulu (phone: 521-2911), which also houses such events as horse and dog shows and wrestling and boxing matches on an irregular basis.

Hawaii's best-known surfing competitions are held during the Pro Tour season in December. The three major events of the Corona Triple Crown are the *Hard Rock Café* competition (late November to early December), the *Billabong Hawaiian Pro* (early December), and the *Marui Masters* (mid- to late December), all held at North Shore beaches. Other events also crop up frequently during the prime winter surf season, and good noncompetitive surfing is available just about any time the surf is up, particularly off North Shore or Makaha beaches.

Other aquatic events that attract spectators are the *Waikiki Annual Rough Water Swim,* in which men, women, and children of varying levels of ability race from Sans Souci Beach, on the Diamond Head side of Kapiolani Park, to Duke Kahanamoku Beach, in front of the *Hilton Hawaiian Village,* sometime during September; and the *Transpacific Yacht Races,* which start at San Pedro, California, on July 4 and reach the finish line at Diamond Head sometime between July 12 and 24, depending on the class of boat. Yachts race in odd-numbered years, multihulled boats such as catamarans and trimarans in even years.

Windsurfing competitions are also held throughout the year off Diamond Head Beach, where the ample lookouts from Diamond Head Road and Kailua Beach Park provide spectators with excellent viewing.

The island's golf classic is the *Hawaiian Open International Golf Tournament,* usually held in February at the ritzy *Waialae Golf and Country Club,* 4997 Kahala Ave., Kahala (phone: 734-2151). Many people come to the *Hawaiian Open* for the aesthetic pleasure of watching the world's greatest golfers ease little white balls over what some experts consider Hawaii's finest greens. Others come simply because it is the only way they will ever be admitted to these hallowed grounds, where membership is as keenly prized by some as inclusion in East Coast social registers.

Head out to Mokuleia on the North Shore any Sunday between March and August to catch first-rate polo at the *Hawaii Polo Club,* 68–411 Farrington Hwy., Waialua (phone: 637-7656). Local teams often pit themselves against mainland or foreign competition, and Prince Charles is among those who have played in exhibition matches here. Food is available, or you can bring a picnic basket. Admission to the polo grounds is $5.

Somewhat more esoteric events are outrigger canoe races and regattas held at various island beaches in the summer (check local newspapers) and off Haleiwa Beach during the *Haleiwa Sea Spree* in February; windsurfing and sailing regattas that take place off Diamond Head Beach and Kailua Beach; cockfights, held at times and places that can be discovered only by personal inquiry; and darts tournaments, which take place occasionally at *Anna Banana's* bar, 2440 S. Beretania St., Honolulu (phone: 946-5190).

FOR THE PARTICIPANT

Bicycling – Except for parts of the desolate lava trail around Kaena Point, where you have to push a bike for a while, the Oahu coast is ideal for bicycling. There are no traumatic hills, and except for the northern corner of the Waianae Coast, food and refreshment are never too far away. All the best beaches and many sights of interest, such as the Bishop Museum and Waimea Falls Park, are accessible by bike. Some easy half-day or day rides out of Waikiki are Hanauma Bay, Sea Life Park, Makapuu Beach, the Kahala beaches, and Pearl Harbor. The routes through central Oahu climb from both north and south up to the central plateau, and unless you're in top condition, they would require walking a few miles. However, there is little to attract the tourist along these routes, and people coming to Haleiwa, for instance, from Waikiki via the Windward Coast might wish to return the same way. Two cautionary notes: Traffic on all the coast roads, especially on the Windward Coast and Southeast Oahu, is bad, and bike lanes, even though they do exist, are few. Thefts and vandalism of bicycles have been reported all over Oahu; the North Shore and the Waianae Coast seem to be spots where bikes and sometimes their riders are especially vulnerable.

For casual weekend outings with reliable guides, contact *Hawaii Bicycling League,* PO Box 4403, Honolulu, HI 96813, for a schedule of its programs and excursions. Information about them is usually available in bike shops. Bicycles may be rented from *Aloha Funway Rentals,* 1984 Kalakaua Ave., Honolulu (phone: 942-9696). If you're planning a stay of several months, check *Goodwill Vocational Training Centers,* where there are occasionally good bargains in standard secondhand bikes. Two locations are in downtown Honolulu: 780 S. Beretania St. (phone: 536-4115); and 2028 Dillingham (phone: 842-1000).

Boating – Although dozens of operators are anxious to sail you down to Pearl Harbor or along the Waikiki shore with a mai tai in hand, surprisingly few places offer boat rentals or instruction. *Froomes Sailing Company, Inc.,* 789 Kailua Rd., Kailua (phone: 261-2961), specializes in catamaran rentals and lessons as well as windsurfing rentals. Bareboat Hobie Cat rentals and instruction are offered from *U-Sail Rental* (phone: 946-0130) in front of the *Hilton Hawaiian Village. Royal Aloha Cruises* (phone: 941-0345), *Jada Yacht Charters* (phone: 955-0772), and *Honolulu Sailing Company* (phone: 235-8264) offer skippered yacht charters.

Body-Surfing – The Diamond Head end of Prince Kuhio Beach in the 2400 block of Kalakaua Ave. offers some of the best body-surfing in Waikiki. Kalama Beach, in Kailua between Kalaka Place and Kaione Place where large surfboards are forbidden, is another favorite spot. Makapuu Beach, on Kalanianaole Highway just beyond Koko Head, is one of the loveliest places on Oahu to while away an afternoon, and it is also the most famous body-surfing beach on the island. Although Makapuu lies between two rocky points, there are no exposed rocks on the beach in the summer (they do appear after the erosion caused by the winter surf), and there is no offshore reef. These conditions mean that when you ride in on a strong but slow-rolling wave, you land — with luck, not too heavily — on firm sand. Here again a caveat is in order: Easy as it might look when you see people performing nonchalantly all around, if you have no experience of body-surfing, this is not the place to learn. Those waves are not always the gentle giants they appear to be. Note that body-surfing here in the winter is lethal and that boards — except for the small *paipo* kind — are forbidden at any time of the year.

Fishing – Au, ahi, ono, mahimahi, opakapaka, aku: If these names are music to your ears, head for the Kewalo Boat Basin on Ala Moana Boulevard across from the Ward Warehouse. Here you will find boats ranging in size from 35 feet to over 60 feet available for charter by the day, half day, or for several days. They are chartered mostly by groups of six and sometimes more, but it is not unusual to be able to buy one or two shares in a cruise. If you're not quite sure what you want, your best bet is to go to the basin in the late afternoon when the boats return and talk to passengers and owners to decide who is offering the trip that suits you the best. If you are commandeering the complete boat, then the outing is tailored according to your needs. Among the better-known operations, all of which supply tackle and bait (lunch and beverage may be supplied at extra charge), are *Island Charters,* Kewalo Basin (phone: 536-1555); *Coreene C's Sport Fishing Charters,* Kewalo Basin (phone: 536-7472), whose deluxe vessel the *Coreene C* once brought back to shore a 1,805-pound marlin, the largest ever caught off Oahu; and *Sport Fishing Hawaii* (phone: 536-6577), which has "party" boats for up to 18 people. If you love deep-sea fishing but have a tendency toward seasickness, opt for the *Kono,* Kewalo Basin (phone: 531-0060), the only gyro-stabilized boat for charter in Honolulu. Catches from the *Kono* are consistently impressive if rarely record-breaking. Pokai Bay, on the Waianae Coast, and Haleiwa, on the North Shore, are other places where you can find charters.

At Haleiwa you will also find people fishing for mullet from the bridge across the Anahulu River. At Kaiaka Bay, about a half mile west, crabs can be found where Paukauila Stream empties into the ocean. At Kaaawa, on the Windward Coast, people seek out squid with spears. Pole fishing is popular all along the Waianae Coast, at the Haleiwa beaches, and along the North Shore between Waialee Beach and Kaihalulu Beach. Oio (bonefish) and moi (threadfish) are some of the catches you might make. For information on fishing in Hawaii, get a copy of the monthly *Hawaiian Charter Fishing Guide* by writing PO Box P, Kailua-Kona, HI 96745 (phone: 325-6171; 800-367-8014).

Golf – If you're serious about golf in Honolulu, you move to Kahala or Diamond Head, fill out an application form for the *Waialae Country Club,* 4997 Kahala Ave. (phone: 734-2151), and wait for a member to die so that you can move up a place on the waiting list. It has the most prestigious greens and the swankiest 19th hole on Oahu, and people have been known to divorce and remarry just to be able to say they belong. Non-members have to make do with the 15 other courses on the island that are open to the public (regardless of pedigree or bank balance), but require greens fees of anywhere from $2 to $60 (cart included). In addition to the municipal, private, and resort golf courses, several of the military facilities on Oahu have their own. If you're glued to Waikiki, the place to head for is the recently regroomed *Ala Wai Golf Course,* 404 Kapahulu Ave. (phone: 296-4653), constructed on what once were waterlogged taro fields. *Ala Wai* is very flat and not particularly challenging. However, it is a pleasant place to stand around looking at the Koolau Range and Diamond Head, which is what a lot of people do while waiting to start on this very busy course. Statistics for the course are: 18 holes, 6,474 yards, par 71. Other municipal courses include *Pali Golf Course* (18 holes, 6,604 yards, par 72), 40-050 Kamehameha Hwy., Kaneohe (phone: 261-9784), which is the one you look down on from the Pali Lookout; and *Kahuku Golf Course* (9 holes, 2,700 yards, par 35), Kahuku (phone: 293-5842), which is right on the ocean in the northeast section of the island, but has neither a pro shop nor carts. At press time, several new courses were being planned.

Two resorts with first class golf are the *Sheraton Makaha Resort* (phone: 695-9511) and the *Turtle Bay Hilton* (phone: 293-8811). The *Sheraton Makaha Resort Country Club* course (18 holes, 6,400 yards, par 72) straddles the low, rolling hillside between the imperious walls of the Makaha Valley. It is bisected by the Makaha Stream and has reputedly the highest stroke rating in Hawaii. If you hear shrieking here, it's not the pro making critical comments but peacocks looking for attention in the undergrowth. The championship course at the *Turtle Bay Hilton* (18 holes, 6,400 yards, par 72) is another oceanside challenge. Although the terrain here is basically quite flat, course architect George Fazio designed subtle traps and elevated greens on landfill that make this course far more interesting than it might appear. Fazio also had the task of diminishing some natural impediments, notably those imposed by the northeast trade winds, which buffet these shores during the winter. Thanks to his careful planning, you play downwind most of the time. Both resorts have fully equipped pro shops. The *Makaha Valley Country Club* (phone: 695-9578), adjacent to the *Sheraton Makaha Resort,* was formerly a private enclave but is now open to the public (the course is 18 holes, 6,251 yards, par 71). *Hawaii Kai Championship Course* and par 3 holes of the *Hawaii Kai Executive Course,* both at 8902 Kalanianaole Hwy. (phone: 395-2358), have magnificent views of the Kaiwi Channel to distract you. There is a pro shop attached and lessons are available (Championship course: 18 holes, 6,350 yards, par 72; Executive course: 18 holes, 2,542 yards, par 54). At *Mililani Golf Club* (18 holes, 6,360 yards, par 72), Mililani Town (phone: 623-2222), instruction is available for the whole family. Other courses include: *Moanalua Golf Club* (9 holes, 2,972 yards, par 36), 1250 Ala Aolani (phone: 839-2411), on the *ewa* (west) side of Moanalua Valley, near the bubble gum pink Oahu landmark, Tripler Army Medical Center; the *Olomana Golf Links* (18 holes, 6,003 yards, par 72), 41-1801 Kalanianaole Hwy., Waimanalo (phone: 259-7926); and *Pearl Country Club* (18 holes, 6,491 yards, par 72), 98-535 Kaonohi St., Honolulu (phone: 487-3802), where you need to call for a starting time. At press time, work was underway on the first of several 18-hole courses at the *Ko Olina* resort near the Ewa district, west of Honolulu; completion is slated for mid to late 1990.

Golf tours, which include in their cost hotel pickup, clubs, greens fees, and carts, are available from *Kato's Golf* (phone: 947-3010) and *Alii Golf* (phone: 735-0060). *Alii Golf* requires a minimum of five golfers.

Hang Gliding – *The Fall of Icarus* is the name of a painting by Pieter Brueghel the Elder, and modern Icaruses still occasionally fall to their death along the Windward Coast in spite of the steadily increasing amount of know-how and streamlined equipment available. The ridges above Sea Life Park are a popular takeoff point in southeastern Oahu, and when the wind conditions are right, colorful airborne flotillas drift between Kailua and Makapuu Point. If you want to have a go, *Tradewinds Hang Gliding Center* (phone: 396-8557) has certified instructors who urge beginners from sand dunes and lead advanced fliers soaring over the *palis.* Tandem flights with a certified instructor are also offered.

Hiking – It is entirely possible to see and appreciate Oahu's coastline by car, assuming that you stop here and there to savor the beaches and the mountain peaks more fully. To penetrate what remains of "hidden Oahu" — the rain forests, a crater or two, and the back reaches of Makaha Valley — walking is the only way. Many of the trails that are marked on maps belong to the federal government or the military or are privately owned. All the hikes referred to below require only will power, varying degrees of stamina, a good pair of hiking boots, and in some cases, supplies of fresh water. (Diamond Head also requires a permit for groups of 25 or more.)

Manoa Falls: This is the most accessible and one of the easiest trails in the Honolulu area, leading through dense, brooding rain forests in the mountains and valleys that can be seen from Waikiki. On either side of the trail, which for part of the way is a stone footpath, are flaming ti leaves, brilliant ginger, mountain apple, hau trees, and colorful thimbleberry and passion fruit vines. You can cool off by dangling your feet in Manoa Stream, at the bottom of the falls, though if the rains have been particularly heavy — 200 inches in 1 year is not unheard of — it is wise to stand clear in case boulders come tumbling over the cataract. To reach the trail, drive to the end of Manoa Road just past Paradise Park and the Lyon Arboretum. Park close to the chain strung across the road; the trail begins on the other side of it in front of a high stone wall.

The escorted tours of *Action Hawaii Adventures* (phone: 944-6754) feature hikes to Manoa Falls.

Diamond Head: Just about everybody knows what it looks like from the outside, but not many people have explored it from within. The crater was a major installation in the defense of the Pacific in World War II and is still part of Fort Ruger and used by the Hawaiian National Guard. Bunkers, shelters, and gun redoubts are still in evidence, and part of the relatively easy climb up to Point Leahi, the highest point on the crater rim, leads you through gun emplacements and up steel stairways and ladders. From the top, the view of Honolulu, Waikiki, and the ocean is memorable. The crater is open from 6 AM to 6 PM daily. To reach the trail head, drive up Monsarrat Avenue into Diamond Head Road and take the right turn into the crater just beyond the junction with Makapuu Avenue. The trail begins at the parking area by the firing range in the middle of the crater and is paved much of the way.

Mauumae Trail: This hike is for the physically fit. It takes about 6 hours and runs along the crest of Mauumae Ridge to an elevation of almost 2,500 feet through groves of koa and ohia trees reminiscent of the Big Island. Around the tree trunks you will see the small white flowers of the *kopiko* shrub, and here and there are dense growths of red *ieie* and wildernesses of tropical ferns. You may even glimpse Kaau Crater, seen by few islanders and fewer tourists. These southeastern reaches of the Koolau Range also have abundant birdlife, and you will most likely see Japanese white-eye (small and greenish, with yellow throat and broad white ring around the eye), apapane (deep red with black wings and tail), and amakihi (yellowish green with a curved bill). If you are lucky, you may catch sight of an elepaio (brown uppers, white hindquarters, cocked tail) or a shama (shiny black with a reddish brown belly, white hindquarters, and a black and white tail). If you don't see the shama you may hear it; its song is lovely. The trail starts at Maunalani Circle at the top of Wilhelmina Rise.

Some other Oahu hikes are Makaha Valley: Easy trails lead up to the back reaches of the valley from the *Sheraton Makaha,* where instruction is available. On these trails, partridge and wild turkey can be heard and/or seen. However, construction planned for the valley may soon inhibit hiking. Koko Head Cliff Walk: A rocky shelf between the ocean and the road leads from Hanauma Bay to the Blowhole. It is a beautiful, 2-mile seaside ramble above tidal pools and past caves. Waves along the coast can be very deceptive even on calm days, and someone has to keep an eye on the surf at all times. If you're walking alone, that means you. This trail is not recommended for children. Makua Gulch: A pool of refreshing mountain water awaits you at the end of this densely overgrown canyon on the northern windward slopes of the Koolau Range.

If you want to hike Oahu with people familiar with the island's trails, check with the *Hawaiian Trail and Mountain Club,* PO Box 2238, Honolulu, HI 96804 (phone: 247-3922), or with the Hawaiian chapter of the Sierra Club, PO Box 11070, Honolulu, HI 96828 (phone: 946-8494), both of which conduct hikes at fairly regular intervals at a small fee for non-members. Before venturing forth, you might read Craig Chisholm's *Hawaiian Hiking Trails* (Touchstone Press; $9.95), which is jammed with facts and makes delightful reading whether you set foot on a trail or not.

Horseback Riding – Some of the best riding on Oahu is up into the wilderness in the little-known back reaches of Makaha Valley: The *Sheraton Makaha* (phone: 695-9511) conducts hour-long escorted rides for guests as well as the public. The *Turtle Bay Hilton* (in Kahuku; phone: 293-8811) offers its guests escorted rides through palm and ironwood groves along beautiful deserted beaches. In the southeast of the island, lessons are available from *Koko Crater Stables,* 408 Kealahou St., Honolulu (phone: 395-2628). The *Kualoa Ranch,* 49-560 Kamehameha Hwy., Honolulu (phone: 237-8515), features 1- and 2-hour trail rides into the undeveloped valleys that stretch inland from the Windward Coast.

Hunting – Wild pig, wild goat, pheasant, quail, partridge, and wild turkey are all present on Oahu. There are 12 designated hunting areas on the island, most fairly inaccessible, but there are no guides or tourist services available for the visitor who would like a day's rough shooting. Hunting activities and the issuing of licenses are controlled by the State of Hawaii Department of Land and Natural Resources, Conservation and Resources Division, 1151 Punchbowl St., Room 330, Honolulu (phone: 548-5919).

Kayaking – *Go Bananas,* near Waikiki, at 740 Kapahulu Ave. (phone: 737-9514), features accredited guides from the American Canoe Association on its Oahu day tours by kayak. During summer months, a sister company, *Oceanic Adventures,* offers escorted neighbor island kayak excursions. *Ocean Sports Hawaii* (phone: 946-6133) has hourly, half-day, and full-day rentals from its shop at 1735 Kalakaua Ave., Honolulu. *Twogood Kayak Hawaii,* 46-020 Aalaloa St., Suite B-6, Kailua (phone: 235-2352), offers lessons ($25) and rentals ($20 for a half-day, $25 full day, and $40 weekend). Car racks are also available for rentals ($12); equipment delivery and pickup in Waikiki costs $25. *Ocean Kayak* (phone: 239-9803), in windward Kahulu, offers half-day rentals for $10, full-day rentals for $20 (no Waikiki deliveries). Closed Sundays.

Parasailing – *Aloha Parasail* (phone: 521-2446) will transport its clients from Waikiki hotels to its takeoff site in Kewalo Basin. Another parasail company is *Waikiki Beach Services* (phone: 924-4941).

Polo – The *Hawaii Polo School* (phone: 637-7656) offers private instruction on the grounds of the *Hawaii Polo Club* and packages that include lessons, play, horses, equipment, and accommodations in a cottage at the *Mokuleia Beach Colony,* adjacent to the polo field. Cost per student is $90 for a 1½-hour lesson, $2,400 for the week-long package.

Scuba Diving – Hanauma Bay, a marine life conservation park, is a good place for beginners. The coral formations, marine plants, marine life, and shells here are more interesting than those found along the Waikiki reefs. An illustrated board on the beach shows you the best spots for diving and what you can expect to find. Several dive shops along the bay operate Mondays through Fridays. Another good spot for beginners is Sans Souci Beach, Waikiki, just *ewa* (west) of the *Kaimana Beach* hotel. More experienced divers can choose more glamorous locations. Divers off Manana Island, popularly known as Rabbit Island, off the Windward Coast, can descend to 60 feet to examine the corals covering the Koolau basalt on the ocean bottom. Fantasy Reef, off Waialae Beach at Kahala, is accessible only by boat. Divers like to come here to see giant sea turtles and watch huge manta rays show off by swimming upside down and turning somersaults. There is more good diving at Laie Beach, on the northern section of the Windward Coast, especially in the reefs between Laie and Laniloa Point. You may find lobster ambling around here as well as the usual dazzling array of tropical fish. In the summer, when the ocean thereabouts is very calm, Haleiwa Beach can be rewarding for the diver.

There are a number of professional operations in Honolulu to help the diver and the would-be diver. Among the best known are *Dan's Dive Shop Inc.,* 660 Ala Moana Blvd., Honolulu (phone: 536-6181), and *Waikiki Diving,* 420 Nahua St., Honolulu (phone: 922-7188), both of which offer instruction for ingenues and brush-up courses for those with some experience. *Aquaventure* (phone: 734-2211) offers in-pool introductory lessons and charter dives from the *Kahala Hilton.* Free van transfers are provided to and from Waikiki. *South Seas Aquatics,* 1050 Ala Moana Blvd., Honolulu (phone: 538-3854), offers two-tank dives off the Waianae Coast out of Waianae boat harbor. Divers can explore coastal sea caves and inspect a World War II boat that rests on the sandy bottom 85 feet below the surface. All these operators make Waikiki hotel pickups and returns. The *Leeward Dive Center,* 87-066 Farrington Hwy., Maili (phone: 696-3414), explores some of the most fascinating waters along the rocky north Waianae Coast.

Guests at the *Turtle Bay Hilton*, Kahuku (phone: 293-8811), can avail themselves of free scuba instruction in the hotel pool. Those who take to the pastime can arrange for ocean dive tours (for certified or non-certified divers) through the LRS Pool Services desk at the hotel.

Snorkeling – This is not the poor or timid man's version of scuba diving, but a quite separate experience — gentle, meditative, and occasionally thrilling. Hanauma Bay, once again, is the paradise among snorkeling spots on Oahu. Friendly fish really will rub noses with you, though enticing them with a crust of bread or cookie crumbs is a no-no even though the habit appears to be growing. Check the display board on the beach for the best snorkeling areas. In Waikiki, Sans Souci Beach is the best place for snorkeling. The North Shore beaches, deadly to all but the most expert surfers in the winter, are ideal for snorkeling on calm summer days, especially Waimea Bay Beach, Sunset Beach, and Pupukea Bay Beach. At Pupukea, from a panoramic vantage point on the surface of the lovely tidal pools known collectively and erroneously as Shark's Cove, you can glimpse some quite large fish cruising idly over the sponges on the ocean bottom. Kahe Beach Park and Nanakuli Beach, off the Farrington Hwy. on the Waianae Coast, provide interesting snorkeling right along the shoreline. If you are a snorkeling buff, it might be worth comparing experiences of the windward side of the island, with its abundant offshore reefs, with those of the Waianae side, where offshore reefs are extremely scarce.

Hanauma Bay day trips are offered by *Snorkel Hanauma Bay* (phone: 955-5680), *Hawaii Snorkeling* (phone: 944-2846), and *Blue Water Divers* (phone: 955-1066). All three companies include hotel or condo transfers and equipment. In addition, most beach hotels in Waikiki and many off-beach hotels rent snorkeling equipment to guests. *Waikiki Beach Services* (phone: 924-4941) is one of a number of equipment rental concessions along Waikiki Beach. *Captain Bob's* (phone: 926-5077) departs Kaneohe Bay for a picnic snorkel with the Windward Coast as a backdrop.

Surfing – This is Oahu's top "glamour" sport, the one that brings visitors to the islands the way skiing brings them to Colorado and grouse shooting to Scotland. In the popular imagination, Waikiki Beach is, along with Bondi Beach near Sydney, Australia, one of the two most famous surfing spots in the world. Hawaiian royalty surfed here generations ago, and the 2- to 5-foot waves that are standard along the celebrated shoreline for much of the year are perfect for novices and amateurs. On the few days in the summer when they reach 15 feet, Waikiki's waves should be avoided by all but experts. There are many concessions on the beach that rent surfboards and have licensed instructors on hand. *Beach Boys Inc.* (phone: 923-0711; ask for beach services) and *Waikiki Beach Services* (phone: 924-4941) both offer equipment rental and lessons for surfing, jet skis, outriggers, and so on. A major drawback for surfers on Waikiki Beach is that it is almost always crowded. The nearest beach off the strip that is safe enough for the casual surfer is Ala Moana Beach Park, just *ewa* (west) of the Ala Wai Canal between the ocean and the 1200 block of Ala Moana Boulevard. Farther afield, Haleiwa Beach Park, in the 6200 block of Kamehameha Highway, on the North Shore, is good for beginners when the surf is low between April and October. Kalama Beach, reached by the public right of way at the end of L'Orange Place or Kalaka Place, off North Kalaheo Avenue in Kailua, is one of the most beautiful surfing spots on Oahu for novices and casual surfers. Board surfing, except on *paipo* boards less than 3 feet long, is forbidden on Kalama Beach between Kalaka Place and Kai One Place. Expert and champion surfers head for Makaha Beach and Yokohama Beach, Farrington Hwy. on Oahu's Waianae Coast, which have some of the most impressive surf in Hawaii during the winter, and for such notorious North Shore spots as Sunset Beach, Ehukai Beach Park, home of the legendary Banzai Pipeline, and Waimea Bay Beach Park, all of which are along the Kamehameha Highway east of Haleiwa.

If you're traveling without equipment, *Local Motion Surfboards*, 1714 Kapiolani

Blvd., near the Ala Moana Shopping Center in Honolulu (phone: 955-7873), sells and rents used surfboards. The store also has experts on duty to advise newcomers on what particular kind of equipment suits which particular area. Surfers who are pretty sure of what they want in terms of size, shape, weight, and skegs (fins), should try one of the following businesses in Honolulu, all of which supply custom surfboards along with whatever esoteric details may be requested: *Blue Hawaii,* 1960 Kapiolani Blvd. (phone: 947-5115); *Downing Hawaii,* 3021 Waialae Ave. (phone: 737-9696); or *Hawaiian Island Creations,* Ala Moana Shopping Center (phone: 941-4491).

Swimming and Sunning – High surf and strong currents are characteristic of every beach on Oahu at some time or another. It may not be very romantic or particularly intrepid, but the smart thing to do is to stick to beaches where there are lifeguards. If you're uncertain about the water conditions on any particular day, ask them; they can tell you whether those gently rolling waves are disguising a mischievous (or worse) current. Other hazards to look out for are surfboards; rare raids by Portuguese man-of-war jellyfish when the wind is in the right direction; and coral, a living organism that can cause nasty gashes and infections. Sharks pose no threat in Hawaiian waters except under the most unusual conditions.

Waikiki Beach, from Duke Kahanamoku Lagoon in front of the *Hilton Hawaiian Village* to the Outrigger Canoe Club at the Diamond Head end, is the most popular — and one of the safest — swimming areas on the island. The area in front of Waikiki Beach Center is considered ideal for the casual swimmer. Queen's Surf Beach, a few hundred yards south of Waikiki Beach Center, is popular because it has lawns behind it on which to relax after exercising. *Kamaainas* like Ala Moana Beach Park. On the windward side of the island, Kailua Beach Park, at the very end of Kailua Rd. in Kailua, is a beautiful white strand that slopes gently into deep waters that are calm most (but not all) days of the year. At Kalama Beach, also in Kailua, the shoreline is steeper and the currents stronger; however, for experienced ocean swimmers, there should be no problem. The bonus here is the absence by law of all surfboards (except the small, *paipo* kind) within a restricted area of about a half mile. Farther north, Kahana Bay Beach Park is another place where a gentle slope to deeper waters makes for safe, pleasant bathing. When the waters are quiet in the summer you can swim at Ehukai Park, home of the Banzai Pipeline, and at Waimea Bay on the North Shore; then, later, at home, you can say "I swam there!" as the huge winter surf rolls across your television screen. For a quite different experience, hike up to Sacred Falls from Plantation Road, which turns off the Kamehameha Highway between Punaluu and Hauula. At the end of the hour-long trek, at the bottom of the falls, there is a lovely swimming hole that can be downright bracing.

Tennis – There are public courts at 40 places around Oahu, all under the supervision of the County of Honolulu Department of Parks and Recreation, Tennis Division, 3908 Paki Ave., Honolulu, HI 96815 (phone: 923-7927), which will supply a complete list of addresses to anyone requesting it with a stamped, self-addressed envelope. Public courts in the Waikiki area are: *Ala Moana Park,* 1201 Ala Moana Blvd., 10 lighted courts; *Diamond Head Tennis Center,* 3908 Paki Ave., 9 courts; and *Kapiolani Tennis Courts,* 2748 Kalakaua Ave., 4 courts. Play is on a first come, first served basis. *Honolulu Tennis Club,* 2220 S. King St. (phone: 944-9696), has 4 courts and an instructor for lessons.

Waikiki hotels with tennis facilities are the *Hawaiian Regent,* 2552 Kalakaua Ave. (phone: 922-6611), with 1 court, professional instruction, and a pro shop; the *Outrigger Malia,* 2211 Kuhio Ave. (phone: 923-7621), with 1 court; and the *Pacific Beach,* 2490 Kalakaua Ave. (phone: 922-1233), with 2 courts. The *Ilikai,* in Waikiki at 1777 Ala Moana Blvd. (phone: 949-3811), has complete tennis facilities, with a resident pro, a pro shop, 4 day courts, 1 lighted court, and 1 lesson court, and offers instruction for singles, couples, or groups. Outside Waikiki, the *Sheraton Makaha* in

Makaha (phone: 695-9511) has 4 courts, a pro shop, and professional instruction; and the *Turtle Bay Hilton* in Kahuku (phone: 293-8811) has 10 courts (4 lit for night play) operated by Peter Burwash International, which provides a director for single or group instruction.

Water Skiing – The novice to the advanced water skier will find fine opportunities in the Koko Marina Lagoon in Hawaii Kai by contacting the *Water Ski Center* (phone: 395-3773).

Windsurfing – After racquetball, windsurfing may be the fastest growing sport in the US. Kailua Beach Park and Diamond Beach Park see most of the action; you can occasionally spot equipment designers and practice teams testing new equipment here. *Windsurfing Hawaii,* 156C Hamakua Dr., Kailua (phone: 261-3539), has a wide selection of boards for people just learning as well as for windsurfing whizzes. The same organization runs the *Kailua Beach School,* which promotes windsurfing tours for beginners and advanced sailors on the Windward Coast, where whales are sometimes spotted, and has a 3-hour introductory course. Private lessons ($25 an hour) are also available for people eager to master the skill of wave jumping. *Aloha Windsurfing,* in Waikiki at 437 Launiu St. (phone: 926-1185), also rents windsurfing equipment in addition to providing lessons and conducting full-day tours from Waikiki to Kailua ($40; $47 with lesson).

AROUND THE ISLAND

Oahu looks vaguely like a square with an appendage off the lower right-hand corner. It has six distinct geographic areas: the southern flatlands, including the Ewa district, Pearl Harbor, and Honolulu; southeast Oahu, a triangle, with Honolulu, Kailua, and Koko Head forming its three points; the wet and very green narrow strip known as the Windward Coast in the east; the North Shore; central Oahu, a broad valley between the Koolau Range in the east and the Waianae Mountains in the west; and the Waianae Coast, on the dry, leeward side of the Waianae Mountains. The highest point in the Koolau Range is Puu Konahuanui, at 3,105 feet, and the tallest peak in the Waianaes is Kaala, at 4,025 feet. The words *north, south, east,* and *west* are heard on Oahu, but the island has some special terms to indicate directions that are not just picturesque but are in constant daily use. The two that are common throughout the islands are *mauka,* which means inland or toward the mountains (from Waikiki, for instance, the Ala Wai Golf Course is *mauka* the Ala Wai Canal; "go *mauka* along Kapahulu Avenue to the golf course"); and *makai,* toward the sea (from the golf course, Waikiki is *makai* of the Ala Wai Canal; "go *makai* along Kapahulu Avenue to Waikiki"). Two terms that are used only on Oahu and more precisely in the Honolulu area are *ewa,* which indicates west (Ewa is a district west of Honolulu); and Diamond Head, which is Honolulu talk for east. (TheBus goes *ewa* along Kalakaua Avenue; "walk two blocks Diamond Head.") Between Diamond Head and Koko Head, east becomes "Koko Head"; west is either still *ewa* or Diamond Head. It is not nearly so difficult as it sounds and is really rather exotic, one of the traditions on Oahu that has not been tainted by commercialism.

Waikiki

From ancient times, Oahu's chiefs made Waikiki something of a royal playground. Then, in the early 19th century, Kamehameha I, the warrior King, built a *pili* (grass shack) on Waikiki Beach for his favorite wife, Queen Kaahumanu. This lovely and serene stretch of sand, with its backdrop of coconut groves, mysterious rainbows, and the romantic Koolau Mountains, was already a favorite swimming and surfing spot for Oahu's *alii* (nobility) long before Kamehameha conquered the island. Subsequent monarchs built cottages; and eventually two hotels, the white, New England–style *Moana* and the raffish and roseate hacienda-style *Royal Hawaiian,* both still flourishing, were constructed to accommodate the mainlanders who had been attracted by Mark Twain's *Letter from the Sandwich Islands* and Isabella Bird's *Six Months in the Sandwich Islands.*

Servicemen who knew Hawaii only in the uncertain days of World War II tell of the long and lonely stretches of beach that remained in Waikiki even then. The great building boom started in the 1950s, and today the *Royal Hawaiian* and the *Moana* are dwarfed and obscured by concrete high-rises that have mushroomed around them, with dozens along the beach and Kalakaua Avenue alone. The coconut groves that used to merge with the taro fields and swamp between the beach and the mountains are all but gone. The swamp in turn has been drained, and Waikiki is now defined on its *ewa* (west) and *mauka* (inland) sides by the Ala Wai Canal, a moat shaped like a hockey stick, with the handle pointing toward Diamond Head and the blade into the Yacht Harbor across from Ala Moana Park. The canal and Diamond Head provide Waikiki with neat boundaries encompassing an area about 2 miles long and a half mile wide.

This small space, chock full of hotels, condominiums, and shopping malls, is for many people what Hawaii is all about. It has been compared to Coney Island, Miami Beach, Babylon, and Paradise. It is none of these, though it does have touches of them all, especially the first three. This may be the island tropics, but Waikiki is every bit an urban resort — a situation that prompted the city and state to create landscaped pedestrian malls on both sides of Kalakaua Avenue at a cost of $10 million. In preparation for the accelerated competition predicted for the coming decade, nearly half a billion dollars more has recently been poured into upgrading Waikiki's numerous hotels.

First, it should be said that the mountains, which are never far away and seldom out of sight, the rainbows, the constant presence of Diamond Head, and the often spectacular sunsets are reminders that there is something more special about the place than just the high-rises that line Kalakaua and Kuhio Avenues. There is an occasional touch of drama, class, or elegance; a glimpse inside the *Hyatt Regency, Royal Hawaiian, Hilton Hawaiian Village, Sheraton Moana Surfrider,* or *Halekulani* will confirm that. There are also a half-dozen restaurants in the area that can deservedly be labeled first class — a claim that can be made for few other tropical resort areas in the US — and there are quiet, sophisticated places where intimacy is possible to the accompaniment of soft music. There are narrow streets where tall coconut palms grow, not straight and sentinel as city planners might like them to be, but slightly bent and wobbly. And then there are the beaches, safe for swimming, where waters are usually clear and smooth. There are the pedicabs, operated by young men and women who will pedal visitors from one end of Waikiki to the other for a negotiable price; the nightly sails from Fisherman's Wharf to Diamond Head, in which rainbow-sailed boats catch and start in the breeze against the sunset; and the dazzling cascades of bejeweled lights as seen from the *Sheraton Waikiki's Hanohano Room; Annabelle's* and the *Top of the I,* atop the *Ilikai;* or *Nicholas Nickolas,* atop the *Ala Moana Americana.*

Then there is the other side — seamy, commercial, and aesthetically offensive. Street-cruising prostitutes peddle their wares. Touts offer a tour, luau, and extravaganza tickets at one-third the regular price, the snag being that beforehand the buyer must attend a cocktail party where time-sharing accommodations are being pushed. And the shopping malls often feature a mix of designer boutiques and kitsch souvenir shops with strictly schlock merchandise masquerading as Hawaiian artifacts. After a few days or a week of such disappointments, Waikiki may no longer seem a Polynesian paradise.

Beaches – Waikiki consists of not one but a series of beaches, stretching from Duke Kahanamoku Beach on the *ewa* (west) fringe of Waikiki to Sans Souci Beach at the Diamond Head end of Kalakaua Avenue. Swimming is good for almost the entire length of the beach, the exception being from the western end of Kuhio Beach Park to the Kapahulu Wall, an easily identifiable landmark along the shoreline. Some features of the beaches, going from east to west, are these: At Duke Kahanamoku Beach, in front of the *Hilton Hawaiian Village,* there is a manmade lagoon of clear waters with a soft sandy bottom. Fort DeRussy Beach Park, just beyond, is a famous sunning spot for military personnel staying at the *Hale Koa,* a hotel for resting and retired servicemen and their families. The next small stretch of sand is called Gray's Beach, with a swimming area known as Gray's Channel, which has long been a favorite spot of *kamaainas* visiting Waikiki. The palm-fringed strand running from the two original hotels and now called the Royal Hawaiian Beach is the most famous stretch of sand in Hawaii. Canoeing, snorkeling, and sailing are just as popular here as swimming or just plain lolling in the sun. At Kuhio Beach Park, farther on, a wall has been built parallel to the beach to retain sand. Although the eastern end here is good for swimming, the wall has a slick covering of marine growth and is best avoided, the nonchalant youngsters running up and down it notwithstanding. At the War Memorial Natatorium in the Kapiolani Beach Park center, there is a 100-meter saltwater swimming pool, which has been closed for several years and faces an uncertain future. Just beyond, at Sans Souci Beach, the reef-sheltered waters draw weekend crowds of *kamaainas.* With Diamond Head as a backdrop, for many Sans Souci represents Waikiki at its best.

Fort DeRussy Army Museum – Weapons used by ancient Hawaiians, weapons captured from the Japanese, and weapons used by US soldiers in campaigns from the Spanish-American War to the Korean War are on display here. In addition, there are uniforms worn at various times by US forces as well as uniforms worn by the enemy. The most fascinating items are the Hawaiian weapons made in times long past from sharks' teeth and the blowups of the Honolulu newspapers describing the early days of the US involvement in World War II following the invasion of Pearl Harbor. Closed Mondays. Kalia Rd. (phone: 438-2821).

International Market Place – Open-air stalls and open-fronted stores dominated by a huge banyan tree are some of the features that lure people to this famous shopping mall. Occasionally there are mimes and puppeteers here as well as Polynesian mat weavers, and hammerers of gold and silver. If you are somewhat retiring, you may find the place Bohemian; if you are Bohemian, you will find it rather tame. At press time, the site was being considered for a major convention center. 2330 Kalakaua Ave. (phone: 923-9871).

Royal Hawaiian Hotel – This place is still lively, even though most of its garden has been usurped by the architecturally characterless *Sheraton-Waikiki* next door and the view of its façade obliterated by the Royal Hawaiian Shopping Center. The theme is pink inside as well as out, and there is an overdose of rose this-and-that everywhere. It is worth a visit to see through the haze of time how travelers to Waikiki lived 50 years ago. 2259 Kalakaua Ave. (phone: 923-7311).

Sheraton Moana Surfrider – Waikiki's oldest hotel (it opened in 1901 and was listed on the National Register of Historic Places in 1972) has been returned to Victorian elegance following a $50-million restoration. The result is a match for the nearby *Royal Hawaiian* in terms of quality and historic appeal of its period pieces. Mementoes from the Moana through the decades are displayed on the second floor. 2365 Kalakaua Ave. (phone: 922-3111).

Honolulu Zoo – It's not a major zoo, but millions have been spent to upgrade and re-landscape this 42-acre preserve. It's easily accessible and a good place to see some unusual animals, such as Galápagos tortoises, and a fine collection of rare Asian birds. Admission fee. Kapiolani Park (phone: 923-7723).

Waikiki Aquarium – A seaside setting, with Diamond Head in the background, adds to well-displayed tanks and exhibits ranging from the exotic chambered nautilus to the history of fishing in Hawaii. The newest addition is the outdoor Touch Tank exhibit. Admission fee. In Kapiolani Park, 2777 Kalakaua Ave. (phone: 923-9741).

Kapiolani Park – This 220-acre park separating Waikiki from the small residential area on the southwest side of Diamond Head is famous for its joggers, rose garden, golden shower trees, and for the free Kodak Hula Show (phone: 833-1661) that takes place Tuesdays through Fridays at 10 AM. In addition, look for the distinguished-looking red-crested, gray-mantled Brazilian cardinal birds, who strut fussily around the park, reluctant to acknowledge the presence of human beings. Other quite untouristy sights are the small, carefully tended garden plots where fruit, vegetables, and flowers are grown. City farmers are assisted in their efforts by the manure that is made easily obtainable by the nearby zoo (phone: 971-2500).

SHOPPING: Waikiki shopping is done, with few exceptions, in hotel arcades and malls. Many of the latter have an architectural or commercial theme, usually Oriental or Hawaiian, and are occasionally outdoors. The emphasis is on aloha- and other resortwear; vacation sundries such as lotions, beach towels and mats, and dark glasses; and Polynesian handicrafts and other gift items. Mixed in are some boutiques that carry famous international names like Courrèges and Gucci, and high-fashion sportswear. In general, it's a bit on the mundane side — gaudy, commercial, and overdone. It could be said that when you've seen one banyan-shaded bazaar selling seashell leis, you've seen them all, but browsing can nonetheless be fun. It is worth noting that prices are generally steeper in Waikiki than in the Ala Moana Center and in the Pearlridge Center. At *Woolworth's,* for example, a pair of running shorts that costs $16 in the Kalakaua Avenue store might cost only $14 at Ala Moana. Family-style grocery shopping for those people living in condominiums is not very convenient unless you're near Hobron Lane or the large supermarket on Kuhio off Kaiulani. The best bet if you're staying for a while is to head to a supermarket outside Waikiki for decent prices and quality produce. The basics are also available in many places described as sundry stores, but at outrageous prices. The *ABC* stores, with locations all over Waikiki, are the best places for buying suntan lotion, picture post-cards, and liquor. The major merchandising centers with a selection of stores worth noting include the following.

ROYAL HAWAIIAN SHOPPING CENTER

This ultramodern, 3-story arcade of boutiques and restaurants covers 6½ acres. The shopping center (phone: 922-0588) runs along the south side of Kalakaua Avenue east from Lewers Street in front of the *Sheraton* and *Royal Hawaiian* hotels. This is where some of Waikiki's best shops have moved, including an outlet for luggage and related wares at *Louis Vuitton* (phone: 926-0621), *Chanel* (phone: 923-0255), and the equally appealing *Les Must de Cartier* (phone: 923-5889).

Andrade – This branch of the famous Honolulu chain specializing in good men's, women's, and children's wear has something else besides — a *Friendship Store* of the People's Republic of China, where you can find cloisonné ginger jars; velvet slippers with dragon designs in beads and sequins; handwoven, lacquered bamboo trays; and some ravishing silver filigree ornaments (phone: 926-1211).

Center Art Gallery – The store has signed prints by Chagall, Dali, and some other prolific printmakers, but its specialty is pictures by celebrities such as Elke Sommer and Red Skelton. If you would like an original painting of Woody Woodpecker commanding an outrigger canoe by his creator Walt Lantz, hurry on over (phone: 926-2727).

The Little Hawaiian Craftshop – For one of Hawaii's best collections of carved wood objects and museum-quality reproductions of Hawaiian sculpture, try this store. It's also known for handicrafts made from such materials as nuts, gourds, bones, whales' teeth, and seaweed, and for jewelry, ornaments, and "conversation pieces" made from cowrie shells (phone: 926-2662).

McInerny – This small department store is one of the best places in town for designer clothing for men, women, and children (phone: 926-1351).

Real Estate Showcase – The place to get an idea of what it costs to buy a piece of paradise. Displays highlighting condominium options on all islands make for interesting browsing and comparing. The Japanese are the big buyers here (phone: 926-5677).

W. H. Smith – Formerly *Hilo Hattie's,* this company features alohawear to suit every shape, size, and taste — including the lack of it. There are other *W. H. Smith* stores in Waikiki and statewide (phone: 926-1476).

Yokohama-Okadaya – The chief reason for stopping in this international gift shop is its fine collection of designer leather goods (phone: 922-5731).

WAIKIKI SHOPPING PLAZA

The merchandise in this complex at 2270 Kalakaua Avenue (phone: 923-1191) has to compete with a 5-story water display that is part fountain and part Plexiglas sculpture. There are a few shops of interest as well as some fine restaurants on the upper floors. Among the stores worth a look:

Betty's Imports – The largest of the semi-wholesale outfits on the fifth floor, it offers real bargains on all kinds of jewelry and imported bric-a-brac, often at prices 30% to 50% lower than at street-level shops (phone: 922-3010).

Waikiki Calls – A free hula show is performed daily at 6:15 and 7:45 PM on the fourth floor of the shopping plaza (no phone).

Lowe's Rare Coins – If you're numismatically inclined, this an interesting place to browse (phone: 923-3372).

Sawada Golf – Fill all your golf needs at this large golf shop (phone: 923-0144).

Something Different – For an unusual souvenir, the "Incredible Machine" will transfer a photographic image to lucite plaques, dishes, mugs, and more, while you wait. Prices range from $10 to $30 (phone: 926-0775).

Villa Roma – It has a nice selection of contemporary women's fashions (phone: 923-4447).

Waldenbooks – Most of the sundry stores have pulp romances and spy novels, but if it's the new Paul Theroux or John le Carré you're after, head here. The shop receives shipments barely days after mainland stores, and if you're staying a month or so, the staff will order anything not in stock (phone: 922-4154).

Yokohama-Okadaya – It's a second branch of the Japanese retailer and features high-priced sportswear by Cerruti and Fila, as well as fine luggage and leather goods (phone: 922-5731).

HEMMETER CENTER

Probably better known as the shopping arcade of the *Hyatt Regency* hotel, it has a rather classy decor. The first three floors of the *Hyatt* complex are dominated by more than 70 shops that surround a three-tier waterfall and pool. A fashion show is held each Wednesday at 4 PM outside *Harry's Bar* beside the pool. Hemmeter Center is at 2424 Kalakaua Ave. (phone: 922-9292).

Chapman's – A rare find in Waikiki, it has good men's clothing, including such helpful basics as lightweight cotton slacks (phone: 923-7010).

Circle Gallery – A comprehensive selection of serigraphs, lithographs, and other graphics by Erté and other, lesser-known artists (phone: 923-6040).

Coral Grotto – If it's coral jewelry you're after, this shop (part of a chain) is known for its quality merchandise. The rings are particularly lovely — in pink, black, and gold coral — and start at about $50 (phone: 923-3454). There's another shop in the Ala Moana Shopping Center (phone: 955-6760).

Cotton Cargo – This shop offers a refreshing change from alohawear, featuring 100% cotton fashion for women. The clothes have style; most are imported from India, Bali, Turkey, Greece, and Central America (phone: 923-5811).

Gucci – The only outlet of this exclusive chain in the islands, it carries the usual fine line of leather goods (phone: 923-2968).

KING'S VILLAGE

This pastel complex of quaint townhouse-style buildings and cobblestone walkways at the back of the Hemmeter Center and the *Hyatt Regency* hotel is designed to resemble urban Honolulu in the days of the 19th-century monarchs. The result is slightly reminiscent of Disneyland, although the *Rose and Crown Pub* (phone: 923-5833), with its horse brasses, etched-glass mirrors, and timber beams, manages to be a fair replica of an English country pub. The Changing of the Guard occurs nightly at 6 PM.

Alfred Shaheen – This is one of five locations of this well-known Honolulu fashion house, where the range of possibilities extends from ultrafeminine slinky evening clothes to simple daytime dresses (phone: 923-5920).

Cal-Oahu Fabric – One of the most comprehensive selections of fabric to be found in Waikiki, with everything from brilliant florals to subdued Oriental motifs (phone: 922-4072).

Kitamura's Oriental Arts, Crafts, and Antiques – The eclectic selection here reflects its name, with some interesting finds that include extravagant kimonos and obis (phone: 926-8006).

WAIKIKI TRADE CENTER

An architecturally distinctive office building at 2255 Kuhio Ave. (the juncture of Kuhio and Royal Hawaiian), it has several stories of shops and restaurants. *Bebe* (phone: 926-7888) features ultrahigh-fashion clothing designs for women, while *C. June Shoes* (phone: 926-1574) offers a marvelous selection of chic footwear. *Video Vacation Camera Rental* (phone: 924-4003; 800-342-7310) features a full range of video supplies available for purchase or rentable by the day or the week.

WAIKIKI BUSINESS PLAZA

Head to the seventh and eighth floors of the complex at 2270 Kalakaua Ave. to shop at discount jewelry stores that offer 30% to 50% off retail prices. While some shops sell only to the trade, the *Hawaiian Jewelry Exchange,* Suite 701 (phone: 922-5541), and *Eureka M,* Suite 709 (phone: 923-5633), offer a wide selection of costume jewelry to the public — at real bargains.

ELSEWHERE IN WAIKIKI

Bailey's Antique Clothing – A wide selection of one-of-a-kind aloha shirts, including "silkies" from the 1940s and 1950s. The best of the batch are priced at $400 and up. 2051 Kalakaua Ave. (phone: 949-8172).

Le Cadeau – All the best names in leather accessories, from Yves St. Laurent to Givenchy, are here at prices likely to shock the uninitiated. 2354 Kalakaua Ave. (phone: 923-6373).

Duke's Lane – In this alley are a couple of dozen narrow stalls teeming with leis made from plumeria, seashells, kukui nuts, and plastic; carved ivory; fancy, embroidered Oriental slippers; Chinese-style cloisonné; tapa wall hangings; and coral jewelry. Much of the merchandise is without distinction. Between Kalakaua Ave. and Kuhio Ave. (no phone).

Hawaiian Holiday Macadamia Nut Factory – It's hard to avoid the temptation to sample some of the delicious cookies, candies, and cakes, all made with — guess what? — macadamias. The cookies are particularly good. Gift packaging for those with a shopping list. 2098 Kalakaua Ave. (phone: 942-7798).

International Market Place – Famous for its huge banyan tree, it's a bustling, noisy bazaar of shops and booths, including South Seas and Hawaiian products, such as bamboo and rattanwork, baskets woven of *lau hala* or pandanus leaves, and tikis, platters, and bowls carved from monkeypod and other woods. Almost every store has its racks of alohawear and shelves of straw hats, and you'll find that quality, styles, and prices vary little from place to place. Numerous kiosks are draped with earrings, necklaces, and bracelets made of shell and semiprecious stones, including amethyst, coral, jade, opal, puka, and so on. You can bargain with these dealers, and very often a feigned disinterest can drop the asking price by half. At press time, the marketplace was being considered for the site of a major convention center. 2301 Kalakaua Ave. (phone: 923-9871).

Kuhio Mall – Behind the International Market Place is this relatively unchic and unrenowned collection of shops with, nevertheless, very attractive prices. If plans for a convention center come to pass, the mall will also be eliminated.

Rainbow Bazaar – A collection of 30 or so boutiques selling ethnic handicrafts and antiques from Polynesia and Asia. On the whole, it is expensive, but several shops worth a browse include the *Pagoda Shop* (phone: 944-2935) and *China Treasure* (phone: 946-5752). There is also a substation of the post office here (phone: 949-4321). Rainbow Bazaar is at Hilton Hawaiian Village (phone: 949-4321).

NIGHTLIFE: "The most fabulous array of shows outside of Las Vegas," Waikiki publicists like to tell you. Maybe, but if it's stars you're after, better try Las Vegas or Atlantic City. Nightlife in Waikiki usually begins with a drink on your lanai and an exquisite sunset, followed by excellent pupus for dinner. Down in the cocktail lounges there is almost always a pianist, guitarist, or, if it's a classy place, a harpist. Many restaurants discourage conversation by providing live background music. A prime exception is the *Halekulani*'s *House Without a Key* (2199 Kalia Rd.; phone: 923-2311), where mellow Hawaiian music and hula complement the Waikiki sunset. The *Gangplank Lounge* in the *Sheraton Moana Surfrider* (2353 Kalakaua Ave.; phone: 922-3111) features live entertainment and dancing nightly. There's piano music during dinner at the *Hanohano Room* of the *Sheraton Waikiki* (2255 Kalakaua Ave.; phone: 922-4422). A lively crowd frequents *Esprit* bar, with nightly music from 9 PM to 1 AM. *Poolside* provides a Hawaiian sunset serenade from 6:30 to 8:30 PM. Backed by the Betty Loo Taylor Trio, popular island singer Jimmy Borges performs mellow ballads nightly at the *Paradise Lounge* of the *Hilton Hawaiian Village,* Fridays and Saturdays starting at 8:30 PM (2005 Kalia Rd.; phone: 949-4321). For the twentyish set, the action is at *Moose McGillicuddy's* (310 Lewers St.; phone: 923-0751). On the outskirts of Waikiki, the *Hard Rock Café* (1837 Kalakaua Ave.; phone: 955-7383) has established itself as an "in" spot with the twenties and thirties crowd. Lots of mingling and noise at the bar.

Headliners in Hawaii usually mean entertainers who have made their name in the islands. The most famous is Don Ho, who has been performing at Waikiki's top showplace, the *Hilton Dome* in the *Hilton Hawaiian Village,* since late 1981. Ho's performances can be sickly and erratic and sometimes downright unpleasant. They are best on Fridays and Saturdays, when he attracts a good number of *kamaainas* who will request songs that the stranger does not know. Also, Charo stars in a good, Vegas-style revue at the *Hilton Hawaiian Village*'s *Tropic Room,* evenings except Sundays. Dinner and cocktail seatings available. Another Waikiki favorite is the Society of Seven, a group performing a mix of contemporary music and comedy at the *Outrigger Waikiki* showroom (2335 Kalakaua Ave.; phone: 923-0711). Check the entertainment guides for details. The Brothers Cazimero, Roland and Robert, are also very popular. They have a great respect for the music of the islands and their show in the *Royal Hawaiian*'s *Monarch Room* (phone: 923-7311) is one of Hawaii's best. Again, check newspapers and guides to find out where they are appearing. Jazz fans head for *Trapper's* at the *Hyatt Regency* to hear Noelani Cypriano and Trilogy perform every night but Sunday (2424 Kalakaua Ave.; phone: 922-9292). Fans of stand-up comedy can head to the Honolulu Comedy Club Tuesdays through Saturdays at the *Top of the I* at the *Ilikai* hotel. Reservations necessary; $10 cover (177 Ala Moana Blvd.; phone: 922-5998).

Waikiki's Polynesian spectaculars (dinner, luau, or cocktail options) provide Hollywood-cum-Broadway versions of Pacific island music and dance and are usually of most interest to first-time visitors to the islands. The best location is the beachside luau and revue at the *Outrigger* hotel (2335 Kalakaua Ave.; phone: 923-0711), Tuesdays, Fridays, and Sundays. At the *Sheraton Princess Kaiulani* (2342 Kalahaua Ave.; phone: 922-5811) there is a nightly show, and the *Royal Hawaiian* (2259 Kalakaua Ave.; phone: 923-7311) is the site for a luau and revue on Sundays. *Voyage* is the latest variation on the theme. Presented in the third-floor theater of the *Waikiki Shopping Plaza* (corner of Kalakau and Seaside Aves.; phone: 922-6600), it is a multimedia music and dance revue that traces the migrations of the early Polynesians, complete with elaborate costumes and sets. The dinner show ($32) is designed to permit diners to coordinate their meals with one of the three show times (6:30, 8:15, or 10 PM) by eating at one of three nearby restaurants; cocktail seating is also available ($15).

Dinner cruises have been part of the Waikiki scene for years. *Rainbow Cruises* (2005

Kalia Rd.; phone: 955-3348), operating out of the *Hilton Hawaiian Village,* offers dinner nightly ($39) and champagne breakfast daily ($19.50) aboard its highly visible catamarans with rainbow sails. *Paradise Cruises* (phone: 536-3641) leaves from Kewalo Basin (hotel pickups are provided), and offers drinks and food during the sail back along Waikiki Beach to Diamond Head. *Aikane Catamarans* (phone: 522-1533) and *Wind-jammer Cruises* (phone: 521-0036) also offer popular sunset sails, with drinks, dinner, and all-too-often noisy entertainment.

Another Waikiki and islandwide tradition is the luau, an ancient Hawaiian ceremony of cooking a pig in an *imu,* an earthen pit lined with lava rock and heated by burning kiawe wood. The pig is stuffed with red-hot rocks, wrapped in wet ti and banana leaves, and covered with earth. Other ingredients such as yams, taro, fish, breadfruit, and whatever is available are placed in the *imu* beside the pig. Hours later, the pig is removed, at which time it is referred to as kalua pork. Removing the pig from the *imu* is a ceremony in itself, often accompanied by songs. There are a number of commercial luaus that include the removal ceremony and a torchlighting ritual, a heavy meal of pork and accompanying traditional foodstuffs, "all you can drink," and Polynesian entertainment. In Waikiki there's a Monday luau at the *Royal Hawaiian* hotel (2259 Kalakaua Ave.; phone: 923-7311). Other luaus take place on beaches out of town but with pick-up buses serving all the Waikiki hotels. At the *Paradise Cove Luau* there is an *imu* ceremony, torchlighting ritual, beachfront *hukilau* (communal net fishing), Hawaiian arts and crafts displays, and a Polynesian review (phone: 973-5828). *Paradise Cove* and *Germaine's Luau* both take place on beaches near Ewa, about 40 minutes from Waikiki (transportation provided). *Germaine's* features a net-throwing demonstration during which, for a brief moment, there's the splendid sight of a fishing net extended in silhouette against the late evening sky. Before the removal of the pig, there is also a procession, with young people modeling costumes worn by ancient Hawaiian royalty. In the Polynesian extravaganza that follows, the audience is invited to participate in various dances and songs in an exhibition that may turn even strong stomachs after a generous number of free mai tais and blue Hawaiis (phone: 949-6626).

For a taste of Hawaii's *paniolo* (cowboy) tradition, the twice-weekly *Hawaiian Hoe-Down Country Barbeque,* held Tuesdays and Thursdays at the *Olomana Ranch* in Waimanalo, starts with a hotel pickup and continues with an all-you-can-eat selection of pulehu ribs, teriyaki chicken, live country-and-western music, and more. Country-and-western entertainment and *paniolo* hula set the pace in the lovely setting at the base of the towering *pali* cliffs (phone: 259-9300 or 737-3812). Sea Life Park (phone: 923-1531) has exhibits and shows from 7 to 10 PM on Thursday, Friday, and Sunday evenings. At the Bishop Museum (phone: 946-3859), a state-of-the-art planetarium show is presented at 7 PM Fridays and Saturdays; admission $2.50. Pack a picnic and seat yourself on the lawn for one of the symphonic, jazz, or Hawaiian shows often presented at the *Waikiki Shell* (box office phone: 521-2911), with Diamond Head as a backdrop. Gates open at 5:30 PM; showtime is usually 7:30 PM. When the moon is full, consider the free escorted walks at Waimea Falls Park (phone: 638-8511).

For something a little more sophisticated, visit the *Spats* disco, which has a kind of swank Bonnie and Clyde atmosphere, in the *Hyatt Regency* (2424 Kalakaua Ave.; phone: 922-9292), or *Annabelle's,* atop the *Ilikai,* where, apart from the glitter of the decor, you can also enjoy the glitter of Honolulu spread out below (1777 Ala Moana Blvd.; phone: 949-3811). Those who prefer their music loud and rocking can head next door to *Wave Waikiki,* a popular dance spot that tends to draw a young crowd (1877 Kalakaua Ave.; phone: 941-0424); others are *Bobby McGee's Conglomeration* (2885 Kalakaua Ave.; phone: 922-1282); *Cillys* (1909 Ala Wai Blvd.; phone: 942-2952); *Pink Cadillac* (478 Ena Rd.; phone: 942-5282); and *Rumours* at the *Ala Moana Americana* (phone: 955-4811). The newest and most extravagant addition to the disco scene is the

$5-million *Majaraja Restaurant and Disco,* in the Waikiki Trade Center, 2255 Kuhio Ave. (phone: 922-3030). *Hula's,* an open-air disco, the centerpiece of which is a light-festooned banyan tree, attracts a crowd of both sexes and sexual persuasions (2130 Kuhio Ave.; phone: 923-0669). At neighboring *Hamburger Mary's,* the crowd is definitely gay (phone: 922-6722).

 CHECKING IN: "We've lost our hotel," a young couple was heard to lament on TheBus one night. Was it the *Surf* or the *Surfrider* for which they were looking, the *Surfsider* or the *Outrigger Surf?* Not long ago, most hotels in Waikiki (apart from the older *Royal Hawaiian* and *Moana* and a handful of modern luxury hotels, such as the *Hyatt Regency*) not only sounded the same, they looked the same, inside and out. With several hundred million dollars spent to upgrade the individual hotels, this is no longer the case, and room quality overall is generally excellent. Standard accommodations consist of double beds or twins; pastel-colored decor; thick wall-to-wall carpeting; wicker armchairs and a table; a TV set; and a lanai, or balcony. Then there are the views which could be, in descending order of desirability and price, of the ocean, Diamond Head, or the mountains. (This is all in the eye of the beholder; the sun rising behind Diamond Head is a pretty inspiring sight, and the rainbows that splay over the mountainsides on many an afternoon can be quite spectacular.)

When making reservations, think carefully about what's most important to you. As a rule, if you plan to spend a lot of time in your hotel, choose a more expensive room with something to look at outside. If all you need is a dormitory while you sunbathe and explore, far less expensive accommodations will likely do nicely. Expect to pay $250 and up for a double room in a hotel listed as very expensive, between $145 and $245 in a hotel listed as expensive, from $60 to $140 in a property listed as moderate, and under $60 in a hotel listed as inexpensive. Unless otherwise stated, all rooms in these categories will include a lanai or terrace, though the size and the view will vary. As elsewhere in the islands, most hotels and condos offer high-season (late December to Easter) and low-season rates.

There are also condominiums in the Honolulu area, many of which are available for short-term rentals. Most offer front-desk services, restaurants, and daily maid service. And while most condos are a few blocks from the beach, nothing in Waikiki is beyond easy walking distance. The condominiums listed below are all within a 15-minute walk of the ocean; the most convenient store for groceries is the *Food Pantry* supermarket on Kuhio, off Kaiulani. With 24-hour advance reservations, *Gray Line* limousines (phone: 834-1044) will make condo pickups for $5. *Airport Motorcoach* (phone: 926-4747) offers $5 airport shuttle service.

The main attraction of a condominium is economic: For a "superior double" — a large 1-bedroom apartment with a living room in which there's a sofa bed — expect to pay around $90 to $125 a night. Unless otherwise stated, the same rate applies for one to four people, though there is often a nominal (under $10) charge for each person after the first two. Thus, it's possible for a family or two couples to save up to 60% over the price of comparable accommodations in a hotel, and for stays extending into weeks or months, the savings are even higher.

Note that some condos, especially those used to long-term renters, do not have telephones, although almost all have jacks for easy phone installation. Telephones are obtained by going to the nearest Phone Mart, picking up the equipment, obtaining a number, and filling in the relevant forms. Service usually starts in less than 24 hours. The nearest Phone Mart to Waikiki is in the Ward Warehouse shopping mall, across from the Kewalo Boat Basin on Ala Moana Boulevard.

Bed-and-breakfast establishments are another option. *Bed & Breakfast Goes Hawai-*

ian, published by *Bed & Breakfast Hawaii* lists nearly 40 such private homes where tourists are welcome. For a copy of the guide, send $8 to Bed & Breakfast Hawaii, PO Box 449, Kapaa, HI 96746 (phone: 822-7771). *Bed & Breakfast Honolulu* (phone: 595-7533; 800-367-8047, ext. 351) and *Pacific-Hawaii Bed & Breakfast* (phone: 262-6026) also list Oahu accommodations.

All telephone numbers are in the 808 area code unless otherwise indicated.

HOTELS

Halekulani – This contemporary mid-rise incorporates the old Lewers home, which served as the original hotel. Among its features are 456 rooms, a library, and an open-air, oceanfront lounge — *House Without a Key* — featuring Hawaiian music and fine views of Diamond Head and sunsets. Its restaurants, *Orchids* and *La Mer*, are among Honolulu's best. The hotel, designed to reestablish Waikiki as a destination for the carriage trade, is the essence of contemporary elegance. This is a hotel for which the adjective "luxury" is no exaggeration. 2199 Kalia Rd. (phone: 923-2311; 800-367-2343). Very expensive to expensive.

Hawaii Prince – Waikiki's newest luxury hotel is the second Hawaii property for Japan's Prince Hotel chain (the other is on Maui). Attention to detail, carefully prepared cuisine, and panoramic views of the neighboring Ala Wai Yacht Tower are the main justifications for top-of-the-scale rates. Located on the western edge of Waikiki, it is just a short walk from Ala Moana Beach and Waikiki Beach. 1697 Ala Moana Blvd. (phone: 800-321-6284). Very expensive to expensive.

Hilton Hawaiian Village – With close to 2,600 rooms and 22 acres, it is Hawaii's largest hotel, as well as the western terminus of Waikiki Beach. Standing between the Duke Kahanamoku Lagoon and the beach, it boasts a colorful shopping center, its own post office, and a catamaran that offers both day and night cruises. The Rainbow Tower, famed for its 30-story rainbow mosaic, and the Tapa Tower, with 250 corner suites, have the best views. The Alii Tower features its own pool and full concierge services. The village has lots that visitors want from a Hawaiian vacation — pools, beaches, fine dining, luaus, and Polynesian extravaganzas featuring Don Ho — but lacks the peace and serenity of rural Oahu. Fridays it's "Aloha Friday," with crafts displays, hula dancing, a fashion show–brunch, and a luau-style dinner from 5 PM at the *Rainbow Lanai.* 2005 Kalia Rd. (phone: 949-4321; 800-445-8667). Very expensive to expensive.

Hawaiian Regent – Just across the road from the beach, the two tall towers possess little architectural distinction. The interiors, however, are a bit more appealing, with inner courtyards paved in tile and marble, and an outdoor-café atmosphere in the main lobby. The Ocean Terrace pool area is also inviting, and the rooms are large and comfortable. There are several first class restaurants in the hotel, including the prestigious *Third Floor,* which underwent a renovation in 1988 that included the addition of a 6,000-bottle wine room. *The Library,* where there's not a book in sight, has some unusually good soft music starting at 8:30 PM. 2552 Kalakaua Ave. (phone: 922-6611; 800-367-5370). Expensive.

Sheraton Moana Surfrider – This beautifully restored Victorian hostelry has been standing at the edge of the Waikiki surf since 1901. Until its exotic neighbor, the *Royal Hawaiian,* was opened in 1927, the *Moana* was the only hotel in the area. Brass headboards, white wicker chairs, antique lamps, and Victorian armoires adorn many of the rooms. These touches, and in many cases a ceiling fan, manage to make you forget the more modern iconography of Waikiki outside. When making reservations, it is wise to specify a room in the old building, if that is what you want, as the Surfrider wing is more contemporary in style and decor. 2365 Kalakaua Ave. (phone: 922-3111; 800-325-3535). Expensive.

Holiday Inn Waikiki Beach – Although the rooms here provide the standard *Holiday Inn* level of style and comfort, this hotel boasts magnificent views of the ocean and Diamond Head. It also has a terrific site: just outside the hustle-bustle of the strip, next door to Kapiolani Park and the Honolulu Zoo, and across the street from the loveliest stretch of Waikiki Beach. Its *Captain's Table,* an easygoing eatery that looks out at the sea, is a good place to sample your first mahimahi. 2570 Kalakaua Ave. (phone: 922-2511; 800-877-8666). Expensive to moderate.

Hyatt Regency – The two octagonal towers atop the ritzy Hemmeter Center are a visual landmark among the concrete blocks along Kalakaua Avenue. The Great Hall, with its outdoor tropical garden, 3-story waterfall, and massive hanging sculpture, is a sightseeing spot in its own right. Each of its 1,234 rooms is handsomely furnished, and the art on the walls is invariably worth looking at. In the suites, which feature some exceptional antiques, there are also original oil paintings. Guests in the Regency Club, as the 39th- and 40th-floor accommodations are known, have their own private, complimentary bar and a concierge. The pool deck is one of the most attractive in Honolulu, and the bars, cafés, and restaurants in the complex — they include *Bagwell's* restaurant, *Trapper's* (a jazz club), and *Spats* restaurant and disco — are among the very best in Waikiki. The service here is exemplary. At the Hemmeter Center, 2424 Kalakaua Ave. (phone: 923-1234; 800-228-9000). Expensive to moderate.

Ilikai – This 3-pronged hotel on the *ewa* (western) edge of Waikiki includes Waikiki's best tennis facilities, with 6 courts and pros available to provide instruction. The open area at the lobby level has pools, terraces, and fountains. The beach, Duke Kahanamoku Lagoon, and the yacht marina are just a stone's throw away. The 800 rooms are among the most spacious in Waikiki, and some have kitchenettes. Atop the hotel sits *Annabelle's,* a disco reached via a spectacular ride in an exterior elevator that opens up vast panoramas of the Pacific as you ascend. 1777 Ala Moana Blvd. (phone: 949-3811; 800-367-8434). Expensive to moderate.

Outrigger Reef – With 800 rooms, this is one of the largest moderately priced hotels in Waikiki. All rooms and public areas have recently been upgraded, resulting in somewhat higher rates. Popular with young couples and singles traveling in pairs, it's right on the beach, with most of the rooms facing either toward Diamond Head or across Fort DeRussy Beach Park to the ocean. Guests here seem to use their lanais more than those at any other hotel in the neighborhood; it's a friendly sight. 2169 Kalia Rd. (phone: 923-3111; 800-367-5170). Expensive to moderate.

Pacific Beach – Standing on the site of the summer home of Queen Liliuokalani, this property is famous for its 280,000-gallon indoor oceanarium, which can be viewed from the hotel's bars and restaurants. Along with the swimming pool, there are tennis courts, shuffleboards, and a Jacuzzi. A good buy. 2490 Kalakaua Ave. (phone: 922-1233; 800-367-6060). Expensive to moderate.

Royal Hawaiian – "The Pink Lady," as this flamingo-colored, 6-story landmark of Spanish-Moorish design is best known, is flanked by 2 other Sheraton properties that seem to stand in an adversary, rather than a neighborly, stance. And indeed, rumor has it along the beach that there are entrepreneurs who would not object to seeing the Lady deposed in favor of something more modern (and anonymous). Never mind. While it lasts — and one hopes it will last a long time — this is one of the two grand old hotels in Waikiki (the *Moana* is the other). The pink color scheme runs, perhaps a smidgin too obviously, throughout the hotel. Most of the rooms have either a pink sofa, quilt, or drapes. Usually it works, sometimes it doesn't. In any case, once away from the bustle of the lobby, which attracts 10 times more spectators than guests, this remains the most charming hotel in Waikiki. Reservations through the Sheraton Waikiki, 2259 Kalakaua Ave. (phone: 923-7311; 800-325-3535). Expensive to moderate.

Sheraton Waikiki – The largest hotel in Waikiki — 1,852 rooms — until it was surpassed by the *Hilton Hawaiian Village* in early 1982, the *Sheraton* still has the greatest number of units in one building of any hotel on the beach. Lanais on the Pacific side loom over the ocean as precipitously as a cliff. It's a splendid sensation if you don't suffer from vertigo, and the sunsets can be memorable. Happily, subtle tans and casually tropical styling have replaced the garish greens and floral designs that made the rooms and lobby rather hard on the eyes. The *Sheraton* has all that's expected from a big hotel: There is never a dearth of taxis, it's a pickup point for every major tour operator, TheBus stops nearby, and there is just about every kind of restaurant you could crave, except a truly first class one. 2255 Kalakaua Ave. (phone: 922-4422; 800-325-3535). Expensive to moderate.

Aston's Waikiki Gateway – Looking like an unfinished pyramid, it stands sentinel at the western end of Kalakaua Avenue, about 5 minutes' walk from the beach. Rooms, which tend to get smaller the higher up you go, have recently been renovated. Its restaurant, *Nick's Fishmarket,* is one of Honolulu's most famous. 2070 Kalakaua Ave. (phone: 955-3741; 800-367-5124). Moderate.

Ilima – Near the Ala Wai Canal, about 3 blocks from the *Royal Hawaiian Beach,* it offers the additional convenience of full kitchens in all rooms, as well as a restaurant, cocktail lounge, sauna, and pool. 445 Nohonani St. (phone: 923-1877; 800-352-6686 in California, 800-421-0767 in other states). Moderate.

Outrigger Prince Kuhio – Quietly set on Kuhio Avenue, just 1 block from the beach, it manages to feel like a small hotel despite its 620 rooms on 37 floors. There are a maximum of 18 rooms to a floor, and each room is individually decorated and furnished, with its own wet bar and marble bathroom. The lobby is a graceful and airy place where complimentary coffee is poured from a silver samovar every morning. Rooms high on the Diamond Head side have stunning views of the crater. The top 3 floors are part of the exclusive Kuhio Club. 2500 Kuhio Ave. (phone: 922-0811; 800-367-5170). Moderate.

Waikiki Beachcomber – Whether you look toward the ocean, Diamond Head, or downtown, the lanais of the *Waikiki Beachcomber* are a pleasant spot for breakfast or cocktails. For the price, its rooms are surprisingly large, with separate dressing areas and capacious closets, and their layout and color scheme give them a feeling of coolness and comfort. The lobby has facilities for booking tours, and the hotel is a short walk from the beach. 2300 Kalakaua Ave. (phone: 922-4646; 800-622-4646). Moderate.

Reef Towers – Although it is hard to believe that a street of concrete blocks can have character, the section of Lewers Street between Kalia Road and Kalakaua Avenue does — it's narrow and shaded by very tall, spindly coconut palms. One of the concrete blocks is the *Reef Towers.* Though gorgeous vistas are not a selling point here, some people find it an excellent buy. Rooms with kitchenettes are available. 227 Lewers St. (phone: 923-3111; 800-367-5170). Moderate.

Waikiki Parc – Recently opened by the same Japanese company that owns the neighboring *Halekulani,* this hotel focuses its attention on service and high-tech features like computer-coded room locks on its 298 rooms.. It's an easy walk to Waikiki Beach, a fact that isn't immediately obvious from its towering proximity to the *Halekulani* and the *Sheraton Waikiki.* 2198 Kalia Rd. (phone: 921-7272; 800-422-0450). Moderate.

Waikiki Shores Apartments – By a stroke of luck, this apartment hotel stands next to the Fort DeRussy Army Museum and has an unobstructed view across the museum grounds. From each wide lanai there is a panorama of both ocean and mountains. Studios convert easily from living to sleeping accommodations, and suites have very comfortable, bright, and "homey" living rooms. Linens, cooking utensils, and dishes are provided. There are fully equipped kitchens and weekly maid service. Cost and location combine to make this one of the best buys on the beach, especially for families. 2161 Kalia Rd. (phone: 926-4733; 800-367-2353). Moderate.

Waikikian – For many returning visitors, the torches that blaze outside each night signal that they are once more entering the fabled resort area. More torches line the narrow path that passes between the Polynesian cabanas that are the hotel's salient feature. These are decorated in Hawaiian motifs, with ceiling fans, rattan carpets, exposed timber ceilings, and wooden lanais, all contributing to the South Seas atmosphere. Some units also have kitchenettes. An adjacent 6-story contemporary building offers more conventional accommodations. The beach, a romantic lagoon, and a particularly attractive palm-fringed poolside area with a popular outdoor café called the *Tahitian Lanai* complete the amenities. 1811 Ala Moana Blvd. (phone: 949-5331; 800-367-5124). Moderate.

Hawaii Dynasty – Set on the extremely busy Ala Moana Boulevard, on the western perimeter of Waikiki (where the high-rises are), this property is within walking distance of the beach and the more hectic attractions of Kalakaua strip. The accommodations are large but not luxurious, and the swimming pool is one of the biggest in Waikiki. 1830 Ala Moana Blvd. (phone: 955-1111; 800-421-6662). Moderate to inexpensive.

Outrigger Edgewater – This small hostelry manages to look more like a seaside apartment house than a hotel and exudes an air of calm and quiet. For those who find the hurly-burly of large establishments either intimidating or just plain exhausting, this is the ideal spot at an ideal price. An added attraction is the *Trattoria,* a well-regarded Italian restaurant. 2168 Kalia Rd. (phone: 922-6424; 800-367-5170). Moderate to inexpensive.

Outrigger Waikiki Village – Brightly decorated with an emphasis on greens and blues, this member of the Outrigger chain is popular with young couples making a first visit to Hawaii. The poolside area is, if anything, busier than many others in the district, considering that the ocean is just 2 blocks away. Perhaps what attracts so many is its underwater viewing area. Some rooms have kitchenettes. 240 Lewers St. (phone: 923-3881; 800-367-5170). Moderate to inexpensive.

Pleasant Holiday Isle – Right in the heart of Waikiki and just a block from the beach, this is a compact hotel where both the decor and the service are casually cheerful. This, plus reasonable rates, more than compensates for the fact that from most of the lanais, the view is less than indelible, and the street noise is occasionally audible. 270 Lewers St. (phone: 923-0777). Moderate to inexpensive.

Quality Inn Waikiki – Just 1 block from 220-acre Kapiolani Park at the foot of Diamond Head, it has always enjoyed a good reputation for service and comfort. Some rooms in the older Diamond Head Tower and all the rooms in the newer Pali Tower have kitchenettes, although the newer accommodations tend to be larger and more subdued in decor. There are 2 swimming pools for people who find the 3-minute stroll to the beach too strenuous. 175 Paoakalani Ave. (phone: 922-3861; 800-228-5151). Moderate to inexpensive.

Royal Islander – Another stopping place where smallness is an advantage. The front desk personnel usually manage to remember guests' names. Recently renovated rooms are on the small side, though not oppressively so, and each has a lanai, refrigerator, and coffee-making facilities. Street noise may prove bothersome. The property is now managed by the Outrigger chain and is opposite the *Reef* hotel, behind which is the beach. 2164 Kalia Rd. (phone: 922-1961; 800-367-5170). Moderate to inexpensive.

Viscount Waikiki – Overlooking Fort DeRussy and Ala Moana Boulevard, it offers complimentary indoor parking with shopping, restaurants, and the beach minutes away. 1850 Ala Moana Blvd. (phone: 955-1567; 800-255-3050). Moderate to inexpensive.

Royal Grove – This is a small apartment hotel with personality. Like the *Royal Hawaiian,* it is painted pink. There are very comfortable, cheerful studios as well as 1-bedroom units. Although the ocean, a block and a half away, is visible from some of the lanais, many people prefer to look out on the pool and tropical gardens. All rooms have air conditioning and kitchenettes. There is maid service but no room service. 151 Uluniu Ave. (phone: 923-7691). Inexpensive.

Waikiki Surf – This is one of the "finds" of Honolulu. In a semi-residential part of Waikiki, it's friendly, clean, decorated in blue and green, quiet, and delightfully inexpensive. Some rooms have kitchenettes. Perhaps best of all, the 288-room *Waikiki Surf* has two companions — the 102-room *Waikiki Surf East* (422 Royal Hawaiian Ave.) and the 110-room *Waikiki Surf West* (412 Lewers St.) — owned and run by the same very friendly people. The original *Waikiki Surf* is at 2200 Kuhio Ave. (switchboard for all three properties: 923-7671; 800-367-5170). Inexpensive.

CONDOMINIUMS

Aston Waikiki Beach Tower – With only four 2-bedroom apartments to a floor, this is Waikiki's most exclusive rentable condominium. The views, particularly on floors 25 to 40, are magnificent, with large lanais offering front-row seats as the sun slides into the Pacific. Another prime asset is privacy — the perfect antidote to the street energy of Waikiki. Full concierge service, with the beach just across the street. 2470 Kalakaua Ave. (phone: 926-6400; 800-922-7866). Very expensive to expensive.

Waikiki Sunset – Given the facilities, good-looking accommodations, and location just 2 blocks from the beach, this place is an authentic bargain. Besides swimming in the large pool, guests can play tennis or shuffleboard. Daily maid service. 229 Paoakalani Ave. (phone: 922-0511; 800-367-5124). Expensive to moderate.

Foster Tower – For location alone — right across Kalakaua Avenue from the beach — this is one of Waikiki's better buys. All rooms have color television sets, and on the property are a restaurant, pool, and shops. No maid service. 2500 Kalakaua Ave. (phone: 523-7785; 800-367-7040). Moderate.

Island Colony – Another luxury high-rise looking out on the Koolau Mountains and the canal, it is decorated with bleached-wood furniture, light brown walls and textiles, and beige carpets, giving it a pleasantly restful appearance. It also has a restaurant, pool, sauna, and hydromassage facilities, as well as shuffleboard. Daily maid service. 445 Seaside Ave. (phone: 923-2345; 800-367-5124). Moderate.

Pacific Monarch – Close to the Kings Alley shopping bazaar and a few minutes from the beach, the property offers spectacular views from its upper-floor 1-bedroom and studio units and the rooftop pool area. Laundry facilities and daily maid service. 142 Uluniu Ave. (phone: 923-9805; 800-367-6046). Moderate.

Royal Kuhio – Two blocks away from the beach and the International Market Place, it has upper-floor units that offer some of the best views of Diamond Head in Waikiki. On the 7th-floor deck, there are barbecue facilities, a pool, and shuffleboard. Weekly maid service. 2240 Kuhio Ave. (phone: 923-1747; 800-367-5205). Moderate.

Waikiki Banyan – One of the largest condos in Waikiki, it's a short walk from the beach, zoo, and the Ala Wai Golf Course. The living rooms are handsomely decorated and have attractive breakfast counters that separate them from the kitchen. The building contains a sauna, a large recreation area with tennis courts and a swimming pool, laundry facilities on each floor, and daily maid service. From the top floor on the Diamond Head side you see beyond the crater to Maunalua Bay. 201 Ohua Ave. (phone: 922-0555; 800-367-8047). Moderate.

Waikiki Lanais – With its attractively furnished 1- and 2-bedroom apartments on one of Waikiki's quieter streets, this well-maintained condominium features a mix of vacation rentals and full-time residences that adds to its appeal, as does its location near the beach and the commercial heart of Waikiki. 2452 Tusitala St. (phone: 531-7595; 800-367-7042). Moderate.

EATING OUT: The culinary surprise in Waikiki is the number of good continental restaurants and the scarcity of good steak houses. Seafood houses of varying quality are abundant, as are familiar fast-food names. Tucked away in hotels on Kalakaua and Kuhio avenues and on various side streets are Italian, Chinese, Japanese, Korean, and Polynesian restaurants — even a couple of English pub–style places serving fish and chips and steak and kidney pie. What is impossible to find is a restaurant of note serving Hawaiian food (the few in Honolulu that do are dealt with in the *Greater Honolulu* section). With some notable exceptions, the best restaurants are not right on the beach, and most of the ones that are serve indifferent food and watered-down drinks. As a rule, dress is informal — which means alohawear, not bathing suits — and some tonier spots "prefer" gentlemen to wear jackets. A couple insist on it. For a meal for two, excluding wine, tips, and drinks, expect to pay more than $60 in a place listed as expensive; between $25 and $55 in a place listed as moderate, and under $25 in an inexpensive place. (*Note:* For a discussion of dining within a short distance of Waikiki turn to *Eating Out*, DIAMOND HEAD.) All telephone numbers are in the 808 area code unless otherwise indicated.

Bagwell's – Luxury is the watchword here, with sculpted and etched glass and rich pastel hues combining to create a chic tropical atmosphere made all the more appealing and private by semicircular banquettes and raised dining platforms. The service is first class and, although always conscientious and friendly, it sometimes reaches a point where it can seem choreographed. The presentation is every bit as appetizing as the food itself, which includes such distinctive entrées as double breast of roast duck in a purée of island bananas, and broiled lamb chops dressed with a sauce of red bell peppers and caramelized garlic cloves. There is also a good selection of cheeses (unusual in Honolulu) and a distinguished wine list. Jackets are not necessary, but the atmosphere is such that a gentleman may feel more comfortable wearing one. Open daily for dinner. Reservations advised. In the Hyatt Regency Hotel, 2424 Kalakaua Ave. (phone: 922-9292). Expensive.

Bali by the Sea – Contemporary elegance, enhanced by a mix of cool whites and Mediterranean pastels, sets the scene for seaside dining. The food is excellent, with appetizers like coquille of shrimp and scallops with ginger sauce, enticing entrées such as Kaiwi Channel opakapaka with fresh basil, and a concluding irresistible dessert tray. Open daily for dinner. Reservations advised and valet parking is available. Hilton Hawaiian Village Rainbow Tower, 2005 Kalia Rd. (phone: 949-4321). Expensive.

Chez Michel – The same Michel who lent his name to the *Colony Surf* hotel also created *Chez Michel*. He's retired, but the restaurant remains popular. Just outside the *Hilton Hawaiian Village* end of Waikiki in Eaton Square, it is lush with plants and heavily accented in French decor. The menu is varied, well prepared, and nicely presented. 444 Hobron Lane (phone: 955-7866). Expensive.

La Mer – The distinctive menu suits one of Hawaii's most refined restaurants. Start with an appetizer of grilled filet with steamed asparagus and orange sauce, then move on to roast duck with cherries marmalade and port wine sauce. The service is excellent and the decor an appealing blend of Oriental styles. Open daily from 6 to 9:30 PM. Reservations necessary. Halekulani, 2199 Kalia Rd. (phone: 923-2311). Expensive.

Nicholas Nickolas – Find dining amid soft lights and elegant at this place atop the 40-floor *Ala Moana Americana* hotel, which affords magnificent views. The extensive menu focuses on both American and continental specialties, ranging from veal to lamb, with pasta, soups, salads, and catch-of-the-day entrées in between. Open daily from 5:30 to 11:30 PM, with live entertainment from 9:30 PM to 2:30 AM weekdays, to 3:30 AM on weekends. Reservations necessary. 410 Atkinson Dr. (phone: 955-4466). Expensive.

Nick's Fishmarket – This is one of the best fish restaurants in Honolulu. Don't let the earthy name confuse you; *Nick's* is a plush establishment with individually controlled lighting systems for those customers seated at banquettes and rather too many staffers per customer. Live Maine lobsters are available at substantial cost, but this is also the ideal place to sample fresh island fish, such as *opakapaka, mahimahi,* and *ulua.* The combination seafood Louis salad is enormous and beautifully prepared. Open daily for dinner. Reservations necessary. In the Waikiki Gateway Hotel, 2070 Kalakaua Ave. (phone: 955-6333). Expensive.

Third Floor – One of the top restaurants in Honolulu, it has consistently won prizes for its cooking. Guests dine in a setting of high-backed rattan chairs with red velvet cushions, strolling musicians, a carp pool, and a fountain. Among the house specialties are medallions of veal *forêt noire* and rack of spring lamb. For dessert there are Polynesian fruits with kirsch, followed by well-made Irish coffee. Open daily for dinner; there is a $15 minimum charge. Reservations advised. In the Hawaiian Regent Hotel, 2552 Kalakaua Ave. (phone: 922-6611). Expensive.

Bon Appetit – Perhaps Honolulu's best French restaurant, it has the look of an elegant bistro in the French provinces with its caned-back chairs and light pink linen. The menu is imaginative and includes an unusual scallop mousse, bouil-labaisse, and snails in puff pastry. The daily three- and four-course dinners are especially well priced. Closed Sundays. Reservations advised. In the Discovery Bay complex at 1778 Ala Moana Blvd. (phone: 942-3837). Expensive to moder-ate.

Furusato – There are two branches of this Japanese restaurant in Waikiki. Each has its own menu and ambience; both are comfortable if not elegant. The kitchens generally offer a range of steaks, seafood, and sushi. Open daily for lunch and dinner. Reservations advised. Hyatt Regency (phone: 922-4991) and Foster Tower condominium (phone: 922-5502). Expensive to moderate.

Golden Dragon – Perhaps Hawaii's most elegant Chinese restaurant, the food happily lives up to the surroundings. One specialty, Imperial Beggar's chicken, is wrapped in lotus leaves with spices, then cooked for 6 hours inside a sealed clay pot to retain natural juices and flavor. Another specialty is the Peking roast duck, and be sure to leave room for pastry chef Gale O'Malley's celestial desserts. Thanks to the exquisite decorative flourishes, dining indoors is as appealing as alfresco. Reservations advised; valet parking available. Hilton Hawaiian Village Rainbow Tower. 2005 Kalia Rd. (phone: 949-4321). Expensive to moderate.

Hy's Steak House – Entering *Hy's* is like walking into a magnificent Victorian private library, full of velvet chairs and etched glass. But the gleaming brass broiler inside a glassed-in gazebo, where steaks and chops are prepared with loving care, demonstrates that it is something more. Although the menu indicates that chicken and seafood are available, the main attraction is steak, which is merely superb. Open daily for dinner. Reservations advised. 2440 Kuhio Ave. (phone: 922-5555). Expensive to moderate.

Matteo's – Low lighting, pleasant decor, and high-backed banquettes all conspire to make this restaurant a place for quiet dining. The service is good, as is the food, which includes such highly recommended dishes as calamari, chicken, and veal. Open daily for dinner, from 6 PM to midnight; the bar is open until 2 AM. Reservations advised. In the Marine Surf Hotel, 364 Seaside Ave. (phone: 922-5551). Expensive to moderate.

Orchids – Sliding French doors that open onto a green lawn and expansive views of Diamond Head and the sea are a perfect backdrop for crisp white linens and tables elegantly set with silver, crystal, and fresh flowers. Breakfast is a highlight, as is the Sunday brunch, though lunch and dinner are also first rate. Reservations necessary. Halekulani, 2199 Kalia Rd. (phone: 923-2311). Expensive to moderate.

Baci – Linens, flatware, and crystal harmonize with the chic decor to provide an appropriate setting for the Italian specialties. Meals are complemented by a fairly priced selection of bottled wines. Open for lunch and dinner daily. Reservations advised for dinner and lunch groups. Ground level, Waikiki Trade Center, 2255 Kuhio Ave. (phone: 924-2533). Moderate.

Great Wok – Cantonese-style Chinese cuisine is prepared at your table, and the menu features such delicately flavored specialties as 1000 Happiness Lobster and Blush of Empress Shrimp. Open daily from 5:30 PM. Reservations advised. Royal Hawaiian Center (phone: 922-5373). Moderate.

Monterrey Bay Canners – The Waikiki branch of this restaurant, located in the *Outrigger* hotel, offers a limited number of alfresco tables that take full advantage of the beachfront location. The best bet on the menu is one of the catch-of-the-day specials, which are reasonably priced and delicious. 2335 Kalakaua Ave. (phone: 922-5761). Moderate.

Richard's Stuffed Potato – Despite its name, this inconspicuous eatery with indoor and patio seating is most notable for the delicious meat, fish, and pasta dishes prepared by the owner-chef. Bring your own beer and wine, easily obtained at a nearby convenience store, and be prepared for a bit of a wait for dinner to reach the table. Open daily except Sundays. No reservations. 2109 Kuhio Ave. (phone: 922-0102). Moderate.

Seafood Emporium – Flavorful food makes up for the relative austerity of decor that recalls New England; clearly, the pleasure here is not in adornment but in eating. Open daily for lunch and dinner. Reservations advised for dinner. Royal Hawaiian Shopping Center, 2201 Kalakaua Ave. (phone: 922-5547). Moderate.

Sergio's – Excellent Italian and continental specialties include a full range of pasta, plus veal, chicken, and shrimp in a variety of styles. Open daily for dinner. Reservations necessary. 445 Nohonani St. (phone: 926-3388). Moderate.

Siam Inn – There has been high praise for this Thai restaurant in the heart of Waikiki, where imported spices and fresh local produce and seafood are combined to advantage. Normally fiery Thai dishes are prepared with Western tastebuds in mind. Open daily for lunch and dinner. Reservations unnecessary. 407 Seaside (phone: 926-8802). Moderate.

Spats – Dinner in a well-known disco might not sound very promising, but don't let what goes on after 9 PM deter you from coming here. The decor recalls a rather lavish speakeasy, with beveled glass, highly polished wood, and waiters in cutaways and suspenders. Try the chicken *alla cacciatore* or shrimp *all' aglio e olio* (with garlic and oil). Fettuccine Alfredo is the star attraction among the pasta. Open daily. Reservations advised for dinner. In the Hyatt Regency hotel, 2424 Kalakaua Ave. (phone: 922-9292). Moderate.

Trattoria – The chef doesn't overload the menu with tomato paste, and many dishes are cooked *al burro* — delicately, in butter — instead of doused in olive oil. The lasagna in this charmingly decorated restaurant is well worth tasting. So are *cotoletta di vitello alla parmigiana* and *pollo alla Romana.* The cannelloni Milanese is definitely a "don't miss." Open daily. Reservations necessary on weekends. Outrigger Edgewater Hotel, 2168 Kalia Rd. (phone: 923-8415). Moderate.

Hard Rock Café – The Honolulu branch of this trendy international chain attracts a young crowd out to be part of "the scene." Food is good, crowds are standard day or night, and the noise level is decibels higher than that which allows comfortable conversation. But, then, that's intended to be part of the appeal. Guitars of famous rockers are part of the decor, as are other blasts of rock 'n' roll memorabilia, and patrons come as much to buy T-shirts and other signature souvenirs as to eat or drink. Valet parking. Open daily from 11:30 AM to midnight. No reservations. 1826 Kalakaua Ave. (phone: 955-7383). Moderate to inexpensive..

It's Greek To Me – The setting amid the shops of the Royal Hawaiian Center is more convenient than charming, but the food is recommended for quality, price, and the speed with which you're served. Open daily from 9 AM to 10:30 PM. Reservations necessary. On the ground floor of the Royal Hawaiian Center (phone: 922-2733). Moderate to inexpensive.

Bavarian Beer Garden – Bratwurst, knockwurst, sauerkraut, and warm German potato salad are among the house specialties. So, too, is dancing to a 5-piece Bavarian band on the largest dance floor in Waikiki. Open nightly from 5 PM to 1 AM. Third floor, Royal Hawaiian Shopping Center (phone: 922-6535). Inexpensive.

Caffé Guccini – The warm welcome at this low-key café is followed by fine pasta, rich cappuccino, and tempting desserts. Guests may bring their own wine or beer, but there's also a full bar. Open daily from 3 to 11:30 PM. Reservations unnecessary. 2139 Kuhio Ave. (phone: 922-5287). Inexpensive.

Diamond Head

Like the Rock of Gibraltar, Table Mountain at Cape Town, and Sugar Loaf in Rio de Janeiro, Diamond Head is immediately recognizable, not only to sailors and airline navigators but to armchair travelers all over the world. Contrary to popular understanding, its name has nothing to do with its shape. It was christened Diamond Head by British seamen who mistook the calcite crystals they found there for diamonds. The older Hawaiian name is Leahi, brow of the ahi, or yellow-fin tuna, which it resembled in the imagination of early Hawaiians. Anyone who has seen the effigies of knights in the crypts of English and Norman churches will find a distinct likeness between them and the silhouette of the crater as seen from the high windows of Waikiki at dusk.

In geological terms, Diamond Head is a formation resulting from the titanic explosions that occurred when water came into contact with hot lava rising from a fissure 400,000 years ago, and it has been at peace, volcanically speaking, for 150,000 years.

Today, Diamond Head is a National Natural Landmark and a state monument. A road off Diamond Head Road between Makapuu Road and 18th Avenue leads through a tunnel onto the eerie floor of the crater, much of which today forms part of Fort Ruger and is used by the Hawaiian National Guard. To get a closer look at the terrain and at the pillboxes, gun emplacements, and warrens of tunnels built as an integral part of the Pacific defense systems in World War II, you can hike from the parking lot near the firing range through the kiawe and keahole trees to the viewing area at Point Leahi, 760 feet above sea level, the highest spot on Diamond Head. Depending on your physical condition, this should take between 30 minutes and 1 hour. The route leads along a gently graded, but occasionally rough, trail dug into the hillside. The most difficult patches have concrete steps and balustrades to make the going easier. Through a short tunnel and up 99 steps, you arrive at a gun emplacement. Beyond, three spiral staircases and a steel ladder lead up to the crater rim and a fine view of Honolulu, Waikiki, and the mountains.

Diamond Head's varied birdlife provides an interesting diversion for those making the climb, for it is an unofficial sanctuary for a number of cage birds, strangers to the islands, that have escaped or been released from captivity and have proliferated inside the crater and on its slopes. Species to look for include the yellow-fronted canary, the red-eared waxbill, the saffron finch with its perennial look of surprise, and the white-cheeked, pink-billed Java sparrow. Probably the most easily recognizable is the pin-tailed whydah, which, with its long, graceful tailfeathers and its black and white plumage, looks like a Dominican friar with a long train. While these birds add a dimension of color to the somewhat muted hues that characterize the crater most of the year, it should be noted that their presence among the native bird population is not without hazards, including hybridization, competition for food, and the introduction of disease.

The ocean side of Diamond Head, from Kapiolani Park to Black Point, is Honolulu's Gold Coast, the most fashionable, expensive, and exclusive few acres in Hawaii. The State of Hawaii has been able to obtain some property here and there, creating several vest-pocket parks. Most of the narrow ribbon of land between the outer edge of the crater and the sea is still privately owned, its cliffside and beachside villas of considerable luxury protected by high walls overrun with hibiscus, bougainvillea, poinsettia, and royal poinciana. This is where the estate of the heiress and socialite Doris Duke is located, where Jacqueline Onassis brought the younger Kennedys for a summer, and where Dorothy Lamour sometimes comes for Christmas. Today much of the money that fuels expensive home construction is Japanese.

Easy access to the cliffs and narrow beaches on the ocean side of Diamond Head is possible from Beach Road, which turns off Diamond Head Road near the lighthouse. At Diamond Head Beach Park you will find divers fishing among the segmented reefs, though casual swimming is not recommended. Swimmers should try Kaalawai Beach, near Black Point, where volcanic lava flowed into the sea several hundred thousand years ago. There is public access from the end of Kulamanu Place, also off Diamond Head Road. Watch for net-throwing fishermen, who still practice their graceful craft in these parts.

 SHOPPING: The Kahala Mall (phone: 732-7736) provides a nice selection of shops, including *Liberty House* (phone: 941-2345); *Long's Drugs* (phone: 732-0784); *Waldenbooks* (phone: 737-9550); and a costume-jewelry kiosk called *Riches* (phone: 737-3303). Kilohana Square, at 1016 Kapahulu Ave. just before Kapahulu Ave. meets the H-1 freeway, offers several excellent antiques stores. Among them: *As Time Goes By* (phone: 732-1174), where jewelry, paintings, and silver are showcased; *Max Davis* (phone: 735-2341), where high-quality Oriental antiques are the thing; and *Carriage House* (phone: 737-2622), where the mix is European, Oriental, and American.

 NIGHTLIFE: Residents of Diamond Head are rarely seen in nightclubs and never at extravaganzas or luaus. If you're not joining them for a civilized evening at home, then you might spot them at the symphony or the ballet. *Bobby McGee's Conglomeration* (Colony East, 2885 Kalakaua Ave.; phone:

922-1282), a mixed bag of stained glass, fringed velvet canopies, Tiffany lampshades, and plush banquettes, has dinner and dancing each night — the latter occasionally bordering on disco.

CHECKING IN: There are just a few hotels in the Diamond Head area, and prices are generally the same as in Waikiki. Expect to pay around $165 and up for a double in a hotel listed as expensive, from $80 to $160 at a place listed as moderate; and under $75 at an inexpensive place. All telephone numbers are in the 808 area code unless otherwise indicated.

Colony Surf – A true Hollywood-style condominium right on the beach, it is one of the most delightful places to stay in Honolulu. Apartments are decorated in the plush, off-white tones that many people associate with seaside living. There are no lanais, but large windows with glorious views. Kitchens are modern and fully equipped, and there is daily maid service and adequate laundry facilities. The lobby is small and elegant and chiefly famous for being the entrance to *Michel's* restaurant. Studios with lanais and kitchenettes are available in the adjacent *Colony East* hotel, which is owned and operated by the same company at the same address. 2895 Kalakaua Ave. (phone: 923-5751; 800-252-7873). Expensive to moderate.

Diamond Head Beach – This 14-story structure on the beach was completely refurbished in 1982 to make it one of the more attractive places in terms of price and location in Honolulu. Units range from hotel rooms to 1-bedroom apartments. Rooms are smallish but comfortable, with good-sized lanais. Although there is little in the way of a lobby and no shops, pool, or tour desks, these are available close by, in the *New Otani.* 2947 Kalakaua Ave. (phone: 922-1928; 800-367-6046). Expensive to moderate.

New Otani Kaimana Beach – The location is the thing here: on the Diamond Head side of Kapiolani Park, just a few minutes away from Waikiki by foot or bus. The beach is right outside, and beautiful reefs are within easy snorkeling distance. A hotelwide renovation and refurbishing was completed in 1988. The terrace restaurant overlooks the beach and is edged by (and named for) large hau trees. Oceanside rooms have stunning views. Families seem to like the *New Otani,* and women traveling alone have found it a friendly, hospitable, and safe haven. 2863 Kalakaua Ave. (phone: 923-1555; 800-421-8795). Expensive to moderate.

EATING OUT: The dinner tab in Diamond Head will generally run a bit higher than in Waikiki. For a meal for two in the restaurants listed below, $60 and up is expensive; $25 to $55 is moderate; and under $20 is inexpensive. This does not include wine, tips, or drinks. All telephone numbers are in the 808 area code unless otherwise indicated.

Michel's – At most beachfront restaurants in Honolulu, the cooking takes a back seat to the view. Not here. For a start, the decor does not suggest a mere extension of sand and ocean. The dining room is elegant and subdued. Although there are occasionally deft local touches, such as prosciutto served with papaya, most of the dishes tend to be classic. Even the *opakapaka* is served Véronique style with a champagne sauce added. Jacket required for dinner. Reservations necessary. In the Colony Surf Hotel, 2895 Kalakaua Avenue, Diamond Head (phone: 923-6552). Expensive.

Miyako – Shabu shabu–style cooking (meat, vegetables, and seafood prepared in boiling water at the table) has the emphasis here. Seating is either in the main dining room with its rooftop, oceanside views, or in small tatami rooms where guests sit on mats on the floor. Two days' advance notice will procure the special Kaiseiki dinner of 7, 8, or 9 courses, all making use of the freshest produce, fish, and seafood available that day. Open daily for dinner. New Otani Kaimana Beach Hotel, 2863 Kalakaua Ave. (phone: 923-1555). Expensive to moderate.

Willows – This is one of the most famous restaurants in the state, and *the* place to sample traditional Hawaiian dishes. The celebrated poi supper offers many of these, including poi itself, steamed *laulau,* sweet potato, chicken luau, and lomilomi salmon. If all this seems too exotic, the curry dishes, leavened with coconut milk, are superb. This is also the perfect place for wearing an aloha shirt or muumuu for the first time; the rural tropical atmosphere of palm trees and thatched roofs seems to call for it, and strolling musicians provide the perfect accompaniment. Open daily. Reservations necessary. 901 Hausten St. (phone: 946-4808). Expensive to moderate.

Hau Tree Lanai – The food is good, but the beachfront setting, especially at breakfast or at dusk, is its own reward. 2863 Kalakaua Ave. (phone: 923-1555). Moderate.

Keo's Thai Cuisine – This is a fine place to sample Thai cuisine, which can be flavorful and fiery, although the kitchen will prepare milder versions of its hot specialties if requested. Mint-flavored spring rolls make a delicious appetizer, and cold sweet tea is a good accompaniment for the spicier dishes. The setting is elegant and nearly drenched in orchids; the crowd, Honolulu's cognoscenti. Reservations necessary. 441 Kapahulu Ave. (phone: 737-8240). Moderate.

Phillip Paolo's – Set in an eclectically decorated private home, a 5-minute drive from Waikiki, the Italian specialties by owner-chef Phillip Paolo Sarubbi earn this restaurant the high praise it receives. Daily specials complement standard features like fettuccine Vigario (pasta with mushrooms and spinach in light basil cream sauce) and shrimp Parmigiano. 2312 Beretania St. (phone: 946-1163). Moderate.

Bernard's of New York – Typical New York deli offerings — from delicious cheese blintzes to matzo ball soup to lean pastrami, and a weekend brunch — are the main reasons for heading this way. Near the University of Hawaii Manoa Campus, 2633 S. King St. (phone: 946-7477). Inexpensive.

Midtown Honolulu and the Ala Moana Center

This busy area — bounded by the ocean, by Ward Avenue on the *ewa* (western) side, Beretania Avenue on the mountain side, and Kalakaua Avenue and the Ala Wai Canal on the Diamond Head side — is the center of Oahu's communications and shopping. The Ala Moana Shopping Center, and to a lesser extent the Ward Warehouse Shopping Center, attract people from all over the state. Ninety percent of the islands' radio and TV news is relayed from the studios here; TheBus terminal at Ala Moana is the busiest on Oahu; and close to Kewalo Boat Basin are two of Hawaii's most famous restaurants. In addition, in this area are Ala Moana Park, the beach park most popular with Honolulu residents, and the *Neal S. Blaisdell Center* (Kapiolani Blvd. and Ward Ave.; phone: 521-2911), which is the scene of wrestling, basketball, and boxing events, rock concerts, and boat and automobile shows. The *Blaisdell Center*'s concert hall on South King Street is also the home of the *Honolulu Symphony Orchestra.*

Ala Moana Center – At this marketplace of the central Pacific can be seen Asians, Australians, and South Seas Islanders as well as Frenchmen, Britons, Germans, and plenty of locals indulging in that ritual that seems to unite people the world over — shopping. It's the perfect place for people watching, with fountains, statuary, and pools to relax by. And it's not just tourists who parade past: Ala Moana Center is the main terminus on Oahu for TheBus, so many island people come through as well. (For discussions of the individual stores, see *Shopping.*) Ala Moana Blvd., opposite Ala Moana Park (phone: 946-2811).

Ala Moana Park – This 76-acre recreation area was once a swampland of bulrushes, duck ponds, and islets of coconut palms and kiawe trees. Later, part of it was the city dump. Today, Ala Moana is the favorite city beach of Honolulu residents partly because of its safe swimming areas (do not venture out into the boat channels, however) and partly because it is easily accessible and away from the main hotel complexes. However, Ala Moana's beach is hard-packed sand, probably because it's manmade. The paths are very popular with Honolulu's fanatical joggers, and there are picnic tables, tennis courts, a bowling green, and six softball fields. The adjacent Aina Moana Park, also known as Magic Island, affords a good view of the yachts sailing in and out of the Ala Wai Yacht Harbor across the narrow canal in Waikiki as well as a sheltered swimming beach. Between Ala Moana Blvd. and the ocean.

Contemporary Arts Center – Originally housed in the offices of the Hawaii Newspaper Agency (where it now maintains a satellite gallery), it moved to its own premises on the lower slopes of Tantalus in 1988. Top-quality, changing exhibits highlight today's best artists in a variety of disciplines. Among the 500 artists whose works are featured are Andy Warhol, Robert Arneson, and Deborah Butterfield, as well as Hawaiians Madge Tennet, Jean Charlot, Satoru Abe, and Isami Doi. Notable is David Hockney's *L'Enfant et les Sortileges,* a three-dimensional work housed in its own pavilion, based on the English pop artist's sets and costumes for Ravel's 1925 opera. Open from 10 AM to 4 PM Mondays and Wednesdays through Saturdays; noon to 4 PM Sundays. Admission $3; Thursdays free. 2411 Makiki Heights Dr. (phone: 526-1322).

Honolulu Academy of Arts – For anyone who has ever been daunted by the sheer magnitude of the Metropolitan Museum of Art in New York or the National Gallery in Washington, DC, this human-sized enclave of civilization and coolness will come as a revelation. It is possible within a couple of hours or so to savor the cultures of the West and the East without becoming mind-boggled with strange images and arcane facts. Paintings from the Italian Renaissance and Impressionist works from 19th-century France form part of the Western holdings. From the Far East there are screens, lacquerwork, and wood block prints from the 17th century. Segna di Bonaventura's *Madonna and Child* (14th century) is one of the earliest Renaissance paintings in the academy's collection. From Japan there is an ink and color handscroll dating from AD 1250. John Singleton Copley and William Guy Wall are among the several American painters represented here. Closed Mondays. 900 S. Beretania St. (phone: 538-1006).

Kewalo Boat Basin – The gleaming white hulls, polished mahogany, uniform masts, and endless bright blue tarpaulins on the boats in the Ala Wai Boat Harbor at Waikiki's western end tend to make it look like a boatyard in aspic, as though a visitor from outer space had read a book on how to construct one and couldn't get the details quite right. The Kewalo Boat Basin reminds you what boats are supposed to look like — slightly shabby and sailed in. The few remaining sampans that work out of Honolulu bring the day's catch back to the marina here, destined ultimately for the pans and broilers of *John Dominis* and *Fisherman's Wharf* restaurants in the neighborhood and other eating houses farther afield. This is also where the tour boats set off for trips along the coast to Diamond Head and Pearl Harbor.

Maui Divers Jewelry Design Center – A million dollars was spent on the museum-quality displays and to create the tour, which starts with an 8-minute video explaining the diversity of Hawaii's corals and follows with a look at the jewelry manufacturing plant where the coral is designed, cast, polished, and assembled. After the tour, you'll have a chance to spend from $150 to $15,000 on the results. Open Mondays through Fridays from 9 AM to 3 PM; admission $3. Near Ala Moana Center, at 1520 Liona St. (phone: 946-7979).

 SHOPPING: In midtown, most shopping means a visit to the Ala Moana Center, Ward Warehouse, or the Ward Centre.

ALA MOANA SHOPPING CENTER

A major expansion in 1989 upped the number of stores in this complex to 220, including large mainland operations such as *Sears* and *J. C. Penney,* plus a food court with more than 20 fast-food specialty restaurants. The center also has the main TheBus terminus on Oahu. The No. 8 bus leaves for and comes from Waikiki every 10 minutes, and the No. 20 bus stops here on the Airport-Waikiki run.

Banana Republic – The Hawaii branch of this outfitter of the urban adventurer is a good place for well-made, sanely priced, all-cotton clothing, as well as a location to find the unusual — especially if it's travel-related (phone: 955-2602).

Chocolates for Breakfast – The women's clothing sold here is often elegant, sometimes daring, and occasionally counter-chic, but always sophisticated. For the pure of heart there are muslins that *look* innocent enough (phone: 947-3434).

Crack Seed Center – Preserved seeds and fruits, including dried cherries, plums, ginger, and lemon peel are featured (phone: 949-7200).

Emanuel Ungaro Boutique – Haute couture for men and women (no phone at press time).

Foot Locker – It bills itself as America's Most Complete Athletic Store, and it might be right (phone: 944-8390).

Hale Kukui – Candles from all over the world, including scented, dripless, and/or smokeless varieties. Charming candle-powered windmills and unusual Hawaiian Christmas decorations are also featured (phone: 949-6500).

Honolulu Book Shop – One of the largest and most comprehensive in Hawaii (phone: 941-2274).

Iida's – This shop specializes in things Japanese, from bronze statues to porcelains to back massage rollers. It's fun to explore just to see what's being offered; there're some good gift ideas, too (phone: 946-0888).

Liberty House – Hawaii's leading department store, of which you will find a token version in hotels on all the major islands. The emphasis is on middle-of-the-road men's, women's, and children's fashions — not quite designer creations, but not simply aloha-wear, either. The Ala Moana store also has housewares, toys, books, and so on. Visits to more than a dozen *Liberty House* stores indicate that the staff is on the whole more than usually helpful (phone: 941-2345).

La Maison du Chocolat – Chocoholics beware. The temptations are many at this ground-level specialty shop (phone: 944-1116).

MCM – Offering the finest in German leather goods, this shop takes its initials from designer Michael Cromer of Munich (no phone at press time).

Michel's Baguette – Here's the perfect place to stop for coffee, pastries, or croissants in the midst of an excursion to Ala Moana. Ocean side, ground level (phone: 946-6888). Inexpensive.

North Beach Leather – From coats to dresses, pants to accessories, everything you might want to wear made of leather — with high-fashion design and price tags to match (phone: 949-6719).

Otsuka Gallerie – The works of Japan's Hisashi Otsuki are worth seeing, even if the price tags are high (phone: 947-8844).

Pocketbook Man – Perhaps Hawaii's most complete selection of luggage and handbags, with some very elegant choices, is here (phone: 949-3535).

Polo/Ralph Lauren – At three times the size of the designer's original shop in Ward Center, this shop carries a full collection of the Polo designs (no phone at press time).

Prides of New Zealand – We mean lambs, and when the cuddly little beggars are slaughtered, their skin is used for stadium rugs, car seat covers, toys, and golf club warmers. Golf club warmers? In Hawaii? Anyway, you'll find it all here (phone: 944-5590).

Products of Hawaii – Hawaiian perfume, Hawaiian tiki carvings, Hawaiian *lau hala* mats, Hawaiian-designed greeting cards are sold here — as advertised. It's a good spot to do all your souvenir shopping at one time (phone: 949-6866).

Ross Sutherland – About 90% of the menswear available in Hawaii is not really suitable for the mainland. If you forgot to pack something for a quick return to Nob Hill, North Michigan Avenue, or Wall Street, this is one of the few places in the state that can help you out of your predicament (phone: 946-2888).

Sharper Image – This adult "toy" store is bound to have something to please, be it products of high-tech electronics or space-age imagination. The prices are neither low nor ridiculous (phone: 949-4100).

Tahiti Imports – Polynesian fashions for women, a lot of them quite classy in their brief way, are sold here. The *pareu,* in simple and elegant designs, can be turned into intriguing cover-ups and skirts (phone: 941-4539).

Vis à Vis – It's perhaps Hawaii's trendiest clothing and accessories emporium, with much that's worth a second look, particularly when sale prices are in effect. From rhinestones to plastics, denim to linen, this shop will provide a glimpse of what's hot in the fashion world (phone: 973-7365).

Waterford/Wedgwood – Here is a complete selection of England's finest porcelain and crystal (no phone at press time).

WARD WAREHOUSE

The Ward Warehouse, on Ala Moana Boulevard opposite the Kewalo Boat Basin, is a 2-story complex of 70 boutiques and restaurants constructed from stout timbers painted brown. A lot of people come here just to sip fine coffee at *The Coffee Works* and to munch on candy from *Fudge Works.*

Artists Guild – On display and for sale are superior Hawaiian arts and crafts. Among them: prints, drawings, woven goods, and scrimshaw with nautical etchings (phone: 531-2933).

The Extra Dimension – Beautiful silk flowers and arrangements are made in this shop with the same traditional techniques used in Japan (phone: 521-5512).

Future Heirlooms – As the name implies, this store sports collectibles worth considering such as beautifully stitched Hmong quilts, Indian and Chinese jewelry, and Balinese wood carvings (phone: 531-0065).

Neon Leon – What started as a neon lighting specialty shop has become a place to find inexpensive, offbeat, humorous gifts, plus one of Hawaii's best selections of humorous greeting cards (phone: 545-7666).

Waldenbooks – Offers a wide selection of best sellers and coffee-table titles, including several shelves of Hawaiiana (phone: 533-2711).

WARD CENTRE

On Ala Moana Boulevard, across the street from Ward Warehouse and from Ala Moana Beach Park, Ward Centre features a selection of upscale shops. *Pappagallo* (phone: 536-6443) carries classic women's resortwear. *Allison's Wonderland* (phone: 521-8697) is home to one of Hawaii's finest selections of children's books and toys. At *Hands of the World* (phone: 531-2300), an interesting selection of hand-crafted jewelry, clothing, and crafts from all over the world will be found, while the items featured at the *Willowdale Gallery* (phone: 536-2080) are of the antique sort, most hailing from Europe. Some popular eateries here are *Monterey Bay Canners,* which features kiawe-wood charcoal-broiled fish (phone: 536-6197); *Chez Sushi* (phone: 536-1007) is self-explanatory; *Il Fresco,* with fine Italian specialties (phone: 523-5191); *Compadres,* a spacious, plant-filled place serving Mexican fare (phone: 523-3914); and *Mary Catherine's,* which serves delicious coffees and desserts (phone: 531-3525).

 NIGHTLIFE: *Rumours,* at the *Ala Moana–Americana* (phone: 955-4811), is one of Honolulu's more popular discos and gears itself to a slightly older, more sophisticated crowd. *TGI Friday's* (950 Ward Ave.; phone: 523-5841) has a lively bar, while the much quieter and more relaxed *Horatio's* (1050 Ala Moana Blvd.; phone: 521-5002) features young island musicians who perform contemporary music on weekends. For just plain mingling, *Monterey Bay Canners, Compadres,* and *Ryan's* at Ward Centre are crowded and lively, and the latter features live guitar and steel drum music.

 CHECKING IN: Midtown is not too close to the "action" in Waikiki, so few tourists stay in the area. That, in itself, may add to the area's appeal for some. Expect to pay $90 and up for a double in a hotel listed as expensive and from $45 to $85 in one listed as moderate. All telephone numbers are in the 808 area code unless otherwise indicated.

Manoa Valley Inn – This may be Hawaii's most complete bed-and-breakfast facility, with 7 bedrooms in a beautifully restored turn-of-the-century Manoa Valley home, and it is highly recommended. Rates include an ample continental breakfast, afternoon pupus, and sunset cocktails. Bus connections to Ala Moana center, and from there to all other parts of Oahu, are available. About 2 miles from Waikiki, at 2001 Vancouver Dr. (phone: 947-6019). Expensive to moderate.

Ala Moana – Bright, sunny rooms in lively tropical colors and just about every kind of hotel service imaginable are two of the things that help this 36-story property compensate for not being close enough to the Waikiki beaches to be in the swing. The hotel's size can sometimes be a disadvantage: Although the room staff and managers seem very helpful, a somewhat impersonal feeling pervades. 410 Atkinson Dr. (phone: 955-4811; 800-367-6025). Moderate.

Pagoda – Some people prefer to keep away from "the strip," but still within striking distance of Waikiki's sands. This is one place to fulfill both aims. A block and a half north of the Ala Moana Center, it's quiet and pleasant, with an informal staff that is surprisingly professional. On the hotel grounds is an attractive tropical garden with a pond of over 3,000 beautifully colored carp as well as the *Pagoda Floating Restaurant,* which is quite popular with residents. 1525 Rycroft St. (phone: 941-6611; 800-367-6060). Moderate.

 EATING OUT: Although not as diverse as the restaurants in Waikiki, there are a number of good places in the Ala Moana–Midtown area, among them *John Dominis,* one of the most famous in Hawaii. For a meal for two, excluding wine, tips, and drinks, expect to pay more than $60 in a place listed as expensive, between $25 and $55 in a place listed as moderate, and under $25 in an inexpensive place. All telephone numbers are in the 808 area code unless otherwise indicated.

John Dominis – One of the best restaurants in Honolulu, albeit expensive, at the end of an unpromising street of warehouses and light industries on a promontory overlooking the Kewalo Basin and the Pacific. Inside the dining room, at a central island lavishly laden with fruits of the sea, a chef shucks oysters, steams clams, and makes broth. In saltwater pools spiny lobsters and fresh local fish clamber and swim around. This is an ideal place to sample island seafood: *ono* (wahoo), *onaga* (red snapper), and *opakapaka* (white snapper) are all available in season. The *cioppino* (stew) of seafood and fresh fish cooked in tomatoes, herbs, and spices is unbeatable. Open daily for dinner. Reservations necessary. 43 Ahui St. (phone: 523-0955). Expensive.

Andrews – The steamed clams in herbs and spices and the veal dishes are particularly noteworthy at one of Honolulu's less touted Italian restaurants. Linens, crystal, and silver set the tone for a relaxed evening in pleasant surroundings. Open daily for lunch and dinner. Reservations advised. Ward Centre, 1200 Ala Moana Blvd. (phone: 523-8677). Expensive to moderate.

Café Cambio – Contemporary northern Italian cuisine combines with southern highlights like *cioppino* and an *antipasto misto.* The owner is from Turin, which helps make *Café Cambio* the real thing. Open for lunch weekdays and dinner daily; closed Mondays. Reservations necessary for lunch only. 1680 Kapiolani Blvd., adjacent to the Kapiolani Theater (phone: 942-0740). Moderate.

Compadres – Delicious Mexican food, a comfortable setting, and good prices make this a hit at Ward Center (phone: 523-1307). Moderate.

Fisherman's Wharf – Tuna and charter boats tie up at the dock beside this seafront restaurant with a nautical atmosphere. Open daily. Reservations unnecessary. 1009 Ala Moana Blvd., Kewalo Basin (phone: 538-3808). Moderate.

Il Fresco – High-tech design and tables set with crystal and linen fit its location in the chic Ward Center. A varied menu features blackened *ahi* (tuna) and pasta. Ward Center (enter on Auahi St.; phone: 523-5191). Moderate.

Horatio's – The nautical decor is most appropriate in this tavern overlooking the Kewalo Boat Basin. Among the house specialties worth trying are mahimahi stuffed with shrimp and crab, and beef Wellington glazed with Madeira sauce. Freshly baked Russian rye bread accompanies each entrée. Open daily. Reservations necessary Fridays and Saturdays. Ward Warehouse, 1050 Ala Moana Blvd. (phone: 521-5002). Moderate.

Yanagi Sushi – Two Tokyo-style sushi bars serve a sushi lover's abundance of specials. The atmosphere is upbeat, the decor simple but appealing, and the sushi first-rate. Open daily. Reservations necessary. 762 Kapiolani Blvd. (phone: 537-1525). Moderate.

Orson's – Downstairs is a coffee shop called the *Chowder House,* which serves fresh salads as well as seafood; upstairs, a dining room decorated with beautifully stained woods offers more fine seafood. Open daily for lunch and dinner. Reservations advised. Ward Warehouse, 1050 Ala Moana Blvd. (phone: 521-5681). Upstairs moderate; downstairs inexpensive.

Ryan's Parkplace – Popular for its pasta, vegetable, and fish dishes, desserts, and coffee. Open daily; dinner only on Sundays. Reservations advised. Ward Warehouse, 1050 Ala Moana Blvd. (phone: 523-9132). Moderate to inexpensive.

TGI Friday's – The Honolulu version of the New York original features antique furnishings, a friendly bar, and surprisingly good food at modest prices (especially for the enormous portions served, which can easily be shared). Best known for its potato skins, this eatery also serves an array of quiches, omelettes, salads, desserts, and more. It's always lively and usually noisy. Open daily. No reservations. 950 Ward Ave. (phone: 523-5841). Moderate to inexpensive.

China House – The cavernous dining room of this Honolulu favorite is often full. If shark fin or bird nest soup is your thing, you can have it here. Four varieties of the former and three of the latter are offered. The dim sum is famous throughout the island and is served daily from 11 AM to 2 PM. Open daily. Reservations advised. At the top of the ramp from Kapiolani Blvd. in the Ala Moana Center (phone: 949-6622). Moderate to inexpensive.

Big Ed's Deli – This is the place to head if you've got a craving for New York–style pastrami or corned beef. Popular with the lunch crowd, it's much easier to go at dinnertime. Open daily from 7 AM to 10 PM. Reservations unnecessary. In Ward Center (phone: 536-4591). Inexpensive.

Downtown Honolulu

It may come as a surprise to many people, but there is a Honolulu outside the beaches and huge, windowed gravestones that line Kalakaua Avenue in Waikiki. Even if the hotels and restaurants were not there, Honolulu would thrive as a marketplace between the Far East and Australia and the United States and as the capital of a fascinating island state with a cultural past as singular as any in the Union. The high-rises housing famous corporations along Bishop Street and the surprisingly elegant promenade of the Fort Street Mall bear witness to Honolulu's importance as a Pacific marketplace and communications center. Iolani Palace and the Iolani Barracks remind us of the state's royal and independent past. The four-masted *Falls of Clyde* is a memento of the days when trade with the Sandwich Islands meant several weeks at sea, not just a few hours in the air. The city's contemporary status as the legislative and executive center of the 50th state is represented by some of the most handsome government buildings in the US, while other structures reflect the religious affiliations of their builders — Catholic, Anglican, and Congregational. There are also small enclaves of Filipinos, Koreans, and Japanese, but more significant, the city has a Chinatown, small by the standards of those in the great port cities such as San Francisco and Singapore, yet still carrying the flavor of the days when people from an exotic land came to a new place, bringing with them their traditions, dress, and cuisine. Although Hawaii managed to escape the exigencies of the British imperium, there is a distinct post-colonial feeling about downtown Honolulu in the formal 19th-century buildings around renovated Merchants Square and the hacienda-style C. Brewer and Company building, with its charming walled garden.

Downtown Honolulu — for our purposes an area bordered by Ward Avenue on the Diamond Head side, the Kapalama Stream on the *ewa* (west) side, the Lunalilo Freeway on the mountain side, and the ocean on the remaining side — leads from one culture to another and from one era to another in a matter of minutes, always with plenty of places for a bite or a sip in between. And, despite efforts to alter the ambience of areas like Hotel Street — with its recently added potted flowers and trees and its mall-style seating — the heart of downtown Honolulu retains its feel of being a sailor's port.

Aloha Tower – In the old days, when first class travel meant elegant, steam-belching liners, this was what you looked for as you entered Honolulu Harbor. It was the scene of swaying hips on lithe, olive-skinned girls handing out leis and kisses to pale-faced *haoles*. Today a few luxury liners make use of its piers, including *American Hawaii Cruises*' SS *Independence* and SS *Constitution* and *Aloha Pacific*'s SS *Monterey*, which dock here each Saturday. The 10th-floor observatory is still the best place to get a perspective of the city from the airport to Diamond Head, although the rapid mushrooming of high-rises can hardly be said to have improved the view. One curious phenomenon is the extraordinary sight of Honolulu Harbor as reflected in the green glass towers of the Grosvenor Center. The effect is that of a vast Japanese mural, full of stylized mountains, clouds, seascapes, boats, and cranes. The tower also affords a bird's-eye view of every deck, nook, and cranny of the few liners that still visit the port. The tower is scheduled for restoration as part of the planned redevelopment of Honolulu's old port. At the bottom of Fort Street Mall (phone: 537-9260).

Chinatown – Chinatown is on the easternmost fringe of downtown and spills across the Nuuanu Stream into Aala Triangle Park, where reverend Oriental sires can be seen playing checkers and mah-jongg or just enjoying the shade of the banyan and monkey-pod trees. The real business of the community takes place on the Diamond Head side of the stream. Here, in open-air meat, fish, and vegetable markets with their esoteric produce, you will find elderly people who still dress in the costume of their native or ancestral land. You will also find barbershops with lady barbers and herb shops that dispense age-old medications for all manner of illnesses, some of them probably contracted in this neighborhood on the previous night. This is also the traditional "sin" quarter of Honolulu, known to generations of sailors and other military personnel who subsequently settled in respectable suburbs with mortgages, station wagons, and probably some fond memories. Sleazy pool bars and live sex shows compete with family-style chop suey houses for customers. A walking tour of Chinatown takes place on Tuesdays at 9:30 AM, starting from the Chinese Chamber of Commerce, 42 N. King St. (phone: 533-3181). It stresses the daytime cultural and business background of the community rather than the nighttime activities, includes a visit to the famous Temple of Kuan Yin (Goddess of Mercy), and ends with an optional luncheon at the neighborhood's most famous restaurant, *Wo Fat*.

Iolani Palace – "The only royal palace on American soil," you will constantly be told. This large, gray, somewhat overly rococo building was completed in 1882, when King David Kalakaua, a hedonist and a wag, took up residence. After the Merry Monarch's death, the house fell to his sister, Queen Liliuokalani, who was deposed in 1893 and lived there as a semi-prisoner until 1895. Currently, it is still being restored to its former glory. Inside, the mansion has a grace that the outside does not quite achieve. The great Corinthian columns, the koa staircases, and the substantial chandeliers gleam, and eventually replicas of the original furniture will restore some life to the empty, elegant rooms. The Iolani Barracks, a sort of Disneyish replica of a Scottish baronial castle, was removed stone by stone from its original site and now stands in the palace grounds. Guided tours of the palace are conducted Wednesdays through Saturdays between 9 AM and 2:15 PM. The tours should be booked at least a day before, but since they are often sold out for several days in advance, reserve early. The fee for the 45-minute tour is $4. At the junction of King and Richard Sts. (phone: 538-1471 for information; 522-0822 for reservations).

Mission Houses Museum – These frame houses, built in 1821 from lumber that came around the Horn from Boston, used to be a school and a minister's home as well as a mission. They contain furniture and artifacts more reminiscent of New England than Hawaii as well as a rare archive of the islands' history. In the print house, constructed from coral, is a replica of the original printing press used to produce religious tracts and primers for schoolchildren, mostly in Hawaiian. On Saturdays, the Living History program populates the mission grounds with volunteers dressed in 19th-century garb. Open daily from 9 AM to 4 PM; tours offered daily from 9:30 AM to 3 PM. Admission $3.50. 55 S. King St. (phone: 531-0481).

Kawaiahao Church – This church likes to think of itself as the Westminster Abbey of Hawaii, and indeed, those remnants of the old Hawaiian royal and princely families who have retained their Congregational faith do occasionally use the church for baptisms, marriages, and funerals. It is the oldest church in Honolulu, built in 1842 on the site of Hawaii's first mission, which was a thatched-roof hut standing close to an ancient and sacred *hao* (spring). Tall *kahilis* (feather-decorated staffs symbolic of royalty) placed on either side of the altar testify to its distinguished past. It was here that King Kamehameha III used the expression *Ua mau ke ea o ka aina i ka pono* ("The life of the land is perpetuated in righteousness"), which is now the state motto. If you would like to hear a church service with Hawaiian hymns (the one at 10:30 AM is best), this is the place. 957 Punchbowl St. (phone: 522-1333).

Judiciary Building (Aliiolane Hale) – Originally built in 1874 as a palace for Kamehameha V, the building is Iolani's match for regalness. It was never used as a royal dwelling, however, although David Kalakaua used to trip the light fantastic here at receptions every once in a while. The recently restored interior has brought to fuller light some very beautiful stained glass, but the building is still best known for the statue out front of King Kamehameha the Great. It is a replica of the original which was lost in an Atlantic storm en route from Italy, but was later recovered and now stands in Kohala on the Big Island, not far from Kamehameha's birthplace. The Honolulu statue is decorated each July 11 with 40-foot leis. At King and Mililani Sts.

Hawaii State Capitol – It is such a pleasure to come across an attractive government building, and the pleasure here is increased by the simple, formal layout of its grounds. The capitol is a massive structure whose cantilevered concrete ribs separated by glass mosaic tiles manage to suggest the form of a volcano and the rhythm of the ocean. Koa wood from the Big Island lines most of the interior, and in the house and senate chambers many pieces of art, including fabrics, rugs, and wall coverings, are patterned after tapa designs in the Bishop Museum. None of these, however, is quite so riveting or as meaningful as the squat, bronze figure of the immortal Joseph de Veuster, Father Damien, sculpted by Marisol Escobar, which stands on the mountain side of the building or the statue of Queen Liliuokalani at the building's other entry. S. Beretania St.

St. Andrew's Cathedral – This is the seat of the Episcopalian bishop and is relentlessly Norman in style. Its outstanding feature is the front wall, a 24-by-55-foot stained glass window showing Christ with a selection of his saints and some Anglican luminaries, which manages to be modern without displaying any sign of artistic ambition. Kamehameha IV and Queen Emma were the church's patrons and among its early congregation. Beretania St. at Queen Emma St.

Our Lady of Peace Cathedral – Oddly enough, this Catholic church is less ornate than its Protestant counterpart and seems to retain a cool and airy feeling even in summer. It is chiefly famous as the place where Father Damien was ordained in May 1864 before starting the pilgrimage that led him to the leper colony on Molokai. Fort Street Mall at Beretania St.

Hawaii Maritime Center – The four-masted square-rigger, the *Falls of Clyde,* and the voyaging canoe *Hokulea,* both riding at anchor at Pier 7, provide the focus of activities at this museum. The captain's quarters of the *Falls of Clyde* form a nautical masterpiece of teak, birch, and mahogany fittings and furnishings, all set off by an abundance of red velvet upholstery. In contrast, visitors also see the cramped crew's quarters typical of 19th-century shipboard life. The *Hokulea* may not be boarded, but it is berthed to permit viewing from three sides. This now famous voyaging canoe has been used on several occasions to journey between the islands of Polynesia by means of stellar navigation in order to study the migration routes used by the earliest Hawaiians. A children's "hands-on" museum is housed in the Kalakaua Boathouse; other exhibitions relating to Hawaii's maritime past, including a library and photo archive, are at Aloha Tower. Open daily 9:30 AM to 4 PM. All-inclusive admission $6. At Pier 7, adjacent to the Aloha Tower and off Ala Moana Blvd. (phone: 536-6373).

Foster Botanic Garden – Some 20 acres of exotic plants and trees can be found in this arboreal enclave, one of six sites across the island that make up the Honolulu Botanic Gardens. This organization is attempting to propagate plants and trees from different environments around the world in appropriate parts of Oahu. The warm, humid climate of downtown Honolulu favors the growth of orchids, and the Lyn Orchid Garden is a popular spot, where these flowers range from the tiny *(pleurothallis)* to the large *(grammatophyllum)*. Orchids from both the Old and the New World grow here in rocks, on the ground, and, most exotic, on trees. Among the unusual trees are the cigar box tree from the Amazon area, which used to provide wood for cigar boxes curiously more aromatic than the tree's flowers; the sausage tree, from West Africa, the gourd-like fruit of which resembles a sausage; and the double coconut palm, which bears nuts weighing up to 50 pounds. A fascinating glimpse of the earth's past can be experienced in the Prehistoric Glen, where you will find primitive plants that thrived in the Coal Age. Fossils of these plants provide us with fuel, medicine, and fertilizer, even with plastic and paint. The gardens offer a useful view of the history of flora. And the sad-looking orchids along the garden fence that lines the freeway, devastated by gasoline fumes, tell us something about our progress. Among other importees in the garden is the Indian mongoose, discovered now and again peering from a rock. Open daily from 9 AM to 4 PM. Admission $1.50. N. Vineyard Blvd. (phone: 533-3214).

Dole Cannery Square – The 60-year-old cannery has been transformed into a visitor attraction, complete with restaurants, a consumer pavilion of Dole products and logo gifts, and shops. A visit here begins with a 10-minute multi-image presentation about the heritage of the pineapple in Hawaii, followed by a 45-minute tour of the cannery and free samples of pineapple and juice. Afterwards, browse through the shops and the exhibits depicting Dole's early days and the evolution of agriculture in Hawaii. Shuttle service (50¢) links the cannery to Waikiki. Open daily; tours are conducted every 15 minutes from 9 AM to 4 PM; shuttle operates from 8:30 AM to 3 PM. Admission $5. 650 Iwilei Rd., just west of downtown, off Nimitz Hwy. (phone: 531-8855).

 SHOPPING: The building-by-building restoration of downtown Honolulu has stimulated the opening of several galleries, antiques emporia, and quite browsable shops in the midst of a persisting honky-tonk atmosphere. It's an eclectic combination that makes a daytime walk downtown interesting. At *Pauahi Nuuanu Gallery,* 1 North Pauahi St. (phone: 531-6088), the emphasis is on Hawaiian arts ranging from wood carving to feather leis to Niihau shell jewelry. Long-established *Lai Fong,* 1118 Nuuanu St. (phone: 537-3497), features Oriental antiques and bric-a-brac, while *Robyn Buntin,* 900A Maunakea St. (phone: 523-5913); *Bushido,* 936 Maunakea St. (phone: 536-5693); *Garaku-ta Do,* 938 Maunakea St. (phone: 955-2099); *Mills Gallery,* 701 Bishop St. (phone: 536-3527), and *Mary Roberts,* 19 N. Pauahi St. (phone: 533-7179), take a high-brow approach to decor with some of Hawaii's best European and Oriental antiques. *Pegge Hopper Gallery,* 1164 Nuuanu St. (phone: 524-1160) presents the the pricey output of this artist's palette, and *Waterfall Gallery,* 1160A Nuuanu St. (phone: 521-6863), features graphics, jewelry, and collector's quality ceramics. The offerings run from practical to kitschy at shops like *Bo Wah Trading Co. Liberty House* has a downtown branch at 1032 Fort St. and a reduced-price merchandise outlet, the *Penthouse,* actually at street level at 1 N. King St. (phone: 941-2345), where some real bargains can be found. *Lily's Lei Shop,* 1104 Maunakea St. (phone: 537-1297), and *Jenny's Lei Shop,* 1151 Maunakea St. (phone: 521-1595), are two of a number of shops downtown that specialize in the traditional Hawaiian art of lei making, with a larger and better-priced selection than that found in Waikiki.

NIGHTLIFE: Most people who earn their bread and butter in downtown Honolulu head for home around sundown. They may linger for a drink in the new pub-like bars around Merchant Square, but few stay for dinner, although Restaurant Row has become its own draw, with several restaurants and a very popular rock 'n' roll disco, *Studebaker's* (phone: 526-9888). The music jumps the decades, and every now and again the staff takes to the table tops to dance. Some of the Chinese and Filipino families who live or have relatives in the neighborhood can be seen until 8 or 8:30 PM, but after that, the people on the streets are either looking for each other or for some kind of substitute for each other. Hotel Street comes alive after 10 PM, when motorcyclists come by and sit on their decorated two-wheelers, watching and talking. Servicemen idle along the street, in and out of bars where the gender of the inhabitants can be indefinite at first glance and where a pool game can lead to bloodshed. The too-few cops assigned to the area, not quite out of sight, stay on the alert all night. Determined nightbirds can listen to rock at the *Swing Club* (35 N. Hotel St.; phone: 536-7864) and the *Shindig* (1140 Maunakea; phone: 531-1572), or watch the striptease at *Hubba Hubba* (25 N. Hotel; phone: 536-7698).

CHECKING IN: Downtown's only option is the 26-room *Town Inn,* which offers the basics at appropriate rates of $35 a day without air conditioning, $37 with it. Weekly rates are also available. Located just beyond Chinatown at 250 N. Beretainia St. (phone: 808-536-2377).

EATING OUT: Except for a couple of restaurants in Chinatown, downtown Honolulu used to be a culinary wasteland. It is still not exactly a diner's paradise, but some spots have better than average food, ambience, and service. And with the rise of the new Restaurant Row (500 Ala Moana Blvd. at South St., on the Waikiki edge of downtown), things are definitely looking up. Lunchtime has traditionally been busier and livelier than dinnertime, but Restaurant Row is changing that trend. For a meal for two, excluding wine, tip, and drinks, expect to pay $60 or more at a restaurant listed as expensive, $30 to $55 in a place listed as moderate, and $20 or less in an inexpensive place. All telephone numbers are in the 808 area code unless otherwise indicated.

Waikiki Trolley operates a shuttle between Restaurant Row and Waikiki (50¢).

Black Orchid – Tom Selleck and the owners of *Nick's Fishmarket* have teamed up to manage this new restaurant, serving American cuisine — both indoors and alfresco. There's also a dance floor and a large, beautifully designed lounge. Open weekdays for lunch, daily for dinner. Reservations advised. Restaurant Row (phone: 521-3111). Expensive.

Ruth's Chris Steakhouse – Some of the best filet and New York steak in town. Restaurant Row (phone: 599-3860). Expensive.

Café Che Pasta – Homemade pasta is only part of a menu that includes fresh grilled fish, calamari, and other nouvelle-style dishes. *Che Pasta*'s original eatery in Kaimuki established the good reputation that's maintained at this downtown branch. Open Mondays through Fridays until 8 PM for lunch, snacks, and dinner. Reservations advised. 1001 Bishop St. (phone: 524-0004). Moderate.

Murphy's Bar and Grill – A pleasant eatery in the revitalized Merchant Square area and a good choice for people who are tired of exotic restaurant grub. From potato skins to salads and pasta, the menu offers many tasty specials. Live sports events are beamed in courtesy of a satellite dish. Open Mondays through Saturdays for lunch; dinner to 9 PM. Reservations advised. 2 Merchant St. (phone: 531-0422). Moderate.

Sunset Grill – The style is California-casual; the food is cooked over kiawe wood to provide a distinctive flavor. Specialties include chicken, veal, lamb, and fish with rotisserie, oven, and grill preparations. Open for lunch and dinner daily, breakfast on weekends. Reservations unnecessary. Restaurant Row (phone: 521-4409). Moderate.

Wo Fat – This granddaddy of Chinese restaurants in Honolulu will soon be 100 years old. Hong Kong chicken, beef in oyster sauce, and Wo Fat noodles draw people here from all over the island for lunch and dinner. Open daily. Reservations advised. 115 N. Hotel St. (phone: 537-6260). Inexpensive.

Chinese Cultural Plaza – Though not quite as successful as planned, this ethnic enclave does offer a wide range of good Oriental restaurants and cuisines — Cantonese, Hakka, Mandarin, or Mongolian barbecue — as well as shops purveying Oriental bric-a-brac that are fun to browse through. Off S. Beretania and River Sts. Inexpensive.

Greater Honolulu and Pearl Harbor

Most of what you see when you fly into town is Greater Honolulu, a sprawl of freeways and suburbs between the spines of the two mountain systems that dominate the island. To the west is the Waianae Range, which almost completely locks in leeward Oahu. To the east is the long and much-photographed Koolau Range, whose central ridges form the Honolulu watershed. Concentrated along the flatlands of the Koolau is downtown Honolulu, with its tall towers at the ocean end of Bishop Street and Fort Street; the low-rising structures along Kapiolani Boulevard behind Ala Moana; and then the Tombstone Mile of Waikiki, its rows of concrete skyscrapers along Kalakaua and Kuhio avenues frowned on by Diamond Head at the eastern end.

Greater Honolulu arches around these points from blue-collar Pearl City to gold-plated Kahala with fingers of domestic urban developments, some abysmal and some magnificent, penetrating the once-pristine valleys in between. Through the sparse coconut palms that managed to survive the busy pavements of Waikiki you can see the distant mansions and villas high up in the narrow, dark green clefts, many of them the homes of the men and women who pilot the fortunes of large mid-Pacific corporations and at least one that has served as a stateside residence for ex-President Marcos of the Philippines.

In some ways, driving along the Lunalilo Freeway from Pearl Harbor to Kahala is like driving along any other American highway that separates the business and entertainment sections of the city from its suburbs. There are the same gas stations, the same low-slung warehouses and industrial buildings, the same pizza parlors and hamburger joints. But here you have in addition strange, wrinkled folds in the mountains, like flesh that has stayed too long in hot water; moody clouds that hang over sharp mountaintops; rainbows, sometimes three at once, diminishing in brilliance the farther away they are; and along the highway the directions to bases, forts, reservations, and cemeteries, which remind us that this is where many of our fathers, sons, brothers — yes, and sisters and mothers — stood watch in defense of the mainland.

Pearl Harbor – It is surely impossible to come here and remain unmoved. Most military monuments tend toward the vainglorious and self-serving. This one is reflective, sober, and serene. Orange buoys mark the bow and stern of the USS *Arizona*, which blew up and sank during the Japanese attack on the morning of December 7, 1941, "a day which will live in infamy." Parts of the battleship's superstructure, eroded by seawater and barnacles, still appear above the waterline. Somewhere in the ship, 1,102 officers and men of the navy and marine corps are entombed. Spanning the sunken hull is the 184-foot-long Arizona Memorial, a covered white concrete bridge sinking slightly in the middle to represent initial defeat, but firm and solid at both ends to signify ultimate victory. The memorial is divided into three parts: the museum room, containing the ship's bell; the assembly area, which can hold 200 people; and the shrine, where the names of those who died aboard the ship are inscribed on a large marble tablet. The American flag, which flies above the memorial, is not in fact anchored in the monument but in the structure of the battleship itself.

There are two ways of visiting the shrine, by sea and by land. If you come by sea, chances are that you will want to take one of the boats that leaves the Kewalo Basin opposite the Ward Warehouse on Ala Moana Boulevard. The Pearl Harbor Cruise, at 9:15 AM and 1:15 PM, operated by *Paradise Cruise Ltd.* (350 Ward Ave., Suite 210; phone: 536-3641) and *Hilton Hawaiian Village*'s *Rainbow I*, which departs Waikiki at 1 PM, both follow a route along Battleship Row and past the flag and plaque above the USS *Utah*. Visitors taking a commercial cruise are not permitted to land on the Arizona Memorial, however. To do this, you must take the land route to the Visitors' Center, which is operated by the National Park Service. You then transfer to a US Navy launch for the trip to the memorial's dock. Although coming via land is less social than the sea voyage, with its drinks and snacks, it is in the end more informative. Here, as elsewhere in the US, the National Park Service and its personnel prove that they are among our foremost national treasures. Each day as many as 3,000 visitors pass through the center, which can get crowded, with hour-long waits for the boat to the memorial not uncommon. Rangers show a movie describing the attack and answer questions about the historic event and current operations at Pearl Harbor. A bookshop has souvenirs, among them model kits of the *Arizona* and copies of the front page of the *Honolulu Star-Bulletin* reporting the invasion. The center also houses the *Arizona*'s anchor and chain. TheBus Nos. 50, 51, and 52 (marked Wahiawa), which leave from Ala Moana Center, and No. 20 (Airport), which leaves from Waikiki, pass the gate to the memorial. *Airport Motorcoach* (phone: 926-4747) operates a shuttle between the memorial and Waikiki ($2).

USS *Bowfin*/Pacific Submarine Museum – Adjacent to the Arizona Memorial Visitor Center, the *Bowfin* provides a first-hand glimpse of the confining reality and technological innocence of World War II submarines. Submarine-related artifacts are displayed in the recently opened museum. Open daily; admission $4 (phone: 423-1341).

Bishop Museum – The Bernice Pauahi Bishop Museum is the formal name of this famous collection of Pacific anthropology and natural history, founded in memory of Princess Pauahi, the last direct descendant of the Kamehameha chieftains, by her husband, Charles Reed Bishop. The central building, in a somewhat pompous Romanesque style reminiscent of Scottish baronial mansions dating from Queen Victoria's reign, was constructed from lava rock with interiors made of koa wood. Outside there is a dome-topped modern science center with a planetarium and telescope. The most famous single exhibit in the museum is a 55-foot-long sperm whale, which weighed 22 tons alive. It hangs from the ceiling in the 3-story, galleried Hawaiian Hall, which displays artifacts reflecting Hawaii's rigidly structured pre-European past, the influence of European merchants and mariners in the 19th-century kingdom of Hawaii, and the influence of the various immigrant groups who have made Hawaii their home. Long feathered capes and helmets in the vivid red and yellow colors that symbolized chieftainship recall the first of these eras. The second stage is represented by thrones and decorations that show how closely the court at Honolulu tried to copy European courts, especially that of Queen Victoria at Windsor. The third development is captured in 19th-century photographs of the early Portuguese, Chinese, Japanese, and Philippine immigrants. The Hall of Hawaiian Natural History contains 16 exhibits depicting Hawaii's geological origins and its biological heritage. They show how some of the plants and animals that are endemic to the islands developed the idiosyncrasies of form and behavior that make them unique. The most famous example of these is the nene goose, Hawaii's state bird, whose ancestry and progress are fully described. In addition, there are materials from elsewhere in Polynesia, such as carvings, masks, tikis, tools, tapa cloths, and ceremonial clothing, indicating how the traditions of the various islands are connected. The museum shop sells books, pictures, and reproductions based on Hawaiian and Pacific island themes. Hawaiian dance is performed daily at 1 PM in the *Atherton Hale,* where traditional crafts are demonstrated from 9 AM to 3 PM. Open Mondays through Saturdays and the fourth Sunday of each month from 9 AM to 5 PM. Adjacent to the museum is a state-of-the-art planetarium, with 2 different shows offered daily at 11 AM and 3:15 PM; evening shows on Fridays and Saturdays at 8 PM. Admission $4.75. 1525 Bernice St. (phone: 848-4129).

Pacific Aerospace Museum – Located in the main lobby of Honolulu International Airport, this innovative museum traces the progress of aviation. Allow some time before check-in to check it out. Honolulu International Airport (phone: 531-7747).

Queen Emma's Summer Palace – Nuuanu Valley was Honolulu's first suburb. *Nuuanu* means "cool heights," and it was up here that Queen Emma, the wife of Kamehameha IV, chose to build a charming, white-frame house with generous verandas in order to escape the summer heat. She called it Hanaiakamalama. It originally had six main rooms and was surrounded by spider lilies, Castilian roses, and *maile* bushes. A major extension was added in 1869, when Queen Victoria's bad-tempered second son, Alfred, Duke of Edinburgh, was expected (he never showed). This room now houses a fascinating collection of Victorian furniture, which, except for the *kahilis* (feather-decorated staffs symbolic of royalty) that stand sentinel on either side of the door and in other spots around the room, might easily convince you that you are in Boston or London. Among smaller artifacts restored to the house — thanks to the efforts of the Daughters of Hawaii, who administer the building — are an ornate British clock, a tiny tortoiseshell brooch set in a lace handkerchief, and a beautiful necklace of tiger's claws set with seed pearls in rolled gold, a wedding gift to Emma from an Indian maharajah. There are also many mementos of Hawaii's other royalty. The palace is just one of many mansions that sprung up in the valley among the ferns, hibiscus, and ginger. Today, some of them are occupied by institutions, many with religious affiliations, that have introduced even more plant and tree life to the area, including banyans, monkeypod, kukui, mangoes, African tulips, bamboo, and eucalyptus. Open daily from 9 AM to 4 PM. Admission $4. 2913 Pali Hwy. (phone: 595-3167).

Punchbowl (The National Memorial Cemetery of the Pacific) – The ancient Hawaiians called this crater Puowaina, the Hill of Sacrifice, and the name rings true today. More than 30,000 American servicemen and servicewomen are buried here, among them 22 recipients of the Medal of Honor, as well as a civilian, the famous war correspondent Ernie Pyle (his grave number is D109). In addition, more than 26,000 names of servicemen missing in action are listed on marble walls called the Court of the Missing. Every day, but especially on Sundays, visitors and islanders come with leis and small bunches of flowers or blossoms to place against individual graves. Services are held here on Memorial Day and Veterans' Day, and there's an especially moving and popular one at dawn on Easter Sunday, when people by the thousands show up to honor the dead. Puowaina Dr.

Tantalus Drive – Starting on the *mauka* (inland) side of Puowaina Drive and Punchbowl, Tantalus Drive passes through the swank suburb of Makiki Heights before making its relentless, zigzag way almost to the tip of 2,013-foot Mt. Tantalus. This peak, formed millions of years ago from a volcanic fire fountain of *lapilli* (glassy black lava fragments) and ash, is today covered with a tropical rain forest dense with ginger, eucalyptus, mountain apple, and bamboo trees. In the clefts and gulches that scar the mountainside, amid the profusion of flowers, taro, passion fruit vines, and avocado, banana, and guava trees, you may catch sight of a wild pig. You will certainly glimpse some of the city's most beautiful and dramatically sited houses perched on steep cliffsides, in some cases with garages on the top floor and the living quarters below. High on the mountain, at Kalaiopua Place, Tantalus Drive becomes Round Top Drive and descends in dizzying swerves down the Diamond Head side to Puu Ualakaa State Wayside. A road off the drive leads to the summit of Puu Ualakaa — known in English as Round Top — 1,048 feet high. The view of Honolulu and the surrounding valleys from this point is famous.

Manoa Valley, Paradise Park, and the Lyon Arboretum – This is another favorite residential area, where many of the attractive homes are owned by descendants of the early American settlers who came to the islands in the 19th century.

At the south end of Manoa Road, which runs the length of the valley, is the famous Punahou School, built in 1841, largely of lava rock, for the children of the missionaries. Halfway up the valley, a short side road to the left leads to the restoration of the Little Grass Shack that once was home for Robert Louis Stevenson. At the north end of the road is Paradise Park, 3737 Manoa Rd. (phone: 988-6686), a luxurious 15-acre garden where the rainfall averages over 160 inches a year. There is a giant walk-through aviary, a hau tree jungle, bamboo groves, and — the prime reason for a visit — more than 500 rare and exotic birds, some of which have unfortunately been taught to do tricks. Although many of the birds are quite dazzling and the flora is interesting, this is not the true Hawaii, but a version of it for tourists. Open daily from 10 AM to 5 PM. A free shuttle links the park to Waikiki hotels, twice daily (phone: 988-2141). Admission $7.50.

For a more authentic and undeniably gorgeous glimpse of tropical Oahu, visit the Lyon Arboretum. Operated as a research garden by the University of Hawaii, it consists of more than 200 acres of both landscaped and wild rain forest. Open weekdays from 9 AM to 3 PM, with tours offered several times monthly. 3860 Manoa Rd. (phone: 988-3177).

Kahala – If humid, forested hillsides don't appeal to you but you're thinking of settling down in Honolulu, perhaps you should head here. This wealthy community consists mostly of sybaritic ranch houses in small, beautifully kept gardens. Honolulu is, on the average, the most expensive city in the Union when it comes to buying a house and — the estates of Diamond Head aside — this is its most expensive community. Naturally, it has much to offer. It is drier than the mountains; it has a long, narrow beach that is excellent in spots for surfing, snorkeling, and swimming; and it has the poshest golf and country club on Oahu, the exclusive Waialae Country Club, which even the denizens of the luxurious *Kahala Hilton* may not enter unless they are members or guests of members. Another singular feature of Kahala is, along Kealaolu Avenue, what is probably the longest hibiscus hedge in the world, part of the fence that keeps the hoi polloi from the club grounds.

 SHOPPING: The largest shopping center outside Ala Moana is at Pearl Ridge off the Kamehameha Highway at Kaonohi Street. There are more than 90 stores here, among them, *J. C. Penney, Liberty House,* and *Sears.* The main attraction of the shopping center, which is off the beaten track for most tourists, is the monorail that makes a loop through the parking area.

The Kahala Mall is a smaller, upscale alternative that includes shops like *Koala Blue,* which sells artistic, casual cottonwear (phone: 735-0200), and *Riches,* purveying earrings and more earrings (phone: 727-3303).

NIGHTLIFE: Danny Kaleikini sings every night except Sunday in the *Hala Terrace* room of the *Kahala Hilton* (phone: 734-2211). He is not as famous as Don Ho, and is considerably less brash, but his personal style with simple Hawaiian melodies is preferred by many *kamaainas* and visitors.

CHECKING IN: The only option is the *Kahala Hilton,* where double rooms start at about $180 a night and go steeply upward. All telephone numbers are in the 808 area code unless otherwise indicated.

Kahala Hilton – Operated by Hilton International (which is now run by Britain's Ladbrooke group), this is one of the chain's prime showpieces. Queen Elizabeth II spent a couple of nights here, and King Juan Carlos of Spain came for part of his honeymoon with Queen Sophia. The main structure of this lavish hostelry is 12 stories high and overlooks a glorious 800-foot stretch of beach that loses nothing by being manmade. Additional beachside bungalows and a 2-story wing watch over a large lagoon in which dolphins, turtles, and penguins cavort. Rooms in the main building have charming semicircular lanais decorated with bougainvillea. Although the room furnishings and decorations are obviously expensive, the bed headboards and the lamps never quite manage to lose the Hilton look. The lobby, however, is an absolute masterpiece — with handsome chandeliers and a stunning circular carpet — that manages to look plush and airy at the same time. Guests are greeted with chilled pineapple, and an orchid is laid on each pillow when beds are turned down in the evening. Besides ocean and pool swimming, the hotel provides kayaks and snorkeling equipment and can arrange deepsea fishing and scuba diving. European efficiency at the executive level and island good humor at the service level are the keynotes here. They work together like a charm. 5000 Kahala Ave., Kahala (phone: 734-2211; 800-367-2525).

EATING OUT: Prices in Greater Honolulu are about on a par with those in Waikiki. For a meal for two, excluding wine, tips, and drinks, expect to pay more than $60 in a place listed as expensive, between $25 and $55 in a placed listed as moderate, and under $25 in an inexpensive place. All telephone numbers are in the 808 area code unless otherwise indicated.

Maile – Guests descend through a minor jungle of anthuriums, yellow heliconia, and orchids into this restaurant beneath the lobby of the *Kahala Hilton,* where kimono-clad waitresses provide expert, unobtrusive service. The award-winning menu includes roast duckling Waialae (with bananas, peaches, litchi, and oranges) and fresh island chicken (poached in white wine with tarragon). Local fish treated somewhat exotically here include *mahimahi* glazed with banana and served on creamed mushrooms and baked *kumu* with fennel and a dash of Pernod. A classical guitarist or a pianist plays during dinner. Live dance music begins at 9 PM. Open daily for dinner only. Brunch is served Sundays on the *Maile Terrace.* Reservations necessary. Kahala Hilton, 5000 Kahala Ave., Kahala (phone: 734-2211). Expensive.

Pearl City Tavern – This Japanese-American restaurant is famous for its Monkey Bar, at the back of which is a long glassed-in alley where denizens of the simian world prance and preen playfully. The Japanese dishes here tend to be better than the American, and the teriyaki and tempura are especially good. The middle-aged waitresses are downright motherly. Open weekdays for lunch, daily for dinner.

Reservations necessary. 905 Kamehameha Hwy., Pearl City (phone: 455-1045). Expensive to moderate.

Castagnola's – A New York–style Italian restaurant that has drawn rave reviews from the day it opened in the Manoa Marketplace. Delicate flavorings make for some good veal, pasta, and seafood dishes. Open daily except Sundays for lunch and dinner; lunch only on Mondays. 2752 Woodlawn Ave., Honolulu (phone: 988-2969). Moderate.

Che Pasta – A casual café with good food. Pasta, veal, and chicken dishes are the specialties. Open weekdays for lunch and dinner, weekends for dinner only. Reservations unnecessary. 3751 Waialae Ave., Honolulu (phone: 735-1777). Moderate.

Hala Terrace – A *Kahala Hilton* restaurant and a lovely lunchtime spot. Sit in the shade and watch the Pacific across one of the loveliest beaches on Oahu. Meals here are on the light side, so it's worth ordering vichyssoise or a spring salad to start with. Elegant sandwiches are the main item on the menu, in addition to which there are daily specials such as Kahuku prawns, which are delicious. Open daily for breakfast, lunch, and dinner. Reservations advised. Kahala Hilton, 5000 Kahala Ave., Kahala (phone: 734-2211). Moderate.

Pottery Steakhouse – People actually throw and fire pottery here, and many of the eating and drinking utensils are made in the workroom-cum-boutique in the front of the restaurant. Steaks are properly aged, juicy, and flavorful. Mahimahi, cooked till it is too dry at many restaurants, is still moist when it reaches the table here. Handmade pottery is made and sold — as well as used here: If you choose the Cornish game hen, you get to keep the pot in which it was cooked. About a 10-minute drive from Waikiki. Open daily for dinner only. Reservations advised, especially on weekends. 3574 Waialae Ave., Honolulu (phone: 735-5594). Moderate.

Southeast Oahu

A favorite short ride out of Honolulu is the triangular drive around Oahu's east end, taking the Pali Highway, Route 61, up the Nuuanu Valley through the Nuuanu Pali Tunnel and making a right turn onto Route 72, the Kalanianaole Highway. This road brings you through Waimanalo, past Koko Crater and Koko Head, through Hawaii-Kai, and back into town. In the hills on either side of the road through Nuuanu Valley, above the churches, schools, convents, and graveyards that mark this as one of Honolulu's early suburbs, there is a herd of wallabies running wild, descendants of a group that escaped from a crate in the dockyards over 70 years ago en route from Australia to the mainland. If this is the only trip you are making outside the city, stop at the Nuuanu Pali Lookout, with its long romantic view north along the Koolau Range and the Windward Coast. Beyond the lookout, as the highway begins its southern progress, you come into a world of dramatic lava rock coastline, jagged cliffs, and clear waters covering endlessly fascinating reefs.

Waimanalo Beach – This sandy demi-paradise stretches for over 3 miles around the curve of Waimanolo Bay, making it the longest continuous beach on Oahu. Bellows Beach, as the northern part is known, is part of a military complex and therefore open only on weekends and certain holidays. The gentle but always active surf here makes it popular with people just learning to board- and body-surf. Occasionally, when the wind is in the right direction and if you have an inclination for marine life, you can spot Portuguese man-of-war jellyfish in the area. These are best not examined too closely since they impart an unpleasant sting. Farther south is Sherwood Forest, the popular name for Waimanalo Bay State Recreation Area. It received its nickname about 20 years ago when it became well known for some decidedly un-Robin-Hood-like petty criminal activities in the dense groves of ironwood trees at the back of the beach, activities that have since been curtailed. At Kaiona Beach Park, farther on, you can see a rock wall that, according to legend, was constructed by a chief of the district who was especially devoted to turtle meat. Each time a turtle was caught, so the story goes, it was deposited in the pool enclosed by the rocks for the chief's sole use.

Kaupo Beach Park – This long and narrow beach south of the Waimanalo beaches is generally quite safe for swimming. It is a perfect place to relax and look longingly at two offshore islands, Kaohikaipu Island and Manana Island, commonly known as Rabbit Island, recalling its days as a rabbit farm. Today, both are bird sanctuaries, and from the shore of Oahu you may catch a glimpse of a venturesome red-tailed *koae-ula* or a friendly white tern.

Sea Life Park – Porpoises, whales, and penguins ham it up here several times a day in the entertainment part of what is a serious marine life research project at Whalers Cove. A major attraction is the Hawaiian Reef Exhibit, a 300,000-gallon tank, 3 fathoms deep and 70 feet across, in which a Pacific reef is re-created with the exotic plants and animals that would be found in the real thing. A spiral ramp winds around the tank so that visitors can observe from above the surface all the way to its depths. Clear water and direct sunlight make the denizens of this fantasy world easily visible. Manta rays and 6-foot sharks nose the glass walls of the tank, and hundreds of multicolored fish create dazzling patterns. On the reef bottom, you can see creatures that never venture to the surface and are normally not visible even to snorkelers or casual divers. The newest addition to the park is the Rocky Shores intertidal pool. Also noteworthy is the whaling museum with its excellent 19th-century artifacts. For kids, seal and sea turtle feeding and the show put on by trained porpoises and killer whales are likely to be highlights. Open daily: Mondays through Wednesdays, and Saturdays from 10 AM to 5 PM with the last complete series of shows starting at 3:15 PM; Thursdays, Fridays, and Sundays until 10 PM, the last shows beginning at 7:15 PM. Off Kalanianaole Hwy. at Makapuu Point (phone: 259-7933). Admission is $8.50 for adults, $6.50 for juniors (7–12 years), and $2.75 for children (4–6 years).

Makapuu Beach – This idyllic spot backed by sand dunes and black lava cliffs is the most famous body-surfing beach on Oahu, so famous that board-surfing is prohibited by law. The huge and elegant waves here are, however, lethal during the winter and even in the summer should be toyed with only by extremely experienced body-surfers. It's safer and easier to lie back, relax, and watch the hang gliders make their aerial parabolas as they catch an eddy in the air currents.

Halona Blowhole – On Kalanianaole Highway just below Koko Head Crater, there is a lookout from which you can see a natural sea geyser that spouts water in a decidedly impertinent fashion through a submerged lava tube. If the waves aren't providing the right kind of water pressure, all you see are the lava cliffs and delicious blue ocean, but if the sea is accommodating, just to the right of the lookout is a small, rock-girt beach called Halona Cove, which is not good for swimming, but perfect for getting a tan.

Hanauma Bay Beach Park – The Elvis Presley epic *Blue Hawaii* was made here. The swimming is good, especially in the sandy bottom part called the keyhole, and the snorkeling is excellent. The bay, an extinct volcanic crater flooded by the ocean, is a state marine conservation area. No fishing of any kind is permitted, nor is the removal of any kind of land or marine life. As a result, many of the fish gliding among the coral reefs are largely unafraid of man and will nuzzle swimmers and divers cautiously. Tall cliffs surround the bay in a horseshoe-like formation and tall coconut palms provide shade. Hanauma Bay Road leads down to the clifftops from Kalanianaole Highway where it crosses Koko Head. Snorkeling equipment is available at the beach pavilion, but it is often not of the best quality. Gear may be rented from *Blue Water Divers* (phone: 955-1066), *Hawaii Snorkeling* (phone: 944-2846), and *Snorkel Hanauma Bay* (phone: 955-5680). These companies also offer escorted day trips, but only a limited number of escorted dives are allowed. It may also be necessary for divers to make their own arrangements for getting here, but once they've arrived they find it hard to leave.

Hawaii-Kai – If you have any interest in how paradise will look once planners have been allowed in, come to Hawaii-Kai. It's a conglomeration of small houses tucked inside neat little gardens, townhouses in unharmonious proximity, condominiums, and a marina that looks as though it were copied from a Hollywood backlot. True, there are the mountains in the background, the ocean nearby, and a scattering of palm trees, but the result is nevertheless depressing.

 SHOPPING: A branch of *Liberty House* is in the Koko Marina Shopping Center (phone: 941-2345), in case you have forgotten your bathing suit en route to the southeastern beaches. The same 2-story wooden complex also contains the *Suyderhoud Water Ski Center,* which provides all that's needed for that activity (phone: 395-3773); and the misnamed *Cosmopolitan Fashion Shoppe,* for ladies who find the bikinis at *Liberty House* too puritanical (phone: 395-4269).

 CHECKING IN: There are no recommended hotels in this area; see *Diamond Head* or *Waikiki* for nearby accommodations.

 EATING OUT: Expect to pay $55 or more for dinner for two (drinks, wine, and tip not included) at a restaurant listed as expensive, and from $25 to $50 at a place listed as moderate. All telephone numbers are in the 808 area code unless otherwise indicated.

Dockside Plantation – It seems that owning restaurants in Hawaii has become a favorite pastime for celebrities, and Dolly Parton is a partner in this one. *DP*'s specializes in continental items: fresh local seafood and steaks. Dining is either inside or on-deck. Open daily for lunch and dinner. Reservations advised. Hawaii-Kai Shopping Center, Lagoonside (phone: 395-2930). Expensive to moderate.

Roy's – Owner Roy Yamaguchi combines Oriental and continental styles for first-rate results. 6600 Kalaniaole Hwy., Hawaii-Kai (phone: 396-ROYS). Expensive to moderate.

Swiss Inn – This is the domain of ex–*Kahala Hilton* chef Martin Wyss, and the crowds tell the story. From simple dishes like wiener schnitzel to the delightful *émince de veau zurichoise* or trout caprice (with mushrooms and bananas), your tastebuds are in for a treat. Closed Mondays. Reservations necessary. Nui Valley Shopping Center, 5730 Kalanianaole Hwy. (phone: 377-5447). Moderate.

Windward Oahu

Standing in a regimental grove of papaya trees or glancing along a row of purple blooms on a vanda orchid farm, it is sometimes possible to forget the ocean on this side of the island. What cannot be ignored, however, is the long, dark green arras, with its mysterious folds formed by the precipitous windward side of the Koolau Range. For mile after mile, the fortress-like face of these fluted cliffs stretches along the eastern side of Oahu. After heavy rains, these numberless clefts are adazzle with ribbon-thin waterfalls in a display that would make even the most convinced skeptic believe that the mountains are enchanted.

Most people on this side of the island live in Kailua, a Honolulu dormitory town, and Kaneohe, where there is a big marine air corps station. Farther north are small settlements of *kamaainas* who have been here for generations and *haoles* and Honolulu residents who have built vacation homes along the beaches. Although there is a highway from Honolulu, Route 61, into Kailua, and another, Route 63, into Kaneohe, any semblance of a network of roads ends abruptly at Kahaluu. The only road north from there is the windward section of the Kamehameha Highway, winding along the coastline beneath towering *palis* and around bays. On the right as you drive north you will see boats bobbing on the water, a tie-line anchoring them to the stilts of small wooden cottages that have the Pacific for a basement. Here and there you may spot a fisherman ankle deep in water preparing to spear an octopus. On the left, between the crenelated outline of the mountains and the highway, are small farms with haphazardly growing banana trees and methodically planted acres of papayas, taro, orchids, anthuriums, and all the other exuberant paraphernalia of nature's green moments that send writers scurrying to the thesaurus looking for synonyms for the word *lush*.

Nuuanu Pali Lookout – Although barely 15 minutes from downtown Honolulu, the lookout offers a spectacular grandstand view of the vast green arena known as Windward Oahu. Kailua, Kaneohe, the ocean, the farms, twin tunnels that penetrate the mountains, and the dramatic northern sweep of the Koolau *pali* are all here at one glance. The wind on the lookout is famous, and you learn in one gasp why this side of the island is called the windward side. Even on a rainswept day, when the view is reduced to zero, the experience can be awesome. At the edge of the viewing rampart you are suddenly face to face with a cloud that is being held back by the cliffs on either side. It is rather like stepping outside an airplane in flight. Legend has it that Kamehameha the Great fought a battle here during his conquest of Oahu and sent hundreds of island warriors tumbling down the *pali* to their deaths when they chose to perish rather than submit. Their bones, the legend continues, lie by the thousands in the valleys below. It is a pious story and one you will hear repeated frequently by tour guides. Historians, however, have failed to verify the incident and the sound you hear is likely to be not the wail of the glorious dead but the wind. The Pali Lookout is reached by a side road off the Nuuanu Pali Highway, Route 61, close to the ridge of the Koolau Range. A turnoff closer to Honolulu onto the old Pali Drive brings you to the same destination by a more interesting route, along which you get some idea of what a suburb would look like surrounded by jungle.

Kailua – The beach park is the main attraction of this otherwise featureless town. The beach is wide and sandy, with excellent swimming, and is very popular with windsurfers. The park is divided into two parts by the Kaelepulu Canal. On the north side of the canal, you can walk to the end of the park and along the beaches that form the backyards of some enviable and expensive homes. On the south side, a stroll up to the pink pillar that marks the gateway to the exclusive community of Lanikai makes a pleasant diversion. From the bluff there is a good view across to the Mokulua Islands, home of the Christmas Island shearwater.

Kaneohe – The Kaneohe Bay Drive from Kailua brings you through an attractive suburban community with beachside and cliffside houses surrounded by colorful gardens. The ocean floor here is shallow and somewhat rocky and marvelously endowed with coral reefs. A glass-bottom boat, the *Coral Queen,* makes hour-long trips over the reefs five times a day from Heeia Kea Boat Harbor, just off Kamehameha Highway (phone: 235-2888; if no answer, call again, as the boat may be out). The sights from this boat might include some wonderful coral formations, such as flowery cup coral and gorgonian coral, as well as brazenly decorative fish and other marine animals with names like damselfish, long-nose hawkfish, spotted puffers, Moorish idols, lionfish, and regal slipper lobster. Cost is $7.50. Close to the pier is the ancient Heeia fishpond, a 12-foot wall enclosing 88 acres of ocean where fish were "farmed" for food for several hundred years.

Haiku Gardens – Haiku Valley was a favorite resort of the ancient Hawaiians. Nowadays *kamaainas* and visitors come here to wander by the spectacular lily and tropical fish ponds and through bamboo groves and to wonder at the unruly loveliness of the flowers, plants, and tropical trees all around. The restaurant on site is open daily, except Mondays, for lunch and dinner. Sunday brunch runs from 10:30 AM to 2:30 PM. 46-336 Haiku Rd., Kaneohe (phone: 247-6671).

Valley of the Temples – The star attraction in this memorial park is the replica of the famous Byodo-In Temple of Kyoto, Japan. Graceful and ornate and set in a classic Japanese garden with peacocks and swans, the temple has something else going for it too — the dramatic *pali* in the background. Open daily from 9 AM to 4:30 PM. Admission $1.50. 47-200 Kahekili Hwy., Kaneohe (phone: 239-8811).

Kualoa Regional Park – A favorite Windward Coast spot for picnics and swimming, the beach is rather narrow but long and sandy and has a beautiful view of the mountains and Kaneohe Bay. Oahu's most famous island, Mokolii, also known as Chinaman's Hat, is just offshore. When the tide is especially low, it is possible to walk the 500 yards to the island, which, although not a bird sanctuary, is a haven for several species including the frigate bird.

Sacred Falls State Park – The god to whom these falls are sacred was known as Kamapuua, the deity of swine, who could change himself into a pig or a man at will. To reach the falls, you have to hike for more than a mile along an uphill trail that is rocky in places and is best avoided in wet weather, when it becomes unpleasantly muddy. Portions of the trail follow the stream bed; for those anticipating a casual stroll — it's not! En route you will find kukui nuts, Java plums, and mountain apples. At the trail's end, in a 50-foot-wide ravine, the falls drop for 87 feet against the ever-present brocade of the green Koolau Range. The pool at the bottom of the falls is an idyllic place for swimming — cool, refreshing, and romantic. But if you have been bathing in the balmy Pacific just an hour or so before, the temperature may leave you breathless at first. From the Kamehameha Hwy. take Plantation Rd., which turns off between Punaluu and Hauula, to the trail ahead.

Hauula Beach Park – Although at first the ironwood trees along the shoreline may seem this beach's most important feature, if you happen to be here early in the day during July and August, you can witness a colorful natural phenomenon. On the ground under the many hau or beach hibiscus trees in the area, you will see red flowers that have fallen the previous night. The trees themselves will be in bloom with bright yellow flowers, which will by nightfall turn to a russet color, then later, bright red, and fall off. Photographers professional and amateur have been known to spend a day here photographing the transformation, a pastime that can be delightfully combined with picnicking and swimming in an ample, walled-in area on the beach.

Mokuauia Island – Who can resist an island, and when you are on a largish one such as Oahu, who can resist a smaller one like Mokuauia, also known as Goat Island? You can wade over from Kalani Point, off the Kamehameha Highway, through water that is sometimes waist deep but is shallow on calm days at low tide, allowing for safe and easy transit. There is a delightful small sandy beach crescent on the leeward side of the island that is good for swimming when the currents are not strong, but perhaps the main pleasure here is in quietly observing the ornithological life. Mokuauia, like most Windward Coast offshore islands, is a state bird refuge, and among the more common black noddy, brown noddy, wedge-tailed shearwater, and brown booby, you may catch a glimpse of a masked-faced booby, with its nun-like hood and black tail, and the distinguished-looking gray-backed tern, with its severe black head, white forehead and throat, and clerical gray tail. Distantly, against the sky, you may even spot a black-footed or a laysan albatross indulging in some effortless and extremely graceful aerodynamics. Mokuauia is a couple of miles north of Laie and the Polynesian Cultural Center, which are discussed in a separate section by that name.

Senator Fong's Plantation and Gardens – Hawaii's first elected state senator pays a flowery tribute to the presidents under whom he served. A 3-mile, 40-minute guided tour by open-air minibus begins at the visitors center in Eisenhower Valley, and covers Kennedy Valley, where over 15 varieties of sugarcane grow; Johnson Plateau of fruit and nut orchards, encompassing over 75 edible plants and trees; Nixon Valley, with the traditional gardens of Hawaii's main ethnic groups (Chinese, Japanese, Filipino, and Hawaiian); and Ford Plateau, which features a pine garden. The 725-acre plantation, just recently opened to the public, is lush with wiliwili, bougainvillea, oleander, plumeria, hibiscus, palms, fern, bamboo, and other flora; bananas are harvested here for commercial use; and Dendrobium orchids are grown in a 20,000-pot hothouse. Senator Hiram Y.L. Fong, now retired, and his family manage the place. Open daily from 9 AM to 7 PM. Admission $6.50 adults, $3 children; under 5 free. Located in Kahaluu, a mile from the junction of Kamemeha (83) and Kahekili Hwys., at 47-285 Pulama Rd. (phone: 239-6775).

SHOPPING: Kailua and Kaneohe shopping centers have food marts to fill the refrigerators of these suburban communities, and at Kailua there is a branch of *Liberty House,* with its line of men's, women's, and children's clothing (phone: 941-2345). *Long's,* a statewide drugstore chain that sells most of the merchandise you find in any five-and-dime as well as pharmaceuticals and photographic equipment, has stores in the Kailua Shopping Center (phone: 261-8537) and in the Kaneohe Shopping Center (phone: 235-4511). Along the highways, a number of ramshackle stores sell papayas, pineapples, mountain apples, bananas, and occasionally some well-made local artifacts. These colorful stores offer a genuine glimpse of what is left of rural Oahu. Hawaiian artists display their works each Sunday in the *Pali Painter's Sidewalk Show,* in the 43-600 block of Kailua Rd., Kailua.

NIGHTLIFE: Mostly it's the lapping of the waves on the sand and the pounding of the surf on the reefs. If you like a mixture of Hawaiian and contemporary music with a country flavor, try *Pat's at Punaluu* (phone: 293-8502), which tends to become lively on Friday and Saturday nights; the beat turns romantic and contemporary on Thursdays and Sundays. For disco, go to *Fast Eddie's* (52 Oneawa St., Kailua; phone: 261-8561) nightly from 8 PM to 4 AM, or the *23rd Step* (274 Kuulei Rd.; phone: 261-4146), where live bands and theme evenings often prevail. Closed Tuesdays.

CHECKING IN: There is not much by way of tourist accommodations on the Windward Coast. People wishing to stay here for a month or more may find it worthwhile to check the *Honolulu Advertiser* and the *Honolulu Star-Bulletin* for home and condominium rentals. *Bed and Breakfast Hawaii* (phone: 822-7771; 800-367-8047, ext. 339) lists several rooms and houses for rent along this stretch of the Oahu coast. All telephone numbers are in the 808 area code unless otherwise indicated.

Pat's at Punaluu – Although all the units here are privately owned, between 30 and 40 of them become available at various times of the year, often for long periods. Each is individually decorated. The building is right on Halehaha Beach, which is good for swimming, snorkeling, or just plain beachcombing. (It is sheltered from the heavy surf by a lovely reef.) There is a freshwater swimming pool and a full gym for those wanting a workout and sauna. Maid service is offered twice a week. *Pat's at Punaluu,* a restaurant and cocktail lounge, is adjacent. Rates start at about $50 for a studio, with a discount for stays of 3 days or more. A private beach cottage is also available. 53-567 Kamehameha Hwy., Hauula (phone: 293-8111).

EATING OUT: Dining outside Honolulu is on the whole a less than memorable experience, and although the windward side of the island isn't quite the culinary semidesert that western Oahu appears to be, only *L'Auberge* at Kailua is worth the trip just for the cooking. The chief ingredient of the others is either the setting or the view. Expect to pay $55 or more for dinner for two (drinks, wine, and tip not included) at a restaurant listed as expensive, from $25 to $50 at a place listed as moderate. All telephone numbers are in the 808 area code unless otherwise indicated.

Crouching Lion – Named for the rock formation above it, this restaurant is just across the road from Kaaawa beach. From the luncheon room watch the waves lap the white sand while you dine on mahimahi, burgers, steak teriyaki, or sandwiches. The main dining room, decorated in a Hollywood baronial style, contains a huge fireplace that is occasionally put to use to dry out the humid air. Dinner specialties include Slavonic steak, a favorite with the *kamaainas.* Open daily for lunch and dinner. Reservations advised. 51-666 Kamehameha Hwy., Kaaawa (phone: 237-8511). Expensive to moderate.

Haiku Gardens – Dining on the lanai at *Haiku* you take in the rain forest, gardens, and the Koolau Range. The house specialty is spareribs cooked over kiawe charcoal; steaks and seafood are also served. Sunday brunch, 10:30 AM to 2:30 PM, is a specialty. Closed Mondays. Reservations advised. 46-336 Haiku Rd., Kaneohe (phone: 247-6671). Expensive to moderate.

L'Auberge Swiss – It is a pleasant and unexpected surprise to find this bistro in an uninteresting part of downtown Kailua. The restaurant resembles a small country inn with checkered tablecloths and simple wooden chairs. The menu is substantial, with veal, beef, chicken, and fish prepared in a variety of continental styles. There is also a full range of appetizers and desserts to round out the menu. *L'Auberge* is a 25-minute drive through the Pali Tunnel from Waikiki. Open Tuesdays through Saturdays from 6 to 10 PM, Sundays from 5:30 to 9 PM. Reservations advised. 117 Hekili St., Kailua (phone: 263-4663). Moderate.

Buzz's Original Steakhouse – A good spot to visit for typical steakhouse fare — steaks, seafood, and salad bar. Seating is either indoors or alfresco, and the service rates among the friendliest in Hawaii. Dinner only. Reservations advised. 413 Kawailoa Rd., Lanikai (phone: 261-4661). Moderate.

Pat's at Punaluu – If *Pat's* were any closer to the ocean it would be in it. There is a shack-like charm to the place that has made it popular. Kahuku shrimp, mahimahi in a beer batter (sautéed or grilled), and guava-glazed lamb are house specialties. Open daily for breakfast, lunch, dinner, and Sunday brunch from 11 AM to 3PM, with Hawaiian entertainment. Reservations advised for Saturday dinner. 53-567 Kamehameha Hwy., Hauula (phone: 293-8502). Moderate.

Bueno Nalo – The coconut wireless (as the local grapevine is called) gives this casual eatery high marks for its Mexican cooking. Guests bring their own wine and wait for tables. Open daily except Mondays, from 5 to 9 PM. 41-865 Kalanianaole Hwy., Waimanalo (phone: 259-7186). Inexpensive.

Polynesian Cultural Center

"A living museum of seven primitive South Sea villages" is how the promotional material describes this 42-acre cultural endeavor of the Hawaii branch of Brigham Young University in the Mormon community of Laie. Here, students from the Hawaiian Islands, Fiji, Samoa, Tonga, Tahiti, the Marquesas, and Maori New Zealand reproduce the skills, music, meals, ceremonies, and rituals of their homelands in fastidiously replicated South Seas villages, an activity for which they are appropriately rewarded with credit toward graduation and salaries for tuition and board. The center can be toured with guides in a festively decorated tram and by canoe on the canals that run through the villages. It is only on foot, however, that you can fully savor the flavor of each community.

Near the southern end of the complex is an Orientation Center; from this point it is best to proceed north to the Tonga Village. Here Tongan women demonstrate *ngatu,* the fashioning of the tapa cloth for which Hawaii is famous. Don't miss the Tongan House, where the walls are lined with weathered tapa decorated in clay-brown tones with ancient Tongan symbols and the floors are covered with *lau hala* carpets and pillows. In the separate kitchen is an *imu* (earth oven) and a huge, cool-looking banana leaf prepared to serve as a dining table for a meal of pig, yams, and tapioca. In the Tahiti Village, a little farther on, serenely beautiful Tahitian girls make shell leis and grass skirts quite unlike those you will find for sale in the open-air bazaars of Waikiki. The adjacent Marquesas Village, a complex of six wooden houses with thatched roofs shaped like a narrow, upside-down "V," has a Chief's House, a house for the women and children, and a small temple with wooden tikis of tribal gods outside. Probably because it is almost totally surrounded by a wall, which in early times served as a fortification, this is easily the most successful replica in the center. "Villagers" like to point out the pictures of warriors, who are completely and elaborately tattooed. Obviously, the young Marquesan males on duty here have not felt it necessary to take authenticity this far. Crossing the bridge to the Hawaiian Village, you come to the most popular spot in the center, possibly because this is in a sense the host village. The Chief's House here boasts a raised bed with a beautiful feather cover and *kahilis* (feather-decorated staffs symbolic of royalty) on either side. You can also learn how poi, a Hawaiian and Polynesian staple, is made. Working at a low wooden table supported by a broad frame woven from pandanus leaves, a Hawaiian student pounds down a taro root. The powdered root, which is rich in vitamins and minerals, is diluted slightly with water and allowed to ferment in order to produce an acid that acts as a preservative. Poi is one of the essential ingredients of a luau. The Fiji Village, next door, is for many people the most attractive. The Chief's House is a large, handsome building divided into four separate rooms, one each for his family, his counselors, visiting common folk, and for the chief himself. His bed is covered with a splendid carpet, only slightly more luxurious than the carpet at the foot of his bed, where his current favorite slept. The walls of the rooms are formed of tapa cloth made from the bark of mulberry trees and printed with designs that appear to tell a story. Outside, Fijian music is played on bamboo pipe organs. An impressive sight in the Maori Village, just to the north, is the 40-man canoe used for coastal raids. You can learn to play the stick game *tititorea* here, although it is more amusing to watch the Maori experts themselves, who make it look like a minor juggling act. The great charm of the Samoa Village, a little farther north, is watching young ladies perform the Mauluulu dance.

In the Carver's Shop, students are reconstructing and making replicas of artifacts of all the islands. If you are lucky, you may even be present when they are carving out a war canoe, a sight that can be quite diverting.

Access to the center is available on an admission-only basis ($25) that covers the villages and the *Pageant of the Long Canoes* at the *Hale Aloha Theater*. The Voyager package ($37) lets you tour the grounds on your own and also includes a buffet dinner and seating at the *This Is Polynesia* revue; the personalized Ambassador Passport package ($62) adds an escorted tour of the grounds and preferential seating for the show. The Alii Luau is held nightly at 6 PM, and can be purchased separately for $15, as a $5 add-on to the Voyager package, or as an option on the Ambassador Passport package. With a cast of 150 performers from all the islands, the revue is the highlight of a visit to the center for many people. It is by far the most authentic South Seas show on Oahu since it seriously tries to represent the spirit and rhythm of the individual islands and is performed by youngsters who appear for the most part to be dedicated to their traditions.

The question remains whether the whole experience of the center works. The answer has to be equivocal. Yes, because having participated, you'll come away with an understanding of life in the various communities that's different from facts in a book. And no, because real communities change while these remain static. The young men talking about baseball in the Samoan village and the young lady humming a Jacques Brel song in the Tahitian village bring a life to those places that is lacking when they are "performing" their daily functions. The shows, for all their authenticity, remain just that and lack the real purpose — placating a god, celebrating a marriage — that true ritual demands. Nevertheless, it should be added that the center is, after Pearl Harbor, the most popular tourist attraction outside Waikiki.

Souvenirs are sold in *The Marketplace*. The merchandise ranges from hula sets with plastic leis and parchment calendars with Polynesian zodiac signs to some quite good tapa wall hangings from Tonga. In between, you can find some presentable bracelet charms made from a variety of materials, such as jade, whale's teeth, and ivory. The *Gateway* restaurant serves a dinner buffet of salad, chicken, spareribs, rice, and desserts that can best be described as acceptable. The buffet is included in the center's $37 package price. This being Mormon territory, there is no liquor, wine, or beer, but there is lemonade. The center, which also offers a worthwhile trip to the grounds of the Mormon Temple, is closed Sundays (phone: 293-3333; in Waikiki, 923-1861).

The community of Laie outside the center is chiefly known for its long beach. Since it is protected from heavy surf by an offshore reef, it is good for swimming and occasionally suitable for body-surfing. From Laie Point, at the end of Naupaka Street, you can watch two pretty small islands defend themselves against the Pacific surf. On rough days it can be quite a sight.

The *Laniloa Lodge* hotel (55-109 Laniloa; phone: 293-9282 or 800-367-8047, ext. 359), just outside the main entrance to the Polynesian Cultural Center, has small, pleasant rooms for about $60 and up for two people. The rooms around the swimming pool are more attractive because the tiny lanais are shaded by tall palms. An adjacent restaurant serves various kinds of chicken, hamburger, and similar items. Again, there is no booze. TheBus makes a stop on its round-the-island runs at the entrance to the center. Most bus tour companies have a special Polynesian Cultural Center package leaving from Waikiki.

North Shore

"The face of this country is uncommonly beautiful," wrote Captain James Cook in his diary for 1784. He was referring to the North Shore of Oahu, an area that can be simply defined as between Kahuku Point, a protuberance in the swampy northeast corner of the island, and Kaena Point, a rocky cape in the northwest. The shoreline in between is the most famous in the world for surfing. It recedes gently to the north face of the Koolau Range in the east, the low-lying land between the ocean and the mountains supporting truck farms and small ranches. West of Haleiwa, the coastal lowlands behind Mokuleia, the old Dillingham Ranch, and the present Dillingham Air Force Base rise dramatically up the northwest arm of the Waianae Mountains, dominated by Mt. Kaala, which at 4,025 feet is the highest peak on Oahu.

In the lowland crescent between the two mountain ranges live some 10,000 inhabitants — small farmers, ranchers, a few fishermen, and people employed by the military, the COMSAT communications center near Pupukea, and the *Turtle Bay Hilton.* The recession of the late seventies and early eighties put many people out of work on the North Shore, and although they are not nearly so frequent as on the west coast of Oahu, there have been incidents of muggings and car thefts.

Nevertheless, well-to-do residents of Honolulu and the mainland still come to their holiday homes along the beaches. You see these properties mainly from Waialee to Haleiwa, sometimes standing on a plot adjacent to a wartime Nissen hut with a corrugated iron roof that has been converted into full-time living quarters. And since nature, unlike man, has few favorites, both types of homes seem to be surrounded with an abundance of swaying palm and ironwood trees, bougainvillea, hibiscus, and, in the winter, poinsettia.

Sunset Beach – This 2-mile-long sandy beach, averaging 200 feet in width, is one of the most attractive — and notorious — on Oahu. In the summer, swimming close to the shoreline and away from the lava rock outcrops is quite safe; swimming in the winter, when high-wave surf competitions are held, can be dangerous. Aficionados of

Sunset have given different sections of it special names. The Pipeline, in front of Ke Nui Road, the residential strip that runs parallel to the Kamehameha Highway, is an area where waves form the famous tubes familiar to many people. They are spectacular to look at, very dangerous, and have in some cases proven fatal even to championship class surfers. Banzai Beach — reputedly named when an observer watching a surfer attack a particularly challenging wave called out "Banzai!" — is just a little farther west and is identified by a small group of rocks called the Banzai Rocks. Both sections of the beach have the same superbly graceful waves that climb into arcs and fall into curls. They also have a lovely view of the northwest fringes of the Waianae Mountains sinking modestly to a cape at Kaena, which, during a cloud-studded sunset, can make you gasp.

Pupukea Beach Park – The offshore coral reef here provides a memorable display of pounding surf in the winter and forms the perimeter of fascinating tidal pools in the summer. Both sights and seasons lend themselves to the photographer.

Puu o Mahuka Heiau – Here at Oahu's most famous temple are three separate enclosures, one of which contains a structure that was probably an altar where human sacrifices were performed. From the *heiau,* there is a lovely view of Waimea Bay, inlet, and beach park and of the square stone belfry of St. Peter's and St. Paul's Catholic Mission Church, which, in spite of looking like an Italian chapel tower, was once part of a rock-crushing plant.

Waimea Falls Park – This 1,800-acre canyon, with its lovely falls, rock-girt swimming pool, botanical gardens, and 7½ miles of hiking trails, is undoubtedly Oahu's most attractive tourist development. Even with its buses with well-informed guides, the park manages to remain low key. The ancient Hawaiian games and sports that are demonstrated on the lower meadow by experts and novices do not obtrude on the visitor who wants to walk casually among the exotic plants and trees. Excavated house sites and fishing shrines remain much as they were found and have not suffered the monstrous reconstructions so beloved by developers of theme parks. Although many of the plants have been introduced from other parts of the tropics, one of the main functions of Waimea Falls Park is to preserve and propagate Hawaii's endangered flora. Among the trees here is the only known kokia cookei still in existence. Other attractions include two wild boar caught in the Waimea Valley; two wild donkeys from the Big Island, where they are known as Kona nightingales and can occasionally still be spotted on the wooded hillsides south of Kailua-Kona; peacocks; and, a special favorite, a pond with huge Amazon water lily pads that look like round, green tea trays. On nights when the moon is full, the park offers escorted moonlight tours (free). For people taking TheBus No. 52 marked Wahiawa/Kaneohe from Honolulu, there is a 15-minute walk to the Falls Visitor Center from the Kamehameha Highway stop. The delightful hike runs through the lower part of the canyon along Kamananui Stream. Open daily from 10 AM to 5:30 PM. Admission is $8.50 for adults, $5.25 for juniors (7–12 years), and $1.75 for children (4–6 years). 59-864 Kamehameha Hwy. (phone: 638-8511).

Waimea Bay – Waimea was the home of several thousand people until 1894, when a flood destroyed homes, taro patches, livestock, and people, leaving the area desolate for many years. Nowadays there are still more visitors than residents, and they come to visit the falls and the beach park. Swimming here in the summer is wonderful, but in the winter it can be dangerous. Experienced surfers come here in December and January to test their prowess against waves that can rise as high as 25 to 30 feet, and spectators come by the hundreds to watch them.

Haleiwa – During the late 1960s and early 1970s, mainland hippies "discovered" Haleiwa, much to the chagrin of the islanders who were raised with its charms. Today, in spite of a growing number of specialty shops, it still manages to retain the feeling of being small-town Hawaii. Suburban villas facing the ocean make it too big to be a slumbering tropical village, and there aren't quite enough decorative clapboard shopfronts to compare it to cattle towns in the Old West, yet it does have character. This can be witnessed each day in the *Sea View Inn* restaurant and bar (66-011

Kamehameha Hwy.; phone: 637-4165), where residents are found exchanging gossip in tones loud enough to fascinate visitors and muted enough to prevent their hearing any real information.

On Kamehameha Highway diagonally across from Kewalo Lane is the Liliuokalani Church and Cemetery. In the church is the perpetual clock of Queen Liliuokalani, who had a summer home close by along the Anahulu Stream in the late 19th century. The clock, which hangs on the back wall of the church, has seven dials and seven hands. They indicate the months, days of the week, the week of the year, the day of the month, phases of the moon, and, against a dial using the 12 letters of the Queen's name, the hours of the day. In the cemetery are gravestones dating from the 1830s.

Haleiwa Beach Park is one of the very few places on the North Shore where swimming is safe almost year-round, though here as elsewhere it is wise to check the water conditions before going in. *Hale'iwa* means "home of the frigate bird," and occasionally these large, elegant fliers can be spotted off the north coast — but always in flight, in spite of the name. The Kamehameha Highway turns south at Haleiwa to proceed across central Oahu to the south coast and Honolulu. A secondary road, Route 82, continues on along the coast past Mokuleia and joins Route 930, which eventually becomes a four-wheel-drive track leading to Kaena Point, the island's extreme northwest tip.

Mokuleia – The Dillingham family used to have a ranch in this quiet corner of northwest Oahu. Today, the Dillingham Air Force Base is the most visible tenant, although the polo fields here have attracted such luminaries as the Duke of Edinburgh, the Prince of Wales, and that polo-playing junkie, the Maharajah of Jaipur. Digging in the sand for shells is a favorite family pastime, as some exquisite specimens can occasionally be found. It is possible to travel beyond Mokuleia to Kaena Point, but the road is difficult and narrow and best suited to hikers.

SHOPPING: Change is coming to Haleiwa, with new restaurants and shops in place for resort growth on the North Shore. Haleiwa holds on to its old-town feel, but country stores like *Matsumoto's* and *Aoki's,* where shaved ice and T-shirts were king, now compete with upscale shops and galleries.

Charlie's Country Store – Apart from the distressingly familiar souvenirs, this store also sells excellent books on the flora and fauna of the islands. In Waimea Falls Park, 59-864 Kamehameha Hwy. (phone: 638-8525).

Deeni's Boutique – Good for beach towels, bikinis, and muumuus, especially when there's an "odd lot" table. 66-079 Kamehameha Hwy., Haleiwa (phone: 637-9871).

Fettig Art Gallery – Large and colorful paintings of Hawaiian rural and maritime scenes. 66-030 Kamehameha Highway, Haleiwa (phone: 637-4933).

Kukui Nuts of Hawaii – This is the place where kukui nuts are transformed into shiny black and brown leis. Also available: an array of products, from lotions to shampoos, created from healthful kukui oil. 66-935 Kaukonahua Rd., between Haleiwa and Waialua (phone: 637-9889).

Outrigger Trading Co. – Inside *Jameson's by the Sea,* this small shop specializes in handcrafted Hawaiian-made pottery, glass, wood, etc. 62-540 Kamehameha Hwy., Haleiwa (phone: 637-4737).

Pacific Island Arts – An appealing selection of local artists' works. North Shore Marketplace (phone: 637-7880).

Platinor – Oriental art and antiques, many from owner Engelbert "Angelo" Klockner's collection. In the lobby of the Turtle Bay Hilton (phone: 293-8777).

NIGHTLIFE: *Steamers* (in the Haleiwa Shopping Plaza; phone: 637-5071) turns into a lively disco Thursdays, Fridays, and Saturdays between 10 PM and 1:30 AM. The *Bay View* at the *Turtle Bay Hilton* (phone: 293-8811) features live entertainment most evenings.

CHECKING IN: The largest and virtually the only modern hostelry along the North Shore is the *Turtle Bay Hilton and Country Club.* At press time, plans for construction of a second hotel at Turtle Bay, along with additional condominiums and a second 18-hole golf course, were announced. There are a few condominiums at Mokuleia Beach, but these are usually let only on fairly long leases. All telephone numbers are in the 808 area code unless otherwise indicated.

Turtle Bay Hilton and Country Club – Just about everything that you could possibly want on a vacation. There are miles of beautiful beach, including the idyllic, tiny Kuilima Cove, one of the few places on the North Shore where you can swim year-round. In addition, the hotel offers golf, tennis, scuba diving, snorkeling, and horseback riding. The rooms are large and on the whole quite elegant, with large lanais. Winter, when it is damp and cloudy, may not be the best time to visit if you are looking for a placid ocean and a deep tan, but once you have been lulled to sleep by the pounding surf along the Kuilima beaches, any other sleeping aid will seem ineffectual. The range of accommodations here is wide, from bay-view rooms to ocean-view rooms to separate cottages, cabanas, and executive suites. Rates start at about $130 for a double room and climb. Off the Kamehameha Hwy., at Kahuku (phone: 293-8811; 800-445-8667).

Kuilima Estates – Studio, 1-, 2-, and 3-bedroom condominiums adjacent to *Turtle Bay*'s expansive golf course provide another North Shore option with full resort amenities. Daily rates start at $50 ($80 in high season); maid service is available at extra charge. Full kitchens, washer/dryers, color TV sets are included. PO Box 899, Kahuku, HI 96731 (phone: 293-2494; 800-422-4744).

Ke Iki Hale – Set on an acre and a half of palm-fringed beachfront amid ironwood and palm trees, these cottages contain 1 or 2 bedrooms, full kitchens, and large picture windows. Recreational facilities include a volleyball court, barbecues, and picnic tables overlooking the water. Cottage rates start at $100 daily; cleaning is extra. 59-579 Ke Iki Rd., Haleiwa (phone: 638-8229).

EATING OUT: Again, the options are few and far between. For a meal for two, excluding wine, tips, and drinks, expect to pay more than $50 in a restaurant listed as expensive, between $20 and $45 at a place listed as moderate, and under $20 in an inexpensive eatery. All telephone numbers are in the 808 area code unless otherwise indicated.

Cove – At this restaurant in the *Turtle Bay Hilton and Country Club,* diners at window tables gaze out at the white foam and deep blue water of Kuilima Cove as they sample the seafood and various international dishes. Reservations necessary. Open daily for dinner. In the Turtle Bay Hilton and Country Club, off Kamehameha Hwy., Kahuku (phone: 293-8811). Expensive.

Jameson's by the Sea – The setting downstairs is quite casual, while upstairs is a bit more elegant, but both provide *Jameson's* popular baked stuffed shrimp, fresh catch-of-the-day, or steak and chicken specialties. Popular with North Shore residents and Honolulu day-trippers. Open daily for lunch and dinner. Reservations advised. 62-540 Kamehameha Hwy., Haleiwa (phone: 637-4336). Expensive to moderate.

Steamer's – Yet another seafood house paying homage to the butcher-block table. Sashimi, *poki* (raw fish, onions, and tomatoes), and steamer clams with tomatoes and onions are favorites, although there are also more substantial dishes, and all can be savored either indoors or on the deck. Open weekdays for lunch and dinner, weekends for dinner only. Reservations advised. In the Haleiwa Shopping Plaza (phone: 637-5071). Expensive to moderate.

Proud Peacock – At Waimea Falls Park, the pride of this restaurant is a beautiful mahogany bar made in Scotland in 1814. From the terrace you can throw tidbits to the peacocks in the garden below and see some of the hundreds of rare trees and plants that stretch up to the falls and beyond. An all-you-can-eat barbecued rib special is served Tuesday and Wednesday nights; prime ribs, steaks, and seafood are nightly specials. Open daily. Reservations advised. In the Waimea Falls Park, 59-864 Kamehameha Hwy. (phone: 638-8531). Moderate to inexpensive.

Rosy's Cantina – Good-quality Cal-Mex specialties, and above-par service. Haleiwa Shopping Plaza (phone: 637-3538). Moderate to inexpensive.

Kiawe-Q – Chicken, ribs, burgers, and fish flavorfully grilled over kiawe wood, Hawaiian barbecue–style. Haleiwa Shopping Plaza (phone: 637-3502). Inexpensive.

Pizza Bob's – One of Oahu's better pizza parlors. Open daily from 11 AM to 10 PM. Reservations advised. Haleiwa Shopping Plaza (phone: 637-5095). Inexpensive.

Central Oahu

Two main roads climb from the North Shore onto the Leilehua Plateau and converge in the middle of the island at Wahiawa. To the east is the Kamehameha Highway, which turns south at Haleiwa as Route 82, and to the west is the Kaukonahua Highway, or Route 99, an extension of Route 930 from Mokuleia. Kuakonahua Highway meanders along the foot of the northeast slopes of the Waianae Mountains, overlooked by Mt. Kaala. The Kamehameha Highway, the quicker and more popular route, makes an easier climb onto the 1,000-foot plateau, passing first through wide fields of sugarcane. Then, about 4 miles north of Wahiawa, the pineapple fields start, miles of them, stretching out on either side of the highway like a vast carpet of light green stripes (the plants) with dark brown stripes (the rich earth) in between. These long, narrow rows are as neat and precise as soldiers on parade — as indeed they should be in a region that is controlled almost completely by the US military.

Ever since James Dole, a New Englander like so many *haole* pioneers, opened the first cannery in 1899 to market the fruit growing on his property, pineapples and Hawaii have been synonymous. Today, the state produces 45% of the total world crop. You can sample the fruit at the recently modernized and expanded Dole Pineapple Pavilion from 9 AM to 5:30 PM daily (64-1550 Kamehameha Hwy., not far from Wahiawa; phone: 621-8408). The fruit is sold in chunks and occasionally, if there is an abundance, visitors may buy whole pineapples. At the Pineapple Variety Garden (a little closer to Wahiawa, at the junction of Kamananui Road and Kamehameha Highway, and operated by Dole's chief competitor, Del Monte), there are displays of more than 20 kinds of *bromeliads,* the botanic term for pineapples. You will recognize the one that looks like a large hand grenade. Those with huge cactus-like tops and others that are scarcely bigger than a golf ball may not be so familiar.

Wahiawa itself is almost totally devoid of charm. It may once have been a picturesque plantation town, but today it is a seedy commercial center with small supermarkets, chain food outlets, and unpleasant bars where fights between *haole* military personnel and *kamaaina* residents are not uncommon and sometimes fatal. Just before entering Wahiawa, at the northern side of Whitmore Avenue, a dirt track road leads through pineapple fields to the

Kukaniloko Birthstones, where the wives of ancient Oahu chieftains came to bear their children to the sound of chants and the ripple of drums. In the same place, the child's umbilical cord was cut and hidden with much ritual and solemnity. There are more sacred stones in the center of Wahiawa at 108 California Avenue. These Healing Stones, as they are known, are set in a crude concrete shelter that barely makes it as a temple. Legend has it that the stones are two sisters from Kauai who flew here and were, literally, petrified by a superior deity. There are still people who firmly believe that the stones have healing powers. Ti leis, flowers, and candles are almost always left in front of them. At 1067 California Avenue is the temple of another culture, the Hongwanji Mission, where you will find an impressive Buddha carved from Japanese cypress and painted with gold leaf. The Wahiawa Botanical Gardens (1396 California Ave.; phone: 621-7321) is a 27-acre retreat of tropical trees, plants, shrubs, and ferns that makes a nice shelter from the sun on a hot summer day. Open daily from 9 AM to 4 PM. Just west of Wahiawa opposite the reservoir is Schofield Barracks. If you have seen *From Here to Eternity* or *Tora! Tora! Tora!* you may recognize the setting. It was through the Kolekole Pass in the Waianaes west of Schofield that the Japanese made their devastating flying raid over the barracks on December 7, 1941. The *Tropic Lightning Museum,* on the barracks grounds, exhibits artifacts and weapons from wars dating from 1812 through World War II and Korea to Vietnam. It is open Wednesdays through Sundays and is reached via the Macomb Gate entrance on Wilikina Drive.

There are three routes south from Wahiawa. The H2 expressway, which skirts the suburb of Mililani, is the fastest; it ends at the junction with H1 at Pearl City. Route 99 passes through Mililani, a completely suburban development of comfortable houses, wide streets, and attractive shade trees. The most interesting feature here is the modern Catholic Church of St. John, with its stark granite altar, cement walls, and sculptures depicting the 14 Stations of the Cross. These and the bronze statues of the Virgin Mary and St. John make the church worth a visit (95-370 Kuahelani; phone: 623-3332). Route 99 also meets H1 at Pearl City. The most interesting road into town from Wahiawa is Route 75, which turns off Route 99 just south of Schofield Barracks and passes through upland pine fields, lowland sugar plantations, and below the dark green backdrop of the Honouliuli Forest Reserve on the windward side of the Waianaes. A short detour leads to the old Japanese community of Kunia, famous for its orchids and its spring display of *ikebana* flower arranging. Route 75 also hits H1 just *ewa* (west) of Waipahu.

 CHECKING IN: At press time, work was underway on the destination resort known as Ko Olina. Plans included a 1990 opening of the resort's first 18-hole golf course, and several marinas and a hotel to follow in late 1990 or early 1991.

 EATING OUT: *Kemoo Farm* – This popular eating place just across from the barracks has been a restaurant since 1935. It's a great *kamaaina* favorite, recommended by islanders for its fresh stuffed trout, roast duck with macadamia nut dressing, home-baked breads, and fresh vegetables. Shaded by eucalyptus trees, the restaurant sits on the banks of manmade Lake Wilson, part of the Wahiawa Reservoir. One of the most famous musicians in the state, Charles K. L. Davis sings here for the *kamaaina* luncheon on Sundays from 11 AM to 2 PM. His forte is old Hawaiian songs, and when he performs the restaurant is usually jammed, making reservations advisable (call the day you're coming). Two people can eat heartily here for under $40, drinks and tips not included, but add $11 per person for the Davis show. Closed for dinner on Mondays. 1718 Wilikina Dr. (phone: 621-8481). All telephone numbers are in the 808 area code unless otherwise indicated.

Western Oahu

This side of the island belongs to the people of Oahu. Except for a few *haoles* who huddle in the fortress-like condos and resorts of Makaha Valley, the coast in the lee of the Waianae Mountains is relatively free of tourists and tourist amenities. Along the Farrington Highway, which runs *ewa* from Honolulu and turns northwest just beyond Makakilo City and then goes almost due north where it meets the ocean at Kahe Point, restaurants are few and shopping facilities confined to a couple of supermarkets and the occasional mom-and-pop store. This is the dry, leeward side of the island, where the days are usually hot and dusty and the light brown Waianae hillsides are textured with plants, shrubs, and scrub of a lusterless green. After a rainstorm these deep valleys with their steep cliffs are transformed: New vegetation springs to life and new leaves appear on old plants. The area never achieves the outrageous verdancy of the east coast, but for a few hours there is a springlike sparkle all around.

Since for the most part this is not resort or vacation country, it is the best place to get some idea of what Oahu would look like had it not been "discovered" by the military and the jet-age tourist industry. People around here are more likely to own a pick-up truck than a station wagon. The few roads that penetrate the broad valleys lead to poultry farms, small flower plantations, and truck farms. The highway is lined with picturesque churches sometimes in need of a coat of paint and tumble-down houses built on stilts in order to provide some breeze and with wooden stoops for watching the famous Waianae coast sunsets. In the winter these ramshackle dwellings are surrounded by flamboyant poinsettias. In some yards, penned in by wire mesh, you can see small plots of ground where roosters strut, not the kind that awaken midwestern farmers, but nasty, demonic-looking creatures bred for battle. Cockfighting *(haka moa)* was a favorite sport among the ancient Hawaiians and is still popular today in some parts of the island, especially in western Oahu. Old-fashioned luaus are held here, too, the kind that start early in the morning and continue till late at night. These are usually family affairs celebrating weddings, birthdays, and christenings. And although the Hawaiian family is often extensive, including uncles, aunties, and cousins with no apparent blood connection, outsiders from the mainland are not likely to be invited, especially if they are known to be spending a month behind the social barriers of Makaha Valley or a week in a Waikiki hotel.

Feeling between the west coast residents and the people they consider intruders has sometimes run high in the past, with muggings and vandalism of property frequent if not commonplace. Things have improved considerably in recent years. The current major danger while visiting western Oahu beaches is that of drowning in waters where strong currents and undertows prevail from October to April. Still, what is dangerous for the swimmer can be a boon for the surfer, and Makaha Beach, the most famous on the Waianae coast, has been the site of the International Surfing Championships since 1952. Many people who have never been to the islands may recall seeing this coast on television or in the movie *Hawaii*, filmed just north of Makaha at Makua Beach in 1965. Farther north still, beyond Keawaula Beach, known as Yokohama Bay, the Farrington Highway ends, and the terrain from here to Kaena Point is a coastal wilderness of rocky coast and sand dunes, which encompasses a nature preserve that's closed to vehicular traffic.

Kahe Beach Park – Where the southwestern tip of the arc formed by the Waianae Mountains meets the ocean is a beach park of low rocky cliffs with kiawe trees in the background. It's not a good place to swim, but it's an excellent spot for pausing to glance north at the shapes and shades of the coastline and the mountains. Even if you venture no farther, you will have seen the Waianae coast.

Pokai Bay Beach Park – This is one of the few beaches where swimming is safe all year and also one of the few safe anchorages in times of heavy surf. If you like to sit and watch boats bobbing on placid waters in the curve of a mountain-backed bay, stop here for a picnic lunch. A *heiau* (temple) from Polynesian times sits on the bay's eastern promontory. For snorkeling or scuba, contact *Leeward Dive Center* (phone: 696-3414).

Makaha Valley – While driving along the Farrington Highway, you suddenly see to your right a broad valley with modern high-rises clinging to the towering cliffs on its north side. It's no mirage, just the most developed resort area outside Waikiki. Ten miles up the valley at the head of Makaha Stream stands Mt. Kaala, at 4,025 feet the highest peak on the island. Dominating the northern ridge is Puu Keauu, 2,650 feet, and on the south side, Puu Kawiwi, 2,975 feet. Although parts of the valley have been irrigated and turned into golf courses and manicured lawns around the condominiums, much of it remains a wild, rocky, and arid land of shrubs and berry bushes where you may spot wild turkey, chukar partridge, red-necked pheasant, peacocks, and the more mundane Japanese white-eye.

A few miles up the valley, accessible only by foot or the resort's escorted horseback rides, is the Kaneaki Heiau, a 17th-century chiefs' temple restored by the *Makaha* resort and the Bishop Museum. The temple was originally dedicated to Lono, the god of agriculture and, unlike most other *heiaus* on Oahu, it contains two thatched huts in addition to the usual platforms. One hut was used for meditation, the other to house instruments of ritual. Sometime between 1795, when Kamehameha the Great conquered Oahu, and 1812, when he established his kingdom of Hawaii, Kaneaki became a *luakini heiau,* place of human sacrifice. Today, all that disturbs the silence of the grass huts, two prayer towers, and sacrificial altar is the gurgle of the Makaha Stream and an occasional flurry of birds. Permission to visit the site can be obtained from the front desk of the *Makaha* resort. Makaha Beach, at the mouth of the valley, is wide and sandy in the summer, and when the surf is calm the swimming is superb. In the winter, heavy surf erodes the sand and turns the beach into a steep narrow strip.

Yokohama Beach – The beach takes its name from the number of Japanese fishermen who used to pole fish from the attractive rocky ledges embedded along the shoreline. If you have rented a car, do not attempt to go farther than the Farrington Highway, which ends here; the road to Kaena Point is only for hikers with stout boots. Even then, the going can be rough. What you can see from Yokohama Beach — stark patches of mountain, sky, ocean, and the surf pounding on the rocks — gives you a good idea of the desolation that lies beyond, which, it must be said, many people rave about, particularly at sunset.

Kaena Point Natural Area – The sand dunes of Oahu's westernmost tip have been set aside to preserve the endangered plants, birds, and sea life native to the area. Once limited to four-wheel-drive vehicles, the roads that once wound their way from Haleiwa and Makaha to the point have been closed to all but pedestrian traffic; on foot, it's less than half a mile either way.

SHOPPING: Most of the shopping in this area is for food and household supplies in the Waianae Mall Shopping Center (86-120 Farrington Hwy.; phone: 696-2690), where you will find a *Big-Way Supermarket* (phone: 696-4271), *Pay n' Save Drug Store* (phone: 696-6387), and, for itinerant gourmets, a *Burger King* (phone: 696-8000), *Pioneer Chicken* (phone: 696-6433), *Red Baron's Pizza* (phone: 696-2396), and *Dave's Ice Cream* (phone: 696-9294). Athletic wear and equipment are available at the *West Course Shop* of the *Sheraton Makaha Resort,* Makaha Valley Rd. (phone: 695-9544).

NIGHTLIFE: Basically it amounts to conversations among visiting main-landers about the weather. If this doesn't interest you, *Rusty's Coast Café* (87-064 Farrington Hwy.; phone: 696-6345) has entertainment one weekend a month, and the *Fogcutter* (84-111 Orange St.; phone: 695-9404) features contemporary Hawaiian music weekend evenings. Also try the *Sheraton Makaha Resort* for contemporary music (84-626 Makaha Valley Rd., Makaha; phone: 695-9511).

CHECKING IN: Accommodations on this side of the island are concentrated at Makaha, either on the beach or in the valley. In island terms, it's considered quite a long way from everywhere, although it is in fact only 40 minutes from the airport and just over an hour from Waikiki. Shops are few, and entertainment is based largely on daytime activities. If you like bright lights and kicking up your heels, forget it. Except for the *Sheraton Makaha* resort, the places listed are condominiums and usually require a stay of 2 or more nights (since people come here for exercise and rest, it is hard to see why anyone would bother to come just for a single night). All telephone numbers are in the 808 area code unless otherwise indicated.

Makaha Beach Cabanas – From the oceanside lanais of this modest-looking condo-minium building, you have the feeling that you could dive straight down into the surf, the water is that close. All the rooms are simple and clean, almost (but not quite) spartan. There are cooking facilities and equipment. Weekly rates start at $255 ($305 in high season). 84-965 Farrington Hwy. (phone: 696-2756).

Makaha Shores – The 40 rental units in this 6-story apartment complex on a beautiful white sand beach come with fully equipped kitchens and lanais. From the upper floors on the ocean side there's a grandstand view of champion surfers during the season. As the apartments are often occupied by their owners, there are pleasant individual touches in the decor that make them usually less impersonal than hotel rooms. No maid service. Rates start at around $300 a week for a studio ($350 in high season). A minimum stay of 1 week is required. 84-265 Farrington Hwy. (phone: 696-9511).

Makaha Valley Plantation – About a mile up Kili Drive from Farrington Highway and Makaha Beach, this condominium complex consists of 2-bedroom units in 3-story townhouses. Some of the accommodations have been decorated by their owners; others come with standard but not unattractive rattan and bamboo fixtures. All have wall-to-wall carpets; a sofa and armchairs; a dining suite; a large, well-equipped kitchen area; and comfortable beds. There are 2 swimming pools, tennis, and golf; meals are available at the *Sheraton Makaha Resort,* a few minutes away by car. Rates start at around $55 ($70 in high season) a night for two. Minimum stay: 3 nights. 84-718 Ala Mahiku Dr. (just off Kili Dr.), Makaha (phone: 695-9758).

Makaha Valley Towers – Because the apartments in this completely unexpected high-rise on the north side of the Makaha Valley are privately owned, they are all individually decorated, occasionally with some taste. Generally only 40 or so of the 500 units are available for rent, and these rent out rather quickly during the high season. If you are lucky enough to get one on an upper floor, the views are stupendous. Rates for studios and 1- and 2-bedroom units start at about $300 ($350 in high season) a week. Preferred minimum stay is 1 week, but daily rates from $50 are available. At the northern terminus of Kili Dr. (phone: 695-9055).

Sheraton Makaha – The cottages at this resort are among the most attractive accommodations on Oahu, handsomely furnished in bold tropical motifs set off by cut flowers and plants and surrounded by well-tended lawns and groves of blossoming trees. The 2 beautiful golf courses have a resident pro to help those whose game is not quite up to championship standards. There are also tennis courts, riding stables, a croquet lawn, a large swimming pool, and a beautifully restored *heiau* (ancient Hawaiian temple). From its elegant patio you can see the ocean a mile down the valley. Perhaps the only drawback is its distance from the ocean, although to compensate, the resort offers a complete beach program of scuba, snorkeling, swimming, even canoeing in an outrigger, all supervised by experts who know the caprices of the waters around here. Rates start at around $100 for a double. 84-626 Makaha Valley Rd., Makaha (phone: 695-9511; 800-325-3535).

 EATING OUT: People searching for gastronomic nirvana will have to look elsewhere. Fast-food outlets aside, there are only a few restaurants along the coast; for a meal for two, expect to pay about $50 in a place listed as expensive, $25 to $45 in a moderate place, and under $25 in an inexpensive place, not including wine, tips, or drinks. All telephone numbers are in the 808 area code unless otherwise indicated.

Kaala Room – In this elegant dining room of the *Sheraton Makaha Resort,* the menu hints at *cuisine minceur* but not to the point of dogma. They have a pleasing way with simple, sautéed mahimahi, baked salmon Mauna Kea, and for something slightly more exotic, prawns are cooked in a Pernod sauce. The atmosphere here is semi-formal, though this does not extend to a jacket and tie for men. Ask for a table with a view down the valley to the ocean, and dine at sunset, when the sinking sun casts a lovely glow over the linen and sparkling crystal and flatware. Open Sundays through Thursdays from 6 to 9 PM, Fridays and Saturdays to 10 PM. Reservations advised. In the Makaha Resort, 84-626 Makaha Valley Rd., Makaha (phone: 695-9511). Expensive to moderate.

Rusty's Coast Café – Standing below a scorched Makaha coast cliff and overlooking lovely Maili Beach, this eatery is contructed from rough timber decorated with hurricane lamps, ship ladders, ceiling fans — and rusty harpoons. The service is casual but pleasantly polite. Open daily for lunch and dinner. Reservations advised. 87-064 Farrington Hwy., Maili (phone: 696-6345). Moderate.

THE BIG ISLAND OF HAWAII

The Big Island sends visitors looking for superlatives. It is, as its name implies, the largest island in the Hawaiian chain, with an area of some 4,000 square miles. Geologically it is the youngest, at just over one million years, and the dormant volcano Mauna Kea, 13,796 feet, is the highest point in the Pacific basin and arguably the tallest mountain in the world — when measured from its base, 18,000 feet below the ocean's surface. Hilo, located on the east coast, is one of the wettest towns in the US, with a rainfall of nearly 140 inches a year. In addition, the southwest Kona Coast is the only area in the nation where coffee is grown, and the ranges of Waimea support one of the largest herds of Hereford cattle in the world.

Next come the contrasts: Sweltering in the humidity of a Hilo afternoon or bathing in the clear waters off the Kona Coast, you can glimpse a snow line high up on the volcanoes and see at one glance several different climates ranging from tropical to temperate to subarctic. In less than an hour you can travel from ravines of rampant jungle to arid lava fields, from intricate green paths ablaze with exotic blossoms and fruits to vast tracts of nothing but serried grass. Although there is a dearth of good beaches on the island, among those that exist are some with jet black sand. It is this richness of topography and flora and fauna that tempts some people to refer to the Big Island as a miniature continent.

Travelers arrive on the Big Island either at Keahole Airport outside of Kailua-Kona, which is served by direct flights from the mainland, or at General Lyman Field, just outside Hilo, the county seat. A deepwater harbor has made Hilo a marketplace since the days when clippers from San Francisco carried sugar from the Hamakua coast plantations to California and around the Horn to the East Coast. Today, Hilo is probably better known for the orchids and anthuriums grown in cultivated fields to the south of the city which give the Big Island another of its nicknames, the Orchid Isle.

North of the city lies the Hamakua coast, a plateau of sugar plantations where water from the top of Mauna Kea has etched out gulches of astonishing beauty, each with its own waterfalls and tropical wilderness. Straddling the mountains between the east and west coasts are the cattle ranges of Waimea, home of ranches, rodeos, and the Hawaiian cowboy, known as a *paniolo*. This is hunting country, too — the territory of wild pigs and goats and a fine sampling of game birds. The ranches stretch north from Kamuela-Waimea through the rolling green Kohala Mountains to the cape at the island's tip. This northernmost part of the island is also the oldest, coming into existence when the Kohala volcano spewed its first rocks from the ocean in the Cenozoic era.

The Kona and Kohala coasts dominate the Big Island and the town of Kailua-Kona dominates the coast. Hawaiian royalty chose this area as a retreat during the 19th century and no one since has seen fit to quarrel with their excellent taste. Kailua-Kona, in contrast to Hilo, barely 40 miles away as the crow flies, averages less than 30 inches of rain a year and is famous for cloudless blue skies that smile over the wide-open spaces of the Mauna Kea and Hualalai escarpments. Accommodations for latter-day visitors include hotels and condominiums ranging from unpretentious to extravagant, particularly to the north of Kailua-Kona, where expansive resorts rise from once-barren — now lushly landscaped — grounds, with a world-class selection of golf, tennis, and seaside facilities.

The road south from Kailua-Kona leads through coffee groves and macadamia nut groves, past old run-down farmsteads graced with varicolored bougainvillea to Hawaii Volcanoes National Park, the island's most famous and fascinating tourist attraction.

The two active volcanoes here, Mauna Loa and Kilauea, attract not just tourists but also scientists, photographers, and journalists. Fortunately, the eruptions are so carefully monitored that fatalities are rare, and park rangers and scientists from the observatory are usually able to predict their size and extent and the path the lava will take. This normally allows spectators — and there are often thousands of them — to witness without danger one of the most dramatic natural phenomena imaginable.

Even when the volcano is quiet there is plenty to see. There are acres of desert where nothing grows and where ropy *pahoehoe* lava makes shapes across the landscape that seem to have emerged from Hades. There are steam vents constantly hissing forth sulfur and other odors from the earth's bowels, and on the eastern side of Kilauea are forests of giant ferns that make visitors feel they are walking through a chapter from *Alice in Wonderland.* The most recent series of eruptions, which started in 1986 and were still underway as we went to press, were the first in years to destroy private homes, and observers believe that the goddess Pele, who according to legend makes her home in the Kilauea Crater, has been angered by recent Big Island development. They predict that she will one day emerge in a great explosion of lava that will form yet another island in the sea, and recent underwater activity to the southeast of the Big Island dramatically supports these believers.

SOURCES AND RESOURCES

TOURIST INFORMATION: The Hawaii Visitors Bureaus at 180 Kinoole St., Suite 104, Hilo (phone: 961-5797), and at 75-5719W Alii Dr., Kailua-Kona (phone: 329-7787), have complete information on hotels, restaurants, sports, tours, museums, and activities. Open from 8 AM to noon, 1 to 4:30 PM, weekdays only.

My Island B&B (PO Box 100, Volcano, HI 96785; phone: 967-7216) and *Bed & Breakfast Hawaii* (PO Box 449, Kapaa, HI 96746; phone: 822-7771) can book bed-and-

breakfast accommodations in Big Island homes. A trio of top-quality bed-and-breakfast establishments in Kamuela is available from *Upcountry Hideaways* (PO Box 563, Kamuela, HI 96743; phone: 885-4550; 800-634-4022). Bed-and-breakfast rates start at $40 for two.

Local Coverage – The Visitors Bureaus also have copies of *This Week Big Island, Hawaii Island Guide,* and *Harry Lyons's Kona Coast,* which are published weekly and available free of charge. The *Big Island Drive Guide,* with maps, itineraries, and other information of interest to visitors, is distributed free to anyone renting a car. The *Hawaii-Tribune-Herald,* published in Hilo, and *West Hawaii Today,* published in Kona, both cover international, national, and local news. The *Honolulu Advertiser* and *Honolulu Star-Bulletin* are also available.

Telephone – The area code for Hawaii is 808.

GETTING AROUND: On this largest of the Hawaiian islands, distances correspond to those in the smaller northeastern states. Consequently, if you wish to spend any time exploring outside Kailua-Kona, Hawaii Volcanoes National Park, and Hilo, you will certainly need a car. The island has two main airports: Keahole Airport, built on hardened lava about 9 miles north of Kailua-Kona, serves the Kona Coast, the Kohala district, and Kamuela-Waimea (which also has a small airfield served by Aloha IslandAir); General Lyman Field, on the outskirts of Hilo, provides access to Hilo and Hawaii Volcanoes National Park. Two inter-island lines fly from Honolulu to Kona and Hilo on a regular basis: Hawaiian Air and Aloha Airlines.

Taxi – Available in Hilo at the airport; radio-dispatched taxis are available from *Hilo Harry's* (phone: 935-7091). Major hotels know of individual owners with whom they like to deal and can usually find a cab within 10 minutes. Most taxi operators offer individual tours at prearranged rates. On the Kona side, the airport is usually well supplied with cabs, and they can be summoned from all major hotels. *Marina Taxi Association* in Kailua-Kona has drivers who are expert in local or all-island trips (phone: 329-2481). The fare from Hilo to hotels on Banyan Drive is about $7. The fare from Keahole Airport to Kailua-Kona runs around $15; to Keauhou-Kona, add another $6 to $8.

Bus – The bus terminal in Hilo is in downtown Mooheau Park at what also serves as a hangout for derelicts. It is merely a ticket office with outside seating facilities for those waiting. Buses serve Hilo residential areas and, to a limited extent, the surrounding area. Fares start at 75¢, and exact change is required. There are daily buses from Hilo to Naalehu-Kau, Pahoa, Honokaa, and to Kealia-Kona via Kailua. The fares are graded according to distance. The $6 fare from Hilo to Kealia, the longest route possible, has to count as one of the most extraordinary transportation bargains in the US. The buses are slow, but the company is fascinating and the scenery wonderful, and the ride is a good way to get an authentic taste of the island. Information is available from the County of Hawaii Transit Agency, 25 Aupuni St. (phone: 935-8241). Bus schedules are available at the terminal. The bus to Hilo leaves Kealia at 5:45 AM and the Mokuaikaua Church in Kailua-Kona at 6:40 AM, after stopping at the *Kona Surf* and other hotels along Alii Drive. There's a rest stop at Kamuela, upcountry. At press time, shuttle service from Keauhou to Kailua-Kona had been discontinued, with the possibility of a return to service under consideration.

Car Rental – Essential if you want to explore the island without a guide, though it can be difficult to choose from among the dozens of companies in the business. Major national firms such as *Avis* (phone: 329-1745), *Budget* (phone: 935-7293), *Dollar* (phone: 329-2744), *Hertz* (phone: 329-3566), and *National* (phone: 329-1674) are represented at both Hilo and Kona airports; also found are such regional companies as *Honolulu Rent-A-Car* (the least expensive; phone: 329-7328), *Phillip's U-Drive* (phone:

329-1730), *Robert's Hawaii* (phone: 935-2858), and *Tropical* (phone: 935-3385). *Manini Rental Cars* (phone: 885-7296) offers rentals from Kamuela Airport.

If you want to ride up to Mauna Kea or down the hair-raising track into Waipio Valley, four-wheel-drive is mandatory, not only because of the difficult terrain, but because most car rental contracts prohibit off-road or Saddle Road use, leaving renters fully responsible for towing charges should they be required. Four-wheel-drive vehicles can be rented in Kona from *Hertz* (phone: 329-3566), and, in Hilo, from *Harper* (phone: 969-1478), which does allow Mauna Kea summit and Saddle Road drives. The available inventory is limited, making advance reservations a must. The dry, lordly ranges of the west side of the Big Island are ideal for riding in convertibles, although heavy winter rain can make ragtops a liability in Hilo or along the Hamakua coast. *Hertz, Budget, Dollar, National,* and *Tropical* offer convertibles.

Mopeds/Bicycles – A great way to see the Kona Coast roads at all times of the year and the Hamakua coast roads in the dry season, though not suitable for visiting the volcanoes or the Kohala Mountains. *Rent Scooters* (phone: 329-3250) has mopeds in the Kona area. *Dave's Triathlon Shop* (phone: 329-4522) rents mountain bikes and 12-speed bicycles.

SIGHTSEEING TOURS: Bus or Van – *Gray Line* will pick you up either in Hilo (phone: 935-2835) at your hotel or the airport, or in Kailua-Kona (phone: 329-9337) at your hotel for tours around the island or to Hawaii Volcanoes National Park. Guides taking tours through the park are well versed in geology. *Akamai Tours* (phone: 329-7324) covers the island in air conditioned minibuses leaving from Kona Coast hotels. The Kohala Historical Tour, which takes about 4 hours, provides an informative glimpse of that comparatively remote region. *Polynesian Adventure Tours* (phone: 329-8008) offers a full-day itinerary of Big Island highlights. *Kona Coast Activities* (phone: 329-2971) staffs a kiosk in the *Kona Inn* shopping center for a wide range of activities and tours. *Hawaii Untouched* (phone: 329-2944) has a 5-hour West Hawaii tour that features outrigger canoeing and snorkeling; hotel pick-up and barbecue lunch are also included. Price is $35.

Jeep – The Jeep or van ride from the Waipio Valley Lookout on the Hamakua coast north of Honokaa takes you down a steep, winding cliff road into an enchanting valley that resembles a jungle hideaway. Reservations can be made through the Waipio Valley Shuttle, Hwy. 24 at Waipio Valley Lookout (phone: 775-7121), for the 1½-hour tour ($20). *Waipio Valley Wagon Tours* (phone: 775-9518) starts its outing in a four-wheel-drive van, but transfers passengers to a mule-drawn wagon for a tour of the valley. *Paradise Safaris* (phone: 322-2366) offers an exciting Starfari four-wheel-drive excursion, taking seven passengers to the summit of Mauna Kea in a comfortable Suburban wagon on a tour that starts midday and ends between 10 and 11 PM. Warm parkas and drinks are provided, but passengers are advised to bring their own light meals. West Hawaii hotel and condo pick-ups are included in the $80 charge.

Helicopter or Plane – When one of the volcanoes is erupting, an aerial tour is particularly worthwhile, with departures from Hawaii Volcanoes National Park via *Volcano Heli-Tours* (phone: 967-7578) and *Io Aviation* (phone: 935-3031), from Hilo with *Hilo Bay Air* (phone: 969-1545) — which also offers several other tour itineraries — and from helipads along the Kona Coast. *Kenai Helicopters Hawaii* (phone: 329-7424) and *Papillon Helicopters* (phone: 883-8808) operate from separate helipads at Waikoloa, while *Kona Helicopter* (phone: 329-0551) departs Keahole Airport, *Mauna Lani,* the *Kona Surf,* and *Kona Village.* All feature tours that range from 1 to 2 hours, at rates that start at $125. *Papillon* offers a half-hour introductory flight for $95.

Even when there's no volcanic activity, the Big Island's landscape is impressive, on aerial tours that include flightseeing over the 14,000-foot summit of Mauna Loa, the dramatic Kohala Coast cliffs, and a coastal trip over colorful and historic Kailua-Kona and Puuhonua o Honaunau. *Big Island Air* (phone: 329-4868) leaves from Keahole Airport on a series of aerial tours aboard fixed-wing Cessna aircraft at about half the cost of a helicopter tour.

Boat – The volcanic reefs of the Kona Coast provide some dramatic viewing from the floor of a glass-bottom boat. *Capt. Cook VII* (phone: 329-6411) leaves Kailua Pier each day at 8:45 AM for a 3-hour cruise down to Kealakekua Bay. The cruise is accompanied by a narrator and divers who surface occasionally with some marine specimens for examination. *Captain Beans' Cruises* (phone: 329-2955) operates the *Tamure,* a stylized Polynesian catamaran. The *Tamure* makes Kealakekua Bay cruises at 8:30 AM, midday glass-bottom boat sailings, and evening dinner sails that feature an open bar, all the steak you can eat, and Polynesian song and dance. The enthusiasm of *Beans'* personnel is contagious, inevitably drawing guests into the partying. The *Intuition* (phone: 329-8783), a 26-foot Excalibur sloop, departs the *Hyatt Regency Waikoloa* on skippered private party sails at $125 for 2 hours or $275 for a full day, carrying up to six passengers. *Captain Zodiac* (phone: 329-3199), who pioneered zodiac rafting along the Na Pali Coast of Kauai, now offers a 4-hour motorized raft trip that departs from Honokahau Harbor and heads south for Kealakekua Bay, where passengers can snorkel and snacks are provided. The $45 trip includes visits to sea caves en route.

Submarine – *Atlantis Submarine* (phone: 329-6626) submerges 155 feet below the surface in a state-of-the-art submarine with portholes. During the hour-long excursion, visitors view reefs and the large schools of multi-hued fish, attracted by a scuba diver with edible handouts. Depending on the fishes' appetite level and the clarity of the water (usually good), the submersion can prove either interesting or adventurous, although it's a bit pricey at $58. Groups depart the *Atlantis* office in the *King Kamehameha* hotel for the Kailua Pier, where they take the 5-minute boat trip to the submarine.

 SPECIAL EVENTS: *The Mauna Kea Ski Meet,* a 4-day competition, is one of three ski events that take place between February and May. *Paniolos* — Hawaiian cowboys — compete in traditional rodeo events during the *Waikoloa Rodeo* in the middle of February. The *Merrie Monarch Festival,* named for Hawaii's last King, David Kalakaua, is Hawaii's premier hula competition and is celebrated in April in Hilo with flower shows, a hula contest, and pageants re-creating King David's court. *May Day,* May 1, sees everyone on the Big Island wearing leis, aloha shirts, and muumuus. *Kamehameha Day,* June 11, is observed with a procession down Alii Drive in Kona in which each island is represented by a princess wearing the ancient *pau,* a full skirt worn by female horseback riders. The same day, the King's statue at Kapaau is decorated with strands of leis. A major celebration among islanders of Japanese extraction are the *O-Bon festivals,* held from late June to September. During this period, Buddhists wearing kimonos and happi coats dance around a central tower to the music of songs, drums, and flutes in an area decorated with shrubs and lanterns. July 4 sees *paniolos* assemble in Waimea for one of three annual rodeos (the others take place Labor Day and Memorial Day). In August, canoes compete in the *State Championship Canoe Regatta* in Hilo Bay. *Aloha Week* is celebrated on the Big Island in early October, with ceremonies using the music and dance of old Hawaii. In October or November, 4 days are set aside for the *Kona Coffee Festival* at Kailua, when you can tour coffee farms and taste some of the entries in a coffee recipe competition. October is also the month of the grueling *Ironman World Triathlon* competition, which combines a 2.4-mile rough-water swim, 112-mile bike race, and 26-mile run.

 SPORTS: The Big Island is one of those rare places where visitors can proceed from skiing on a mountaintop to snorkeling in tropical waters in just about 2 hours — in minutes if transporation is via helicopter. The activities that attract most sports enthusiasts, however, are deep-sea fishing, golf, tennis, and hiking, for which the Big Island appears to be custom-made. The Kona Coast will undoubtedly become your headquarters if you are dedicated to a particular sport. The few good beaches there embellish this side of the island, and the dry climate and seemingly endless sunshine give it an unfair advantage over the humid, frequently cloudy east coast when it comes to scoring tourist points. If golf or tennis is your thing, the large resort hotels such as the *Mauna Kea Beach, Mauni Lani Bay, Hyatt Regency Waikoloa, Royal Waikoloan,* or the *Kona Surf Resort* may be what you want. Deep-sea fishing enthusiasts usually head for Kailua-Kona, close to the dock next to the *King Kamehameha* hotel, where most charter boats pick up their passengers. Hikers often head for the *Volcano House* (phone: 967-7321) in Hawaii Volcanoes National Park, which has some of the most interesting trails on the island.

Bicycling – Alii Drive from the *King Kamehameha* hotel in Kailua down to Keauhou Bay makes a lovely, leisurely 8-mile bike ride past hotels, private homes, condominiums surrounded by extravagant tropical plants and blossoms, and small, palm-ringed beaches. Cyclists can be seen struggling along the road that climbs up to Waimea, but such jaunts are only for the fit and truly determined. In Hilo, Banyan Drive and Bayfront Highway are both flat but can be quite busy with motor traffic. The beaches and coves along Kalanianole Avenue are easily accessible by bicycle. If you didn't bring a bike with you, ask the front desk at your hotel where you might rent one. *Red Sails Activities* at the *Hyatt Regency Waikoloa* (phone: 885-1234) offers a 14-mile downhill bicycle run from upcountry Waikoloa to Anaehoomalu Beach, where a picnic lunch is served. The 3-hour run costs $50. *Backroads Bicycle Touring* (phone: 415-895-1783; 800-553-2573) circles the Big Island at an easy pace in the course of its escorted, multi-day bicycle tours.

Deep-Sea Fishing – Connoisseurs claim that big game fishing along the Kona Coast is among the best in the world. Tuna, mahimahi, wahoo, and barracuda are some of the fish you can do battle with in sight of land. Marlin weighing more than 1,000 pounds have been caught in spots less than an hour's boat ride from the pier at Kailua. Since 1958, the Hawaiian International Billfish Tournament has been held here each summer, usually at the end of July or the beginning of August, attracting anglers from all over the world. Half-, 1-, and 2-day charters are available through *Kona Coast Activities* in the Kona Inn Shopping Village (phone: 329-2971) or the *Kona Charter Skippers' Association,* 75-5663 Palani Rd. (phone: 329-3600), both of which will put you aboard a 6-passenger boat; some full-day charters include food and drink, but most require that you buy your own. Half-day charters are also available. Several dozen independent charter boats operate out of Kona at rates that sometimes can be negotiated at less than booking service prices. If you want to sail out of Honokohau Harbor, just north of Kailua, take the *Omega* (phone: 325-7859), which has boats available for charter and sharing. Several boats also depart from Kawaihae Harbor for a full day's fishing in the calm waters between Keahole Point near Kailua and Upolu Point at the island's northernmost tip. This trip often affords passengers a marvelous view of the Haleakala Volcano on Maui. The *Hawaii Charter Fishing Guide* (free), available at numerous locations, provides comprehensive fishing information.

Golf – On the Big Island, players can tee off on a mountainside, right at the ocean's edge, or on the rim of a volcano. The most publicized golf course (recently "softened") is the one at the *Mauna Kea Beach* hotel (phone: 882-7222), wrought by the senior Robert Trent Jones from a wilderness of lava and scrub. Mauna Kea number 3 is notorious for the Pacific Ocean and some craggy cliffs that always somehow manage to interpose themselves between the middle tees and the green. Statistics for the course are: 18 holes, 6,365 yards, par 72. Close by is the *Mauna Lani Bay* resort (18 holes, 6,109 yards, par 72), which closely rivals (some say exceeds) *Mauna Kea* in terms of design and challenge (phone: 885-6655). It is actually a golf course–cum–Japanese garden, built at a cost of $8.5 million. The sixth tee here is separated from the green by a rocky inlet often awash with surging, mocking surf. On the *Waikoloa Beach Golf*

Course (phone: 885-6060), designed by Robert Trent Jones, Jr., one plays among some famous Hawaiian landmarks, including ancient petroglyph fields (18 holes, 5,810 yards, par 70). In the same neighborhood is the *Waikoloa Village Golf Course* (phone: 883-9621), which was ranchland before being transformed, once again by Jones Junior (18 holes, 6,142 yards, par 72). A second beach course, which is scheduled to open in early 1990, is a showplace designed by golfer Tom Weiskopf (18 holes, 6,913 yards, par 72), with six lakes and enough sand traps to provide a real challenge. *Keauhou-Kona Country Club Golf Course* (Alii Dr., about 8 miles south of Kailua; phone: 322-2595) can occasionally be tough (18 holes, 6,329 yards, par 72). The first 9 holes of a second 18-hole course are also open for play. The course at the *Volcano Golf and Country Club* (Hawaii Volcanoes National Park; phone: 967-7331) may be the only one in the world that owes its green appearance to fallout from a volcanic eruption — it was ash from a 1924 upsurge that fertilized this once-barren area (18 holes, 5,969 yards, par 72). Additional courses include *SeaMountain at Punaluu* (phone: 928-6222; 18 holes, 6,106 yards, par 72); *Hamakua Country Club,* Route 19, Hamakua (phone: 775-7244; 9 holes, 2,505 yards, par 33); and *Hilo Municipal Golf Course,* 340 Haihai St. (phone: 959-7711; 18 holes, 5,991 yards, par 72).

Hiking – The ideal way to appreciate the wide variety of scenery, animal life, and plant life on this island is to explore it on foot, either on short walks or overnight treks. When and where to go and how to behave so as not to disturb the island's singular physical (and social) environment are answered by the Hawaii Geographic Society, PO Box 1698, 217 S. King St., Honolulu, HI 96806 (phone: 538-3952), which offers a packet of maps and leaflets with suggestions and warnings for $5. Most hikers visiting the island for the first time like to make for Hawaii Volcanoes National Park. Hiking trails here range from a ½-hour stroll to a 3- or 4-day trek to an overnight adventure. The 3.2-mile trail from the *Volcano House* to Halemaumau is probably the most popular, passing through dense fern forests before arriving at the crater's lava rock floor. The Devastation Trail, a surrealistic landscape of ashes and scarred trees, is a favorite short walk. The 7.2-mile Halape Trail, leading down to a rugged lava beach, is the most popular in the Kau Desert. The trail up Mauna Loa Summit is one of the most ambitious on the island. It normally takes 3 to 4 days round trip and means staying at the Red Hill Cabin, 10,000 feet up Mauna Loa's slopes. Check-in is at park headquarters (phone: 967-7311), 7 miles from the trail head, where overnight hikers have to sign up for permits. People making 1-day or shorter trips often like to stay at the *Volcano House* (phone: 967-7321), a rustic inn with such amenities as baths and a cocktail lounge. Advance reservations are essential. Outside the park, the most popular hiking is on the Waipio/Waimanu Valleys Trail, which starts at the Waipio Valley Lookout at the end of Route 240 north of Honokaa. This involves walking through true wilderness across a remote, romantic valley where thousands of Hawaiians once lived, up the northwest *pali* (cliff) of the Waipio Valley, and across numerous gulches to Waimanu. En route you'll see wild pigs, birds native to this area, butterflies, waterfalls, and a paradise of exotic trees. Permission to camp in Waipio Valley can be obtained from the Hamakua Sugar Company in Paauilo (phone: 776-1211). Less rigorous, perhaps, but also more appealing and more probable for the day-tripper are the short trails at Captain Cook Monument and at the City of Refuge, on the Kona Coast south of Kailua, while a walk through the mountainside roads that link Honaunau with the small town of Captain Cook provides a memorable glimpse of pastoral, ramshackle houses in lovely, haphazard gardens and a feeling of the quiet and calm of life as it was led here 30 or 40 years ago.

Horseback Riding – A Hawaiian cowboy, called a *paniolo,* is your guide if you are lucky enough to be a horse-riding guest at the *Mauna Kea Beach* hotel stables in Waimea (phone: 885-4288). Riders crisscross the high, open ranges of the Parker Ranch on 1- and 2-hour rides at $21 an hour for both guests and non-guests. *Waikoloa*

Stables, Kamuela-Waimea (phone: 883-9335), conducts riders over 10,000 acres of South Kohala hillside through areas where it is possible to come across wild goats and wild donkeys. *Ironwood Outfitters* (phone: 885-4941) in Waimea offers a 2½-hour morning mountain ride, with by-the-hour escorted rides in the afternoon. This company gives experienced riders the chance to do some real riding, as well as spend some quieter time on the trail. *Waiono Meadows* (phone: 329-0888) offers 1- and 2-hour trail rides from upcountry stables in Holualoa, 5 miles above Kailua-Kona. Fees run $17 for an hour's ride, and $30 for 2 hours.

Hunting – The sparse grasses and low scrub of the western side of the island remind some travelers of East Africa. Wild boar is the most exciting prey here, although hunters go after wild goats and sheep as well. On private lands, these can be hunted year-round. The season for game birds starts in early November and lasts till the end of January. Prey in this category includes partridge, wild turkey, quail, and several kinds of pheasant. Guests from the *Mauna Kea Beach* hotel hunt on the Parker Ranch. Eugene Ramos of *Hawaii Hunting Tours,* Paauilo (phone: 776-1666), arranges 8- to 10-hour forays across private lands looking for pigs, sheep, and goats. The company will rent guns and ammunition. A license ($15 for out-of-staters) and a permit (free) to enter certain state or county lands are required. Both are available from the State of Hawaii Conservation Enforcement Division, PO Box 936, 75 Aupuni St., Hilo, HI 96720 (phone: 961-7291), and from several agents on the island whose names, addresses, and telephone numbers are available from the Hilo office. Licenses must be purchased in person.

Parasailing – *Kona Watersports* (phone: 329-1593) offers parasailing with a raft take-off and landing in the usually calm coastal waters of Kailua-Kona. A padded harness and floatation device help calm nervous initiates. From several hundred feet up, the courageous get magnificent views of Kona and Haulalai.

Skiing – No kidding: While you are happily snorkeling in clear blue 83F waters down at Kona in mid-January, somewhere in the snow you see in the distance through swaying palm trees people are skiing. Up on Mauna Kea from December to early May (and sometimes as late as July) there are slopes attractive enough to draw beginners, experts, and the foolhardy. It's easy to get short of breath at these altitudes — 11,000 feet and above — and badly sunburned if you are not careful. There are no lifts and a four-wheel-drive vehicle is necessary to reach the slopes. *Hertz* (phone: 329-3566) and *Harper* (phone: 969-1478) can supply the the vehicles, but you'll need someone willing to drop skiers at the summit and then pick them up at the end of a run. Call the Hawaii Visitors Bureau in Honolulu (phone: 923-1811) for current information on summit skiing.

Scuba Diving and Snorkeling – The reefs along the Kona Coast make these particular activities a rare delight. At Mahukona Beach, on the west coast of North Kohala, good visibility permits you to see a wide variety of exotically colored and sometimes quite tame fish. At Puako, off Route 19 about 10 miles south of Kawaihae, you enter the water from the boat ramp. The water here is shallow and there are fascinating coral formations. The depth of the water makes it more interesting to snorkelers than to divers. Anaehoomalu Beach also has good snorkeling close to the rocks. Old Airport Beach is the best place for scuba diving within walking distance of Kailua. Follow the Old Airport Highway, which swings left around the north side of the *King Kamehameha* hotel and leads right to the shore. You can snorkel in the shallow lagoon that forms part of the hotel's backyard. South of Kailua are good scuba diving and snorkeling at Pahoehoe Beach Park and Hookena Beach Park.

If you are planning to snorkel or dive independently, you can rent equipment from *Kona Watersports* (phone: 329-1593) or buy it from *Big Island Marine* on Alapa Street in the Kailua Industrial Complex (phone: 329-3719). Larger resort hotels, such as the *Mauna Kea Beach* (phone: 882-7222) and the *Royal Waikoloan* (phone: 885-6789), rent snorkeling equipment. In Keauhou, the *Fairwind* (phone: 322-2788) rents snorkel gear as does *Jack's Diving Locker* (phone: 329-7585), which also offers a full dive series, from beginner to certified. *Kamanu Charters* in Kailua (phone: 329-2021) offers a 3-hour cruise aboard its sailboat, the *Kamanu,* 3 times daily — at 9:30 AM, 1:45 PM, and at sunset — for 6 or more passengers. *Sea Breeze Cruises* (phone: 326-1311) sets sail from Kailua Pier at 9 and 11:30 AM and 2 PM on 2-hour snorkel sails. *Gold Coast Divers* (phone: 329-1328) takes a maximum of six passengers for 4-hour scuba and snorkeling trips aboard 26-foot power boats, each with a skipper-instructor; it offers certification courses and has trips for certified divers. *Captain Nemo's Ocean Sports* (phone: 885-5555), in the *Royal Waikoloan* hotel, has daily scuba and snorkeling cruises aboard the 42-foot *Me A'u,* which leaves Anaehoomalu Beach daily at 8:30 AM and also offers an afternoon cocktail cruise on most days. *Dive Makai* (phone: 329-2025), *Jack's Diving Locker* (phone: 329-7585), *King Kamehameha Divers* (phone: 329-5662), *Sandwich Isle Divers* (phone: 329-9188), *Sea Dreams Hawaii* (phone: 329-8744), and *Sea Paradise Scuba* (phone: 322-2500) feature 1- and 2-tank shore and boat dives that start at $40. Enthusiasts can pursue full certification in five ½-day programs that start at between $300 and $350. The 55-foot *Sun Seeker* takes scuba divers down the western coast of Hawaii; contact Paul Warren, 78-134 Holua Rd., Kailua-Kona, HI 96745 (phone: 322-6774).

Surfing – Not a major sport on the Big Island since the reefs are too dangerous and the surf is quite tame by North Shore Oahu standards. But there are surfing waves year-round at Honolii Beach Park, 4 miles north of Hilo, and surfers are occasionally seen just outside the Wailuku River Estuary, at the foot of Kaiulani Street in the old part of the town. The best surfing on the Kona Coast is at Waiulua Bay, off Route 19 about 3 miles south of Kawaihae, and at Kealakekua Bay, 13 miles south of Kailua at Napoopoo.

Swimming – Just about every major and most smaller hotels on the island have a swimming pool; this is because not many hostelries, even those at the water's edge, are near a substantial beach. The best swimming beaches are on the island's northwest coast between Anaehoomalu Bay and Kawaihae. Here as elsewhere on the island caution has to be exercised regarding strong currents and rough surf. The rule is, if the water is not what you're used to or think you can handle, stay out. Anaehoomalu Beach itself is one of the most beautiful on Hawaii. It is off Route 19, about 25 miles north of Kailua-Kona. Hapuna Beach, 3 miles south of Kawaihae just off Route 19, a great favorite with islanders, is easily accessible and beautifully looked after. North of the main beach (a short hike) is a second, less crowded beach. At Spencer Beach Park, kiawe and coconut trees surround a grassy area at the back of the beach. The swimming conditions here are among the safest on the island, and there are shower and toilet facilities. Spencer Beach is at the southern end of town on the Kawaihae coast. Closer to Kailua is Honokohau Beach, where islanders and visitors defy the law and come to expose naked bodies to the sun. Being a nude beach, it takes a little reaching: Take Route 19 north a couple of miles out of Kailua, then take the left turn to Honokohau. Park by the small boat harbor and walk north about one-third of a mile. You'll know when you're there. In Kailua itself there is a charming small beach on the ocean side of the *King Kamehameha* hotel. At White Sands Beach, 5 miles south, the sands sometimes disappear, washing away with the tide, leaving lava rock beneath; when the sands are there, this is an idyllic spot for good, safe swimming. Kahaluu Beach Park, close to the *Keauhou Beach* hotel, is another popular small beach with picnic areas and bathroom facilities. In South Kona there is good swimming at Napoopoo Beach Park, 13 miles from Kailua, and at Hookena Beach Park, about 26 miles south. Both have picnic facilities and are ideal places for a meal alfresco. You can enjoy the buoyancy of the ocean without its hazards in the manmade tidepool at Harry K. Brown Beach Park in Puna. The black sand beaches in this neighborhood are very seductive, but swimming from them is perilous, to put it mildly. Two popular spots in Hilo are Leleiwi Beach Park and Onekahakaha Beach Park, both just off Kalanianaole Avenue. Neither has much sand, and swimming is limited to days when the surf is calm. The pool at the *Hoolulu Swim Stadium* (Kuawa and Kalanikoa Sts.; phone: 935-8907) is Olympic-size and open to the public from 1 to 4 PM and 6 to 8 PM weekdays, 10 AM to noon and 1 to 4 PM on weekends.

Tennis – There are dozens of public tennis courts on the Big Island, with the largest concentration in Hilo. *Lincoln Park, Lokahi Park,* and *Panaewa Park* are some of the locations. The eight courts at *Hoolulu Park* (phone: 935-8213) include three indoor courts, which cost $2 per hour ($4 after 4 PM), and five outdoor courts, which are free. There are five public courts at Kailua, four of them at *Old Airport Beach Park,* one in *Kailua Playground.* Other places with courts include *Kamehameha Park,* Kohala; *Honokaa Park,* Honokaa; and *Waimea Park* in Kamuela-Waimea. Public courts are under the jurisdiction of the County of Hawaii Department of Parks and Recreation, 25 Aupuni St., Hilo (phone: 961-8311). In addition, many of the hotel courts are open to the public for a fee. They include, in Hilo, those at the *Naniloa* (phone: 969-2033); in Kailua, the *King Kamehameha* hotel (phone: 329-2911) and the *Kona Hilton* (phone: 329-3111); and at *SeaMountain at Punaluu* (phone: 928-8288). The *Hilton,* the *Kona Surf* (phone: 322-3411), and the *Royal Waikoloan* (phone: 885-6789) all have tennis pros on hand. There is also a tennis pro at the *Mauna Kea Beach* hotel (phone: 882-7222), but play is limited to hotel guests and club members, and on a space-available basis for non-guests at $20 per hour.

AROUND THE ISLAND

The Big Island is dominated by Mauna Kea, which rises 13,796 feet above sea level, and Mauna Loa, 13,680 feet. Measured from their bases beneath the sea they are the tallest mountains in the world, both rising over 32,000 feet above the ocean floor. Between them, the two volcanoes give definition to the island's six main areas: Hilo and its district, which nestles among the gentle inclines where the two mountains meet; Hawaii Volcanoes National Park and the adjacent Kau area, which straddles Mauna Loa down to the ocean in the south; the Kona and Kailua coasts on the island's west side; the upcountry Kamuela-Waimea district on the "saddle" between the Mauna Kea and Kohala volcanoes; the Kohala on Mauna Kea's northwest slopes; and the Hamakua coast, extending from Waipio Valley in the northeast to Hilo.

Hilo

Hilo, the largest town on the island and the county seat, is a place for travelers rather than tourists. Its attractions as a resort are few. What beaches there are are small and relatively hard to find, and the winter climate can be wet, with daily rainfall that adds up to 133 inches a year. Even Banyan Drive, where most of the hotels are, manages to look run-down. But for anyone in a Graham Greene frame of mind, the very seediness of the place becomes a virtue. Most of the extensive waterfront area was washed out in two *tsunamis* (tidal waves) — one in 1946, the other in 1960 — and is now a somewhat unimpressive public park. But the parts of the old town that remain, especially in the few blocks that straddle the Kilauea Avenue–Mamo Street junction, are a fascinating blend of frontier town and colonial waterfront architecture with wooden façades and elegant trimming that could often do with a coat of paint. Still, people come and stay here for months at a time at places like the old *Hilo* hotel downtown and make the weekly pilgrimage a few blocks down to the waterfront to watch a solitary cruise liner monopolize the skyline between the two points that mark the corners of crescent-shaped Hilo Bay. During the week, meanwhile, an old-fashioned pattern of commerce makes the city one of the most exotic in the US, its 1940s appearance and pace notwithstanding. There are still soda fountains with spinning stools, and Chinese preserved-fruit shops stand among Japanese *mochi* (rice cakes) shops, thrift stores, saddlers, and swap shops, where you may find a delightful, uncomputerized world in which calculations are done by hand or even abacuses. Although the incursion of shopping malls situated on the outskirts of town had begun to draw business away from downtown, a modest revival of this area is underway, centering on the shops and restaurants on Keawe Street. Just outside town are orchid and anthurium farms, vast fields of sugarcane, and macadamia nut groves that reach up toward the peaks of Mauna Kea where, in wintertime, the snow line is clearly visible.

Banyan Drive – Hilo's hotel row is lined with these odd denizens of the arboreal world, each one named for a celebrated American from various walks of life. Babe Ruth and Cecil B. De Mille are among those selected for this singular honor.

Liliuokalani Gardens – If you are allergic to formal public gardens, don't let that deter you from visiting this lovely, small park close to Banyan Drive. The gardens are landscaped around a Japanese teahouse in the Edo style, and footpaths meander across ponds and graceful bridges and past stone lanterns and pagodas.

Suisan Fish Market – Just off the Bayfront Highway where the Wailoa River meets the ocean, the market is a 5- or 10-minute stroll from the Banyan Drive hotels. Compared to the vast fish markets of Pusan and Marseille it is small, but that is its charm. Here you may find, depending on the weather and season, mahimahi, opakapaka, tuna, and many other varieties of fish destined for the table. The action begins around 7:30 AM, when traders and fishermen start to bargain in English, Japanese, Hawaiian, and a local mixture, all of which adds up to pidgin English.

Coconut Island – Reached by a small footbridge from Banyan Drive, this palm-fringed islet in Hilo Bay, surrounded by interesting, low black rocks, is probably the pleasantest picnic spot in town.

Rainbow Falls – The Banyan Drive shuttle stops at this spot in the Wailuku River Park, about 5 minutes from downtown. The best time to see it is in the early morning, preferably after a heavy rainfall, when the sun's rays throw a dazzling rainbow over the pool below. Just above the falls, the river churns in a series of rock-bound pools called the Boiling Pots.

Lyman Mission House and Museum – Another stop on the Banyan Shuttle, the museum part of the complex, opened in 1973, has pictures, artifacts, and traditional clothing of all the peoples who have made the Big Island their home as well as a collection of minerals relating to the island's geology. Just as interesting is the Mission House itself, once the home of the Lymans, a missionary family from New England who came to the islands in the 1830s. The house, with its four-poster beds, quilts, pianola, and "puddled" glass brought from Boston, would be believable as the home of Louisa May Alcott's Little Women in Massachusetts. It is only after close examination of the koa floors and doors and the ohia wood furnishings that you realize you are somewhere more exotic. Individual tours with well-informed guides are available. Open daily, except Sundays, from 9 AM to 5 PM. 276 Haili St. (phone: 935-5021).

Onekahakaha Beach – About 3 miles from Hilo on the south shore of the bay lies this strip of white sand with a tidal pool and picnic facilities. On Kalanianaole Ave., toward Leleiwi Point.

Flower Gardens – Hilo's reputation for being one of the wettest cities in the US lends it one advantage: The public and private gardens in the area burst with luxuriant blooms most of the year. Commercially grown orchids and anthuriums are the city's chief source of income. There are a number of places where you can watch lei makers, examine arrangements of fresh flowers and displays of dried flowers, or simply stroll among many varieties of exotic flowers. Some nurseries are designed to give the impression of being ornate formal gardens; a few are open to the public. The most extensive is *Nani Mau Gardens Inc.,* 421 Makalika St. (phone: 959-3541), with 20 acres and over 2,000 varieties of orchids as well as anthuriums and red ginger. There's also *Hilo Tropical Gardens,* 1477 Kalanianaole Ave. (phone: 935-4957), with 2 acres of orchids and other tropical plants; *Orchids of Hawaii* 2801 Kilauea Ave., off Hwy. 11 (phone: 959-3581), open weekdays only; and *Hirose Nurseries Inc.,* 2212 Kanoelehua Ave. (phone: 959-4561). Among the numerous anthurium nurseries in the nearby Pahoa district are *Anthuriums of Pahoa* (phone: 965-8247) and the *Hata Farm* (phone: 966-9240). Both will ship boxed flowers to the mainland.

Hawaii Tropical Botanical Garden (phone: 964-5233) provides one of Hawaii's loveliest garden settings on magnificent coastal acreage, complete with waterfalls, pools, palm forest, and flowers in exotic and authentic profusion. The garden is on the 4-mile-long scenic route that traces the original Hamakua Coast road. First stop is at the old church that now serves as an office. From here there is a shuttle down to the gardens, then a self-guided tour takes visitors through the primeval landscape. Open daily, 8:30 AM to 4:30 PM.

 SHOPPING: The *Prince Kuhio Mall,* a few miles from downtown, features *Liberty House, Sears, Long's Drugs* (good prices on film), a supermarket, and more. *Honsport,* 111 E. Puainako, (phone: 959-5816) has the Big Island's most complete selection of athletic gear, from backpacks to swimsuits. Partially destroyed by *tsunamis* several times, downtown Hilo has until now suffered a 20-year-long decline. But downtown's distinctive ambience and a growing number of new shops have triggered a modest revitalization focused on residents as much as on visitors. In the streets of downtown Hilo there are functional restorations and shops with unretouched character, particularly along Keawe Street.

Basically Books – Lots to look through, including an admirable collection of Hawaiiana. 169 Keawe St. (phone: 961-0144).

Chocolate Bar – Danger for those with a mania for chocolate. Made fresh in the shop daily, including a visually and tastefully delicious selection of "sushi" with coconut for rice and sweets for the seaweed and filling. 98 Keawe St. (phone: 961-5088).

Cunningham Gallery – Hawaiian prints and artwork are the theme. 116 Keawe St. (phone: 935-9122).

Futon Connection – In addition to the custom-made mattress-like futons, there's lots to appreciate, including silk kimonos and pajamas, and Bali wood carvings — all examples of beautiful craftsmanship. 104 Keawe St. (phone: 935-8066).

Hawaiian Handcrafts – The Hawaiian wood products focus on the large selection of koa wood bowls. Inventive and unusual, with some beautiful pieces at reasonable prices. 760 Kilauea Ave. (phone: 935-5587).

Hilo Hattie's Fashion Center – This clothing store chain is famous across the islands for its muumuus, tropical tops, swimsuits, T-shirts, and alohawear. At this branch, however, the staff not only wants to show you what they have, but also how they make it. Tours are offered and pickups at Hilo area hotels can be arranged at no charge. 933 Kanoelehua St. (phone: 961-3077).

The Most Irresistible Shop in Hilo – This is the place to pick up an elaborate doll's house or a wood-burning stove, if that is what you're hankering for. There are also handsome koa wood bowls, lace napkins, toys, wall decor, jewelry, and some especially fine greeting cards "suitable for any occasion." 110 Keawe St. (phone: 935-9644).

Serendipity Bookshop – A nice selection of books, including many on the lore of Hawaii. 2100 Kanoelehua (phone: 959-5841).

 NIGHTLIFE: Most people go to bed early in Hilo, restaurants are usually closed by 10 PM, and only a few bars remain open after 11 PM. Exceptions are the Friday and Saturday night disco at the *Naniloa* (phone: 969-3333), which runs to 2 or 4 AM, and *Reflections* in the Hilo Lagoon Center (phone: 935-8501), where dancing to live and recorded music can be found Wednesdays through Saturdays until 1 AM, and the *Menehune Lounge* of the *Hilo Hawaiian* hotel (phone: 935-9361), where happy-hour pupus run from 4 to 6 PM, and live music and dancing continue until 11 PM nightly. For the rest, just about all the entertainment available takes place in cocktail bars from 4:30 to 6:30 PM and in dining rooms between 7 and 9 PM. *Uncle Billy's Steak and Seafood Restaurant* in the *Hilo Bay* hotel (phone: 935-0861) offers a twice-nightly hula dinner show at 6 and 7:30 PM, which is popular with both *kamaainas* and visitors. Rock groups from Honolulu occasionally make forays into Hilo's *Civic Auditorium* (Manono St.; phone: 935-8213). And the *Crown Room* at the *Naniloa* (phone: 969-3333) often features Hawaii headliner shows.

 CHECKING IN: Hilo's emergence around 1980 as a hub for Hawaiian tourism and Big Island commerce has proven short-lived: No longer are there direct flights to Hilo from the mainland, and several of the hotels that were built in anticipation of a boom have closed. Quiet, sometimes seedy, this is Hawaii beyond the hoopla of tourism — aside from the hotels that line Banyan Drive, and even they are a comfortably pleasant retreat from the typical resort environment. Prices in Hilo are the lowest in Hawaii. Over $100 for a double room in the expensive category; $50 to $95 in a place listed as moderate; and under $45 in an inexpensive place. Aside from low rates, the beauty of the surrounding countryside and the proximity to Hawaii Volcanoes National Park make Hilo a good base for a bit of relaxed exploring. All telephone numbers are in the 808 area code unless otherwise indicated.

Naniloa – Recently renovated and upgraded, this is Hilo's best hotel. It stands on a spur of Hilo Bay, and its neatly trimmed gardens wrap gracefully around small lagoons and extend to the water's edge. The adjacent 9-hole golf course has been upgraded, and new restaurants offer American, Japanese, and Chinese food. Many of the accommodations are suites with expansive views of Hilo Bay and Mauna Kea. There are 2 oceanside pools, one of which is part of the hotel's health spa, and 4 tennis courts, lighted for night play, adjacent to the golf course. Service is both competent and friendly. 93 Banyan Dr. (phone: 969-3333; 800-367-5360). Expensive to moderate.

Hilo Bay – Rusticity is the watchword here. The 2-wing hotel is built alongside a narrow carp pool lined with hala, bamboo, and palm trees. The lobby is a collage of thatchwork and rattan. A few rooms overlook the bay; all have air conditioning. Ground-floor rooms that open onto the tropical garden are the best bet. Kitchenettes are available for a small supplement. 87 Banyan Dr. (phone: 935-0861; 800-367-5102). Moderate.

Hilo Hawaiian – There is a beautiful view of tiny Coconut Island in Hilo Bay from the large, open terrace of the *Hilo Hawaiian*. Marine blue is the predominant color in the rooms, most of which have patriotic red, white, and blue striped bedspreads. There's a good-size swimming pool and a pleasant dining room, the *Queen's Court*, overlooking the bay and Mauna Kea (see *Eating Out*). 71 Banyan Dr. (phone: 935-9361; 800-272-5275). Moderate.

Dolphin Bay – In an old residential part of Hilo shaded by palm trees and surrounded by tropical vegetation, this 18-room apartment hotel is much favored by people who have to make extended stays. There is no room telephone service, no bar, no restaurant, no swimming pool; and desk fans provide whatever cool air there might be. But the rooms are pleasant, all have kitchenettes, and the managers are quite delightful. In the front yard is a banana tree from which guests are invited to help themselves. 333 Iliahi St. (phone: 935-1466). Moderate to inexpensive.

Waiakea Villas – This is the only part of the lovely Waiakea resort that remains as a hotel. The setting is still pleasant, although nothing like it once was (but neither are the prices, which have fallen by half). Studios with kitchens and 1-bedroom suites are available, there is a deli for lunch and dinner, and Hilo is easily accessible. 400 Hualani Rd. (phone: 961-2841; 800-367-7042). Moderate to inexpensive.

Country Club – Perhaps the most outstanding thing about this hotel is the friendliness of the staff. Rooms are decorated in a standard Polynesian style. Most have refrigerators, and a few on the ocean side of the building have decent views. 121 Banyan Dr. (phone: 935-7171). Inexpensive.

Hilo – There has been a hotel on this site in downtown Hilo since 1888. Slightly seedy, the *Hilo* has clean, comfortable rooms that are more functional than decorative, plus a swimming pool, cocktail lounge, and a fine restaurant, the *Fuji*. The front-desk staff is very helpful. 142 Kinoole St. (phone: 961-3733). Inexpensive.

Lanikai – A small, island-style hotel with a restaurant and lounge, 3 blocks from downtown. 100 Puueo St. (phone: 935-5556). Inexpensive.

 EATING OUT: The chefs of Paris, Rome, and New York have nothing to fear from their colleagues in Hilo. There are some acceptable restaurants, however, and one, the *Fuji*, where the cooking and presentation are particularly good. If you favor people watching, remember that restaurants here tend to be at their busiest between 11:30 AM and 12:30 PM and between 6:30 and 8 PM. A meal for two, excluding wine, tips, and drinks, will cost more than $40 in a place listed as expensive, between $20 and $35 in a moderate place, and under $20 in an inexpensive place. All telephone numbers are in the 808 area code unless otherwise indicated.

JD's Banyan Broiler – This simply decorated, quasi-Polynesian shack is a half-open affair next to an ornamental carp pool. Steaks are the specialty, but there are also some popular dishes such as Kal bi ribs and the fresh catch of the day. Open daily for dinner. Reservations advised. 111 Banyan Dr. (phone: 961-5802). Expensive to moderate.

Nihon Saryo – This small Japanese restaurant serves patrons at sushi and teppan bars, as well as at tables. The food is good, the design of gray marble and brass appealing. Open daily for breakfast, lunch, and dinner. Group reservations necessary. In the Naniloa Hotel, 93 Banyan Dr. (phone: 969-3333). Expensive to moderate.

Queen's Court – A Friday night seafood buffet is the attraction here. Though it's at the *Hilo Hawaiian* hotel, it's also very popular with residents, and reservations are necessary. Open daily for breakfast, lunch, and dinner. In the Hilo Hawaiian Hotel, 71 Banyan Dr. (phone: 935-9361). Expensive to moderate.

Roussel's – Hilo may seem a surprising place to find Cajun cooking, but even more surprising is the quality of this menu, which includes soft shell crab "Rising Sun," Louisiana-style boiled shrimp in a zesty Créole sauce, and melt-in-your-mouth trout prepared in a variety of innovative styles. The brothers who own *Roussel's* are Louisiana born and bred. One of Hawaii's finest restaurants and a real find.

Closed Sundays. Reservations advised. 60 Keawa St. (phone: 935-5111). Moderate.

Shokoen – Cantonese cuisine is the specialty, and comfortable decor makes this a good choice if you're craving Chinese food. Open daily for lunch and dinner. Group reservations advised. In the Naniloa Hotel, 93 Banyan Dr. (phone: 969-3333). Moderate.

Uncle Billy's – This is nothing if not Polynesian, with its grass roof and abundance of tapa, batik, and bamboo. The menu is filled with steak and seafood dishes and combinations of both. Breast of chicken, marinated in wine and herbs and barbecued, is a great favorite. The mahimahi sautéed and topped with macadamia nuts is popular with adventurous mainlanders. Open daily. Reservations unnecessary. In the *Hilo Bay* hotel, 87 Banyan Dr. (phone: 935-0861). Moderate.

Fuji – Unlike the rather austere hotel of which it is a part, the restaurant provides a comfortable setting of natural woods and hanging plants. Service — by waiters and busboys in traditional attire — is excellent. The beef and vegetable teppenyaki are highly recommended; the sashimi is delicate and tasty; and the tempura dishes arrive in a gossamer-thin batter retaining the flavor of what's inside. The place is something of a tradition with local Japanese families. Open daily, except Mondays, for lunch and dinner. Reservations advised. In the Hilo Hotel, 142 Kinoole St. (phone: 961-3733). Moderate to inexpensive.

KKTEI – It's a real find for the Hilo visitor, with ample portions of tasty Japanese and American foods and very reasonable prices. A popular spot with residents. Lunch and dinner daily; Sundays, dinner only. Reservations unnecessary. 1550 Kamehameha Ave. (phone: 961-3791). Moderate to inexpensive.

Nihon – A panoramic view of Hilo Bay is the backdrop for this restaurant and sushi bar, which specializes in sukiyaki and shabu shabu–style presentation at your table. Closed Sundays. Reservations advised. 123 Lihiwai St., across from Liliuokalani Gardens (phone: 969-1133). Moderate to inexpensive.

Bears' Coffee – Downtown's deli and espresso bar provides a good place for lingering over breakfast or lunch. This is where Hilo folks go to mingle. No reservations. Closed Sundays. 106 Keawe St. (phone: 935-0708). Inexpensive.

Ken's Pancake House – It's a lot more than the name suggests: Though the pancakes are delicious, the extensive menu, late hours, and local crowd are equal attractions. You know you've been in Hilo when you eat at *Ken's,* and it's a short drive (or walk) from Banyan Drive hotels. Open 24 hours a day, 7 days a week. 1730 Kamahameha Ave. (phone 935-8711). Inexpensive.

Koreana – Barbecued beef, chicken, and pork are the specialties here. Or maybe it's the free *pupus* (snacks) offered nightly in the lounge that motivate a visit. An interesting ethnic perspective of Hawaii few visitors experience. Open daily for lunch and dinner. Reservations unnecessary. 200 Kanoelehua Ave., in the Waiakea Square Warehouse (phone: 961-4983). Inexpensive.

Sun Sun Lau – Many locals consider this Hilo's best Chinese restaurant. The mostly Cantonese menu includes such dishes as pineapple shrimp. Closed Wednesdays. Reservations advised. 1055 Kinoole St. (phone: 935-2808). Inexpensive.

Hamakua Coast

From the air, this northeast section of the Big Island looks like a peaceful, rolling plateau, carpeted with sugarcane and dotted here and there with sleepy, one-street villages — "one-horse towns" they would be called on the mainland. Where the land abruptly embraces the ocean, the airborne traveler sees small, indented slashes of green.

From the road, these verdant slashes turn out to be small jungle canyons referred to as gulches, each with its own waterfall and a few acres of rain forest clinging to treacherously steep slopes.

Even from the main highway, Route 19, which stretches north the 49 miles from Hilo to Waipio, there are gorgeous views of lacy cascades in emerald ravines. But wherever there are side roads leading down to the shore (remnants of the old Mamalahoa Highway), there are even greater rewards. These narrow lanes cross old wooden bridges and small waterfalls that have cut their way through the hillside to form stone arches. They pass by small, simple wooden cabins, the homes of the mostly Japanese and Filipino plantation workers whose forebears came to work in the sugar fields at the end of the 19th century. Eventually, they lead down to rocky coves where black volcanic rocks stand like jagged gravestones against a milk-blue sea. To savor the full flavor of the Hamakua coast, it's necessary to explore places right on the shore as well as some a little farther inland.

The first stop traveling north from Hilo might possibly be Akaka Falls State Park, at Honomu, 15 miles north of the city, where you turn off the highway onto a small road, Route 220, which climbs for close to 4 miles through cane fields to the park, a 66-acre forest preserve of huge fan-shaped bamboo trees, plumeria, banana trees, orchids, heliconia, azaleas, ferns, bird of paradise flowers, ti plants and giant philodendrons with 2-foot leaves. Paths wind through the dense growth to the falls themselves, the lofty, ribbon-thin Akaka Falls, 442 feet high, and the lowlier, thinner Kahuna Falls, which drop a mere 400 feet into the icy bedrock pool below. Hawaiian legend has it that this is where the god Akaka fell to his death. Two smaller waterfalls farther down the gulch and crossed by one of the meandering pathways are named for his mistresses, Lehua and Maile, who turned into waterfalls when they were unable to quench their tears after Akaka's death.

Nearly 12 miles beyond the Honomu turnoff Route 19 reaches Laupahoehoe, where a small winding road leads down to Laupahoehoe Point. This narrow peninsula jutting out into the Pacific Ocean is a finger of lava — the name actually means "leaf of lava" — covered with grass and shaded by tall coconut palms, with tables and barbecue grills for picnickers. It is an ideal spot for examining the structure of the coastline, since it is one of the few places where one can see the ocean side of the cliffs and spot the gulches without going out to sea. A monument at the water's edge commemorates 20 children and three teachers who died when the 1946 tidal wave rolled over their school, which used to be part of the village located here. After the last *tsunami,* the town chose to rebuild at its present upcountry site rather than along the coast.

Kalopa State Park, 13 miles north of Laupahoehoe and 2 miles up the side of Mauna Kea off Route 19, is a native forest reserve covering some 615 acres of mountainside and narrow ravines. Elevations in the park range from 2,000 to 2,572 feet. Marked trails and tags identifying various types of trees and plant life make a visit to the park ideal for the casual visitor or for someone wishing to examine the native flora and fauna in greater depth. Some simple trails to follow include the Nature Forest Trail, a 0.7-mile hike through the heart of an ohia rain forest with a ground cover of at least a dozen varieties of fern, and the Planted Forest, with groves of eucalyptus, silk oak, paper bark, ironwood, and tropical ash. A hike through the Kalopa Gulch Trail System offers the visitor a rare opportunity to penetrate the precipitous slopes of a Hamakua coast gulch. The io (Hawaiian hawk) and aakuu (night heron) may be spotted. At dusk the opeapea (Hawaiian hoary bat) can be glimpsed hunting for insects. The park has picnicking and camping facilities, and there are four "group cabins" housing up to eight people in dormitory accommodations. The price for two people is around $12; reservations are essential (phone: 961-7200). For information, write to: Hawaii State Parks, PO Box 936, Hilo, HI 96720.

Just before reaching downtown Honokaa, Route 19 veers left toward Kamuela-Waimea. An extension of the highway, Route 24, stretches north to Kukuihaele and the Waipio Valley through this pleasantly old-fashioned plantation town, forming its main street. Honokaa is known as the macadamia nut capital of the world. Lime, peach, loquat, and rose apple trees adorn the front and back yards of the town, recalling the Portuguese ancestry of many of the inhabitants. The main street is lined with charming pastel shops. Signs on shop doors give some idea of the casual pace of life in this region: "Gone to the dentist" or "I'm at Charley's." There are two handsome frame churches on the main street, the United Methodist and Our Lady of Lourdes. The *Hawaiian Holiday Macadamia Nut Company* (Lehua St.; phone: 775-7743) sells its products from 9 AM to 6 PM each day; candy making and nut processing can be seen at selected times. Call for current information. The *Honokaa Club* (Rte. 24 in downtown Honokaa; phone: 775-0678) has a restaurant serving inexpensive Japanese and American food (open for breakfast, lunch, and dinner) and clean, spartan rooms that smell strongly of disinfectant. It is not for the faint of heart, but it is a bit of small-town Hawaii, with singles for $24, doubles for $26.

The town and surrounding area have a justifiable reputation as a good place for picking up artifacts made from local materials. Just off Route 19 in Honokaa at *Kamaaina Woods* (phone: 775-7722) you can see vases, bowls, and other objects being made by craftsmen working in koa, mango, milo, and Norfolk Island pine. *Waipio Woodworks,* in nearby Kukuihaele (phone: 775-0958), sells pottery, sculpture, and woodwork made only by native Hawaiian craftsmen. Ceramics and stained and blown glass are another specialty; lovely old-fashioned wooden cradles on rockers are also carried.

Route 24 ends 10 miles beyond Honokaa at the Waipio Valley Lookout. Here, from a height of 900 feet, you can glimpse one of the few accessible valleys on the *pali* coast of the northeast Kohala Mountains. "Accessible," however, is a relative term, since the only road to the valley floor zigzags down the mountainside for a mile at grades reaching 26% and angles of up to 45°. A four-wheel-drive vehicle is essential for the ride, but even those travelers who have one would be well advised to make a visit with either the *Waipio Valley Shuttle* (phone: 775-7121), which conducts a 90-minute excursion along the streams and taro patches of the valley floor, or *Waipio Valley Wagon Tours* (phone: 775-9578). The shuttle departs on the hour daily from 8 AM to 4 PM, using Land Rovers for the journey. Tours cost $20 per person; tickets can be purchased at *Waipio Woodworks,* but call in advance for reservations. Wagon tours depart at 9 and 10:30 AM and 1 and 2 PM for a 2-hour visit that starts with a four-wheel-drive van ride to the valley floor, where a mule-drawn wagon takes over. Add $5 to the $25 charge and the 10:30 AM departure can be extended an hour to allow time for a short hike or a swim.

The road down the precipitous cliff can be awesome if roller-coaster-type gradients and twists are not your thing, and once down in the valley the ride can be bumpy and escorted by mosquitoes. What, then, are the compensations? For one, Waipio is spectacularly beautiful; for another, it retains the aura of old Hawaii, and guides make Waipio's natural and Polynesian history come vividly to life.

When a Protestant missionary, the Reverend William Ellis, came to the valley in 1823, there were 1,325 inhabitants farming plantations of taro, sugarcane, and bananas. Just 40 years earlier, King Kamehameha the Great had been assigned his warrior god in the valley, which still contained a *heiau,* or temple. Because of its royal associations, it became known as the Valley of the Kings. Today, about 50 people live here. Since World War II, two tidal waves and a major flood that brought rocks and debris down the steep cliffs have destroyed the taro crop. Some farmers have returned to start over, including several of the few pure-blooded Hawaiians left in the islands. Outsiders have taken an interest, too. A Philadelphia financier planned and built a restaurant that you can see as you approach the valley's bottom. He never opened it: Hawaii County residents and officials thwarted him, and today it stands empty except for a caretaker. The government was also here briefly when it selected the valley as a suitable site for training Peace Corps volunteers and built replicas of Bornean, Filipino, Malayan, and Nepalese huts for them to live in. However, time and nature have undone most of what was built.

Once on the valley floor, the Jeep travels along dirt tracks that are little more than mud, fording the Wailoa Stream just before it reaches the sea and driving up riverbeds against fast-flowing water. Along the black sand beach, outrigger canoes in many colors lie under the ironwood trees. All around, there are bananas, noni apples, guavas, and grapefruit; occasional remnants of sugarcane fields; and along the tracks, wild orchids and hibiscus. But the chief glory of the valley is its waterfalls: Hilawe, 1,300 feet high, and Nanaue, a series of cataracts that drop from pool to pool, two of which are easily reached and safe for swimming. There are hiking trails throughout the valley, one of which leads into the next valley north, Waimanu, an uninhabited place famed for its groves of hala trees, wild mountain apples, and wild pigs. The trail is about 9 miles long, climbs steeply up cliffs, and is recommended only for people with some hiking experience.

Waipio Valley even has its own motel — of sorts — for anyone who wants to spend the night, or week, in the splendid isolation of the valley. Admittedly, it's not for everyone: The *Waipio* motel imports its drinking water from Hilo; has no electricity (the three cozy bedrooms are lit with kerosene lamps), one cold shower, Coleman stoves and kitchen utensils but no refrigerator; and the nearest place to get food is the aptly-named *Last Chance Store,* a mile away in Kukuihaele on Route 24 (phone: 775-9222), which is accessible from the valley only by shuttle Jeep (stocking up before making your descent is not only advisable, it's essential).

But daybreak makes it all worthwhile. From the porch you can watch the sun come up over the not-so-distant cliffs, illuminating the taro patch and riot of fruit trees only steps away. Or watch the sunrise from the black sand beach, a 20-minute hike on a dirt path strewn with fallen guavas, where there's a good chance of meeting up with a black and white cow or peaceful horse. All this can be experienced at the cost of $10 per person, per night — and Tom Araki, the taro farmer who runs the motel, might throw in a starchy purple slab of boiled taro to accompany your dinner. Reservations should be made at least 3 weeks in advance (write the Waipio Motel, 25 Malama Pl., Hilo 96720; phone: 775-0368 or, if you get no answer, 935-7466).

Kamuela-Waimea

Whether you arrive from Hilo via the subtropical Hamakua Coast or from Kona over the sparse and arid grasslands of Waikoloa, Waimea comes as a surprise. Suddenly there are meadows of soft green grass and dark green trees, white Victorian frame houses with gingerbread trimmings that recall New England. White picket fences surround gardens where camelias and magnolias bloom, and fresh, temperate-zone vegetables grow in neat rows. Farther off, in fields bordered by hardwood trees, horses and cattle graze.

This is ranch country, the home of the 225,000-acre Parker Ranch, which boasts one of the largest Hereford herds in the world on one of the largest private ranches in the United States. Parker Ranch was started by the present owner's great-great-great-grandfather John Palmer Parker, a Massachusetts sailor who jumped ship here in the early part of the 19th century. Parker went to work for Kamehameha, rounding up cattle that had gone wild on the Big Island. Eventually he accumulated a herd for himself, which he settled on land given him by Kamehameha III in 1847. From this beginning grew the vast spread that now exists. To assist him, Parker imported cowboys from Latin America who were referred to early on as *Españolas* — the Spaniards — a word that the Hawaiian tongue adapted to *paniolos.* Today the land on which cattle graze is called paniolo land and the beef they produce, paniolo beef, even though native Hawaiians, Japanese, Chinese, Filipinos, and Caucasians now work alongside the descendants of the original cowboys. Several rodeos held every summer in Waimea prove that this pastime is as popular here as in the western part of the mainland. The most important ones are held on Labor Day, July Fourth, and Memorial Day.

Parker Ranch Visitor Center and Museum – Start with the 15-minute film about the ranch and its history, then proceed to the museum, where you will find clothes and furnishings belonging to the original Parker as well as artifacts used in ranching more than 100 years ago, such as bridles, bits, and some particularly vicious-looking forceps for delivering calves. A smaller section of the museum has a collection of materials relating to the famous Hawaiian Olympic swimmer and champion surfer Duke Kahanamoku. Open Mondays through Saturdays, 9 AM to 3:30 PM (phone: 885-7655).

Historic Parker Ranch Homes – Richard Smart, owner of the Parker ranch, has opened to the public his historic family home, *Puuopelu,* along with *Mana,* the home built in 1847 by his great-grandfather, John Palmer Parker. As an unexpected surprise, Puuopelu is also a small gallery that includes Smart's fine collection of French Impressionist paintings (Chagall, Degas, Pissaro, Renoir). The gallery is open Mondays through Saturdays from 10 AM to 3 PM. Two tours that include these homes are also offered. The 3-hour Paniolo Country Tour departs the Pukalani stables, now transformed into a small museum, and makes its way across ranchland to the original upcountry site of Mana before heading for the historic homes tour. Cost of $34 includes a barbecue lunch; departures are at 9 AM and noon on Tuesdays, Thursdays, and Saturdays. The 2-hour Shuttle Tour departs the stables and includes a stop at the visitor center museum as well. Cost is $15; departures are at 9 AM to 3 PM. Tickets for both may be purchased at the Parker Ranch Visitor Center (phone: 885-7655).

Imiola Congregational Church – This charming New England–style church on the east side of town dates from 1857. The koa wood interior and the koa bowls that serve as chandeliers are especially handsome (phone: 885-4987).

Kamuela Museum – If you can imagine the spacious attic of a particularly favorite but slightly eccentric aunt, then you have some idea of the flavor of this museum. Few attics, however, yield treasures as rare as some to be found in this wildly eclectic collection. Ancient Hawaiian relics and robes, medals, and insignia from the days of the monarchy appear to form the nucleus of the holdings, but there is much else besides, such as German and Japanese weapons from World War II, old English and German china, rare lithographs of Old Masters, specimens of Hawaiian rocks, jewelry, priests' vestments, and rare books. Harriet Meyers Solomon, who owns the museum with her husband, is a descendant of the founder of the Parker Ranch and has to be counted among the museum's major delights. You will find a chat with her as rewarding as the collection itself. Open daily 8 AM to 5 PM. At the junction of Rts. 19 and 20 (phone: 885-4724).

Saddle Road/Mauna Kea Summit – Route 20, also called the Saddle Road, links east and west Hawaii over the plateau between Mauna Kea and Mauna Loa. Although it is the shortest route between Hilo and Kona, it is slow going in rainy weather, since portions of the road just outside of Hilo are unpaved. Most rental car companies specifically list the Saddle Road as off-limits, which means they are not responsible for towing or repair charges incurred while traveling on this route. *Harper* (phone: 969-1478) is the exception. Though *Hertz* (phone: 329-3566) also rents Jeeps, it provides no coverage for off-road travel. The Saddle Road's chief attraction is that it provides access to the road to Mauna Kea's summit observatories, a state-of-the-art complex that now includes eight major telescopes. The road is paved 9,000 feet above sea level to Hale Pohaku, where dormitories and support services for observatory staff are located. Of more interest to visitors is the recently opened Onizuka Center for International Astronomy (phone: 961-2180), open Fridays from 1 to 6 PM and 7 to 9 PM, Saturdays from 9 AM to 2 PM and 4:30 to 6 PM, and Mondays from 1 to 5 PM. Exhibits explain the work being conducted atop Mauna Kea, while putting this great volcanic mountain in a Hawaiian context. Tours of the summit itself (nearly 14,000 feet above sea level) depart from the site of the University of Hawaii's 88-inch telescope Saturdays and Sundays at 2:30 PM. Visitors must reach the summit on their own (four-wheel-drive is almost a necessity). On Saturday nights from 6 to 10 PM a group of 30 are given a chance to look through the university's 24-inch telescope for a bit of first class star gazing. Children under 16 are not allowed on the summit tours, and those with heart or respiratory problems are advised against going any higher than Hale Pohaku, where a small, high-quality telescope makes star gazing possible (Mondays through Fridays). Reservations are required (phone: 935-3371). Weather conditions atop Mauna Kea are quite unpredictable, so warm clothing is essential, and come prepared, as no gas, food, or lodgings are available.

Astronomy aside, a visit is also worthwhile just for the majesty of the setting: The mountainsides, streaked with red and amber at dawn and the haunting shadows at sunset, are more than memorable. Apart from the song of the lark and a glimpse of California quail, large three-ringed pheasant, and brown-black chukar, there is also the possibility that you will spot wild pigs, wild goats, and Hawaii's very own bird, the nene goose. Or you may simply want to go skiing, which is why people come here from as far away as Japan between December and May, although skiing at these altitudes — above 10,000 feet — can be very strenuous.

Hale Kea – Translated as White House, this turn-of-the-century wood frame home, built by the former manager of the Parker Ranch, A. W. Carter, is now open to visitors. Aside from the main house, which now features shops and a restaurant, there are gardens, a blacksmithy, and several interesting shops (see *Shopping*) housed in accompanying outbuildings.

 SHOPPING: *Alihi Creations Scrimshaw* – This is primarily an outlet for local craftspeople working with gold, bronze, and feathers to create some unusual jewelry and decorations. The owners are the Big Island's only scrimshanders, and you can watch them at their trade in the store. Parker Ranch Shopping Center (phone: 885-7737).

Nikko – Relocated to the Hale Kea complex, owner Murthi Vinay'aga continues to offer one of the most eclectic selections of artworks in the islands. The emphasis has shifted from Oriental antiques, and the store is now a showplace for contemporary glasswork, pottery, woodwork, painting, lithographs, and more. Hale Kea, on Route 19 (phone: 885-7661).

Paddock Shop – Boots, belts, buckles, chaps, ten-gallon hats with beautiful feathered bands made from the plumage of game birds — in fact, anything the well-dressed cowpuncher could possibly want is available here. This is another outlet for local craftspeople, some of whom work on the premises. The staff is charming, even if you're just browsing. Parker Ranch Shopping Center (phone: 885-4977).

Waimea General Store – Napkin rings, candleholders, egg cups, and boxes in a variety of shapes beautifully tooled from many native woods including koa, ohia, kiawe, and mamani are on sale here. They are made by Waimea craftsman Larry Trombly, a retired electronic engineer who sells his work nowhere else. Canvas shopping bags with Hawaiian designs and typical boutique items such as potholders, tea towels, and aprons are among the extensive inventory here. Route 19, across from the Hawaii Prep Academy Campus (phone: 885-4479).

Yugen – Mostly expensive custom-designed clothing in hand-dyed batik material — worth a second look. On Route 19, in the Hale Kea complex (phone: 885-7007).

 NIGHTLIFE: Eating dinner at the *Parker Ranch Broiler* and listening to Hawaiian music in the *Waimea Corral* is about it (phone: 885-7366). However, things can get lively at *Cattleman's Steak House* (phone: 885-4077) where the bar features dancing to live entertainment, weekends until 1:30 AM.

 CHECKING IN: There is nothing glamorous in the way of accommodations up here on the prairie, but there are two quite comfortable places in the $35 to $65 price range. Lodging is also available at three bed-and-breakfast establishments where accommodations will run between $45 and $120 a night. For information about bed-and-breakfast establishments in Kamuela, see *Tourist Information.* All telephone numbers are in the 808 area code unless otherwise indicated.

Kamuela Inn – An old favorite in early motel style, but cleaner looking and more comfortable than ever since its revamping a couple of years back. The green of the surrounding hills is astonishing on the morning after a rainstorm. Kitchenettes in some units; continental breakfast included. Route 19 (phone: 885-4243).

Parker Ranch Lodge – This is the newer of the two Hamalua coast lodging places, neatly furnished, with a kitchenette in each unit. The more expensive rooms are hung with textiles and oil paintings. There are tennis courts and riding stables in the vicinity and complimentary Kona coffee in the morning in the TV lounge. Route 19 (phone: 885-4100).

 EATING OUT: Given the extensive bovine population around here, beef understandably figures prominently on any menu, but rarely to the exclusion of seafood. The restaurants listed will feed two people for between $25 and $50; drinks and tips are extra. All telephone numbers are in the 808 area code unless otherwise indicated.

Cattleman's Steak House – Steaks are the specialty here, with lunch served on weekdays and dinner every night (phone: 885-4077).

Edelweiss – Owner and chef Hans Peter Hager has created a restaurant that's the perfect lunch stop on an upcountry tour and worth a drive from the Kona Coast for dinner. The mostly continental menu focuses on veal dishes and wursts, though daily specials may be more exotic: Edelweiss papaya, for example, is a half papaya filled with fresh scallops and Stroganoff sauce, then baked. Lunch and dinner daily, except Mondays; dinner reservations advised. Closed Mondays and the month of September. Route 19 (phone: 885-6800).

Merriman's – Recently opened by Peter Merriman, a former chef at the *Mauna Lani Bay* hotel, this restaurant earns high praise for its light, contemporary American regional specialties using island-grown herbs, produce, poultry, meat, and fish. Open for dinner daily, brunch on Sundays. Reservations necessary. On Route 19 in Opelu Plaza (phone: 885-6822).

Parker Ranch Broiler – The bar here, called *Waimea Corral,* is straight out of *Annie Get Your Gun,* with opulent Victorian decor and red velvet chairs. The dining room, on the other hand, recalls "As the World Turns." It is suburban and inoffensive, with koa paneling surrounding some oil paintings. The specialty, predictably, is beef, and whether you decide on New York sirloin, London broil, or a wineless and herbless *paniolo* stew, it is very good. Open daily, except Sundays, for lunch and dinner. Reservations advised. Parker Ranch Shopping Center (phone: 885-7366).

Kohala

Although destination resorts are now found along the coast of the Kohala district, few tourists penetrate the mountainous peninsula that forms the northern part of the Big Island. When they do, however, they find that it is here that the Hawaii of half a century ago, sleepy and unhurried, lives on.

The area is rich in the history of both native Hawaiians and those people who settled here in more recent times. There are *heiaus* — ancient temples — and at the very northern tip of the island, the birthplace of King Kamehameha I. Handsome, simple churches recall the arrival of the missionaries from the mainland, who came with little save zeal as baggage, and cemeteries in the northeast corner salute the memory of the Chinese (mostly from Hakka province) and Japanese immigrants who came to work in the five sugar plantations that once dominated the economy of Kohala.

Geographically, there are two distinct regions. On the eastern, rainy side of the peninsula, wild ravines, gorges, valleys, and waterfalls are densely covered by rain forest that is periodically gaudy with exotic blossoms and heady with their fragrance. Unfortunately, these areas are off-limits, except to hikers with special permits; they're a paradise to be glimpsed from the air on a helicopter tour, perhaps, but probably never explored.

On the western side, the Kohala Mountains drop in a lordly sweep down to the parched Kawaihae coast, where little grows but pili grass, kiawe trees, and prickly pear cactus. Still, this side of the island also has a grandeur in the same way that the arid, open spaces of West Texas have, although there is a bonus here in that the sparse, rocky terrain meets a brilliant blue sea.

Dividing the two regions is a lesser one that blends with both. This is the high-country prairie, bisected by Route 25, which runs north from Kamuela-Waimea to Hawi. The bracing 20-mile drive along this road takes the traveler, with climbs and swoops, through cattle country, past ranches standing amid sweet grass and fennel, behind windbreaks of eucalyptus and Norfolk pine at an exhilarating altitude somewhere between 2,000 and 3,000 feet.

Hawi, the Big Island's northernmost town, provides a point of entry to the Hawaii of the plantation era, where colorful old houses stand next to rustic general stores and the derelict remains of busier times.

Just a few miles east of Hawi on Route 27 is Kapaau, where taro patches and a pandanus forest — and a considerable increase in the humidity — indicate that you are on the wet side of the island. The pride of Kapaau is the gilt and bronze statue of Kamehameha the Great, of which the version in downtown Honolulu is merely a replica. The original Kapaau statue was sculpted in Italy in 1879–80. On its journey to Hawaii it was lost in a storm in the South Atlantic. Years later, an American sea captain discovered it in a junk shop in Port Stanley in the Falkland Islands and brought it to Hawaii. Kapaau's other monument is the Kalahikiola Congregational Church, built under the supervision of the Reverend Elias Bond. This white edifice with its bright red roof stands with Protestant simplicity amid trim lawns. To build it, parishioners spent 6 years hauling rocks on their shoulders from nearby ravines and taking coral from the ocean to mix with cement for making mortar. Farther into the mountains lies Halawa, where there was once a flourishing opium den not far from a charnel house, two traditional symbols of life (and presumably death) in the Chinese province of Hakka. Their former denizens now lie beneath the sod on the hillside that slopes down the Halawa Valley, their resting places marked by lichen-covered burial stones. Even farther into the dense greenery that carpets this part of the world is Niulii, where an old Japanese graveyard is partly hidden by pandanus trees. Around here you will still find waterlogged terraces of taro and sweet potatoes grown as they were before the arrival of the Europeans.

A mile and a half beyond Niulii, the road comes to an abrupt end at the

Pololu Valley Lookout. From here you can see the valley floor 300 feet below and 'look down the northeast coastline, where dark shadows along the cliffs hint at hidden gorges full of luxuriant foliage and indigenous birds exotic to both ear and eye. The dirt trail to Pololu is easy to navigate, and if the surf looks relatively calm, you could take a swim. As elsewhere on the Big Island, beware of strong currents.

Leaving Hawi to the west, a side road, Route 271, makes a loop off Route 27 before rejoining it a few miles farther on at Puakea Ranch. Route 271 passes Upolu Point, the northernmost tip of the island, and tiny Upolu Airport before reaching Mookini Heiau, just a few hundred yards from King Kamehameha's birthplace. Part of this road is a dirt track that after a heavy rainstorm is suitable only for four-wheel-drive vehicles.

From Puakea Ranch, Route 27, known as Akoni Pule Highway between Hawi and Kawaihae, turns south along the arid Kawaihae coast. From Kapaa Beach, which has no sand but excellent fishing and snorkeling, there is a spectacular view of Maui across the Alenuihaha Channel. The Mahukona Beach Park, a mile farther south, is also without sand, but here again the fishing is very good, especially for big redeye, threadfin, mullet, papio, and menachi.

At Lapakahi State Historical Park, a little south of Mahukona, is one of the few non-royal historical sites in Hawaii. Lapakahi is a 600-year-old seaside village partly restored by archaeologists. It is open daily for guided or self-guided tours through gnarled and thorny kiawe trees to sites once occupied by houses, the village canoe shed, and guest shelters. Marked stones indicate which were used as a fish shrine or as a *papamu,* a board for playing *konane,* the old Hawaiian form of checkers. Just off Route 27 toward the beach (phone: 889-5566, but not between noon and 2 PM).

Archaeological work is also in progress at the Puukohola Heiau, just off Route 27 at Kawaihae. Established as a National Historic Site in 1972, the *heiau* looms impressively above its 224-by-100-foot platform between the ocean and the highway. It was built in 1791 by King Kamehameha in honor of the war god Kukailimoku, following a prophecy that if he did so his victories over his rival kings and other islands would be secured. Kamehameha himself supervised the thousands of workers who built the massive, stone-lava structure. On the day of its dedication he slew his chief enemy, who was present at the ceremony, and offered the unsuspecting guest as a sacrifice to the god. The observation that after these events the King did indeed become ruler of all Hawaii is intended to be chronological, not moral. Open daily 7:30 AM to 4 PM (phone: 882-7218).

Kawaihae marks the southern outpost of the Kohala Peninsula. Until the port was constructed to handle outgoing eucalyptus and sugar products, it was possible to see cattle from the mountain ranches herded out to sea and forced to swim through the surf to boats waiting to carry them to the abattoirs of Oahu. Today you can watch them filing through gates onto barges tied up at the jetty. Ironically, it is also where cattle and horses first landed on the Big Island in 1803. For something to eat in Kawaihae, the garden terrace of the *Harbor Hut,* on Route 297, just off Route 19 (phone: 882-7783), is a good place to get the feel of a lazy Kohala afternoon. The large menu encompasses burgers, sandwiches, steaks, and seafood, along with a good selection of imported beer.

Modern times are making inroads, however, as the Kohala coast resorts draw increasing numbers of visitors. *Harringtons* (phone: 882-7997) in the plantation-style Kawaihae Shopping Center, caters to the upscale, with stylish decor and a menu that features fresh steamed clams, calamari, oysters on the half shell, fresh fish, steak, chicken, and prime ribs. Dinner for two ranges between $30 and $40. At the *Polihali Bar,* in the Kawaihae Shopping Center (phone: 882-7076), there's live music or disco on Thursdays, Fridays, and Saturdays.

South from Kawaihae, Kohala's west coast emerges as a flat lava plain. Geologically a part of the extinct Kohala Volcano, the Kohala Coast resorts are not really an extension of the resort-lined coast centered on the historic Kona district and the town of Kailua-Kona.

Kailua-Kona

For arrivees at Keahole Airport, the first glimpse of the Kona Coast can seem rather bleak. The Queen Kaahumanu Highway, which stretches 35 miles from Kawaihae to Kailua, crosses vast acres of lava wasteland with nothing but sparse grasses and shrubs for texture. Along the shoreline, however, there is a thin ribbon of palm trees, and here and there down the highway, bushes of bougainvillea in various shades of purple, pink, red, orange, and white leaven the barren landscape. Unlike the damp, eastern side of Mauna Kea, where the mountain is cut through with ravines and precipitous *palis,* the dry, western slope is gentle and generous, the roads and highways that traverse it at altitudes varying from a few feet to over 1,000 feet have views of the ocean that can add up occasionally to an almost implausible grandeur.

In recent years, the stretch of coastline running through the South Kohala region, about 20 miles from Kawaihae to Kaupulehu, has come to be referred to as the Kohala Coast. While a handful of resorts dot this coast that was more or less desolate until the 1960s, it is still a virtual wilderness compared with the explosion of hotels, motels, and resort condominiums that characterize the Kailua-Kona district to the south — a contrast that many visitors find welcome. The growing popularity of the more isolated Kohala Coast resorts has set a second stage of development in motion, with new hotels, condominiums, and resort facilities planned in the next couple of years.

Visually, the country south of Kailua is more of a collage. There are groves of coffee trees, with white blossoms in the spring and glistening red berries in the fall, and macadamia nut plantations and terraces of mangoes that give some variety and definition to the terrain. Nestled between banana and papaya trees are ramshackle houses built on stilts with wooden stoops and corrugated iron roofs. Up in the hills of Hualalai, the 8,271-foot volcano that forms the backdrop to Kailua, you can travel upcountry by Jeep to within braying distance of wild donkeys — Kona nightingales, as they are known.

And all along the beautiful shore are spots intimately connected with Hawaiian royalty and history: Kamehameha's royal compound at Kamakahonu, on the grounds of the present-day *King Kamehameha* hotel; Kamehameha III's birthplace close by the spot that is now Keauhou boat harbor; and a half dozen or so *heiaus* (temples) — among them, the Hikiau Heiau at Kealakekua, where Captain Cook was honored as a god. There are sandy beaches along this stretch of coast, too, though the number varies with the season because of occasional heavy winter surf that washes sand away from the lava rocks. Invariably, the sand returns. (White Sands Beach on Alii Drive is also known as Disappearing Sands Beach for this reason.) Where there is no sand, the shoreline can be even more fascinating. Just a few steps off the drive at any number of places between Kailua and Keauhou will bring you upon tidal rock pools — worlds in miniature where exotically colored and striped fish, fussbudget crabs, and other marine life are confined between high tides.

The Kona district is generally thought of as the area along Alii Drive — the Nobles' Drive — which starts at the *King Kamehameha* hotel in the north and ends 8 miles away at Keauhou Bay. The southern portion of the drive is lined with condominium developments and private houses and is a favorite walking and biking route. The variety and color of the bushes, trees, plants, and flowers along here gives one the impression of passing through a spectacular private garden.

At the center of the Kona Coast and at the north end of the drive is Kailua; it clusters around that stretch of the road that starts at the *King Kamehameha* hotel and ends at the *Kona Hilton,* a distance of just over a mile. This was a royal haven in the 19th century, and the small but gracious Hulihee Palace and the Mokuaikaua Church where royalty worshiped stand opposite one another on Alii Drive, still lending a sense of distinction to the community that the resort town shopping arcades have not totally destroyed. Another important element of the Kailua landscape is the sunset, which, swift though it may be by most mainland standards, usually manages to be outstanding.

There are no skyscrapers in Kailua and no flashing neon lights, so evenings tend to be low key, a time for strolling, window shopping, or dining to quiet music on a flare-lit wooden terrace at the ocean's edge.

NORTH OF KAILUA

Holualoa and Upcountry – In addition to the coastal highway, there is a beautiful upcountry road that provides more than 30 miles of panoramas from 2,000- to 3,000-foot elevations. The drive is worth the time and allows for visits to small upcountry towns, like Holualoa, and Kona's famous coffee farms.

Ellison Onizuka Pavilion – At press time, an open-air museum at Kona's Keahole Airport dedicated to Ellison Onizuka, the Big Island–born astronaut who was killed in the explosion of the space shuttle *Challenger,* was still in the planning stages.

Hyatt Regency Waikoloa – The 65 acres landscaped with pools, lagoons, and waterfalls; the grand-scale architecture; and enough artwork to fill a fair-size museum are an attraction in their own right. Priced at $365 million, the *Hyatt Regency* is not only the most expensive hotel ever built in Hawaii, but also the most elaborate and extravagant, with motor launches and trams to shuttle you from here to there and back again. The property is worth a look if you're interested in the shape of things to come, although it doesn't have much to do with things Hawaiian.

Mauna Kea Beach Hotel – One reason for visiting this latter-day Shangri-la off Route 19, 35 miles north of Kailua, might be to see how the other half lives. A less worldly reason, however, is to look at its art collection. It consists of more than 1,000 art treasures, most of them antiques from the Pacific and Asia. A 7th-century Indian Buddha carved from pink granite and standing in the hotel's north garden is the outstanding piece. It comes from Nagappattinam in South India and sits in meditation atop a black granite pedestal, casting a serene eye on the foibles and frivolity all around. In the third-floor lounge is another piece of more than usual significance: the Pacifica Bell Collection, a series of antique bells from Japan, Ceylon, Singapore, and Cambodia. Japanese lacquered screens, painted masks, three-legged Indian storage chests, a hand-carved Buddhist altar from Thailand, Tongan war clubs, and Solomon Islands dance wands are some of the other things that might catch your eye. The collection of 29 original hand-stitched Hawaiian quilts is especially appealing.

Hapuna Beach State Park – When Laurance Rockefeller built the *Mauna Kea Beach* hotel, he donated the beachfront at neighboring Hapuna Bay to the state to be developed as a public park. The park, about a mile south of the *Mauna Kea,* has since become one of the Big Island's most popular, with an attractive beach, good swimming (although conditions may be hazardous), and rental cabins ($7 per shelter, which can accommodate one to four persons) on the grounds. Contact the Department of Land and Natural Resources, PO Box 936, Hilo, HI 96729; phone: 961-7200.

Puako – About 31 miles north of Kailua and 4 miles south of the *Mauna Kea Beach* hotel, take the coastward turn off Route 19 to Puako. Near the end of the road, past house 153, is a trail that leads through clouds of dust and groves of kiawe trees to a petroglyph field. Here, carved in ropy *pahoehoe* lava, are primitive figures of men and animals. Something special to look for are the round circles circumscribing a dot, which are supposedly where the umbilical cords of newborn babies were deposited so that tribal clairvoyants could predict the infants' destinies.

KAILUA

Kamakahonu and the Ahuena Heiau – Standing at the back of the *King Kamehameha* hotel beside a small beach is the site of Kamakahonu, where Kamehameha the Great spent his last years governing all the Hawaiian islands. The rebuilt Ahuena Heiau (temple) and an authentic *hale* (house) surrounded by canoes and tikis are part of the itinerary offered in the King Kamehameha historical tours given by Aala Akana, whose considerable knowledge of the area comes a close second to her obvious affection for the place. The tour (offered weekdays) includes artifacts in the hotel's lobby and corridors, where ancient surfboards, musical instruments, and weapons are on display (phone: 329-2911).

Kailua Wharf – Just off Alii Drive next to the *King Kamehameha* hotel. Actually it's just a stone jetty, but it serves as Kailua's rialto, where you can be sure of meeting friends if they are somewhere in Kona — and where you can make friends if they are not. Around 5 PM the charter fishing boats come back to the pier with their proud (or cowed) parties, and most nights you can see landlubbers kneeling in front of lordly, defeated marlins, having their pictures taken. Later, tourists and islanders, glasses in hand and hearts pinned to sleeves, bathe themselves in the rays of the setting sun.

Hulihee Palace – It looks like a simple, late Victorian vicarage on England's Isle of Wight with its spacious rooms and vaguely gothic window frames. In fact, it was the summer residence of Hawaiian chiefs and kings from 1837 on. It is simple and handsome, and though the koa four-posters and armoires date from the stifling Victorian era, it still stays delightfully airy. No other house on the coast is quite so handsome, nor quite so lovingly tended. Tours daily from 9 AM to 4 PM (phone: 329-1877).

Mokuaikaua Church – This and Hulihee Palace across the road are the two focal points of old Kailua, and long may they flourish. Between them, they lend an air of benign dignity to the village and stand watch against possible architectural horrors. The church was built in 1837 of rock mortared with coral and has interior koa beams. The spire can be seen for miles and for many people symbolizes the heart of the Kona Coast.

Little Blue Church – Also known as St. Peter's, it is on a lava-strewn beach 4 miles south of Kailua on Alii Drive at Kahaluu Bay. If you are used to very ornate Catholic churches, this one will surprise you. Inside, it is bare except for a plain crucifix without a figure, in front of which a small bunch of bright red anthuriums is usually placed. This flash of color in the middle of austerity sums up the Kona Coast, where blossoms of outrageous gaudiness flourish amid an often forbidding landscape.

Kealakekua Bay – On southbound Route 11 in Captain Cook is a junction where the main highway swings east (left) and a secondary road leads off to the right. Known as the Napoopoo Road, it snakes down from Route 11, almost doubling back on itself, through avocado groves and trees heavily laden with mangoes and bright yellow papayas and eventually through acres of rough lava scrub before reaching the small township of Napoopoo, which gives its name to the lovely beach park along the shore. Napoopoo's few houses are partly hidden by arbors of luxuriant foliage often adazzle with blossoms. The stone walls surrounding them are latticed here and there with night-blooming cereus. Kealakekua Bay is famous for its clarity, and its abundant sea life, easily visible to swimmers and snorkelers, is of such variety that the park has been turned into a marine preserve where fishing is forbidden. The bay is usually so tranquil that it is sometimes hard to remember that this is where European man had his first dramatic misadventure with the Polynesian. Here Captain James Cook made his second landing in the Sandwich Islands, as they were then newly known, on January 17, 1779. At first Cook was greeted as a god (Lono in the Hawaiian pantheon), and in due deference the natives bowed their heads and hid their faces as he passed. On February 4, Cook and his two ships, the *Discovery* and the *Resolution,* set sail, but less than a day out of the bay they ran into a winter storm off the Kohala coast in which the *Resolution*'s foremast was damaged, forcing them to return to Kealakekua. Seeing that Cook's property was vulnerable, like that of any other mortal, the natives were less in awe of him than before. One night, the *Discovery*'s cutter was stolen, and Cook and a party of Royal Marines went ashore to take the local chief, Kalaniopuu, hostage. Enraged by this apparent arrogance, a party of native warriors attacked Cook and his companions with daggers, stones, and clubs, killing the captain and four of his followers. It is interesting to note that one of Cook's companions at Kealakekua was the notorious Captain Bligh, who later commanded the *Bounty.* A monument to Cook, a 27-foot obelisk, stands on the north side of the bay at Kaawaloa. It is best seen from one of the boats that sail daily to the spot from the pier at Kailua. If you want to get closer, take a four-wheel-drive vehicle or walk down the road that starts at a right turn about 100 feet along the Napoopoo Road from Route 11. The turnoff is signaled by the giant jacaranda tree that stands at the junction. The paved road that leads down to Napoopoo continues south, parallel to the coast, to the City of Refuge; it crosses a terrain full of nothing but air and sunshine, lava rocks and wispy grasses, and the sound of the ocean, which for many people is enough.

Kona Coffee Mill and Museum – This is the place to see at first hand what happens to all those red berries growing on the coffee trees that line some of the hillsides. You can watch coffee being dried, raked like mulch to turn it over so that all sides reap some of the sunshine, and being cleaned and graded. The museum part is really an overgrown boutique with cases of photographs showing what Kona coffee country looked like in the early 20th century. There are also examples of antique roasters and coolers. The main attraction, however, is the free sample of Kona coffee, which many experts agree is as fine as that grown under similar climatic conditions in Kenya. A pound or two of coffee will generally cost more here than in supermarkets along the coast. Napoopoo

Rd. between Napoopoo and Honaunau, off Rte. 11. Open 8 AM to 4:30 PM daily (phone: 328-2511).

St. Benedict's Church, Honaunau – On Route 16, which spirals up from the City of Refuge to Keokea on Route 11, a small country road leads off to the left. Barely 100 yards from the turnoff, standing on a foliage-clad rise next to a serene, pastoral grave-yard, is a wooden edifice with a decorative, turret-like spire known all over the island as the Old Painted Church. Although the lacy, gothic fretwork on the porch is more ornate than that generally found on other island churches, it is a mere overture to the inside. The interior walls are vividly painted with religious scenes, some using Hawaiian motifs. Pillars decorated with painted scrollwork blossom into painted palm trees at the top. The wall behind the altar seems to be a gothic apse, which turns out to be a *trompe l'oeil* painting based on the nave of the Spanish cathedral of Burgos.

Puuhonua o Honaunau, the City of Refuge National Historical Park – Route 160 branches off Route 11 at Keokea and leads to the City of Refuge, but the undulating road that crosses the sparsely grassed lava moors girded by the Pacific can be more interesting. Even if restorations tend to leave you cold, don't let that deter you from visiting this one. The natural environment of lava beach and palm trees has been left largely intact, and parts of the 6-foot-thick walls, built of lava rock and locked in place without mortar, and some of the formidable tikis — monstrous wooden idols — are handcrafted copies of the 16th-century originals. The coves, rock pools, and tidal lagoons here are lovely, but there is a solemnity about the park that is communicated even by the park ranger as he recalls what the place meant to his Hawaiian ancestors. In the Hawaii that Captain Cook found existed laws of *kapu,* an index of forbidden behavior. It said, for instance, that commoners might not walk in the footsteps of royalty and that women were forbidden to eat with men. Flouting a *kapu,* it was believed, led to catastrophe, which in this case might mean a lava flow or tidal wave. However, the ancient traditions held that a person reaching a *puuhonua* (place of refuge) could be purified by a priest and reinstated in normal society. Noncombatants in tribal battles and defeated warriors could also find sanctuary here. The refuge at Honaunau, where there are two *heiaus* dating from before 1550 and one built in 1650, was one of these and is today the best preserved and restored on the Big Island. It is not necessary to be fascinated by the philosophical aspects of the island's history to enjoy the City of Refuge. Canoes wrought as they were 200 years ago, the game of *konane* (checkers) set out on a rock on the beach, and *kamaainas* weaving mats and carving tikis are sufficient to hold the attention. The grounds are open from 7:30 AM to midnight and the visitor center from 7:30 AM to 5:30 PM (phone: 328-2326).

SHOPPING: The shopping scene has come to dominate Kailua in Lahaina-esque fashion. Most shops are not worth a special mention, although there are some exceptions in the small malls that now line Alii Drive. The Kona Coast Shopping Center on Palani Road opposite the Kailua-Kona Post Office and the Keauhou Shopping Village on Alii Drive have stores selling just about anything you'll find in a suburban shopping mall, including liquor, food, and aspirin. Some of the more interesting shops for visitors are on the road from Kailua to the City of Refuge, an upcountry swing that takes you through Kainaliu, Kealakekua, Captain Cook, and Honaunau. Some distance north of Kailua, approaching Kawaihae, the *Mauna Lani, Mauna Kea,* and *Waikoloa* resorts have antiques shops, galleries, and boutiques aimed at wealthy buyers.

KING KAMEHAMEHA HOTEL

Hawaiian Traders – One of two branches in the neighborhood (the other is at the *Kona Surf* hotel), this shop specializes in fine wood products, etched glassware, and some interesting leis of Niihau shells, all made in the state (phone: 329-2246).

Jafar – An eclectic array of Art Deco glass lamps, paperweights, and acrylic jewelry by local artists, along with fashionable men's and women's clothing (phone: 329-5563).

Liberty House – If Kona is your first stop in Hawaii, then this may be your first glance at this Honolulu chain of ready-to-wear apparel for guys, gals, and kids. The quality tends to be good, the prices by mainland standards high (phone: 329-2901).

Lani's Floral Shop – Not just fresh flowers but also leis and interesting arrangements of dried flowers that can be mailed back home for you (phone: 329-2551).

Shellery – The place to get shell-shock if ever there was one: Here you'll find shell jewelry, shells inlaid with silver and gold, shell statuary, shell ashtrays and ornaments, and just plain shells (phone: 329-2911). Another *Shellery* shop is in the Kona Marketplace.

KONA MARKETPLACE

This shopping center is just across the road from Kona Inn Shopping Village.

Middle Earth Book Store – Floor to ceiling books, calendars, and related goods. It's a lot better than your average resort bookshop; here you really have some options. 75-5719 Alii Dr. (phone: 329-2123).

World Square Theater – An option for that rare rainy day or for an evening out, this moviehouse offers good first-run films (phone: 329-4070).

SEASIDE MALL/KONA BANYAN COURT

Across the road from the *King Kamehameha* hotel.

Kona's Finest Woods – The name may go a bit overboard, but some nicely crafted pieces can be found among the less unusual bric-a-brac that lines the shelves (phone: 329-1765).

The Sandal Basket – Actually adjacent to the mall, this shop sports an impressive selection of casual shoes and sandals. 75-5707A Alii Dr. (phone: 329-1969).

Unison – Silk-screened sweatshirts and T-shirts are found here, well designed (phone: 329-2343).

KONA INN SHOPPING VILLAGE

Farther along Alii Drive, this shopping center has been converted from a famous old hostelry. There is a good-looking seaside restaurant here, and the walkways between the stores are made of timber.

Big Island Hat Company – From caps to dapper straw weave hats — and everything in between (phone: 329-3332).

Competitive Edge Triathlon Center – As the name implies, it stocks just about anything you need for running, swimming, or bicycling, whether you plan to enter Kailua's annual triathlon or not (phone: 329-8141).

Fare Tahiti Fabrics – Not long ago it seemed as if every other shop in Hawaii sold fabrics, though today there aren't many left that do. This is one that does, and it offers the whole spectrum — from tacky to tasteful (phone: 329-2015).

Jim Bill's Gemfire – Owned by well-known jewelry designer Jim Bill, this is probably as close as many will ever come to a pirate's treasure trove. There are literally thousands of loose gems here — rubies, emeralds, topaz, and so forth — that you can have mounted to your own or Bill's design (329-4838).

Kona Bay Trading Company – Oriental porcelain — some of it especially good and gently priced — and imported bags of eelskin or leather are the highlights (phone: 329-4076).

Kona Kai Farms – This shop has a nice selection of culinary gifts as well as an outdoor coffee bar that serves fine coffees (Kona and otherwise) and pastries (phone: 329-2262).

Original Maui Divers – No, the name's not a mistake; it simply refers to the coral found off the Maui coast. Pink coral, the more common black coral, and freshwater pearls are what to seek out here (phone: 329-9442).

KEAUHOU SHOPPING VILLAGE

The shops and restaurants at the shopping village of the Keauhou resort provide a range of resort shops and galleries as well as basics like a supermarket — useful for condo dwellers along the southern half of Kona's resort coast. Just off Alii Dr., by the turnoff for the Kona Surf.

Collectors Cottage – All sorts of collectibles, from limited edition plates and porcelains to dolls and music boxes (phone: 322-3154).

Henri's – Fine candies — including more than 40 varieties of chocolates, plus jams, teas, and locally produced honeys and coffees are the lure (phone: 322-2321).

Logo Shop – If the Keauhou logo demands remembrance, here's the place to go (phone: 322-9211). There's a post office sub-station here, too.

Possible Dreams – A high-end card and gift shop with browse-worthy crystal, porcelain, and other collectibles (phone: 322-3292).

Showcase Gallery – Original art by names like Robert Lyn Nelson, Pegge Hopper, and Herb Kane; posters; and Hawaiian-made crafts (phone: 322-9711).

KAILUA ENVIRONS

Country Store Antiques – An interesting variety of affordable antiques can be found at this small shop in Captain Cook; perhaps you'll spot a bargain or two. Rte. 11 (phone: 323-3005).

Grass Shack – Yes, Virginia, there is a little grass shack in Hawaii. It's up in Kealakekua and has koa wood bowls, tapa cloth, tikis, jewelry made from black coral and jade, and kukui nut leis. Rte. 11 in Kealakekua (phone: 323-2877).

Hale O'Kula/Studio Seven Galleries – A fine selection of gold jewelry, ceramics, wood sculpture, and lithographs can be purchased here. On Rte. 18 in Holualoa (phone: 324-1688 or 324-1335).

Kona Coffee Roasters – In addition to the Kona coffee roasted and brewed on the premises, a range of gourmet treats are found at this shop in Kainaliu, 8 miles south of Kailua on Rte. 11. Look for the bright blue awning (phone: 322-9196).

Little Gallery – Housed in a restored church, it features batik, ceramics, paintings, and other works by Kona artists and craftspeople. On Rte. 18 in Holualoa (no phone).

MAUNA LANI BAY HOTEL

Connoisseur's Gallery – Contemporary fine arts from sculpture to painting are well represented at this gallery in the hotel lobby (phone: 885-7244).

Gallery of the Pacific – On a par with the neighboring Miller collections, this shop focuses on contemporary painting and sculpture. 2 Mauna Lani Dr. (phone: 885-5757).

Herman F. Miller Museum and Gallery – One of the better antiques shops on the Big Island, and also among the best in Hawaii. The better pieces, many of museum quality, were imported from the Orient by owner Herman Miller during the 1920s and 1930s, and are quite expensive. On the resort drive that leads from Kaahumanu Hwy. to the hotel. 2 Mauna Lani Dr. (phone: 885-7779).

 NIGHTLIFE: Happy hour on the Kona Coast is early by mainland standards, starting for most people at 4 PM, though for others it never seems to end — it's that kind of place. Musical entertainment runs from 5:30 to 10 PM in the *King Kamehameha*'s *Billfish Bar* (phone: 329-2911), and there's Hawaiian music Tuesdays through Saturdays from 5:30 to 9:30 PM at the *Nalu Terrace* of the *Kona Surf* (phone: 322-3411). The *Surf*'s *Puka Bar* also features nightly Hawaiian music. At the *Royal Waikoloan* (phone: 885-6789) there's entertainment after 10 in the *Vanda* lounge and piano music to accompany dinner on the *Royal Terrace*. Sunset devotees sidle down to the Kailua pier, drinks and lovers in hand, to participate in the ancient ritual of watching the orange disc disappear over the horizon. Luaus are a favorite with tourists, and on the Big Island they seem to be less contrived than on Oahu. There are luaus at the *Royal Waikoloan* (phone: 885-6789) on Sundays; at the *Mauna Kea Beach* hotel (phone: 882-7222) on Tuesdays; at the *Kona Hilton* (phone: 329-3111) on Mondays, Wednesdays, and Fridays; and at the *King Kamehameha* (phone: 329-2911) on Sundays, Tuesdays, and Thursdays. *Mauna Kea*'s luau features Hawaiian music and dance performances (Hawaiian music is also a nightly feature in the hotel's *Café Terrace,* where complimentary *pupus* are served with cocktails). At *King Kamehameha,* the luau takes place in the shadow of the Kamakahonu restoration, where you eat by torchlight and watch a musical pageant, partly on the water, called *Hawaii Through History.* (*Note:* Since luaus are not offered every night, it's best to call ahead for the schedule in order to fit one in to your Kona visit.) *Captain Beans' Cruises* (phone: 329-2955), which offers ocean bottom-viewing cruises during the day, also runs a nightly dinner cruise that leaves the Kailua Pier at 5 PM and returns at 7. When the food is cleared away, scantily clad young ladies shake and gyrate on the dining tables to vaguely Hawaiian rhythms in a performance that would have perplexed their ancestors and outraged the missionaries. Male passengers, their inhibitions adrift in the limitless liquor that is part of the tab, are invited to join in the "fun." The resulting exhibition is one that usually manages to offend the prudish and the sophisticated in equal measure.

Conversation can be found in the bar of the *Ocean View Inn* (phone: 329-9998), the Kona Coast's neighborhood tavern, until around 10 PM most evenings; there is talk about football or baseball, depending on the season, in the bar of *Quinn's* restaurant (phone: 329-3822) and at Don Drysdale's *Club 53* (phone: 329-6651). At the oceanfront *Jolly Roger's* (phone: 329-1344), there's dance music nightly. The *Eclipse* (phone: 329-4686); *Mitchell's,* in the Keauhou Shopping Village (phone: 322-9966); and *Spats,* at the *Hyatt Regency Waikoloa* (phone: 885-1234), disco till 2 AM, 7 nights a week, in settings that would not disgrace New York's East Side. Walking along Alii Drive between the pier and the shopping village on a night when the moon is full is an affair to remember.

 CHECKING IN: Because of the scarcity of sandy beaches on the Big Island, the few hotels or condominiums that have access to them tend to be very expensive. However, the success of more reasonably priced hostelries along Alii Drive, from Kailua to Keauhou Bay, proves that acres of sand are not absolutely essential for drawing visitors. For many people, the warm, dry climate, the historic appeal of Kailua-Kona, and a swimming pool on the rocks or in a landscaped garden seem to work quite well. Some places do have pocket-sized beaches adjacent or nearby, but the charm of most seagirt properties lies in the access they afford to intriguing rock pools and excellent snorkeling.

Those planning to stay a week or more on the Big Island will find a Kona Coast condo both convenient and a good bet financially as it will allow day-trip access to Kohala, Waipio, or Hawaii Volcanoes National Park, along with the luxury of eating at home or in Kailua-Kona. In selecting a condominium, be sure to specify the facilities needed to meet your personal needs and preferences. Although some are quite luxurious, well located, and well appointed, others are far simpler affairs, perhaps across the highway from the coast. Before sending a deposit, it is wise to find out if daily maid service, telephone, laundry, food shopping, restaurants, tennis, and the like are readily available.

There are four price categories for accommodations along the Kohala and Kona coasts. The *Kona Village, Mauna Kea, Mauna Lani Bay,* and and *Hyatt Regency*

Waikoloa fall into a class of their own: very expensive, with rooms that begin at about $225 a day. Otherwise, expect to spend $160 for two in hotels listed as expensive, $75 to $155 in a place categorized as moderate, and under $70 for an inexpensive hostelry. All telephone numbers are in the 808 area code unless otherwise indicated.

Kona Village Resort – This very special place 15 miles north of Kailua consists of 125 "beachcomber *hales*" which are scattered along the beach and lagoon. Accommodations are styled after the thatch-roofed huts found in the Pacific islands. Although equipped with beds, baths, coffee makers, and refrigerators, the more intrusive aspects of modern life — telephones and television sets — have been blissfully excluded. The resort is built around one of the few palm-shaded beaches on the island. Guests can snorkel, swim, sail Sunfish; rent fishing equipment; play tennis, volleyball, ping-pong; or learn to shinny up a palm tree at no charge. Deep-sea fishing and scuba diving charters are also available. The daily rate includes breakfast, lunch, and dinner. Friday nights there's a good luau. Box 1299, Kailua-Kona, HI 96745 (phone: 325-5555; 800-367-5290). Very expensive.

Mauna Kea Beach – This princely establishment, now operated by Westin Hotels, was founded by Laurance Rockefeller as one of his luxurious Rockresorts. It stands above a crescent-shaped bay adjacent to one of the best sandy beaches on the Big Island. Flagstone terraces lined with tall pillars enhance the hotel's appealing open-air layout. Lofty coconut palms tower over carp pools in the hotel's atrium. But perhaps the most outstanding feature of the *Mauna Kea* is the art and antiques collections which give the corridors, landings, and walkways the atmosphere of a highly accessible museum. Rooms are elegant, though simple, and spotlessly clean. Chairs and bed frames have been made for the hotel in natural-colored wickerwork; bedspreads and cushions are brightly colored; the floors are polished brick. The lanais are large enough for a chaise longue, armchair, and table and chairs for dining, and views are memorable. The hotel is surrounded by an 18-hole golf course designed by Robert Trent Jones, Sr., and there is a 13-court tennis park. Also available are excellent swimming, snorkeling, and windsurfing from the beach, fishing and scuba diving from the hotel's own 58-foot catamaran, the *Island Voyager,* and transportation to the stable at Parker Ranch. Tariffs at the *Mauna Kea* are MAP (including breakfast and dinner) during the winter, and EP (no meals) — with a MAP option — the rest of the year; sports activities, except for special packages, are extra. The property's lordly condominiums, straddling the periphery of its golf course, may also be rented, with free use of hotel facilities, beginning at a mere $400 per day. Off Queen Kaahumanu Hwy. at Mauna Kea Beach, near Kawaihae (phone: 882-7222; 800-228-3000). Very expensive.

Mauna Lani Bay – This 351-room luxury hotel, which opened in February 1983, is designed to appeal to the same monied clientele that frequents the nearby *Mauna Kea Beach.* Most guests who recently sampled both properties say this is the more elegant enclave. More than $70 million was spent building luxurious, extra-large bedrooms, a 10-court tennis garden, a health club, 4 restaurants, including a version of Honolulu's well-known *Third Floor* (see *Eating Out*). There is also a manmade beach. A walking trail skirts the sea as well as fish ponds restored from centuries past and the golf course, which is considered one of the best and most beautiful in the islands — lush fairways surrounded by jagged black lava rock, with the sparkling Pacific Ocean as a backdrop. MAP option available. PO Box 4000, Kohala Coast, HI 96743 (phone: 885-6622; 800-367-2323). Very expensive.

Mauna Lani Terrace – Adjacent to the *Mauna Lani Bay* hotel, these luxurious 1-, 2-, and 3-bedroom units are in low-rise buildings that face nicely landscaped grounds providing direct access to the sea and two nearby beaches. Among the on-property amenities are a pool, Jacuzzi, sauna, and barbecue facilities. Mauna Lani Resort (phone: 885-4944; 800-882-4252). Very expensive.

Hyatt Regency Waikoloa – Costing more than $360 million to build, this 1,244-room resort complex is both the largest hotel on the Neighbor Islands and the most expensive yet to be built in Hawaii. It is a mega-resort by the same developer who built the *Hyatt Regency Maui,* the *Westin Kauai,* and the *Westin Maui,* and it shows: the 62 oceanfront acres have been landscaped to include manmade canals, waterfalls, and lagoons. The main wings of each of the 3 separate towers house a collection of works of art that can be enjoyed by strolling along the mile-long walkway that links them. Ocean views are available from 85% of the rooms, all of which have access to such amenities as 8 tennis courts, numerous swimming pools (the largest of which covers three-quarters of an acre), a health spa, racquetball courts, and 7 restaurants. Transportation around the property is provided by trams and a fleet of passenger boats; shuttle service links the hotel with nearby golf courses, the third of which is still under construction (completion slated for 1990). This hotel is meant to be an attraction in and of itself, which suggests that it will be far from the quiet getaway that some Hawaii-bound visitors seek. As dramatic as it is, it doesn't have much to do with Hawaii. Waikoloa Resort, Waikoloa (phone: 885-1234; 800-228-9000). Very expensive to expensive.

Mauna Lani Point – In a lovely oceanfront setting adjacent to the sumptuous fairways of the Mauna Lani golf course, the 1-, 2-, and 3-bedroom apartments are distingushed by their quality furnishings. Other attractions include a pool, Jacuzzi, and barbecue area. 2 Kaniku Dr., Kohala Coast (phone: 885-5022; 800-642-6284). Very expensive to expensive.

Aston's Royal Sea Cliff – Artful architecture and landscaping combine to make this one of the Kona Coast's more elegant condo options. Two oceanfront pools, one saltwater, one fresh; a Jacuzzi; and a large sauna are on-property extras. So is a location just a couple of miles south of Kailua-Kona. Studio, 1- and 2-bedroom apartments with seasonal rates. 75-6040 Alii Dr., Kailua-Kona (phone: 329-8021; 800-922-7866). Expensive.

Aston's Shores at Waikoloa – The prime oceanfront setting, with easy access to the beach, makes this elegantly furnished condominium worth considering. On-site facilities include pool, Jet-Spa, and tennis; apartments have cable-television link-ups. Full resort facilities are nearby and a car is recommended. Waikoloa Resort, Waikoloa (phone: 885-5001; 800-922-7866). Expensive.

Casa de Emdeko – A Kona favorite because of its large living rooms, marble baths, and lanais overlooking gardens that are full of tropical flowers. The waterfront side of the building has been filled in with sand and a lava wall built along the ocean's edge to make a sun trap. There are barbecue facilities, a sauna, and 2 pools. 75-6082 Alii Dr., PO Box 1071, Kailua-Kona (phone: 329-6488 or 800-367-5168). Expensive to moderate.

Kanaloa at Keauhou – This is surely one of Hawaii's most pleasant condominium properties. Beyond the entrance security gates are oceanfront pools, tennis facilities, and a clubhouse. Well-priced 1-, 2-, and 3-bedroom apartments are private, spacious, elegantly furnished, and include Jacuzzis. One of the better buys on the Kona Coast. 78-261 Manukai (phone: 322-9625; 800-367-6046). Expensive to moderate.

Kona by the Sea – Built on the grounds of an old estate, this low-rise condominium takes full advantage of its setting: the pool and Jacuzzi are surrounded by landscaped grounds and a line of palms that front the sea. There is also a second seawater pool and an excellent restaurant on the premises. 75-6106 Alii Dr., Kailua-Kona (phone: 329-0200; 800-922-7866). Expensive to moderate.

Kona Hilton – Although the rooms have a certain feeling of *Hilton* standardization about them, the compensation is a good-sized, attractive lanai, so constructed that a guest cannot see or be seen from above or below (it also serves as an extra outdoor room, especially if you are lucky enough to have a corner room). Other assets include its tennis facilities; the smallish ocean-fed pool, handsomely screened from the full force of the main by dramatic black rocks; and its proximity to Kailua. Entertainment in the lobby area includes some voracious carp and a parrot with less dialogue than Calvin Coolidge. The friendly staff is helpful. Alii Dr., Kailua-Kona (phone: 329-3111; 800-445-8667). Expensive to moderate.

Royal Waikoloan – Not only is the broad, sandy beach a lure here — it's one of the nicest on the island — but there's also a palm-fringed lagoon, the kind that's more commonly constructed on a Hollywood back lot. The public areas are a series of indoor-outdoor terraces, their lines softened by an abundance of tropical greenery. Old Hawaiian art objects are sprinkled throughout the hotel, which has 528 rooms and 20 lagoon suites, each with its own lanai. Two 18-hole golf courses are open to guests, one directly adjacent and one in the Waikoloa village. Tennis and horseback riding are also available. Taking its name from the Tahitian gardenia, the *Tiare* dining room provides a backdrop of polished koa wood, etched glass, and soothing harp music for its French and continental cuisine. It is a good but somewhat overpriced resort. Off Queen Kaahumanu Hwy. at Anaehoomalu Bay, Waikoloa (phone: 885-6789; 800-537-9800). Expensive to moderate.

Keauhou Beach – On a historic site, the *Keauhou Beach* adjoins the remains of an ancient *heiau* complex and a reconstruction of the summer cottage of King Kamehameha III as well as some beautiful rock pools. The exterior of the hotel is famous for the cascading bougainvillea that surrounds it, and the rooms within are comfortable, with panoramic views. 78-6740 Alii Dr. (phone: 322-3441; 800-367-6025). Moderate.

King Kamehameha – Built on a historic site, chosen by Kamehameha I as his royal retreat, the *King Kam* keeps a historian on staff who gives tours of the hotel and its fabled surroundings, including the *hale* and reconstructed temple on the adjacent tiny beach. The walls of the hotel's shopping center are lined with the ancient artifacts used in athletic contests and war, among them, *ulu maika* (stone pitching disks), *pahee* (darts), and *panaiole* (bow and arrows). The lobby contains a mural by island artist Herb Kane showing King Kamehameha at nearby Kamakahonu Bay. The rooms are more than usually bright and cheerful, especially those facing the ocean. All have Pacific blue carpeting, bamboo-patterned bedspreads, and a touch of rattanwork. There are 4 tennis courts on the premises. The location may be of even greater interest to deep-sea fishermen because the small wharf where bill-fishing charter boats tie up is next to the building. Luaus are held Tuesdays, Thursdays, and Sundays. 75-5660 Palani Rd., Kailua-Kona (phone: 329-2911; 800-367-5170). Moderate.

Kona Surf – Architecturally one of the more interesting hotels along the coast, this building has 4 wings, each named for a different Hawaiian island. An abundance of art in the form of tapestries and prints lines the corridors. Landscaped rock pools and tropical gardens are a tourist attraction in themselves. All rooms have queen- or king-size beds with lanais and interesting Hawaiian wall hangings. Golf and tennis facilities adjoin the hotel. There are 2 swimming pools and good snorkeling in the bay. A well-priced hotel option. Alii Dr., Keauhou-Kona (phone: 322-3411; 800-367-8011). Moderate.

Waikoloa Villas – About 25 miles north of Kailua-Kona, located near the golf course of the sprawling Waikoloa resort area, this 104-condominium complex compensates for its relative remoteness and distance from the beach with a beautiful ranchland setting. To reach the complex, take the Waikoloa turnoff on Route 19 and drive east 6 or 7 miles (phone: 883-9588; 800-367-7042). Moderate.

Aston Islander Inn – The subdued orange and tawny brown of the decor here are in marked contrast to some of the gaudy trim found along Alii Drive. Turn-of-the-century architecture and a beautifully shaded pool area bring a relaxing, mellow touch to this popular condo. Accommodations consist of studios; those with kitchenettes are available on request and cost $5 extra. There is daily maid service and telephones in rooms. This is a good buy, particularly during off-season. Alii Dr.; PO Box 1239, Kailua-Kona, HI 96740 (phone: 329-3181; 800-922-7866). Moderate to inexpensive.

Keauhou Resort Condominiums – Five acres of lush tropical gardens surround the condominium's 1- and 2-level townhouses. Lanais have timber balustrades and outdoor carpeting, which make them more like another room than a balcony. Most face the ocean, and all have an abundance of bougainvillea trailing toward the roof or the lanai below. Light greens and primrose yellow make most rooms look as fresh as springtime. There are 2 swimming pools, and the famous Keauhou-Kona golf course, a 6,800-yard, par 72 championship affair, forms the resort's backyard. 78-7039 Kamehameha III Rd., Kailua-Kona (phone: 322-9122; 800-367-5286). Moderate to inexpensive.

Kona Bay – Right in the heart of Kailua and around a pleasant courtyard and pool, the *Kona Bay* is actually a remaining wing of the lovely old Kona Inn, now, alas, a shopping center on the waterfront across the road. The rooms here are simple and clean; some have kitchenettes and all have TV sets. For price, comfort, and convenience, this is a very attractive option. 75-5739 Alii Dr., Kailua-Kona (phone: 329-1393; 800-367-5102). Moderate to inexpensive.

Sea Village Resort – Pleasantly decorated rooms with some better-than-average wickerwork furniture and handsome wooden lanais make the units in this condominium among the most attractive here. Oceanside accommodations have particularly fine views. Continuous-cleaning ovens, dishwashers, and washer-dryers cut down on housekeeping time. Maid service is provided once for stays of 7 nights or longer, more frequently at extra cost; there is no room telephone service. A Jacuzzi and swimming pool are pleasantly situated on lava rocks just above the ocean. 75-6002 Alii Dr., Kailua-Kona (phone: 329-1000; 800-367-5205). Moderate to inexpensive.

Kona Seaside – It would be hard to be more centrally located in Kailua than at this small, simple hotel. High standards of cleanliness and efficiency apply here, and for low-budget travelers this is an address worth remembering. Alii Dr., Kailua-Kona (phone: 329-2455; 800-367-7000). Inexpensive.

Kona Riviera Villa – The 13 units of this oceanside condo are well maintained by their individual owners, each of whom visits fairly frequently. Each unit has a lanai, most with ocean views, and fully equipped kitchens. A 3-day minimum stay is required, with a discount offered on month-long stays. Weekly maid service. 75-6124 Alii Dr., Kailua-Kona (phone: 329-1996). Inexpensive.

Kona Tiki – A small, modestly furnished hotel right on the water's edge — the kind of place you remember nostalgically when you have graduated to something grander. Delicious Kona coffee and rolls are served free of charge on the oceanside terrace. Some units have tiny kitchenettes. There is no room telephone, and a minimum stay of 3 days is required during high season. The managers are delightful. Alii Dr., PO Box 1567, Kailua-Kona, HI 96745 (phone: 329-1425). Inexpensive.

Kona White Sands Apartment Hotel – This condominium has only 5 units, and they are often booked a season in advance. While not luxurious, they are very comfortable and have huge picture windows with views over the ocean, across the road, deserving extravagant praise. This is the kind of place where you might want to spend a month or two. It is close enough to Kailua to provide sufficient amusement and just far enough away — about 4 miles — to avoid the hustle-bustle. No maid service. Alii Dr. at White Sands Beach, PO Box 594, Kailua-Kona, HI 96740 (phone: 329-3210; 800-553-5035). Inexpensive.

EATING OUT: No one who comes to the Kona Coast would want to miss the opportunity of eating within sight and sound of the ocean. In Kailua-Kona alone there are at least eight restaurants where this is possible, and a couple more nearby. On the other hand, the two best restaurants in Kailua have no water view — they compensate with fine food. In general, a meal for two, excluding wine, tip, and drinks, will run more than $75 at a place listed in the very expensive category, from $50 to $70 in a restaurant listed as expensive, $20 to $45 in a moderate place, and under $20 in an inexpensive eatery. All telephone numbers are in the 808 area code unless otherwise listed.

Water's Edge – From an extravagant breakfast buffet ($12) to fixed-price dinners ($75), the operative word here is straightforward elegance. The restaurant faces a large lagoon for water's-edge seating. Specialties — rack of lamb *provençale,* duck *à la orange,* and tournedos Rossini — make for Big Island cuisine at its most haute. Open daily for breakfast and dinner. Jackets and reservations necessary at dinner. Hyatt Regency Waikoloa (phone 885-1234). Very expensive.

Batik Room – This two-tiered dining room in the *Mauna Kea Beach* provides an eclectic collection of Middle Eastern decor to complement its fine menu. The fragrance of the fine curry specialties is just an initial olfactory hint of the tastes to follow. Also offered are classics such as veal Oscar, tournedos of beef, and châteaubriand. Service is good, and the low noise level permits easy conversation. Open daily for dinner. Reservations necessary. Mauna Kea Beach off the Queen Kaahumanu Hwy., just past Hapuna Beach (phone: 882-7222). Expensive.

Donatello's – One of Hawaii's best Italian restaurants, the ambience is pure Mediterranean, the service impeccable. Unlike some restaurants where pretense outpaces results, just about everything tastes as good as it reads on the menu, which includes northern Italian specialties like perfectly tender *calamari fritti* as an appetizer, linguine *al pescatore* (a perfect mix of mussels, scallops, and clams) and other pasta, pizza (with artichokes or, perhaps, smoked *pancetta*), and entrées ranging from *saltimbocca* to *ossobuco alla milanese* (veal shanks braised with vegetables, white wine, and tomatoes). Open daily for dinner. Reservations necessary. In the Hyatt Regency Waikoloa (phone: 885-1234). Expensive.

Gallery – The food served supports the rave reviews it so frequently garners. The menu includes such entrées as chicken and shrimp stir fried with mint and chilies and served on taro leaves, or fresh scallops and black beans with garlic, ginger, and sake. The chef will also prepare the catch of the day in any style requested. Those with a less adventurous palate will find fine versions of more standard offerings, such as succulent, grilled lamb chops with a mango glaze. Dinner daily; reservations advised. At the Racquet Club of the Mauna Lani Bay Hotel (phone: 885-7777). Expensive.

Third Floor – Modeled on the popular Honolulu restaurant of the same name, it features some of the Big Island's best continental cuisine, with an emphasis on fresh seafood. High-back wicker chairs and strolling musicians give it a casual elegance. Dinner daily; reservations necessary. At the Mauna Lani Bay Hotel (phone: 885-6622). Expensive.

Eclipse – This restaurant doubles as a disco (open nightly 10 PM to 1:30 AM) and sports a neo-disco decor — a lot of chrome and colored lights that create a dappled effect while you dine. Considering the ambience, the food, mostly steak and seafood, is surprisingly good. The service is slow but friendly. Open for lunch weekdays, dinner daily. Reservations advised. Across from Foodland on Kuakini Hwy., Kailua-Kona (phone: 329-4686). Expensive to moderate.

Fisherman's Landing – Plenty was spent to make this large restaurant tropically elegant. The menu includes catch of the day specials, *paella,* and New Orleans-style blackened fish. Open daily for lunch and dinner. Reservations advised. In the Kona Inn Shopping Village (phone: 326-2555). Expensive to moderate.

Imari – Elaborately Japanese in style, the specialties include sukiyaki beef, shabu shabu chicken and beef, and *yosenabe* seafood, all cooked tableside, with *teppanyaki* and *kaiseki* dinners as well. An elegant place to go Oriental. Open daily, except Tuesdays, for dinner. Reservations necessary. In the Hyatt Regency Waikoloa (phone: 885-1234). Expensive to moderate.

Jameson's – The first neighbor-island branch of this popular Oahu eatery has taken over the old *Dorian's* and made a few changes in the menu and decor. Now the atmosphere is tropically casual, the furnishings contemporary rattan. Catch-of-the-day specialties are a good bet, but meat and poultry dishes are also on the menu. Open weekdays for lunch, daily except Sundays for dinner. Reservations advised. Alii Dr. at Magic Sands Beach, Kailua-Kona (phone: 329-3195). Expensive to moderate.

Kona Inn – This attractive open-air restaurant and bar boasts a decor dominated by beautifully carved koa wood and a fine vista of Kailua Bay through a silhouette of palms. The food's as tempting as the view, ranging from seafood to steaks to prime ribs. Open daily (lunch and dinner) to 1 AM. Reservations advised. Kona Inn Shopping Center (phone: 329-4455). Expensive to moderate.

Beach Club – The eclectic menu ranges from blackened fish "on a painted plate," artistically designed with three sauces (*beurre blanc,* raspberry, and pesto), to ancho chiles stuffed with goat cheese, to Cajun-style three-mushroom pasta. Should you be in the mood for something a bit less exotic, try the grilled fish. Whatever you choose, it's likely to be well prepared and presented. Open Tuesdays through Saturdays for dinner. Reservations advised. In Kona by the Sea condominiums, Alii Dr., Kailua-Kona (phone: 329-0290). Moderate.

Chart House – The newest addition of this island chain featuring a selection of fish, beef, and seafood entrées. Dinner daily; no reservations. On Alli Drive, in the Waterfront Row shopping complex, Kailua-Kona (phone: 329-2451). Moderate.

Kona Ranch House – There are two rooms here, of which the Lanai Room, with brass ceiling fans and white latticework, is by far the more elegant. Steaks, from island-reared cattle, and fish from local waters are faultless. Salads taste as fresh as they look, and the *Ranch House* serves what may be the best breakfast in Kona. Open daily from 6:30 AM to 9 PM. Reservations advised. At the intersection of Kuakini and Palani Hwys., Kailua-Kona (phone: 329-7061). Moderate.

Old Kailua Cantina – Tasty Mexican meals are served in surroundings that emphasize the sea: Dried starfish dot the stucco walls; vividly colored fish and coral glide and sway in a huge tank; and most tables offer a view of Kailua quay, just across the street. Oyster shots — raw oysters served with tequila and salsa in a shot glass — are one of the menu's more inventive touches. Open for lunch and dinner daily. Lunch reservations advised. Across from Kailua pier on Alii Dr., Kailua-Kona (phone: 329-0788). Moderate.

Phillip Paolo's – A neighbor-island branch of the popular Honolulu restaurant of the same name. The food is flavorfully Italian. Open daily for lunch and dinner. Waterfront Row, Alii Dr., Kailua-Kona (phone: 946-1163). Moderate.

Poo Ping Thai Cuisine – This may be the best Thai restaurant on the Big Island. The decor is sparse, the food spicy (though you can order milder versions of anything on the menu). Soups, curries, and noodle dishes are prepared using Thai vegetables and spices grown by the owners in the Kona garden. At the Kona Inn Shopping Center (phone: 329-2677). Moderate.

Pottery Steakhouse – Like its sister steak house in Honolulu, this is a place with a gimmick. Samples of the potter's art through the ages are displayed in the dining room. If it all sounds just a touch too cute for your palate, take heart: the steaks are juicy and cooked precisely to order — a rare phenomenon in this part of the world — and the concomitant specialty, mushrooms sautéed in wine sauce, is excellent. The menu also includes stir-fried seafood, and ribs. Open daily from 6 to 10 PM. Reservations advised. 75-5995 Kuakini Hwy., Kailua-Kona (phone: 329-2277). Moderate.

Quinn's – One of the few spots on the Big Island where it is possible to dine after 10 PM. (Dinner and sandwiches are served until 1 AM.) It is popular with the kind of crowd that favors singles bars. The main dining area is an outdoor patio where scallops, shrimp, and steaks are consumed by people who seem mostly to be repeat customers. Open daily for lunch and dinner. No reservations. Opposite the Hotel King Kamehameha on Alii Dr., Kailua-Kona (phone: 329-3822). Moderate.

Aloha Café – Located in the historic Aloha Theater, 8 miles south of Kona, this place is especially great for breakfast, serving Kona coffee, freshly prepared espresso, and cappuccino; coconut, papaya, and pineapple smoothies; and homemade banana muffins alongside the fine omelettes. Open daily. Hwy. 11, Kainaliu (phone: 322-3383). Inexpensive.

Ocean View Inn – If you were to canvass repeat visitors to Kailua about their favorite restaurant, odds are they would root for the *Ocean View*. It is large, noisy, and entirely devoid of decorative charm. Not the slightest effort has been made to exploit the view of the ocean and harbor just across the road. But it is always full, most of the time with people from the Kona and Kohala area who use it as a kind of eating club. The vast menu lists dishes of Hawaiian, Chinese, Japanese, and American persuasion with various mongrel combinations available. The cooking will never win any prizes, but on the other hand, it's hard to believe that anyone ever complains since portions are ample and the booze, by Hawaiian standards, is liberally poured. And for character and color, it merits an A plus. Closed Mondays. Right in the heart of Kailua on Alii Dr. (phone: 329-9998). Inexpensive.

Sibu – The setting is like a street café, the food tastefully Indonesian, with specialties like Balinese chicken (flavored with tarragon, garlic, and onions), satés, and curries. Wine and beer available. Lunch and dinner daily. No reservations. Under the large banyan by the seawall in Banyan Court shops (phone: 329-1112). Inexpensive.

Wurst Place – The place to head if it's after hours and you're hungry. Featured is a local menu with specialties like short ribs, pork chops, and mushroom chicken. Open until 3 AM most nights. No reservations. North Kona Shopping Center (phone: 329-1166). Inexpensive.

Hawaii Volcanoes National Park and Environs

Make no mistake about it, the goddess Pele is alive and well in Hawaii Volcanoes National Park, the most popular tourist attraction on the Big Island. The Kilauea Caldera, where she resides deep inside the Halemaumau Crater, erupted no less than 30 "major" times between January 1984 and December 1986, making Kilauea and Mauna Loa, the 13,680-foot-high "long mountain" farther up in the park (whose eruption in 1985 caused the evacuation of Hilo's western suburbs), the most active volcanoes in the world. Since records were begun 200 years ago, they have between them covered nearly

200,000 acres of land with lava, destroying trees, plants, animals, houses, and occasionally even people in the process. Generally, however, eruptions are not life threatening, and it is possible to predict with some accuracy where the lava will flow. Volcanic activity is monitored around the clock by seismographs at the Hawaii Volcanoes Observatory (call 967-7977 for eruption reports) on the western edge of the caldera, where visitors can watch them recording the minor tremors that take place each day — and the occasionally more violent tremors that indicate that Pele is restless. These safety precautions and easy accessibility have given Kilauea the nickname "the Drive-In Volcano," where people may come and watch glowing lava beside newsmen, photographers, volcanologists, geophysicists, geochemists, and geologists from around the world. Several years ago they might even have found themselves rubbing shoulders with the nation's most famous astronauts, who were brought here to give them a taste of the terrain they would face on the moon. At the recently opened Jaggar Museum (open 8:30 AM to 5 PM), adjacent to the new Hawaii Volcanoes Observatory on the rim of Halemaumau Crater, visitors can check seismic charting, speak with personnel, and learn a bit of the science of Hawaiian volcanology from displays. It is also possible to view the recently hardened lava that has been adding acreage to the Puna coast (and destroying dozens of homes in the process) since 1986, when flows began from the Kilauea East rift zone. Since then, thousands have hiked (illegally and against the advice of civil defense and park officials) the half-mile-plus distance from where lava covered Route 13 near Kalapana, to watch as molten lava flows into the sea. At press time, large sections of the newly formed coastline had begun to collapse into the sea, making these coastal hikes all the more dangerous. This ongoing eruptive series is the longest recorded in the 20th century.

Generally, however, there is no sun-red lava burgeoning from the earth's bowels, although the steam and sulfur hissing from vents inside the crater and on the surrounding mountain ridges hint at something more sinister. Certainly you sense that there is endless activity taking place beneath your feet and that the *terra* may not always be *firma*.

But steam vents and moonscape are not the whole story. The park is also a nature reserve of tropical black sand beaches, humid rain forests and fern jungles, temperate-zone acres of shrubs high up on Mauna Loa, and woods full of wild orchids, birds, and butterflies. A major delight for anyone examining the seemingly barren lava has to be the glimpse of exquisite amaumau and kupukupu ferns breaking through fissures as though determined to declare a perpetual springtime in the midst of the surrounding desolation.

The Wahaula Visitor Center, at the Kalapana entrance to the park (open from 8:30 AM to 5 PM), has brochures and leaflets and a museum of artifacts used by the ancient Hawaiians, with visual and sound tapes explaining their life and customs. At press time, ranger-led tours were departing from the center daily, except Saturdays, at 1 PM to visit the site of recent coastal volcanic activity. Until lava from several early 1987 eruptions blocked the road, the center provided a useful stopping-off point for travelers taking the coastal drive through Puna from Hilo on Route 13. Check with the visitor center for the status of this road. If the road is closed, a Hilo return requires a trip back up the Chain of Craters road to Park Headquarters.

The best place to get a compact and comprehensive picture of the park is the Kilauea Visitor Center (open from 7:45 AM to 5 PM; phone: 967-7311), where maps and books are available to show you the roads and trails around the park, and where there is a film each day, on the hour from 9 AM to 5 PM, explaining how volcanoes in general are formed and how they behave and showing footage of the eruptions that began in 1986 and which continue as we went to press.

Some terms used in the film and literature that you may wish to memorize are: *aa,* dark, cindery, rough lava; *caldera,* the open, depressed, bowl-like area at the summit of a volcano (Kilauea Caldera is one, Mokuaweoweo Caldera on top of Mauna Loa is another); *ejecta,* cinders and other matter thrown up during an eruption; *fumarole,* a vent emitting steam, sulfur, or other matter; *kipuka,* an island of soil and vegetation surrounded but untouched by lava; *olivine,* semiprecious chrysolite, greenish yellow in color, often found among cinder fallout; *pahoehoe,* smooth, shiny lava that covers the ground in thick folds, often resembling solidified molten lead; *volcanicity,* the underground volcanic makeup of a country or area.

The Kilauea Visitor Center is close to the *Volcano House* hotel (phone: 967-7321), where you will almost certainly want to make your headquarters, whether you are visiting just for one day or for several. Bring a jacket or sweater, since at these altitudes (*Volcano House* stands at 4,077 feet) the air can get chilly, and in the winter there is snow on the summit of Mauna Loa.

It is possible to get some idea of the volcanoes and their environment by taking the 11-mile drive around the Kilauea Caldera from *Volcano House* and back again. But only by exploring some of the trails on foot can you truly appreciate the area and its wonders. Aerial tours of the park, the East rift zone, and the lava flows are offered by *Volcano Helitours* (phone: 967-7578).

Chain of Craters Road – This 27-mile drive from the Wahaula Visitor Center to the Kilauea Visitor center was reopened in 1979; parts of it had been inundated by lava during a 1974 eruption. Stretches of the old paved road can still be seen between fingers of lava. The new road passes several pit craters dating from prehistoric times, as well as more recent *pahoehoe* lava fields, which sometimes seem to resemble deformed heads and bodies and have inspired comparisons with scenes from Dante's *Inferno.* Once providing coastal access back to Hilo via Keaau, Route 13 was covered in several places by a series of lava flows in 1986. The Wahaula Visitor Center remains open, and the site of the flow is a new visitor attraction, although through-traffic to Hilo was impossible at press time.

Crater Rim Drive – This road circles the Kilauea Crater in an 11-mile sweep from the Kilauea Visitor Center. It passes verdant rain forest, bleak desert, recent lava flows that gleam in the sun, and areas piled high with pumice from recent eruptions. The road is dotted with well-marked trails and parking areas overlooking significant parts of the park, among them, Kilauea Iki (Little Kilauea) Crater, Halemaumau Crater, and, from the Umekahune Bluff overlook, Kilauea Caldera from its northwest side.

Thurston Lava Tube – A drive of just under 4 miles from *Volcano House* brings you to this trail, ¼ mile long, through the most accessible lava tube on the Big Island. The tube was formed when the outer crust of a layer of flowing lava cooled while lava inside that was still molten continued to flow. Eventually the hot lava flowed right through the cool, leaving this tube-like crust, 450 yards long and from 10 to 20 feet high. All around the tube is the celebrated Fern Jungle, a humid wilderness of ohia trees surrounded by giant hapuu ferns and smaller ferns. Two native birds to look for in this neighborhood are the iiwi, a bright vermilion specimen with black wings and an orange-yellow beak, and the amakihi, identified by its blend of yellow and olive green plumage. They are often sighted among the brilliant red blossoms of the ohia, which provide them with a rich source of food. In midsummer, kahili ginger produces an almost overwhelming fragrance in the Fern Jungle.

Kipuka Puaulu – About 2 miles west of *Volcano House.* Take Route 11 west to Mauna Loa Strip Road; the park is a little way up the road on the right. A walk around the 1.1-mile loop of this enchanting *kipuka* illustrates vividly how an island of plants, birds, and insect life survives surrounded by hostile-looking petrified lava. The trail takes you through open meadows and forest studded with koa, ohia, mamani, soapberry, and kolea trees. Hawaiian raspberries, *akala,* grow in abundance along the trail. The wonderful birdlife this unusual ecosystem supports accounts for its English name, Bird Park. An extremely comprehensive exhibit at the *kipuka* entrance is worth examining.

Steam Vents and Sulfur Banks – A short, leisurely walk along the edge of Kilauea Caldera from *Volcano House* brings you to some billowing steam clouds caused by rainwater seeping into Kilauea's seething underground oven and bursting out through vents on the rim. Just a little way beyond are volcanic fumaroles emitting foul-smelling sulfur gases from the same nether regions. To reach it, you pass through a lovely forest of sandalwood, ohia lehua, and ferns.

Halemaumau Trail – The round-trip distance between *Volcano House* and the end of this trail is 6.8 miles. A steep climb down from the inn leads through dark gorges covered with vegetation into the bare, deserted Kilauea Caldera and across fresh lava flows to the Halemaumau overlook, where you can peer down into the mysterious realms where Pele dwells. If you want to walk one way and be deposited or picked up by car, there is a parking area close by on Crater Rim Road.

Devastation Trail – In 1959, an eruption in Kilauea Iki sent pumice, ash, and other ejecta shooting 1,900 feet into the air. An ohia forest on the same spot was almost completely buried. The few trees that remained were scarred and scattered and bleached by the sun. Here and there stubby bushes and brilliant yellow flowers have pushed their way through the debris, giving haphazard touches of color to this macabre landscape. A boardwalk .6 mile long crosses the area to prevent wear and tear on boots and shoes. The way to the trail is marked from Crater Rim Road and from Crater Rim Trail.

Puna – East of Hawaii Volcanoes National Park and south of Hilo, the Puna district is served by Route 13, which extends to Kalapana. The link to the Wahaula Visitor Center is now made only via the Chain of Craters Road. Check with the Park Visitor Center (967-7311) for information on road conditions and openings. In this area are acres of vanda orchid and anthurium farms, most of which are open to visitors. At Lava Tree State Park, on Route 132 just 2.7 miles southeast of Pahoa, you can witness the bizarre aftermath of a volcanic eruption that took place around 1790. At that time molten lava flowed through what was a dense forest of giant ferns and large ohia trees. The first waves of lava cooled and hardened around the base of the trees and plants while lava behind it built upon the first wave until there were as many as five layers. As molten lava drained away downhill or into holes in the ground, a series of grotesque pillars of petrified lava were left behind, some of them resembling unfinished tikis. Farther along Route 132 is a 420-foot-high cinder cone, the site of the village of Kapoho, which was inundated by *aa* lava in the eruption of 1960 (no lives were lost). At Kaimu, where Route 13 meets the coast, you will find the longest black sand beach on the island, lined with picture-postcard palm trees, the trunks of which are often lashed by the dangerous surf. A few miles farther along Route 13, at Kalapana, is one of the Big Island's famous painted churches, the Star of the Sea, which is decorated simply and charmingly with biblical scenes. Some 8½ miles beyond Wahaula on the same road, just before you come to the lava roadblock formed by the 1972 eruption, a sign indicates the Puuloa petroglyph field. From the parking area you can take a 15- to 20-minute stroll toward the beach along a dusty trail, at the end of which can be found some of the oldest petroglyphs in the islands, depicting man in a variety of pursuits, weapons, fish, and a wide range of seemingly abstract symbols.

The Kau District – On the southwest flank of the park lies Kau, a tranquil farm district whose roadsides are lined with weather-beaten rural houses surrounded by bougainvillea and eucalyptus trees. Traveling along Route 11 out of the park, you pass through fields of cattle-feeding grasses dotted here and there with yellow mamani trees and white *alahee,* a variety of coffee plant. At Punaluu there is another black sand beach. A few miles beyond Waiohinu is a left turn off Route 11, which leads to what the Hawaiians call Ka Lae (South Point). Here, at 18.58° north of the equator, is the southernmost tip of the US. This is also the site of some of the earliest Polynesian settlements (5th and 6th century) in Hawaii. For generations this has been a favorite fishing ground, even though the catch has to be hauled up over 50-foot cliffs. These are studded with the ancient iron rings used by fishermen for mooring their boats. A 3-mile hike east along the coast will bring you to Green Sand Beach, a strand formed of ground olivine particles. Just beyond the turnoff to South Point, Route 11 veers north through South Kona to Kailua.

Kau Desert – "There's no there there," Gertrude Stein is reported to have said about Oakland, California. And if the Hawaii that you seek is made up of white sands, palm trees, and women dancing the hula, then that might be your reaction to the Kau Desert, the area lying southwest of the Kilauea Caldera, between Route 11 and Chain of Craters Road. If, on the other hand, you are looking for one of the most unusual encounters with geography you are ever likely to experience, then it is here. The southwestern deserts of the mainland US, with their sparse grasses and cacti, seem a jungle compared to this. For acre upon acre there is nothing — *nothing* — but ropy, *pahoehoe* lava lying in folds, hot, shiny, and barren. Other areas consist simply of cinder parks of *aa* lava, where every step you take sends you walking through a calf-high cloud of dust. Astronaut Neil Armstrong walked here before setting foot on the moon to get some idea of the conditions he would face when he made one small step for mankind. On the desert's perimeters, between the smooth lava at its center and the shrub and grasslands that surround it, you will find Pele's hair, a thin golden substance, in the holes and fissures. Legend has it that when Pele was rampant, she would tear out her hair, scattering it to the winds, and that it would be caught in clefts and on trees. The geological version is more mundane. It states that this odd variety of natural glass is a by-product of drops of very liquid lava — known, to complicate the matter, as Pele's tears — ejected into the air. The tears take on a teardrop shape before solidifying, while the threadlike traces they leave in their wake cool quickly into hair-like strands. Something else that relieves the texture of the desert at its edges is the appearance of whitish lichen — "Hawaiian snow" — which is the first thing that will grow on new lava.

To the traveler newly arrived from Hilo, less than 40 miles away, where it rains on average more than 130 inches a year, this aridity is astonishing. Even more remarkable is the sight of low, dense clouds dissipating their moisture on the northeastern slope of the caldera so that *Volcano House,* visible from many parts of the desert, has 100 inches of rain a year, while where you stand barely 20 inches fall.

Just inside the park's western boundary and marked with a trail sign on Route 11 is one of the few phenomena in the desert involving man: One day in 1790 a bizarre eruption of gas and dust asphyxiated a band of warriors who were crossing the desert on their way to do battle with the troops of Kamehameha the Great. A brief and altogether freakish rainstorm followed the eruption, turning the dust into damp clay so that those warriors attempting to escape left footprints behind. Footprints Trail, just under a mile long, leads to the site of this scramble, where some of the prints can still be seen, encased under glass to preserve them. It is a reminder that it is not wise to fool with Pele.

 SHOPPING: Housed in the original *Volcano House,* the *Volcano Art Center* (phone: 967-7511) specializes in Hawaiian painting, sculpture, prints, and needlework. The artifacts available are among the finest in the islands. Bowls made from koa wood, quilts, watercolors, and oil paintings merit particular attention. In the *Kilauea Visitor Center* (phone: 967-7311) at the Hawaii Volcanoes National Park are posters, dramatic slides of the volcano in eruption, and a good selection of books concerning the park and its flora and fauna.

 NIGHTLIFE: *Uncle George's,* the *Volcano House* bar (phone: 967-7321), provides a place to relax. When Pele, the goddess of the volcano, is acting up in Halemaumau Crater, the view from *Uncle George's* can be spectacular.

 CHECKING IN: Perhaps because Hawaii Volcanoes National Park is so easily reached on a day trip from Hilo or Kona, accommodations are scarce. The three available places are usually heavily booked, and reservations are essential. *Volcano House* handles reservations for the park's cabins at Namakani Paio. These sleep four and cost $24 per night. Only one blanket is provided, which may leave you chilly. All telephone numbers are in the 808 area code unless otherwise indicated.

Volcano House – Although it is often mobbed by day with visitors using the bar and restaurant as a base for exploring the park, at night *Volcano House* takes on the air of a rustic lodge that in recent years has begun to look a bit worse for wear. A fire usually is kept burning in the large lobby fireplace, attracting occasional guests. *Uncle George's* bar provides another relaxing setting. Although none of the 37 rooms is large, they are all generally comfortably furnished and warm (it can be nippy up here at night). The view from the rooms overlooking the crater is memorable. There are no television sets and no swimming pool, but there is a sauna fed by steam vents from the volcano. Around $70 to $82 for a double. Advance reservations advised, particularly for crater-view rooms. Hawaii Volcanoes National Park (phone: 967-7321).

Kilauea Lodge – Located in Volcano Village, 1 mile from the Kilauea Visitor Center of Hawaii Volcanoes National Park, this large, rustic inn, built in 1938 as a YMCA retreat, is now a noteworthy bed-and-breakfast establishment. Each of the 4 rooms are spacious, decorated with flair, with its own theme and bath, fireplace, and view of the fern forest or garden. Priced at $65 per night, double, including a sizeable breakfast of Punaluu sweetbread French toast, pancakes, or eggs. Advance reservations are advised. PO Box 116, Volcano, HI 96785 (phone: 967-7366).

Colony One Condominium at Sea Mountain at Punaluu – Between the black sand and lava Kau coastline and sprawling ranchlands that climb up to Mauna Loa, this condominium complex of cottages is built, furnished, and decorated in a style that might aptly be described as rustic chic. There are tennis courts, a golf course, and a swimming pool, and the situation is ideal for those who like hiking or fishing (you won't run into many other people doing either). Daily maid service is by request and involves a surcharge; rates are based on a 2-night minimum stay. From $63 to $133 for a double. Just off Rte. 11 between Pahala and Naalehu at Punaluu; PO Box 70, Pahala, HI 98777 (phone: 928-8301; 800-367-8047, ext. 145).

EATING OUT: Dining is limited to five possibilities. In the moderate category, expect to pay $40 and up for a dinner for two and under $30 in inexpensive. Drinks and tips are not included. All telephone numbers are in the 808 area code unless otherwise indicated.

Black Sands – A typical range of steak and fish highlights the menu for both lunch and dinner daily. Open daily. Dinner reservations advised. A lagoonside setting and proximity to Punaluu Black Sand Beach provide appeal (phone: 928-8528). Moderate.

Kilauea Lodge – This is the place to head for dinner if you're near the national park between 5:30 and 9 PM. The dining room, with its commanding fireplace and rustic mood sets the tone. Seafood Mauna Kea and chicken Albert are among the specialties. Desserts, like ohelo berry or liliko'i chiffon pie, are something to appreciate. Closed Mondays. Reservations advised. Old Volcano Rd. (phone: 967-7366). Moderate.

Ka Ohelo Room – The *Volcano House* has a simple dining room, with tables set with warm, deep yellow linens and candles. Dinner is usually a bit more complex than the luncheon smorgasbord: The menu includes the usual Hawaiian chicken, and the prime ribs are quite good. There's also a very reasonably priced all-you-can-eat soup and salad bar special. Open daily, by reservation only. Last seating at 8:30 PM. Volcano House (phone: 967-7321). Moderate to inexpensive.

Sea Mountain Broiler – The resort's golf clubhouse serves breakfast and lunch daily, and dinner on an irregular basis (call for information). Reservations unnecessary. It's a good choice for a midday stop on a day trip between Hilo and Kona (phone: 928-6222). Moderate to inexpensive.

Volcano Store Diner – Breakfast starts the day at 8 AM, with snack-bar hamburgers and sandwiches plus lunch plate specials available until 4 PM. Open daily. On Old Volcano Hwy., attached to the Volcano Store (phone: 967-7707). Inexpensive.

MAUI

No one spends much time on Hawaii's second largest and third most populated island before discovering that its residents consider themselves tops in any contest. *Maui no ka oi,* the local saying goes — Maui is the best — and they can tick off some facts to prove it. Maui is the fastest-growing island in the Hawaiian chain. Its population has increased over the years to more than 85,000 and, after Oahu (Honolulu), it is the most popular tourist destination of all the neighbor islands, playing host to over 2 million visitors annually. This is the place where, only a few years ago, the well-to-do drew lots for the privilege of buying very special condominiums at prices starting at $200,000, and this is one of the places where the well-to-do want to be — Maui has more millionaires per capita than either Palm Springs or the French Riviera. Obviously, *Maui no ka oi* is no mere expression of diehard chauvinism. There must be something to it.

One answer is Maui's topography, which accounts for scenery so beautiful that the Polynesian demigod Maui — who is credited with having fished all of the Hawaiian islands up from the sea — is thought to have called this one home. Geologists have their own version of events, however. The 729-square-mile island is actually formed by two massive volcanoes. West Maui, with its 5,788-foot summit, Puu Kukui, was the first to form, and because of this, the West Maui mountains appear more deeply eroded and more rugged than East Maui, scarred with age and all but impassable. By comparison, the younger and larger land body of East Maui looks almost wrinkle-free from a distance, its broad-based height often camouflaged by a cover of cloud. But appearances are deceiving, because East Maui is the massive 10,023-foot volcano Haleakala, whose crater is the centerpiece of a national park. Haleakala is now dormant, but while it was still growing, enough lava washed down its slopes to back up at the base of West Maui and form a central isthmus, which joined the two. According to one explanation, Maui's sobriquet, the Valley Isle, comes from this central valley, which is now covered with fields of sugarcane bending in the wind.

Just where Maui chose to rise from the ocean floor also contributes to its beauty. Visitors to West Maui find the stunning presence of the West Maui mountains — their lower reaches swathed in more fields of bright or pale green sugarcane, their higher elevations twisting to gray-green peaks that lose themselves in smoky clouds — an unforgettable backdrop to their days. But the views in the other direction — of Molokai, Lanai, and Kahoolawe looming so close offshore at times, their medley of greens turned to blues that mimic the intervening sea — are equally heart-stopping images. Drive the length of Maui's western coasts from the top of West Maui, where ribbons of red dirt thread through neat, frosty green plantations of pineapple, to the end of the road on East Maui, and an island is almost always with you, the

next one gathering substance as the first one disappears. If the demigod Maui did fish them from the sea, it was only yesterday, because the colors are as fresh and clean as wet paint.

Other colors accent the basic blue-green scheme — frothy white on the crest of a wave and bleached gold in strips and scallops at the edge of the water; hot, tropical reds of anthuriums in a garden or of royal poincianas lining a driveway; the pink, yellow, and white of plumeria. Sometimes the accents are surprising, as when the air cools upcountry on the slopes of Haleakala and the fields of pineapple and sugarcane give way to flower farms of carnations and protea. Higher up, in the crater, the colors are ashen and muddy, at most streaked with red and yellow mineral tints and dotted here and there with the metallic leaves of the silversword plant. It is not at all unusual to see a rainbow on Maui, as though Mother Nature were keeping the palette always close at hand.

That all of these beauties still exist on the most developed of the neighbor islands is because development has come only very recently to Maui, most of it in an environmentally conscious age. It could have been otherwise. Maui was the island "between" during the 18th century, its chiefs at war nearly constantly with those of the Big Island and of Oahu for hegemony over the entire inhabited chain. In the end, the Big Island chief Kamehameha emerged the victor after defeating his last significant rival, Maui's chief Kahekili, in a decisive and exceedingly bloody battle in the Iao Valley in 1790. (The pivotal event in this valley, which reaches into the center of West Maui's volcano, is for some the true reason Maui is known as the Valley Isle.) Kamehameha then began to transform the west coast village of Lahaina — up to that point the playground of Maui's *alii* (high chiefs) — into a political center of his united Hawaiian kingdom. Though he himself spent little time here, his "favorite" wife, Queen Kaahumanu, and his "sacred" wife, Queen Keopuolani, did make Lahaina their base, and his sons and successors, Kamehameha II and Kamehameha III, carried on much of the government here. Fortunately for the fate of Maui, the latter transferred the government to Honolulu during the 1840s.

Lahaina, nevertheless, had been transformed into something else in the meantime: a provisioning station for America's Pacific whaling fleet. From the 1820s through the 1860s, Lahaina Roads was crowded with whaleships riding at anchor, and the Lahaina waterfront was crawling with seamen aflame with liquor and lust and living by the dictum "No God west of the Horn." Lahaina's newly arrived Protestant missionaries struggled to prove otherwise and met with reasonable success. The problem of debauchery shrank to manageable proportions with the end of whaling; the Hawaiian Royal Family converted not only to Christianity but also to the alien idea of democracy, and the missionaries themselves, having come to do right, as the saying goes in Hawaii, "did right well" — especially in temporal matters.

The sons of the missionaries were prominent in Maui's next economic phase, which belonged to agriculture and primarily to sugar. Two in particular, Henry P. Baldwin and Samuel T. Alexander, founded a dynasty on sugar, and today Alexander & Baldwin Inc. is one of Hawaii's Big Five companies, the largest private owner of land on Maui, and its subsidiary Hawaiian Commercial and Sugar Company — whose cane fields cover the central valley — is the largest sugar plantation in the state. Sugar, as well as the growth of the pineapple industry and cattle ranching, provoked a drastic change in the makeup of Maui's population. More labor was needed than the island's declining indigenous population could provide, so during the last quarter of the 19th century, Chinese, Japanese, and Portuguese workers were brought in, followed by great numbers of Filipinos in the 20th century. Along with the native Hawaiians and the early New Englanders, all of these ethnic groups are honored in a tribute to the island's melting pot, the Kepaniwai Park and Heritage Gardens in the Iao Valley.

Maui's resort boom began over 2 decades ago when Amfac, the biggest of the Big Five, opened the first of the super developments, the Kaanapali resort, on the coast of West Maui a few miles above Lahaina. Hotels, condominiums, and facilities for every conceivable kind of vacation activity materialized on land that was (and still is) bordered by photogenic cane fields that had been only marginally productive. With the 1970s came two more planned resorts: Kapalua, surrounded by the pineapple fields of the Maui Land and Pineapple Company on the northwest corner of West Maui, and Wailea, an Alexander and Baldwin project that turned a wasteland of kiawe trees on the coast of East Maui golf-course green. The Makena resort, adjacent to Wailea, followed in the 1980s. Condominiums have sprung up along the coast of Kihei, northwest of Wailea, and also along the coast north of Kaanapali, through Honokowai and Kahana to Napili. And old Lahaina, whose population has doubled since 1980, is in its third incarnation as the island's major tourist attraction. Royal Hawaii is nearly a century past, and the only whaleboats nowadays are the ones filled with tourists out for a closer look at the humpbacks who make the waters off Maui their winter home.

Tourism now employs more than 50% of Maui's wage earners, few of whom could afford to buy a prime coastal condominium, but most of whom still greet visitors with the authentic welcome that demonstrates the spirit of aloha is still alive. Some deplore the changes of the last 20 years and point to old Hawaii as it once existed — and still endures in the quiet East Maui ranching district of Hana, practically devoid of tourist facilities and reachable only by determined driving along the most taxing paved road on the island. But most visitors will probably conclude that, with few exceptions, Maui has been successful at placing topnotch accommodations in settings that remain sublime, a mix that can provide such unforgettable experiences as a Valley Isle sunset witnessed in the privacy and comfort of one's own ocean-view lanai. As white clouds with silver linings turn to gray clouds outlined in pink, becoming formations as palpable as the neighboring islands in the sea, and as the ripples on the slate surface of the water shimmer behind the profiles of palm trees, you, too, may agree that *Maui no ka oi* — Maui is the best.

SOURCES AND RESOURCES

TOURIST INFORMATION: The first source of information most visitors encounter is the attendant at the State Visitor Information kiosk (phone: 877-6431) in Kahului Airport. Run by the State Department of Transportation and stocked with brochures on activities, sights, and hotel and condominium accommodations, the kiosk is open daily from 6 AM to 9 PM. A bit farther off the path beaten by newly arrived travelers is the Maui Visitors Bureau, which functions as a branch of the Hawaii Visitors Bureau. The office (380 Dairy Rd., Kahului) is open from 8 AM to 4:30 PM, Mondays through Fridays (usually closed for lunch from noon to 1 PM). Prospective visitors who need help with particularly problematical requests would do best to write ahead (mailing address: PO Box 1738, Kahului, Maui, HI 96732), but those on the spot are welcome to call (phone: 871-8691) or to drop in for assistance and brochures on everything from car rentals to windsurfing.

Bed & Breakfast Hawaii, PO Box 449, Kapaa, HI 96746 (phone: 822-7771; 800-367-8047, ext. 339), provides information about bed-and-breakfast establishments on Maui and the other Hawaiian islands. Individual bed-and-breakfast lodging reservations are also taken by Jody Baldwin, who operates a lovingly restored 60-year-old home called *Kilohana* in upcountry Kula (378 Kamehameiki Rd., Kula, Maui, HI 96790; phone: 878-6086). Natalie Powell runs an establishment that serves a full breakfast in rural Ulumalu (455 Kapuai Rd., Haiku, Maui, HI 96708; phone: 572-7692), and Denise Champion operates *Haikuleana,* near Hookipa, a top windsurfing spot (69 Haiku Rd., Haiku, Maui, HI 96708; phone: 575-2890).

To check out just about anything that's bookable on Maui, drop by Tom Barefoot's *Cashback Tours* (626 Front St., Lahaina; phone: 661-8889). Tom has created an informative circular file system that helps visitors make educated choices from among helicopter tours, snorkeling trips, and other, more offbeat, excursions. All reservations earn a 10% discount off published rates.

Local Coverage – The local newspaper, the *Maui News* (25¢), is published weekdays. It's the place to find out what Maui is really talking about — local news, sports, weather, plus the tally of births, deaths, marriages, divorces, and building permits.

The island is also well supplied with free publications written with the tourist in mind. These can be found at the airport, in hotel and condominium lobbies, at shopping centers, on car rental counters, and anywhere else the distributor suspects the wandering eye of the tourist might alight. Two of the most prominent are *This Week Maui,* which comes out on Fridays, and the weekly *Guide to Maui,* published on Thursdays. All of them contain maps, tips on sightseeing, shopping, dining, and entertainment, and a number of coupons for discounts on goods and services. Similarly, the *Maui Drive Guide,* revised four times a year and distributed free to anyone who rents a car on the island, contains most of the above information along with more specific maps and instructions for drivers. Many hotels also distribute informative pocket-sized *Beach Guides* on Kaanapali, Lahaina, and Wailea-Kihei.

For guidebooks, picture books, books on Hawaiian flora and fauna, crafts, food, history, legend, and the language, consult the Hawaiiana sections of the island's bookstores. *Upstart Crow & Co.,* in Lahaina's The Wharf shopping center, and branches of *Waldenbooks* at the Whalers Village shopping complex in the Kaanapali resort and at Kaahumanu Center in Kahului have broad selections. Robert Wenkam's lusciously illustrated coffee table book *Maui No Ka Oi* (Rand McNally; $29.95) can be bought here. The text deals with Maui and the other islands of Maui County — Molokai, Lanai, and Kahoolawe — and combines history, anecdote, and personal observation by someone who has been writing about Maui for 40 years. Another coffee table offering well worth considering is Rita Ariyoshi's profusely illustrated, award-winning *Maui On My Mind.*

Telephone – The area code for Hawaii is 808.

GETTING AROUND: Maui has very little in the way of public transportation, so you will have to arrange wheels, wings, or something waterborne yourself. If you arrive on the island by air, you'll land at one of Maui's three commercial airports. Kahului Airport (phone: 877-0078) is the main airfield, the only one that can accommodate a commercial jet. It is served by Aloha Airlines, Hawaiian Air, Aloha IslandAir (a sister company to Aloha Airlines), and Air Molokai. Aloha IslandAir uses the commuter terminal at the Diamond Head end of the international terminal; Air Molokai flies from its own small terminal off Lagoon Drive. Both fly smaller planes that provide good flightseeing opportunities en route. American, Delta, Hawaiian, and United also fly to Maui from the mainland. Aloha IslandAir and Hawaiian Air serve Kapalua/West Maui Airport (phone: 669-4866), located between the Kapalua and Kaanapali resorts. For those bound for either resort or for Kahana or Napili, this airport provides a logical — not to mention beautiful — alternative to often-overcrowded Kahului. Hana Airport (phone: 248-8208), a tiny terminal outside Hana in East Maui, is served by Aloha IslandAir.

Bus – The *Gray Line Airporter* (phone: 877-5507 for reservations) provides service between Kahului Airport and Lahaina, and Kaanapali. The fare is $8.30 per person between Kahului and Lahaina or Kaanapali. *Trans Hawaiian Services* (phone: 877-7308) runs shuttles from the airport to Lahaina and Kaanapali daily from 8:30 AM to 6 PM. The one-way fare is $9 and reservations are required. The Kaanapali Trolley, looking like an old-fashioned, green, two-car trolley, runs through the Kaanapali resort daily from 7 AM to 11 PM, making stops at hotels, condominiums, the Whalers Village shopping complex, the golf clubhouse, and the Kaanapali station of the Lahaina-Kaanapali and Pacific Railroad. From 9 AM to 5 PM, the trolley offers free links between the resort and Lahaina. In addition, the trolley meets flights into and out of the Kapalua/West Maui Airport. In the Wailea resort area, the complimentary Wailea shuttle links hotels, condominiums, the shopping village, and sports facilities, making the rounds every 15 to 20 minutes from 6:45 AM to 10 PM. Kapalua's shuttle does not have a regular schedule, but is on call between 6 AM and midnight and upon request provides free transportation between hotels and the Kapalua/West Maui Airport.

Taxi – One of Maui's several cab companies, *Mita, Inc.* (phone: 871-4622), is conveniently stationed at Kahului Airport. If your hotel is not taking care of your transfer from the airport and if you are not renting a car, expect the fare from Kahului to a Lahaina or Kaanapali hotel to be about $35 to $40 per car (up to six people) and to an address in Kihei, Wailea, or Makena to be between $15 and $25. Once you've settled in, either consult the phone book or have your hotel call you a cab. Most taxi companies provide private sightseeing tours as well as regular service.

Car Rental – The rental counters of almost a dozen companies are in a line just outside the terminal of Kahului Airport. These include large national companies such as *Alamo* (phone: 871-6235), *Avis* (phone: 871-7575), *Budget* (phone: 871-8811), *Hertz* (phone: 877-5167), and *National* (phone: 871-8851); statewide or regional companies such as *Dollar Rent-A-Car* (phone: 877-5578), *Rainbow Rent-A-Car* (phone: 661-8734), and *Tropical Rent-A-Car* (phone: 877-0002); plus some smaller companies such as *Andres* (phone: 877-5378), *Sunshine* (phone: 871-6222), and *Trans-Maui* (phone: 877-2611). Bargain basement companies — *Klunker's* (phone: 877-3197) and *Word of Mouth Rent-A-Used-Car* (phone: 877-2436), for instance — cluster in the Dairy Road–Puunene Avenue area. Still more names can be found in Lahaina and Kihei. Several companies also have rental booths at Kapalua/West Maui Airport, or they will pick up customers at the airport for a short transfer to rental outlets. These include *Avis* (phone: 661-4588), *Budget* (phone: 661-8721), *Dollar* (phone: 667-2651), *Hertz* (phone: 661-3195), *Sunrise* (phone: 661-5646), and *Tropical* (phone: 661-0061). During the peak winter and summer seasons, cars may be in short supply, so it is advisable to make a reservation. During the rest of the year, special rates are often offered on a day-to-day availability basis. Hana Airport rentals are available through *Dollar* (phone: 248-8237) at the *Hana-Maui* hotel (phone: 248-8211). In fact, most hotels and many condos on Maui have car rental desks in their lobbies for those who decide, after arrival, that they would like to have a car. (For the toll-free numbers of many of the above car rental firms, see *Touring by Car,* GETTING READY TO GO).

With the exception of portions of the Hana Highway, a tourist attraction in itself, the roads that most visitors will encounter on Maui are well paved. The island map in the *Maui Drive Guide* (free to anyone renting a car) shows those that are not and are, therefore, off limits to rental car drivers. Though native drivers have been known to kick up the dust along these stretches in almost anything that moves, visitors should negotiate them only in a four-wheel-drive vehicle, available from *Adventure Unlimited Jeep* (phone: 877-6626), as well as from *Budget* and *Hertz.* Again, reserve well in advance, and be sure that the vehicle you get is indeed of the four-wheel-drive variety rather than two-wheel.

Bicycle Rental – *Go-Go Bikes Hawaii,* 30B Halawai Dr., #5, Lahaina (phone: 661-3063), rents bicycles and mopeds by the hour, day, or week. Pickup and delivery service applies to West Maui only, and at the full rate (although seasonal discounts may be available); a credit card or $100 in cash is required as a security deposit, and reservations are advisable. A paved bike path leads from Lahaina to the Kaanapali resort and on to Kapalua, but other parts of the island can present difficulties. High-speed winds in the central valley, for instance, make the going exceedingly rough for bikers.

 SIGHTSEEING TOURS: Bus or Van – Nearly all hotels and many condominiums have tour desks that will book guests on escorted sightseeing tours around the island. In case yours doesn't, contact one of the major tour companies — *Gray Line Maui* (phone: 877-5507), *Robert's Hawaii Tours* (phone: 871-6226), *Trans Hawaiian Maui* (phone: 877-7308), or *Akamai Tours* (phone: 871-9551) — and count on spending anywhere from $20 to $50 per person for a 5- to 10-hour outing, which may or may not include meals. Standard half-day and full-day itineraries visit Kula, Haleakala Crater, Wailuku, Iao Valley, and Lahaina in various combinations, whereas the drive to Hana is always a full day in length. *Akamai*'s 15-passenger van specials include a daily Sunrise at Haleakala trip, which starts with a hotel or condo pickup in the wee morning hours. Another worthwhile option is their off-the-beaten-path circuit of the West Maui Mountains. *Trans Hawaiian* features a full-day tour of Hana in 11- or 14-passenger vans. Their Haleakala Sunrise offers a light breakfast at the summit.

Helicopter/Plane – This is hardly inexpensive but it's the only way to penetrate many of the valleys of the Valley Isle to see them in all their otherwise hidden splendor. The most popular rides fly through Haleakala Crater, out to Hana, and over the Seven Pools in East Maui, or along the West Maui coast and beyond the barrier of the West Maui mountains. Costs for a 20-minute to 1½-hour flight range anywhere from $85 to $325 per person. *Maui Helicopters* (phone: 879-1601) has three itineraries taking off from Kahului, and its Panoramic Journey, which takes in Haleakala, Hana, and the Seven Pools, is particularly popular at $135 for 55 minutes aloft. Maui's largest helicopter-tour company, *Papillon Helicopters* (phone: 669-4884), operates a variety of tours departing from a heliport near Kapalua and Kahului Airport. *Papillon*'s 2-hour Haleakala Sunrise tour includes a continental breakfast stop in Hana ($220); its hour-long Sunset tour features the north coast of Molokai and the mountains of West Maui ($180). Papillon also offers All-Day Hana, an excursion that includes lunch at the *Hana Ranch* and 5 hours with a rental Jeep for $325. *Kihele Maui Tours* (phone: 871-2555) offers aerial day tours to the Big Island aboard a 10-passenger Beechcraft. Tours include volcano-watching itineraries with narrated ground segments from $129 to $149. *Sunshine Helicopter* (phone: 871-0722) leaves from Kahului Airport for West Maui tours at $49 (20 minutes) and $75 (30 minutes), East Maui tours to Hana for $99 (45 minutes), and an hour-long tour that includes Haleakala Crater, verdant Kipahulu

Valley, and the Kaupo Gap ($135). *Kihele Maui Tours* (phone: 871-2555) offers 2- to 2½-hour flightseeing tours that depart Kahului Airport for the Big Island's volcanoes. Cost is $129; an additional $20 gets you a ground tour.

Boat – Non-snorkelers can get a firsthand look at the fascinating underwater world through the viewing ports of the glass-bottom boat *Lin Wa* (phone: 661-3392). Done up to resemble a Chinese junk, the *Lin Wa* cruises out of Lahaina five times daily, offering those aboard a chance to view plenty of coral. If the fish are shy, a scuba diver bearing edible gifts coaxes them into the range of vision.

Cruises to the neighboring islands of Lanai or Molokai or both — usually costing about $60 to $90 per person for a full day out — are among the many other popular seagoing excursions from Lahaina Harbor. The Coon family of *Trilogy Excursion* (phone: 661-4743) sails to Lanai, Mondays through Fridays year-round, taking up to 40 people on the 50-foot *Trilogy,* the 55-foot catamaran *Trilogy II,* and the 55-foot *Trilogy III* for $110 per person. Breakfast is served; then there's time for fishing, snorkeling, swimming, a barbecue at Manele Bay, and a 1½-hour van tour of the island before returning to Lahaina in the late afternoon. *Aloha Voyages* (phone: 667-6284) heads to Lanai on Mondays, Wednesdays, and Fridays aboard the 85-foot, 49-passenger schooner *Machias* on a 6-hour sail that includes a continental breakfast and a barbecue lunch ($50). On Tuesdays, Thursdays, and Saturdays, the *Machias* goes to Molokai for a full day that includes snorkeling, a glass-bottom boat tour, kayaking, windsurfing, and a van tour ($80). *Captain Zodiac* (phone: 667-5351) sails to Lanai aboard 14- and 15-passenger motorized rafts on half- ($50) and full-day ($90) tours. Both itineraries include snorkeling; full-day itineraries circle the island and land for lunch. *Ocean Activities Center* (phone: 879-4485) departs Lahaina for Lanai on half- ($55) and full-day ($85) snorkeling excursions aboard the *Manutea*. Full-day sails feature a land tour and lunch at the *Lanai* hotel. *Genesis Charters* (phone: 667-5667) will customize an inter-island itinerary for up to six passengers aboard the 48-foot sailing ketch *Genesis* or the 38-foot sloop *Mareva*. Overnight charters (priced at $600 per day for two, $700 for three or four, with a maximum of six passengers) are another option. These and other sails from Maui can also be booked through *Aloha Activity Center* at the Whalers Village, Kaanapali (phone: 667-9564), or *Maui 800* in Kahului (phone: 877-2748; 800-367-5224). *Maui Kayaks* (phone: 874-3536) offers escorted half- and full-day kayak tours along the Maui coast. Snorkeling gear is provided.

Another operator, *Club Lanai* (phone: 871-1144) offers a full-day excursion to Lanai aboard one of its two catamarans. The $70 fee covers the sail, a barbecue buffet with open bar, snorkeling, windsurfing, kayaking, and volleyball at the 8-acre beachfront retreat, which also provides plenty of deserted beach for wandering. Catamarans also depart Lahaina Tuesdays through Saturdays for a Stardust Dinner Cruise from 6 to 8 PM ($50), and a Night Club Cruise with open bar from 9 to 11 PM ($20).

The object of the snorkel sail is not to tour the neighbor islands but to see their glorious coastlines — and Maui's — from the water, explore the underlying coral reefs, and swim, sun, or simply enjoy the sail itself. The price tag can begin at $25 per person for 2 hours adrift and go up as high as $80 or $90 for a full day of sailing with a picnic lunch included. Sunset cruises, generally about 2 hours long, average $20 to $35 depending on whether the sun goes down to a cocktail toast alone or is memorialized with a full dinner. The 36-foot sloop *Scotch Mist* and 50-foot *Scotch Mist II* carry, respectively, 6 and 19 passengers on half-day snorkel sails and sunset sails from Lahaina Harbor (phone: 661-0386). A number of skippers do one or the other type of cruise aboard smaller boats taking no more than six people at a time. Among these boats are the 58-foot *Seasmoke* which sails from Kaanapali Beach (phone *Captain Nemo's:* 661-5555), and the *Pardner* (phone: 661-3448) and *Alihilani Yacht Charters'* *Makani Wiki* (phone: 661-3047), both sailing out of Lahaina Harbor. Farther up the coast, at Kaanapali, *Sea Sails* (phone: 661-0927) departs from its beach shacks at the *Sheraton*

Maui, the *Royal Lahaina,* the *Westin Maui,* the *Kaanapali Beach* hotels, and the *Kaanapali Shores* and *Sands of Kahana* condominiums for picnic/snorkel sails to Honolua Bay and sunset cocktail sails. In addition, the *Hyatt Regency* (phone: 667-7474) has its own catamaran, the *Kiele V,* and offers snorkel as well as sunset cocktail sails. Catamarans also depart from the beach at the *Kapalua Bay* hotel (phone: 669-5656) on picnic and sunset cocktail sails.

The Kihei-Wailea coast of East Maui doesn't offer quite the number or variety of cruises for visitors as the West Maui coast, but some eye-filling adventures are possible here, too. The crescent-shaped volcanic islet of Molokini, lying offshore between Maui and the island of Kahoolawe, is a marine conservation district famed for clear waters and a multitude of fish and corals, and is a favorite destination of picnic and snorkel sails. The *Maui Sailing Center* (phone: 879-5935) has two snorkel sails daily to Molokini aboard boats departing from Maalaea Harbor. The *Pacific Whale Foundation* (phone: 879-8811) can take up to 30 passengers aboard the 40-foot cruiser *Sea Sport,* which makes a daily half-day Molokini snorkel trip from Maalaea Harbor. The *Sea Sport* also departs Lahaina on half-day Reef Adventures, continental breakfast served and snorkel gear provided. The *Ocean Activities Center* (phone: 879-4485) — with a store at the Wailea Shopping Village and offices at the Cannery in Lahaina, the Kamaole Shopping Center, the *Mana Kai Maui,* the *Stouffer Wailea Beach Resort,* and the *Inter-Continental Maui* hotels — operates the 65-foot catamarans *Wailea Kai* and *Maka Kai,* which can take 75 to 100 passengers on half-day picnic and snorkel sails departing daily from Maalaea Harbor. (The *Wailea Kai* takes snorkelers on its Molokini sails; for more on snorkel/scuba trips, see *Sports.*) Sunset cocktail cruises are also popular on this coast; the *Wailea Kai* does one out of Maalaea Harbor, and so do others. The *Maui Prince* hotel (phone: 874-1111) operates a half-day catamaran sail to Molokini that features on-board continental breakfast, lunch, and an open bar.

Most of the above excursions are offered year-round, but in the winter a new twist appears. From December through April, many a picnic/snorkel sail turns into a whale watch — in fact, it almost seems, during this time, that a cruise by any other name does not exist. The most informative whale watch by far is the 2½-hour benefit cruise ($25) sponsored by the *Pacific Whale Foundation* (Kealia Beach Plaza, 101 N. Kihei Rd., Suite 25, Kihei, Maui, HI 96753; phone: 879-8811), a nonprofit research, conservation, and education organization. Conducted by foundation experts aboard *Whale One,* a 53-foot power cruiser, it departs Maalaea harbor daily during the season (tickets are available through the *PWF* and other vendors). The *Pacific Whale Foundation* also departs Slip II in Lahaina Harbor for whale watching cruises as well as a daily sunset cruise. If missed, the only recourse is to watch for the whale lecture on your hotel's activities board (*PWF* lecturers make the rounds of Maui hotels and some condominiums, appearing in major ones regularly) and then take a commercial whale watching cruise. Though not specialists in whale lore, *Seabird Cruises* (phone: 661-3643), *Windjammer Cruises* (phone: 667-6834), *Scotch Mist* (phone: 661-0386), and others also do whale watches. The cruises depart from Lahaina (not necessarily every day), take 2½ hours, and cost $20 to $25 for adults (children, half price). The *Ocean Activities Center* (phone: 879-4485) and *Kihei Sea Sports,* in the Kihei Town Center (phone: 879-1919) and at Rainbow Mall (phone: 879-4188), do whale watches out of Maalaea Harbor.

Train – The *Lahaina-Kaanapali and Pacific Railroad* (phone: 661-0089; 800-367-4753) operates the Sugarcane Train between Lahaina and Kaanapali six times daily. Round trip is 12 miles and takes about an hour; fare is $7.50 for adults, $4.50 one way (half price for children). Various excursions can be purchased together with the train ride (see *Kaanapali to Kapalua*).

SPECIAL EVENTS: During February and March, the *Maui Marine Art Expo,* at the *Inter-Continental Wailea,* presents the work of numerous prominent artists in a variety of media, all with a marine theme. Runners may watch or participate in the *Maui Marathon,* which begins in Wailuku and ends in Lahaina, and is usually scheduled for early March. In late March the *Miss Maui Pageant* is sponsored by the Jaycees in the *Baldwin Auditorium,* Wailuku. The *Marui–O'Neil Invitational Windsurfing Competition* takes place at Hookipa Park in early April; the Sunday on or before May Day is the date for an island-wide lei competition at the *Inter-Continental.* On June 11, Maui participates in the statewide celebration of *King Kamehameha Day* with a parade of floats and marching bands in either Lahaina or Kahului. *Paniolos* (Hawaiian cowboys) compete at calf-roping, bronco-busting, and steer-wrestling in an old-fashioned *Rodeo* held at *Oskie Rice Arena* in the upcountry town of Makawao over July Fourth. In mid-July, the Jaycees sponsor their *Carnival* at the *Kahului Fairgrounds;* and in August runners compete in the new *Run-to-the-Sun Marathon,* an exhausting 37½-mile race from Kanaha Beach Park to the summit of Haleakala. *Aloha Week* — that statewide festival of parades, pageants, luaus, dances, crafts demonstrations, canoe races, and sports competitions — takes place in Maui during September or October. The *County Fair,* held in October at the *Kahului Fairgrounds,* has the standard flower and produce displays, arts and crafts exhibits, and livestock shows. Late October–early November sees the *Aloha Classic Windsurfing Championships* at Hookipa Park, as well as fishermen from all across the islands participating in the *Annual Lahaina Jackpot Fishing Tournament,* headquartered in Lahaina's historic waterfront hostelry, the *Pioneer Inn,* offering a tempting purse for the heaviest marlin. Lahaina takes *Halloween* very seriously — expect shop clerks, waiters, and waitresses to be wearing something outlandish. And Kaanapali is the center of Maui's own festival, *Na Mele O Maui,* a potpourri of Hawaiian arts and crafts, music, and dance, and the high point of early November. The PGA-coordinated *Isuzu Kapalua International,* in November, is a highlight of Maui's annual series of golf tournaments. And November or December sees the *Michelob Polo Competition* at Makawao.

SPORTS: Since sunshine, sand, and the sea lure most visitors to this as well as to the other islands, it's only natural that much of Maui's active sports life takes place on the shore and in the water. Tennis is also a big draw, and golf courses actually preceded many of the major resort hotels. The following is a rundown of these and other possibilities.

Bicycling – The 38-mile road that winds its way from the 10,023-foot summit of Haleakala to the coast (at Paia) provides cyclists with a half-day escorted excursion. Three firms operate bicycle tours on fully equipped mountain bikes that take the downhill momentum without speeding out of control, which makes the tours a suitable option for just about anyone comfortable on a bicycle. *Pacific Island Cruisers* (505 Front St., Lahaina; phone "Cruiser Bob" at 667-7727) offers a sunrise ride that includes champagne and a midday run for $89; *Maui Mountain Cruisers* (542 Keolani Pl., Kahului; phone: 572-0195) and *Maui Downhill* (333 Dairy Rd., Kahului; phone: 661-8889) charge $79 and $84, respectively. Hotel or condo pickup is included, as is continental breakfast.

Boating – The vast majority of boats bobbing up and down in Lahaina Harbor and elsewhere around Maui are dedicated to picnic/snorkel sails, sunset cocktail trips, sightseeing cruises, whale watching expeditions, and other seagoing excursions in which you'll be a passenger. These are discussed in *Sightseeing Tours (By Boat).* Due to insurance difficulties, there are no longer any bareboat charters in Hawaii. But *Seabern Yachts,* PO Box 1022, Lahaina, Maui, HI 96761 (phone: 661-8110), at Berth 64 in

Lahaina Harbor, has two sailboats that can be rented, either on a sharing basis or for private, skippered charters by the hour, half day, full day, or week. Each boat measures 42 feet, and charters range from $40 per hour to $250 for a half day, and run $450 for a full day. The most popular 7-day route goes up the West Maui coast, crossing the Pailolo Channel to Kaunakakai on the south coast of Molokai, to Manele Harbor on Lanai, and then back to Maui. Sailing lessons can be provided en route.

The *Maui Sailing Center,* Kealia Beach Village, 101 N. Kihei Rd. (phone: 879-5935), has boat rentals on Maalaea Bay. The center monitors its sailors, requiring them to stay in a designated sailing area on the bay, never more than 2 miles from shore, and it has a chase boat for emergencies.

Most hotels have a catamaran or two for rent. In the Kaanapali resort, *Sea Sails* (phone: 661-0927), which operates water sports desks at the *Sheraton Maui,* the *Royal Lahaina,* the *Westin Maui,* and the *Kaanapali Beach* hotels and at the *Sands* and *Kaanapali Shores* condominium, rent Hobie Cats at $30 for the first hour and $20 per hour thereafter, with lessons available for $10. The *Maui Marriott* (phone: 667-1200) rents an 18-foot, 2- to 3-passenger (plus captain) Prindle for $40 an hour, and the *Hyatt Regency* (phone: 667-7474) rents 16-foot Hobie Cats for $45 an hour.

Camping and Hiking – While Maui has numerous hiking trails of varying degrees of difficulty — among them, those at Honokowai Valley, Iao Valley, Kanaha Pond Wildlife Sanctuary, Keanae Arboretum, La Perouse Bay, Polipoli Springs State Park, Waikamoi Ridge, Waimoku Falls, and Waianapanapa State Park — the trails that lead into the floor of Haleakala crater, the island's dormant volcano, are unmatched in beauty and solitude. For overnighters there are three cabins and two campgrounds within the crater and another campground just inside the park entrance. More detailed descriptions of the two major trails into the crater, Halemauu and Sliding Sands, are given in the section of this chapter entitled *Haleakala National Park.*

Ken Schmidt of *Hike Maui* (PO Box 330969, Kahului, Maui, HI 96733; phone: 879-5270), guides a variety of day and overnight hikes to Maui's most scenic and interesting locales. Schmidt is well versed in Hawaiian flora, fauna, geology, and history, and his trips emphasize how best to relate to the environment. Day rates range from $50 to $90 and include lunch; overnight rates are $300 each for the first two people signed up for the hike, $100 for each person thereafter, include camping gear and meals. Groups are limited to six.

Fishing – The islands of Maui, Lanai, and Kahoolawe form a triangle that is brimful of fish waiting to be caught, though they'll put up enough of a fight to satisfy any sportsman. Fishing is a year-round activity, but the biggest prize, the Pacific blue marlin, which is generally caught off the southeast coast of Lanai, is most likely to be hooked in the fall. Other species to try for are ono (wahoo), caught throughout the year; mahimahi (dolphin fish), caught small in summer and larger in winter, and ahi (yellowfin tuna), aku (skipjack tuna), and kawakawa (oceanic bonito or false albacore), all most abundant in summer. No license is required for saltwater fishing in the State of Hawaii.

Charter boats are as plentiful as a school of fish in Lahaina and also in Maalaea. They usually accommodate up to six people and are available on a private or share basis for a full 8-hour day or a 4-hour half day, sometimes for a 6-hour day. All gear is provided, though the fishermen bring their own food and beverages. The average cost (you'll find them higher and lower) of a private charter on Maui is $550 for a full day and $350 for a half day, whereas the cost of a shared charter ranges from $100 to $125 per person for a full day and from $60 to $75 for a half day. If you're interested in sharing, most operations will organize a share boat for you if given a day or two notice in the winter, more time in the slower spring and fall seasons. If there are non-fishing members in your party, investigate the larger boats; some, while taking only six fishermen, are licensed to carry more than six passengers and will take them at half price. Remember that Hawaiian skippers keep costs down by selling the catch, so unless you come to some arrangement beforehand (they're usually very understanding about this), you'll be given only a few filets for your very own.

Among the charter captains and companies operating out of Lahaina, all available on a share or private basis for a full or half day, are *Aerial Sportfishing Charters* (phone: 667-9089), *Lahaina Charter Boats* (phone: 667-6672), *Luckey Strike Charters* (phone: 661-4606), and *Finest Kind Sportfishing* (phone: 661-0338). *Fishing Charters Lahaina* (phone: 667-7548) represents three boats, booking them on a full-day basis only. Outside Lahaina, contact the *Ocean Activities Center*, Wailea Shopping Village (phone: 879-4485), which operates the *No Ka Oi III* on fishing charters out of Maalaea Harbor. The *Aloha Activity Center*, with offices at Kaanapali's Whalers Village (phone: 667-9564; 800-222-4856), can also book fishing charters.

Those interested in joining the fishermen seen along the beaches and rocky coasts of Maui should check the phone book for fishing supplies stores; the salespeople can usually be counted on for advice on how it's done in Hawaii, where to go, and what you might expect to catch.

Hang Gliding – Hawaii's constant trade winds and mountains make for ideal hang gliding conditions. The Paia-based *Maui School of Hang Gliding* (PO Box 1119, Paia, Maui HI 96799; phone: 579-8077) offers 3- to 4-hour lessons for $50, and 45-minute tandem flights from the summit of Halekala to Kihei beach for under $100.

Golf – It may be a challenge to keep your eye on the ball, because one thing almost all of Maui's golf courses have in common is the distractive power of their scenery.

In the Kaanapali resort, the *Royal Kaanapali Golf Courses* (phone: 661-3691) consist of two 18-hole championship courses, one of which, the North Course, has been seen on TV in various tournaments, including a stop by the LPGA tour. Designed by Robert Trent Jones, Sr., the course begins close to the Pacific and climbs gently up the West Maui mountains, and from the upper holes, especially the 12th, the view of the neighboring islands of Lanai and Molokai is stunning. Royal Kaanapali's South Course, designed by Arthur Jack Snyder, slopes more gently mountainward, encountering, along the 5th fairway, the route taken by tourists aboard the Lahaina-Kaanapali and Pacific Railroad's sugarcane train. Greens fees at either course are $75, which includes a mandatory $20 cart fee. (A reduced twilight rate goes into effect between 2 and 6 PM.) Rental clubs are available at $18.

At Kapalua, the *Kapalua Golf Club* (phone: 669-8044) offers another pair of spectacularly scenic 18-hole courses, and work is underway on a third. The older and more relaxed of the two is the Bay Course, designed by Arnold Palmer, with two holes — the 4th and the 5th — on a lava peninsula stretching dramatically to the blue sea. The newer Village Course, designed by Palmer and Ed Seay, climbs 720 feet into the mountains, and it's rapidly gaining a reputation as the most demanding course in Hawaii. The higher elevation also enhances the view, making vistas of pineapple fields, Cook pines, and the island of Molokai across Pailolo Channel, quite simply, matchless. Greens fees of $85 per player ($55 to Kapalua resort guests) include mandatory cart rental, and there is an afternoon rate (for play between 2:30 and 6 PM) of $45. Club rental is $16.

The two championship golf courses of the *Wailea Golf Club* (phone: 879-2966), called the Blue Course and the Orange Course, are both designed by Arthur Jack Snyder and both are set on the lowest seaside slopes of Haleakala. Here again it's a case of the older (Blue) course being the more forgiving. On the Orange Course, 4-foot-high lava rock walls, manmade but of unknown origin (they may be the remains of a 16th-century King's highway), run through the fairways — they lie along holes 5–10 and 13–18. Other distractions include *heiaus* (ancient temples), a natural rock garden, wiliwili trees, and views of the islands of Kahoolawe and Molokini. Prime time to play here is early morning, when the sun makes its dramatic entrance over Haleakala. Greens fees for guests at the Wailea resort are $30 low season, $50 high season; for the public the rates are $50 and $80, respectively. Club rental is $15; pro shop open daily.

There are other courses to play on Maui. The Makena resort features the 18-hole *Makena Golf Course* (phone: 879-3344), 2 miles south of Wailea. Designed by Robert Trent Jones, Jr., it, too, includes some ancient stone walls, though they don't come into play as they do at Wailea. Greens fees at Makena are $65, including a cart. The recently opened 18-hole *Silversword Course,* 1345 Piilani Hwy. (phone: 874-0777), charges a $40 greens fee that includes cart, and offers a $30 twilight rate from 2:30 to 6:30 PM in summer. Clubs rent for $14. The course, on an often windy hillside overlooking Kihei, is a bit rough around the edges by Maui standards. The upcountry location of the 18-hole course of the *Pukalani Country Club,* 55 Pukalani St., Pukalani (phone: 572-1314), provides views from on high of the island's central valley with the ocean on both sides, of the back of the West Maui mountains, and up to Haleakala. Greens fees are much lower here, too ($20 for a shared cart), as they are at the *Waiehu Municipal Golf Course* (phone: 244-5433), 18 holes next to the ocean north of Kahului. Greens fees are $15 weekdays, $20 weekends. Cart rental (optional) is $12, clubs $8.50. It's off Hwy. 340, 5 miles north of Kahului. The *Maui Country Club,* 48 Nonohe Pl., Paia (phone: 877-0616) has a private (relatively unscenic) 9-hole course open to the public Mondays.

Horseback Riding – Some of Maui's best scenery is beyond the paved highway, and a guided trail ride astride a four-legged mode of transportation isn't a bad way to see it. The cost is about $10 to $15 per person per hour, though longer excursions with extras such as a picnic lunch or dinner can cost more.

On West Maui, the 2 hours spent riding with the *Kaanapali Kau Lio Riding Stables* (PO Box 10656, Kaanapali, Maui, HI 96761; phone: 667-7896) will take you several miles above the cane fields and into the mountains behind the Kaanapali resort, where you'll have a panoramic view of the shoreline and the islands of Lanai and Molokai. Riders can arrange to be picked up and returned to Kaanapali-area hotels and condos. *Rainbow Ranch* (PO Box 10066, Lahaina, Maui, HI 96761; phone: 669-4991) offers mountain and plantation rides from stables situated between Kaanapali and Kapalua. For beginner to experienced riders, the 1- to 3½-hour rides cost from $20 to $60.

Two outfits in East Maui run day-long trail rides into Haleakala crater. Tours include lunch, groups are limited to seven people, and reservations should be made at least a week in advance. *Pony Express Tours* (PO Box 535, Kula, Maui, HI 96790; phone: 667-2202) charges $120 for a full-day tour, $80 for a half-day tour (both include lunch); and *Thompson Ranch* (RR 2, Box 203, Kula, Maui, HI 96790; phone: 878-1910) charges $120 for a tour of the crater, $185 on overnights. Less arduous 1½- and 2½-hour rides, with gentler upcountry scenery, are also offered for $25 and $45 on the lower slopes of Haleakala at 3,200 feet. Two-hour private rides are $35 per person. In Wailea/Makena, *Makena Stables* (7299 S. Makena Rd., Kihei, Maui, HI 96753; phone: 879-0244) offers upcountry rides from $50 to $115 on Ulupalakau Ranch lands. Their 5½-hour ride to the Tedeschi Vineyards includes lunch. From the Kaupo side, *Charley's Trail Rides and Pack Trips* (c/o Kaupo Store, Hana, Maui, HI 96713; phone: 248-8209) will take you into the crater on an overnight adventure that begins in the morning with an 8-hour trip up the Kaupo Valley and includes dinner, night lodgings in a National Park Service cabin or campground, and a chance to see the sun set as well as rise over Haleakala. Rides for two to three people cost $200 per person, including food; for four to six, the cost is $150 with food or $125 if you bring your own. Reservations a month in advance are advised.

In the Hana district, riding is one of the major allures of the *Hana-Maui* hotel (phone: 248-8211), which has its own stables and organizes breakfast rides, cookout rides, sunrise and moonlight rides, rides by the hour, lessons, and many other variations at varying prices (no rides on Sundays). Priority is given to hotel guests, but non-guests are welcome. *Adventures on Horseback* (PO Box 1771, Makawao, Maui, HI 96768; phone: 242-7445) features personalized 5½-hour excursions that depart from Halawa

Bridge on the Hana Highway at 10 AM. Daily rides are limited to six participants, and include a waterfall swim and a picnic stop for $110.

Jet Skiing – On Kaanapali Beach, contact *Kaanapali Beach Jet Ski* (phone: 667-9740), which offers jet ski rentals (with lessons) for $35 per half hour, $55 per hour, and 2-passenger wave runners at $65 per hour. *Pacific Jet Ski* (phone: 667-2066) also offers jet ski rentals at $35 per half hour, $50 per hour. On Maalaea Bay, the *Maui Sailing Center* (phone: 879-5935) rents jet skis at $30 per half hour, $40 per hour.

Parasailing – *Parasail Hawaii* (phone: 661-5322) offers instruction by the hour ($42.50).

Snorkeling and Scuba Diving – The shores of the Valley Isle compare favorably with those of any of the other Hawaiian islands; in fact, they offer some of the best underwater sites in the state. In the vicinity of Lahaina, one of the spots favored by both divers and snorkelers is Cemetery, north of Wahikuli State Park (and just out from a cemetery). South of Lahaina, the shallow reef at Olowalu provides good snorkeling and diving (about ¾ mile south of the general store rather than north of the store, where the surfers congregate), and still farther south, about ¾ mile past the Scenic Lookout on Highway 30, a dirt road leads to Wash Rock, a popular diving site. The Kaanapali resort has Black Rock, the lava cone on which the *Sheraton Maui* stands. It's ideal for either snorkeling or diving, the fish are tame enough to be fed by hand, and it's very convenient. Kapalua Beach, also extremely easy to find and endowed with a public parking lot, provides moderately good diving and snorkeling, and because of the loveliness of the beach, it would be worth a visit even if the underwater view were only fair. North of Kapalua, Honolua Bay (turn off Hwy. 30 onto the dirt road about 1½ miles north of D. T. Fleming Beach Park and after Slaughterhouse Beach) is the number one surfing spot on Maui, but as part of a coastal marine life preserve it also has excellent snorkeling and diving, particularly around the reef on the right.

The western coast of East Maui becomes interesting to snorkelers just below Kamaloe Beach Park III, in Kihei, and it's better in the morning than in the afternoon. Keawakapu Beach, near the *Mana Kai Maui,* is another morning spot. When the sea is calm, snorkeling is good in the rocky areas of Mokapu Beach (in front of *Stouffer's Wailea Beach*), excellent at Ulua Beach (between *Stouffer's Wailea Beach* and the *Inter-Continental*), and good again at Wailea Beach and Polo Beach (south of the *Inter-Continental*). From Kamaole Beach to Polo Beach, all six have the paved parking areas and other conveniences characteristic of beach parks. Five Caves, between Polo Beach and Makena Beach (but before the turnoff to Ulupalakua), is known for excellent scuba diving and snorkeling in caves below offshore rocks — which are reached by a long swim, however — and Makena Beach itself (see *Swimming and Sunning* for how to find it) has excellent snorkeling around the Puu Olai cinder cone. Farther south, via a dirt Jeep trail, the rocky shores of the Ahihi-Kinau Natural Area Reserve, which runs from Ahihi Bay across Cape Kinau to La Perouse Bay, do not always allow easy access to the ocean, but the snorkeling and diving are well worth the effort.

Guided trips to nearby islands are another feature of diving on Maui. Experienced scuba divers can visit the underwater lava caves known as the Lanai Cathedrals, Mokuhooniki Rock off Molokai, and Becks Cove, off Kahoolawe, whereas everyone from the novice snorkeler to the certified diver turns up at Molokini, a volcanic islet whose crescent shape protects a great diversity of fish and coral between East Maui and the island of Kahoolawe. *Blue Water Rafting,* PO Box 10172, Lahaina, Maui, HI 96761 (phone: 879-RAFT), conducts snorkeling and whale watching cruises via motorized raft to the outer reef of Molokini. Departures take place at 7 and 10:30 AM from the Kihei Launch Ramp.

Beach activities concessions at most hotels have masks, fins, and snorkels for rent, occasionally with free instruction if necessary. Numerous excursion boats take passengers — anywhere from 6 to 100 people at a time — on snorkel sails, some directly from beaches in front of hotels, but most from Lahaina or Maalaea harbors. Prices range from $20 per person for a 2-hour sail up to $105 for a full-day sail, equipment included. Many such excursions feature snorkeling time along with time for swimming and sunning, a picnic on a beach, and perhaps some neighbor island sightseeing, and are listed under *Sightseeing Tours (Boat)*.

Maui has a number of full-service dive shops that rent and sell snorkel and scuba gear, though most shops will rent scuba equipment to — or refill tanks for — certified divers only. Intensive, usually 5-day, courses that lead to certification by *PADI (Professional Association of Diving Instructors)* and/or *NAUI (National Association of Underwater Instructors)* or *NASDS (National Association of Scuba Diving Schools)* are given by several outfitters, including, in Lahaina, *Central Pacific Divers,* 780 Front St. (phone: 661-8718), which also offers introductory dives for non-divers; refresher dives for certified but inactive divers; and two- and three-tank trips to Lanai or Molokini for certified divers. *Dive Maui,* Lahaina Marketplace (phone: 667-2080), also has 4- and 5-day certification courses and dives for beginners or certified divers, as do *Lahaina Divers,* 710 Front St. (phone: 661-4505), and *Scuba Schools of Maui,* 1000 Limahana Pl., Suite A (phone: 661-8036). *Kapalua Beach Activities,* beachfront at the *Kapalua Bay* hotel (phone: 669-4664), offers daily catamaran snorkel sails, as well as full scuba rental, lessons, and excursions. In the Kihei area, contact the *Maui Dive Shop,* in the Azeka Place Shopping Center (phone: 879-3388). In Wailea, the *Ocean Activities Center,* in the Wailea Shopping Village (phone: 879-4485), offers one- and two-tank dives, but no certification courses. The average price of a 4-day certification course is $250, and the price of a dive, whether introductory or refresher, local or inter-island, is anywhere from $65 to $85.

Surfing – Maui is not as well endowed with surf sites as Oahu, but then, neither is any other place in the world. Nevertheless, many consider Honolua Bay, on the northern coast of West Maui, one of the best surfing spots in Hawaii, certainly the best on Maui. On a good winter day, there are waves up to 15 feet, perfect tubes, and spectators watch from the cliffs above the rocky beach. Honolua is the next bay north of Slaughterhouse Beach (see *Swimming and Sunning*), accessible by dirt road off Highway 30. Other West Maui beaches that attract winter surfers are Windmill Beach and Honokohau Bay, both beyond Honolua and, because of a shallow bottom at one and submerged boulders and powerful currents at the other, both to be approached with extreme caution. Hookipa Beach Park, on the north coast of East Maui, probably has Maui's second best surf, and it's as well known as Honolua in the annals of surfing because the contemporary sport on Maui was born here. It's also as much of a surf-watching spot as Honolua, easily visible off Highway 36 just east of Paia and equipped with parking areas and picnic pavilions. This is a year-round site, though the spectacular waves — again up to 15 feet — occur in winter. Because of dangerous currents, however, Hookipa is definitely only for the experts.

On Maui's southern shores, the surf is best in the summer. Maalaea Bay, on the south side of the central valley, provides a very popular site, Maalaea Rights, considered the best break on the south shore, and though it is better in summer, there is winter surfing here, too. Maalaea Mudflats, another summer spot on the bay, is good at medium to high tide, but should be avoided at low tide because of a hazardous reef. Southeast of Maalaea, Kalama Beach Park, about midway down the Kihei coast on the western shore of East Maui, attracts its share of summer surfers; in the other direction, Olowalu, on the West Maui shore about midway between Maalaea and Lahaina, has reasonably good surfing year-round (the exact spot is ½ mile north of the village general store). In Lahaina, where the elite of pre-*haole* Hawaii rode the *papa he naru* (the wave sliding board), there are summer breaks both to the north and south of the harbor, anywhere from 2 to 10 feet.

West Maui has several places to rent surfboards and Boogie boards (a shorter surfboard), including *Central Pacific Divers,* 780 Front St., Lahaina (phone: 661-8718), and *Hobie Sports,* in Kaanapali's Whalers Village (phone: 661-5455). *Sea Sails* rents only surfboards at the *Sands of Kahana* condominiums (phone: 669-0400), and Boogie boards exclusively at the *Kaanapali Beach* hotel (phone: 661-0927). *Lightning Bolt,* in the Kahului Shopping Center (phone: 877-3484), rents surfboards by the day and has a very economical weekly rate. In the Kihei and Wailea areas, *Kihei Sea Sports,* in Kihei Town Center (phone: 879-1919), rents Boogie boards, and at Rainbow Mall (phone: 879-4188), they rent beginner surfboards. *Tradewinds Deli* in Maalaea (phone: 242-9161) rents Boogie boards. On Maui, surfboards generally rent at $15 to $20 per 24-hour day, and Boogie boards at $5 to $10; a deposit is usually required.

Swimming and Sunning – Nearly all and certainly the best of Maui's approximately 33 miles of beach are on West Maui and on the southwest coast of East Maui, appropriately in the same general areas with the greatest concentration of resort hotels and condominiums. Quite a number of them are beach parks, equipped by the county with paved parking areas, picnic tables and pavilions, showers, and restrooms, but they are not necessarily crowded, though the most popular ones may be on weekends. Be wary of the water at remote, deserted beaches, and even more wary if you come across a well-frequented beach, with island families ensconced thereon, but no one in for a swim. Surf conditions — and the appearance — of many beaches undergo changes from time to time, making caution always necessary.

The Lahaina area of West Maui is not overly endowed with good beaches, though it does have some picturesque ones; in fact, a stunning view of the islands of Lanai or Molokai or both is part of the beauty of all the beaches from Lahaina to Kapalua. Launiupoko State Park and Puamana Park along Highway 30 south of Lahaina both have views of Lanai across the Auau Channel guaranteed to comfort the eye, but neither is notable for swimming or sunning. The beach of Lahaina town, in the vicinity of the *Lahaina Shores* hotel, is negligible, which explains the popularity of Wahikuli State Park, along Highway 30 between Lahaina and Kaanapali, and Hanakao's Beach Park, adjacent to the Hyatt. Both are equipped with paved parking areas, picnic pavilions, barbecue grills, restrooms, and showers, and while most of the shoreline is edged in boulders, small beaches allow access to good swimming.

Kaanapali Beach is West Maui's showcase, a 2-mile length of golden sand that fronts the hotels and condominiums of the Kaanapali resort and then extends north another mile to Honokowai. There's plenty of room for everybody here, though the beach is widest where it snuggles up to Black Rock toward the center, an excellent snorkeling area. Swimming is very good, with only two provisos: Watch for the red warning flags put out by the hotels when the surf is heavy, and watch your children, because the bottom does drop quickly to depths over one's head. Access to the beach is via condos, hotels, or the Whalers Village shopping complex.

North of Kaanapali are two near-perfect crescents of sand curving between rocky points, both with picture-postcard views of Molokai. The first is the beach at Napili Bay, backed by condominiums hidden among palm trees, which detract little from its loveliness though they do create a parking problem (every space within a reasonable distance of the Hui Drive or Napili Place public rights of way seems to be marked for residents only). The waters of Napili are usually gentle, especially in the summer, as are the sparklingly clear aquamarine waters of the smaller beach fringing Kapalua Bay, the next bay north. Kapalua Beach (formerly Fleming Beach) is beautiful and it is easily reached (turn off Highway 30 near the Napili Kai Beach Club) and has a public parking lot and restrooms.

Two more well-known beaches are north of Kapalua. The popular D. T. Fleming Beach Park, on Honokahua Bay, is longer and wider than either Kapalua or Napili, and the peace inspired by its graceful backing of ironwoods and still another view of Molokai is hard to disturb even though you may have neighbors on the sand. The park has full facilities — picnic tables, barbecue pits, restrooms, and a parking area — and it has plenty of space for sunning, but heed the sign that says it's unsafe for swimming even though you may see people in the water. Currents are dangerous here, and there have been drownings. Slaughterhouse Beach, the next beach along Highway 30, is also a dangerous beach for swimming, particularly in winter, and you'll have to be something of a mountain goat to reach it (but then so will others). After passing the first Blow Horn sign (to warn pineapple trucks coming down private roads to the right), you'll see cars parked at a clearing on the left. The beach — also known as Mokuleia — is below, a pocket of sand nearly enclosed by low cliffs.

Considering the wealth of beaches elsewhere, there is no need to search out those in the Kahului area, but bear in mind if you are staying in Kahului that there are better local beaches than the one on the harbor by the hotels. Beaches are few and far between en route to Hana — the coast is mostly high and low sea cliffs — and in Hana, there are only two main beaches — Hana Beach Park, the safest swimming beach in the district, and Hamoa Beach, where the *Hana-Maui* hotel has its private facilities. But the western coast of East Maui is quite another thing — almost one uninterrupted stretch of sand from Maalaea Bay down to its southern tip beyond Wailea. About 3 miles at the northern end are called Maalaea Beach, a favorite with joggers because of the hard-packed sand, but also a good swimming and sunning beach as long as you arrive early in the morning. By noon, the wind howling across the central valley will blow you straight out to Kahoolawe.

Another 6 miles of the coast, which can also become windy in the afternoon, is known as Kihei Beach, a fairly loose term that describes any beach along South Kihei Road not otherwise named. There is no shortage of pale, soft sand here, Kahoolawe and Lanai can be seen offshore, and the view of the seacoast curving north to the West Maui mountains is a grand final touch. A great deal of this stretch is lined with condominiums, and if you are not staying in one of them, your acquaintance will probably be limited to the easily accessible sections set aside as parks. Kamaole Beach Parks I, II, and III are the most popular and apt to be crowded on weekends. Kamaole Beach Park I, in the 2300 area of South Kihei Road, is a lovely, long, wide beach equipped with picnic tables, showers, restrooms, and a paved parking area. Moving south, Kamaole Beach Park II has lost its parking lot and some facilities to a storm, though the beach remains. Kamaole Beach Park III, still farther south, has a playground for children, making it the most popular of all, even though its beach is the smallest. Children should be watched carefully at all three beaches (the water becomes deep rather quickly), but otherwise swimming is safe, periods of heavy surf and kona storms excepted.

The gap between Kihei and Wailea is bridged by Keawakapu Beach, a sugary soft expanse of sand lapped by translucent water. It begins at a lava point off South Kihei Road and extends ½ mile south to another lava point inside the Wailea resort, this latter portion constituting the first of the fabulous five Wailea beaches. (The beach can be reached either from the right of way where South Kihei Road meets Kilohana Road or from inside the resort.) Mokapu Beach, in front of *Stouffer's Wailea Beach* hotel, and Ulua Beach, between *Stouffer's Wailea Beach* hotel and the *Inter-Continental Maui,* are two smaller crescents, both set off by the verdant landscaping of the resort behind them, while the fourth of the five, Wailea Beach, is a glorious, long, and wide one backed by kiawe-covered dunes south of the *Inter-Continental.* By the time you reach the fifth, Polo Beach, you'll conclude it's just another pretty strand, only more secluded because it is the farthest from resort activity. Swimming is excellent at all five (and the bottom drops gently), access is clearly marked from the main road inside the resort, and all have paved parking lots and paved walks to the sand.

Pressing on past Polo Beach, there is what some consider the most beautiful beach on Maui, very long and wide, with clear waters and a view of Kahoolawe and Molokini in front, steep mountain and kiawe trees behind, and sand up to your ankles. The beach, first known as Oneloa, meaning "long sands," or Puu Olai, from the cinder cone to its right, then Hippie Beach because of the community that took up residence in the late 1960s, is now known as Makena Beach or Big Beach, to distinguish it from Little Beach, the next cove north. Reached only by walking around Puu Olai, Little Beach is Maui's foremost (but unofficial) nudist beach. Nude sunbathing is prohibited by state law, and recent police raids and arrests have discouraged total-body tanners. Be careful of Makena during heavy surf, and don't leave valuables in the car; the beach is not deserted, as the debris at its back will attest.

Tennis – Most hotels and the larger condominiums have one or a few courts, in some cases for guests only, in others open to the public. Three island installations are outstanding: The *Wailea Tennis Club* (phone: 879-1958) is not only the largest tennis complex in the state, it is also the only one with grass courts, 3 of them. In addition, there are 11 Plexipave courts (3 with lights) and a well-stocked pro shop. Tennis director Joe Violette and two assistant pros give private lessons and hold clinics on request. Court fees range from $12 per person per hour for a Plexipave court ($10 for Wailea guests) to $15 per hour for grass. At press time, the addition of a tennis clinic, to be operated by the Grand Champion tennis organization, was also in the works. The *Royal Lahaina Tennis Ranch* (phone: 661-3611, ext. 2296), in the Kaanapali resort, has 10 Plexipave courts (6 with lights), 1 stadium court, and a pro shop. Peter Burwash International offers group and private instruction, a tennis clinic, and round robin play. All-day court fees are $6 per person, per court, for guests of the *Royal Lahaina* and $9 for others. Fees guarantee 1 hour of play, the rest on a space-available basis. Night play is $2 additional. The *Kapalua Tennis Garden* (phone: 669-5677) provides 10 Plexipave courts, 4 lighted. Private and group lessons are available; clinics and round robins are scheduled according to demand. Play is $8 per person per day for guests of the *Kapalua Bay* hotel or the *Kapalua Villas;* others pay $9 per person per day, with 1 hour guaranteed and space available the remainder of the day.

Maui also has a number of county courts run by the Department of Parks and Recreation (phone: 244-9018) where play is free. They're in several areas frequented by visitors, but the top ones are the 5 lighted Laykold courts at the *Lahaina Civic Center* (phone: 661-4685), across Honoapiilani Hwy. from Wahikuli State Park, north of town. They operate on a first-come, first-served basis from 7 AM to 9:30 PM daily. Other county courts are in Kihei, Hana, Pukalani, Makawao, Wailuku, and Kahului.

Waterskiing – *Maui Water Ski,* at 104 Wahikuli Rd. in Lahaina (phone: 661-5988), has lessons and towing time available for up to five skiers. Rates start at $25 for 15 minutes to $75 for an hour. *Lahaina Water Ski* (phone: 661-5988) takes skiers offshore Kaanapali from the *Hyatt Regency Maui.*

Windsurfing – The newest water sport on Maui is growing by leaps and bounds. Experienced board sailors congregate along the north shore, between Kanaha Beach Park east of Kahului and Hookipa Beach Park east of Paia, where the Maui International Grand Prix of windsurfing is held and where wind conditions are ideal year round. *Sailboards Maui* (430 Alamaha St., Kahului; phone: 871-7954) sells windsurfers and rents them at $30 per 24 hours, and $175 per week. Private lessons in advanced techniques can be arranged. Two hour-long courses, one introductory ($25), one advanced ($20), are given by the *Maui Sailing Center* (Kealia Beach Village, 101 N. Kihei Rd.; phone: 879-5935). Straight rentals range from $19 an hour to $80 for 8 hours. The center supervises its windsurfers as it does its other sailors; all must stay within its designated sailing area on Maalaea Bay. Jet skis and 2-passenger wave skis are available at $50 and $60 a hour, respectively. *Sea Sails* (phone: 667-2525) rents windsurfers for $20; instruction is also offered. A motorized viewing board that takes the effort out of snorkeling ($25 an hour), is also available. The *Kaanapali Windsurfing School* (phone: 667-1964) offers rentals and lessons from a beachfront location south of the *Hyatt;* rates begin at $15 an hour and $25 for 2 hours. *Kapalua Beach Activities* (phone: 669-4664) offers lessons and rentals by the hour and for longer periods.

More and more hotels are adding windsurfing to their sports rosters. In the

Kaanapali resort, *Sea Sails,* with desks at the *Sheraton Maui,* the *Royal Lahaina,* the *Westin Maui, Maui Marriott,* and *Kaanapali Beach* hotels and *Kaanapali Shores* condominiums, rents windsurfers. In Wailea, the *Ocean Activities Center* rents windsurfers at its *Stouffer's Wailea Beach* and *Inter-Continental Maui* hotel outlets. Hotel rentals cost between $25 and $35 for the first hour, which includes instruction, then drop, sometimes to half price, for additional hours without instruction. *Nick's Aquasports* (phone: 661-1234) operates out of the *Hyatt Regency* at Kaanapali with windsurfers, snorkels, and Boogie boards.

AROUND THE ISLAND

Maui looks something like the head of a steer facing east. The head is East Maui, the ear is West Maui, and where the ear is attached is the central isthmus, or valley, connecting the two. Kahului Airport is just east of the twin towns of Wailuku and Kahului, the administrative center and port respectively, on the northern coast of the central valley. Highway 38 (380 on some maps) crosses the valley north to south and meets Highway 30 above the small harbor village of Maalaea, on Maalaea Bay, which is the valley's southern shore. Highway 30 then proceeds west, circling the outer edge of West Maui in a clockwise direction, passing Lahaina, the Kaanapali resort, the condominium strips of Honokowai, Kahana, and Napili, and the Kapalua resort, beyond which the paved road ends. The interior of West Maui is mountainous, partly unexplored.

East Maui is the larger landmass, dominated by the dormant Haleakala volcano. From Kahului, one main route leads south (Hwy. 35 or 350) across the central valley to the condominium strip of Kihei and the Wailea resort, which occupy East Maui's western coast. Another main route (Hwy. 37) leads inland southeast from Kahului, climbs the lower slopes of Haleakala, then veers around them through a district known as the Kula uplands or upcountry, while a branch road zigzags to the crater at the top. The third main route from Kahului leads east (Hwy. 36), most of it in poor condition, and follows East Maui's northern coast to the village and district of Hana, at the snout of the hypothetical steer. Highways 37 and 36 actually form a loop around East Maui, but a portion of the loop on the southern side is unpaved.

Lahaina

This old waterfront town began the 19th century as the residence and playground of island *alii* (high chiefs), gradually assumed importance as the political center of the early Hawaiian kingdom, became the whaling capital of the world almost overnight, then almost as quickly sank into the oblivion from which it has only recently awakened to become Maui's prime tourist hub. Its main thoroughfare, Front Street, is lined with brightly painted (or unpainted), weatherbeaten frame buildings. They are almost all storefronts where visitors can become tropically clad *wahines* (women) and *kanes* (men), swathed in Hawaiian garb and leis of seashells or kukui nuts; or they are restaurants and bars where these same visitors can watch the sunset over mai tais and a meal of mahimahi, opakapaka, or other fish brought in with the day's catch. If nothing about the town seems terribly serious today, it must be said that it never was a very stuffy place.

Remnants of Lahaina's royal past are few. The village had already been a watering place for Maui's *alii* class for centuries before Kamehameha the Great arrived to spend the year in 1802, well after the last of the battles that assured his eventual rule over a united Hawaiian kingdom. During that year — usually taken as the date he established Lahaina as his capital — Kamehameha made his headquarters in the Brick Palace, built for him by two foreigners a few years earlier and the foundations of which can still be seen off Front Street behind the library. The Brick Palace, with four rooms and two floors, was the first Western building in the islands, but the King is said to have found it confining and lived in a grass house next door instead.

Kamehameha did not remain on Maui, but the two most important of his 21 wives, Queen Kaahumanu and Queen Keopuolani, both from Maui, spent most of their time here, as did the three royal children — Prince Liholiho, Prince Kauikeaouli, and Princess Nahienaena. The main residence of Liholiho, who became Kamehameha II, was an island in a pond that used to exist at the corner of Shaw and Front streets, now marked only by a clump of palm trees in Maluuluolele Park; and while Kauikeaouli, who became Kamehameha III, spent a good part of his reign building a European-style palace of coral block — Hale Piula, or the House of the Tin Roof, which he never finished — he, too, preferred to live in what he called his private apartments, a grass house on the same little island behind the palace.

The diaries and letters of the missionaries are the best testimony of Lahaina's style of life in those days. The royal surfing grounds were in front of Princess Nahienaena's grass house, just south of today's small boat harbor, and they were well frequented, according to one missionary, who recorded that the surfboard was "an article of personal property, among all the chiefs — male and female, and among many of the common people." Another wrote of seeing the King (in this case, Kamehameha III), his wife, and others coming from the King's taro patch, which was next to the Brick Palace: "They were without shoes and stockings and hats and with a large wreath of maile and no more clothes than necessary. They were happy as any children playing in summer showers. The company had just come from performing one of those ancient acts of community interest, teaching the people the dignity of labor."

Protestant missionaries — the Reverends Charles Stewart and William Richards were the first — arrived in Lahaina in 1823 at the invitation of Queen Keopuolani, who was the first Hawaiian chief to convert to Christianity. Almost simultaneously another set of newcomers, also mainly New Englanders, was rapidly growing from a trickle to a horde. Whalers working the lucrative sperm whale grounds off Japan began to arrive in Hawaii in 1819, and soon they discovered the safe anchorage of Lahaina's open roadstead — less enclosed than a harbor, easy to approach and leave with any wind that blew — and the abundant fruit, vegetables, and Irish potatoes grown upcountry at Kula. The town suddenly became the most important provisioning stop for America's Pacific whaling fleet, and it is not difficult to picture the wide eyes of the missionary Dr. Dwight Baldwin, who noted: "Ten days since we had two whaleships, next day ten came in, and the next day six. From that time to this, scarce an hour but we have seen from one to half a dozen coming down the channel — 50 ships now here." Lahaina had become the whaling capital of the world. When traffic was at its peak, in 1846, 429 whaleships came to call; that same year, the town census recorded 882 grass houses, 155 adobe houses, 59 houses of wood or stone, and a population of only 3,557 people.

While replenishing their stores, the whalers also replenished themselves and it was their R&R activities that created all the fuss. Multiply a possible 50 ships at anchor by an average crew of 25 to 30 men sprung from long months of confinement and it is easy to see why the missionaries invented the muumuu. And not only the missionaries were concerned about temptations in their ersatz Garden of Eden. Maui's governor from 1823 until his death in 1840 was the high chief Hoapili, counselor to the first two Kamehamehas, the husband of the widowed Queen Keopuolani, and, like her, a Christian convert. Hoapili struggled mightily to maintain law and order, banning brothels and grog shops and putting a *kapu* (taboo) on ships and their crews, thus prohibiting native women from swimming out to visit them. His efforts were badly received from the start. In 1825, one ship put into port and the crew discovered that women were not allowed aboard and that the grog shops were closed. During the ensuing riot, the life of the Reverend Mr. Richards, suspected as a moving force behind the cleanup campaign, was threatened. Two years later, another riot ended with the crew of the whaler *John Palmer* firing a few cannonballs into the same reverend's yard. Soon this tropical paradise had a curfew, a fort, and a jail; still, the problem was only resolved when the whaling era ended.

Lahaina declined as whaling declined. The discovery of oil in Pennsylvania in 1859 was the beginning of the end, the loss of whaleships to Civil War blockades contributed further, and the loss of what was left of the fleet in the ice off Alaska in 1871 was the final blow. The effect of the missionaries was more lasting. They had been instrumental in establishing schools, the most important of which, Lahainaluna, was the first high school west of the Rockies when it opened in 1831. A few years later, a printing press on its grounds was turning out the first newspaper west of the Rockies, in Hawaiian. Mr. Richards, who had instructed Queen Keopuolani in the faith, became an adviser to Kamehameha III, whom he instructed in the study of democracy; and after issuing a declaration of rights and an edict of religious toleration, the young King signed Hawaii's first written constitution in 1840. The representative body thus constituted met in Lahaina for a few years until the government was moved to Honolulu, a transfer Kamehameha accomplished gradually over the course of the decade. His successor, Kamehameha IV, rarely visited Lahaina.

Few people, in fact, came to Lahaina until the 1960s, when the Kaanapali resort opened, a few miles north, and tourists began to flock to Maui. At the same time, the federal government designated much of the town a National Historic Landmark, inspiring the citizenry to undertake an ongoing project of restoration. What remains of the old is not difficult to visit since the town is only a few blocks deep, and while it is about 2½ miles long, most of the points of interest are on or just off a half-mile stretch of Front Street. Sightseeing should take only 2 hours or so, except for those entranced by window-shopping, and it should be done in the morning, before the accuracy of the name of the town — Lahaina means "merciless sun" — becomes all too apparent. The County of Maui Historic Commission publishes a brochure, "Lahaina: A Walking Tour of Historic and Cultural Sites," that can be picked up at the Baldwin House Museum during a visit.

Banyan Tree – As much a center of attraction in Lahaina as the *Pioneer Inn* next to it, the banyan tree is as good a place as any to begin a walking tour and an equally good place to end one. Planted in 1873 to commemorate the 50th anniversary of the arrival of the Protestant missionaries, this tree of Indian origin has grown and grown, propping itself up when necessary by sending aerial roots downward from its many horizontal branches and turning them into subsidiary trunks to support continued expansion. By now, the banyan looks like a grove of trees and covers two-thirds of an acre — quite a lot of much-needed shade in a town as sunstruck as Lahaina. Tourists and islanders alike take shelter on park benches beneath the boughs, mynah birds congregate topside, and though signs everywhere warn against climbing the tree, nothing prevents young children from swinging on the hanging tendrils that have yet to take root. In the middle of the block bounded by Front, Hotel, Canal, and Wharf Sts.

Pioneer Inn – Across the street from the banyan tree, this hotel is the most famous manmade landmark in town. It opened in 1901, too late to accommodate the whalers, but still in time to put up travelers disembarking from the inter-island steamers plying the Lahaina Roadstead. These must have been an equally rowdy crew, judging from the rules of the house posted right from the beginning by the reception desk; to wit: "Women is not allow in you room. If you wet or burn you bed you going out. You are not allow to gambel in you room. You are not allow in the down stears in the seating room or in the dinering room or in the kitchen when you are drunk. You must use a shirt when you come to the seating room." The dark green wooden structure with the white-trimmed ground-floor arcade and second-story veranda all around is today actually two buildings — the old wing facing the harbor and, behind, a new wing, added in 1966 and looking as authentic as the original. Even if you're not staying at the hotel, you can soak up some of its atmosphere by visiting the *Snug Harbor* "dinering" room or the *Old Whaler's Grog Shop* bar, both in the old section. Hotel and Wharf Sts. (phone: 661-3636).

Carthaginian – Imagine every boat in the harbor rigged like this one and discover a picture of Lahaina in its heyday. What is now the *Carthaginian* left German shipyards in 1920 as a two-masted schooner, was converted to diesel power by Swedish owners, and for most of its life hauled cargo through the Baltic Sea. Bought in 1972 by the Lahaina Restoration Foundation, it underwent an intensive transformation, and by 1980 it had been turned into a replica of a 19th-century square-rigger, the only true-rigged brig in the world. The *Carthaginian* replaces another square-rigged vessel that was moored here (and featured in the film *Hawaii*) until 1972, when it broke up on a coral reef en route to a Honolulu dry dock. The sails are still to come for the *Carthaginian,* but in the meantime, the ship serves as a floating museum; its exhibits include the continuous showing of two videotapes on whales, phones on which to hear recorded whale songs, and an old whaleboat found preserved in Alaska in 1973. Open daily from 9 AM to 4 PM. Admission $2; children free with parents. The Whale Report Center on the dock beside the *Carthaginian* keeps tabs on when and where whales have last been spotted and is the place to ask where next to look for these slow-moving creatures. Lahaina Harbor, directly in front of the *Pioneer Inn* (for information on the *Carthaginian* or to report a whale, phone: 661-8527).

Wo Hing Society – Built by immigrant Chinese plantation workers in 1912 as a residence and social hall for indigent bachelors, the Lahaina Restoration Foundation has given this building new life, as a museum on Chinese culture and its links to Maui. Particularly interesting are the films — shown throughout the day on a large screen — depicting the impact of Chinese immigrants on the island's culture. Open Mondays through Saturdays from 9 AM to 4:30 PM; Sundays from noon to 4:30 PM. 858 Front St. (phone: 661-5553).

Hauola Stone – A Hawaii Visitors Bureau warrior marker along the sea wall to the right of the *Pioneer Inn* and the *Carthaginian* points to several rocks in the water below. There is not much to see, but the most chair-shaped one was thought by the Hawaiians to have healing powers. They had only to sit in it and let the waves washing over them restore them to health. At your back are the foundations of Kamehameha the Great's Brick Palace and the site of the King's taro patch.

Courthouse – The Lahaina Courthouse was built in 1859 of wood and stone taken from the European-style palace that Kamehameha III had raised for himself not far away and never completed. Kamehameha's palace — Hale Piula, or the House of the Tin Roof — had already been converted into a courthouse in 1848, but 10 years later, a strong wind put an end to its usefulness and the rubble was transported here to become the new Lahaina Court and Custom House and Government Offices. Today, the building houses the District Court and offices, plus galleries of the Lahaina Art Society on the ground floor and in the basement (in the basement gallery, paintings are hung in the cells of the former jail). Open daily from 10 AM to 4 PM. Wharf St., in front of the banyan tree.

Old Fort – By the time the courthouse appeared, the fort had already been and gone. The two corners of the fort wall, now on the courthouse grounds at the Canal Street and Hotel Street intersections of Wharf Street, were reconstructed in 1964 to provide some reminder of the former landmark. The fort was built in about 1832 in an effort to restore some semblance of law and order to the R&R activities of visiting seamen, who had rioted more than once in the past upon putting into port and finding that the native women were prohibited from coming aboard and that the grog shops in town were closed, too. While the fort stood (until the early 1850s), a curfew was also in effect, and every evening at sundown a soldier stood on the ramparts beating a drum to warn all sailors ashore to return to their ships. The fort once had an inventory of 47 cannons, but the four guns now pointed at the tame fleet of pleasure boats in Lahaina Harbor were never among them. These four are believed to have come from a Russian ship that sank in Honolulu Harbor in 1816. Wharf St.

Holy Innocents Episcopal Church – As you go south on Front Street, passing Kamehameha III School on the right, this small church, dating from 1927, will also be on your right. Stop in for a look at the Hawaiian madonna on the altar, the triptych of Hawaiian scenes below it, and the other paintings in a tropical mode. Princess Nahienaena's grass house and Kamehameha III's palace, Hale Piula, were once both in this vicinity, between Front St. and the sea.

Waiola (formerly Wainee) Church and Cemetery – The first Christian services on Maui took place outdoors in June 1823, shortly after the arrival of the Protestant missionaries. It was not until 1828, however, that construction began on Wainee Church, the first stone church to be built in the islands. When it was finished in 1832, it was large enough to seat 3,000 people, though not substantial enough to survive the elements. In 1858, the same wind that damaged Kamehameha III's palace blew the steeple and part of the roof off Wainee. Then, in 1894, the whole church was torched by mobs protesting the abolition of the monarchy and the annexation of Hawaii by the US (the reverend at the time favored both developments). A subsequent church succumbed first to fire and then to a whirlwind, so that the present small, cream-colored, shake-roofed church, its name changed from Wainee to Waiola (Water of Life), dates only from 1953. The cemetery next door, surrounded by pink, red, and white plumeria trees, contains the graves of Hawaiian royalty and commoners and of missionaries and their children as well as many unmarked graves. Entering from the Waiola churchyard, a faded wooden sign points to the Royal Tomb, where two large headstones are enclosed in a black wrought-iron fence. Here lies Queen Keopuolani, wife of Kamehameha I, mother of Kamehameha II and Kamehameha III, and the first of the Hawaiian chiefs to convert to Christianity. Her daughter, Princess Nahienaena, is also buried here as is Governor Hoapili, another convert. As Governor of Maui from 1823 to 1840, he was an ally of the missionaries and the real power behind the banning of grog shops and brothels that so inflamed the early whalers. Wainee St., around the corner from Shaw St.

Hongwanji Temple – The white, slatted structure with the three gray outer-space turrets — on the left as you continue north along Wainee Street — is the church of Lahaina's largest Buddhist congregation. The Hongwanji sect has been meeting here since 1910, but the building dates from 1927.

Hale Paahao (Old Prison) – Until this prison was built, rowdy sailors were locked up inside the old fort on the waterfront. By 1852, rowdiness had evidently accelerated to an unprecedented degree in Lahaina (the gold rush was blamed for a second great influx of foreigners and the lack of moderation in their behavior) and a new prison was begun, built by the prisoners themselves. First came the wooden prison house (the small brown building that looks more like a little chapel), then the massive prison wall of coral blocks taken from the walls of the old fort, which the prison replaced. In 1988, Hale Paahao was taken apart and reconstructed, with the addition of on-site storyboards. Open daily from 9 AM to 4 PM. Prison Rd., just off Wainee St.

Episcopal Cemetery and Hale Aloha – You can return to Front Street by proceeding north along Wainee Street and turning left at Dickenson Street. En route, on the left side of Wainee, is the Episcopal Cemetery, where Walter Murray Gibson, King David Kalakaua's principal adviser during the 1880s, is buried, and if you walk into the cemetery, you will be able to see something of Hale Aloha (House of Love) behind it. This church meetinghouse, completed in 1858 and restored in 1988, was built to commemorate Maui's safe deliverance from the scourge of a smallpox epidemic that had decimated Oahu 5 years before.

Maria Lanakila Church – The large church on the corner of Wainee and Dickenson streets is a 1928 replacement and replica of a previous one on the spot, built in 1858. An even earlier church, built in 1846, was Lahaina's first Roman Catholic house of worship. Next to the church is its cemetery, and next to that, a sign points out the Seamen's Cemetery — though only one or two slabs remain of the many that were here when the plot was in use in the 19th century.

Masters' Reading Room – In 1833, work began on what is today Maui's oldest building, the money for which came from both the Protestant mission and an assortment of ships' captains. Upon completion, the ground floor served as the mission storeroom, and the reading room upstairs was where seamen could engage in more seemly R&R activities than those that had previously strained relations between the islanders and rowdy ships' crews. The Lahaina Restoration Foundation (phone: 661-3262) is housed in the building, which is not open to the public. Corner of Dickenson and Front Sts.

Baldwin House Museum – This plastered and whitewashed coral stone house was built in 1834–35 by one of Lahaina's early missionaries, Ephraim Spaulding. From 1836 to 1868, however, it was the home of Dr. Dwight Baldwin, a missionary who was also a doctor, and his family, which grew to include six children. Through the years, the house was crowded not only with Baldwins but also with a constant parade of visitors and guests — missionaries, whaling captains, the minister's flock, and the doctor's patients. The building has been restored, furnished with period pieces (English and local), and is now a museum run by the Lahaina Restoration Foundation. The rooms open for viewing include the living room with the family's Steinway piano, the dining room set with their imported china, the master bedroom with the koa wood four-poster bed, the bathroom with the first toilet brought to Maui, the boys' bedroom with superfluous bed warmers, and the dispensary, where there is a copy of Dr. Baldwin's Hawaiian medical license, allowing him to charge $50 for "very great sickness," $40 for "less than that," $30 for "a good deal less," and so on. Note the small park next door. The home of the Reverend William Richards used to be on this spot, and this is where those cannonballs fell in 1827, fired by sailors who suspected Richards of having been the instigator of Governor Hoapili's morality drive. Museum open daily from 9:30 AM to 4:30 PM. Admission charge $2; children free with parents. Front St., beside the Masters' Reading Room (phone: 661-3262).

Lahaina Jodo Mission – This Japanese cultural park is too far from the center of Lahaina to be included in a walking tour, but its very distance makes it a peaceful place to visit. A small sweep of grass, pebbles, and walkways is encircled by pink and white oleander bushes and dominated by the great bronze Buddha, unveiled in 1968, on the hundredth anniversary of Japanese immigration to the Hawaiian islands. Neither the white pagoda with the three red-trimmed roofs, a memorial to the dead, nor the tiny brown and white temple is open to the public, but you can walk up the steps to the temple and peer in at its lovely flowered ceiling. Another structure houses the temple bell. Ala Moana St., near Mala Wharf.

Lahainaluna School – Also too far away to include in a walking tour, this could be the object of a short drive that will take you 2 miles uphill behind Lahaina but not as far as the giant L etched onto the summit of Mt. Ball (you'll be treated to the broadest possible view over the town and the Lahaina Roadstead on the way down). The L, freshly limed twice a year to keep it visible, stands for Lahainaluna, and though the campus may not appear unusual, the school is. When it was opened by the American Board of Commissioners for Foreign Missions in 1831, it was the first secondary school west of the Rockies. Not only did the initial students, who came from mission schools all over the islands, have to build their own facilities and grow their own food, they also had to manufacture their own textbooks; Hawaiian had become a written language only a few years before, and most of the early pupils were natives. By 1834, the first newspaper printed in Hawaii (and in Hawaiian) was coming off the press at Lahainaluna, and soon Hale Pai (the printing house) was turning out histories, grammars, dictionaries, and other books, many of them first editions, that are still important to the study of Hawaiian history and culture. The school introduced a boarding program almost from the start, and though it became part of the public school system in the 1920s and is now West Maui's only public high school, it still has students who board. Traditional and vocational courses — carpentry, auto repair, agriculture, horticulture, and, lately, aquaculture — are offered, and just as the early students mixed the academic with the practical by necessity, today's boarders must fulfill a work requirement, usually farmwork (in the past they've even run their own dairy). Instruction has been in English since 1877, but the preservation of native culture is an important part of the school's heritage, as can be seen at the end of each school year on David Malo Day, when the students put on a program of song, dance, and ancient Hawaiian sports. The pageantry remembers Lahainaluna's most famous alumnus, a member of the first class who became a teacher and a preacher and who, as the author of the classic work of history and anthropology *Hawaiian Antiquities,* is considered to be the first Hawaiian scholar. The campus is open to the public, but if school is in session and you want to do more than drive through, stop by the vice principal's office first.

Hale Pai – The oldest building on the campus of the Lahainaluna School, Hale Pai (House of Print) has been restored to be a museum devoted to Hawaiian printing. Open to visitors Mondays through Fridays from 10 AM to 4 PM. No admission; donations accepted. Lahainaluna Rd. (phone: 667-7040).

Omni Theater/Hawaii Experience – The giant domed screen provides a three-dimensional view of Hawaii's natural and human history. *Hawaii: Islands of the Gods* is artistically filmed and sensitively written. Years in the making, and 45-minutes in the showing, it's well worth considering at $5.95 ($3.95 for children aged 2 to 12). Shows daily from 10 AM to 10 PM. 824 Front St. (phone: 661-8314).

SHOPPING: A short walk through Lahaina should be enough to convince anyone that shopkeeping is, if not the town's only business, at least one of its main ones. The stores jammed the length of "downtown" Front Street leave room for little else except, perhaps, restaurants, and Lahaina has several shopping centers to boot. The most conspicuous of the latter is The Wharf, an assemblage of many shops and a few restaurants in a three-tiered rustic wooden structure across Front Street from the banyan tree. Most of what is for sale at The Wharf is meant to entice the visitor, whereas the merchandise at the Lahaina Shopping Center, a more prosaic agglomeration of stores and parking spaces farther north along Front Street, tends to satisfy the utilitarian needs of the islanders. Here are the post office, supermarket, variety market, drugstores, hardware stores, banks, and fast-food outlets as well as clothing stores appealing to various levels of taste. Between these two, a small indentation along Front Street of no more than several shops around a paved brick court is referred to as the Lahaina Market Place — not the same thing as Lahaina Square, which is behind the Lahaina Shopping Center and something of a continuation of it. At the southern end of town, are the shops and restaurants of 505 Front Street, in a setting reminiscent of an old-fashioned New England town. The latest addition to Lahaina's commercial offerings is the mix of shops and restaurants at the expansive Lahaina Cannery, about one mile from downtown, in the direction of Kaanapali. This 50-store complex, built in the style of the pineapple cannery that was originally located here, features *Long's Drugs* and *Safeway* as its anchor tenants, with a secondary focus on visitor-oriented shops and services, including an *Ocean Activities Center* office.

A final note: The Wharf is the Lahaina location of *Liberty House,* the most ubiquitous of Hawaiian stores. Like many of the other branches on Maui, it is a specialty store carrying, above all, a line of women's and men's resortwear of reliable quality.

Apparels of Pauline – This boutique has been here for a decade catering to women who wish to slip into the aloha spirit but don't want to look as though a missionary had dressed them. Among the best-sellers are lots of silks, in languorous dinner dresses, loungewear, and sarongs; cotton kimonos imported from Japan; and oversized T-shirts hand-painted on Maui. Lahaina Market Place, just off Front St. (phone: 661-4774).

The Bakery – It's a bit out of the way, but worth the trip, especially when the pastries and cakes are hot from the oven. 991 Limahana Pl. (phone: 667-9062).

Claire the Ring Lady – Her name is Claire Edwards, and the cases in her shop are filled with trays of coral, opals, garnets, jade, topaz, lapis, pearls, amethysts, and peridots, to name but a few. Other trays hold gold and silver settings of her own design. Choose stone and setting, and Claire, who learned her trade in Florence, Italy, will fashion your very own ring. 858-4 Front St. (phone: 667-9288).

Crazy Shirts – Only one of Hawaii's many T-shirt shops and only one of *Crazy Shirts'* three locations on Maui. The outlet on Front Street is noteworthy not simply for the T-shirts but because it contains a museum of whaling artifacts and the figurehead of a helmeted warrior salvaged from the 1972 shipwreck of the *Carthaginian I* on the Lahaina reef. 865 Front St. (phone: 661-4775); The Wharf (phone: 661-4712); and Lahaina Cannery (phone: 661-4788).

David's – Low-cost Maui-abilia — T-shirts, shorts, sweatshirts, and Lahaina's best collection of "greeting" cards make it worth a visit. 815 Front St. (phone: 661-4009).

The Gallery – Perhaps Hawaii's best and most expensive antiques store, geared to Lahaina's well-heeled yachting crowd, it's especially notable for its Oriental collection and worth a visit, if only to browse. 716 Front St. (phone: 661-0696).

High as a Kite – Here you'll find soaring scimitars, rainbow deltas, and spinnakers; dragon kites and fighter kites; kites in the shape of birds, handmade and painted in China; plus kite kits to make a few contraptions you'd swear would never fly but do. 703 Front St. (phone: 661-3159).

Lace Secrets – A fine selection of intimate lingerie, designer swimwear, and women's sportswear is sold here. 505 Front St., Suite 303 (phone: 661-5720).

Lahaina Camera Center – Not only film and processing, but underwater and 35mm camera rentals and repairs are available here, as well as binoculars for whale watching during the winter. Lahaina Shopping Center, Front St., across from the post office (phone: 661-3306).

Lahaina Printsellers – As much a museum as a shop, this unique store in the historic Old Seamen's Hospital (ca. 1832) offers one of the best collections of antique prints and maps found anywhere. Especially tempting is the excellent collection related to Polynesian Hawaii and the early explorers like Cook and La Perouse. 1024 Front St. (phone: 667-7843).

Lahaina Scrimshaw Factory–Pier 49 – Both collectors and the merely curious will find the largest selection of scrimshaw on Maui in the 6 stores of the *Lahaina Scrimshaw Factory.* A roster of resident scrimshanders produces most of the work, which is carved or engraved less and less on the teeth of the sperm whale (protected by the Endangered Species Act of 1973, which prohibits the importation of whale products, though teeth on hand at passage may still be used) and more and more on fossilized walrus tusk. While it is possible to spend as little as $5 for a fossil walrus ivory charm, it is also possible to spend several thousand dollars for a larger, weightier, more intricately carved piece. 845 Front St. (phone: 661-8820) and at the Lahaina Cannery (phone: 661-3971).

Luana's – Sells resortwear for women and men, plus its own brand of Hawaiian print bikinis (tops and bottoms sold in separate sizes), to which can be added a *lavalava* (a short hip skirt) or a sarong to match. In addition, there are caftans, aloha shirts, shorts, pants. 869 Front St. (phone: 667-2275); and The Wharf (phone: 661-0651).

The Mail Room – Packing, giftwrapping, and shipping for what you don't want to hand-carry back home. Lahaina Shopping Center (phone: 661-5788).

Maui Mad Hatter – Stacked hats cover every bit of wall space and more hats hang from the ceiling — straw hats from China and the Philippines, panamas from Ecuador, *lau halas* from the South Pacific islands, and more. The feathered hatbands, jewel-like in color and velvety in texture, are exquisite examples of the Hawaiian craft. The Wharf (phone: 661-8125).

South Seas Trading Post – This shop, which looks like a small but veritable museum of South Seas imports, stocks anything from a Marshall Islands stick chart (actually a map, with sticks showing navigation routes and cowrie shells showing the islands) to "naif" paintings by Balinese children, Tongan tapa cloth, and rare shell leis from Niihau. Objects are carefully labeled, so you know what they are and whence they came. 851 Front St. (phone: 661-3168).

Superwhale – A children's boutique that is *the* place for teeny bikinis, miniaturized muumuus, saucy small T-shirts, and dolls clad in hula skirts. The Lahaina Cannery (phone: 661-3424) and three other stores on Maui.

Surf Sports – If it relates even remotely to the sea, it's here. The selection of surf and beach paraphernalia includes stuff to keep you covered up, or uncovered if you prefer. 736 Front St. (phone: 661-0698).

Village Gallery – Turn up Dickenson Street past the Masters' Reading Room and the parking lot to reach this spare contemporary showroom with the anachronistic Victorian chairs and sofa. The gallery has oils, watercolors, prints, and mixed media by some of the finest Hawaiian artists. 120 Dickenson St. (phone: 661-4402).

Waterfront Gallery – The emphasis here is on coral, pearls, scrimshaw, and gold, with many an interesting piece on display. 825 Front St. (phone: 661-3124).

 NIGHTLIFE: Neighbor islanders are early to bed and early to rise, and it might strike mainlanders from locales less close to nature that nightlife on Maui takes place prematurely, too. It begins at sunset, or just before, and in Lahaina, sunset watching is the ritual that kicks it off. To participate, make your way to any bar with an unobstructed view west — those of *Kimo's,* the *Oceanhouse,* and the *Lahaina Broiler* restaurants, all on the *makai* (ocean) side of Front Street, are especially nice spots, and on the opposite side of the street, *The Keg* also has a clear view over the seawall out to the blue.

The *Old Lahaina Luau* ($37) is offered Tuesdays through Saturdays, at a beachfront setting adjacent to the shops at 505 Front St. (phone: 667-1998). With its focus on traditional hula and costume, the attention to authenticity makes this one of Hawaii's better luaus. While prime ribs, chips and dips cater to mainland tastes, island favorites like grilled mahimahi, shoyu chicken, pulehu ribs, lomilomi salmon, and poi are also served.

After dinner or the luau, the evening proceeds with, perhaps, a stroll, and while this part of the night is in progress, Lahaina's main drag crawls with pedestrians making their way randomly up one side of the street and down the other, with frequent enough crossings-over to slow the bumper-to-bumper traffic to well below the 15 mph speed limit. Because many stores stay open late, some of this promenade is nothing more than straightforward window-shopping, and by about 10 PM, when stores are closed and most restaurants are serving their last customers, the town begins to close down for the night. Only a few spots persevere to rend the nocturnal peace, and night owls who haven't checked their papers beforehand will be able to find them by keeping their ears open. The loudest sound is liable to be coming from *Moose McGillicuddy's,* 844 Front St. (phone: 667-7758), where disco — or its live equivalent — reigns in Lahaina. The bands attract a mostly young crowd (few over-30s here), who appreciate the top-40 format. Another favorite nightspot with islanders is the *Old Whaler's Grog Shop,* just inside the swinging doors off the lobby of the *Pioneer Inn* (phone: 661-3636). Decked out with captain's chairs, whaling artifacts, and other nautical paraphernalia, the bar is the late afternoon haunt of habitués who drop in from the waterfront, and by the time the live music begins at 8:30 PM, the joint is ready to jump — to the rhythms of bluegrass or jazz — until closing between midnight and 2 AM. *Longhi's,* 888 Front St. (phone: 667-2288), is also a good place to stop in for an after-hours drink; weekends, there's often live music and dancing in the elegant second-story lounge. *Blackie's Bar,* at Blackie's Boat Yard on Honoapiilani Hwy. (phone: 667-7979), is the place to go for jazz Mondays, Wednesdays, Fridays, and Sundays from 5 to 8 PM. (You won't have trouble finding *Blackie's* — it's in a big house with a bright orange roof, shaped like a hexagon and built on stilts, on the main highway between Lahaina and Kaanapali.) At the *Whale's Tale,* 666 Front St. (phone: 661-3676), singers join the piano music provided from 5:30 to 10:30 PM. (From noon to 7 PM, live guitar music offers a pleasant escape from Lahaina's afternoon heat.) The *Tiger,* 730 Front St. (phone: 667-7003), offers the best live music in town; country and Hawaiian shows are performed daily from 9:30 PM to 12:30 AM. The place also draws football fans to watch "Monday Night

Football" during the season. *Club Lanai* (phone: 871-1144) sets to sea nightly at 8:45 for a 2-hour live music and dancing sail aboard the 70-foot *Kaulana* ($20). There's also Hawaiian music at the *Old Lahaina Café,* 505 Front St. (phone: 667-1988), from 8:30 PM to midnight.

 CHECKING IN: Lahaina is the center of a great deal of the action in West Maui, but most people do not make it their headquarters, mainly because the town itself is without a proper beach. In addition, it tends to be hot, its backdrop of steep West Maui mountains cutting off the trade winds that do begin to ruffle the palms only a few miles up the coast. Thus, most of the hotel and condominium building has taken place north of Lahaina, where beaches and trade winds coincide, and those wishing to stay in the old whaling capital itself have a somewhat limited choice. In the suggestions below, expect to pay $80 to $130 to accommodate two people in places listed in the moderate category, $40 to $65 in places listed in the inexpensive category. All telephone numbers are in the 808 area code unless otherwise indicated.

Lahaina Shores – This is Lahaina's major resort condominium and the only place to stay if you want to be both in town and directly on a beach. The 200-plus units occupy one 6-story building topped by a penthouse, and though the building is modern, the white columns and balustrades of 6 rows of lanais give it a fanciful antebellum look. The rooms — studios or 1-bedroom units, ocean or mountain views — are more prosaic, but still pleasant, with TV sets, phone, and air conditioning. A swimming pool and a Jacuzzi are on an Astroturf-covered patio, but just a few steps farther over real grass and you are on the beach, albeit a narrow one, just south of the harbor. Shops and restaurants are next door at the Whaler's Market Place, 475 Front St. (phone: 661-4835; 800-367-2972). Moderate.

Maui Islander – Located several blocks back from Front St., this low-rise apartment complex offers both hotel and condominium accommodations. While not fancy, the comfortable facilities include tennis courts and a pool. 660 Wainee St. (phone: 667-9766; 800-367-5226). Moderate.

Plantation Inn – The 21 rooms and suites of this beautiful, Victorian-style hotel are situated just a block from Front St. and the ocean. *Gerard's* (see *Eating Out*) is located in the hotel and provides the breakfasts that are included in the cost of a room. Other attractions include the pool and the warm aloha supplied by owners/managers Jim and Lina Patterson. 174 Lahainaluna Rd. (phone: 667-9225; 800-433-6815). Moderate.

Pioneer Inn – This waterfront hotel has been a Lahaina landmark since 1901 (see *Special Places*), and it is wonderfully evocative of former times. The atmosphere begins in the tiny lobby of the original wing, replete with grandfather clock, plate rails, and a stairway that leans and creaks past a lovely stained glass window on its way to the rooms. Not everyone appreciates the stamp of yesteryear in the accommodations, however: makeshift closets, rooms without bath or with baths not quite up to snuff (showers only), ceiling fans and screen doors, but no air conditioning. Rooms in the new wing, added in 1966, are air conditioned and an improvement in other respects, too, including their distance from the *Old Whaler's Grog Shop,* a lively bar and meeting place next to the lobby in the old wing. Restaurants on the premises are the *Snug Harbor Dining Room,* the open-air *South Seas Patio,* and the *Harpooner's Lanai,* serving breakfast and lunch on the side porch. There are no TV sets, nor private lanais, but rooms in the old wing have access to the 2nd-story veranda from which to view Lahaina Harbor, while those in the new wing open on individually railed sections of veranda overlooking the swimming pool, the banyan tree, or Front Street. 658 Wharf St. (phone: 661-3636). Inexpensive.

EATING OUT: Most restaurants in Lahaina — and on Maui in general — fall into two categories: the broiler type, where the menu stresses steaks, seafood, and one or two fresh fish-of-the-day selections; and everything else; that is, those specializing in French, Italian, or some other national cuisine — almost anything except authentic Hawaiian (though most restaurants include a few Polynesian preparations on the bill of fare). Chances are good that the prices will run a bit higher than back home. Expect to pay $60 or more for the average meal for two in any restaurant listed below as expensive and anywhere from $30 to $55 in any restaurant listed as moderate. An inexpensive listing means under $25 for two — and none of the above guidelines includes drinks, wine, or tip. There is a fourth category of eatery, the fast-food outlet, where you can spend a lot less for hamburgers, pizza, fried chicken, yogurt with toppings, and certain Oriental specialties.

The dress code is very relaxed on Maui. In no restaurant listed below would a man in an aloha shirt or comparable neat sportswear, or a woman in a simple cotton dress, skirt and blouse, or T-shirt, feel out of place at dinner. Casual dress does mean something on the formal side of shorts and rubber thongs, however, though even these usually will be fine at lunch.

All telephone numbers are in the 808 area code unless otherwise indicated.

Chez Paul – The unlikely setting of this worthy French restaurant is the village of Olowalu: what looks like a general store, a barn of corrugated tin, and, in between, *Chez Paul*'s homey, trellis-trimmed front porch. Inside, too, it looks like a mom-and-pop operation at a country crossroads, with no more than 15 tables and no decor to speak of beyond the clean white and green color scheme. Yet the food belies all this simplicity. Begin with the homemade pâté, move on to the duck à l'orange, a regular on the menu, or try the *poisson du jour* — which is and also isn't simply another way of saying fresh fish of the day. Open for dinner nightly. Reservations necessary. Hwy. 30 at Olowalu, 6 miles south of Lahaina (phone: 661-3843). Expensive.

Avalon – This is the star among Maui's new restaurants. Well prepared and beautifully presented are the wok-charred veal chops, broiled Omaha corn-fed beef with shitake mushrooms, and fresh steamed clams with black bean sauce, among other choices. Open daily from 11 AM to midnight. Reservations necessary. 844 Front St. (phone: 667-5559). Expensive to moderate.

La Bretagne – With its front yard full of plumerias blooming, this looks much like a private home, and the feeling of being *en famille* is even stronger once you've stepped into the parlor (with good reason — the place is run by a family). Dining tables are covered with linen prints, and each guest sits in the padded comfort of an armchair upholstered in flowered cretonne. Victorian lamps, their globes painted with roses, light the scene, and floral drapes, antiques, and oil paintings complete it. The food is French, including onion soup and escargots among the appetizers. Many of the specialties are based on local fish and produce — such as seafood in puff pastry and Cajun prawns — and there is also a changing menu that includes veal, lamb, and duck entrées. Desserts, focusing on pies and pastries, are a specialty of the house and are as fine as everything else on the menu. Open for dinner daily. Reservations advised. Off Front St., facing Maluuluolele Park (phone: 661-8966). Expensive to moderate.

Chart House – It's way, way north of the section of Front Street that could be called the beaten track, but word of mouth among visitors has made this a hit nonetheless. The building is Polynesian rustic, resembling a longhouse, but the food is no-nonsense steaks, seafood, or a combination of both, plus the best-selling prime ribs. Portions are generous, as is the salad. Open for dinner daily. No reservations. 1450 Front St., at the junction of Front St. and Hwy. 30 (phone: 661-0937). Expensive to moderate.

Gerard's – Chef-owner Gerard Reversade has created one of Maui's finest restaurants with a menu that changes daily, taking advantage of what's freshest in the way of seafood, meats, and produce. The results are memorable, be they appetizers like wild mushrooms in puff pastry or calamari with lime and ginger; entrées like *opakapaka*, tournedos *au poivre* or in lobster sauce; or luscious desserts. The ambience is a French-Hawaiian hybrid. Open daily for breakfast, lunch, and dinner. Reservations advised. In the Plantation Inn, 174 Lahainaluna Rd. (phone: 661-8939). Expensive to moderate.

Longhi's – This immensely popular Italian restaurant attracts an arty crowd that contributes as much to its cabaret atmosphere as the white and black cane-back chairs and the black-and-white checkered floor. The fellow who pulls up a chair next to your table and begins the good-humored recitative is the waiter, and the litany he's reciting is the menu, so pay attention — it's the only one you get. Homemade pastas are the ticket here, too, though you can also have fish, chicken, veal, steak, or eggplant *alla parmigiana*, and all this is still merely a prelude to dessert. When the time comes, a tray laden with calories will sweep over the heads of the crowd, and if the array is confusing when it reaches eye level, rest assured that the mocha chocolate cheesecake will not disappoint. Open for breakfast (with some delicious fresh pastries), lunch, and dinner daily. No reservations. 888 Front St. (phone: 667-2288). Expensive to moderate.

Oceanhouse – Along with *Kimo's* and *Lahaina Broiler*, this is one of Lahaina's oceanfront favorites. Here it's the dining room downstairs on the edge of the water, while the bar is upstairs, open to the breeze on three sides. The latter is a delightful place to be at sunset and even more so after dark, when the sight of the floodlit waves rippling toward the foundations is mesmerizing. The *Oceanhouse* serves lobster with black bean sauce, filet mignon, chicken Claudia (with Parmesan and lemon butter sauce), beef teriyaki, and barbecued ribs — with or without the salad bar — and it has perhaps the friendliest service anywhere in this very friendly town. Open for lunch (upstairs at the *Seafood Café*) and dinner daily. Dinner reservations advised. 831 Front St. (phone: 661-3359). Expensive to moderate.

Kimo's – One of the three popular waterfront restaurants, *Kimo's* is a bit more sophisticated than the other two, and it is one of Lahaina's better values. Begin with a drink under one of the huge white canvas umbrellas on the open deck downstairs, and when the sun has definitely set, move on to the indoor-outdoor dining room upstairs. A basic mix of steaks, seafood, and local fresh fish of the day is served, each order with a zestfully seasoned house salad, rice, and freshly baked breads. The Polynesian chicken (marinated in a sauce of soy and ginger) and Koloa pork ribs (glazed with plum sauce in the manner of Koloa, Hawaii) are island specialties, and the hula pie (macadamia nut ice cream in an Oreo cookie crust, topped with chocolate fudge, whipped cream, and macadamia nuts) is legendary. Open daily for dinner; daily except Sundays for lunch. Reservations advised. 845 Front St. (phone: 661-4811). Moderate.

Kobe Steak House – The sushi bar is the real draw, but the Teppan-style cooking provides another reason for this restaurant's popularity with locals and visitors alike. Dinner served until 10 PM daily. Reservations advised. 136 Dickensen St. (phone: 667-5555). Moderate.

Lahaina Broiler – You'll spot this by the 100-year-old monkeypod tree, growing right through the roof. The *Lahaina Broiler*, run by the same people who run the *Pioneer Inn* and its restaurants, is one of three local favorites, all on the waterfront. It's every bit as viewful as the *Oceanhouse* and *Kimo's* and a lot more exposed to the elements. The bar and dining area are on one level, which is well nigh wave-pounded sea level. Steak, prime ribs, and fresh fish of the day are the menu mainstays. Open for breakfast (7 to 11 AM), lunch, and dinner daily. Reservations advised for dinner. 885 Front St. (phone: 661-3111). Moderate.

Tiger Asian Cuisine – Choices range from Japanese sushi to pupu platters to Korean barbecue. The decor is appealing, the food satisfying. Open daily from 11 to 2 AM. Dinner reservations advised. 630 Front St. (phone: 667-7003). Moderate.

Alex's Hole in the Wall – The premises are up one flight of stairs and smallish, yes, but despite the faintly pejorative air to its name, this restaurant, run by the Didio family, is a spic and span and decorous place that manages to strike the right balance between liveliness and intimacy. The menu, too, offsets some of its more expensive veal dinners with a selection of economical spaghetti dinners, while the linguine with white clam sauce is a middle-of-the-road favorite of many a repeat customer. The pasta is made daily. Open for dinner only; closed Sundays. Reservations advised. Wahie La., off Front St. (phone: 661-3197). Moderate to inexpensive.

Sam's Beachside Grill – California-casual in style, with a wonderful oceanfront setting. The menu ranges from delicious homemade soups and hamburgers to steamed clams and catch-of-the-day specialties. Open daily for lunch and dinner. Reservations advised. 505 Front St. (phone: 667-4341). Moderate to inexpensive.

Sunrise Café – The fresh-baked daily French pastries and coffees are worth a gourmand's attention. The place is owned and operated by the folks from *La Bretagne.* Open daily from 5:30 AM to midnight. No reservations. 693-A Front St. (phone: 661-3326). Inexpensive.

Kaanapali to Kapalua

So many of the visitors to Maui point their rented cars in the direction of West Maui that, left to their own devices, the Toyotas could probably make the trip themselves (and do it better, without any wrong turns near the airport). West Maui's gold coast of hotels and condominiums begins 4 miles north of Lahaina at the Kaanapali resort and ends some 10 miles farther north at another resort, Kapalua. In between are what local fancy and a few maps still refer to as towns, though to the uninitiated they look like a single, barely interrupted string of condominiums and homes lining both the *mauka* (inland) and *makai* (ocean) sides of the coastal road. Do not picture the concrete canyon of Waikiki, however, because the resorts at each end were planned to enhance, not overwhelm, their natural setting, and the structures between the two are sufficiently varied — here aggressively prominent, there shrinking in leaf-covered seclusion — not to blot out the view, which on West Maui, with its clean sweep from mountains to cane fields to sea, is always extraordinary.

The Kaanapali resort is a 500-acre playground containing six hotels (almost all the hotels on West Maui), five condominium complexes, two golf courses, a shopping center, and an excellent whaling museum, all arranged along 3 miles of choice sandy beach divided in half by a volcanic lava cone called Puu Kekaa (Black Rock) and laced together by a system of neat, tree-lined driveways. Guests may not realize it, but the complex, which opened in 1962 with only a golf course and an embryonic hotel in operation and a second hotel on the way, was Hawaii's first planned resort, the prototype of an idea that no longer seems unusual, though it certainly was back in the 1950s when first proposed.

Before its development, Kaanapali was an unproductive piece of scrubland at the foot of a more productive sugarcane plantation, both owned by

Lahaina's Pioneer Mill Company. During the late 19th and early 20th centuries, a sugarcane train traveled between Lahaina and a boat landing next to Black Rock. Cut cane was hauled to Lahaina; raw sugar was hauled from Lahaina and loaded onto tugboats at Black Rock and carried out to waiting ships. Pioneer eventually switched the sugar-loading operation to Lahaina, and it and its parent company, Amfac (American Factors), one of Hawaii's Big Five, began to think of a better use for the beach area. Two decades later, Kaanapali is still growing, with construction of new condominiums with more planned, including a cultural center; the only reminder of the old days is the Lahaina-Kaanapali and Pacific Railroad, a replica of an old-fashioned sugarcane train that now puffs its way along a pleasure route behind the hotels.

Kaanapali's beach stretches north beyond the limits of the resort as far as Honokowai, then disappears and reappears at intervals as sandy parentheses in the otherwise rocky coastline. The holiday condominiums lining the coastal road north are more consistent. The coastal villages of Honokowai, Kahana, and Napili are really an example of suburban sprawl pulled lengthwise, Honokowai turning into Kahana at the "S" in the road, Kahana turning into Napili in the vicinity of beautiful Napili Bay. Napili Beach is the first of two particularly lovely beaches, and Kapalua Beach, which edges Kapalua Bay around the next bend in the coast, is the second. Kapalua Beach is surrounded by the exquisite scenery of another of Maui's planned resorts, Kapalua, set on 750 panoramic acres formerly used to grow pineapples. Kapalua was the brainchild of the Maui Land and Pineapple Company, and its central features — the *Kapalua Bay* hotel, several condominium communities, two golf courses, ten tennis courts, and a small shopping center — all came into being during the 1970s. Work is underway on another condominium complex and plans for a second hotel have been announced.

Although the face of West Maui has in recent memory been sculpted by Amfac, Maui Land and Pineapple Company, and other Hawaiian business interests, the area has a pre-*haole* history as well. The road that circles West Maui (Highway 30) is still called Honoapiilani Highway, recalling the 16th-century chief Piilani, who built the first road here. Honoapiilani means "the bays of Piilani," and a drive along Highway 30 from Kaanapali to beyond Kapalua will take you past all six of the bays — Honokowai, Honokeana, Honokahua, Honolua, Honokohau, and Hononana — associated with him. And Puu Kekaa, according to ancient belief, was a sacred spot from which souls of the dead leaped into the spirit world. It was also the spot from which Maui's last chief, Kahekili, who ruled at the end of the 18th century and excelled at the sport of cliff jumping, made several of his most daring leaps. That he survived, defying death in more ways than one, reinforced his authority over his subjects. Today, the jump is repeated every evening at sundown at the *Sheraton Maui,* which sits astride Black Rock, and though the feat is less risky in thoroughly modern Maui, it can still raise a few goose bumps.

Lahaina-Kaanapali and Pacific Railroad – That is, the Sugarcane Train, an oil-fired turn-of-the-century steam locomotive and three open passenger coaches that now carry tourists on a pleasure excursion through golf courses and cane fields, across a

400-foot-long trestle, past views of the seashore and Lanai on one side and of the West Maui mountains on the other. The train puffs along 6 miles of 36-inch narrow-gauge track, portions of which follow the roadbed of the original cane haul line that ran between the cane fields of Kaanapali and Lahaina's Pioneer Mill from the 1880s to the early 1950s. Both of the railroad's engines — *Anaka* and *Myrtle* — were built in 1943 for a quarry in Ohio, and both have been rebuilt to resemble vintage sugarcane locomotives — circa the 1880s in the case of *Anaka,* about 1910 for *Myrtle.* The custom-made coaches are patterned after cars made in England in the late 19th century for a passenger train on the island of Hawaii. The LK & PRR makes six round trips daily between the Puukolii Boarding Platform and the Lahaina Station, with an interim stop at the Kaanapali Station. A one-way ride takes about 25 minutes, during which time the conductor delivers some facts and figures on the subject of sugarcane, plays the ukulele, and sings. The trip costs $5 one way, $8 round trip (half price for children aged 2 to 12), and various combination tours — such as a glass-bottom boat ride in Lahaina Harbor ($19); a Historic Lahaina itinerary, which includes admission to three museums ($12.50); and a viewing of the film *Hawaii: Islands of the Gods* on a 180-degree screen at the *Omni Theater* ($13) — are possible. The Kaanapali Trolley serves the Kaanapali Station, and a free railroad bus provides transportation between the Lahaina Station and the waterfront. The Puukolii Boarding Platform is across the highway from the *Royal Lahaina;* the Kaanapali Station is above the *Maui Eldorado* condominiums, and the Lahaina Station is 1½ blocks north of the intersection of Honoapiilani Hwy. and Lahainaluna Rd. (phone: 661-0089).

Whalers Village Museum – This is *the* place to visit if you want to know more about whales and the history of whaling. The bleached skeleton of a sperm whale, looking for all the world like a giant piece of modern art, is suspended above sculptured models of whales, porpoises, and dolphins, and a ceramic tile floor map places the major whaling grounds and ports of call. Cases full of artifacts and illustrations detail every aspect of whaling, from the construction of the ship to setting out on the voyage, life at sea, and the hunting, killing, and processing of the whale. There are tools used in sail making, harpoons, some rather horrific-looking instruments used by a ship's surgeon, and whale products — antique lamps filled with whale oil, walking canes with whale ivory handles, whale ivory letter openers, rolling pins, and pie crimpers. Scrimshaw is an important part of the collection; in fact, along with the larger Pacific Whaling Museum on Oahu, the best examples of old scrimshaw remaining in the Hawaiian islands are on view here. You'll see materials for scrimshaw, comparisons of 19th-century scrimshaw with reproductions and examples of modern scrimshaw, plus some unusual pieces such as a scrimshawed ostrich egg and the jawbone of a sea lion scrimshawed with a portrait of George Washington. Open daily from 9:30 AM to 10 PM; no admission charge. Whalers Village, Kaanapali Resort (phone: 661-5992).

SHOPPING: Almost everyone staying in West Maui eventually makes a shopping trip into Lahaina; the salty old town has the greatest concentration of vendibles in all the Valley Isle and no less an inclination to commerce than when whalers walked the streets to replenish their ships. Visitors don't have to make the trip, however, because almost equal opportunities to browse and buy exist closer to their Kaanapali-Kapalua homes-away-from-home. There is, first of all, Kaanapali's Whalers Village Museum and Shopping Complex. There shops stock necessities as well as gifts, souvenirs, and clothing, and stay open till 9 or 10 PM daily. Hotels in the Kaanapali resort have lobby shops, and some have substantial shopping arcades that aim to do much more than sell guests on Hawaiian shirts. Foremost among these are the promenades at the *Hyatt Regency* and the *Maui Marriott* as well as that of the *Westin Maui.* Several miles to the north at Kapalua, the first-rate Kapalua Shops practice their version of not-for-the-stingy seduction. On Mondays and Thursdays from

8 AM to 1:30 PM, the farmers' market in Kahana features locally grown produce (including sweet Hana corn and Molokai watermelon), fresh baked breads and cookies, and low prices.

WHALERS VILLAGE MUSEUM AND SHOPPING COMPLEX

A recent upgrade of the complex has seen the addition of numerous name shops. Among them: the *Sharper Image* (phone: 661-7061), *ACA Joe* (phone: 667-2282), *Benetton* (phone: 661-8188), and *Esprit de Corps* (phone: 661-4400). Shops of a more homegrown style include the following:

Bebe's – One of several shops on Maui, this branch features women's contemporary fashions of bright colors and easy-to-wear styles (phone: 661-0444).

Hobie Sports – Bright and upbeat, this shop carries a wide range of water sports equipment as well as beach fashions, beach chairs, and all kinds of beach accessories (phone: 661-5455).

Island Tan – Your nose will know where you are before you enter, with fragrances of tuberose, frangipani, pikake, and other tropical flowers wafting from within. This store sells tanning lotion and skin care products (all made with aloe vera), and original Hawaiian fragrances (phone: 667-9077).

Ka Honu Gift Gallery – The local and South Pacific handicrafts include lots of wood carvings; bowls of koa, milo, hau, mango, and monkeypod; and shell leis from the island of Niihau. Browse among the large selection of Christmas ornaments (phone: 661-0173).

Lahaina Printsellers Ltd. – This gallery specializes in antique maps and prints of Hawaiian and South Seas scenes. Among the unusual inventory are engravings from the folio of illustrations that accompanied the official account of Cook's third voyage, as drawn by James Webber, the artist assigned to travel with Cook, and as cut into plates and published (1784) by the Admiralty in London. Other beautiful prints from diverse sources document paradises when they were truly unspoiled (phone: 667-7617).

Lahaina Scrimshaw Factory – After seeing the rare old pieces on display in the Whalers Village Museum, stop here to admire more modern (most of them) examples of the art of scrimshaw. The *Lahaina Scrimshaw Factory* has a roster of resident scrimshanders producing work on whale's teeth and fossil walrus ivory for its four stores on Maui. Charms begin at $5; large, museum-quality pieces are an investment (phone: 661-4034).

Liberty House – The Whalers Village branch of the department store chain carries men's, women's, and children's clothing; cosmetics; and some gift and souvenir items (phone: 661-4451).

Painted Lady – Here find a wonderful selection of hand-painted women's wear and accessories (phone: 661-5383).

Silk Kaanapali – This shop features one of Hawaii's best selections of fashionable silks (phone: 667-7133).

Waldenbooks – Besides all the latest paperbacks, this branch of the well-known chain provides a selection of Hawaiiana — and Mauiana — from guidebooks to folklore (phone: 661-8638).

HYATT REGENCY

Center Art Gallery–Hawaii – It may be the best stocked and classiest of all the art galleries in the islands, with a good selection of original paintings, lithographs, and sculpture by both American and European artists (phone: 661-1200).

Chapman's – This men's store sells jackets, blazers, slacks, shirts, and shoes in subdued color schemes, with only a very few, very quiet aloha shirts (phone: 661-4121).

Collections – This upscale division of *Liberty House* features an excellent selection of high-fashion women's wear (phone: 667-7785). There is also a branch at a nearby *Westin Maui* (phone: 661-5083).

Elephant Walk – Ceramics, batiks, glassware, and other items handcrafted by Hawaiian artists are among the featured collectibles and knickknacks (phone: 667-2848).

Hawaiian Island Gems – Everything (or nearly) is made of gold or ivory. Among the more interesting items are reproductions of 19th-century Hawaiian coins and Hawaiian heirloom jewelry. Bracelets and rings in this series are hand-engraved and can be enameled either with your own name in Hawaiian or as is, with a Hawaiian term of endearment (phone: 667-7788).

Lloyd and Carver – Luggage, briefcases, wallets, and ladies' handbags by French and Italian designers make up the bulk of this shop's merchandise. Swiss watches and jewelry of the only-one-piece-out-of-the-case-at-a-time variety are sold, too (phone: 667-7789).

Postmark Maui – Some of it may be tacky, but some of it isn't, and at any rate, it's all made on the island, and for lovers of Maui, that may well be enough. Gifts and a wide array of souvenir trinkets, useful and otherwise (phone: 661-3408).

Sandal Tree – The name is clear: men's and women's footwear appropriate to the clime and the place; and for the opposite extreme, straw hats with feathered hatbands (phone: 661-3495).

KAPALUA

By the Bay – Quite the nicest shell shop on Maui has shells and corals from Hawaii and the rest of the Pacific. Large, lovely, pale blue coral from the Indo-Pacific; white branch, lettuce, and trumpet corals from the South Pacific; bright orange Hawaiian sea fans; and sprigs of Maui black coral make such an enticing show of the premises that all but collectors may overlook the tinier specimens, including the precious wentletrap, or spiral staircase shell, coveted by the Dutch in the 19th century. Also distinctive shell jewelry (phone: 669-5227).

Distant Drums – It sells a small museum's worth of handicrafts, artifacts, antiques, and jewelry from Hawaii, the Pacific islands, New Guinea, Indonesia, and Asia (phone: 669-5522).

Kapalua Shop – The resort logo decorates towels, glassware, scarves, men's and women's sportswear, luggage, eyeglass cases, kimonos, and so on Sometimes the Kapalua name appears unobtrusively in print, but mostly the butterfly is flying alone (phone: 669-4172).

Longhi's – High style and high prices are equally apparent in the clothes (both men's and women's), jewelry, collectibles, and crafts that make browsing a pleasure. Stop by at the right time, and refreshments and piano music are included (phone: 669-5000).

Mandalay – Despite its name, the cottons and silks in this shop come from Thailand. There are long caftans, short dresses, smocks, blouses, and jackets for women, and a few shirts for men (phone: 669-6170).

Michele's – Elegant dresses and accessories for women. *Michele's* sells the sort of clothing you might pick off the designer racks back home and could wear to dinner at Kapalua's *Bay Club* or *Veranda.* It's not the place to come for Polynesian styles (phone: 669-6943).

Reyn's – This shop features both its own line of shirts, slacks, and swim trunks and sportswear by other manufacturers. The company pioneered reverse-print men's clothes — made with the bright right side of the fabric inside — more than a decade ago, and the look has become a Hawaiian classic (phone: 669-5260).

Superwhale – Much like its sister store in the Whalers Village, this boutique includes appealing handmade quilts, custom outfits, and artwork for a child's room (phone: 669-5282).

MAUI MARRIOTT

This hotel in the Kaanapali resort opened with a *Liberty House* (phone: 667-6142), selling men's and women's clothing and some accessories, while the adjoining *Suits Me* (phone: 667-6132) is a *Liberty House* specialty shop carrying swimwear for men and women. Clothing for men only is at *Buck's For Men* (phone: 667-7801), which sells much more than swim trunks. The *Maui Marriott* logo on sportswear, beach gear, and other articles is available from *Hawaii I.D.* (phone: 667-1200, ext. 66717); masks, flippers, Boogie boards, rafts, and suntan products are sold at *Sun and Surf* (phone: 667-9302). Two jewelry stores, *Jewels by Cellini* (phone: 661-5594) and *Jewels by Andrade* (phone: 667-1967), are in place with eclectic selections; and *Lahaina Scrimshaw* (phone: 661-3145) is perhaps the most attractive of the *Lahaina Scrimshaw Factory* outlets on Maui.

 NIGHTLIFE: With any number of hotel and restaurant bars strategically placed so that sight lines lead straight out to the Pacific and the offshore islands of Lanai or Molokai, sunset watching is as important here as in Lahaina. The most unusual observance takes place at the *Sheraton Maui* (phone: 661-0031) just before sunset, when a hotel employee in native dress appears brandishing fire, lights a line of tiki torches running the length of Black Rock promontory, throws his lei into the sea, and then dives from the cliff himself. Though the leap is not impressively high, it can be affecting, because the ritual recalls the ancient Hawaiian belief that Black Rock (its real name is Puu Kekaa) was a "soul's leap," a place where the souls of the dead left Earth to rejoin the spirit world. The hotel's high *On the Rocks* restaurant is a splendid wide-screen vantage point for watching Kaanapali sunsets, but the *Sundowner Bar* by the pool is the best place to be for the torchlighting ceremony.

The grounds of the *Sheraton Maui* are also the site of the *Aloha Activity Center*'s *Aloha Luau,* one of the few daily, old-style luaus (meaning that guests see the kalua pig come out of the *imu,* the underground oven in which it has been steaming all day) on Maui. The entertainment includes a Polynesian show, which reaches its peak with the appearance of the Samoan fire dancer. The luau goes on at 5:30 PM — so beachfront sunset watching is included, too. At press time it cost $36 for adults, $19 for children. (Check with the *Aloha Activity Center* at the Whalers Village, or call 667-9564.)

The *Royal Lahaina* (phone: 661-3611) has a competitively priced nightly luau, featuring traditional foods like Kalua pig and haupia (coconut pudding), as well as a variety of salads. The hour-long Polynesian revue is held on a beachfront lawn, and the luau runs from 5:30 to 8:30 PM, timed to take in the sunset. A musical revue, *Maui, Moonlight, and Magic,* is presented in the *Discovery Room* of the *Sheraton Maui* (phone: 661-0031) at 8:30 nightly except Tuesdays, for a $5 cover charge with dinner, or $15 for cocktails only. At the *Westin* (phone: 667-2525), *Cooks at the Beach* features a three-choice dinner buffet ($17) accompanied by live Hawaiian music, from 5 to 7 PM daily (no reservations). The *Hyatt Regency* (phone: 667-7474) features the Drums of the Pacific dinner show on the *Sunset Terrace* ($24), with cocktail seating ($22) at 7 PM daily, except Sundays and Thursdays.

The Kaanapali resort has two popular discos, *Spats II,* at the *Hyatt Regency,* where the dancing goes on till 2 AM nightly in a cavernous space reminiscent of the gaslight era, and the *Maui Marriott*'s handsome *Banana Moon,* with two handkerchief-size dance floors, quite a few cozy seating areas conducive to conversation, and a backgammon bar. More mellow music for dancing is played in various hotel rooms around the resort, including the *Royal Ocean Terrace* at the *Royal Lahaina* and outdoors at the *Pavillion Courtyard* of the *Hyatt Regency* (nightly). Best for relaxed listening are the

Tiki Terrace of the *Kaanapali Beach, Maui Marriott*'s *Makai Bar,* and the *El Crab Catcher* restaurant at Whalers Village. For the early bird, the *Westin Maui* serves cocktails alfresco at its *Beach Bar* to the sounds of a Hawaiian trio, and its *Villa Restaurant Lounge* hosts contemporary jazz from 7 PM to midnight.

Beyond the Kaanapali resort, nightlife is less active, though there are possibilities. The *Kapalua Bay* (phone: 669-5656) offers dancing to a piano-led trio in *The Garden,* nightly except Sundays, from 8 PM to midnight. The dinner show at the *Napili Kai Beach Club* (in the *Seahouse Restaurant;* phone: 669-6271) is an unusual demonstration of Hawaiiana, Fridays only, put on by children of the hotel staff. Tickets sell out quickly to *Napili Kai* guests, but you can reserve leftover seats. A Hawaiian trio holds forth with music for dancing on other nights in the same restaurant. There's nightly dancing to live contemporary and country music at the *Kahana Keyes* restaurant (phone: 669-8071) in the *Valley Isle Resort* condominiums at Kahana.

 CHECKING IN: The greatest concentration of hotels and condominiums on Maui is found along the Kaanapali-Kapalua coast. North of Kaanapali, the beach narrows and gradually gives way to stretches of lava rock coast and shallow reef-lined waters that make swimming more difficult. At both Honokawai and Kahana, clusters of condominiums overwhelm the small beaches, but Napili's low-rise properties are better suited to their surroundings, taking advantage of a mix of rocky promontories and beach-lined bays. If you have just arrived from Honolulu, these accommodations may seem comparatively high priced. Expect to pay $250 and up for a double room in a place listed in the very expensive category, from $150 to $240 in expensive, $85 to $145 in moderate, and from $60 to $80 in those classed as inexpensive. There may be a slight drop in the rates off-season, which, for some properties, includes summer. The hotels below have air conditioning, a phone, a TV set, and a private lanai for every room; and while all the units in the condominiums listed are similarly endowed with the latter three amenities, they are air conditioned only as stated (the farther north you go, the less air conditioning occurs; most people find it unnecessary). Some condominiums charge extra for maid service, a few require a 3- or 4-day minimum stay, and some do not accept credit cards. All telephone numbers are in the 808 area code unless otherwise indicated.

Hyatt Regency – One of the sightseeing attractions of West Maui, and sooner or later everyone drops by for a look. An outsider won't see the 815 rooms — all decorated in subdued tones of peach to beige to mauve — which are dispersed in three 7- to 9-story towers, but the real razzle-dazzle is open to all. To begin with, there's a multimillion-dollar collection of Asian and Pacific art spilling out of teak, glass, and brass lobbies onto the grounds. And these — about 20 acres — are not only landscaped with Japanese and tropical gardens, but waterscaped, too, with streams, waterfalls, pools, and bridges around the centerpiece swimming pool, a free-form extravaganza crossed by a swinging footbridge, fed by a 130-foot water slide, and divided in two by an upcropping of rock that sends waterfalls tumbling over the swim-in or walk-in bar in its middle. Exotic birds, which glide, flutter, and perch throughout the property, are tended by a staff ornithologist. Other amenities, in addition to the beachfront location, include a 55-foot catamaran, tennis courts, a health club, a promenade of shops, some of Kaanapali's most popular restaurants (see *Eating Out*), and a disco. The major thing questionable here is the high level of activity, which, because of frequent conventions (not to mention the scads of regular visitors), can become fairly frenetic, especially around the pool. Furthermore, the complex doesn't really have anything to do with Hawaii; it is instead a resort unto itself. At the southern end of the Kaanapali Resort (phone: 661-1234; 800-228-9000). Very expensive to expensive.

Kaanapali Alii – This is one of Maui's best condo properties, with beautifully landscaped grounds, a large pool area adjacent to the beach, and nicely designed and furnished apartments. Kaanapali Resort (phone: 667-1400; 800-642-6284). Very expensive to expensive.

Kaanapali Shores – Maui's largest condominium complex combines the advantages of both condo and hotel. High-rise (mostly 9 stories), the 463 units zigzag along a horseshoe that faces the sea and encloses nicely landscaped grounds. Public areas are stylish, with marble floors and contemporary works of art, while the decor upstairs reverts to the comfort of cane, rattan, and splashy prints. Studios, 1-, and 2-bedroom units are air conditioned, spacious, well maintained, and fully equipped; guests can avail themselves of the 24-hour front desk, and the activities desk, which organizes a week-round schedule of diversions. In addition, there are tennis courts, a putting green, a sundry store, the poolside *Beach Club* restaurant, and an oceanfront location just past the northern end of Kaanapali Beach (although reef-lined shallows may inhibit swimming here). 100 Kaanapali Shores Pl. (phone: 667-2211; 800-922-7866). Very expensive to expensive.

Kapalua Bay – If the *Hyatt* is the southern boundary of West Maui's vacationland, this is its northern anchor, though the two properties are distinctively different. *Kapalua Bay* specializes in a far quieter, more restrained and stylish brand of luxury, with no glitzy gimmicks, but no less eye appeal. Its lobby is strikingly handsome: a 3-story open space through which birds fly amid the hanging vines as though it were the great outdoors. Recently refurbished at a cost of $10 million, the hotel's fewer than 200 rooms (alike in size and decor, with generous bathrooms and his-and-her sinks) are on multiple levels of two main wings that extend seaward from the lobby like outstretched arms, one of them all but touching the exquisite crescent of Kapalua Bay beach. Views from the rooms vary, but the entire 18-acre property, with its acres of manicured lawns, occupies some of the island's most splendid topography. Equally renowned are the Kapalua kitchens, which supply 3 restaurants (see *Eating Out*). Pools (including a new one that is an abstract copy of the resort's butterfly and pineapple logo), golf and tennis at the resort's 2 courses (a third is underway) and 10 courts, a variety of water sports and other activities (from *ikebana* to kite flying), and an adjoining shopping arcade add to the picture. The hotel offers both MAP and EP year round. 1 Bay Dr., Kapalua (phone: 669-5656; 800-367-8000). Very expensive to expensive.

Kapalua Villas – The *Kapalua Bay*'s neighbors at the Kapalua resort. Unlike most condominium complexes, this is not a compact grouping of units on a limited lot; rather, it looks like an exclusive residential community spread out over vast verdant green acreage sloping to the sea, with breathtaking views part of most bookings. The *Bay Villas* are clustered closest to the water, the *Ridge Villas* are higher up across the highway, and the *Golf Villas* are tucked behind the Bay Course facing a panorama of the Pacific Ocean and the island of Molokai in the not-too-far distance through lines of neat Cook pines. Units — 1- and 2-bedroom sizes — are indeed luxurious, with high beamed ceilings, large bathrooms, and tiled kitchens. Guests have access to 3 beaches, several pools, the resort's golf and tennis facilities, room service, and they can sign up for any of the activities offered by the hotel. 500 Bay Dr., Kapalua (phone: 669-5656; 800-367-8000). Very expensive to expensive.

Embassy Suites at Kaanapali – Hawaii's first all-suite hotel, this recently opened 413-unit property is situated on 7½ acres of beachfront directly north of the Kaanapali resort. With condominiums a well-established option in Hawaii, the all-suites concept is a less dramatic shift from traditional accommodations. Each suite provides 800 square feet of living space, and the hotel amenities include pool, restaurant, lounges, and a beach-services pavilion. A 12-story waterfall adds a tropical touch to the landscaped atrium in what is otherwise designed in a Spanish

Mediterranean style. 100 Kaanapali Pl., Kaanapali (phone: 661-2000; 800-462-6284). Very expensive to expensive.

Maui Marriott – What meets the eye here is something of a wide V formed by two 9-story guest wings connected by a 4-story lobby, paved in brick and landscaped with orchids, palms, and fountains. Between the buildings and the beachfront are grassy lawns and gardens and 2 swimming pools edged in rock. The hotel's tiered main dining room, the *Moana Terrace,* faces the gardens, and so does the more intimate *Lokelani Room,* done up to resemble a plantation living room of the last century (for a third restaurant, see *Eating Out*). Add several bars, a good-looking disco-nightclub, an arcade of 20-plus shops, 5 tennis courts, water sports, and a full activities program (including poi pounding) to keep guests happy. Most rooms have good ocean views, but overall the hotel doesn't have quite the pizzazz of other hotels in the same price category. Kaanapali Resort (phone: 667-1200; 800-228-9290). Very expensive to expensive.

Westin Maui – The $155 million spent to transform the old *Maui Surf* into the 762-room *Westin Maui* has added a new showpiece to the Kaanapali resort, featuring Maui's largest pool area, a multi-level affair complete with waterfalls, islands, slides, and grottoes. Artworks (to the tune of $2 million) grace the public areas, which are among Hawaii's most appealing, designed to provide both elegance and privacy. A lovely promenade winds past shops and the lush landscape that surrounds the pool. The hotel benefits from its central location on Kaanapali's South Beach, which allows it to offer a full water-activities program. Other amenities include a complete health spa, free to guests, and excellent food in its 6 restaurants and lounges. Kaanapali Resort (phone: 667-2525; 800-228-3000). Very expensive to expensive.

Whaler – The two stark white 12-story blocks that face each other over the swimming pool and Jacuzzi look as though they could as easily have sprouted on the Mediterranean — balconies, flower boxes, et al. The *Whaler* comprises 360 spacious garden-view, ocean-view, or oceanfront units, from studios to 2-bedroom suites, many smashingly decorated in wicker and Polynesian prints, all air conditioned. A 24-hour front desk operates in the lobby, and tennis courts, an exercise room, a sauna, a mini-market, and the beach are right out front, but guests interested in further activity must venture beyond the enclave. Restaurants and shopping at Whalers Village next door. Kaanapali Resort (phone: 661-4861; 800-367-7052). Very expensive to expensive.

Kaanapali Beach – The fact that this is the smallest and the least expensive hotel in the Kaanapali resort complex does not mean its guests choose it by default. It has a friendly feeling, perhaps more homespun than elsewhere, that recommends it. The hotel, with 4 wings of 3 or 6 stories, is shaped like a horseshoe facing the beach, with a paved patio, lawn and garden, and a pool in the form of a whale among the enclosures. The 433 rooms are pleasant but not lavish, and there are stores, a coffee shop, and the *Tiki Terrace* restaurant, not to mention the beach shack for water sports rentals and tennis privileges at the *Royal Lahaina.* Kaanapali Resort (phone: 661-0011; 800-657-7700). Expensive.

Maui Park Inn – This new, Aston-managed property consists of 72 studios and 216 single-bedroom units, each with complete kitchen facilities, lanai, ceiling fans, and cable television. It's set north of Kaanapali, on 5 acres across from Honokowai Beach Park. 3626 Lower Honoapiilani Hwy. (phone: 808-669-8098; 800-92-ASTON).

Napili Kai Beach Club – It calls itself a hotel, one of the few in the condominium strip stretching beyond the Kaanapali resort to Kapalua. The rooms, however, have kitchenettes (smaller than those in the standard condo), and room service is not offered. Right on the beach, its 136 rooms spread in 8 buildings (2-story maximum) that creep along the north edge of beautiful Napili Bay; to reveal the view, you have only to slide open the shoji panels to your lanai — an appealing Japanese touch. There are 5 swimming pools, 2 tennis courts, and 2 putting greens on the property, and the *Kapalua Golf Course* is just across the road. There's dancing at the beachfront *Seahouse* several nights a week, a weekly mai tai party, and a weekly Polynesian show. No credit cards accepted for the room tab. 5900 Honoapiilani Rd. (phone: 669-6271; 800-367-5030). Expensive.

Sheraton Maui – The other of Kaanapali's two original hotels, this one sits on the resort area's most striking spot — atop and around Black Rock promontory, a volcanic cone whose existence gave the *Sheraton* a nice expanse of beach and two levels on which to build its lobbies, restaurants, and bars. Garden Tower, Cliff Tower, the Ocean Lanai wings at the back of the rock, and the low-slung cottages at sea level have all been recently refurbished and are architecturally striking, too, an ensemble of circles and vine-draped lunettes. An open restaurant and bar are down by one of the hotel's 2 pools (the one surrounded by Astroturf), but for a truly panoramic view, take the elevator or the cliffside walk up to the window-walled *On The Rocks Bar* and *Discovery Room* and enjoy sustenance. Handsome bedrooms (435), a catamaran shared with neighboring resort hotels, tennis courts, luau, and the best snorkeling in the resort off the rock. Kaanapali Resort (phone: 661-0031; 800-325-3535). Expensive.

Maui Eldorado – Were it not for a slice of the *Royal Kaanapali Golf Course,* this, too, would be a beachfront condominium. As it is, there's a fair bit of fairway in front of it, and while the path that weaves through the green to the *Eldorado*'s own beach cabana is a lovely walk, an electric cart makes the trip hourly to spare guests the effort. The condominium consists of 200-plus air conditioned studios to 2-bedroom units in 12 low (2-story) buildings, exceedingly well-manicured grounds, 3 swimming pools, and little else. No restaurants or distracting activities, though the amenities of the Kaanapali resort are all around you. Kaanapali Resort (phone: 661-0021; 800-367-2967). Expensive to moderate.

Napili Point – The strength of this condominium is its extraordinary long and narrow position running the length of a high point of land separating two bays, and the panorama from almost any lanai on the property is a sight to be seen. The handsome strip of low units is on two levels, fronted by a strip of lawn that drops off to boulders, but around the point a footpath leads to the beach at Napili Bay. Rooms — 115 1- or 2-bedroom units — are attractive, and there are 2 pools, barbecue grills, and picnic tables on the grounds, but for the rest, nothing is planned except peace and quiet. A sundry store is nearby. 5295 Honoapiilani Hwy. (phone: 669-5611; 800-922-7866). Expensive to moderate.

Royal Lahaina – On Kaanapali's northern stretch of beach, this is one of that resort area's two original hotels. Its 514 rooms — in both the 12-story Lahaina Kai Tower and in the 24 two-story cottages between the beach and the golf course — have recently been refurbished and renovated. Walk around the manicured grounds and you'll come across 3 pools, 3 restaurants (*Chopsticks,* with a well-priced international, all-appetizer menu; *Moby Dick's* for seafood; and the *Royal Ocean Terrace* for more standard fare and a lavish Sunday brunch), a nightly luau, beachside outlets for a number of water sports, Jacuzzi, and the biggest drawing card, the *Royal Lahaina Tennis Ranch,* which has 11 courts and a stadium and is managed by Peter Burwash International. Kaanapali Resort (phone: 661-3611; 800-227-4700). Expensive to moderate.

Mahina Surf – This small gem of a condo is for those who wish to be left to their own devices. Three 2-story buildings enclose a green lawn that sweeps down to boulders at the edge of the ocean, and beyond a good-sized swimming pool, outdoor barbecue, palm trees, plumerias, bougainvillea, and banks of ginger, there is no further distraction. The 56 1- and 2-bedroom units have been individually — and nicely — decorated by their owners. You'll sun on the grass, snorkel off the rocks, but for something sandy, you'll get in the car and head up or down the road a bit. Grocery shopping is about ½ mile away; maid service is extra. Minimum stay: 3 nights, with discounts for stays of 7 nights or longer. 4057 Lower Honoapiilani Rd., in the Honokowai area (phone: 669-6068; 800-367-6086). Moderate.

Maui Kaanapali Villas – A 200-unit mix of mostly low-rise hotel room and condominium accommodations in an excellent location on the Kaanapali's quiet North Beach. The nicely landscaped, well-maintained grounds surround 3 swimming pools and add a luxurious spaciousness not typical of Kaanapali properties. 2805 Honoapiilani Hwy. (phone: 667-7791; 800-922-7866). Moderate.

Polynesian Shores – Two doors from the *Mahina Surf* and its twin in all but a few respects. This time there are 52 1-, 2-, and 3-bedroom condominium units in those 3 low wings, the pool amid the plumerias is slightly smaller, and there is the wistful addition of ironwood trees where the sweep of lawn meets the sea. A wooden deck built out over the boulders is the place for barbecuing and sunset watching, and a wooden staircase nearby leads down to a tiny, mostly rocky beachlet, good for snorkeling but not for sunning. Rooms, again individually decorated, are well above average, and it is probably for this that the *Polynesian Shores* costs somewhat more than its neighbor. Maid service is not provided. Monthly rates are available. Minimum stay: 3 nights. 3975 Honoapiilani Rd. (phone: 669-6065; 800-433-6284). Moderate.

 EATING OUT: Since almost everything in the Kaanapali-Kapalua strip has been created with the tourist in mind, there is certainly no shortage of places to eat, and there are many, many more eating options than those listed below. The choice of food — continental, Italian, basic steakhouse — is much as in Lahaina and the price range also is much the same. Expect to pay $50 or more for the average meal for two (without drinks, wine, or tip) in a restaurant listed as expensive; $30 to $45 in a place listed as moderate; and $20 to $25 in an inexpensive restaurant. The area does differ from Lahaina in two respects, however. For one thing, though the prevailing mood is still casual, there are more places where you won't feel out of place if you want to dress up, and several that strongly suggest you do. Another difference is the dearth of fast-food outlets. Those pinching pennies will find more to choose from back in town. All telephone numbers are in the 808 area code unless otherwise indicated.

Bay Club – The *Kapalua Bay*'s reputation for fine food can be tested in any of its three highly praised restaurants, and the *Bay Club* is one of them, though it's actually a bit away from the hotel on a lava rock peninsula at the far end of Kapalua Beach. In appearance, the dining room is exceedingly well bred — pine walls with koa trim, rattan furniture cushioned in fresh batik prints, but no superfluous detail to distract from the open-air view. Lunch is relaxed (the restaurant even has a pool), with pasta, catch of the day, omelettes, sandwiches, salads, or a heaped plate from the salad bar to choose from; but dinner is a quiet, very softly candlelit and refined occasion to partake of the specialties of seafood, steaks, lamb, or veal. Open daily. Reservations necessary. Kapalua Bay Hotel, Kapalua (phone: 669-5656). Expensive.

Garden Room – Another of the *Kapalua Bay*'s restaurants. The reason most nonguests have beaten a path to the door is the Mayfair Luncheon Buffet, the greatest temptation to excess since an invite from Lucullus. A fruit table, two salad tables, a cheese tray, four hot entrées with vegetables, potatoes, and rice (one day's selection: lamb curry with full garnish, island fish meunière with macadamia nuts, roast veal in cream sauce, pork tofu) and approximately 20 feet of pies, cakes, and pastries (plus wax porpoises, swans, and nene geese) are all yours at the price at press time of $16.50 a head. The Mayfair Buffet is served Sundays from 10 AM to 2 PM. A somewhat more modest breakfast buffet is served on other days from 6:30 to 10 AM ($12.50). Reservations advised. Kapalua Bay Hotel, Kapalua (phone: 669-5656). Expensive to moderate.

Nikko Steak House – Diners sit with others at teppan tables (which have a grill set in the middle) nibbling appetizers, sipping miso soup and sake, until the chef arrives to bedazzle with his demonstration of the martial art of cooking. Knives flash and chop onions in midair, lobster tails pop from their skins, steaks fall into a dozen slices by sleight of hand alone. The chef cooks it all in front of you, fills your plate, and exits to applause, bowing. Don't worry if you've no room left for dessert — the fried ice cream is not so much a delicacy as a curiosity. Open for dinner daily. Reservations necessary. Maui Marriott, Kaanapali Resort (phone: 667-1200). Expensive.

Plantation Veranda – The third restaurant at the *Kapalua Bay* and the most intimate. Pegge Hopper's handsome murals of Hawaiian women are a modern note, but for the rest, this indoor spot is meant to be reminiscent of the veranda of an old plantation house, thus the old-fashioned multi-paned windows facing the courtyard, the hooked rugs, the Windsor chairs, and the pewter service plates. Here, "home cooking" includes caviar for an appetizer, and among its best-selling entrées are fresh fish of the day poached with saffron and tomatoes or spring lamb on marinated eggplant with port wine sauce. The wine list, a long one, features California wines. Open for dinner daily. Reservations necessary; so are jackets. Kapalua Bay Hotel, Kapalua (phone: 669-5656). Expensive.

Sound of the Falls – A grand entrance down a wide and lovely flight of lighted steps is an apt preparation for the elegant dining room that awaits. With much of the dining area in open air, a guest is treated to views of a waterfall, flamingoes, and palm-studded pools. Perhaps a bit on the pretentious side, the menu nonetheless promises fine food, and doesn't disappoint in quality upon serving. The confit of duck salad with scalloped artichoke and oriental mushrooms in a light walnut dressing is a delight. The wine cellar is one of Maui's best, with more than 200 choices. Soufflés are created in a wide variety of flavors (Grand Marnier, coconut, and chocolate being but three), and the loving table-side preparation of numerous dessert cakes provides a dramatic closing note for dinner. Open daily for dinner. Reservations necessary, as are collared shirt, dress slacks, and shoes for men. Westin Maui (phone: 667-2525). Expensive.

Swan Court – The fine dining room of the *Hyatt Regency* has its entire façade open to the air, the mauve and dusty rose carpeted floor a mere three flagstone steps above the water of a lagoon. Guests enter by descending a grand staircase at the back, take their seats, and watch the swans glide by as though in a fairy tale. Roast duck, roast rack of lamb, châteaubriand, seafood, and the Nettings of the Hukilau (fresh catch of the day) are typical items from the continental menu. Open for breakfast and dinner daily, and if you opt for the latter, remember the staircase and dress accordingly (collared shirt, dress slacks and shoes for men). Reservations advised. Hyatt Regency, Kaanapali Resort (phone: 667-7474). Expensive.

Lahaina Provision Company – The name conjures up visions of a dusty warehouse or a folksy general store, which is unfortunate, because this open-air restaurant looking out over the rock upcropping in the *Hyatt Regency* pool is quite slick and smart. The green tile floor shines, as does the green upholstery of the rattan chairs, and so do the leaves of innumerable potted plants. The fare is basic — steaks, chops, seafood — but come dessert, diners are directed to fill a bowl with ice cream and do their own thing at a copper counterful of chocolate toppings. It's called the chocoholic bar and is offered in the evening only. Open for lunch and dinner daily; reservations advised. Hyatt Regency, Kaanapali Resort (phone: 667-7474). Expensive to moderate.

Lokelani – It's an elegant dining room, with tinkling piano music, candlelight, pictures of old Hawaii, and antique china and lamps. The menu, while not especially innovative, always features well-prepared and beautifully presented old favorites: appetizers such as sashimi and shrimp lumpia; entrées such as veal Marsala and sautéed scallops. Open for dinner daily. Reservations advised. Maui Marriott (phone: 667-1200). Expensive to moderate.

Maui Rose – The terrine of capon with fresh morels as an appetizer, pizza topped with eggplant or Canadian scallops, and Upcountry pheasant stuffed with wild mushrooms as an entrée are some of the more unusual offers at *Embassy Suites'* fine dining establishment. Open for dinner daily. Reservations advised. 100 Kaanapali Pl. (phone: 661-2000). Expensive to moderate.

Moby Dick's – The name tells the tale: This eatery specializes in all manner of seafood, from Australian lobster tails to island prawns and the catch of the day. Open for dinner daily; reservations advised. Royal Lahaina (phone: 661-3611). Expensive to moderate.

Peacock – The former Kaanapali golf clubhouse has become an elegant restaurant. Magenta napery set with brass service plates and wicker chairs in fanciful shapes hint of the Near and the Far East. The menu includes such specialties as rack of lamb and veal dishes. Alohawear is fine. Open for lunch weekdays, dinner daily; reservations advised. 2550 Kekaa Dr., Kaanapali Resort (phone: 667-6847). Expensive to moderate.

Chopsticks – Maui's first restaurant dedicated to "grazing," with a selection of appetizer-sized portions that allow diners to enjoy samplings of Chinese, Japanese, continental, and Polynesian specialties all in one sitting. Open daily for dinner; reservations advised. Royal Lahaina (phone: 661-3611). Moderate.

El Crab Catcher – Like the *Bay Club,* this is a seaside restaurant with a pool. At lunch, you'll probably sit outside (the stretch of beach up front is a place where islanders like to see and be seen). Later, as the sun sets, white tablecloths appear, and the mood progresses from easygoing to rather romantic, you can retreat to the glassed-in (partly) main dining area yet still be comfortably alfresco. The restaurant specializes in seafood, fresh local fishes of the day in particular, but the beer-steamed Alaskan king crab legs have been highly praised, too. Open daily for lunch and dinner; reservations advised. Whalers Village, Kaanapali Resort (phone: 661-4423). Moderate.

Grill & Bar – Though it's between the Tennis Garden and the Golf Club at Kapalua, the *Grill & Bar* is run by *Kimo's,* of Lahaina, rather than by the *Kapalua Bay.* This handsome redwood pavilion has windows all around to allow a view of the golf course and the bay, and given its setting, it's at once elegant and sporty. Come in tennis togs (but no cut-off jeans) if you wish, even at dinner; and then, order no more than a cheeseburger, if that's all you want. For others, there's the very thick and very good Portuguese bean soup, entrées ranging from pasta and salads to steak and lobster, and a dessert of hula pie or Amaretto creme caramel. Open daily for lunch and dinner; reservations advised. Kapalua (phone: 669-5653). Moderate.

Seahouse – This open-air spot right on Napili Beach has a back wall of lava rock sprouting orchids and ferns, a palm tree or two growing up through the roof, and an adjoining bar from which to watch the sun set splendidly over the bay. The ambience is tropical and the menu continental, with emphasis on seafood and light entrées. Open for breakfast, lunch, and dinner daily; mellow Hawaiian music for dancing Mondays through Thursdays, and Saturdays. On Fridays local children put on a Hawaiian show. Reservations necessary. Napili Kai Beach Club, 5900 Honoapiilani Rd. (phone: 669-6271). Moderate.

Market Café – One part of this is the market, a grocery for gastronomes selling wines and spirits, pastries, meats, and cheeses. The rest of it is a rather stylish café of crisp green and white striped tablecloths, booths, and bentwood chairs. The ample menu includes everything from teriyaki beef to fried chicken, Italian dishes, and seafood. The sandwiches are huge, bursting with fresh and flavorsome ingredients; there are a dozen variations on the coffee; and as for the beer, imbibers can read through a long list of brands before getting from Anheuser-Busch to Watneys. This is an indoor, air conditioned eatery, open from 8 AM to 9 PM daily. No reservations. Kapalua Shops (phone: 669-4888). Moderate to inexpensive.

Rusty Harpoon – An informal eatery behind the shops in Whalers Village in an unassuming frame structure that lets in the air and lets out sounds of much conviviality and the frequent tinkling of a piano. Sandwiches, salads, and chili are lunchtime options; at dinner, Kal bi ribs, fresh island fish, stir-fried chicken, and pasta dishes are the specialties. Open for breakfast, lunch, and dinner daily. Reservations necessary for parties of 6 or more. Whalers Village, Kaanapali Resort (phone: 661-3123). Moderate to inexpensive.

Ricco's Old World Deli – For casual evening meals, this is the place to go — sit indoors or out, choose from a list of 46 domestic and imported beers, and tuck into a pizza or a homemade meatball or Italian sausage sandwich. Open daily from 10 AM to 10 PM. Reservations unnecessary. Whalers Village, lower level (phone: 661-4433). Inexpensive.

Kihei, Maalaea, Wailea, and Makena

When the Kaanapali resort opened on West Maui in 1962, there was precious little on the arid leeward side of East Maui but wasteland and forests of gnarled and thorny kiawe trees. Protected by the mass of 10,023-foot Haleakala, Kihei and Wailea receive less rainfall per year than any other coast on Maui, and it was only after resort ventures began to evolve elsewhere that endless, rainless, sunny days and an edging of virgin beaches all the way from Maalaea almost to La Perouse Bay connected in anyone's mind and turned it to thoughts of resort development. Now the coastline from Kihei to Makena is the second most important resort area on Maui and is beginning to give the Kaanapali area some competition.

But Maalaea/Kihei and Wailea/Makena are a study in contrasts. Kihei was the first to grow, and it does, like Topsy, along either side of South Kihei Road, from one end to the other, a distance of approximately 6 miles. Drive the length of this main thoroughfare and you will have seen it all: clusters of condominiums, a hotel or two, some restaurants, a few shopping centers, plus other by-products of life in society — the bank, the post office, the real estate office. Because its growth came about haphazardly, the result of the independent actions of many landowners and developers, Kihei is often held up as a patently poor example, a model of what not to do in development.

Kihei, however, also has its partisans, who point to those 6 miles of almost uninterrupted golden sand, apt to be windy in the morning, at least north toward Maalaea, but not likely to be obscured by clouds or saturated with raindrops. Views of Kahoolawe, of Lanai, and of the crevassed green glory of the West Maui mountains grace the shore, and even if it is often blocked by a bulwark of buildings, the water's edge can be reached via rights of way, several beach parks, or from a condominium lanai. Though the area as a whole strikes some as an unsightly mix, Kihei has individual condominium complexes as lovely as any on West Maui — and they cost less. Kihei is also less sophisticated than Kaanapali and, because many more natives of Maui live on this side of the island, more homespun. Chockablock as everything is, in Kihei you'll rub shoulders — on the beach, at the gas station, in the grocery store — with as many *kamaainas* as visitors.

Southeast of Kihei, Wailea and Makena are, on the other hand, totally planned resorts, designed by architects and landscape artists down to the last street sign and palm tree. In 1970, Wailea was only a bright idea in the corporate mind of the landowner, Alexander & Baldwin, one of Hawaii's Big Five. Two years later, there was a golf course; a second golf course followed, along with a tennis center, four condominium villages, a shopping center, and two first class hotels. Wailea is eloquent testimony to what the simple garden-variety sprinkler can do: What was once 1,450 acres of kiawe scrubland is now 1,450 acres of rolling green velvet, resulting in such a visible distinction between Wailea and its northern neighbor that any announcement at the entrance is superfluous. Wailea also has five splendid beaches among its blessings and has been applauded for making access to them via paved roads, parking areas, and paths as easy for the public as it is for resort guests, even easier than it was before development.

Wailea's resort amenities equal those of Kaanapali and Kapalua, but neither it nor Kihei can claim the diversity — of restaurants, nightlife, shopping — of West Maui (which is a 45-minute drive away). Nor does the area have its own sightseeing attractions beyond its beaches. Upcountry is just "upstairs," but Kihei-Wailea residents must take the same route via Kahului that everyone else does, because only a rugged dirt road (closed at press time) links the two areas directly. More beaches, including the popular mile of sand at Makena, stretch south from Wailea. A four-wheel-drive vehicle is necessary to get as far as Cape Kinau, formed by the lava flow from Haleakala's last eruption in 1790 and now a nature preserve, or La Perouse Bay, named for the French explorer who landed there in 1786, the first European to set foot on Maui. Much easier to reach, actually, is the tiny islet of Molokini, offshore halfway between Maui and Kahoolawe. The exposed part of a volcanic cone, its crescent shape harbors so many kinds of fish and coral that it has been declared a marine conservation district and is the object of snorkeling and diving expeditions from both Kihei and Wailea.

Opened in August 1986, the *Maui Prince* is the first hotel of the neighboring Makena resort. Owned by Japan's Seibu Corporation and operated by Tokyo's Prince Hotels, the understated yet elegant resort features an 18-hole golf course (with a second 18 holes underway), restaurants, and tennis courts. Among its assets are good service and easy access to nearby Makena beaches.

SHOPPING: There are more than six main shopping centers in the Kihei and Wailea area. The smallest, Kihei Town Center, along South Kihei Road, with its supermarket, *McDonald's*, and a few assorted shops, has less of interest to the visitor than either the Azeka Place Shopping Center, which is to the north along South Kihei Road, or the Wailea Shopping Village, in the Wailea resort to the south. The newer Rainbow Mall and Kamaole Center in the heart of Kihei's condominium row, offer gift shops, beach boutiques, and several restaurants, mostly of the fast-food variety.

The Azeka Place Shopping Center is a large and busy place thronged with residents buying gas and running in and out of the post office, the bank, the supermarket, the hardware store, the florist, and the health food store. In addition, it has several clothing stores, including the Kihei branch of *Liberty House* (phone: 879-7448), and a store or two selling gifts and souvenirs. The Wailea Shopping Village has branches of several shops found elsewhere on the island, most notably the browse-worthy collection at *Lahaina Printsellers* (phone: 879-1567), as well as a few exclusive shops like *Native* (phone: 879-3075), with a fine selection of fine-woven, hand-printed fashions. The shopping village presents free Polynesian entertainment Tuesdays at 1:30 PM (phone: 879-4465); bring a camera. Open Tuesdays and Fridays from 2 to 5 PM, *Maui's Farm Market* on S. Kihei Rd. (by the *Suda* store) offers locally grown produce, fruit, breads, pastries, at low prices.

Alchemists' Garden – With Austrian crystal palaces and Egyptian fragrances and all sorts of exotic imports, this shop is one of Maui's most interesting. The owners also issue an extensive mail-order catalogue called *Pieces of Dreams*. Azeka Pl. (phone: 879-6126).

Mango Club – A good, though small, selection of men's and women's fashions, from high-style shorts to shirts. Hand-screened shirts by the Balinese designer Baik Baik are featured, along with a large selection of collectible aloha shirts and some interesting antique and reproduction jewelry. Kamaole Shopping Center (phone: 879-6898).

Paradise Fruit – A craving for fruit can be satisfied here at any time of day or night — it's open 24 hours. Pineapples, papayas, and Maui onions are packaged to travel home intact; also available are such Hawaiian favorites as Maui potato chips, Kona coffee, and tropical jams and jellies. By *McDonald's*, off S. Kihei Rd. (phone: 879-1723).

Rainbow Connection – This particularly nice gift shop has beautiful silk-screen prints, a vast supply of imaginative and colorful mobiles and wind chimes, dishes, Christmas tree decorations, and locally handcrafted gift items such as carved Koa wood whales and dolphins. Azeka Place (phone: 879-5188).

Sea and Shell – The selection of specimen shells, mounted shells and coral, and jewelry made of shells, as well as decorative ceramics and wind chimes, makes this shop worth a special look. Wailea Shopping Village (phone: 879-1116). Four other outlets owned by the same family are at the *Hyatt Regency* at the Kaanapali resort (phone: 661-8967); in Lahaina (phone: 667-9074); at Kapalua Shops, where it is known as *By the Bay* (phone: 669-5227); and at Whalers Village (phone: 661-3730).

Superwhale – A children's boutique, only one of several locations on the island. It turns ordinary children into *keiki* in no time. Wailea Shopping Village (phone: 879-3636).

Vagabond – A good source for canvas bags, tote bags, beach bags, backpacks, and luggage. Otherwise, it's just another clothing store for men and women. Azeka Place (phone: 879-3060).

Wow Swimwear – Men's, women's, and children's bathing suits and beachwear, especially in large sizes. This store and *Wow*'s other store in Kahului's Maui Mall are also the only places on Maui to buy bikini tops and bottoms in separate sizes, though the Kahului branch has the larger selection. Azeka Place (phone: 879-1448).

NIGHTLIFE: The Kihei-Wailea-Makena area is not exactly overcrowded with hot spots, which is one of the reasons why the route north to Lahaina and Kaanapali sees such heavy evening traffic. At the *Inter-Continental Wailea,* there is live music for dancing nightly in the partly open-air *Inu Inu Lounge* (phone: 879-1922), which stays awake until 1 AM. On Sundays and Mondays the tempo is disco; Tuesdays through Saturdays the music is live. The *Stouffer Wailea Beach*'s nightspot, the *Lost Horizon* (phone: 879-4900), with pillars in the shape of palms and taro-leaf motifs on the walls, has undergone a change of heart from disco to live music, and is open nightly until 1:30 AM.

The *Inter-Continental* hosts a Tuesday night luau billed as Maui's merriest. The setting, a grassy oceanfront lawn, is certainly one of the nicest in the Islands. Dinner and Polynesian show cost $39. Kihei's *Maui Lu Resort* features a popular luau on Saturdays, currently priced at $32 for adults and $19 for children. The luau begins at 5 PM with the requisite lei greeting and the sipping of cocktails while the oven is uncovered rock by hot rock and the pig triumphantly removed. A buffet meal and a Polynesian revue follow. *Jesse's Luau Polynesia* (1945 S. Kihei Rd.; phone: 879-7227) is held Sundays, Wednesdays, and Fridays, with an open bar, all-you-can-eat buffet, and a musical revue featuring Jesse Nakaoka and his hula troupe. Beginning at 6 PM with the *imu* ceremony, in which a pig is taken from the underground oven, it runs until 9 PM, and the cost is $39 ($20 for children under 12). Nearby, on Mondays and Thursdays at *Stouffer Wailea Beach Resort,* the luau also features the *imu* ceremony and a musical revue for $38.

Elsewhere in Kihei, there's disco dancing Wednesdays and Thursdays, contemporary and live music Fridays through Sundays from 9:30 PM until 2 AM at the *Luigi's* in the Azeka Place Shopping Center (phone: 879-4446). *Kihei Seas Restaurant* has a piano bar with dancing from 6:30 to 11 PM and rock videos from 11 PM to 2 AM nightly. It's in the Rainbow Mall, near Kamaole Beach I (phone: 879-5600).

Best bet at Wailea is the *InuInu Lounge* at the *Inter-Continental.* Drinks at sunset, followed by a snack at East Maui's first sushi bar (5:30 to 8 PM) and dancing that starts at 9 PM are the reasons. Sunday is swing night at the *InuInu,* which presents a musical revue of sounds of the 1930s and 1940s, from 5 to 7:30 PM. No cover. *Lost Horizon,* at the *Stouffer,* attracts a younger crowd from 9 PM to 1 AM (closed Sundays). Makena's *Maui Prince* provides a landscaped courtyard in which a string quartet edifies with the works of Mozart and other masters. Nightly performances begin at 7 PM and continue until 9:30, when the music segues to the sounds of contemporary piano. In the hotel's *Molokini* lounge, there's music Tuesdays through Saturdays.

 CHECKING IN: Though the price categories remain the same for this area as for West Maui, on the whole it costs a bit less to stay here. Most properties have high- and low-season rates, with high season running mid-December to mid-April. In the listings that follow, very expensive means $250 and up double occupancy, expensive means $150 to $240, moderate is from $85 to $145, and inexpensive is from $45 to $80. All condominium units have full kitchens, and whether condominium or hotel, all rooms have private lanais and phone service unless otherwise stated. Hotels are air conditioned, most condominiums are not, though the afternoon trade winds that blow along this coast make air conditioning superfluous for most people. Note finally that daily maid service may not be provided free in all the condominiums, that some may require 3 or 4 days' minimum stay, and that some do not accept credit cards. All telephone numbers are in the 808 area code unless otherwise indicated.

Makena Surf – Spacious, nicely decorated 2- and 3-bedroom apartments and a private beachfront setting make this newly opened condominium, the first for the Makena resort, one of Maui's most appealing. On-site facilities include uncrowded tennis courts and a large pool and lounge area. There is a 3-night minimum stay. 3750 Wailea Alanui Dr. (phone: 879-1595; 800-367-5246). Very expensive.

Four Seasons Wailea – The first of two Four Seasons properties underway in Hawaii, it is set to open in November 1989. At 620 square feet each, the 347 guestrooms are among the largest conventional accommodations in Hawaii and, at a $150-million price tag (a record-breaking $400,000 per room), the most expensive. More than 85% of the rooms come with ocean views, and all have oversize closets, deluxe bathrooms, and in-room VCRs, designed to appeal to guests with a longer stay in mind. Large lanais and a spa are other pluses. The accent is Hawaiian, the design and decor first-rate. And taking full advantage of a perfect backdrop, the 7 stories blend with the hillside into which they are built. 3900 Wailea Alanui Dr. (phone: 874-8000; 800-332-3442). Very expensive to expensive.

Maui Prince – The 300 rooms provide the Makena resort with its first hotel, and the Prince Hotel chain with its first property in the US. It is adjacent to one of a string of Makena beaches, isolated at the end of the road, where its authentic elegance is all the more unexpected. Three restaurants pamper tastebuds with traditional Japanese and eclectic American cuisine. At night the sounds of Bach or Mozart fill the central courtyard. During the day the same courtyard echoes with the sound of running water from a series of falls and pools. Available are 6 tennis courts, 2 pools (a bit small, but nicely located), golf, and horseback riding. Almost all rooms have full or partial ocean views. 5400 Makena Alanui Rd. (phone: 874-1111; 800-321-6284). Very expensive to expensive.

Stouffer Wailea Beach – Of the two hotels in Wailea, this is the smaller and the slightly more formal. With the exception of a low oceanfront wing (the only thing that comes between the hotel and Mokapu Beach), its 350 rooms are arranged in a 7-story, 3-pronged structure whose grand entrance is flanked by reflecting pools and bold sculptured concrete walls depicting the god Maui. Equally bold, but elegant nonetheless, are the public areas beyond, strewn with splendid carpets and hung with huge fabric murals that are contemporary works of art. Still farther back, the sloping 15-acre grounds make use of streams, waterfalls, bridges, and tropical plantings — the latter doing so well that many an ocean view has turned into a garden view (rooms with mountain views are also available). The hotel's *Raffles'* restaurant is highly praised, the activities program is a strong one (from hula lessons to windsurfing), and all the resort's sports facilities are close at hand. Wailea (phone: 879-4900; 800-9-WAILEA). Very expensive to expensive.

Wailea Condominiums – What the *Kapalua Villas* are to West Maui, these are to East Maui — condominium communities designed for the most luxurious, yet unobtrusive, kind of vacation living. *Wailea Ekolu* village consists of rows of 2-story redwood buildings behind flowering trees on a slope above the Blue Golf Course, from where they have wonderful seaward views. *Wailea Ekahi,* also with low buildings, is lavish with bamboo, Manila, and traveler's palms and plumeria, and it slopes, too, right down toward Keawakapu Beach. The most exclusive village, *Elua,* is on Ulua Beach between Wailea's two hotels. There are 8 pools among the villages, and of the 594 units, about one-third can be rented — anything from a studio to a gorgeous 2- or 3-bedroom townhouse with cathedral ceilings. A minimum stay of 3 nights is required. Vacation Resorts/Wailea, 3750 Wailea Alanui Blvd., Wailea (phone: 879-1595; 800-367-5246). Very expensive to moderate.

Maui Inter-Continental Wailea – With 600 rooms, this is nearly twice as big as its Stouffer neighbor, and though it occupies not much more acreage, it feels anything but crowded. In fact, if you stay in one of the many scattered low structures that account for half the quiet, swank rooms, you may want to drop a trail of breadcrumbs for a while to find your way around the garden paths. Otherwise, rooms are in a 7-story tower next to the lobby, which is a long, open-air, mall-like affair divided into intimate seating areas by pillars, fountains, potted greens, and exotic tropical plants showing up nicely against the basic white stucco. Recently upgraded, the hotel has several restaurants, including *La Perouse* to compete with nearby *Raffles'*, 3 pools, a jogging path, and a location on a rock and morning glory–edged headland between Ulua and Wailea beaches. Sports-minded fans find it just as activities-conscious as the *Wailea Beach* but a bit more relaxed in atmosphere. Investigate reasonable off-season rates here. Wailea (phone: 879-1922; 800-367-2960). Expensive.

Maui Hill – First impressions are reminiscent of Spain, because the condominium buildings that curve up the hillside are topped by the sort of red tile roofs that so often shines in the Mediterranean sun. The pillared and arched balconies, with the wrought-iron railings that shade each unit, are downright hacienda-like, though they're actually Hawaiian lanais. Buildings are no more than 2 or 3 stories high, and the 1- to 3-bedroom units (140 all told) come with well above average furnishings (including koa cabinetry in the kitchens), 2 baths, and most have grand ocean views. The grounds — nicely landscaped, yet too new to be lush — contain a large pool, tennis and shuffleboard courts, a putting green, barbecue facilities, and nothing else — you cross the road and walk along a bit to get to the beach. 2881 S. Kihei Rd. (phone: 879-6321; 800-367-5124). Expensive to moderate.

Kamaole Sands – There are ten 4-story buildings clustered around the pools and tennis courts (free court time for guests) at this property across the road from Kamaole Beach Park III. Available are 1-, 2-, and 3-bedroom units, with a children's pool, barbecue areas, and individual washers and dryers making this a good family choice. The only extra that's missing here is air conditioning, which now and again can be a blessing, although the trade winds usually make it unnecessary. 2695 S. Kihei Rd. (phone: 879-0666; 800-922-7866). Expensive to moderate.

Koa Resort – This condominium winner is made up of five 2-story buildings holding a total of 50-some units whose lanais tumble with bougainvillea and face a spacious central lawn–cum–putting green as smooth as velvet. The rattan- and bamboo-furnished rooms — units have from 1 to 3 bedrooms — are spacious, too, and as beautiful as any in a Maui condominium. Nothing more than an occasional cocktail party is planned, but to compensate, the swimming pool is large, and there are tennis courts, shuffleboard courts, barbecue facilities, and a Jacuzzi. The nearest beach is across the road. 811 S. Kihei Rd. (phone: 879-1161; 800-367-8047, ext. 407). Expensive to moderate.

Mana Kai Maui – Basically a condominium run as a hotel; and though the interiors are humdrum and the building — one high-rise block of 8 stories — not very handsome, consider these points in its favor. First, the location, smack on the curving far end of the same beach that runs all the way to Wailea, needs no apologies. Second, each 2-bedroom, 2-bath apartment can be split into a 1-bedroom, 1-bath unit with kitchen and a lanai overlooking the sea and a no-kitchen, no-lanai hotel unit facing the back; the latter, though small, are of interest to those on a tight budget. Third, a rental car with airport pickup comes with both hotel and condo units. On the property are a swimming pool, general store, beauty salon, apparel shop, a branch of the *Ocean Activities Center* for water sports, a bar, and a restaurant (see *Eating Out*). 2960 S. Kihei Rd. (phone: 879-1561; 800-525-2025). Moderate.

Hale Kamaole – Another attractive condominium choice on the *mauka* (inland) side of South Kihei Road. The 180-plus units are staggered in low lines around a lawn containing plumeria, a few tall palms, and walkways edged in ixora, oleander, and bougainvillea. More flowers hang on trellises between the lanais.

Units of 1 and 2 bedrooms are individually decorated, and the 2-level, 2-bedroom ones are especially nice. Phones in selected units only, 2 swimming pools, a tennis court, and barbecue grills. Directly across the road, another sweep of grass ends in a small beach that is an extension south of Kamaole Beach Park III. Ask about off-season discounts. 2737 S. Kihei Rd. (phone: 879-2698; 800-367-2970). Moderate to inexpensive.

Maui Lu – This Kihei hotel lacks the sophistication of its counterparts in Wailea and the rooms are not flashy, but when it says it remembers "the good times of old Hawaii," it means it. The Saturday night luaus are part of it, but the key seems to be the many Hawaiian employees, whose spirit of *ohana* (family) strikes the visitor here more than elsewhere. The best of the 170 rooms on the extensive, heavily palmed grounds are the superiors in the 3-story wooden wing (Haleakala views), which repeats the architectural theme of the hotel's Polynesian longhouse-style restaurant, and the deluxes in the waterfront units across the road (where there are beachlets and access to a longer, sandier beach past the property. Most of the amenities — pool, tennis, hula lessons — of a resort hotel. 575 S. Kihei Rd. (phone: 879-5881; 800-922-7866). Moderate to inexpensive.

Nani Kai Hale – You could hardly pay less for condominium accommodations than what you'd pay for a studio unit here. The 6-story rectangular building takes up nearly the whole property (the ground floor is parking), the only green area is a small lawn in back (with a good-sized pool, picnic tables, and barbecue grill, however), but the location is on the beach and the sand stretches for miles. Larger units are available (the high front 1-bedrooms definitely have a view), and room-and-bath-only hotel units are possible, too. Phones can be put in for long-term residents. Maid service available. No air conditioning. Minimum stay, 7 nights during peak season, 3 nights off-season. Ask about off-season discounts. 73 N. Kihei Rd. (phone: 879-9120; 800-367-6032). Moderate to inexpensive.

EATING OUT: The area won't overwhelm you with the number and diversity of its restaurants, but there are good places to eat nonetheless. In Kihei, they occur intermittently along the length of South Kihei Road; in Wailea, there are a few free-standing eating spots in addition to the restaurants and coffee shops in the hotels. As elsewhere, expect to pay $50 or more for the average meal for two in a restaurant listed as expensive; $30 to $45 in a place listed as moderate; and $20 to $25 in an inexpensive place — drinks, wine, and tip not included. For fast food and other budget eateries, scout Kihei's shopping centers — Azeka Place and Kihei Town Center primarily. Finally, the dress code for Kihei and Wailea is on the whole casual, the two top hotel restaurants excepted. All telephone numbers are in the 808 area code unless otherwise indicated.

La Perouse – The glint of wineglasses, silver, and candlelight, paneled walls and padded banquettes, pastry carts and flaming desserts, impeccable, all but heel-clicking service (the reverberation might interfere with the classical piano music) — this is the *Maui Inter-Continental Wailea*'s most refined dining room. The menu stresses seafood (such as Pacific snapper with crab and dill, or sautéed scallops with black beans and cucumber), but other, more land-oriented, possibilities adorn the menu as well. To begin the meal, the *callaloo* (crab) soup is sublime. Open for dinner nightly; reservations advised. Collared shirts required for men. Maui Inter-Continental, Wailea (phone: 879-1922). Expensive.

Prince Court – Both the food and the prices may raise eyebrows at the main dining room of the *Maui Prince*. The theme is American cuisine, but with entrées such as Hawaiian prawns, lobster, and scallops in a saffron sauce with wild rice and pecans, and broiled Kansas sirloin steak with grilled pumpkin and roasted new potatoes, diners quickly realize that American cuisine has been given a new meaning here. The pleasant setting is complemented by the strains of Bach or Mozart drifting in from the string quartet playing in the courtyard outside. Service is superb, and the food is as good as it is creative. Open daily for dinner. Reservations advised. Maui Prince, Makena (phone: 874-1111). Expensive.

Raffles' – What *La Perouse* is to the *Inter-Continental Wailea*, *Raffles'* is to *Stouffer Wailea Beach*. The *Raffles* hotel of Singapore inspired this fine dining room, which mixes Oriental carpets, polished teak floors, Chinese ceramics, and rattan furnishings with stuffed armchairs, creamy swag curtains, and chandeliers, thereby pulling off a look of burnished British colonial elegance. Hawaiian standards such as mahimahi or opakapaka (served in six styles) appear on the menu, as do roast rack of lamb with diablo sauce and filet mignon (have this with fresh mushrooms). The chocolate mousse is scrumptious; otherwise, choose dessert from the pastry cart or the chocolate Grand Marnier soufflé. The service here, too, is impeccable. Open for dinner nightly and for Sunday brunch; reservations advised. Collared shirts or jackets suggested for men. *Stouffer Wailea Beach Resort,* Wailea (phone: 879-4900). Expensive.

Fairway – It's in the Wailea Golf Clubhouse between the Orange and Blue courses, and quite panoramically placed so that you sit high up over the sea, either outside on a paved patio surrounded by a tropical hedge or inside behind sliding glass panels in a sporty ambience of brown wood and leather. Entrées include Polynesian chicken, steaks, chops, prime ribs, fish and seafood, and a salad bar smorgasbord stocked with lots of cold cuts in addition to greens, making it a popular main course. Open daily for breakfast, lunch, and dinner; reservations for dinner advised. Wailea Golf Club (phone: 879-4060). Expensive to moderate.

Island Fish House – If uku (gray snapper) is among the fresh fish of the day, don't pass it up and do have it sautéed as the chef suggests. He does an excellent job with other fish, too, and the bowl of chowder you may choose for a starter is also very good. The restaurant is indoors and not in a particularly scenic location, though you can look through the many large picture windows and watch the sunset over Kalama Beach Park. Inside are soft lights, sweet music, and an easygoing atmosphere verging on elegance. A few steak and chicken dishes; an extensive list of white wines. Open for dinner daily; three-choice early-bird dinner from 5 to 6 PM. Reservations necessary. 1945 S. Kihei Rd. (phone: 879-7771). Expensive to moderate.

Wailea Steak House – There's no more romantic place to dine from Kihei to Wailea. If you sit at one of the outermost tables, your gaze will travel over a pond on the Blue Golf Course, above a line of treetops, to Kahoolawe and the setting sun. Then darkness falls, lights come on beneath the trees around you, the pond shimmers like a mirror, and the mood is set. The restaurant structure, originally the golf clubhouse, has won awards for architecture and landscaping, probably because its indoor and outdoor areas flow so smoothly from one to the other, and the whole, camouflaged by palms, clinging vines, and a headdress of bougainvillea, is so very much at home in the environment. This is a classy steakhouse with a classic (steaks, seafood, fish) steakhouse menu. Open for dinner daily; reservations advised. Wailea Iki Dr., above the Wailea Shopping Village (phone: 879-2875). Expensive to moderate.

Chuck's Steak House – Except for the many stained glass windows in flower patterns, the restaurant is entirely clad in redwood, so it's definitely not the place for outdoor dining or a view. Inside, plants hang, candlelight flickers, and golden oldies and more recent tunes play softly, creating a pleasantly mellow atmosphere all the same. Part of a chain that's well represented elsewhere in Hawaii (there's another at Kaanapali), *Chuck's* serves steaks, ribs, fish, and seafood, and has the added attraction of an excellent salad bar. Cheesecake or the ice cream and cookie crust concoctions known as mud pies and dirt pies are the desserts. Open for lunch (except Sundays) and dinner daily; early bird specials from 5:30 to 6:30 PM. No reservations. Kihei Town Center (phone: 879-4489). Moderate.

Kihei Prime Rib House – This handsome second-story room with the high-beamed ceiling is dominated by original oil paintings and several very large carvings done by master woodcraftsman Bruce Turnbull. It's known, naturally enough, for its prime ribs dinners and for its salad bar, replete with Maui onions, but a few other entrées — Polynesian chicken, teriyaki steaks, seafood brochette, shrimp, and fresh fish — also appear on the menu. Get to the restaurant early enough for the Early Bird Special (between 5 and 6 PM), and you can have the prime ribs or the fish at a substantial reduction. Open for dinner daily; reservations advised. Kai Nani Village, 2511 S. Kihei Rd., Kihei (phone: 879-1954). Moderate.

Lanai Terrace – The attractive decor and delicious food both make this restaurant a fine choice; alfresco dining is an added plus. Although the best buy is the daily buffet — a tempting assortment that may include steamed clams, stuffed lamb-chops, or Cajun mahimahi — the evening menu offers such specialties as lamb curry and peppered steak. Either way, a meal is aptly culminated with a wonderful selection of pies, cakes, and flambéed desserts. Breakfast (6 to 11 AM), lunch, and dinner daily; reservations advised. Maui Inter-Continental Wailea (phone: 879-1922). Moderate.

Ocean Terrace – The open-air setting is meditative, with palms overhead and the distant sound of the surf. The food is tasty and priced fairly, with fresh fish — sautéed, charbroiled, or deep fried — and prawns the house specialties. Open daily (weather permitting) for breakfast, lunch, and dinner; reservations advised. At the Mana Kai Maui condos, 2960 S. Kihei Rd. (phone: 879-2607). Moderate.

La Familia – With an emphasis on healthful ingredients, this restaurant serves Mexican dishes that include steak, lobster, shrimp, fish, and chicken fajitas. Mexican tile tables, ceiling fans, and hanging plants make this another attractive rendezvous. Open for lunch, and dinner daily. No reservations. Below the Kihei Prime Rib House, Kai Nani Village, Kihei (phone: 879-8824). Moderate to inexpensive.

Kahului and Wailuku

Most tourists arriving at Kahului Airport jump right into a rented car and head straight for the resort hotels of West and East Maui. Barring a wrong turn somewhere along the airport road, they bypass the town of Kahului completely as well as the adjoining town of Wailuku, though they may return to Wailuku later, on their way into the Iao Valley. This is as it should be, because though Kahului and Wailuku have several features of interest to the visitor, they are not at all resort towns. The greatest concentration of Maui's population lives here (32,000 of the island's total 85,000), and while vacationers count the grains of sand along the golden beaches, it is in the everyday world of Wailuku and Kahului that much of the island's work is done.

Kahului and Wailuku flow so uninterruptedly into each other on the northern coast of Maui's central valley that they appear on the map and in reality almost one and the same. There are those who refer to them as Waikahu, but despite the flippancy, there is a division (the bridge over the Wailuku Gulch) and there is a difference. Kahului, to the east, is the newer of the two. It is a business and commercial center, and in addition to having Maui's only jet airport a few miles out of town, it has Maui's only deepwater port, right in the center of town. The island's mainland-bound sugar and pineapple production sets out from Kahului Harbor, where piers and stacked containers are part of the view from the three tourist hotels and the beach park also on the harbor. Behind them, Kahului's main thoroughfare, Kaahumanu Avenue (Highway 32), runs east and west, the downtown end of it dominated by three large shopping centers, and behind that — a part of town that visitors rarely see — are residential back streets lined with relatively new and pleasant-looking family homes.

Kahului's Kaahumanu Avenue proceeds west and turns into Wailuku's Main Street, and by the time Main reaches High Street, where "downtown" Wailuku is situated, the visitor is already in the foothills of the West Maui mountains. As a result, Wailuku is hillier, leafier, and more picturesque than its eastern neighbor; it is an administrative center and the county seat of Maui County (the islands of Molokai, Lanai, and Kahoolawe are part of the county) as well. While modern government structures such as the State Office Building, the Federal Building, and the 9-story Kalana O Maui — the County Office Building — line one side of High Street (the not so modern 1907 Court House is here, too), the other side is part of the Wailuku Historic District, which includes High Street between Main and Aupini Streets and a compact area toward the mountain. The 19th-century Bailey House, now the Hale Hoikeike museum, and the 19th-century Kaahumanu Church are the most important buildings in this preserve, but the two white, red-roofed buildings with the brightly tiled entryways next to the church add to the picture. Some of Wailuku's side streets have the wooden and tin-roofed charm of many a Hawaiian plantation town, whereas others contain beautifully landscaped suburban hillside homes.

Main Street continues across High Street as the Iao Valley Road, the final alias of Highway 32. This is well along the tourist track and there's a reason for it. Drive along the Iao Valley Road and you are suddenly confronted by the majesty of the West Maui mountains rising in steep, dark green and brown creases on either side of the Iao Stream, their lower slopes covered in the light frosty green of kukui trees that contrasts with the more somber colors above. The route is short and sweet, because 3 miles west of Wailuku, it bumps into the near-vertical crater walls of Puu Kukui, the volcano that gave birth to the island of West Maui. The scenic Iao Valley State Park is the turnaround point.

Kanaha Pond Wildlife Sanctuary – One of the state's most important waterfowl sanctuaries is the stopping place of migratory birds and the home of a great number of Hawaiian coots and stilts. Nevertheless, it may take patience and a pair of binoculars to satisfy your curiosity (the coot is the grayish-black bird with the white bill and frontal shield; the stilt is the one with the long pink legs). The pond is large, shallow, and dotted with grassy clumps, and whatever action takes place can be observed from a shelter at the end of a spit of land extending into the water. Between Kahului Airport and Kahului; the observation shelter is on Hwy. 396 and difficult to find (if you're driving east on Hwy. 32, turn right onto Hwy. 36, then left onto Hwy. 396).

Alexander & Baldwin Sugar Museum – Founded in the 19th century by descendants of Hawaii's early New England Protestant missionaries, Alexander & Baldwin grew to become one of Hawaii's Big Five corporations and Maui's predominant land-owner, having planted tens of thousands of acres to sugarcane. Although the future of the sugar industry in Hawaii has lately been called into question by less-costly foreign production, it was the islands' most important economic resource for nearly a century. This museum demonstrates how and why. Located in the restored home of a plantation manager, and adjacent to a still-active sugar mill at Puunene, it houses carefully researched and well-displayed exhibits that include historic photographs, documents, and artifacts, all providing an overview of the crop's impact on Hawaii. Especially informative is the material on American entrepreneurs like Klaus Spreckels, Hawaii's "Sugar King," and that which deals with the immigrants who were brought in to work on the plantations from such locales as China, Japan, Korea, the Philippines, and Portugal, thereby recasting the demography of Hawaii. Open Mondays through Saturdays from 9:30 AM to 4 PM; $2 admission. A short drive from the airport, on Hansen Rd., Puunene (phone: 871-8058).

Maui Tropical Plantation – The canefields that lead to Waikapu Valley provide a setting for a wide range of tropical crops and flowers. This is the place to go if you want to see what papayas, pineapples, macadamia nuts, and avocados look like while growing. A tram takes visitors on a tour of the grounds. There is a large restaurant and a collection of very touristy shops. Open daily from 9 AM to 5 PM. The $8 admission, valid for 7 days, includes all activities and a tram tour. At sunset a "country party" follows a *paniolo* (cowboy) theme, with a sunset hayride on a horsedrawn wagon, followed by a barbecue dinner and square dancing Mondays, Wednesdays, Thursdays, and Fridays from 5:30 to 8:30 PM. Off Rte. 30 at Waikapu (phone: 244-7643).

Maui Zoological and Botanical Gardens – This is probably worth a special trip only if you have restless children with you. The native Hawaiian plants in the botanical garden are somewhat upstaged by the smallish creatures of various ancestry in the zoological garden, which is actually a children's zoo. There are showy birds, such as peacocks, scarlet macaws, and salmon-crested cockatoos, and an assortment of animals, including spider monkeys and African pygmy goats. Native Hawaiian *pueo* owls, stilt birds, nene geese, and koloa ducks, all endangered species, are represented, and you'll also be able to see examples of the wild boar and feral goats and sheep (these last look like overworked pieces of macrame) that roam Maui's mountain fastnesses. Open from 9 AM to 4 PM daily; no admission charge. Kanaloa Ave., Kahului (phone: 244-3276).

Hale Hoikeike (Maui Historical Society Museum) – Hale Hoikeike means House of Display, and here the 19th-century home of a missionary is used to display a small collection of artifacts that includes items of Hawaiiana dating from both before and after the arrival of *haoles*. The plastered stone house, built in stages between 1833 and 1850, was the home of Edward Bailey, the principal of the Wailuku Female Seminary, which coexisted on the property during the 1840s. Some interesting things can be learned about tapa cloth in the museum's main-floor Hawaiian Room (that only the Hawaiians developed the art of block printing on tapa, and of beating two tapas of different colors together to make the cloth reversible, and of using various plants to give the cloth a sweet scent, for instance). The same room contains pre-Cook weapons, tools, and ornaments (including an ancient "mirror"), whereas the bedroom and sitting room upstairs are given over mainly to missionary-era furniture. A small adjoining structure (formerly the seminary dining room and the only seminary building that still stands) houses a collection of Mr. Bailey's paintings, and no matter what you think of his talent, they do show the Wailuku area as it was in its youth. Open daily from 10 AM to 4:30 PM. Contribution suggested. 2375A Main St., Wailuku, or Hwy. 32, on the left as you head into the Iao Valley (phone: 244-3326).

Kaahumanu Church – Queen Kaahumanu attended services in a temporary church here (actually a grass shack) in 1832 and asked that the first permanent church built on the spot be named after her. The next church was an adobe one that dissolved in the rain, but by 1837 a stone church, the predecessor of the present one, had been erected. Today's white building, dating from 1876, is half the size of the earlier version, but its green trim, the green clock in the steeple, and the cloud-covered mountains in the background make it a much-photographed landmark. Because it is locked most of the time, visitors will not see the stark interior, like an early New England church, unless they sit in the beautiful koa pews on Sundays. At the 9 AM Hawaiian Congregational services, the hymns are sung in Hawaiian. High St. (Hwy. 30), Wailuku.

Kepaniwai Park and Heritage Gardens – This lovely county park in the Iao Valley is a memorial to the Maui melting pot, and the symbol chosen to represent the various ethnic groups that settled here, appropriately enough, is the house. Scattered about the landscaped grounds you'll find a typical early Hawaiian stone-walled and grass-roofed shack, a New England saltbox with a white picket fence, a Portuguese villa with a formal garden, and picturesque Chinese, Japanese, and Philippine dwellings. The park is a pleasant setting for lunch if you want to take advantage of the picnic pavilions provided, but things were not always so peaceful here. It was in the vicinity of Kepaniwai that the forces of Kamehameha the Great defeated the forces of the Maui chief in the decisive battle of 1790. The battle assured Kamehameha of eventual hegemony over all the Hawaiian Islands, but the price paid by both sides was high. So great was the slaughter that the Iao Stream was blocked with bodies (Kepaniwai means "damming of the waters") and the village downstream got the name Wailuku (meaning "bloody river"). Iao Valley Rd. (Hwy. 32).

John F. Kennedy Profile – It might as well be mentioned, because otherwise you'll wonder why all those cars are parked at a curve in the road. The area is called Black Gorge, and if you, too, stop and look up as indicated, you'll see that the natural rock formation does look remarkably like the late president. Iao Valley Rd. (Hwy. 32).

Iao Valley State Park – The Iao Valley Road ends here at the head of the valley, which is actually the erosion-enlarged crater of the volcano that created West Maui. The centerpiece of the beautiful park is an erosional remnant known as the Iao Needle, a green-carpeted spire that rises 1,200 feet from the valley floor (and 2,250 feet from sea level). The walk that begins at the parking lot crosses a bridge over the Iao Stream as it comes rushing down from around the needle, and more paths will take you down to where you can sit on boulders in the water's path if the day is hot or browse through the jungle of plants and sweet-smelling flowers that line it. Other paths and stairs lead up to a shelter that provides a better view of the needle and the surrounding steep valley walls or, in the opposite direction, of the mist-filled valley opening up before you, with Kahului Bay lost in the distance. Iao Valley Rd. (Hwy. 32).

SHOPPING: Kahului has three very large shopping centers all in a row on the *mauka* (inland) side of Kaahumanu Avenue. The Kahului Shopping Center in the middle is the oldest, and busy as it is with residents making their way from the supermarket to the dry cleaner to the auto parts shop (and to the movies at the *Maui Theatre*), it has few specialty shops stocking the kinds of things visitors usually like to buy. To the east of it, the Maui Mall Shopping Center does have some such shops in addition to the more mundane supermarket and drugstore (it also has a *Woolworth's*), but visitors would do best to head directly to the spiffier Kaahumanu Center, the westernmost of the shopping centers and Maui's largest. You won't find anything here that you won't find elsewhere on the island, but if your shopping spree is going to take place in Kahului, this is the place for it. *Sears* is at one end of the complex, and the island's largest *Liberty House* is at the other. The *Holiday Theater* is also here. In Wailuku the shopping is small-town in style, with Market Street providing a surprising selection of stores worth browsing. A few other shops are listed below.

The Artful Dodger's – In a cluster of shops across from the Maui Mall, this is what bookstores and browsing are all about. 55 Kaahumanu (phone: 871-2677).

Honsport – This sporting goods store carries all the necessary equipment for archery, baseball, and basketball, camping, exercising, fishing, golf, hunting, running, tennis, and most other strenuous activities. Kaahumanu Center (phone: 877-3954).

House of Music – Hawaiian tunes are among the records, tapes, cassettes, and sheet music. Guitars and ukuleles are also sold. Kaahumanu Center (phone: 877-2424).

Lightning Bolt Maui – Everything needed for all sorts of watersports, plus accessories and bathing suits. 55 Kaahumanu (phone: 877-2116).

Maui Potato Chip Factory – Maui is famous for potato chips — specifically the "Kitch'n Cook'd" brand turned out at this family-owned factory. The Kobayashi family's success story began in 1957, and by 1978 had made the front page of the *Wall Street Journal,* after which orders poured in from around the world. The factory stubbornly remains a small business, however. Maui merchants get the chips first, then the rest of the state, and a stray bag may make its way to the mainland. If you haven't found them on the local shelves, you can buy them here, 6 or 12 bags to the box. 295 Lalo Pl., off Hwy. 36 in the Kahului industrial area (phone: 877-3652).

Memory Lane – The selection of antiques and collectibles is likely to provide more than one temptation — perhaps a bit of 1930s Hawaiiana. 158 N. Market St., Wailuku (phone: 244-4196).

Things from the Past – A collection of antiques of mixed quality. Best buys: jewelry, stemware, and crystal. 160A N. Market St., Wailuku (phone: 244-8177).

Traders of the Lost Art – Tribal arts of New Guinea, the Philippines, and Oceania. 158 N. Market St., Wailuku (phone: 242-7753).

Wailuku Trading Company – Odds and ends from kitsch to antiques, including vintage postcards and Hawaiiana. 46 Market St., Wailuku (phone: 242-9211).

Waldenbooks – Large and well stocked with best sellers and general books, it also carries many titles that come under the heading of Hawaiiana — books on Hawaiian flora and fauna, history, culture, crafts, the Hawaiian language, and more. In the Maui Mall (phone: 877-0181) and the Kaahumanu Center (phone: 871-6112).

 NIGHTLIFE: The *Maui Theater* in the Kahului Shopping Center (phone: 877-3560) and the *Holiday Theater* in the Kaahumanu Center (phone: 877-6622) feature first-run films. The *Maui Community Theater* (phone: 242-6969) presents excellent live performances in Wailuku's *Iao Theater* on an irregular schedule. At the *Maui Tropical Plantation,* there's a sunset *paniolo* hayride and barbecue from 5:30 to 8:30 PM, Mondays, Wednesdays, Thursdays, and Fridays.

 CHECKING IN: Anyone who stays in a hotel in Kahului expecting the resort of his or her dreams, including a palm-lined shore at the door, is in for a rude disappointment. The beach of Kahului Harbor is very narrow, not very clean, and definitely not what people come to Hawaii for. You can expect to pay about $40 to $60 for a double room in the inexpensive hotel listed below. All telephone numbers are in the 808 area code unless otherwise indicated.

Maui Hukilau/Maui Seaside – Two parts make up this nearly 200-room hotel, which would have to be described as providing clean, adequate rooms to sleep in and a pool to swim in, but no grounds for illusion. The Hukilau wing consists of two long 2-story buildings facing each other across a lawn with palms, breadfruit trees, and the pool, while the newer Seaside wing is a 3-story row behind the Hukilau, away from the pool. The Seaside rooms are reasonably large and air conditioned but lack lanais, whereas some of the Hukilau rooms are air conditioned and all have lanais, though those on the ground floor are less private. The hotel is on the beach, such as it is, and has a restaurant. Kaahumanu Ave., Kahului (phone: 877-3311; 800-367-7000). Inexpensive.

EATING OUT: Since the Kahului-Wailuku area is Maui's workaday world, restaurants with visitor appeal — those that try to provide a pleasant dining experience along with the food — tend to open elsewhere. In addition to the restaurants below, there are sandwich shops, hamburger houses, and pizzerias aplenty in the shopping centers. Price categories in this area do not deviate from the island norm: The average dinner for two in a restaurant listed as moderate will range from $30 to $45 without drinks or tips; in an inexpensive place, about $20 to $25 for two. All telephone numbers are in the 808 area code unless otherwise indicated.

Mickey's – The popularity of the Kihei branch of this restaurant led to the opening of one here in Kahului, which has also drawn good reviews. A steady clientele of businesspeople come to lunch on the fine fish and prime ribs. Lunch weekdays only; dinner Tuesdays through Sundays. Reservations advised. 33 Lono Ave., corner Kaahumanu Ave., Kahului (phone: 871-7555). Moderate.

Siam Thai Cuisine – Very popular, and deservedly so, with Thai specialties like red, green, and yellow Masman curries and spring rolls. Open Mondays through Fridays for lunch, daily for dinner. Dinner reservations advised. 123 N. Market St. (phone: 244-3817). Moderate to inexpensive.

Ming Yuen – The location is fairly unencouraging and — as at many Chinese restaurants — the decor is utilitarian at best. However, the food is quite good (mostly Cantonese, with a bit of Szechwan) and a favorite with the island's cognoscenti. Lunch daily except Sundays and dinner nightly. Reservations advised. 162 Alamaha St., Kahului (phone: 871-7787). Inexpensive.

Sir Wilfred's – An espresso bar with character, serving great coffee, sweets, and sandwiches. Maui Mall (phone: 877-3711). Inexpensive.

Yuri's – The food is local and is concocted into such specialties as poki (raw fish, onions, and shoyu) and squid laua (made with coconut milk). The small-town Hawaii ambience and nurturing aloha welcome blend well to provide a fine meal. Lunch and dinner daily, 1 to 9:30 PM. Reservations unnecessary. 303 N. Market St., Wailuku (phone: 244-3121). Inexpensive.

Upcountry

The trip from Kahului to the summit of Haleakala is an ascent from sea level to 10,023 feet in only 38 miles, an accomplishment possible on no other automobile road in the world. The drive takes about 1½ hours, the latter part of it one twist and turn after another on the hairpin Haleakala Crater Road. But long before the twisting and turning begins, visitors may be surprised at the beauty of the countryside going by, because Maui's upcountry, as the lower slopes of Haleakala are known, is a quiet rural region where sugarcane and pineapple fields give way to pastureland, eucalyptus trees, and clumps of cactus, where cattle graze, horses roam, hibiscus grows wild, jacarandas bloom by the roadside in spring, and the rolling hills are neatly carpeted with cultivated flowers. Because it is always cooler up here (average daytime temperatures are in the low 70s, and at night it's often chilly enough for a cozy fire), many Mauians happily reside upcountry, far removed from the tropics and the spirit of resort life down below.

The uplands include the Kula district, at an average elevation of 3,000 feet, the center of vegetable, fruit, and flower farming on Maui. Rich volcanic soil and the combination of warm days (with Haleakala's cloud cover taking the sting out of the sun) and cool nights makes the area suitable for a variety of crops. The Irish potatoes that the whalers loaded onto their ships at Lahaina and that fed gold rush prospectors in California were grown in Kula, and the sweet, sweet Kula onions you'll taste at salad bars all over the island are grown here, too. So are cabbages, lettuce, tomatoes, carrots, and peas. Carnations are the leader among the flowers — there are some two dozen carnation growers upcountry, the majority of whom send cut flowers to Honolulu to be strung as leis — but proteas, exotic natives of Australia and South Africa (and cousins to the macadamia nut) are the newest blossoms to be cultivated commercially. Growing conditions at Kula not only produce superior proteas, with stronger stems and richer colors, but also cause some varieties to bloom at different times of the year than they would if grown elsewhere, thus giving the Hawaiian flowers an edge in international markets.

Upcountry is also ranch country. The town of Makawao, headquarters of the 20,000-acre Haleakala Ranch, has the tumbledown and dusty aspect you'd expect of cattle country, and every year, over July Fourth, its Wild West heritage bursts forth in a genuine rodeo. Maui's largest ranch, Ulupalakua, has 30,000 acres, about 5,000 head of Hereford and Angus cattle, and a long history besides. According to the story, one James Makee, the captain of a ship tied up at Lahaina, was struck on the head with an ax by a sailor to whom he had refused permission to go ashore. Makee stayed on in Maui to recuperate and in 1856 bought land and began to build what was known then as Rose Ranch, growing sugarcane while his wife grew roses. The Makees lived on a grand scale, and they entertained naval officers and royalty — King David Kalakaua was a frequent guest — lavishly, often heralding their arrival with torchbearers. Later, the ranch became a potato farm, then a cattle ranch, and today, a few of Ulupalakua's acres are planted with Carnelian grapes to form Hawaii's only vineyard. The grounds of Ulupalakua already hold Hawaii's only winery, which produces wine from pineapples and will continue to do so even after the first grape wine is sent to market.

Even without these details of its landscape, Maui's upcountry would be remarkably scenic. From some vantage points the view extends down the hills and across the central valley, where you'll see the coast on both sides and the back of the West Maui mountains. From others, you'll see the entire coastline from West Maui to Wailea, plus the islands of Molokini and Kahoolawe. Some of the marvelous scenery is visible en route from Kahului to Haleakala National Park, but a detour is well worth the trouble. To go directly to Haleakala, take Highways 37, 377 (just above Pukalani), and 378. To detour, stay on Highway 37 past Pukalani. It crosses the Kula uplands (marked on some maps now as the Kula Highway) and eventually reconnects with Highway 377, where you can turn back or continue as far as Ulupalakua Ranch. (Beyond Ulupalakua, Highway 37 becomes Highway 31 and proceeds counterclockwise around East Maui to Hana.) After suffering a landslide, the road was closed, and as of press time, plans for reopening it were uncertain. You can as easily detour around the uplands on your way down from Haleakala, and you can try out a few back roads, too: Some of the most soothing pastoral scenes occur on byways that don't appear on the *Maui Drive Guide* map.

Pukalani – The bedroom community of Pukalani, whose name means "hole in the heavens," is the first town along the route from Kahului to Haleakala and the gateway to the Kula district as well. Pukalani has the only upcountry golf course — and a shopping center, the Pukalani Terrace Center, with a supermarket, drugstore, laundromat, bank, and other stores catering mainly, but not entirely, to residents. The town also has a few places to stop for a cup of coffee or a meal (see *Eating Out*).

Church of the Holy Ghost – Continue along Highway 37 beyond Pukalani and you'll soon see this Kula landmark on a hillside to the left, with the bulk of Haleakala as a backdrop. This octagonal church was built in 1897 for the many Portuguese immigrants brought to Maui to work upcountry as ranch- and farmhands. (Much farther along Highway 37, at Keokea, is St. John's Church, built to serve the Chinese, another important ethnic group among Kula's early farm laborers.)

Maui Agricultural Research Center – Just beyond the Kula Elementary School, a left turn onto Copp Road will take you to the University of Hawaii's Kula experimental station. The first proteas in Hawaii were planted here in the mid-sixties, and by now the Kula station is recognized worldwide as a center of protea research and development. The public is invited to step inside the gates for a look at these unusual flowers, whose varieties include the thumb-sized Blushing Bride and the King, as big as 8 to 12 inches across; the Sugarbush, which pours out its nectar if you tip it over; the Pink Mink, so feathery you'll want to pet it; the Pincushion; and the Hawaii Gold, the first hybrid, developed at Kula. If you do visit the garden — which is also an official All-America Rose Selection (AARS) display garden — you are required to stop by the office, where you will be given a map and asked to sign a risk sheet absolving the university of any blame in case of injury. Open weekdays from 7:30 AM to 3:30 PM. Off Hwy. 37 (phone: 878-1213).

Tedeschi Vineyards and Winery – Highway 37 crosses the western flank of Haleakala as far as Ulupalakua Ranch. Go past the ranch headquarters and you'll see a small plaster and lava rock building that was the jail of Rose Ranch, as it was known when James Makee owned it over 100 years ago and grew sugarcane. Today the jail is the tasting room and gift shop of Hawaii's only vineyard and its only winery. The prime drink is pineapple wine, which, despite its slight pineapple "nose," is surprisingly good. (The gift shop sells two- or three-bottle gift packs ready to be carried onto the plane, but you can also buy it in Maui liquor stores.) The winery has been making wine of juice bought from the Maui Land and Pineapple Company since 1977, but even before that it began to test more than 140 varieties of grapes to find the one that grew best in the upcountry climate at 2,000 feet. Twenty-five acres are now planted with the winner, the Carnelian grape, which produces a sparkling Maui Blanc de Noir and a pale, dry Maui Blush. Tasting room open — with free tours offered — from 10 AM to 5 PM daily. Ulupalakua Ranch, Hwy. 37 (phone: 878-6058).

Kula Botanical Gardens – On the way back from Ulupalakua, the entrance will be on the right, shortly after Highway 37 rejoins Highway 377. The gardens are not large, but they are quite comprehensive and entirely different from the plots of the University of Hawaii experimental station nearby. Here, trees and flowers grow in a more natural setting on landscaped mountain slopes cut by two streams, with a pond at the bottom, bridges to cross, pergolas to walk through, and picnic tables to sit at. The garden has native koa trees and early and late newcomers to Hawaii such as the kukui tree and the Norfolk Island pine. There are bamboo orchids, fragrant gingers, assorted proteas, and many more examples of the plant life you will have seen in hotel gardens and by the roadside and will now be able to identify — provided the specimen has not overgrown its marker. Open daily from 9 AM to 4 PM. Admission charge $3; 50¢ for children. Hwy. 377 (phone: 878-1715).

Sunrise Protea Farm – Upcountry Kula is protea country, and this shop offers a wide selection of this exotic flower for shipment to the mainland. Open daily from 7:30 AM to 5 PM. On Hwy. 377 (phone: 878-2119).

SHOPPING: *Alchemy of Happiness* – Crystals, books, stones, esoterica, and things connected to the spirit suit the store name. 1538 Makawao Rd. (phone: 572-7908).

Hawaii Protea Co-operative – It's the best place to buy proteas; you can carry them home with you or have them sent. They last up to 4 weeks and they dry well. Hwy. 37, on Kula Lodge grounds (phone: 878-6273).

Komoda Store – It's just a little upcountry store, but it's got some extra-buttery pastries and cookies that draw in the locals. 3674 Baldwin Ave., Makawao (phone: 572-7261).

Maui Island Books and Toys – The focus is on children here: If you've got a child in your life, you'll likely find something special. 3643 Baldwin Ave., Makawao (phone: 575-2398).

Maui Moorea Legends – This surprisingly elegant store sells high-style clothing and accessories. All-cotton and handmade leather garments predominate. 3639 Baldwin Ave., Makawao (phone: 572-0801).

Maui Sunburst Farm – At this working protea farm, which has 16 acres of the flowers, you can buy protea at very good prices and take them away with you or ship them to the mainland. Copp Rd., just up from the Maui Agricultural Research Center (phone: 878-1218).

Coconut Classics – Collectibles and antiques, with an emphasis on kitsch, from 1900 to the present. 3647 Baldwin Ave., Makawao (phone: 572-7103).

CHECKING IN: For the most part, only hikers or campers make the upcountry their base, and unless you are a repeat visitor and know what you are doing, take heed. Besides the cabins in Haleakala National Park, there are very few places from which to choose. All telephone numbers are in the 808 area code unless otherwise indicated.

Kula Lodge – Recently renovated and expanded, this cluster of 5 rustic chalet-style cabins are set in a woodsy location on the mountainside. Most are large enough to sleep 4 people; several can accommodate 3 people only. Most have a wooden front porch or lanai, some have fireplaces, none have kitchenettes, but there is a restaurant in the main lodge open daily for breakfast and lunch, and on weekends for dinner. Rates are $87 to $103 for double occupancy. Hwy. 377, on the right going up (phone: 878-1535).

EATING OUT: Because most people come tootling around the mountain quite early in the day, especially if they've been up to watch the sunrise at Haleakala, they're usually looking for a late breakfast, lunch, or midafternoon snack rather than dinner. The restaurant listed as expensive will run $40 or more for two, those listed as moderate run between $20 and $35, while under $20 warrants an inexpensive categorization (does not include drinks, wine, or tip). All telephone numbers are in the 808 area code unless otherwise indicated.

Makawao Steak and Fish House – The setting is comfortable, and the food is good enough to attract a collection of upcountry regulars. This is a restaurant with charm and individuality. Open daily for dinner, daily except Sundays for lunch.

Reservations advised. 3612 Baldwin Ave., Makawao (phone: 572-8711). Expensive to moderate.

Pukalani Terrace – This is a simple, attractive place, with wraparound windows through which you can see the balls popping on the Pukalani golf course, and practically all of Maui that lies westward. Sandwiches, omelettes, and full meals are on the menu, including traditional Hawaiian food. Open daily for lunch and dinner. Reservations advised for groups. Turn right (on your way up) off Hwy. 37 just below the Pukalani Terrace Center. 360 Pukalani Rd. (phone: 572-1325). Moderate.

Casanova's Deli – The place to stop for a great sandwich to eat in or take out. The salads are fresh, the cheeses imported, and the food delicious. Open daily from 8:30 AM to 8:30 PM, Sundays to 7 PM. No reservations. 1188 Makawao Ave. (phone: 572-0220). Moderate to inexpensive.

Kula Lodge – The restaurant at the lodge has windows looking down a wooded slope, with the central valley and the West Maui mountains in the distance. It's open daily for breakfast and lunch, and for dinner Fridays through Sundays (5:30 to 9 PM). Reservations advised. Hwy. 377 (phone: 878-1535). Moderate to inexpensive.

Polli's – The original owner of Wailuku's *La Familia* has another hit in this small Mexican eatery, which serves vegetarian dishes along with more traditional fare. Open daily for lunch and dinner. Reservations advised for groups of 6 or more. 1202 Makawao Ave., Makawao (phone: 572-7808). Moderate to inexpensive.

Bullock's of Hawaii – Some might call it a greasy spoon, but complaints have yet to be heard about the moonburgers (a double hamburger with the works, including a mustard and mayonnaise sauce) or the guava, pineapple, apricot, orange, chocolate, or coffee shakes. Open from 7:30 AM to 3 PM (at press time); a burger plus a shake here costs $5. No reservations. Hwy. 37, just above Pukalani (phone: 572-7220). Inexpensive.

Haleakala National Park

In translation, Haleakala (Hah-lay-*ah*-kah-lah) means "the house of the sun." From some points on the island it does appear that the sun rises directly from the center of Haleakala, but according to legend, the volcano gets its name from an extraordinary feat of the demigod Maui, undertaken once upon a time before ecology was a household word and the environmental impact statement was born. Back in those days, the sun used to rush rather quickly across the heavens, leaving too little daylight for Maui's mother, Hina, to finish her chores, especially the drying of tapa cloth. So one morning, well before dawn, Maui climbed the summit of Haleakala and lay in wait for the sun to come up over the eastern rim of the crater. No sooner had it appeared than Maui lassoed it (by the genitals, according to some versions of the story) and tied it to a wiliwili tree, releasing it only upon the sun's solemn promise to henceforth move more slowly across the sky.

Today Haleakala is the centerpiece of a 27,284-acre national park dedicated to preserving nature's status quo, and visitors who make the sunrise trek to the top of the mountain huddle in the cold behind tripods trained on the eastern rim to capture the sun on film alone. The scene is indeed spectacular.

Standing at the summit, the actual crater in front is only a small part of the panorama. Eighty miles away, the peaks of Mauna Loa and Mauna Kea on the Big Island of Hawaii stand up above the clouds, and as the sun slowly begins to edge the far horizon in red and gold, the earth looks like nothing so much as a giant bowl of whipped cream. Before it rises suddenly and blindingly, forcing the eyes to turn away, you may sense for a moment, at least, what Mark Twain meant when he said he felt "pinnacled in mid-heaven, a forgotten relic of a vanished world."

Curiously enough, from the central valley connecting the two, it is Maui's other volcano, the older and much-eroded Puu Kukui of West Maui, that appears the more precipitous. But Puu Kukui reaches a height of only 5,788 feet, whereas the massive Haleakala, which makes up East Maui, rises more steadily, its summit often deceptively obscured by a wreath of clouds, to 10,023 feet. Its crater — 7½ miles long by 2½ miles wide, 21 miles in circumference, and covering an area of 19 square miles — is a 3,000-foot depression in which the tallest cinder cone, Puu o Maui, stands nearly 1,000 feet high, or about four-fifths the height of the Empire State Building. The extent of Haleakala's crater is due more to erosion than to volcanism, processes that alternated over the course of its life. The volcano once stood 2,000 to 3,000 feet higher than it does today, high enough to catch the moisture of northeast trade winds and cause torrential rains to carve valleys down its slopes. Eventually, the amphitheater-like heads of two of these valleys — the Keanae Valley to the north, the Kaupo Valley to the south — met at the summit, creating one vast erosional scar. Subsequent volcanic activity filled the scar with lava and cinder cones (the result of volcanic material falling back around the vents from which it was blown), causing Haleakala finally to look like a true volcanic crater.

Haleakala's last eruption took place, it is thought, in 1790, a date arrived at (in the absence of any written firsthand account of the event) by comparing the journals of the French explorer La Perouse, who visited Maui in 1786, and the English navigator Vancouver, who visited in 1793. The eruption was forceful enough to send lava down the side of the mountain and add another peninsula to the southwest corner of East Maui in the vicinity of La Perouse Bay. Since then, the volcano has been quiet, but because the last eruption was so recent — at least according to the geological clock — Haleakala is not yet classified as extinct, but dormant.

In 1961, the summit and crater of Haleakala, which had once been part of the Big Island's Hawaii Volcanoes National Park, became a separate national park. And it was enlarged in 1969 by the addition of the Kipahulu District, a 6-mile strip following the Kipahulu Valley east from the crater to Maui's eastern coast near Hana. In both sections, the purpose is to preserve native — any plant or animal that reached Hawaii without the aid of man — flora and fauna that is rapidly being destroyed elsewhere, both by the incursion of man and by the competition of introduced species. Dry forests once covered the lower western slopes of Haleakala, for instance, but they were cleared long ago to make way for grazing cattle, and examples of the trees that grew there have now retreated to less accessible areas of the park. One hundred years ago, the rare silversword, a native plant found only in the higher alpine zones of Hawaii, carpeted the same Haleakala hillside that now contains a small, carefully enclosed stand of them. Hikers who venture to the eastern side of the crater may see the nene, or Hawaiian goose, found only here and on the island of Hawaii. The bird had been extinct on Maui until it was reintroduced in the 1960s in an international preservation effort. Even an endangered Hawaiian seabird, the dark-rumped petrel (*uau*), has taken refuge in the cliffs of Haleakala.

Before setting out for the park, it's a good idea to call 572-7749 for recorded information on weather and viewing conditions. The temperature drops about 3 degrees for every 1,000 feet in altitude, so at the summit it can be 30F (or more) colder than down on the coasts. Most likely, you will be very glad you brought a warm jacket, and if you've come for the sunrise, doubly so. Summer and fall (May through October) are generally better for viewing because they tend to be drier; winter and spring tend to be wetter, and in the winter, it can even snow, at least at the top. The crater is at its clearest in the morning, whereas from midmorning to late afternoon it may be filled with clouds, the result of heat rising from the surrounding land and pushing the volcano's wreath of clouds upward till they pour through gaps in the rim. Sunrise and sunset can both be inspiringly beautiful events, but the sunrise pilgrimage is the traditional one (see *Sightseeing Tours,* SOURCES AND RESOURCES, for guided sunrise tours). Depending on the time of the year, sunrise can occur anytime from about 5:45 to 7:05 AM, and you should arrive at least a half hour before that to catch the first light. The *Maui News* prints the exact times of the next day's sunrise and sunset, and the park's recorded message gives the information as well. If you need more detailed information, call park head-quarters at 572-9306 or 572-9177 (recording). In case of an after-hours emergency, call 572-9221.

The trip from Kahului to the summit usually takes 1½ to 2 hours. Ask at your hotel exactly how long it takes if it's important for you to arrive by a specific time, such as sunrise. Visitors with heart disease, respiratory disease, or high blood pressure are reminded that the altitude may affect them adversely; they should consult a doctor before making the trip and they shouldn't drive alone. Finally, there are no restaurants, hotels, or shops in the park (though there are cabins and campgrounds) as at Hawaii Volcanoes National Park. For places to stop on the way up or down, see *Up-country.*

To reach the park, take Highway 37 (Haleakala Highway) from Kahului and turn left onto Highway 377 (still called Haleakala) above the town of Pukalani. At an elevation of about 3,000 feet you'll bear left again onto Highway 378, or Haleakala Crater Road, and after about 10 miles of switchbacks, the road will deliver you to the park entrance — at an elevation of almost 7,000 feet — where the entry fee of $3 per car, or $1 per van or bus passenger, is paid. From there on, you'll find the following main points of interest, though if you've come to see the sunrise, waste no time in getting to the observation shelter at the summit first.

Hosmer Grove – Just inside the park entrance, a side road to the left leads in less than ½ mile to Hosmer Grove, a campground with picnic tables and a nature trail through a stand of introduced (not native to Hawaii) trees such as North American pine, cedar, juniper, fir, and cypress as well as Australian eucalyptus. The grove honors Ralph Hosmer, a pioneering forester who in the early years of this century experimented with planting foreign trees to replace the native ones that had been cleared to make way for grazing lands, much to the detriment of the island's water supplies. Hosmer planted foreign trees because they grew faster than the native ones, and preserving the damaged watersheds was his overriding concern. Now, the protection of native vegetation, which is lower-growing and has no chance in the competition for light with the tall "exotics," is the park's prime purpose, and it is a sign of success that foreign trees such as these are in the minority within its boundaries.

Park Headquarters – About a mile from the park entrance (open daily from 7:30 AM to 4 PM), this is the place to stop for a comprehensive brochure on the park (if you don't see it, ask for it) and to buy books, slides, and posters. Those intending to use the park's campgrounds must also obtain permits here. Others may want to ask whether any crater rim walks are scheduled. These guided walks, ½ hour to 2 hours long, have been offered in the past (summer months only), but due to staff shortages they may not be offered in the future. Before leaving, go around the building to the pen containing a pair of nene, or Hawaiian geese. It may be one of your few chances to see Hawaii's state bird unless you're planning to hike into the crater.

Leleiwi Overlook – Here, at the first crater lookout point, 8,800 feet up, you might see the Brocken Specter (if conditions are right, that is, with late afternoon sun and clouds in the crater) — your own image projected on the clouds encircled by a rainbow. The name comes from one of the Harz Mountains in East Germany, where the specter also occurs.

Kalahaku Overlook – By all means, stop here. Not only can you look into the barren and blistered world of the crater, but the silversword enclosure is here, one of only two places in the park you're likely to come upon this famous native plant (the other is the Silversword Loop of the Halemauu Trail in the crater). Silverswords take some 7 to 20 years to mature, bloom once, and then die. Before the flower stalk begins to develop in May or June, the plant looks like a great pompom of silver daggers. By July or August, the flower stalk has shot up 3 to 8 feet and is covered with up to 500 individual flower heads of yellow and deep reddish purple, each shaped much like the sunflower to which it is related. Unfortunately, by autumn the plant is dead, and it lies drying on the landscape, as impressive as an old gray mop. The stone wall enclosing the collection of silverswords is meant to keep feral goats and souvenir hunters at a distance.

Haleakala Visitor Center – This glass-fronted observation building at 9,745 feet (yes, it's rounded off to 9,800 feet above the door) is 10 miles from park headquarters. It's open from 8:30 AM to 3 PM, and has been renovated recently. The ranger on duty gives an hourly (9 AM to noon) introductory talk on Haleakala. You can also study the exhibits inside, which explain the geology of the crater. Outside, a footpath leads to White Hill (Pakaoao), a small hill on the crater rim adjacent to the visitor center. A short hike of about 360 yards will take you to its summit, passing stone-walled enclosures used as sleeping shelters by the early Hawaiians.

Puu Ulaula Overlook – The highest point on Maui. The glass-enclosed observation shelter with the 360° view is on top of Puu Ulaula, or Red Hill, which is actually a cinder cone, and the 10,023-foot summit of Haleakala. The building is open 24 hours a day, unattended, and it's the traditional spot from which to watch the sunrise. On a very clear day you can see not only the rest of Maui, but also the islands of Molokai (behind West Maui), Lanai, Kahoolawe, and Hawaii, and on a very, very clear day, even Oahu can be spotted, 130 miles away. The crater before you is less landscape than moonscape, as near perfect a lunar likeness as the earth can muster, and behind you, the five domes of Science City look exactly like any space colony you might have imagined.

Science City (Kolekole) – This research and communications center is outside the park and has nothing to do with it. The installations include solar and lunar observatories of the University of Hawaii, a Department of Defense satellite tracking station, two TV relay stations, and the equipment of a few other tenants. The scene must be admired from afar, however, because Science City is not open to the public.

Hiking and Horseback Riding – There is no better way to experience Haleakala than to descend the crater, and see its rim as skyline and its volcanic curiosities at close hand on all sides. The crater contains 32 miles of hiking trails, which wind past such sites as Pele's Paint Pot, where the usually gray to pinkish hills are colored with reds and yellows from the iron and sulfur imprisoned in the cold lava; Bubble Cave, formed by expanded gases that held their shape while the lava around them hardened; and the 60- to 70-foot-deep Bottomless Pit, blasted through by rising gases, into which ancient Hawaiians threw the umbilical cords of their newborns (supposedly to prevent the infants from growing up as thieves). Making your way east, you'll pass cinder cones splattered with volcanic "bombs" (chunks of lava flung from vents and solidified in midair), cross lava flows, hear the bleating of feral goats, and, if you go to the rainy far eastern end, enter a green and grassy wilderness in considerable contrast to the rest of the crater. Here, Paliku Cabin, one of three crater cabins maintained by the National Park Service, is nestled in solitude among trees and shrubs at the base of a 1,000-foot cliff.

Two main trails lead into the crater from the western side of Haleakala. The Halemauu Trail begins along the highway 4 miles up from park headquarters, and Sliding Sands Trail begins farther up toward the summit, at the visitor center. If you set out along the Halemauu Trail, it is a 4-mile hike to Holua Cabin, another scant mile to the Silversword Loop (a ½-mile detour around some good examples of the plants), and another 1½ miles to the Bottomless Pit and nearby Pele's Paint Pot. Setting out on the Sliding Sands Trail, it's 6 miles to Kapalaoa Cabin and another ½ mile to Bubble Cave, but a popular route for a full-day hike using this trail is to turn off it at the first junction and take the connecting Ka Moa O Pele Trail north, leaving the crater on the Halemauu Trail. The route leads to the Bottomless Pit, Pele's Paint Pot, the Silversword Loop, and Holua Cabin; it is a strenuous one, recommended for hikers in good physical condition only (though it does avoid climbing back up the steep and aptly named Sliding Sands Trail). A less strenuous route for a day's hike is the 8-mile round trip along Halemauu to Holua and back.

No permits are necessary to hike in the park unless you stay overnight, but day hikers are requested to fill in the registration slips found at the trail heads and drop them into the box provided. And before stepping over the edge, hikers should be prepared for any kind of weather — hot and sunny or cold and rainy — with a light raincoat, sun hat, suntan lotion, and canteen as well as proper shoes. Given the distances involved, the terrain covered, and the effect of the altitude, there are no easy strolls in Haleakala.

Trail rides are another way to visit Haleakala. One possibility is a day trip entering the crater from the western side, along the Halemauu Trail or the Sliding Sands Trail. Another is an overnight adventure that begins in the morning and includes an 8-hour trip up the Kaupo Valley before entering the crater in time for sunset. For details on riding expeditions, see *Sports,* SOURCES AND RESOURCES.

Kipahulu District – This section of the park is reached by returning to the north coast of the island, driving the Hana Highway (Highway 36) east to and through the small town of Hana, and continuing 10 miles south beyond it on Highway 31. An arduous alternative route for hikers entails following the trails across the crater, leaving the Haleakala section of the park south through Kaupo Gap, and then continuing on foot, again along Highway 31, from Kaupo village 7 miles east to Kipahulu. Though evidence suggests that the early Hawaiians once used the crater as a short-cut directly to Hana, this is no longer possible, not even for the daring hiker able to negotiate the terrain, because the two accessible sections of the park are separated by a part of it, the Upper Kipahulu Valley, which has been declared a scientific research preserve and closed to the public.

This makes Kipahulu a sort of park within a park, and there is a certain appropriateness to the separation. Where Haleakala is, on the whole, a cold, dry, and desert-like world of ash and cinder cones, most of Kipahulu is like a jungle, with little besides streams and waterfalls to cut the dense, tangled vegetation. Subtropical weather prevails, the humidity is high, and in the upper reaches as much as 250 inches of rain falls yearly to keep things green. Nevertheless, the rain forest is ecologically fragile. It is estimated that 90% of the plant life in the Upper Kipahulu Valley is native Hawaiian, and some very rare birds have been sighted here, too. The nukupuu, a native of Kauai and Maui that at one time was thought to be extinct, lives here, along with the akohekohe, or the crested honeycreeper, found only on Maui and only in this zone. The akohekohe is a member of a uniquely Hawaiian family of birds that evolved long curved bills to sip the nectar from Hawaiian flowers or shorter bills to feed on either nectar or insects. Another honeycreeper, the poouli, was unknown until it was discovered in 1973 in a forest on the northeast slope of Haleakala, its range confined to less than 1,000 acres.

By keeping the Upper Kipahulu Valley off-limits, except for research, its practically untouched ecosystem endures. Thus, the points of interest in the Kipahulu district that are accessible to visitors are in the coastal zone. The best known are the Seven Sacred Pools, a misnomer, because there are more than seven and they are sacred to no one. The pools are caused by the Oheo Stream as it rushes down the hillside, filling depression after depression until it overflows and cascades to the next lower level. Swimming in the pools is a popular activity among visitors, but it can be dangerous. During high water, the stream floods quickly and has been known to carry the unwary straight out to sea.

Makahiku Falls and Waimoku Falls are the objects of hiking trips in this area. The trail begins south of the bridge over Oheo Gulch and follows the left side of the stream up ½ mile to Makahiku Falls, then continues through pastureland and bamboo forest another 1½ miles to the base of Waimoku Falls. In the summer, park rangers conduct hikes as far as Waimoku every Saturday morning (no reservations, but call to make sure the hike is scheduled). For information, call the Kipahulu district office of the National Park Service in Hana (phone: 248-8260; if no answer, try 572-9306).

 CHECKING IN: Overnight camping in the park is permitted only at cabins and campgrounds, and no one may spend more than 2 consecutive nights in any one cabin or campground, nor more than 3 nights per month in the park.

Cabins – The National Park Service maintains three cabins within the crater: *Holua Cabin,* about 4 miles along the Halemauu Trail; *Kapalaoa Cabin,* 6 miles along the Sliding Sands Trail; and *Paliku Cabin,* about 10 miles in along either trail. Each cabin accommodates up to 12 people and will be rented to only one party at a time; rates are $5 per person, with a $15 nightly minimum plus a $2.50 per person firewood fee. Reserve at least 60 to 90 days in advance with first, second, and third choices; write to the Superintendent, Haleakala National Park, PO Box 369, Makawao, Maui, HI 96768.

Campgrounds – There are three campgrounds in the Haleakala section of the park, one at Hosmer Grove and two in the crater near Holua and Paliku cabins. The number of campers is limited to 25 per campground, and the necessary permits are allotted on a first-come, first-served basis at park headquarters. The Kipahulu district's only campsite is the Oheo Campground. No permits are required, but the 3-night limit remains in effect.

Hana and the Hana Highway

Put simply, Hana is a small, remote village on the eastern coast of East Maui reached by the Hana Highway (Highway 36), a scenic drive that follows the northern coast of East Maui, or close to it, for 52 miles from Kahului. But putting it simply does not explain the Hana mystique. The name Hana is usually preceded by the adjective "heavenly," and the appellation is far from hyperbole. Located on the windward side of Haleakala and endowed with more than 70 inches of rainfall annually (much more on the volcano's upper slopes), the Hana area is, for one thing, part dense, luxuriant rain forest, laced with waterfalls, and part open countryside, where cattle feed on meadows that are always green and dewy fresh.

In this setting, old-time Hawaii, at least on Maui, is valiantly making its last stand. The entire district is home to only some 1,800 people, many of them pure and part Hawaiians, and the village of Hana may hold about half that number. The area is agricultural, and because it is isolated and undeveloped, the tranquillity indigenous to rural spots and the simple spirit of aloha characteristic of Hawaiian towns carry on relatively undisturbed — at least for now. Outsiders have taken root in Hana, but they, mostly wealthy and many of them movie stars — such as Burt Reynolds, Carol Burnett, Richard Pryor, and Jim Nabors, all of whom have purchased property here — have come for exactly the peace, quiet, and privacy that Hana offers, and they haven't changed it one bit.

The splendid isolation that endures on this side of East Maui is due, more than anything, to the Hana Highway. This narrow, winding country road was built in 1927, and though paved since, it is so pitted and potholed, and with such ragged edges, that you'll swear it's never once been patched. By unofficial count, it contains 617 curves and 56 one-lane bridges, which explains why the drive of little more than 50 miles takes a resident expert 1½ hours at breakneck speed and everybody else at least 3 hours. The issue of improving "The Road" is a controversial one. You will hear it said that the residents are against it, to keep the tourists out, but the truth is that because road conditions have deterred no one, more recent controversy centers on the state's policy of making short stretches of the road near perfect (such as the last few miles at either end), versus the Hana residents' preference that first aid be applied to the whole course.

Those who want their Maui vacation to be a simple interlude in the country, with the added attraction of a few beaches (but not the best on the island), with no nightlife (because of Haleakala, even the sun sets early here) and no TV (reception is bad), will choose to stay in Hana. For everyone else, the road to Hana itself, and the scenery along it, is the attraction. The route runs through a jungle of subtropical vegetation, winding by damp, fern-blanketed rock walls on one side and hala trees clinging to a cliff on the other. You'll pass koa and kukui trees, mango and breadfruit trees, and, depending on the season, you'll drive over a roadway strewn with fallen guavas and the bruised red petals of the African tulip tree. Even the winding at its worst is leavened by the vision of shaded waterfalls and those one-lane bridges in the inner crooks and by sunny glimpses of sea and coast on the outer elbows. And after you've rounded the last bend to catch the last whiff of ginger or eucalyptus blown in on the breeze, the road will suddenly unwind, the jungle will open up, pastures will come into view, and blazing poinsettias and crotons will announce that you, too, have finally survived the road to Hana.

There are some rules of the road. The first is to get an early start and to keep track of the time. It will likely take at least 3 hours to make the trip, even without stopping at all of the points of interest listed below, and you should be leaving Hana for the return trip no later than 3 PM — it's a dangerous drive in the dark. Fill the gas tank — there's no gas station between the town of Paia and Hana — and stock up on enough food and drink for the duration, because there's no place to grab a bite to eat either. Despite the scenery, keep an eye on the road, keep to your side of it, and drive very slowly around the narrow blind curves. Keep the other eye on the rearview mirror, and when you see traffic backed up behind you, pull over as a courtesy. Though most tourists take the road at speeds ranging from 15 to 30 miles per hour, locals who know it well deserve to be allowed to go on their way. Finally, if you are planning to spend the night in Hana, make sure you have firm reservations before setting out, and if you simply want to get to Hana, consider flying. There is an airport, and your hotel or condominium will pick you up if you arrange it, though unless you also arrange a rental car (through hotel or condo), you'll have no means of getting around during your stay.

Paia – Once a busy sugar plantation town, then a sleepy has-been, Paia is now struggling valiantly to become more than a last-chance stop on the road to Hana. Paint has been slapped from one end of the dusty, sun-bleached strip to the other, a few restaurants have opened or been upgraded, and shops, funky and otherwise, have appeared on the scene. The old Paia Mercantile Building has been restored and converted into the *Paia Arts Center,* with shop and studio space for artists and craftsmen, though natural cosmetics are sold and costumes are rented here, too. Despite this, it still looks as though the stagecoach should be passing through any minute. You will see half of the town if you keep to Highway 36, the other half if you turn right at the crossroads and drive up Baldwin Avenue, which leads to the old sugar mill owned by Henry Perrine Baldwin, one of Maui's 19th-century sugar kings and a founder of Alexander & Baldwin, now one of Hawaii's Big Five. Paia does have the last gas between civilization and Hana and purveyors of box lunches for the trip, so stock up.

About 2 miles east of Paia, you will round a bend and, depending on the time of day, see cars parked on a ledge below. This is Hookipa Beach Park, where contemporary surfing on Maui got its start. The park contains covered picnic pavilions facing out to sea and they, or the unpaved parking areas on the cliffs, are wonderful places to sit and watch the surfers as they streak across the blue with thundering waves at their backs.

Hana Highway – Highway 36 starts out as a fast, wide, smoothly paved road, but once you've hit the 19-mile marker and the sign announces "Narrow Winding Road Next 30 Miles," you'll know you're on your way to Hana in earnest. En route are many places to stop, but the first lookout point is Kaumahina State Park, where another sign reads that you've come 28 miles from Kahului and still have 24 miles to go. The park has picnic tables, barbecue grills, and a splendid view out to sea, down to the small beach at Honomanu Bay, and ahead to the Keanae Peninsula.

A turnoff leading to the peninsula is farther along the road, but before you reach it, the Keanae Arboretum will appear on the right. The arboretum contains sections devoted to tropical plants, Hawaiian domestic plants, and native trees, and it makes an interesting stop (provided you can spare the time). Beyond the turnstile, it is a healthy walk between yellow ginger in the gulch to the left and ferns on the bank to your right before the plantings begin, but if you persevere, you'll be able to see at first hand how taro is grown. Quite a few varieties are planted in the demonstration patches, which are irrigated with the channeled waters of a waterfall that spills from one patch to the next seeking its lowest level (be forewarned: it's a muddy business tiptoeing through taro). The native tree section is best left to another day because the visit involves a 1-mile hike back into the valley.

The Keanae turnoff is a left fork in the road after the arboretum. If you take it, you leave the already narrow Hana Highway to go down an even narrower stretch of paved road that turns into a dirt road leading around the peninsula to a dead end. The peninsula is an ancient lava flow that issued forth from Haleakala, and the waves breaking all around it make its edging of black lava rock fairly shine through the white spray. Somewhat stranded in this location, the village of Keanae is no more than a scattering of houses and a church, a traditional Hawaiian community where taro is grown and where you may still see the villagers pounding the taro root into the diet staple, poi. What part of their domain is not taro field or banana patch or palms is left to grazing cattle, goats, and horses.

Whether you make the Keanae detour or not, you should stop at the small paved lookout on the highway just beyond the turnoff. The view is the classic bird's-eye shot of Keanae as it appears in all the pictures: water-logged taro fields stylized into a neat agrarian checkerboard, the whole peninsula a sparkling expanse of clear, fresh greens projecting into the sea.

An opportunity for another detour occurs farther along when you see the Wailua spur road indicated to the left. It descends into the Wailua Valley and leads through another peaceful, old-time Hawaiian village of taro farmers, while the Wailua Valley Lookout, which you'll come across back on the highway shortly after the turnoff, affords a panoramic view of this second green and taro-patched sweep of loveliness. The pebbled parking area is to the right of the road and the stone stairway leading to the actual overlook on the level above is not easy to find at first, but look for the steps under a clump of overhanging trees. Still farther along, another lookout to the left of the road surveys the same valley.

Puaa Kaa State Park is the next stop. The parking lot is just beyond a one-lane bridge, and from there a pathway will take you back to where a pretty waterfall tumbles into a natural pool (of which a swimmer or two might be taking advantage), then seeps forth as a stream and runs under the bridge and down and out through the valley. The small park contains picnic tables and is full of banana trees and ringed by eucalyptus.

The vista widens over grazing lands just after you've endured one of the remaining unimproved stretches of the Hana Highway, and by the time you see Hana Gardenland on the right — a nursery where tropical plants and seeds are sold — you'll be only 4 easy miles short of the goal. The next "landmarks" on the left are the turnoff to Hana's tiny airport and then the turnoff to Waianapanapa State Park. (Also in the vicinity is a side road to Piilanihale Heiau, the largest of the many *heiaus* (pre-Christian temples) scattered along the coast above and below Hana and reputed to be the largest yet discovered in Hawaii. It is not accessible, however, without a four-wheel-drive vehicle.)

Much larger than the usual wayside park, Waianapanapa contains cabins and campsites in addition to picnic tables. Tent campers must have a permit, which can be issued by any Hawaii State Park office, including the Wailuku branch on the ground floor of the State Office Building in Wailuku, which is open weekdays from 8 AM to 4:15 PM (phone: 244-4354). Cabins are rented through the same office (see *Checking In*). Those passing through may still want to drive in for a look at the park's two main sightseeing attractions: the black sand and pebble beach on Pailoa Bay (be careful of rough currents if you go swimming — it's not always safe even for the best of swimmers) and Waianapanapa Cave, a double cave that is actually a water-filled lava tube overhung by ferns and surrounded by flowers and legend. The legend concerns a Hawaiian princess who is supposed to have taken refuge in a hidden chamber of the cave (reachable only by swimming underwater) while fleeing her jealous husband. He found her nonetheless and killed her, and because this unfortunate event took place in April, it is claimed that every April since then the waters of the cave turn red (some blame the effect on the presence of shrimp). Waianapanapa State Park is also the starting point of a 3-mile hiking trail to Hana. It follows the path of an ancient trail along low sea cliffs, past a *heiau,* and through stands of hala trees, perilously close to the edge at times and all but undecipherable at others.

Just before Hana, Highway 36 divides into a high road on the right and a low road on the left. Either one leads into town, the lower one as Uakea Road, the higher one as the Hana Highway, which goes through town and comes out the other end as Highway 31. Halfway between Waianapanapa and town is Helani Gardens, a 68-acre drive-through park alive with the botanical abundance of the tropics, with all plants fully labeled. The park also features Japanese koi ponds and a luncheon pavilion. Open daily from 10 AM to 4 PM; admission $2 (phone: 248-8274).

Hana – This serene and isolated village has been by turns a battleground, a sugar town, and a cow town. In the war-torn years of the 18th century, before Kamehameha the Great established the united Hawaiian kingdom, the Hana area's proximity to the Big Island gave it enormous strategic importance. As the place from which Maui's chiefs launched their attacks on the neighboring island and where retaliating Hawaiian chiefs began their invasion of Maui, it was conquered and reconquered by one army after another. With the return of peace, other chapters in Hana's history began. In the mid-19th century, the first sugar was planted and numerous sugar plantations came into being that eventually coalesced into the Hana Plantation — later the Kaeleku Sugar Company — and sugar remained the basis of Hana's economy until the period between the two world wars.

Hana quickly turned into a cow town with the arrival of a San Francisco millionaire, Paul Fagan, who foresaw the end of the sugar era and in 1944 bought up 15,000 acres of sugarland. After the last crop was harvested in 1945, he began replanting the property in range grass, imported Hereford cattle from his ranch on Molokai, and called his new spread the Hana Ranch. Because this endeavor was not enough to solve Hana's unemployment problems, Fagan moved just as quickly to build a hotel, which opened in 1946 with his own baseball team, the San Francisco Seals, as the first guests. Millionaire friends followed, and the *Hana-Maui* hotel acquired a reputation as an exclusive retreat for the few, which has stuck. Today, in the post-Fagan era, the hotel is still owned by Hana Ranch Inc. (though the entire enterprise is now owned by Caroline Hunt Schoellkopf, the late H. L. Hunt's wealthiest daughter), and continues to employ a good percentage of Hana's wage earners.

Fagan died in 1960, and the memorial erected in his honor on Mt. Lyons, a cinder cone above the town, is the most panoramic spot in Hana, an ideal place to get your bearings. If the gate is open and it is daylight, don't miss the chance to take the very narrow road that begins behind the hotel and goes through pasture straight up and then around the cone to the cross at the top. From here, the eye takes in one vast seaward roll of green hills and grazing cattle, a view of which the whole of Hana Bay (between Nanualele Point and Kauiki Head) is only a small part, and of which the whole of Hana, with a host of red roofs and every landmark visible, is a still smaller part.

The whole of Hana is the point, because as far as the day-tripper is concerned, the town has few specific sightseeing attractions. Kauiki Head, the cinder cone shaggy with ironwood trees to the right of Hana Bay, figured heavily in Hana's history as a fortress rock, the site of vicious battles between the armies of the Maui chief Kahekili and the Big Island chief Kalaniopuu. It was also the birthplace (ca. 1768) of Queen Kaahumanu, the favorite wife of Kamehameha the Great. Hana Beach Park, also on the right side of the bay, consists of picnic tables and the small beach itself, which offers the safest swimming in the entire district. Hana's community pavilion is the building almost in the shadow of Kauiki just across the road from the park, and at the end of the road is a T-shaped pier. From the end of the pier, there's a broad view of the town as a low line of houses tucked among trees, with two green-carpeted humps (one, Mt. Lyons) as a backdrop and the cloud-covered Haleakala behind all.

Moving inland from Hana Bay, you'll come across Wananalua Church on Haouli Street. The church was built from 1837 to 1857 on the site of an old *heiau.* Across the Hana Highway from it and just a bit south is another focal point, the Hana Ranch Center complex — the ranch headquarters, a bank, the post office, the *Hana Ranch* restaurant, and, nearby, the *Hana Store.* The latter is not the store for which Hana is famous, however — the *Hasegawa General Store,* which figures in a once-popular song by the same name, is on the Hana Highway south of the ranch center (see *Shopping*).

The misnamed (and now often crowded) Seven Sacred Pools (Oheo Gulch) are the major sightseeing attraction beyond Hana. On Highway 31, in the Kipahulu district of Haleakala National Park, the pools are not known to have been sacred to anyone, and more than seven of them are formed by the Oheo Stream tumbling down the valley on its way to the sea, filling depressions at various levels like a string of overflowing champagne glasses. The pools are popular swimming holes (though high water can turn them dangerous quickly), and they are also the starting point of a hiking trail uphill to Makahiku Falls and Waimoku Falls. (For information concerning Saturday morning ranger-conducted hikes to Waimoku, call 248-8260, the Kipahulu district office of the National Park Service, or 572-9307.)

The round-trip drive to the Seven Sacred Pools adds 20 rough miles to a Hana drive. Though not as winding as Highway 36, the road appears twice as narrow and twice as pockmarked, and the trip will take approximately 45 minutes each way. A satisfactory alternative is to drive beyond Hana far enough to sample the peaceful grazing lands on the other side and to see cattle ranging up the slopes of Haleakala and down to the frothy edge of the ocean and, offshore, the tiny island of Alau, with two tall palms standing out like a cowlick on top.

Those who want to go farther will pass Wailua Falls, 7 miles south of Hana, before they get to the pools. And about 1½ miles beyond the pools, just past an old sugar mill on the right, a sign points out the Kipahulu Congregational Church to the left, where Charles Lindbergh — a resident of Hana — was buried in 1974. (Visitors are requested not to trespass on the church grounds.) A little farther, another sign announces a rough road for the next 7 miles. This is the beginning of an unpaved portion of Highway 31 which, over one surface or another, leads around East Maui to Ulupalakua. In Hana, cars can be rented from *Dollar Rent-A-Car* (phone: 248-8237), or the *Budget* at the *Hana-Maui* hotel (phone: 248-8211). Both will provide an airport pickup for customers who are flying in.

SHOPPING: Hana's few stores cater almost entirely to utilitarian needs and, therefore, close by 6 PM. In Paia, however, catering to the visitor is a growth industry. You may want to check out what's new at the *Paia Arts Center,* in addition to the shops below. Warning: You won't really find anything in this area that you won't also find elsewhere, so if you are in a rush, you might just as well save your shopping for later.

Clothes Addict – Casual wear, bikinis, and Maui's largest collection of antique aloha shirts are for sale in this pink building with the flowered awning. 12 Baldwin Ave., Paia (phone: 579-9266).

Hana Gardenland – This nursery sells tropical plants and seeds that can be taken with you or shipped for you. Its many varieties, though naturally immature, are so well labeled that if you've been trying to identify something seen en route, a stop here may solve the problem better than a visit to a botanical garden. Open Mondays through Saturdays from 10 AM to 3 PM. Mail-order catalogue available. Hana Hwy., 4 miles from Hana (phone: 248-8975).

Hana Store – A combination grocery store and five-and-dime. It sells all that you'd expect to find in such stores plus the "Road to Hana Survivor" T-shirt. Hana (phone: 248-8261).

Hasegawa General Store – This is the famous one, the one the song is about, the general store against which all other general stores must measure themselves. Its motto is "Almost everything," which includes groceries, clothing, hardware, souvenirs, liquor, magazines, film, cowbells, Hawaiian moon calendars, movie rentals, and gas. The faded jumble of it all is touching. Hana (phone: 248-8231).

Jaegers – Here are women's casual fashions, with a touch of the exotic in fabrics and styles. 100 Hana Hwy. (phone: 579-9221).

Maui Crafts Guild – Craftspeople display everything from stained glass to photography, basketry to Hawaiian quilts, in this small Paia emporium. 43 Hana Hwy. (phone: 579-9697).

Summer House – Shop here for contemporary women's clothes and accessories with a European flair. 124 Hana Hwy. (phone: 579-9201).

 CHECKING IN: Hana can accommodate only so many people, so whether you plan to stay awhile or are simply unable to face driving the Hana Highway twice in one day, reserve accordingly. Here, the very expensive category means the all-meals-included *Hana Maui,* with rates that start at $416, double. A room for two in a place listed as expensive runs over $90; in a place listed as moderate, $50 to $75; and in an inexpensive place, under $50. All telephone numbers are in the 808 area code unless otherwise indicated.

Hana-Maui – What was already known as an exclusive Hawaiian retreat has been turned into one of the world's unique resorts as a result of a $24-million reconstruction and renovation program. Located on landscaped acres in the heart of Hana Town, the resort is under the aegis of Rosewood Hotels — Caroline Hunt Schoellkopf's company — and it is up to the standard of such other members of the exclusive chain as the *Mansion on Turtle Creek* in Dallas and the *Bel-Air* in Beverly Hills. Low-rise bungalows are framed by flowering plumeria, heliconia, and orchids. Rooms are made luxurious with sunken bathtubs that face private gardens, and are equipped with phone and refrigerator, but no TV sets. Diversions are provided by the heated outdoor pool, tennis courts, pitch-and-putt golf course, beachfront pavilion, stable of horses, and a schedule of activities that includes cookout rides and a weekly luau. Vans, or a rebuilt 1929 Packard, shuttle guests to and from private facilities at Hamoa Beach, 3 miles away, or to and from the airport, and rental cars are also available. The hotel also offers the Sea Cottages, with 2 apartments each, that enjoy panoramic ocean views, large lanais, and individual deckside saunas in which to soak it all up. Note that all rates at the *Hana-Maui* include breakfast, lunch, and dinner. Hana (phone: 248-8211; 800-321-4262). Very expensive.

Hana Bay Vacation Rentals – To rent a fully furnished, fully equipped home for a Hana base, Stan and Suzanne Collins are the people to contact; they handle 10 homes in the town of Hana. Some require a 3-night minimum, others are offered daily. Car rentals can also be arranged. Check for weekly discounts. The reservations office is closed Saturdays (phone: 248-7727). Expensive to moderate.

Hana Kai Maui Resort – Two gray wooden buildings make up this 19-unit condominium — one banked with red ginger and a border of yellow allamandas, the other reached by a bridge over a stream edged in blue ginger. The rooms, while not elegant, were refurbished recently. Each has a large lanai with a table, chairs, and lovely ocean views, which makes for perfect alfresco dining. There are, however, no phones in the units and the lack of air conditioning can prove a discomfort on occasional humid nights. The *Hana Kai* is only a short walk from the coast, where there is a rocky beach and a rough surf: Swimming is not recommended. Uakea Rd., Hana (phone: 248-8426). Moderate.

Heavenly Hana Inn – This small inn looks like something your great-aunt might live in — or run — were she Japanese. It has the air of a private home, hidden behind a Japanese gate hung with Japanese lanterns and guarded by two stone lions. The lobby and lounge area, too, are filled with Japanese knickknacks (plus a piano), but apart from the shoji screens everywhere, the 4 units for rent are less Oriental in their accoutrements. Each has 2 double bedrooms, a tiny TV room, a sit-in kitchen with a small refrigerator but a hot plate instead of a stove, a bathroom with stall shower, and a private porch on the encircling Japanese garden. Also available through the inn are 2 rental homes, one a beachfront cottage with kitchenette. No swimming pool. Airport transportation available at minimal charge with advance notice, however, a car is a practical necessity. On the Hana Hwy., halfway between the airport and town (phone: 248-8442). Moderate.

Waianapanapa State Park – The 12 rustic cabins here are in a forest of hala trees not quite dense enough to blot out the sun. Each has a living room, a bedroom, and kitchen facilities, and each is completely furnished with bedding, towels, and cooking and eating utensils. Prices range from $14 to $30 a day, depending on the number of occupants (the maximum is six people), so make reservations well in advance. The cabins are about 3 miles from Hana but are rented through the Department of Land and Natural Resources, Division of State Parks, PO Box 1049, Wailuku, Maui, HI 96793 (phone: 244-4354). An in-person or mail-in deposit is required. Inexpensive.

EATING OUT: There are restaurants at either end of the Hana Highway, but en route there are only picnic tables, where you'll eat what you've brought with you. (*Picnics,* at 30 Baldwin Avenue in Paia, packs box lunches for the road. It's open daily except Sundays from 8 AM to 3 PM.) Selected restaurants in the Paia area and *all* of the places to eat in Hana are listed below; beyond these, at the Hana end, you'll have to rely on groceries from the *Hana Store* or the *Hasegawa General Store,* on take-out service at the *Hana Store,* or on hot dogs or hamburgers from *Tutu's* lunch counter at Hana Beach Park. Dinner at the very expensive *Hana-Maui* dining room has a fixed price of $50, without drinks or tip. Elsewhere, expect to pay $20 to $30 if the establishment is listed as moderate, and under $20 if it's listed as inexpensive. All telephone numbers are in the 808 area code unless otherwise indicated.

Hana-Maui – Hana's only proper restaurant is this hotel's elegant, spacious dining room. Natural woods and hanging plants, exposed beams, and teakwood tables add up to a wonderful setting for specials that include sizzling whole fish and grilled veal chops. The prix fixe menu features only fresh produce, meats, fish, and poultry. Open for breakfast, lunch, and dinner daily; dinner reservations necessary. Hotel Hana-Maui, Hana (phone: 248-8211). Very expensive.

Mama's Fish House – Some say that Mama serves the best fish on the island, but with so many Maui restaurants serving fish, the statement would be difficult to prove. Mama also serves steaks, seafood, and a chicken dish or two, but if you do have the fish, have it sautéed, the most popular of several styles ranging from poached to baked in tarragon sauce to teriyaki. The restaurant is enclosed, with screened windows along the *makai* (ocean) side looking across a lawn, some low palms, and the break of the surf on Kuau Cove. Open for lunch and dinner daily; reservations advised. Off the Hana Hwy. at Kuau Cove, between Paia and Hookipa Beach Park (phone: 579-9672). Moderate.

Dillon's – From the street, this dusty red building looks like a Wild West saloon tarted up with yellow lace curtains. Inside, the ambience is more Polynesian, and out back there's even a tiny garden of five tables squeezed in among banana trees and a large schefflera. The menu features fresh fish, plus steaks, seafood, and Italian dishes. Open daily for breakfast, lunch, and dinner. Reservations advised. 89 Hana Hwy., Paia (phone: 579-9113). Moderate to inexpensive.

La Vie en Rose – A surprisingly sophisticated little restaurant, whose owners are resettled Basque windsurfers. What the menu lacks in variety it makes up for in quality. Open daily except Tuesdays for lunch and dinner (until 8:30 PM). Reservations unnecessary. 62 Baldwin Ave. (phone: 579-9820). Moderate to inexpensive.

Hana Ranch – Take a humble cafeteria, add windows on the sides, sliding glass doors, and an outdoor dining deck with a noble view of cattle range and coastline, and you'll have an idea what this restaurant is about. Hana's luncheon buffet (11 AM to 3 PM daily) includes hot dishes and a salad bar. Since a lot of the people who've made it to Hana eat here, there is a certain amount of relief-related conviviality in the air. Dinner is served from 6 to 8 PM on Fridays and Saturdays; reservations advised. In the Hana Ranch Center complex (phone: 248-8255). Inexpensive.

Picnics – This is the place for the best box lunches. All pastries and breads are baked on the premises. Open daily from 7:30 AM to 3:30 PM. Reservations unnecessary. 30 Baldwin Ave. (phone: 579-8021). Inexpensive.

Tropical Garden Café – Fresh-baked breads for breakfast and a range of sandwiches, soups, and salads for lunch with indoor and outdoor seating make this a comfortable stop en route to Hana. Open daily for breakfast and lunch. Reservations unnecessary. 120 Hana Hwy., Paia (phone: 579-8422). Inexpensive.

MOLOKAI

The smell and feel of Molokai are, at first rush, pure prairie. The effect upon landing at Hoolehua Airport is not unlike alighting from the single daily plane in a small Texas town. Agriculture and a long horizon are everywhere. A pure plains wind lifts the red dust and brings the dry air into the lungs.

There is, after Honolulu, tangible culture shock. Molokai is Hawaii's unsullied frontier, preserved for the time from the ravages of ambition and the pressures of population by a strange series of events. Coincidence, difficult times, and shrewd design have somehow combined to keep the island's population hovering around 6,000 and the economy almost totally based on the land. Lack of development — and lack of reason for it — has protected almost all of Molokai's virgin beaches, forested mountains, and secluded valleys. Here is a place to leave a footprint that will be marred only by the creeping tide, to swim in a pool at the foot of a waterfall with only a floating ti leaf to bear witness, to find contentment in a trackless forest.

Kaunakakai, the only real town on the entire island, has not a single traffic light. Except for the Polynesian and Filipino faces, it could be any small town in the Southwest, right down to the single storefront street lined with pickups. The whole island, 38 miles long, has a tiny police force whose members until only recently drove their own automobiles in service to the community. From Oahu's Makapuu Point it is but 22 miles across the open water of the Kaiwi Channel to Molokai's Laau Point. The flight from Honolulu to Hoolehua takes less than 30 minutes. Yet these few miles and few ticks of time are the measure of decades.

It is not so much that time has stood still on Molokai, although it most certainly has lagged, as it is that the clock periodically has been broken. Molokai long has been more isolated than most of the seven inhabited Hawaiian islands; only Niihau and Lanai have had less contact with the outside world. The first Hawaiians, Polynesians who, it is calculated, arrived sometime in the 5th or 6th century, at first avoided Molokai. The island did not appear hospitable — its west end dry and barren (thus the Hawaiian name: *molo,* "barren"; *kai,* "sea"), its east end precipitous and choked with jungle. In addition, prevailing winds and currents did not favor voyaging to or from Molokai, the island's leeward shore had no protected anchorages, and its windward coast was isolated by immense cliffs (now regarded as the highest such sea cliffs in the world). Only later were the fertile north coast's valleys and the south coast's lowlands settled.

Kamehameha the Great conquered the island with a great army in a battle fought at Pakuhiwa Battleground on the south shore. The King's fleet of war canoes is said to have stretched for 4 miles. Molokai, however, was a small prize, and Hawaii's history quickly moved on and left it once more quiet.

Add to these factors the potent *kahunas* (priests or magic men of ancient

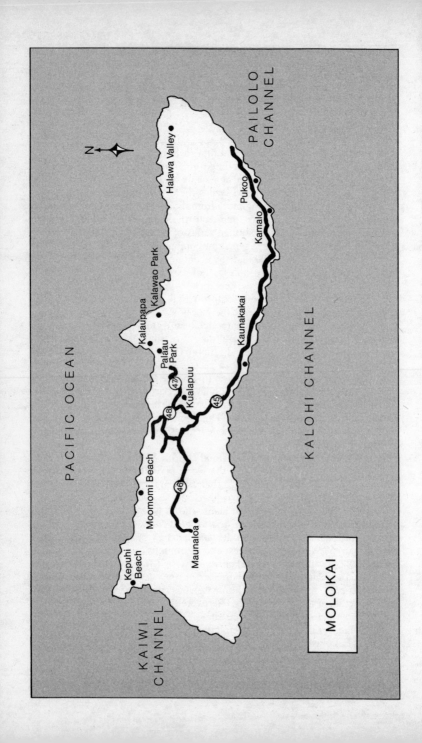

Hawaii), which Molokai apparently had in abundance and of whom every-body else in Hawaii was scared stiff, and Father Damien's Kalaupapa leper settlement, which came much later but tended to put people off, and it is fairly easy to understand why even today Molokai is regarded with some reverence and suspicion.

The missionary families that began to arrive in the early 19th century did little to open Molokai to the world. They were interested in religion and commerce, with one not necessarily taking precedence over the other. The Meyer and Cooke families came to control Molokai, at first planting trees and eventually causing cattle to fatten, pineapples to grow, and payables to accrue. It was their dominion over two-thirds of Molokai, including the best beaches, that preserved the island's natural wonders just as isolation had guarded them in earlier times.

Until 1988, Molokai Ranch Ltd., heir to the efforts of these early families, owned or controlled about half of Molokai, but the company's voice in island affairs and its impact on the island's economy have been even more potent. Del Monte leased its pineapple fields from the company, and 6,000 head of cattle grazed on company pastureland. Green panic and guinea grasses from company land were sold to feedlots and dairies throughout Hawaii. Modern tourism came to Molokai only when the company set aside, and eventually sold, nearly 14,000 acres of prime west end beach and hill land in the middle 1970s for resort and residential development.

There have been a small number of pivotal events in the modern history of Molokai, the first being the introduction of pineapple cultivation during the 1920s. Dole and Del Monte leased huge parcels of rolling land, imported hundreds of Filipino laborers to work the fields, and brought relative prosperity to the island. The sharp-spiked fruit grew in geometrical precision on the entire western half of Molokai and spawned the company towns of Maunaloa (Dole) and Kualapuu (Del Monte). But as competition from pineapples grown in the Orient with far cheaper labor became intense in the 1970s, raising the fruit became less profitable on Molokai. Dole pulled out in 1975 and Del Monte in 1983. Maunaloa, on the west end plateau land, became a relative backwater, even by Molokai standards, despite modest efforts to establish it as an arts and crafts center. Almost everyone agrees that in place of the expired commercial pineapple production diversified agriculture must come — most of the acreage once devoted to pineapples has reverted to pasture, a boon for the reviving cattle herds that were destroyed by state decree in 1987 due to an outbreak of bovine tuberculosis — as must some acceptable level of tourism.

The next epochal event that shaped modern Molokai, after the arrival of the pineapple, was a tidal wave that swept the east end of the island in 1946. At that time, the verdant, peaceful Halawa Valley, which had been inhabited from ancient times, was still home to several hundred residents. Taro grew easily and the fishing was good in lovely Halawa Bay. The water rose gradually and slowly filled the valley, giving the people time to escape, but the *tsunami* receded rapidly, taking almost everything with it. Their homes and possessions lost, the people abandoned their beautiful valley and moved else-where on the island or left it entirely. This was the same tidal wave, says local lore, that spilled into the south shore lagoon in front of Kaunakakai and made it dull, shallow, and unfit for swimming.

Even more significant in terms of the future was the opening, in 1977 (on land formerly owned by the Molokai Ranch Company), of the Sheraton Molokai (now Colony Resorts' *Kaluakoi Hotel and Golf Course*), the first true resort hotel on the island (there were already several smaller hotels near Kaunakakai). The 292-room hotel not only had a lovely beach, but an 18-hole golf course and tennis courts as well. Plans for a 375-room deluxe property at Kaluakoi have been delayed by environmental and cultural concerns. The recent sale of most of Molokai Ranch's west Molokai holdings to Japanese interests may pave the way for future development, although an activist community is likely to bring pressure to restrain building it considers inappropriate to Molokai's rural lifestyle.

Certainly there are wonders sufficient to support far more tourism on Molokai. The island's 260 square miles include glorious (if too often unswimmable) beaches; the jungled 4,970-foot summit of Kamakou, the highest spot on the island; secluded valleys; and sacred groves and fish ponds. There is Palaau Park and its famous Kalaupapa Lookout, which draws the eye down nearly 2,000 feet of sheer cliff to the flat, volcanic, tongue-like peninsula of the remote leper colony that is now safe and open to visitors as Kalaupapa National Historic Park.

But possibly most of all there is about Molokai its ancient Hawaiian past, a mysteriously touched past. Many believe Molokai the most spiritual, the most Hawaiian of the islands — a place of powerful *kahunas,* helpful *menehunes* (little, leprechaun-like people), potent *kapus* (taboos), sacred places, myths, legends, whispers . . . The population includes the largest percentage of pure-blooded Hawaiians of all the Hawaiian islands, save off-limits Niihau. Molokai is an island of many names: In ancient times it was said to be called Puleoo (Effective Prayer). Today it is known as the Friendly Isle, but in the past it has also been the Forgotten Isle and the Lonely Isle. Molokai's direction remains today as unclear as it has for centuries.

SOURCES AND RESOURCES

TOURIST INFORMATION: The Hawaii Visitors Bureau does not have an office on Molokai, so for information contact the main office at 2270 Kalakaua Ave., Honolulu, HI 96815 (phone: 923-1811). The Destination Molokai Association, PO Box 233, Kualapuu, HI 96757 (phone: 567-6255; 800-367-4753), will provide brochures and information. On Molokai, your options are informal and few. Rental car offices at Hoolehua Airport have a useful guidebook and map.

Local Coverage – Also useful is the local newspaper, the weekly *Molokai News.* All the basics are also printed on the restaurant placemats at the *Kaluakoi* hotel, which include capsule descriptions of several tourist sites. The *Kaluakoi* hotel is also a good place to get a verbal rundown; check at the guest relations desk or tour desk in the lobby. A booklet, *Molokai, the Friendly Isle,* is available several places on the island; also worth a look is Phil Spaulding III's booklet *Molokai.* The top of the line in books is the beautifully produced *Molokai, An Island in Time,* by Cooke family member Richard Cooke.

There are several bed-and-breakfast accommodations available on Molokai through *Bed & Breakfast Hawaii,* Box 449, Kapaa, HI 96746 (phone: 822-7771). Among those offering vacation rental accommodations on the east end: Diane and Larry Swenson, Star Rte. 279, Kaunakakai, HI 96748 (phone: 558-8394), Herb and Marion Mueh, Star Rte. Box 128, Kaunakakai, HI 96748 (phone: 558-8236), and the *Honomuni House,* Star Rte. Box 306, Kaunakakai, HI 96748 (phone: 558-8236).

Telephone – The area code for Hawaii is 808.

GETTING AROUND: Connections between Honolulu, Maui, and Molokai are provided by Hawaiian Air, with daily flights on its four-engine, Dash-7 turboprops. But lots of people like the fast service of the commuter lines with their small twin-engine craft; these include Air Molokai and Aloha Island-Air. The *Maui Prince* hotel (phone: 553-5736) operates boat service three times daily between Kaunakakai and Lahaina, Maui; seating is in an air conditioned cabin or on the sundeck. Each way, the trip takes 75 minutes and costs $21.

There is no public transportation on Molokai. Most people arrive on the island by air at the main airport at Hoolehua (there is a small strip at Kalaupapa, mainly to accommodate the sightseeing flights to the leper colony). *Gray Line of Molokai* operates a shuttle service between the airport and hotels and condos (advance reservations required; phone: 567-6177).

Taxi – Save yourself the aggravation and rent a car.

Car Rental – *Avis* (phone: 567-6814; 800-331-1212), *Budget* (phone: 567-6877; 800-527-0700), *Dollar* (phone: 567-6156; 800-352-3923), and *Tropical Rent-A-Car* (phone: 567-6118; 800-367-5140) have booths at Hoolehua Airport, but fleets are small, so it's advisable to reserve well in advance. *Budget* and *Dollar* have off-road vehicles. Note that rental cars may be driven on dirt roads, but renters bear full responsibility for damage or towing.

Bicycles/Mopeds – The *Kaluakoi* hotel is the best bet for rentals. Try the travel desk for bicycles, and the concession at the golf course for mopeds (phone: 552-2555).

SIGHTSEEING TOURS: *Gray Line of Molokai* (phone: 567-6177) and *Robert's Hawaii Tours* (phone: 552-2751) offer half- and full-day van and bus tours of the island, valuable if you're stuck without a rental car but easily duplicated if you've got one.

Mule – *Molokai Mule Ride* mounts daily expeditions on sure-footed mules that clamber down the steep, narrow, 3⅛-mile trail from the cliffs overlooking the peninsula on which the Kalaupapa leper colony settled. The views are stupendous, and the experience itself is breathtaking. Guides meet the mule train at the bottom and conduct a tour of Kalaupapa and the Makanalua Peninsula. A simple picnic lunch is served at lovely Kalawao Park overlooking the sea cliffs of the north coast. The entire tour, including lunch, costs $75 per person. *Molokai Mule Ride* will also book hike-and-ground and round-trip air-and-ground tour visits to Kalaupapa. Contact *Molokai Mule Ride,* PO Box 200, Kaulapuu, Molokai, HI 96757 (phone: 567-6088; 800-843-5978).

Wagon – The horse-drawn *Molokai Wagon Ride* (phone: 552-2555 or 576-6773) includes a visit to the sacred Iliiliopae Heiau as well as a beach stop for a picnic. The genuine Hawaiian hospitality makes this hour-and-a-half ride fly by. At press time, a licensing dispute threatened to curtail wagon-ride itineraries.

SPECIAL EVENTS: A canoe race across Kaiwi Channel from Molokai to Oahu is traditionally held each year during *Aloha Week;* however the area from which the race is launched is usually closed to visitors. A traditional Makahiki — a Polynesian-style Olympics — is held in Kaunakakai in mid-January.

SPORTS: Do not come to Molokai for the swimming, snorkeling, or water skiing. Come instead for the golf, hiking, tennis, hunting, exploring, and relaxing. The greatest concentration of traditional resort sports is found far out at the west end at the Kaluakoi resort, which boasts the island's only top-grade golf course and the best tennis courts.

Boating and Sailing – Sailing is offered at Kaunakakai aboard the 42-foot sloop *Satan's Doll* by *Molokai Charters* (PO Box 1207, Kaunakakai, HI 96748; phone: 553-5852). Options include snorkeling, sunset sails, and day trips to Lanai. Glenn Davis of *Hokupaa Ocean Adventures* (PO Box 141, Kualapuu, HI 96757; phone: 800-567-6255) offers cruises May through September, and the *Alele II* (PO Box 121, Kaunakakai, HI 96745; phone: 558-8319) departs Halawa Valley on the east end for a day-long cruise along the spectacular north coast to Kalaupapa. *Adventure Kayaking International* (PO Box 61609, Honolulu, HI 96822; phone: 988-3913 or 800-634-7537) during the calmer summer months leads kayakers along the same coast, with its spectacular mix of sea cliffs, valleys, and waterfalls. *Whistling Swan Charters* (PO Box 1350, Kaunakakai, HI 96748; phone: 553-5238) sets out on overnight and week-long sails.

Fishing – Although the fishing is legendary at Penguin Bank, off Molokai's southwestern tip, there is presently only one charter boat for hire: the 35-foot, twin-diesel cruiser *Alele II,* which is fully equipped to troll for marlin, mahimahi, shark, tuna, and ono. Remember that the custom in Hawaii is that the captain, not the fisherman, gets to keep the catch. Call Chris Lightfoot (phone: 558-8319) to arrange for charter fishing.

Golf – There are two golf courses on Molokai, but only one is worth playing — and it is well worth it, one of the nicest in the islands. The other is an undistinguished 9-holer. *Kaluakoi Golf Course* (phone: 552-2739), a robust Ted Robinson design, has 18 holes, stretches 6,618 yards and plays to a par 72, and features 5 holes set along the sea. This is a beautiful course, equal to the best in Hawaii, with a complete pro shop, driving range, and practice putting green. It's also right at the *Kaluakoi* hotel, on the western tip of the island. Greens fee is $42, including a cart — $36 for guests — and golf-inclusive packages are available (phone: 552-2555; 800-367-6046). *Ironwood Hills Golf Club,* the Del Monte course in Kualapuu in the middle of the island, has nine holes, 2,790 yards, and par 35. Carts are not available, but it's a lovely walking course. Visitors may still obtain permission to play by calling the Del Monte office (phone: 567-6121) and paying the $5 fee in Kualapuu (there's no clubhouse at the course and rarely anyone there). To find Ironwood, drive up Route 47 toward Palaau State Park and look for a tiny sign that says "Golf Course" on your left.

Hiking – The hiking possibilities on Molokai are quite attractive — particularly up Halawa Valley or along the Wailau Trail across the entire island — but trails are poorly marked, often very difficult, and guides are unavailable. What's more, a few *pakalolo* (marijuana) growers in such isolated areas guard their territories jealously. Secure parking for hikers to Halawa Valley can be found with the *Dupre Dudoit* family (turn right upon gaining the valley floor). The Nature Conservancy owns nearly 3,000 acres of prime mountain rain forest and dry shrubland. A Jeep road intersecting with Route 46, just outside Kaunakakai, leads to the *Kamakou Preserve* which is home to a wondrous array of rare native Hawaiian plants and birds. Most trails were created by wild boar hunters, who still use the property for this purpose. No camping is permitted within the preserve, but there is a campsite just outside the park at the Waikolu Lookout; a permit is required and can be obtained from the Department of Forestry & Wildlife, PO Box 347, Kaunakakai, HI 96748 (phone: 553-5019). It's wise to keep in mind that although the hiking is good, hikers should first be sure to get good local information, directions, and perhaps permission to cross private land.

Horseback Riding – Experienced riders can arrange half- or full-day rides, complete with picnic lunch, by calling *Hawaii Horsemanship Unlimited* (phone: 552-0056).

Hunting – The hunting is very good on Molokai, especially for the small axis deer

(May through October), wild boar, mountain goats, and a whole flock of game birds. Deer were stocked on the island in 1850 by Kamehameha V. As elsewhere in Hawaii, the sport does not come at bargain rates. The guided hunt costs $400 per day for the first hunter, $150 for each additional hunter, and $600 for each axis deer, barbary sheep, or Indian black buck of trophy caliber bagged. Bird hunting isn't quite as dear, however. Ring-necked pheasant, wild turkey, quail, doves, partridge, and other birds may be hunted on the Molokai Ranch's 40,000 acres for a season permit of $300 or $25 per day. The season runs from November through January. A state hunting license ($15) is also required. And be sure to bring your own gear since none is available on the island. For information, contact Molokai Ranch (phone: 552-2767). *Air Molokai* (phone: 553-3636) offers special bird-hunter charters from Honolulu.

Snorkeling – The best diving is at the east end of the island. Halawa Bay is a fine site when swells aren't kicking things up, and a series of coves around the area of Morris Point are fine, too. *Molokai Fish & Dive Corp.* in Kaunakakai (phone: 553-5926), the only place on Molokai to rent or buy snorkeling gear, recommends the area between mile markers 20 and 22 on the east side for snorkeling and scuba diving. Moomomi Beach on the Pali coastline of the north shore is said to offer good diving (but it's on a dirt road, which is forbidden to all but four-wheel-drive vehicles), as does the reef about a mile from shore opposite Kaunakakai. *Molokai Charters* (phone: 553-5852) offers half- and full-day snorkeling trips; the waters of neighboring Lanai are featured on full-day trips. Also contact Glenn Davis of *Hokupaa Ocean Adventures* or Chris Lightfoot (phone: 558-8319). Past the *Kaluakoi* is a series of beaches with easy access and good diving close to shore. Divers must bring their own equipment as no scuba gear is available on the island.

Surfing – Halawa Bay has decent surfing when conditions are right. In the winter, Kepuhi Beach often has huge waves suitable only for experienced surfers, and the action can be watched from the *Kaluakoi* hotel; during the summer, the waves here are too flat. The entire south shore is inside the reef.

Swimming and Sunning – Swimming is a sometimes proposition from the lovely beaches of the west end, but the sunning is fine in this dry area — as long as the wind isn't blowing; better swimming can be found in the isolated lagoons and coves of the east end, but the sun is iffy there. The south shore of Molokai, along which Kaunakakai is located, consists of a shallow, silty, unappetizing lagoon. The *Kaluakoi* hotel is nestled next to Kepuhi Beach, which is extremely photogenic but swimmable only during calm periods in the summer and winter; otherwise, it can be treacherous. The same goes for 2-mile-long Papohaku Beach, said to be Hawaii's longest, which stretches just south of the *Kaluakoi* — it's spectacular, but risky. Both beaches lose much of their sand in the winter, exposing wicked-looking rock and coral formations. Perhaps the best all-around beaches on the island are scattered along the western end of the north shore. The trouble is that only unpaved roads lead to these beaches — Kawakiu and Moomomi (now protected as a nature preserve) are the finest — and the car rental outfits specifically prohibit driving their vehicles off *paved* roads. Possible solutions include ignoring this instruction and hoping for the best (not recommended), or renting an off-road vehicle from *Avis* in Kaunakakai (a better idea). Kawakiu Beach is reached from a turnoff on Route 46 marked with a small sign that announces "Beach Access," and the drive in is a few miles. Moomomi Beach is where paved Route 48 ends and a dirt road about 3 miles long begins. Tricky as many of the west end beaches are to find, those on the east side of the island require even more patience and more than a little intuition. There's a "secret" beach (without a name, apparently) that's known only to islanders — drive along Route 45 until you reach the landmark "neighborhood grocery store," which looks like a roadside fireworks stand, on your left; just past the store on the right, take the dirt road toward the sea, where there's a protected area that's fine for swimming. There are a few more "beaches" on the east end, but they're on a very shallow lagoon. The best deep place to swim here is Halawa Bay, when the wind and swells cooperate.

Tennis – The *Kaluakoi* hotel has four Laykold courts lighted for night play, a resident pro, and a pro shop. These courts, by far the best on the island, are at the south end of the hotel complex near the 8th green of the golf course and are free for guests. *Ke Nani Kai,* next to the *Kaluakoi* hotel, has two courts available for guests, as does the *Wavecrest Resort,* a condominium complex on the east end. The courts at *Wavecrest* are lighted at night. In addition, there are courts at Molokai High School and the Community Center in Kaunakakai.

AROUND THE ISLAND

Molokai is half rolling lowlands, half steep mountains and deep valleys, 38 miles long and between 7 and 10 miles wide; some amateur cartographers say it resembles a shoe or moccasin. There is a central, low-lying saddle; a craggy, wild east end topped by 4,970-foot Mt. Kamakou; and a high, grassy, rolling, tableland in the west. Three volcanoes conspired to build an island of sharp contrasts; erosion then set in, carving volcanic domes into breathtaking cliffs, deeply creased jungle valleys, and cloud-scudded heights. The fish ponds, of which legend says there were 58 in ancient times, lie off the eastern and southern coasts — a few are still visible today. The Makanalua Peninsula, better known as site of the Kalaupapa leper colony and Father Damien's martyrdom, is a 4½-square-mile lava flow protruding from the center of the north shore like a huge, level tongue; it seems almost not part of Molokai at all, it is so isolated. The major village of Kaunakakai, a trading town without a traffic light, pokes its single significant street south toward the reef and at the hump of Lanai, rising 9 miles away across the Kalohi Channel.

Kaunakakai, Central Molokai, and the South Shore

Kaunakakai, Molokai's "capital," is best known for the song written about a supposed individual of some civic note, "The Cock-eyed Mayor of Kaunakakai." Yet Kaunakakai has no mayor; the seat of government is actually on Maui, since Molokai is part of Maui County. Still, Kaunakakai is an important place even though its population probably doesn't exceed 1,000. It was here that Kamehameha V chose to build a summer home. And it is here that everyone on the island comes to shop, eat, drink, and gossip — Ala Malama Street, though it is only 2 blocks long, is the commercial heart of Molokai.

The south shore of Molokai, although important in Hawaiian history for its collection of royal fish ponds, has mostly drowsed in modern times. Apart from Kaunakakai and its underused pier that stretches a half mile offshore in search of deep water, there is little but the historical sights to interest a visitor. In fact, the entire western half of the south shore has only a rough dirt track, and permission must be obtained even then to use it. The eastern part of the south shore is nicely paved, however, and Route 45 rolls past points of historical interest and a picnic ground or two before proceeding into the verdant mysteries of the east end. Central Molokai, above and beyond Kaunakakai, contains the airport and homestead area of Hoolehua, agricultural and pasture lands, the town of Kualapuu, and Palaau State Park, the windswept outlook over Kalaupapa and the staging point for mule expeditions down the sheer cliffs.

Kapuaiwa Grove – Originally a grove of 1,000 coconut palms, said to have been planted for Kamehameha V, beside the lagoon just west of Kaunakakai and across the street from Molokai's famous Church Row (see below), in an area considered sacred. Although there are far fewer palms now, their effect is still striking. Next to the grove is a small park.

Church Row – Six churches and a mission school are lined up in an impressive display of the island's regard for religion just west of Kaunakakai and across Route 46 from the Kapuaiwa Grove. Most of the churches are tiny clapboard affairs and combine on Sunday mornings to produce Molokai's weekly "traffic jam."

Palaau State Park – This cool, whispery park, with trails, a picnic area, and campgrounds, is forested with cypress, koa, ironwood, and paperbark trees on a high bluff over the ocean pounding the northern shore. There's also Kauleonanahoa, the well-known Phallic Rock, which seems anatomically perfect enough and to which ancient Hawaiians attributed magical powers to combat barrenness. But the most famous feature here is the Kalaupapa Lookout, from which the leper colony and its buildings 2,000 feet below can be clearly seen and the totality of its isolation fully comprehended.

Hoolehua – This residential area of homesteads also holds the island's airport. But blink and you'll miss it. At *Purdy's Nuts* (phone: 567-6601 or 567-6495), a small macadamia nut farm, a tour is offered, with a chance to taste and buy afterward. Open daily, 9 AM to 1 PM.

R. W. Meyer Sugar Mill – Recently opened, this excellent restoration of one of Molokai's original steam-run sugar mills (c. 1878) also includes well-documented displays and memorabilia of Rudolph Wilhelm Meyer. The German immigrant settled on Molokai in the 1850s, and his numerous descendants (he reportedly had 110 children) are to be found all over Molokai. Open Mondays through Saturdays from 10 AM to noon, Sundays from 1 to 5 PM. As press time, plans called for an extension of weekday hours: A phone call will give you an update. The $2.50 admission fee includes a tour. On Route 47, between Kualapuu and Palaau State Park (phone: 567-6436).

Kualapuu – Del Monte's former pineapple town was said to have a population of 550 prior to the company's pull-out. Kualapuu Reservoir, visible from the road, is claimed to be the largest manmade rubber-lined reservoir in the world, built to hold 1.4 million gallons to irrigate the pineapple fields. Del Monte maintains the nearby 9-hole *Ironwood* golf course, a walking course available to visitors.(phone: 567-6121).

Sandalwood Pit – More than a hundred years ago, when sandalwood trees grew on Molokai, sailing vessels would come to the island to load the precious cargo. This pit was dug to simulate the size of a ship's hold so the amount of wood could be measured for a single load. The dirt road that leads here forks off from Route 46 and heads bumpily inland several miles west of Kaunakakai before the turnoff to Route 47; be prepared for a tough Jeep ride.

Waikolu Lookout – As long as you've made it to the Sandalwood Pit, you might as well continue along the same rutted track a couple of miles more, where you'll be rewarded with one of Molokai's most inspiring views. The Waikolu Lookout reveals wooded valleys and a 3,000-foot-deep gorge. It's only about 12 miles from the paved road, but it'll seem much more. Beyond Waikolu is a 3,000-acre nature preserve, with several partially obscured trails.

Kamehameha V's Summer House – Just west of the pier outside Kaunakakai is the rubble and foundation of the monarch's getaway during his reign from 1863 to 1872. There's so little left to see that it's a bit difficult to find.

The Pier – The solid concrete structure once used for loading pineapples is one of the island's proudest achievements, yet it seems destined to fall into disuse. It's possible to drive ½ mile out on it.

Kakahaia Park – A pleasant, well-kept beach strip park on the lagoon a few miles east of Kaunakakai and past the *Molokai* hotel. There are picnic tables, grass, and a fine view of Lanai, but not a swimmable beach.

One Alii Park – A bigger park with more facilities and closer to Kaunakakai than Kakahaia. This is one of very few places on Molokai where it's possible to camp. Permits are available in Kaunakakai from the County Parks Office (phone: 553-3221).

 SHOPPING: Resort clothing and tourist trinkets are not common items on Molokai — you're more likely to find farm implements and basic household products. This is particularly true in the Kaunakakai area, where most of the residents come to shop. There are, however, a few interesting exceptions. Molokai kiawe tree honey is an excellent local product.

Imports Gift Shop – For the dedicated browser, a surprising array of souvenirs, jewelry, and ladies clothing will be found here. Ala Malama St. (phone: 553-5734).

Molokai Gift Shop – This well-stocked shop in the *Molokai* hotel has a good selection of Hawaiian print muumuus, aloha shirts, and swimsuits. Also on hand is quite a bit of unusual Hawaiiana. Hotel Molokai (phone: 553-5801).

Molokai Fish and Dive – This is the place to head for Molokai's largest selection of T-shirts and other Molokai-emblazoned souvenirs. Open daily. Ala Malama St. (phone: 553-5926).

Molokai Island Creations – Kaunakakai's most contemporary shop has an interesting selection of women's and children's wear, toys, lingerie, books, hats, jewelry, and more. Ala Malama St. (phone: 553-5926).

Shop 2 – Clothing is sold at this small boutique on Kaunakakai's main street, along with Chinese herbs and other fun-to-browse items. Ala Malama St. (phone: 553-5888).

 NIGHTLIFE: Nightlife in and around Kaunakakai is so limited, it's easy to find. The *Molokai* hotel's *Holo Holo Kai* (phone: 553-5347) features simple guitar-and-voice entertainment next to the bar and restaurant on Thursdays, Fridays, and Saturdays. But the best bet is at the *Pau Hana Inn* (phone: 553-5342), whose bar is *the* place locally, especially on Friday and Saturday nights. There's usually a dance band, and things often get very Hawaiian and sometimes very enthusiastic. Those in search of local color will find it here.

 CHECKING IN: Room rates on Molokai are among the lowest in the islands. A listing of expensive indicates accommodations running $75 or more, moderate hotels cost $40 to $70, and inexpensive prices range from $25 to $40. All telephone numbers are in the 808 area code unless otherwise indicated.

Molokai – The first classy hostelry on the island, opened in 1966. A real Polynesian flavor clings to this place, from the island-style, 2-story wooden buildings to the open bar and restaurant area. The grounds are compact but filled with flowers, coconut palms, and lots of tranquillity, except when a boisterous crowd is at the bar. All rooms have a lanai swing and a refrigerator. There's a small pool that faces right on the unswimmable lagoon. And there's very low-key entertainment on weekends. PO Box 546, Kaunakakai, HI 96748 (phone: 553-5347; 800-367-8047). Expensive to moderate.

Pau Hana Inn – Molokai's oldest hotel seems to have been around forever, but a recent refurbishing has spruced things up considerably. This relaxed, very basic place has a real charm for those who appreciate the native way of doing (or not doing) things. It's so laid back that the *Pau Hana*'s own brochure admits the hotel is "content to do business in an aimless, languid, southseas sort of way." And that goes double. There's an assortment of 39 units with ages and prices that bounce all over the place and amenities reflected in the price. It's on the beach, but the beach is awful so most people opt for congregating around the nice, medium-size pool instead. The hotel is within easy walking distance of Kaunakakai and, as it advertises, it does "cater to *kamaainas,*" as can easily be discerned at the bar and in the restaurant (where prime ribs are the best bet). The *Pau Hana* is truly action central, particularly on Friday and Saturday evenings. PO Box 860, Kaunakakai, HI 96748 (phone: 553-5342; 800-367-8047). Expensive to inexpensive.

Molokai Shores – Here is a very pleasant condominium, opened in 1978, with 101 1- and 2-bedroom units, all with full kitchens, in three 3-story buildings. It's less than 2 miles east of Kaunakakai, and boasts lovely grounds facing an unfortunately unswimmable lagoon. There's a pool, picnic tables, and barbecues, a 9-hole putting green, lots of lawn, laundry facilities, and even a hair salon. But there's no bar, no restaurant, and no grocery store. Maid service is available for an extra charge. A Molokai condo caution is to bring anything fancy with you since Kaunakakai's markets are neither super nor very well stocked with luxury items. PO Box 1037, Kaunakakai, HI 96748 (phone: 553-5954; 800-367-7042). Moderate.

 EATING OUT: The food served on Molokai is unexceptional despite menus that aspire to more discriminating tastes. Expect to pay about $20 to $30 for two people in establishments listed as moderate, less than $20 in an inexpensive place. These prices do not include wine, drinks, or tip. All telephone numbers are in the 808 area code unless otherwise indicated.

Holo Holo Kai – Simple but generally good food is served in this lagoon-front restaurant. Breakfast (try French toast made with Molokai bread), lunch (finished at 1:30 PM), and dinner (a good place for alfresco sunset dining) are offered daily. Catch of the day and teriyaki chicken are the best bets. There's a bar and entertainment Thursdays, Fridays, and Saturdays, and a Sunday buffet from 6 to 9 PM. Open daily. Dinner reservations advised. Hotel Molokai (phone: 553-5347). Moderate to inexpensive.

Pau Hana Inn – Meals are served inside near the fireplace or outside under the huge banyan tree, depending on the season and weather. Breakfast, lunch, and dinner are on a par with Molokai's best. The Portuguese bean soup is fine, though, as are the prime ribs, sautéed shrimp, and catch of the day. The bar is active, especially on Friday and Saturday nights. Open daily. Reservations unnecessary. At the Pau Hana Inn (phone: 553-5342). Moderate to inexpensive.

Hop Inn – The island's Chinese restaurant looks a bit shabby from Ala Malama Street, but the food is good. Open daily to dish out lunch and dinner. No reservations. Kaunakakai (phone: 553-5465). Inexpensive.

Kanemitsu Bakery – This is the source of the wonderful Molokai cheese and onion bread. There are a few tables in back, and breakfast, lunch, and dinner are served. Closed Tuesdays. Reservations unnecessary. Kaunakakai (phone: 553-5855). Inexpensive.

Mid-Nite Inn – The best place to eat on Ala Malama Street in Kaunakakai, although it's really just a simple neighborhood restaurant that closes at 9 PM (no matter what the name promises). Meals are served on Formica tables (wear old jeans if you don't want to seem out of place); the fish, when it is fresh, can be quite tasty. Open daily for lunch and dinner, Sundays for breakfast. Reservations unnecessary. Ala Malama St. (phone: 553-5302). Inexpensive.

Outpost Natural Food – Off Ala Malama Street, good sandwiches and a range of health-related dishes are the offerings here. There's a juice bar, and picnic tables are outside. Open Sundays through Fridays from 9 AM to 6 PM. Makena Pl. (phone: 553-3377). Inexpensive.

West Molokai

It really is, as they say, "out island" here. This is the turf of the *paniolo,* the Hawaiian cowboy — the word is said to be a corrupted form of *Español,* referring to the Mexicans who were the first cowboys to come to Molokai early in this century. Most of the western portion of Molokai is owned or leased by the recently sold Molokai Ranch Ltd. It is largely grazing land or empty spaces awaiting the future, perhaps tourism and residential development. The arid, high tableland that is the dominant feature of West Molokai once was heavily planted in pineapple, but that ended in 1975, when Dole gave up its lease. Molokai Ranch has since planted these fields in hay, which it sells as cattle feed in Hawaii and Japan. There is fine bird hunting upland here, and fringes of attractive beaches, most of which cannot be reached without a four-wheel-drive vehicle (hard to find) and Molokai Ranch permission (difficult to get). On the 6,700 acres of Kaluakoi are the Colony Resorts' *Kaluakoi* hotel, a golf course, and several small condominiums. Kaluakoi and its regulated development, centered around the slow phasing in of tourism and secondary residences, is thought by many to contain the germ of economic salvation for Molokai as the island's agricultural base dwindles; others see it as the initial step in the destruction of the Hawaiian way of life treasured by the people.

Molokai Ranch Wildlife Park – This 800-acre wildlife preserve with more than 300 animals native to India and Africa was begun in 1977 by Molokai Ranch Ltd. to stock and breed exotic and endangered species for the world's zoos and parks. But the business venture turned into something more when guests at the nearby *Kaluakoi* hotel showed an interest in visiting the park. Now there is a very low-key 1½-hour van tour that bumps and lurches into the park and affords glimpses, often close ones, of axis deer, sable antelope, Indian black buck, barbary sheep, oryx, ibex, and zebra — all grass eaters, no predators, who thrive in the dry brush and hills that duplicate so well their native habitat. The office for the tour is at the tour desk of the *Kaluakoi;* the cost is $12 plus tax for adults, $6 for children up to age 12. Kaluakoi Hotel, PO Box 1977, Maunaloa, HI 96770 (phone: 552-2555).

Maunaloa – After emerging in the 1920s as company town for Dole, of pineapple fame, it remained one of the most important towns on Molokai for half a century. Then Dole abandoned its pineapple fields and left Maunaloa in 1975. For several years, the town — left still and nearly empty on a high plateau about a mile from the ocean, yet near the modern development of Kaluakoi — seemed to be dying. But lately it has seen a modest revival thanks to the combined efforts of new arrivals and the few old-time residents. A forlorn post office, a ramshackle general store called the *Friendly Market,* and rows of plantation housing are reminders of the past. This is the end of the paved road — only fields of grass that once were covered in pineapple plants lie beyond.

 SHOPPING: There are three shops at the *Kaluakoi* hotel: *Liberty House* (a branch of the Hawaiian clothing chain), *Molokai Gems* (a jewelry boutique), and *Kepuhi Sundries* (reading matter, liquor, snack foods, and so on). In all of West Molokai, there are only three other shops, all in Maunaloa — *Dolly Hale,* for Hawaiian dolls (no phone); *Plantation Gallery,* with deer-horn scrimshaw, silver jewelry, wood carvings, and Balinese imports (no phone); and the *Big Wind Kite Factory,* whose motto, "Come fly a kite," tells you all you need to know (phone: 552-2364).

 NIGHTLIFE: There is no nightlife outside the *Kaluakoi.* The *Ohia Lounge* (phone: 552-2555) features an active bar and a Hawaiian group that plays during the cocktail and dinner hours.

 CHECKING IN: Room rates in West Molokai match those of the more common destination resorts, particularly at the *Kaluakoi,* where rates start at $95 per room in high season, $79 in low season, and range as high as $185 in high season. For a room at the properties listed below, above $100 is considered expensive, from $75 to $95 is considered moderate. All telephone numbers are in the 808 area code unless otherwise indicated.

Kaluakoi Hotel and Golf Course – Now operated by Colony Resorts, the spiffiest hotel on the island is also the biggest by far — when the 29-acre resort opened in 1977 (as the *Sheraton Molokai*), its 292 rooms immediately doubled the number of accommodations on Molokai. Beautifully set on photogenic Kepuhi Beach (not, however, usually suitable for swimming) with a first-rate 18-hole golf course curling around it, this hotel also has 2 restaurants and a lounge. There's a small free-form swimming pool, 4 lighted tennis courts, and several shops, including a branch of *Liberty House.* Rooms are in 32 1- and 2-story buildings scattered over broad areas of lawn, all nicely decorated in South Seas motifs, all with TV sets (not common on Molokai). Here you will be isolated (a rental car is a necessity, unless you want to make this a retreat) but in comfortable surroundings. PO Box 1977, Maunaloa, HI 96770 (phone: 552-2555; 800-367-6046). Expensive to moderate.

Ke Nani Kai – This resort condominium has 170 1- and 2-bedroom units with full kitchens and lanais offering views across the golf course and beach. There's a pool, Jacuzzi, and 2 tennis courts; a short walk leads to the beach, restaurants, and shops at the *Kaluakoi.* PO Box 126, Maunaloa, HI 96770 (phone: 552-2761; 800-922-7866). Expensive to moderate.

Paniolo Hale – The property is adjacent to the *Kaluakoi* hotel and separated from the beach only by a fairway of the golf course. There are 77 studio, 1-, and 2-bedroom units (although not all are in the rental pool) in a well-designed community of 1- and 2-story structures; all have full kitchens (there's a small market 6 miles away in Maunaloa), and some have indoor hot tubs (extra charge for heating). There is a pool, paddle tennis court, outdoor gas barbecues, and weekly maid service. No restaurant or bar (use the *Kaluakoi's*), and you'll feel lost without a car (phone: 552-2731; 800-367-2984). Expensive to moderate.

EATING OUT: There isn't much to choose from in the way of restaurants on this side of Molokai. In the expensive range, expect to pay about $15 to $20 per person; $10 to $15 at a place listed as moderate; less than that at an inexpensive place — not including wine, drinks, or tip. All telephone numbers are in the 808 area code unless otherwise indicated.

Ohia Lodge – The *Kaluakoi*'s main restaurant, an attractive, high-ceilinged, lodge-like affair above the crashing surf, serves breakfast, lunch, and dinner; most call it the best restaurant on the island, with a decent wine list, a limited but good dinner menu. Open daily. Dinner reservations necessary. In the Kaluakoi hotel (phone: 552-2555). Expensive to moderate.

Paniolo Broiler – This may well be the better of the two *Kaluakoi* restaurants since its pretensions are fewer and the food simpler. There are steak, chop, and fish dishes, and a salad bar. Open for dinner only when hotel occupancies are high. In the Kaluakoi hotel (phone: 552-2555). Expensive to moderate.

Jojo's Café – Decent lunches and West Molokai's least expensive dinners, with 1950s mood and prices. Open nightly until 7:30 PM. Maunaloa (phone: 552-2803). Inexpensive.

The Snack Shop – Near poolside at the *Kaluakoi*. Fast foods (including good burgers) from 11 AM to 5 PM daily (phone: 552-2555).

Kalaupapa and the Makanalua Peninsula

One of the most awe-inspiring sights in all Hawaii is also its most deeply moving spiritual experience. Makanalua is the isolated volcanic tongue of slightly more than 12 square miles spewed out eons ago and separated from the rest of the world by the vigorous sea on three sides and by sheer ocean cliffs said to be the highest in the world on the fourth. This natural prison became an actual one on January 6, 1866, when the first lepers were dumped into the sea and left to drown or begin a harsh existence on the barren peninsula. Leprosy — called *mai-Pake,* the "Chinese disease" — had come to Hawaii sometime in the early 19th century, and the government responded by hunting down and exiling the lepers to the most inaccessible place they could find. The Makanalua Peninsula was it, and the lepers who survived established a crude settlement at Kalawao. Father Damien Joseph de Veuster, a Belgian priest who served in Hawaii, heard of the ugly, lawless colony of condemned people and came here permanently in 1873 to tend the lepers and bring organization and justice. Often called the Martyr of Molokai, Father Damien died of the disease in 1889 at age 49 and one day may be officially canonized a saint: Locally he is already considered one.

The settlement moved to Kalaupapa (once a native fishing village) from Kalawao in 1888, when water was piped in to this more pleasant west side of the peninsula. There are a score of weathered structures, a modern hospital, a kind of general store, and Father Damien's St. Philomena Church, completed in the late 1870s. Kalawao Park, on a beautiful but rugged portion of the peninsula's east coast, is the site of the original colony. The victims of Hansen's disease (the proper term for leprosy) who live on the peninsula today number fewer than 100 (there were 1,200 early in this century), and their condition has been arrested through the use of sulfone drugs, introduced in the 1940s. But they chose to remain at Kalaupapa, which was declared a National Historic Park (phone: 567-9093), although it remains under state control.

There are several ways to reach Kalaupapa. *Air Molokai* (phone: 553-3636) and *Aloha IslandAir* (phone: 567-6115; 800-652-6541 in Hawaii; 800-323-3345 elsewhere in the continental US) fly into Kalaupapa's tiny airstrip from Hoolehua Airport topside on Molokai. *Aloha IslandAir* also flies to Kalaupapa from Oahu and the other Neighbor Islands. Both carriers offer inclusive tour packages (a guide must meet you before you leave the airstrip). It's also possible to hike in, down the steep 3-mile trail from the top of the 2,000-foot cliff at Palaau State Park, but hikers must be experienced and ready for a strenuous climb; before heading down the trail they must have a sponsor who will obtain the required permit from the state's Department of Communicable Diseases and will arrange for a tour guide to meet them at the base of the cliffs. *Damien Tours* (PO Box 1, Kalaupapa, HI 96748; phone: 567-6171 or 567-6675) will arrange a land tour (including a mule ride) for visitors arriving by air or on foot. Usually led by the company's owner and resident curmudgeon, Richard Marks (the third generation of his family to be settled at Kalaupapa), the tours are interesting, informative, and enjoyable. Remember to bring your own lunch.

Most visitors reach Kalaupapa as part of a mule train. From a bluff 2,000 feet above the peninsula, the mule train winds down a 3⅛-mile trail studded with 26 hairpin switchbacks. The view is thrilling and the adventure is, well, stimulating. But be comforted that no mule has yet missed a step. At the bottom, each excursion is met by a tour conductor who is also a Kalaupapa resident for a close look at the settlement. A box lunch is served at Kalawao Park, the site of the original colony. The entire trip takes about 7 hours. Reservations are required as permits must be obtained for you; the minimum age is 16, the maximum weight, 225. Trips begin about 9 AM at the stables near the Kalaupapa Lookout and return around 3:30 PM. The price is $75 per person. Contact Molokai Mule Rides (phone: 567-6088; 800-843-5978 in the continental US).

Makanalua Peninsula and Kalaupapa are not the usual tourist attractions. There are no hotels, shops, or restaurants. Though there is no chance of being exposed to or contracting Hansen's disease, you're not permitted to leave the tour and wander around on your own. No children under the age of 16 are allowed, and none will be seen living here (any children born are raised outside). The experience is a somber yet uplifting one.

East Molokai to the Halawa Valley

It is only about 30 miles from Kaunakakai to the end of Route 45 at the luxuriant Halawa Valley, but it is the distance of time. Every mile farther east takes you a step back into Hawaiian history as the landscape changes gradually from dry and hilly to lush and mountainous. This east end once was thickly populated, at least for Molokai, and was a center of island life. Now things are different. There are few residents, no gasoline, no restaurants, no bars, only a single lonely condo complex. This is the part of Molokai being protected, held back from development and the encroachment of modern ways. There is much sacred here to many Hawaiians, much that is *kapu* — locked and off-limits. It is the mysterious and fascinating part of Molokai.

Places of historical interest are numerous in this east end of Molokai, although many are nearly impossible to find without local help and a few are behind locked gates or otherwise on private land. Heritage is sometimes jealously guarded out here.

Fish Ponds – These traps once supplied fish for royal tables. In the old days it is said there were 58, some perhaps ½ mile long, ringing the east and southeast shoreline. They were built of lava rock and worked by allowing in small fish that, when fattened, would be too large to escape through the chinks in the walls. Historians have speculated that fish ponds existed on Molokai as early as AD 1000, but positive records indicate them in the 15th century. Some ponds have been restored and are in use today — they can easily be seen as you drive along Route 45. Two, Keawanui and Ualapue, are part of a National Historic Landmark.

Halawa Valley – The road ends at the entrance to this beautiful, verdant valley, once the home of many of the island's people. A tidal wave (*tsunami*) forced Halawa's evacuation in 1946, and most of the residents never returned; it echoes with ghosts today. Yet it remains a lovely, tranquil, very tropical place popular with hikers and nature lovers. It's 4½ miles long, and a 2-hour hike that isn't too difficult (there are several streams to ford) leads to Moaula and Hipuapua falls, which cascade 250 feet down into the head of the valley. The freshwater pool at Moaula Falls is cool but safe for swimming, according to legend, if a ti leaf floats.

Kalanikaula Grove (also spelled Lanikaula) – This sacred grove of kukui trees is said to have been planted for a very powerful *kahuna* (priest and magic man) around his grave. Hawaiians say the aura is potent. The grove is on private land just before reaching the Halawa Valley.

Mapulehu Mango Grove – The trees are venerably old in what may be Hawaii's largest mango grove. Plans are in the works to make it something of a showpiece, but for now it's just a wonderful, authentic bit of old Hawaii. In season, try a mango smoothy.

Iliiliopae Heiau – One of the largest religious shrines of ancient Hawaii is more than 100 yards long and nearly 40 yards wide. Only the stone platform and terraces may be seen, but the scale is impressive. It's near Pukoo on private land, yet it's possible to pay a visit. *Molokai Wagon Tours* (phone: 558-8380) includes the *heiau* as part of its 3-hour itinerary ($25).

Kawela – This "city of refuge," similar to the more famous one on the Big Island of Hawaii, was where Hawaiians accused of crimes fled. Little remains today. It's just before Kamalo.

Pakuhiwa Battlefield – The area west of Kamalo is where Kamehameha the Great landed with a force of war canoes said to have stretched for 4 miles. It is here the warrior-conqueror vanquished Molokai. Artifacts of the battle are still found today.

Our Lady of Sorrows Church – Mass is celebrated in this church, which was founded by Father Damien before he moved to Kalaupapa and is now brightly restored. A life-size statue of the Martyr of Molokai is in a screened pavilion next to the church, which is on the inland side of the road at Kaluaaha.

St. Joseph's Catholic Church – Another of Father Damien's churches, a tiny, white clapboard structure, is right next to the road on the lagoon side at mile marker 10 near Kamalo.

Smith and Bronte Landing – Ernest Smith and Emory Bronte made a somewhat less than dignified emergency landing just past the lagoon in a stand of kiawe trees at Kamalo after the first civilian transpacific flight in 1927. A roadside marker notes their ignominious contribution to history.

Moanui Sugar Mill – The ruins of a sugar mill operated between 1870 and 1900 by a Norwegian lie inland a short distance from Halawa. The crumpled stack and rubble can be seen from the road.

Wailau Trail – A rough hiking trail that crosses the entire rugged east end of Molokai from south to north leads to the idyllic Wailau Valley, once heavily populated. Permission must be obtained for crossing private property and grumpy islanders may not be overly pleased by an intrusion — best to get good advice on this trek.

SHOPPING: Nary a single boutique out here.

NIGHTLIFE: You guessed it.

CHECKING IN: The only option is the Wavecrest Resort, with 1- and 2-bedroom apartments which rent from $56 to $86. All telephone numbers are in the 808 area code unless otherwise indicated.

Wavecrest Resort – A 125-unit condominium complex, at mile marker 13 between Kamalo and Pukoo, with 35 1- and 2-bedroom suites, all of which have kitchens and an ocean view, but no maid service. The 5½-acre resort is on the lagoon, but the water is not suitable for swimming or diving. There is a pool, lighted tennis courts, a putting green, and a reasonably well stocked general store, but no restaurant, though a snack bar has opened at the *Neighborhood Store,* several miles away in Pukoo. Things are tranquil indeed at *Wavecrest,* and also neat and orderly; the climate here is considerably more damp than in the central and western parts of the island. Star Rte. 155, Kaunakakai, HI 96748 (phone: 558-8101; 800-367-2980).

EATING OUT: There isn't so much as a snack bar on the entire east end of Molokai. The nearest restaurant is in the *Molokai* hotel, west of Kamalo. (The telephone number is in the 808 area code.)

Neighborhood Store – The snack counter here provides take-out foods for a Halawa Valley picnic, or a place to stop for lunch en route. Stock up. It's the last store on East Molokai. Open from 7 AM to 7 PM daily (phone: 558-8933).

LANAI

Despite its location at the heart of the archipelago, Lanai is the least known of the major Hawaiian islands, with a history of being shunned that stretches back into the mists of Polynesian colonization. The old legends identify Lanai as having been a cursed island, haunted by evil spirits and consequently hostile to men until Kaululaau, the precocious son of a West Maui King, was exiled to Lanai — just 8 miles across the Auau Channel — for his harmful hijinks, such as pulling up breadfruit trees. Kaululaau proceeded either to hunt down and kill or to drive off the demons, and when he'd made Lanai safe, he lit a signal fire to inform watching Maui that Lanai was ready for habitation. The brat became a hero and Hawaiians moved to Lanai.

Apparently, however, not too many came to the vaguely pear-shaped "hump" (the rough English translation of Lanai) of an island 13 miles across at its widest and 18 miles long. Geography did not favor Lanai. The wet mountains of the east side contained precipitous gulches and other largely uninhabitable areas, while the rest of the island was dry, mostly devoid of vegetation and unsuitable for any agriculture. Anthropologists have estimated that the inhabitants of old Lanai never exceeded 1,200 (though some figures estimate as many as 3,000), and populated periods were interspersed with long intervals during which the island was deserted. When Captain James Cook's expedition sailed past the island in the last part of the 18th century (after Cook himself had been killed on the island of Hawaii), it was described in logs as a brown, barren, and inhospitable place. Yet it was on Lanai at Kaunolu Bay that King Kamehameha I (Kamehameha the Great) chose to make his summer home in the early 19th century.

History moved sluggishly, in fits and starts, on Lanai. Battles were fought when Kamehameha and his forces swept through during his conquest and unification of Hawaii; important petroglyphs were left; some old *heiaus* (ancient shrines and temples) were built. A faint ripple was felt in 1854, when a group of Mormons arrived to colonize Lanai and began farming the fertile but arid Palawai Basin — a vast depression that is all that's left of the ancient volcano Palawai, which formed Lanai. But the endeavor failed and the Mormons left a decade later.

It wasn't until 1921, when Jim Dole purchased the entire island (with the exception of a few small parcels granted by Hawaiian royalty to local families) for $1.1 million to raise pineapples, that Lanai began to emerge from its entirely Polynesian past. There had been short-lived attempts to grow sugarcane and raise cattle, but both had been unsuccessful. Pineapples were perfect for the island's climate, however, and grew furiously once water was piped in from the mountains and pumped up from underground. The Palawai Basin was quickly planted in pineapple fields of military precision, turning Lanai into one of the largest pineapple plantations in the world.

LANAI

KALOHI CHANNEL

PACIFIC
OCEAN

AUAU
CHANNEL

● Koele
● Lanai City

Keomuku ●

● Lanaihale
3,370 ft.

44

44

Kaumalapau ✈

441

● Kaunolu

Hulopoe Bay   Manele Bay

KEALAIKAHIKI CHANNEL

Consequently, Lanai quickly became known as the Pineapple Island. Yet the name was deceiving and gave the impression that the place was overrun with the prickly plants when, in truth, Lanai's pineapple fields never exceeded 16,000 of the island's 90,000 acres and now occupy fewer than 14,000. The plain fact is that the Dole Company and the firm that purchased it, Castle & Cooke, preferred Lanai to stay quietly and singularly devoted to the cultivation of pineapples. That is how things have been for half a century on Lanai, at least until recently.

It would be misleading to say that Lanai is changing radically with the advent of mainstream tourism, but the days of isolation — when Lanai's sole accommodations were found in its sole ten-room hotel — have definitely been relegated to times past. The $35-million *Lodge at Koele,* intended for those seeking a luxurious getaway, was, as we went to press, set to open toward the end of 1989; the 250-room *Manele Bay* hotel overlooking Hulopoe Beach will debut then also. Both properties are slated to be under Rockresorts management, although recent sale of the former Rockefeller hotel company leaves the situation a bit uncertain at press time. New private homes and condominiums are also in the works. In addition, the new 18-hole, Arnold Palmer–designed golf course was well on its way to completion.

Castle & Cooke, owner of all but approximately 2% of the island (which is in private hands in the forms of old Hawaiian land grants and recent sales of residential plots), continues to pledge its commitment to maintaining Lanai's agricultural orientation and to preserving the wilderness areas that provide the island with its necessary watershed and some of the best hunting for Mouflon sheep and axis deer in Hawaii. Lanai's people nevertheless tend to view this change as a mixed blessing: Although most seem to welcome the new opportunities that development will provide, others express concern that these changes, however well-intentioned, can only spell the end of a way of life.

However, in spite of the changes that have been put in motion, Lanai maintains the feel of its early plantation days. Pineapple still dominates the landscape, providing revenues for Castle & Cooke and jobs for many of the 2,100 people, predominantly of Filipino extraction, who live here. Only a handful of miles separate Lanai from the tourist bustle of Kaanapali and the rest of West Maui, and several entrepreneurs — notably Andy Kraftsow and his *Club Lanai,* with 8 beachfront acres on the isolated north coast — cross the channel on day trips to take advantage of Lanai's clear waters for snorkeling, scuba, and touring. But, for now, Lanai still remains a true getaway for the adventurous — for those who want to be first . . . or last.

SOURCES AND RESOURCES

TOURIST INFORMATION: The Hawaii Visitors Bureau has no office on Lanai, but information can be obtained from the main office at 2270 Kalakaua Ave., Honolulu, HI 96815 (phone: 923-1811). On Lanai, talk to Glen Oshiro of *Oshiro's* (the gas station, car and Jeep rental agency, and taxi service); the folks at *Lanai City Service* (another gas station and car rental agency); or a ranger with the *Koele Company,* the Castle & Cooke division that manages Lanai's wildlands. The best book for background and insights is *Survey of the Island of Lanai,* by Kenneth Emory; if you can't find it here, try the Bishop Museum in Honolulu. Another good book to consult is Ruth Tabrah's *Lanai. Oshiro's* has a good map, which you'll need.

Telephone – The area code for Hawaii is 808.

 GETTING AROUND: Air Molokai, Hawaiian Air, and Aloha IslandAir offer scheduled flights to Lanai from Honolulu, Maui, Molokai, and the Big Island.

Lanai has absolutely no public transportation. There's a taxi shuttle to and from the airport run by *Oshiro's* (phone: 565-6952) and *Lanai City Service* (phone: 565-7227); and plans are underway to institute a shuttle linking the airport with Lanai's two new hotels (both under construction at press time).

Car and Jeep Rental – Glen Oshiro has a small fleet of Toyota sedans ($28 daily plus gas), four-wheel-drive vehicles ($75 daily plus gas), and assorted other vehicles for hire (*Oshiro's;* phone: 565-6952). Charge card required. Reserve ahead if you want a specific vehicle. *Lanai City Service* (phone: 565-7227) also rents compacts for $31 per day plus gas, and four-wheel-drive vehicles for $85 plus gas. Lanai only has 22 miles of paved roads, so if you want to do more than drive to the beach you'll need a Jeep. (*Note:* At press time, Castle & Cooke plans call for the addition of a fleet of rental cars that could soon replace those of the smaller local businesses.)

SIGHTSEEING TOURS: Again, very little is offered in the way of prepared tours. *Lanai City Services* (phone: 565-7227) offers a daily, 1½-hour van tour that includes Lanai City; however, individuals would do better to rent a car and just follow the map.

Boat – Several Maui-based operators, including *Trilogy* (phone: 661-4743) and *Ocean Activities Center* (phone: 879-4485) offer day sails to Lanai, stopping at Manele Bay with time for snorkeling and sunbathing; both offer 2-hour land excursions as well. Lahaina's *Seabern Yachts* will customize skippered day tours or overnighters to Lanai (PO Box 1022, Lahaina, HI 96761; phone: 661-8110). *Club Lanai* (on Maui; phone: 871-1144) departs Lahaina for its 8-acre preserve on Lanai, where snorkeling, scuba, kayaking, volleyball, and beachcombing on deserted stretches of coast are some of the rewards. Lunch is included.

SPORTS: Lanai offers good swimming, beachcombing, scuba, and snorkeling; fair fishing; superb hunting; and some golf and tennis.

Boating – At press time, no sailboats or powerboats were offered for rent. It seems likely, however, that some will be made available for rentals by the *Lodge at Koele* and *Manele Bay* hotel.

Fishing – No charter fishing boats are available for hire on Lanai. Surf and shore fishing are usually only fair and depend on tides and time of year. Skillful fishermen may be successful with reef fish, divers with lobsters at the north end of the island.

Golf – As of this writing, work was underway on the transformation of the 9-hole *Cavendish Golf Course* into an 18-hole championship course designed by Arnold Palmer. The 9 holes remain open, with the full 18 set for play in mid-1990.

Hiking – Camping is allowed only at Hulopoe. Prepayment is required via the *Koele Company.* Hiking is permitted in certain areas, but discouraged in others — remember, this is practically all private land. The Munro Trail loop of 7 to 8 miles, up and over the ridge of mountains behind Lanai City, is one of the most beautiful hikes in Hawaii. From various viewpoints on clear days almost all of the Hawaiian islands are visible, and the trail leads through lush foliage and past the haunts of axis deer and numerous birds. Just be sure you have a well-marked map — *Oshiro's* has a good one. It's also a good idea to check with hunting sources (see below) to make sure you won't be hiking in a hunting area.

Horseback Riding – The stables affiliated with the new *Lodge at Koele* offer a number of riding options.

Hunting – Lanai is a hunter's paradise. The prized axis deer, a small but treasured trophy animal native to India and imported from Japan in the 1920s, outnumbers humans on Lanai by at least two to one. Mouflon sheep are hunted in August, with two Sundays limited to bow-and-arrow hunting and from two to six Sundays (depending on the sheep population) to high-powered rifle. Hunters are selected by lottery for this popular game opportunity. State lands impose seasons (for seasons, licenses, and requirements, check with the State Department of Land and Natural Resources, Division of Forestry and Wildlife, PO Box 1, Lanai City, HI 96763; phone: 808-565-6688), but there are none for axis deer on the private land of the *Koele Company*. (Trophy axis deer, however, are usually taken between May and November.) Guide service is normally required by the company. The $400-per-day fee includes guide, permit, transfers, and vehicle; there is no "trophy" fee, as often charged. For information: Chief Ranger, Koele Company, PO Box L, Lanai City, HI 96763 (phone: 565-6661). Game birds such as Gambel's quail, chukar partridge, Rio Grande turkey, ring-necked pheasant, and francolin are also hunted on Lanai — get information from the State Department of Land and Natural Resources in Honolulu. Note that there are no outfitters on Lanai. Accommodations for those on guided tours are arranged by the *Koele Company*.

Snorkeling and Scuba – Hulopoe Bay and adjacent Manele Bay (a small boat harbor) constitute the Manele-Hulopoe Marine Life Conservation District, with spear- and boat-fishing prohibited. Generally calm water with many coral formations means superb diving on good days, with visibility in many places along this south coast to 100 feet. Puupehe, a rocky outcropping just offshore, is popular with dive boats from Maui. Other good dive areas, all of which require a four-wheel-drive vehicle to reach, are Kaunolu Bay and Three Stone Bay. The *Manele Bay* hotel offers daily snorkeling and scuba diving trips, with equipment rentals planned — at press time.

Surfing – Rarely is the surf very good. Hulopoe Bay sometimes gets decent waves, as do some stretches of Shipwreck Beach. Lopa, on the east coast, is another hopeful surfing location.

Swimming and Sunning – Hulopoe Bay beach (also called White Manele), 7 miles down a twisting but paved road from the Lanai City, is one of the best in Hawaii. Virtually surfless, except when storms kick up from the south, it has fine, white sand and shower and picnicking facilities. Don't swim anywhere else on Lanai, because of both aesthetics and safety. There is a small, nice campsite at the far end of the small cove — advance reservations are required. Apply to the Koele Company, PO Box L, Lanai City, HI 96763 (phone 565-6661) for permission. Fees are $5 for a permit, $5 per person per night, with a maximum stay of 7 nights.

Tennis – The *Lodge at Koele* features four courts, none of which are lighted. Play after dark will become available upon the opening of the *Manele Bay* hotel in late 1989–early 1990. There are four public courts on 7th Street in Lanai City; two are lighted for night play (stroll over to the electric company and ask them to turn the lights on). The courts are not in great shape but are playable.

AROUND THE ISLAND

Lanai is shaped much like a pear or avocado balanced on its fat end. The lower, plumper portion contains the verdant mountains and gorges as well as the pineapple fields laid out in the depression of the Palawai Basin, while the upper part comprises largely arid, rolling tableland. Lanai City is almost in the exact center of the 140-square-mile island.

Lanai City

This is a company town and looks it: rows of single-story, wooden buildings and houses cluster in a grid pattern around a central park square. The only commercial enterprises on Lanai, outside the new hotels, and plantation and government offices, also surround this square, with the *Lanai* hotel on a low knoll above it. Yet it is an oddly satisfying little town, out of step with both modern times and with the rest of Hawaii. And it seems like a pleasant, if *very* tranquil, place. At 1,650 feet above sea level, Lanai City is above the pineapple fields and below the 3,370-foot peak of Lanaihale, the highest point on the island, and so enjoys an unusually temperate climate enhanced by the huge, old Norfolk pines that shade and cool the town — at night, even in summer, it can be foggy and chill. It was founded in 1923 by Dole and even today shelters virtually the entire island population of perhaps 2,100, almost all connected with the pineapple industry. There is one bar, in the *Lanai* hotel, and it is closed by 10 PM — the sidewalks roll up rather early here, probably because the horn announcing the next day's work will wake everyone up before dawn (except on weekends and holidays).

Lanai City contains little of significance except the quaint, tidy, terribly uncontemporary aspect of the town itself; it is its own kind of time machine.

Ito's Garden – A retired pineapple worker spent his time meticulously putting together a plant and rock garden on the edge of town just a short stroll from the *Lanai* hotel. Mr. Ito is now gone, but his personal statement of tropical flowers and foliage remains.

The Old Plantation Manager's House – It's just above town and has been recently restored, providing a public reception hall and a glimpse of the vanished grand plantation style.

 SHOPPING: The only things you'd want to buy on Lanai are what you've run out of unexpectedly, since there are no local arts and crafts or other kinds of industries. Once they have opened, the shops at the *Lodge at Koele* and *Manele Bay* hotel will be the places to look for resortwear and souvenirs.

Pine Isle Market – This general store combines groceries, booze, and dry goods with a hardware section. 365 8th Ave. (phone: 565-6488).

Richard's – This is another general store and it does have Lanai T-shirts. 434 8th Ave. (phone: 565-6047).

■ **Note on pineapples:** This fruit is difficult to find on Lanai, except growing in the fields. Everyone here is pretty much sick of it so the fresh fruit is simply not for sale; you *will* be able to find canned pineapple and pineapple juice, however. Whenever people feel an urge for pineapple, they simply drive into the fields and pick a ripe one, which is against the law but done all the time anyway. Since pineapples have sharp spikes and pesticides may be used around them, be careful.

NIGHTLIFE: The various hotels are apt to present such low-key entertainment as Hawaiian trios and the like; check with them for schedules. Despite the new trend toward sophistication, things still close early; 11 PM is apt to find most people asleep hereabouts. There are local shindigs and dances if you can find them, and the town's bachelors get together almost nightly to gossip and drink beer, usually around the barbecue behind the electric company. That's the kind of island Lanai is. Starting late afternoon and running until 10 PM, the bar at the *Lanai* hotel (phone: 565-7211) is the hotspot in town, and attracts a usually raucous but friendly mix of locals and visitors.

CHECKING IN: Lanai's accommodations are either rustic or elegant, with nothing in between. Elegant means expensive, and for such accommodations, rates begin at $300 for a double room and run significantly higher. Moderate indicates something in the $60 range. All telephone numbers are in the 808 area code unless otherwise indicated.

Lodge at Koele – Scheduled to open during 1990, this will be Lanai's only upcountry resort hotel. Located adjacent to Lanai City, the plantation era has been incorporated as its theme, and it is well suited to the setting at the base of Lanaihale's mountainous heights. Although not the palm-tree-and-beach variety of Hawaiian surroundings, its charm and authenticity makes it every bit as appealing. The hotel's 102 rooms are situated in garden surroundings and have easy access to the island's only golf course, soon to be extended to 18 holes and brought up to championship caliber. Lanai City (phone: 800-223-7637). Expensive.

Manele Bay – With access to such assets as Lanai's best beach, excellent snorkeling and scuba, and some of Hawaii's sunniest weather, this 250-room hotel will be difficult to leave. It is scheduled to open in 1990 and, between its chic contemporary architecture and decor and its beautiful setting overlooking Hulopoe Beach, is likely to dazzle and delight its guests. Manele Bay (phone: 800-223-7637). Expensive.

Lanai – This rustic clapboard example of authentic Hawaiiana was constructed in 1923 as a boarding house for Dole supervisors and a temporary lodging for visitors. In the course of its existence, it has been the Lanai Inn, then the Lanai Lodge, and is now the *Lanai* hotel. Currently owned and operated by Castle & Cooke, the simple, 1-story frame structure contains 10 rooms, some better than others but all nicely redecorated and all with private baths. The dining room is wood-paneled and cozy and the bar comfortably set on the glass-enclosed lanai. Expect a basic but comfortable room, decent food, and personal attention. Beach towels are supplied for excursions to Hulopoe. PO Box A-119, Lanai City, HI 96763 (phone: 565-7211; 800-624-8849). Moderate.

Private Home Rentals – *Oshiro's* (PO Box 67, Lanai City, HI 96763; phone: 565-6952) can arrange the rental of 3 fully equipped private homes on Lanai. One has 4 bedrooms, can sleep up to 11, and rents for $150 per day, with a 3-day minimum and a 10% discount for stays of a week of more; the other two have 3 bedrooms each and rent for $85 to $95 per day, with a 2-day minimum and the same long-term discount. Lucille Graham runs a comfortable bed-and-breakfast establishment for about $45 a night (312 Mahana Pl., Lanai City, HI 96763; phone: 565-6378).

EATING OUT: At press time, no resort hotel restaurants had actually opened. However, the *Lodge at Koele* is slated to include several restaurants with decor and food consistent with its upcountry plantation theme, and prices of around $50 for two, excluding drinks or tips. The *Manele Bay* hotel intends to cater to the upscale tastes of its projected guests, with restaurants serving haute cuisine and prices that will be equally haute. For the rest of the island, the options are limited to places where a down home atmosphere prevails. Expect to pay $20 to $30 for two, without drinks or tips, at the restaurant listed as moderate; under $15 at the inexpensive establishments. All telephone numbers are in the 808 area code unless otherwise indicated.

Lanai – Good, solid, home cooking in a rustic setting. Expect hearty breakfasts, uninspired lunches, decent dinners centered around meat-and-potatoes dishes. Nothing fancy, certainly, but the homemade apple and macadamia nut pies are great, and there is bar service. Open daily. Reservations advised. Lanai Hotel (phone: 565-7211). Moderate.

Dahangs Bakery – Breakfast and lunch, served in a bright, cheery atmosphere. Closed Sundays. 409 7th Ave. (phone: 565-6363). Inexpensive.

S&T Properties – An unlikely name for a counter service luncheonette, but breakfast and lunch are served. Open daily. 419 7th Ave. (phone: 565-6537). Inexpensive.

Elsewhere on the Island

A number of rewarding tourist sites are spread around Lanai, but be forewarned that most of them will require a sturdy four-wheel-drive vehicle. And even thus equipped, you may find many of the rutted dirt roads impossible to maneuver. It's best to check first at *Oshiro's* (phone: 565-6952) or *Lanai City Service* (phone: 565-7227) to see which roads are passable and then make your plans. For the sake of those unwilling to take the four-wheel-drive plunge, listed first below are those sites reached by nice, civilized, paved roads.

Hulopoe Bay (paved road) – A lovely, white sand beach in a small, protected cove. Not only the best beach on Lanai, it's the *only* swimmable one (most north coast beaches generally front shallow reefs). There are gentle waves, good snorkeling, picnic tables, showers, and a campsite. Even when it's cool and cloudy 1,650 feet higher up and inland in Lanai City, it's likely to be clear, dry, hot, and sunny here. Besides, this is one of the most pleasant beaches in all Hawaii.

Manele Bay (paved road) – This is the bay right next to Hulopoe, a small boat harbor and marina where the tour boats from Maui dock and disgorge their passengers for a few hours at the beach.

Kaumalapau Harbor (paved road) – The pineapples have to leave Lanai from somewhere, and this is it. This pineapple loading port is at its most interesting during the height of the summer picking season.

Munro Trail – George C. Munro was a New Zealander who in the early 1900s was the manager of the ill-fated Lanai Ranch during the cattle experiment phase of the island. But Munro was also an amateur botanist who imported seeds for Lanai's now-signature Norfolk pines from his native land and sowed them (along with those of other trees and plants) along the 7-mile ridge above what is today Lanai City. That ridge is now crowned by a tough trail (and a road suitable only for four-wheel drive vehicles) bearing Munro's name that winds through Norfolk pine, eucalyptus, ironwood, silver oak, and koa trees. From the trail on clear days all the Hawaiian islands except Kauai and Niihau can be glimpsed, along with the deep, spectacular gulches (particularly Hauola and Maunalei) on the wild and rugged east slope. Along the way you will crest the 3,370-foot peak of Lanaihale, the island's highest point. A four-wheel-drive vehicle is a necessity for this exploration, as are detailed instructions on how to find the beginning of the trail.

Luahiwa Petroglyphs – These fascinating rock carvings only a mile or so outside Lanai City off Manele Road (Route 441) to Hulopoe and Manele bays are difficult to find, but you'll be rewarded with some of the best examples of petroglyphs left in the islands. Boulders containing the drawings march up a steep hillside next to pineapple fields and are deeply scratched with likenesses of men, animals, and ships. Getting here means traveling on dirt pineapple roads, so you'll need good instructions.

Garden of the Gods – An unusual, austere tumble of boulders and lava formations near Kanepuu, off the beaten path, about 7 miles from Lanai City. Even with good instructions, it may prove impossible to find. The colors and severe beauty are locally celebrated.

Kaunolu Bay – King Kamehameha I, the warrior King who united Hawaii by force of arms, kept a summer home and built a small village at the southwestern tip of Lanai in the early 19th century. This archaeological site is one of the most interesting in Hawaii, although only stone foundations remain. Next to Kaunolu Village is Kahekili's Leap, where the King, as a test of loyalty and bravery, ordered his warriors to jump 62 feet past a protruding ledge and into the sea. The road here is a very difficult four-wheel-drive-only track.

Shipwreck Beach – The breezy northern coast of Lanai, the portion facing Molokai, is protected by coral reefs and swept by strong currents. Numerous ships have been driven onto the reefs and some hulks remain visible today. The beach stretches for 8 miles, has excellent beachcombing (glass Japanese balls used to float nets are often found), decent diving, and fine lobstering, but the sea is shallow and dangerous. There is a good paved road that leads to the north shore but not along it — for that you'll need a Jeep; a dirt track parallels the coastline westward from the end of the road.

Keomuku Village – If, when you reach the end of the paved road at Shipwreck Beach, you drive straight ahead rather than turning left and then bend eastward along the shoreline, eventually you'll reach the overgrown ruins of the sugar town that was abandoned in 1901 when the irrigation water turned brackish. There really isn't much to see any longer, and the trek in is difficult but perhaps worth it in terms of island history.

Club Lanai – This palm-lined, hammock-hung, 8-acre beachfront preserve is usually reached by catamaran on a 45-minute trip from Lahaina, though it is possible to reach by dirt road via Keomoku. The property, originally the private beach estate of a Honolulu advertising executive, is now managed by the Kraftsow family. A day's outing here might include sea kayaking, beachcombing, volleyball, windsurfing, swimming, and sunbathing on secluded beaches. There's snorkeling at Turtle Reef (non-snorkelers can view the reef life via a glass-bottom boat), and cyclists will find miles of bike trails along beaches and through kiawe forest, where wild turkeys are sometimes spotted. A barbecue is prepared for guests, Hawaiian entertainment provided, and Hawaiian arts and crafts — palm weaving, fish-net throwing, lei making — are taught in a grass shelter on the grounds. A day's outing costs $69 and includes the boat trip from Maui and an open bar all day. For information, contact Club Lanai, 333 Dairy Rd., Suite 201-A, Kahului, HI 96732 (phone: 871-1144).

KAUAI

While the kings of Maui, Oahu, and Hawaii bloodily battled each other for control of the Hawaiian islands, Kauai, the westernmost of the major islands, stayed peacefully out of the fray. Twice, by sheer luck or divine intervention, Kauai was spared invasion by King Kamehameha, who had already subdued — and with no light hand — all the other islands. The first attempt, in 1796, was thwarted by rough seas in the channel between Oahu and Kauai, and the second, 6 years later, by an epidemic of cholera (or perhaps typhoid) that ravaged Kamehameha's army as it waited on Oahu's shores for propitious weather to make the crossing to Kauai. Although Kauai eventually became part of Kamehameha's kingdom, it was as a semi-independent state. Kauai's King Kaumualii, smart enough to realize his people might not be so lucky if the persistent conqueror tried a third time, agreed to acknowledge him as King of all Hawaiian islands, and was so able to keep much of his autonomy.

In many respects, Kauai still retains a sense of separateness from the other islands. Kauai is the Hawaii most visitors seek but never find. Many of its attractions are quaint — a mountain that resembles a sleeping giant, a rubbly wall that is barely recognizable as the Russian fort it once briefly was. Slow to make use of its tourist resources, which are considerable, developers have until recently had a tough go with planning and zoning boards on Kauai. Many are now concerned that the possible demise of sugar and the lure of tourist dollars may be undoing decades of caution. Even low-rise development can be an intrusion if it goes too far, and while Kauai's resort hotels and condominiums are generally well planned and nicely designed, they tend to surrender authenticity in order to service the increasing flow of visitors.

While the population of Kauai is still mostly rural, living in villages where the grocery store and post office make up most of the business district, shopping malls and convenience stores have sprung up, implanting contemporary suburbia in a setting of unparalleled natural beauty. Even the Na Pali coast and Waimea Canyon, once the preserve of hikers alone, now echo with the engines of the helicopters, planes, and motorized boats bringing increasing numbers of visitors to Kauai's primeval wilderness. Conflicts over use of the wilderness have been brewing for years, and access limitations are being implemented. Although tourism and the introduction of taro, guava, papaya, macadamia, and prawn farming have somewhat broadened the island's economic base, sugarcane still dominates the landscape, as it has since the first cane plantation was started at Koloa in 1835. Everywhere you see cane at one stage or another: newly plowed fields waiting to be planted; young seedlings green against the red furrows of earth; mature cane, taller than corn in August. At night, fires burning the leaves off the harvested cane blaze orange

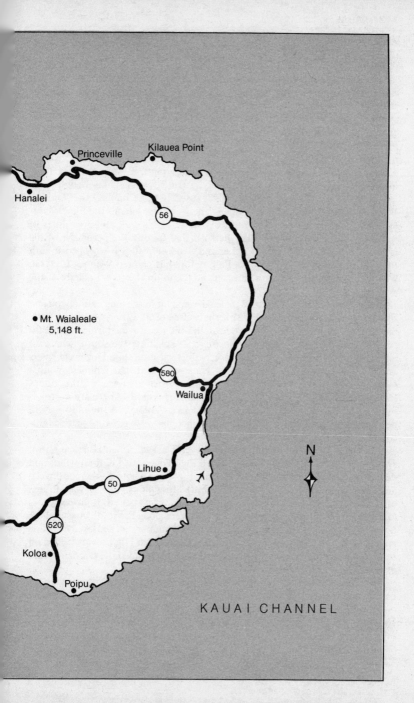

before the dark, impenetrable mountains of the interior. By day, huge cane trucks, stacked to overflowing with the raw stalks, rumble down the roads on their way to one of the four sugar mills on the island.

It was almost inevitable, however, that tourism would eventually overtake cane as the island's chief industry, for Kauai is stunningly and endlessly beautiful. A newcomer is likely to stop at every other bend in the road to admire a beach glistening under the midday sun or an early missionary church sitting small and pious before the majestic wilderness of Kauai's mountains. And while islanders, who have jobs to get to and errands to run, might find all this stopping annoying, they can hardly blame their visitors. There's rarely a view that isn't breathtaking, grand, mysterious, evocative, inspiring, charming, or just plain lovely, a truth Kauaians know best.

The verdancy pervading Kauai has caused it to be dubbed the 'Garden Isle." Along the north shore of this vaguely circular island, the fourth largest in the chain, are the extravagantly beautiful Na Pali cliffs, 14 miles of valleys so steep and narrow that the road that follows the perimeter of the island comes to a dead halt at either end. And almost as if to contrast with the rich and vibrant greens of Na Pali, nature has painted Waimea Canyon, which cuts down the western third of the island, in the pastel palette of the desert.

In the center of Kauai is Mt. Waialeale, remnant of the long extinct volcano that gave birth to Kauai and is still the source of its varied beauty. A little over 5,000 feet high, Mt. Waialeale catches the moist winds from the northeast, feeding the lushness of the north while shielding the south, where an annual rainfall of 20 inches makes for a perfect vacation spot. Dozens of rivers and streams rise on Mt. Waialeale — Hanapepe, Hanalei, Waimea, Wailua — as do countless waterfalls that hang like Christmas tinsel on the mountain's creased slopes. Like Na Pali, Waialeale is remote. There are no roads into the mountains (besides a few private Jeep trails), and the only way to penetrate the cloud-veiled summit is by helicopter or fixed-wing plane flight-seeing, a trip that's heartily recommended.

Quiet little Kauai made the news in November 1982 when Hurricane Iwa, sweeping in from the southwest, battered the island with 110 mph winds and devastating tidal waves. (Niihau, the small private island to the southwest, and Oahu were the only other islands hit.) Miraculously, there was no loss of life on Kauai — Iwa's single victim was a sailor on Oahu. But property loss exceeded $100 million. Damage was most severe along the south coast, where tidal waves washed out roads and destroyed numerous houses, beachside restaurants, and a good portion of the *Sheraton* hotel. High winds ripped off roofs and porches on other parts of the island and denuded the Garden Island of much of its luxuriant vegetation.

The cleanup started immediately. Within days, the main roads were repaired, and within 3 months, all but one of the major south shore resorts were open again. The foliage began regenerating just as quickly. Six weeks after Iwa, fertile Kauai started to bud and bloom again. Except in the stories locals tell, the visitor today will find little evidence of the worst storm in a generation to hit this island.

SOURCES AND RESOURCES

TOURIST INFORMATION: The Hawaii Visitors Bureau is at 3016 Umi St., Rm. 207, Lihue, HI 96766 (phone: 245-3971). The *Kauai Drive Guide,* with excellent maps and other useful information, is one of the best visitor publications. Pick up the guide, which includes good maps and itineraries as well as entries on restaurants, shops, sights, and sports, at most car rental agencies.

Local Coverage – Other useful free visitor publications include *This Week on Kauai* and *Spotlight.* The two local newspapers are the weekly *Kauai Times* and the *Garden Island,* published five times a week. Many hotels and condominiums also offer copies of the excellent *Beach Guide* series on Poipu, East Kauai, and the North Shore. The *Sandwich Islands Quarterly* and *Kauai* feature Kauai in four-color, magazine format.

Telephone – The area code for Kauai is 808.

GETTING AROUND: Several inter-island airlines provide service to Kauai: Aloha Airlines and Hawaiian Air both fly into Lihue's new airport, while Aloha IslandAir has daily service to Princeville Airport at Hanalei. The only major airline with scheduled flights to Kauai via Honolulu is United. While on the island, you can choose one of many modes of travel to see it — bus, car, taxi, boat, rubber raft, or helicopter.

Taxi – All taxis are metered, and because there's a fair distance between sights in Kauai, they're not an economical way to travel. From Lihue Airport to the Wailua area, expect to pay between $13 and $14 (excluding tip); to Poipu Beach, about $25; and to Princeville, around $55. Some reputable services to call: *Garden Island Taxi & Tours* (phone: 245-6161), *Lorenzo's Taxi Service* (phone: 245-6331), and *A-1 Taxi* (phone: 742-7441).

Very convenient and more reasonable is *Shoppe Hoppers* (phone: 332-7272), which provides van service to Lihue Airport ($6) and to shops, from Poipu to Kapaa.

Car Rental – Despite the proliferation of rental companies — nearly a score now — demand can outstrip supply, particularly during the peak winter season and when convention business is heavy. While excess availability discounts may be offered on arrival, it is still a good idea to book in advance, especially for the Jeeps and convertibles that are an increasingly popular rental option for touring the Garden Isle. While many companies have check-in counters at the new Lihue Airport terminal, most cars are picked up at lots nearby, with company vans providing transfers.

Cars here are a bargain, though, and the best way to get around. Although the roads get curvy at the Waimea end and narrow past Hanalei, they are very good in between. In addition to the national chains — *Alamo* (phone: 246-0645), *Avis* (phone: 245-3512), *Budget* (phone: 245-4021), *Dollar* (phone: 245-3651), *Hertz* (phone: 245-3356), *National* (phone: 245-3502), *Rent-A-Wreck* (phone: 245-4755), and *Thrifty* (phone: 245-7388) — there are also regional and local agencies at or near Lihue Airport: *Adventure Rent-A-Jeep* (phone: 245-9622); *Honolulu Rent-A-Car* (phone: 245-8726), at press time offering the cheapest cars on Kauai; *Robert's Hawaii Rent-A-Car* (phone: 245-4008); *Sunshine* (phone: 245-9541 on Kauai; 800-522-8440 on other islands); and *Tropical Rent-A-Car* (phone: 245-6988). Check for daily and weekly specials.

If you fly into Princeville, your choice is more limited — *Avis* (phone: 826-9773) or *Hertz* (phone: 826-7455).

Bicycle/Moped Rental – In the Poipu area contact *South Shore Activities* (phone: 742-6873) for both bicycles and mopeds; in Hanalei call *Pedal & Paddle* (phone:

826-9069) for bikes and mopeds; in the Kapaa area, *Aquatics Kauai* (phone: 822-9213) for bicycles. *North Shore Bike Cruise and Snorkel* (phone: 822-1582) offers a 6-mile escorted bike tour along the North Shore, followed by snorkeling and a beach barbecue ($65).

 SIGHTSEEING TOURS: By Bus – Tour options consist of half-day trips to Waimea Canyon, Hanalei and the North Shore, or Wailua and the Fern Grotto, and are offered by a number of companies. Full-day itineraries usually combine two of these half-day options. Many tours are by van rather than big bus, and most companies will pick you up at your hotel or condo.

One of the best van tours is operated by *Chandler's Kauai Tours* (phone: 245-5675), which offers half- and full-day tours to Waimea Canyon. Full-day itineraries include a boat trip to the Fern Grotto. *Chandler's* also runs special half- and full-day tours to Hanalei and Haena. Another company, *TransHawaiian* (phone: 245-5108), does sightseeing tours to Waimea and Hanalei. *Gray Line Kauai* (phone: 245-3344, 800-367-2420) offers both van and bus tours, as does *Robert's Hawaii* (phone: 245-9558). The most off-the-beaten-path option is the four-wheel-drive excursion into Kauai's magnificent wilderness interior via *Kauai Mountain Tours* (phone: 245-7224). The 5-hour ($55) and 7-hour ($75) tours (with lunch) of Kokee State Park include exploration of upcountry forests and streams, with stops at isolated overviews of the Waimea Canyon. Guides are well-versed in Hawaiiana and provide interesting insights into the Polynesian past and the Hawaiian present. Hotel transfers from various Kauai resorts are included.

A visitor can also hire a car and driver/guide through some of the taxi companies. *Akiko's Taxi,* for instance, charges $25 an hour with a 4-hour minimum (phone: 822-3613). *Gilligans* (phone: 822-0600) offers multi-activity packages that combine ocean rafting and snorkeling, flightseeing by helicopter, and land touring by four-wheel-drive vehicles. *Best of Kauai* (phone: 826-6189) features a full-day excursion that includes a helicopter tour, a visit to the Kilauea Lighthouse and bird sanctuary, and a boat trip to the Fern Grotto ($99).

Boat – Two companies — *Smith's Motor Boat Service* (phone: 822-4111) and *Waialeale Boat Tours* (phone: 822-4908) — ply the Wailua River up to the Fern Grotto. It's a short ride (about 2 miles), and although Hawaiian music and local legend are used to make it interesting, the experience is more a cliché than a true adventure. Numerous companies take visitors along the 19-mile Na Pali coast in an assortment of Zodiac rafts and hard-hull vessels. In most cases, landings are not made, this being conservation property. There are, however, opportunities to enter sea caves and snorkel offshore at several locations. In the winter, strong currents and waves may make the Na Pali coast dangerous for boating, and many companies shift their operations to Kauai's south shore, where the highlights are the magnificent beach and fish at Kipukai and the Spouting Horn.

An unusual boat tour is offered by *Captain Zodiac* (phone: 826-9371), which uses rubber rafts seating up to 15 people to cruise the Na Pali coast and, in the winter, the southeast coast from Nawiliwili to Kipukai. From May through September, there are morning, full-day, and sunset cruises, plus a drop-off service for Na Pali hikers and campers. Prices range from about $45 for the 2-hour sunset cruise to $100 for the 5-hour day trip. For $45 per person, *Fantasy Island Boat Tours* (phone: 742-6636) takes its customized raft from Kukuiula Harbor near Poipu for snorkeling and a visit to Kipukai, perhaps the single most exotic and idyllic bit of the tropics in Hawaii. During the summer months, *Fantasy Island* also offers raft and snorkeling excursions along the Na Pali coast, as do *Na Pali Adventures* (phone: 826-6804) aboard a 24-foot motorized catamaran ($80); *Blue Odyssey Adventures* (phone: 826-9033) aboard 28-foot inflatables ($85); *Paradise Adventure Cruises* (phone: 826-9999), with two tours daily on 22- and 25-foot, 6-passenger Boston Whalers ($75); and *Bali Hai Charters* (phone: 826-9787), which uses 6-passenger rafts and motorized craft for its two tours daily ($55). *Lady Ann Cruises* (phone: 245-8538), *Napali Kauai* (phone: 826-7254; 800-367-8047, ext. 155), and *SeaScapes* (phone: 826-1111) ply coastal waters in motorized pleasure craft, making en-route stops for snorkeling. *Captain Andy's Sailing Adventures* (phone: 822-7833) runs snorkel (with lunch) and sunset tours in a 37-foot trimaran from Kukuiula Harbor.

Helicopter – Without a doubt, the best way to see Kauai is by helicopter, for there's no other way to get close to much of the island, and there's nothing to match the exhilaration of hovering over the jagged cliffs of Na Pali or sweeping into the heart of Waialeale. Several companies fly daily, all charging about $130 for a 50-minute spin around the island. (Check tourist publications for discount coupons.) They are *ERA Helicopters, Inc.* (phone: 245-9555), *Kenai Helicopter Tours* (phone: 245-8591), *Island Helicopters Kauai* (phone: 245-8588), *Papillon Helicopters* (phone: 826-6591), *Menehune Helicopters* (phone: 245-7705), *South Seas Helicopters* (phone: 245-7781), *Kauai Helicopters* (phone: 245-7403), *Bali Hai Helicopters* (phone: 332-7331), *Ohana Helicopters* (phone: 245-5041), and *Jack Harter Helicopters* (phone: 245-3774). In addition to Lihue Airport, there are helipads at Princeville Airport (Papillon), and at the *Westin Kauai* (Jack Harter) at Nawiliwili. *Papillon* also offers several tours that land in the wilderness for a swim and picnic lunch. For photo enthusiasts, *Kauai Helicopters* will add 10 and 20 minutes to tours. Those interested in flightseeing over Kauai and the nearby island of Niihau should contact *Niihau Helicopter* (phone: 335-3500), which departs from Port Allen Airport. Called the "Forbidden Island," the privately owned jewel (Kauai's Robinson family are the owners) until recently has been off limits to all but a select few invited guests (see NIIHAU). Two tours ($135 and $185) are offered Mondays through Fridays. Visitors should not expect to see any Niihauans, however; the single landing on the island is at its isolated north end.

Glider – *Tradewinds Glider* (phone: 335-5086) features 20- and 40-minute glider flights that depart Port Allen and take in the south coast from Poipu to Hanapepe, heading inland (weather permitting) for views of isolated canyons and valleys. Costs range from $75 to $125 for a single, $90 to $150 double.

Jeep – For scenic views of Waimea Canyon by the back roads, *Kauai Mountain Tours* (phone: 245-7224) offers a tour of Kokee State Park in a four-wheel-drive vehicle. There's time to explore upcountry streams and the chance to learn about native and exotic forest flora. A picnic lunch is included.

Plane – For those who prefer the familiarity of a fixed-wing plane or an aerial tour at about half the typical helicopter rate, *Fly Kauai* (phone: 246-9123) offers tours that start at $39. Its circle island tour ($69) is actually a bit more comprehensive than the helicopter options, tying in the south coast in a fly-by that includes Kipukai, Poipu, and Waimea before heading inland for a circuit of Waimea Canyon and the Na Pali coast.

 SPECIAL EVENTS: Waimea marks the anniversary of Captain James Cook's arrival in the Hawaiian islands with reenactments, a parade, parties, and a foot race during the *Captain Cook Celebration* in February. The most special of special events on Kauai is the *Prince Kuhio Festival* in April, honoring native son Prince Jonah Kuhio Kalanianaole, who for many years was the Hawaiian Territory's delegate to the US Congress. There's lots of Hawaiian pageantry, canoe races, and a royal ball to cap the festivities. With the Japanese constituting the largest segment of Kauai's population, *Buddha Day* in early April, celebrating the birth of Buddha, is an occasion for pageants, flower festivals, and dance across the island. On May 1, locals celebrate *Lei Day* with flowers, music, and song. July is a good month to watch Kauai celebrate itself, not the least of reasons being the week-long (July 5-11)

King Kamehameha Celebration, which culminates in a festive parade in Lihue. August brings the *Kauai County Fair,* with exhibits of local foods, flowers, and arts and crafts. The *Miss Native Hawaiian Pageant* happens in September; in late September or early October the *Aloha Week* activities — canoe races, luaus, dances, pageants, and parades — get under way.

 SPORTS: Boating – Most of the boating visitors do on Kauai is as passengers. *Blue Water Sailing* (phone: 822-0525) provides skippered charters aboard its 42-foot ketch at $100 per hour, with a 2-hour minimum. There are no bareboat charters available on Kauai because of insurance problems, but most tour operators offer charters in addition to scheduled tours. *Na Pali Coast Cruise Lines* (phone: 335-5078), *Lady Ann Charters* (phone: 245-8538), *Blue Odyssey Boat Tours* (phone: 826-9033; 800-426-3293), *Sea Kauai* (phone: 826-9886), and *Captain Zodiac* (phone: 826-9371) are among those who offer snorkeling along the Na Pali coast in an armada that ranges from diesel-powered launches to rubber Zodiac rafts. When winter surf is high, tours usually depart the south coast from Nawiliwili, Poipu, or Port Allen. *Captain Andy's Sailing Charters* depart Kukuiula Harbor in Poipu aboard a 37-foot, 20-passenger trimaran for snorkel and sunset cruises along the south coast (phone: 822-7833). *Pacific Safari Cruises* (phone: 822-5156) sets out from Port Allen (pickups are provided from Kukuiula Harbor) in 20-passenger glass-bottom boat tours of south coast reefs, with whale watching an extra in winter. *Sailboards Kauai* at the Kalapaki Beach Center (phone: 245-5955) and *Hanalei Sailboards* (phone: 826-9732) both offer windsurfing rentals and lessons; *Garden Isle Windsurfing* (phone: 826-9005; 800-331-8044) offers lessons only. *Island Adventures* (phone: 245-9662) runs trips up the Huleia River off Nawiliwili Bay (scenes from *Raiders of the Lost Ark* were filmed here) in royaks — 1-passenger, kayak-like vessels. *Kayak Kauai* (phone: 826-1132) rents 2-passenger inflatable kayaks for self-guided excursions ($45 including car rack) or for escorted Na Pali coast trips ($85). *Outfitters Kauai* (phone: 742-9667) departs Kukuiula on kayak trips to Lawai Kai Bay. Both *Aloha Destinations* in Koloa (phone: 742-9773) or *Gilligan's* (phone: 822-0600) can make reservations for a number of water activities.

Camping – Between state and county parks, there are several attractive places to camp on Kauai, from the green forests high in Kokee State Park to the stark beach at Polihale. For permits to camp in state parks, go to the Division of State Parks, 3060 Eiwa St., Lihue (phone: 245-4444); for county parks, to the Parks Permit Section, 4280A Rice St., Lihue (phone: 245-1881). Equipment rentals are available from *Hanalei Camping & Backpacking* (phone: 826-6664).

Fishing – The best season is from May to August, when 100-pound-plus yellowfin tuna is the big catch, but year-round fishing is good, too, with a plentitude of marlin, ono, mahimahi, and bonito. Charter rates run $85 per person for a half day, $145 for a full day, and $400 for the entire boat (holding up to six people) for a half day. Among the operators: *Gent-Lee Fishing Charters* (phone: 245-7504), *Coastal Charters* (phone: 822-7007), *Alana-Lynn Too* (phone: 245-7446) operating from Nawiliwili, and *Sea Fever Sport Fishing* (phone: 826-6815) in Hanalei. *Sport Fishing Kauai* (phone: 742-7013) offers fishing charters from Kukuiula Harbor near Poipu. *Sea Breeze Sport Fishing Charters* (phone: 828-1285) offers less expensive charter rates and departs from Anini or Port Allen. *Bass Guides of Kauai* (phone: 822-1405) provides the guide and the boat to get to private inland lakes where largemouth, smallmouth, and peacock bass can be hooked. Half-day cost is $85 for one person, $125 for two.

Golf – There are five distinctive golf complexes on Kauai: the 27-hole *Princeville Makai Golf Course* and the newly completed 18 holes of the adjacent *Prince Course,* strung through the paradisiacal landscape near Hanalei; the *Kiahuna Plantation Golf Course,* whose 18 holes (18 more to come) wrap around various archaeological sites in Poipu; the Jack Nicklaus–designed 18-hole *Kiele Lagoons* and 18-hole *Kauai Lagoons* courses of the *Westin Kauai,* newest on the island; the 18-hole *Wailua Golf Course,* considered one of the best municipal courses in the country; and the charming 9-hole *Kukui o Lono Park Course,* on a hill from which the ancient Hawaiians signaled fishermen along the south coast.

Hiking – Kauai is a hiker's dream. There are miles of well-marked trails in the state parks at Kokee, Waimea Canyon, and along the Na Pali coast, threading through areas so wild and remote as to challenge the imagination as well as the body. Get maps of trails and good advice from the Division of State Parks (3060 Eiwa St., Lihue, HI 96766; phone: 245-4444), and from the Division of Forestry (same address and telephone number as the Division of State Parks), which maintains trails in forest reserves throughout the island. There are also two excellent guidebooks: *Hiking Kauai,* by Robert Smith (Wilderness Press, Berkeley, CA; $5.95) and *Hawaiian Hiking Trails* by Craig Chisholm (Touchstone Press, Beaverton, OR; $7.95). Both include maps, descriptions, and pertinent commentary on both well-known and less-traveled trails. If the timing is right, you could join one of the Sierra Club's twice-monthly outings. Call the Sierra Club's Hawaii Chapter in Oahu (phone: 946-8494) for local officers' numbers.

Horseback Riding – In Poipu, *CJM Country Stables* (phone: 245-6666) offers escorted rides along the South Shore's wild coastline. The 3-hour Breakfast Ride includes coast and valleys, with a beach breakfast ($55). Midday options are the 1-hour ($20) and 2-hour ($40) coastal rides. Full-day and overnight rides can also be arranged.

Snorkeling and Scuba Diving – The best beaches for these sports are Kee, Haena, and Anini in the north; Anahola and Moloaa in the east; and Palama, Sheraton Caves, and Koloa Landing in the south. Most resort hotels and condominiums provide snorkeling equipment (fins, masks, and snorkel) gratis to guests. If you plan to do a lot of snorkeling, it's worthwhile to ask whether hotels offer this amenity. Otherwise, expect to pay between $5 and $15 a day for snorkeling equipment. Hotels will also arrange for snorkeling or scuba lessons. The *Waiohai* (phone: 742-9511) and *Sheraton Poipu Beach* (phone: 742-1681) hotels, for instance, give a free hour-long mini-scuba lesson in the hotel pool. Dive shops in Koloa, Wailua/Kapaa, and Hanalei feature shore and boat dives at the introductory, intermediate, and advanced levels, although most boat dives are limited to certified divers or to those involved in the 4- or 5-day certification courses that are available. One- and two-tank dives are featured at an average of $55 to $75. Certification courses range from $300 to $350, inclusive of dive time, equipment, and books, while private certification courses range from $400 to $500. A 1½- to 3-hour snorkeling tour will cost about $55, including equipment, and half-day scuba dives cost around $70. Since prices vary so much on package courses, it pays to shop around.

In the Poipu area, *South Shore Activities* at the *Sheraton* (phone: 742-6873) rents snorkel equipment, *Kauai Divers* (phone: 742-1580) and *Fathom Five Divers* (phone: 742-6991) rent snorkel gear as well as offer boat and shore dives, instruction, and courses in diving certification. In the Wailua/Kapaa area, *Ocean Odyssey* (phone: 822-9680), *Get Wet* (phone: 822-4884), *Aquatics Kauai* (phone: 822-9213), and *Sea Sage Diving Center* (phone: 822-3841) all offer escorted dives and certification courses, the least expensive of which is *Odyssey,* with certification courses at $275. *Sea Sage* also rents scuba equipment. Dives and rentals can also be arranged through *Aloha Activities* in Koloa (phone: 742-9773). In Hanalei, *Pedal & Paddle* (phone: 826-9069) and *Sand People* (phone: 826-6981) offer snorkeling equipment rentals.

Surfing – Tyros should stick to the beaches on the east and south side of the island: Anahola, Wailua (across from the *Coco Palms*), Kalapaki, and Poipu. All have steady, gentle waves just right for beginners. More experienced surfers may want to tackle the rougher waves at Kekaha and Polihale on the south coast or at Hanalei Bay and Anini on the north coast. Unless you're an exceptionally good surfer, however, don't surf the

North Shore in winter. Rollers as high as 30 feet make even boats that call this home in other seasons take refuge in the south during winter.

You can rent surf and Boogie boards (a shorter version of the surfboard) from most big hotels and condominium resorts, or from *South Shore Activities* (phone: 742-6873) in Koloa, *Pedal & Paddle* (phone: 826-9069) and *Sand People* (phone: 826-6981) in Hanalei, and *Sea Sage Diving Center* in Kapaa (phone: 822-3841), which also offers instruction. *Sea Sage* is closed Sundays; Saturday rentals include Sunday at no charge. Surfboards rent for between $10 and $16 a day; Boogie boards, between $5 and $10.

Swimming and Sunning – To make it easier to enjoy its miles of beautiful beaches, Kauai County has built numerous beach parks that provide restrooms, showers, and picnicking facilities right next to the water. But there are plenty of other beaches unnamed on maps and unmarked on the road that would make for a lovely day of swimming or sunning, often in solitude.

Starting as far west as civilization will carry you is Polihale Beach — wide, long, bone white, and dry, a good swimming beach with state camping and picnicking facilities nearby. Kekaha Beach, in the southwestern corner of the island, and Waimea Beach, about 5 miles on, are also long, sunstruck beaches with parks. The most popular beach on the south coast is Poipu; "popular," on weekends, can mean crowded.

Since the east coast is the most developed, the beaches here are, naturally enough, the most populous. But they are also ample and easily accommodate the growing number of visitors. Kalapaki Beach, a graceful scimitar of sand on Nawiliwili Bay, is always bustling with both guests of the *Westin Kauai* and residents, who like the protected waters for windsurfing. No more than 15 minutes up the coast is Hanamaulu Beach, as serene as Kalapaki is lively, although swimming here is more difficult because of an offshore reef.

The coast from Lydgate State Park at Wailua River to Kapaa is one long series of beaches that vary from good to very good for swimming, sunning, or splashing around. Those along the several resorts at Wailua and Waipouli tend to get a fair number of bathers, but toward Kapaa Beach Park, roughly midway through the town of Kapaa, the bathers are fewer and, for the most part, local. Some 3 miles north of Kapaa is Anahola Beach, another excellent swimming beach with good picnicking facilities.

The north coast is studded with small and not-so-small beaches that aren't marked on maps and don't have the amenities offered by more popular spots. And although swimming on the north coast, especially in the winter, can be iffy (asking islanders is usually a good way to find out if a beach is safe for swimming), don't pass up those tempting jewels of beaches just because there's no sign pointing the way. Even the better-known North Shore beaches offer a quiet and seclusion few others can boast. Anini Beach, a few miles outside Kilauea; Hanalei Bay; Lumahai Beach, where *South Pacific* was filmed; Haena and Kee beaches, at the end of the road, are all splendid strips of sand, often with few fellow bathers around. Anini, Hanalei, and Haena have showers, restrooms, picnic tables, and barbecue pits. If it's a wilderness setting you want, hike the Kalalau Trail, to the otherwise inaccessible beaches of Na Pali — Hanakapiai, a beach that is often washed out in winter; Hanakoa; or Kalalau, where not only the beach but the whole valley is likely to be yours. Just be cautious when swimming in the coastal waters — that current can be rough, and there have been injuries.

Tennis – If it's a tennis vacation you're after, the best bets are *Kiahuna Plantation,* the *Westin Kauai, Hanalei Bay Resort,* or *Poipu Kai Resort,* all of which don't charge guests court fees and have full-time professional staffs. Other resorts that have good tennis facilities, but do charge court fees (ranging from $4 to $6), are the *Waiohai, Coco Palms,* and the *Princeville Resort.* In addition, many smaller hotels and condominiums have courts, and there are free public courts at Kapaa, Wailua, Lihue, Koloa, Kalaheo, Kekaha, Hanapepe, and Waimea.

Water Skiing – Despite several wide rivers on Kauai, this sport hasn't caught on here, at least with tourists. There's only one company, *Kauai Water Ski and Sports* (phone: 822-3574), that offers it, for $30 per half hour or $60 per hour (not per person but for boat time), on the Wailua River.

AROUND THE ISLAND

The westernmost of the major Hawaiian islands, Kauai looks like a circle drawn by a small child, bulging or concave in spots, but essentially round. Lihue, the county seat and the point of arrival for most island visitors, is on the southeast coast, about 60 miles from Oahu, Kauai's nearest neighbor besides the tiny island of Niihau. Midway up the east coast is the resort area of Wailua. To the north is Hanalei, the wettest and greenest part of the island, and to the northwest, the breathtaking Na Pali coast. Poipu, a popular and growing resort, sits along the island's sunny south coast; and running up the dry west side of the island is the 10-mile-long Waimea Canyon.

Lihue

It's an indication of Kauai's slow pace that Lihue, a populated crossroads on the southeast coast, is the commercial and governing center of the island. With some 4,000 people calling it home, it's just a larger version of the plantation it was to begin with, although new housing and a shopping center on the outskirts of town have given it a more contemporary look. The sugar mill is, in fact, still in the center of town, just across from the shopping center, which, in turn, is next to a little square of state and county buildings. Lihue is also the site of the island's main commercial airport, so most travelers see some of the town even though their destination is one of the resorts up or down the coast. Lihue offers a funky kind of charm, and it has some interesting sights, several good restaurants, and the extravagant *Westin Kauai*.

Kauai Museum – The museum has a permanent natural history collection as well as changing exhibits on current art and culture and a good gift and book shop. There's also a 10-minute, self-operated film about Kauai, which is a good way to get your bearings before exploring the island yourself. Open Mondays through Fridays 9:30 AM to 4:30 PM, Saturdays, 9 AM to 1 PM. Adult admission, $3; children free. 4428 Rice St. (phone: 245-6931).

Grove Farm Homestead – Founded as a sugarcane plantation in 1864 by the son of a Hanalei missionary family, Grove Farm was a flourishing plantation for three-quarters of a century. (The company is still in existence, but moved from this site in the 1930s.) Now the farm — the main house, plantation office, workers' cottages and various outbuildings, orchards, gardens, and pastures — is a carefully preserved museum of early plantation life. The 2-hour tour, conducted by well-informed guides and limited to two or three groups of six (depending on how many guides are available), often sells out, so it's a good idea to call or write for a reservation in advance (PO Box 1631, Lihue, Kauai, HI 96766; phone: 245-3202). One bit of advice to parents: this isn't the place to bring small children since you're on the move the whole 2 hours of the tour. Open Mondays, Wednesdays, and Thursdays, with tours starting at 10 AM and 1 PM. Admission for adults, $3; for children between 5 and 12 years old, $1. Nawiliwili Rd.

Menehune Gardens – A majestic weeping banyan that covers an acre of ground is the centerpiece of this small tropical garden. The guided tour lasts about an hour, but you're free to wander about on your own for as long as you like. The owners, the Kailikea family, also provide visitors with some genuine aloha. Open daily, 8 AM to 4 PM. Admission $3. Nawiliwili Rd. (phone: 245-2660).

Nawiliwili Bay – Well-protected Nawiliwili Bay is one of two deepwater harbors on the island (Port Allen on Hanapepe Bay is the other). A lot of cane is shipped from here, and many fishing and pleasure boats call this home. At the ocean end of the harbor are beautiful Kalapaki Beach and Kalapaki Beach Park. Farther inland, at the mouth of the Huleia Stream, is Niumalu Beach Park.

Alakoko (or Menehune) Fishpond – The pond, off Hulemalu Road to Nawiliwili Bay, is a portion of the Huleia Stream walled off by a 900-foot-long stone wall to create a fish pond. It's nothing much to look at; the interest in it is mostly generated by the legend that it was constructed by the semi-mythical Menehune, who once lived on the island. As the lore has it, the Menehune, like Irish leprechauns, were a race of tiny people possessing supernatural powers and who, in addition, were prodigious workers capable of building the likes of the Alakoko pond in a single night. More likely, the Menehune were the Marquesans, the first inhabitants of Hawaii, who were conquered by the later Tahitians and put to work serving them. (The Tahitian word for "commoner" is very similar to Menehune.)

Wailua Falls – Just north of Lihue is the Maalo Road, which will take you to Wailua Falls, on the southern branch of the river by the same name. The twin falls are lovely to look at, and, for the hardy, there's a rather steep trail down to the pool at the bottom. For the less adventurous, a more accessible pool is some 200 yards beyond the falls.

Kilohana Estate – Standing on some 35 acres of landscaped grounds is the Wilcox House, renovated to look as it did when it was built in 1935 and housing collections of Oceanic and Hawaiian artifacts. There is also a restored section of sugar plantation homes, displays, a selection of shops and restaurants, and a carriage around the grounds pulled by powerful Clydesdales. Off Rte. 50, on the outskirts of Lihue (phone: 245-5608).

Westin Kauai/Kauai Lagoons – With hundreds of landscaped acres, oceanside lagoons, extravagant displays of art, mosaic beachside promenade, pools, and colonnades more reminiscent of Versailles or Las Vegas than Hawaii, the *Westin Kauai* (phone: 245-5050) is an attraction in its own right. Elegant carriages drawn by Clydesdales traverse miles of trails, while canolas (outrigger canoe/gondola hybrids) and a fleet of eight mahogany launches make half-hour tours ($4) of the lagoons, whose small islands are home to kangaroos, wallabies, and monkeys. Both make stops at the resort's lagoonside shopping villages, health spa, and restaurants.

 SHOPPING: Shopping in Lihue improved considerably with the addition of the Kukui Grove Center on Route 50 just south of town. With *Liberty House, Sears, Woolworth, Long's Drugs* (for Kauai's best buy on film), and a collection of shops and restaurants, it's a good place to go for alohawear, beach clothes and supplies, and incidentals.

Worth a visit to the center is *Stones Gallery* (phone: 245-6653), which displays the best of contemporary Hawaiian art — fine silkscreens, etchings, pastels, and oils from artists all over the state. The gallery also has handcrafted koa bowls; baskets, weavings, and tapas from the South Pacific; and, occasionally, Hawaiian quilts. There's a café serving pastries and coffee.

Other shops of interest: *Waldenbooks; Great Gourmet!,* which stocks quality kitchenware and a good selection of cheeses, specialty foods, and California wines; and *Foot Locker,* for running gear that didn't get packed. Some of the more interesting shops at Kilohana (just off Hwy. 50) are *Island Memories* (phone: 246-9380), proffering eclectic collectibles from around the world; *Stones at Kilohana* (phone: 245-6684), affiliated with *Stones Gallery* at Kukio Grove, featuring Hawaiian arts and crafts; and *Kilohana Galleries* (phone: 245-9452), specializing in laser-etched scrimshaw.

The small town of Kapaia, just a few miles away on Kuhio Highway, en route to Wailua and Hanalei, also has a number of shops worth visiting. There's the *Kapaia Stitchery* (phone: 245-2281), featuring Hawaiian print and patchwork quilts, cotton kimonos, fabrics, and needlework. Hanamaulu offers a cluster of old plantation-style buildings that house a variety of crafts shops, including *Isle Tiles* (phone: 822-3850), with its Hawaiian-made ceramic tiles, and the studio where artist Kathy McClelland sells her stained glass wares (phone: 822-5694).

The shops at the *Westin Kauai,* as suits this extravagant showplace, make for interesting browsing and may even tempt a purchase or two, although the prices may inspire caution. Among the most interesting are *Elephant Walk* (avant-garde jewelry, ceramics, and marvelous Kosage kaleidoscopes), *Brendi* (high-fashion jewelry and women's wear), *La Maison du Chocolat* (Godiva, Neuhaus, etc.), and *Le Cadeau* (Andrelux and Martel leather goods). In addition to hotel shops, the resort also features two commercial theme villages, one focused on clothing and accessories, the other on jewelry and arts and crafts. The villages were designed as a visitor attraction in their own right, and can be reached by boat, horse-drawn carriage, or car. Adjacent to the resort, on Nawiliwili Harbor, are the shops and restaurant of the Anchor Cove commercial complex, also under construction at press time.

 NIGHTLIFE: Nawiliwili is the headquarters for nightlife in the Lihue area. *Club Jetty* (phone: 245-4970), on the wharf, is one of the liveliest spots, with a bar popular with merchant seamen, a restaurant, and disco with dancing till 3 AM Wednesdays through Saturdays. The *Westin Kauai* is about as far from *Club Jetty* in mood and spirit as things can get: The *Paddling Club* features disco from 9 PM to 2 AM weeknights, to 4 AM weekends, and the *Colonnade Lounge* presents classical piano and stand-up bass from 5 to 9 PM.

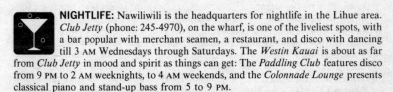 **CHECKING IN:** The only hotel worth mentioning in Lihue is the new *Westin Kauai.* It has taken several hundred million dollars to transform the old *Kauai Surf* into one of Hawaii's most extravagant resort hotels, an 849-room blend of eclectic elegance and contemporary chic. The 1,400-foot beachfront is backed by landscaped lagoons and a Copacabana-style mosaic promenade. Facilities include a large swimming pool complete with waterfalls and 5 Jacuzzis, 36 holes of golf, an 11-court tennis complex (plus a 1,000-seat stadium court), stables, a full health spa (containing everything from Nautilus equipment to raquetball courts), a Japanese garden, a wedding chapel on an island in a lagoon, and theme shopping villages (fashion, jewelry, and arts and crafts). Though smallish and less impressive than the public areas, the guestrooms are nicely furnished, using pastels and white to create a tropical feel. While there's plenty of space to wander about, this is not your quiet Kauai hideaway; it tries to operate at a low-key level, but the decor clearly has been designed for maximum impact and high-powered glamour. With rates that start at $185 a night for a single or double room, it is clearly pitched toward an affluent trade and a healthy proportion of convention business. Glitz is king here, and it's hard to find much Hawaii in these halls. 3500 Rice St., Lihue, HI 96766 (phone: 808-245-5050; 800-228-3000).

EATING OUT: A typical dinner tab in Lihue tends to be substantial, though there are some noteworthy exceptions. For a meal for two, excluding wine, tip, and drinks, expect to pay around $100 or more in the restaurant listed as very expensive, $50 in those noted as expensive, $30 to $45 in a moderate place, and under $25 in an inexpensive eating place. All telephone numbers are in the 808 area code unless otherwise indicated.

The Masters – Elegance in both decor and service is the keynote at the *Westin*'s top dining spot. No less impressive are the creations of its French-trained chefs, with a seasonal menu that includes *pigeonneau à la fricassee champignons sauvages* (squab stewed with wild mushrooms) and *crevettes Malibu* (steamed shrimp seasoned with curry and Malibu liqueur). With some 300 labels, the wine cellar offers a range to satisfy the most demanding palate. Open Tuesdays through Saturdays for dinner only. Reservations advised. Jackets are required for men. In the Spa and Racquet Club at the Westin Kauai (phone: 245-5050). Very expensive.

Inn on the Cliffs – Within the stylish decor, pasta and the day's catch are the house specialties, with a wide variety of familiar and innovative combinations from which to choose. Diners twirl their forks while they enjoy views of Nawiliwili Bay and the *Westin Kauai.* Open daily for lunch and dinner. Reservations advised. At the Westin Kauai resort (phone: 245-5050). Expensive.

Prince Bill's – Tiled floors, blond wood, and soothing pastels create a relaxing setting that is enhanced by panoramic views of Kalapaki Beach and Nawiliwili Harbor. The dinner menu features prix fixe dinners that include hors d'oeurves, appetizer bar, and Caesar salad along with a choice of entrée, such as fresh salmon, double lamb chops, and filet mignon. Also open for breakfast and Sunday brunch. Open daily. Reservations advised. Atop the Surf Tower of the Westin Kauai (phone: 245-5050). Expensive.

Gaylord's – Dining is alfresco, on the veranda facing the grassy lawn that is the back yard of Kilohana, the restored Wilcox mansion. Panoramic views of Kauai's central core of mountains add to the feeling of *la dolce vita*. Sunday brunch is particularly pleasant. Dinner choices include fresh lamb, venison, veal, and chicken stuffed with prawns and cream cheese — overpriced for the quality. Dinner from 5 to 9:30 PM. Reservations necessary. On Kaumualii Highway, 2 miles south of Lihue toward Poipu (phone: 245-9593). Expensive to moderate.

Tempura Garden – An attractive Japanese garden creates a serene atmosphere in keeping with the menu, which features tempura, sushi, and sashimi, all served Kyoto style. There's table seating as well as sushi and tempura bars. Open daily for dinner. Reservations advised. On the grounds of the Westin Kauai (phone: 245-5050). Expensive to moderate.

Casa Italiana – Northern Italian cuisine and a fine selection of homemade pastas are the specialties. Particularly worthy of mention are the garlic and pepper breads, salad bar, and coffees served at the espresso bar. Reservations advised. Closed Sundays. 2989 Haleko Rd., Lihue (phone: 245-9586). Moderate.

Dukes – The owners of *Kimo's* in Lahaina, Maui, have made this a very Hawaiian place. In the boathouse of the *Westin Kauai,* it has a beachfront setting that suits a distinctive collection of racing canoes and paddling memorabilia. The menu is basic and casual. Westin Kauai (phone: 245-5050). Moderate.

JJ's Broiler – Long the leading restaurant of its kind on Kauai, the kitchen serves steaks, steaks, and more steaks — plus the catch of the day, simply broiled. Dinner only, 5 to 9:30 PM. In the Anchor Cove Shopping Complex on Nawiliwili Harbor, adjacent to the Westin Kauai (phone: 822-9782). Moderate.

Barbecue Inn – Halfway down what looks like a deserted street is this popular restaurant. It's short on atmosphere but offers an international menu where yakitori rubs elbows with knockwurst and down-home favorites like pot roast. The food is tasty, and the low price includes everything — soup, vegetables, drinks, and dessert. Open for breakfast, lunch, and dinner; closed Sundays. Reservations unnecessary. 2982 Kress St., Lihue (phone: 245-2921). Inexpensive.

Brick Oven Pizza – Some say it's the best pizza on Kauai. It's certainly the best in Lihue. Open daily. No reservations. Kikui Grove Center (phone: 245-1895). Inexpensive.

Eggbert's – Back when this restaurant was known as the *Egg and I,* it served omelettes only. Now it has added fish, beef, chicken, and pork dishes to its menu and stays open for all three meals. Still, what you come for are the omelettes, which you can get in an almost endless combination of ingredients. Open daily. Reservations advised. 4481 Rice St., Lihue (phone: 245-9025). Inexpensive.

Hamura Saimin – Perfect for those tired of the tourist glitz and ready to experience Kauai as a local. The steaming bowls of noodles and broth are best appreciated when extras like ham, beef, egg, and a dab of hot mustard are added. All the more authentic for being located in the heart of Lihue's old shopping district. Open daily. No reservations. 2956 Kress St. (phone: 245-3271). Inexpensive.

Kiibo – Japanese atmosphere and food: tempura, teriyaki, sukiyaki, and sushi. Open daily except Sundays for lunch and dinner. Reservations unnecessary. 2991 Umi St. (phone: 245-2650). Inexpensive.

Rosita's – Good Mexican food in a California Mexican setting. All the basics, including ample margaritas. Open daily for lunch and dinner. Reservations necessary on weekends. In Kukui Grove Center (phone: 245-8561). Inexpensive.

Hanamaulu, Wailua, and Kapaa: East Kauai's Coconut Coast

Hawaii's royalty, the *alii,* claimed Wailua, midway along the east coast, as their own. It had everything those of regal temperament and expectations could want: a superb beach to indulge their love of sunning and surfing, a stately river that winds through tropical forests hiding grottoes and waterfalls, and dependable weather all year. It wasn't beset by the rain and angry seas that winter brought to the north; nor did it bake in summer, as the south coast did. To the pleasures that nature bestowed, the *alii* added a few of their own. They dug freshwater lagoons to sweeten and fatten up their fish and planted magnificent groves of towering coconut palms. And they kept it all to themselves. Commoners were forbidden, on pain of death, to enter Wailua except at the *alii's* pleasure.

In these democratic times, Wailua is a gracious host to thousands of commoners a year. There's still much of old Hawaii here, if not in buildings, then in legend, and, not surprisingly, the site attracts a fair number of visitors. Happily, the resorts that have grown up around Wailua have used the natural beauty that drew royalty here to good advantage.

The town of Kapaa, Kauai's second largest, is adjacent to Wailua. In recent years they've kind of grown together by way of small shopping malls and development along the Kuhio Highway. Kapaa has some fairly good restaurants, clothing and dive shops, and a stretch of condominiums that front its several miles of white sand beach.

Lydgate State Park – This park at the mouth of the Wailua River is a good place to start a tour of the area's historical sites. Here are the remains of an ancient place of refuge, where Hawaiians sentenced to death for breaking one of the many *kapus* could find sanctuary and where women and children sought safety during war. Nearby is one of the many *heiaus* (temples) along the river, Hikina O Kala, which, like the place of refuge, is now a low stone wall enclosing a coconut grove.

Holoholoku Heiau – Royal mothers traveled to this important *heiau* a mile or so up the north bank of the river to give birth and thereby ensure the royalty of the child. All that's left of the old temple is the birthstone, against which women in labor leaned; the bellstone, which rang to announce the birth of another royal Hawaiian; and a more ominous relic of old Hawaii, a large stone upon which human sacrifices reputedly were made.

Coconut Grove at Coco Palms – Planted in the mid-1800s by a German doctor who wanted to start a coconut plantation, now the center of one of Hawaii's most famous resorts, this serene grove of towering palms has the feel of a public garden, an impression the hotel, happily, does nothing to discourage. Palms have a relatively short life span — about 100 years — and as the original trees grow old, the *Coco Palms* plants replacements in the names of its many illustrious guests. The plaques identifying the trees' namesakes are a record of recent Hawaiian history. In addition to Hawaiian politicians, writers, athletes, and philanthropists, there are representatives of corporate Hawaii. And there are a few distinguished *haoles* too, such as writer James Michener and singer Bing Crosby, who earned honorary citizenship for their fondness for the islands.

Wailua River State Park – A 2½-mile drive up Route 580 leads to Opaekaa Falls and the Wailua River State Park. Continue along Route 580 till it ends, another 3 miles or so, and you'll come to the Keahua Arboretum. Hike along here (the Division of Forestry has a leaflet identifying the tree plantings), picnic, and swim in a secluded swimming hole.

Smith's Tropical Paradise – Smith's is a cross between a garden and a cultural center. Scattered throughout its 23-acre tropical garden are full-scale models of Polynesian, Filipino, and Japanese villages, complete with ducks and chickens — visit them on a self-guided walking tour or via a narrated tram tour. A luau, dance, and music revue, which focuses on the cultural legacy of Polynesia, are offered weekdays ($36). Admission to the park is $3; it's open daily from 8:30 AM to 4 PM. Adjacent to Wailua Boat Marina (phone: 822-4654).

Opaekaa Falls – While this isn't one of one Kauai's largest waterfalls, it is the most easily accessible and certainly lovely. Just 2 miles inland from the Kuhio Highway are several scenic lookouts that offer a view of the falls as well as Wailua River and the surrounding mountains.

Fern Grotto – A cave draped with ferns, this popular attraction is incontestably beautiful. But to get there you have to endure a 20-minute boat ride ($8) during which you're relentlessly entertained with corny tourist jokes. And once there, you share this lovely spot with literally hundreds of others, since two boats leave every half hour. If you *must* go, take the very first cruise and carry a cane so you'll have an excuse to lag behind the crowds. Boats leave from Wailua Marina. *Smith's Boat Tours* (phone: 822-4111) and *Waialeale Boat Tours* (phone: 822-4908).

Kamokila Hawaiian Village – Located on a bend of the Wailua River and accessible via a road adjacent to the Opaekaa Falls lookout, this cluster of Hawaiian grass houses, display areas, and taro patches provides a glimpse of the ancient Polynesian lifestyle, authentically replicated by staff. This reconstruction is near the site of the ruins of an old Hawaiian village. You park by the lookout and are transported by van the last half mile to the riverside village. Plans are in the making for stops by boats en route to and from the Fern Grotto. Closed Sundays (phone: 822-1192).

Coconut Plantation – Between Wailua and Kapaa at Waipouli is the Coconut Plantation, a collection of several resort hotels sharing a rocky beach, a shopping center called the Market Place, and a number of restaurants ranging from fast-food noodle shops to leisurely dining spots.

SHOPPING: A full selection of shops can be found at the Market Place at Coconut Plantation. There's a wide selection of resortwear, jewelry, scrimshaw, wooden bowls, wicker, pottery, other island crafts, and plenty of souvenirs and T-shirts, not to mention 1-hour photo service. Numerous shops and restaurants are also to be found in small shopping malls along the highway and in Kapaa, which has been undergoing a commercial revival, with the restoration of many of its early-19th-century buildings attracting a variety of crafts shops.

Classical Glass – Besides great browsing, there are demonstrations by glass workers Meg and John. Closed Sundays and Mondays. 4523 Niu St., Kapaa (phone: 822-5515).

For Your Eyes Only – Everything you need to shade your eyes from the tropical sun, and fashionably. Coconut Plantation (phone: 822-5922).

Kahn Gallery – A real find, with beautifully — and locally — made ceramics, woodwork, jewelry (including an excellent selection of Niihau shell necklaces), lithographs, paintings, and much more. Coconut Plantation (phone: 822-4277).

Kauai Crafts in Progress – A wide selection of Hawaii-made products, many from Kauai, including food products, jewelry, dolls, and tiles. 1384 Kuhio Hwy. in the heart of Kapaa (phone: 822-7558).

Lady Jane's Company – An interesting selection of quality Hawaiian crafts, including some particularly noteworthy handcrafted wood bowls. 3-4684 Kuhio Hwy., near Hanamaula (phone: 245-1814).

Leisure Living of Kauai – This small apparel store carries a wide range of imported clothing and Hawaiian wear. Coconut Plantation (phone: 822-9802).

Nighten' Gales – Fine handicrafts are imported, mainly from Indonesia: batiks, woven Borneo bags, shell work, and more. 1467 Kuhio Hwy., Kapaa (phone: 822-0595), and *Nighten' Gales II,* 4-1312 Kuhio Hwy., Kapaa (phone: 822-3729).

The Only Show in Town – It's pleasant to browse the selection of antiques and curiosities here. On Kuhio Hwy., just at the bridge on the Hanalei side of Kapaa (phone: 822-1442).

Plantation Stitchery – This small craft shop carries a wide selection of needlecraft supplies and some lovely all-cotton Hawaiian fabrics at about $6 a yard and up. Coconut Plantation (phone: 822-3570).

Plum Tuckered – The collection of hand-crafted crystal, jewelry, and avant garde T-shirts here makes for enjoyable browsing and some good buys. Coconut Plantation (phone: 822-6988).

Tahiti Imports – Here's Kauai's best selection of silk-screened fabrics with a South Seas flavor, including a nice collection of *pareos* (cloth wraps). Coconut Plantation (phone: 822-9342).

The Plant Shoppe – Art with floral themes, on everything from T-shirts to *pareos,* earrings to paintings, plus real plants ready for shipment to the mainland. 1620 Kuhio Hwy., in the center of Kapaa (phone: 822-1422).

Wildflowers – Casual clothing is the specialty here. Coconut Plantation (phone: 822-3981).

NIGHTLIFE: For Polynesian entertainment there is a nightly luau at the *Sheraton Coconut Beach* (phone: 822-3455), Sundays at the *Aston Kauai Resort* (phone: 245-3931), and Mondays through Fridays at *Smith's Tropical Paradise* (phone: 822-4654). All feature typical Hawaiian foods (Kalua pig, lomilomi salmon, and poi) plus a musical revue including the dances of the various

Pacific island groups. The *Coconut Beach* luau is the most popular. There is also a Polynesian revue with family-style dining, Wednesdays through Sundays at the *Coco Palms' Lagoon Dining Room* (phone: 822-4921). The menu is more traditionally American here, highlighting catch of the day and prime ribs for those anxious to steer clear of more exotic culinary offerings. The *Aston Kauai Resort* (phone: 245-3931) also features a dinner show of Polynesian music and dance on Mondays, Wednesdays, Fridays, and Saturdays.

Dance action centers on the *Kauai Hilton*'s *Gilligan's* (phone: 245-1955), where disco reigns 8 PM to 2 AM weekdays (closed Mondays and Tuesdays), to 4 AM weekends. Non-guests must pay a $2 cover charge on weekends.

The *Sheraton Coconut Beach* features quieter dance and listening music 8 to 11 PM nightly in its *Cook's Landing* restaurant (phone: 822-3455). The *Flame Room* at the *Coco Palms* (phone: 822-4921) sets the tone for a relaxing evening with Hawaiian guitar and soft-edged oldies. The *Aston Kauai Resort* (phone: 245-3931) plays host to name entertainment from Honolulu and the mainland.

And if you're in the mood for a film, check the schedule at the *Plantation Cinema* (phone: 822-9391).

 CHECKING IN: For accommodations listed here, $145 and above for two people is considered expensive, $75 to $140 moderate, and less than $75 inexpensive. These figures are based on the tariffs for a typical 1-bedroom condominium apartment or double hotel room. All telephone phone numbers are in the 808 area code unless otherwise indicated.

Kauai Hilton and Beach Villas – Opened early in 1986, this 350-room hotel has incorporated the adjacent 150 condominiums originally run as the *Kauai Beach Villas*. The condominiums are priced a bit higher than the hotel rooms, and they provide full kitchen and laundry facilities as well as a full range of hotel services. The new property features a lovely beachfront setting, several restaurants, including *Midori*, which incorporates continental and Japanese cooking styles, and a 3-section pool complete with waterfalls, Jacuzzis, and sauna. Hanamaulu (phone: 245-1955; 800-445-8667). Expensive to moderate.

Lae Nani – This low-rise luxury condominium complex faces the coast, with tidal pools and a private stretch of beach. The oceanfront pool is surrounded by grassy lawns and landscaped grounds. On the Wailua beachfront (phone: 822-4938; 800-367-6046). Expensive to moderate.

Sheraton Coconut Beach – Farther up the Waipouli Beach is the *Sheraton*, previously the *Holiday Inn Kauai*. The handsome building, with a whitewashed atrium lobby, elevated walkways, and serried terraces, is very slick and modern, and the grounds, which include a nice stretch of beachfront, are lovely. The nightly luau is one of Kauai's most popular. Coconut Plantation (phone: 822-3455; 800-325-3535). Expensive to moderate.

Aston Kauai Resort – The $7 million spent to redesign and refurbish this hotel has transformed it dramatically. The rooms, among the largest hotel accommodations on Kauai, are tastefully decorated in pastel hues with rattan furniture; the cabana units feature kitchenettes. New features include the pool, 2 tennis courts, restaurants, and the lobby. What has been retained — wisely — is the magnificent beachfront setting backed by 10 acres of landscaped grounds. Located at the mouth of the Wailua River. 3-5920 Kuhio Hwy. (phone: 245-3931; 800-922-7866). Moderate.

Coco Palms – On the royal grounds of the *alii* is the hotel that made Wailua a resort destination. It has been the scene of numerous movies (*Blue Hawaii* and *Sadie Thompson* among them) and television shows ("Fantasy Island"), and has played host to celebrities of every rank. It's such an institution that even if you're not staying here you should at least visit. The theme is Polynesian Hawaii, and every night Hawaiian runners race through the coconut grove and across the 3 lovely lagoons in an elaborate torch-lighting ceremony. As for the rooms, they are tastefully decorated in tropical pastels. There's little the *Coco Palms* doesn't offer in the way of activities: tennis, swimming (3 pools, and the beach is just across the street), croquet, billiards, fishing, a museum, a zoo, and, just in case you need it, a thatched wedding chapel amid the coconut trees. Wailua (phone: 822-4921; 800-542-2626). Moderate.

Kauai BeachBoy – A quiet oasis in the middle of Kauai's busiest tourist center. The courtyard opening onto the beach encloses a pool, shuffleboard, volleyball, and tennis courts. The beach is lovely; the rooms, good-sized and well kept, each with a view of the beach from a private balcony. Coconut Plantation (phone: 822-3441; 800-367-8047). Moderate.

Plantation Hale – This pleasant little condominium in the Coconut Plantation complex is just a short walk from the beach. The large 1-bedroom, 1-bath suites have recently been refurbished and include a full kitchen and terrace and sleep up to four. There are 3 swimming pools and a volleyball court on the property. Coconut Plantation (phone: 822-4941; 800-367-6046). Moderate.

Wailua Bay View Condominium – On a slight rise over Wailua Beach and with easy access down, this small condominium couldn't be better located. The 1-bedroom apartments, with full kitchen and balconies facing the beach, are furnished by owners and, therefore, have a pleasing individuality. Each unit has a washer and dryer. There's a 3-day minimum stay. Wailua (phone: 822-3651; 800-367-2912). Moderate.

 EATING OUT: For a meal for two, excluding wine, tips, and drinks, expect to pay around $50 in a place listed as expensive, between $25 and $45 in moderate, and about $20 in inexpensive. All telephone numbers are in the 808 area code unless otherwise indicated.

Kintaro – A typical Tokyo blend of light wood, white rice paper shoji screens, and black trim provides a comfortable setting. The food is well prepared, with nightly specials in addition to teriyaki, tempura, and sushi standards. The fact that *Kintaro* has more than doubled in size since opening several years ago attests to its popularity with both residents and visitors. Dinner only. Reservations advised. 4-370 Kuhio Hwy. (phone: 822-3341). Expensive to moderate.

Sea Shell – An open pavilion right on Wailua Beach, this Coco Palms restaurant has a good selection of seafood specialties and steaks. Dinner only. Reservations advised. Coco Palms Resort Hotel, Wailua (phone: 822-4921). Expensive to moderate.

Bull Shed – As you might guess, this eatery, a little north of Coconut Plantation, specializes in beef and prime ribs, but it also does teriyaki chicken and seafood; its fresh catch of the day is generally delicious. The setting on the water and tropical decor are also nice. Dinner only. Reservations advised for groups of six or more. 796 Kuhio Hwy. (phone: 822-3791). Moderate.

Dragon Inn – Kauai's best Chinese restaurant specializes in Szechwan cuisine. Dinner daily; lunch Tuesdays through Saturdays. Reservations advised. In Waipuoli Plaza (phone: 822-3788). Moderate.

Hanamaulu Café – From the highway, this place doesn't look like anything special, but just head through the main room, which is pleasant enough, and you'll find shoji-screened rooms, tatami mats and on-the-floor seating, plus a lovely garden landscaped around a free-flowing brook and ponds. The food is good, featuring Japanese and Chinese specialties. It's a pleasant place to spend a few hours over dinner. Open for lunch and dinner Tuesdays through Fridays; dinner only Saturdays. Reservations advised. 3-4291 Kuhio Hwy. (phone: 245-2511). Moderate to inexpensive.

Jimmy's Grill – Sand on the floor and a surfer decor create an upbeat — if somewhat noisy — setting for dinners of ribs, fresh island fish, homemade pasta, and hamburgers. Open daily for lunch and dinner. Reservations unnecessary. 4-1354 Kuhio Hwy., in the center of Kapaa (phone: 822-7000). Moderate to inexpensive.

Kountry Kitchen – This small unpretentious restaurant in Kapaa serves tasty food (breakfast, lunch, and dinner) in plentiful proportions. Breakfast is the best bet. Try the omelettes. Open daily from 6 AM to 8:30 PM. No reservations. 1485 Kuhio Hwy., Kapaa (phone: 822-3511). Moderate to inexpensive.

Tropical Taco – This colorfully inviting Mexican restaurant is a good choice for a low-cost, casual dinner. The menu is California Mexican, the food good, the portions well-sized. Open from 11 AM to 9:30 PM daily. No reservations. Kapaa Shopping Center (phone: 822-3622). Inexpensive.

Princeville and Hanalei: The Magnificent North Shore

The standard cliché is "sleepy," and if that includes a fully conscious desire to remain quiet and unhurried, then it fits Hanalei, the northern province of Kauai. North Shore folk have a kind of perverse pride that there's no nightlife to speak of, and it doesn't bother them one iota that their single-lane bridges are too narrow for tour buses. In fact, they prefer it that way, resisting recent efforts to widen the bridges that maintain the North Shore's slow pace. As presently planned, the rebuilt bridges will retain their country appeal.

If in the past Princeville's reputation for quiet and its rather wet winter weather have made the North Shore a less popular overnight destination than the Coconut Coast or Poipu — with their sunny skies — the tropic beauty of the setting and an expanding range of activities and options have begun to draw those who prefer its uncrowded beaches (some of the best anywhere in Hawaii) and sense of Hawaiian authenticity. Still, due to the limited number of accommodations, most visitors see the North Shore on a morning or afternoon swing up the coast by car or van tour, or aboard one of the numerous boats and rafts that provide access to the spectacular wilderness of the Na Pali coast.

Those who linger longer do so to take in the abundance of the riches that nature saw fit to bestow on this corner of the Pacific. For here are a string of white sand beaches splendidly isolated at the foot of towering cliffs, a broad luminous bay backed by mountains whose forms seem to change with the light of day, numerous waterfalls, rainbows, a wide fertile valley of taro fields that serves as a bird sanctuary, and the Na Pali cliffs, jagged and lofty, virtually inaccessible and achingly beautiful.

You can have your nature both ways, too — from the inside of a pup tent on an isolated Na Pali beach or from the unstinting luxury of your own apartment at the Princeville resort. And besides the sports that nature affords — camping, hiking, swimming, surfing, snorkeling, sailing, fishing, horseback riding — are those that require the civilizing hand of man — tennis and golf.

The good life as envisioned by the golf and tennis set is the guiding principle behind the development of the Princeville resort — the North Shore's mix of single-family homes, resort condominiums, and the *Sheraton Princeville* hotel. Development of its second thousand acres has begun. At present, there are 45 holes of golf, a score of tennis courts, a dozen swimming pools, and three good restaurants, not to mention an attractive shopping complex. Even non-golfers can't help but like Princeville. On a rolling plateau overlooking Hanalei Bay, with mountains rising behind it, Princeville is one of the most gorgeously situated resorts in the world.

Kilauea Point – Naturalists gravitate to this craggy point at the northernmost tip of the island for the rare chance of seeing some of the Pacific's seabirds at close range. The point, under the protection of the US Fish and Wildlife Service, is home to the wedge-tailed shearwater, the red-and-white-tailed tropic bird, and the frigate; just across the bay, within easy sight, is a colony of the red-footed booby. There's a good self-guided tour on the point's bird, plant, and sea life. The lighthouse here, out of use since 1967, isn't open to the public. Kilauea Point is open from noon to 4 PM every day but Saturday. No admission charge.

Hanalei Valley Lookout – Just past the entrance to Princeville is a lookout that spreads the treasures of the North Shore before you. In one direction is a patchwork of taro fields cut through by the placid Hanalei River, along which farmers tether their horses without fear of thieving. Seaward is Hanalei Bay, with lips of white beaches and the shrouded Na Pali coast looming beyond. Most of what you see from here is part of the Hanalei National Wildlife Refuge. Taro farmers get special permission to use the land because their fields provide a good habitat for the endangered birds the refuge is meant to protect: the Hawaiian stilt, gallinule, koot, and duck. With binoculars, it's possible to see them from the lookout.

Hanalei – The town of Hanalei stretches from the line of shops on Kuhio Highway toward the bay. Despite recent development, Hanalei retains a lazy charm, exemplified by several historic buildings, a number of older buildings renovated as shops, and a lack of high-rises. Hanalei Beach Park and Pavilion, near the wharf where the Hanalei River enters the Pacific, is a perfect spot for picnicking and swimming. The sunset from the end of the pier is as sublime an experience as a Polynesian sunset should be, and according to residents of many years, repeated exposure doesn't jade the senses to it.

Waioli Mission House Museum – At first glance you might mistake this trim white frame building for a private home. But the house, built in 1841 by early Protestant missionaries, has been a museum for over 60 years, containing furniture and artifacts of the missionary period of Hawaiian history. The guided tour, given Tuesdays, Thursdays, and Saturdays from 9 AM to 3 PM, is an interesting mix of the founding family's history and that of Hanalei. No admission charge. Hanalei town (phone: 245-3202).

The Native Hawaiian Trading & Cultural Center – Until 1981, this site housed the *Ching Young Store,* Hanalei's only general store and a landmark built in the early 1900s. Now it houses a cluster of shops focusing on Hawaiian crafts and a small museum on Hawaiiana (phone: 826-7222).

Lumahai Beach – There's rarely a travel brochure of Kauai that doesn't include a picture of this beach, about 2 miles outside Hanalei town. This is Polynesia, as pictured by Hollywood in *South Pacific,* and although pretty, it's really no lovelier than a number of other beaches that ring the North Shore like a necklace.

Wet and Dry Caves – Just before you come to Haena State Park is the Maniniholo Dry Cave, so called to distinguish it from the Waikapalae Wet Cave a jot down the road or the Waikanaloa Wet Cave farther on. These sea caves, wide-mouthed and shallow, so there's no need for a guide or artificial light to see them, were probably formed when the sea stood at a higher level. Hawaiian legends ascribe them to the work of Pele and other mythical beings.

Haena State Park – This is the terminus for vehicles and the jumping-off point for hikers and campers headed into Na Pali. There's an exquisite little beach — Kee Beach — at the very end of the road, and just around the promontory that curls over it is the Hula Halau Heiau, where Pele was thought to dance and where in earlier times young women came to learn the ancient art of hula. Wade out into the water at Kee and you can see the Na Pali cliffs shimmering in the distance.

SHOPPING: The Princeville Center, low redwood buildings connected by white-railed walkways, is a pleasant place to catch your breath if you're day-tripping to the North Shore. Since it serves a resident community as well as tourists, it's more than a collection of souvenir and gift shops. There is a butcher shop, supermarket, beauty shop, and bank in addition to a well-stocked camera shop; the *Princeville Plantation Store* (phone: 826-9292), selling island handiwork and other gifts; *Toucans* (phone: 826-1471), an enjoyable stop for swimwear, resortwear, and other women's apparel; and the *Mail Service Center* for shipping and fax services (phone: 826-7331).

Also notable are some of the shops in the town of Hanalei, including *Ola's* (phone: 826-6937), which carries a wide range of imaginative gifts and top-quality woodwork, ceramics, dolls, and other crafts, as well as one of Hawaii's best selections of humorous cards; and the Native Hawaiian Trading and Cultural Center (formerly the *Ching Young Store*), including the *Artisans Guild of Kauai* (phone: 826-6441), which showcases the work of local painters, potters, woodworkers, and jewelers at prices usually lower than those in Kauai's resort shops. *Hanalei Camping,* in the new Ching Young Center (phone: 826-6664), not only rents and sells camping supplies, but has available a full range of sporting goods and books on Hawaii. Stop in to browse, and you're likely to find something you want.

About 10 miles southeast of Hanalei, the plantation town of Kilauea features the surprisingly sophisticated *Kong Lung Store,* Keneke St. and Lighthouse Rd. (phone: 828-1822), where gift items include custom-made arts and crafts, clothing, Hawaiiana, antiques, and Oriental objets d'art. It's well worth a stop while en route to the Kilauea Lighthouse. Also of interest are the eclectic mix of imported artworks at the nearby *Artisans International,* 420 Kilauea Rd. (phone: 828-1918), and the collection of Hawaii-themed books at the *Hawaiian Art Museum and Bookstore,* 2488 Kolo Rd. (phone: 828-1309).

Near Kilauea (about 8 miles before Princeville on the Kuhio Highway) is *Moloaa Sunrise* (phone: 822-7552), an open-air shop that features exotic fresh fruits and other Hawaiian delicacies. Try the tropical "smoothies," delicious fruit shakes. *Banana Joe's Tropical Fruit Farm,* in Kilauea, features a similar range of items (phone: 828-1092).

NIGHTLIFE: Your best bet is the *Tahiti Nui* (phone: 826-6277), on the main highway in Hanalei, where most nights there's impromptu Hawaiian entertainment or country-western music, as well as Wednesday and Friday night luaus. Those who want to boogie can try the *Ukiyo Lounge* at the *Sheraton Mirage Princeville* (phone: 826-9644), where there is recorded music 6 PM to midnight weekdays and to 2 AM weekends. The *Sheraton's Lobby Bar* features music between 6 and 10:30 PM. *Charo's* (phone: 826-6422) features a dinner-dance revue that ranges from Hawaiian to Latin at 8:30 PM; a $5 cover charge is added to the dinner bill.

CHECKING IN: For accommodations listed here, $200 and up for two people is considered very expensive; $150 to $195 is expensive; and $75 to $145 is moderate. These categories are based on a typical one-bedroom condominium or double hotel room. All telephone numbers are in the 808 area code unless otherwise indicated.

Hanalei Bay Resort – More like a hotel than the other condominiums at Princeville, this resort has a bustling central area with a full-service front desk, shops, and a restaurant and lounge overlooking 11 tennis courts and a swimming pool. The hotel rooms, studios, and the fully equipped 1-, 2-, and 3-bedroom condominium apartments have terraces opening onto beautifully landscaped grounds, but the rooms have none of the distinctive features found in the other Princeville properties. The resort is just a walk down a paved footpath to the beach, where there's a telephone to summon the jitney if you don't want to walk back. Princeville (phone: 826-6522; 800-657-7922). Very expensive to expensive.

Sheraton Mirage Princeville – This 300-room property, the first hotel at the Princeville resort, serves as a luxury flagship for the Sheraton chain in Hawaii. The views from its tastefully decorated rooms are nothing short of spectacular, taking in the expanse of Hanalei Bay and the first cliffs of the nearby Na Pali coast. The $60 million recently spent to upgrade and redecorate has resulted in elegance throughout the hotel. Paths on various levels lead to an enlarged pool and beach on Hanalei Bay. Guests have access to and preferential times and rates at the resort's tennis and golf facilities. Princeville (phone: 826-9644; 800-325-3535). Very expensive to expensive.

Cliffs – Named for its dramatic setting over the Pacific, it is one of Princeville's more handsome properties. Its big, breezy apartments (from 1 to 4 bedrooms) feature balconies off both the living rooms and master bedrooms and soaring 2-story living rooms with spacious sleeping lofts. And because the design allows the apartment to be divided into single rooms, staying here can be very economical. There's daily maid service, a front desk, a swimming pool, tennis courts, Jacuzzis on the property, and access to Princeville's golf course. The kitchens aren't as well equipped as you might like, but this is only a minor drawback. Request a unit with a telephone if that matters to you. Princeville (phone: 826-6219; 800-523-0411). Expensive to moderate.

Pali Ke Kua – This clifftop condominium offers unexcelled panoramic views. Its 1- and 2-bedroom units (some feature an additional loft) have full kitchen facilities, TV sets, and telephones. There's a pool, and a paved path leads down the Princeville cliffside to a private beach. Princeville (phone: 826-9066; 800-367-7042). Expensive to moderate.

Puu Poa – A sense of privacy pervades this well-priced condominium resort. The 2-bedroom/2-bath apartments are large, with all appliances and even hot tubs; all units feature panoramic ocean views. Maid service is provided every third day on week-long stays. Other amenities include a tennis court, swimming pool, and a pathway to the beach. Princeville (phone: 826-9602; 800-367-7042). Expensive to moderate.

Hanalei Colony Resort – This appealing condominium just a few miles from the end of the road at Haena State Park is a country cousin to Princeville's sophisticated brood. The 2-bedroom apartments are essentially 1 bedroom with a sleeping niche separated by folding louvered doors. But the whole is open, large, and comfortable. Right on the beach (the only North Shore resort that is), it also has a swimming pool and Jacuzzi. What you get in spades here is quiet. There are no telephones or TV sets in the apartments, and you're away from what little community the North Shore can claim. Don't even consider this secluded haven unless you have a car. Hanalei (phone: 826-6235; 800-367-8047, ext. 148). Moderate.

EATING OUT: For a meal for two, excluding wine, tip, and drinks, expect to pay around $80 or more at a place listed as very expensive, $50 and up in a place listed as expensive, between $25 and $45 in a moderate place, and under $25 in an inexpensive place. All telephone numbers are in the 808 area code unless otherwise indicated.

Nobles – The *Sheraton Princeville*'s intimate, elegant dining room goes nouvelle, with food and service to be admired. From appetizers like French goose liver pâté to entrées of venison, abalone, and buffalo, the fixed price menu delivers on taste and presentation. Open Tuesdays through Saturdays for dinner. Reservations advised. Jacket required and available at the door. At the Sheraton Princeville (phone: 826-9644). Very expensive.

Charo's – The seaside setting halfway between Hanalei and Haena and the rattan-and-tile interior are pleasant enough, but the menu, featuring fish, steak, prime ribs, and specialties like shrimp breaded in macadamia nut crumbs, draws mixed reviews. Owned by the entertainer Charo, the place also features dance music nightly, with Latin and Hawaiian sounds in an hour-long show that starts at 8:30 PM and adds $5 per person to the dinner bill. Open for lunch and dinner daily. Dinner reservations advised. Hanalei Colony Resort (phone: 826-6422). Expensive.

Bali Hai – Panoramic views of the surrounding mountains include the profile of famous Bali Hai peak, from which this restaurant at the *Hanalei Bay Resort* takes its name. Breakfast is the best bet, though the lunch and dinner menus are good enough. Dinner reservations advised. Hanalei Bay Resort (phone: 826-6522). Expensive to moderate.

Beamreach – Dark and nautical, this Princeville restaurant offers standard fare — steaks, seafood, and chicken dinners that include salad and vegetables. Dinner only, nightly. Reservations advised. Pali Ke Kua Condominium, Princeville (phone: 826-9131). Expensive to moderate.

The Dolphin – Deliciously prepared fish, steaks, and chicken are the mainstays at this small restaurant on the banks of the Hanalei River. Complete dinners include generous salads served family style, vegetables, and hot bread. Dinner only, nightly. No reservations. Hanalei town (phone: 826-6113). Expensive to moderate.

Hanalei Shell House – A very relaxed place with a beach-shack atmosphere enlivened by hanging plants, it serves fresh seafood (catch of the day prepared in 7 styles), pasta dishes, great macadamia pancakes, and lavish salads bursting with fresh ingredients. Open daily for breakfast (the best on the North Shore), lunch, and dinner. Dinner reservations advised. Hanalei town (phone: 826-9301). Expensive to moderate.

Casa di Amici – In an out-of-the-way setting in the middle of the plantation town of Kilauea (9 miles southeast of Princeville), this Italian restaurant features sliding walls that allow it to enjoy the night breezes. Prices are reasonable, but the food gets mixed reviews. Open daily, except Sundays, for lunch; daily for dinner. Reservations advised. 2484 Keneke St. (phone: 828-1388). Moderate.

Chuck's Steakhouse – A branch of the Hawaiian steakhouse chain, it is worth a visit for its good steaks, prime ribs, teriyaki, and seafood dishes. Dinner daily, lunch on weekdays only. Reservations unnecessary. Princeville Shopping Center (phone: 826-6211). Moderate.

Tahiti Nui – If you want to experience a real Hawaiian luau, skip the elaborate dos put on by the big resorts and come here for the Monday, Wednesday, and Friday night luaus. For $30 you can get the traditional fare — kalua pig, taro, poi, lomilomi salmon, sweet potato — in the company of islanders and in a setting that is distinctly old Hawaii, including traditional Hawaiian musical entertainment. The rest of the week, *Tahiti Nui* serves a selection of chicken, short ribs, shrimp, fresh fish, and plenty of vegetables for lunch and dinner daily. Reservations necessary. The bar, with its wide veranda made for sipping a beer at sunset, is open from 11 AM to 2 AM. Hanalei town (phone: 826-6277). Moderate.

Café Hanalei – The views from the terrace would be worth a recommendation even if the food were mediocre, but it's not. An excellent menu offers a full range of entrées as well as some of the best sandwiches in Hawaii, if it's a light meal you're after. A great place for a relaxed breakfast, also. Dinner served nightly until 10 PM. Reservations advised. Sheraton Mirage Princeville (phone: 826-9644). Moderate to inexpensive.

Café Zelo's – Breakfast includes delicious omelettes and frittatas, while lunch focuses on hefty sandwiches, fresh salads, and specialties like spinach lasagna and stuffed potatoes. Dinner features a Mediterranean menu, with pasta and seafood the specialties. There's also an excellent selection of coffees. Open daily. Reservations unnecessary. Princeville Center (phone: 826-9700). Inexpensive.

Farmer's Market – The perfect lunch stop, serving homemade soups, salads, and sandwiches. Open daily from 9 AM to 9 PM. No reservations. In Kilauea, en route to the Kilauea Lighthouse (phone: 828-1512). Inexpensive.

Jacques' Bakery – Fresh croissants and pastries for a fast breakfast or a midday snack en route. French expatriate Jacques Atlan has created a Kauai tradition here. Milk and fresh coffee are also available. Don't be surprised if you have to wait on line a few minutes to be served. Word of Jacques' baking talent has spread far and wide, despite the out-of-the-way setting in Kilauea. Open daily from 6 AM to 6 PM. No reservations. Oka St. (phone: 828-1393). Inexpensive.

Pizzaburger – This very informal restaurant in the Princeville Center makes good pizza, subs, and other standards of fast food — fries, onion rings, etc. It's a little pricey because of the neighborhood, but one of the few casual places to eat on the North Shore. Open 11 AM to 10 PM daily. No reservations. Princeville (phone: 826-6070). Inexpensive.

Na Pali Coast

Unless you possess extraordinary powers of imagination, it's hard to picture the dazzling beauty of this 14-mile stretch of coast. Wind, rain, and the centuries have cut deep valleys into the windward face of Kauai, leaving sharp pleats of land as lush as they are mysterious. And between the great knuckles of cliffs that jut out into the surf are beaches, pristine and isolated from all but the most determined adventurers.

The Na Pali coast has never offered easy access. Early Polynesians settled in these vertiginous valleys because the formidable natural barriers offered a measure of protection from belligerent neighboring tribes. They've long since departed, and only the remnants of stone-walled taro fields built up in the narrow valleys recall their tenure.

Because there are no roads into Na Pali, most people see it from a helicopter or boat. But a few penetrate its tropical valleys on foot. For day hikers, there's a 2-mile trail starting from Haena Beach Park and ending at Hanakapiai Beach. More experienced backpackers hike the 11-mile trail to Kalalau Beach. But it's a vigorous hike requiring at least one overnight stop at Kalalau, and none but the hardy should attempt it.

Poipu: The Sunny South Coast

It's no surprise that the south coast of Kauai has become one of the most popular spots on the island. Its perpetual sunshine, broad swaths of white sand beaches, calm seas year-round, and exuberant plant life that scents the air with intoxicating fragrance make it irresistible. Poipu, a long, scalloped beach at the southernmost tip of the island, is where the resorts took root, providing such amenities as golf, tennis, good restaurants, and handsome lodgings to complement the area's excellent swimming, snorkeling, scuba diving, and surfing.

But except for the developments at Poipu and the gentrified plantation town of Koloa, sugarcane is still king in the south, and the villages that dot the coast owe their existence to it rather than to tourism. Driving down a road between tall fields of mature cane or following a lumbering cane truck makes the tourist industry at Poipu seem miles and light-years away.

The south coast is hot, too, especially after the shaded cool of Hanalei, and it becomes hotter the farther west you go. The long, treeless beaches of Waimea, Kekaha, and Polihale should be visited before the day heats up.

This coast was particularly hard hit when Hurricane Iwa ripped through the island in November 1982. A number of buildings along the shore — from the resorts at Poipu to the sugarcane town of Kekaha — were simply swept off their foundations by tidal waves. Portions of coast roads were washed out, as was much coastal vegetation.

Recovery has been remarkably fast. Main roads were repaired within days. Resorts cleared the sand and rocks from swimming pools and lobbies, rebuilt rooms, replaced furnishings, and started to reopen 6 weeks after the storm. Replanting began immediately, too, replacing the salt-soaked soil with fresh earth. And the landscape today looks as luxuriant as ever. The only lasting damage done by Iwa was to the reefs off Poipu Beach, which were good spots for snorkeling and scuba diving before the storm.

Koloa – About 3 miles from Poipu's condominiums and hotels on Kaumualii Highway, Koloa was Hawaii's first plantation town, built around a mill that started refining sugar in 1835 — and its residents still plant and harvest sugar cane from surrounding fields or work in the mill a few miles outside town. An artistically appealing and informative monument to Hawaii's sugar workers is found at the entrance to the town, adjacent to the chimney that is all that remains of the plantation's original mill. In recent years, shop-by-shop restoration has made Koloa a popular attraction, outwardly maintaining its plantation town feel, although increasingly compromising its authenticity in the process. Despite an increasingly gentrified façade, however, Koloa remains a charming village of old plantation houses and churches — Protestant, Catholic, and Buddhist — that reflect the diverse origins of Kauai's people.

Poipu Beach – The series of beaches that line the Poipu coast are what attracted resorts to this southernmost portion of Kauai. Shower and toilet facilities are on Poipu Beach itself, attracting a mix of locals and visitors. Hotels and condos provide right-of-way access to the other beaches. Surfers head this way for offshore waves, snorklers for multicolored waters, and swimmers for reef-sheltered waters which can, however, be quite rough on occasion. Hobie Cat rentals and catamaran sails depart from here.

Olu Pua Gardens – Japanese gardens, palms, jungle plants, and orchids are some of the many themes that appear throughout the recently reopened Olu Pua. Tours are offered daily at 9:30 and 11:30 AM and 1:30 PM. Admission charge: $10. Just off Hwy. 50, near Kalahe, en route to Waimea Canyon (phone: 332-8182).

Kukuiula Harbor – This pretty bay about 2 miles west of Poipu has recovered from the damage done by Iwa and is once again the home of many small pleasure crafts as well as a center for water sports.

Spouting Horn – If you have a taste for sea geysers, this fountain — created by waves pushing water through a submerged lava tube — may interest you. A popular visitor attraction, it is reached by a coastal road from Poipu. Nearby hawkers peddle a surprisingly complete selection of well-priced coral jewelry and Niihau shell leis: Shop around and negotiate.

Pacific Tropical Botanical Garden – A research garden to study the prodigious variety of plants that thrive in the tropics, this is also one of the most rewarding side trips you can take on the island. The tour of the 186-acre garden — lasting 2 hours and demanding a comfortable pair of walking shoes — is conducted by a knowledgeable volunteer who from time to time will stop to cut a branch of a plant or tree carefully to let the group get a closer look at it. In addition to the research garden, the tour includes an adjoining private garden which once belonged to John Gregg Allerton, a local patron and millionaire whose family established the First National Bank of Chicago. Allerton, an architect by training, created an exquisite garden on the spot where Queen Emma, the wife of King Kamehameha IV, started one in the last century. There's a serene outdoor "room" walled by tall, thin-trunked trees, a lovely bamboo grove, and an ingenious series of pools, fountains, and waterfalls. Tours of the gardens. are offered weekdays at 9 AM and 1 PM, Saturdays at 9 AM, and Sundays at 1 PM. The tour includes a visit to the grounds of the adjoining Allerton Estate (on weekends the tour skips the beach portion of the estate). Cost is $15, with tours limited to about a dozen people. Call well in advance for reservations or write: PO Box 340, Lawai, Kauai, HI 96765. 2 miles south of Lawai, off Rte. 53 (phone: 332-7361).

Hanapepe Lookout – About a mile and a half before you come to Hanapepe town, stop here to get a panoramic view of the valley. Upvalley are the taro fields; downvalley, the town itself, picturesque clapboard buildings ranging along both sides of the Hanapepe River. Just outside the town, off the main road, is Salt Pond Beach Park, named after the nearby salt ponds that are still harvested.

Waimea – Captain Cook landed here in 1778 at the mouth of the river that carved the magnificent Waimea Canyon. The town was also the winter home of the Kauaian royalty, who, when summer heated up, moved their court to Wailua on the eastern side of the island. There's a plaque to commemorate Captain Cook's landing, a neat little beach park, and the remains of a Russian fort on a point of land opposite the town. Don't waste your time looking for Ft. Elizabeth, built in 1816 by a German adventurer employed by a Russian shipping company; it's not much more than a low wall of red rubble with a tangle of dead-looking trees inside.

Kekaha – Kekaha is the last town of any size before the Kaumualii Highway stops at the western end of the Na Pali cliffs and is as dry as Haena is wet. There's a sugar mill here, and you can pull off the road to watch the cane trucks disgorge their load into what looks like a giant Cuisinart.

Polihale State Park – At the literal end of the road (and a rutted cane road at that) is Polihale State Park, where a ¼-mile-wide beach of bone white sand stretches on for miles nearly unbroken by shade trees. Polihale is a fine beach for swimming and body surfing and a good vantage point for seeing the Na Pali cliffs. You can camp and picnic here, too. But it *is* hot on this side of the island, and there's precious little in the way of shade, manmade or otherwise. Those planning to spend the day should stock up on food and drink ahead of time.

 SHOPPING: In recent years quite a number of shops and restaurants have opened to serve south Kauai's growing number of visitors. A free jitney shuttle links Koloa Town with Poipu's resort hotels and condominiums, also making a stop at the Kiahuna Shopping Village. The *Shoppe Hoppers* van (phone: 332-7272) also provides shuttle service links to south coast locations, including Kukuiula Harbor and the Spouting Horn, for $1.50 per person, and to Lihue for $5 per person (minimum two to the van).

Old Koloa Town

After many quiet years as a lazy plantation town, Koloa has been transformed into a small Lahaina, complete with restored buildings from the turn of the century and earlier, and the usual array of souvenir shops, resort and water attire, activities desks, and restaurants, including *That Tropical Feeling* (phone: 742-9433) for swimwear, *Paradise Clothing* (phone: 742-9454), *Crazy Shirts* (phone: 742-7161), *Koloa Casuals* (phone: 742-7381), and *Fathom Five Dive Shop* (phone: 742-9791). The last holdout from pre-gentrified Koloa is the *Sueoka Store* (phone: 742-1611), a typically small town, all-purpose market. The recent addition of the Koloa Plantation Marketplace is commercial overkill for a small town.

Paintings and watercolors by noted Hawaiian artists are at *The Gallery* at the *Waiohai* hotel, along with delicate Japanese porcelains, scrimshaw, and wood carvings of local birds. The *Gallery* collection also includes some rare Niihau shell leis and some strikingly beautiful leis of peacock and pheasant feathers (phone: 742-9211).

The *Waimea Town Store* carries a bit of everything, as its old general store atmosphere suggests. There are attractive casual clothes at good prices, Hawaiian fabrics, jewelry, and a slew of tasteful inexpensive gifts, such as bath oils, hair ornaments, straw bags, Chinese purses, and stationery.

KIAHUNA SHOPPING VILLAGE

This nicely designed cluster of shops provides Poipu with a commercial core. A free Polynesian revue is offered Thursdays at 5 PM in the center's grassy central courtyard.

Black Pearl Collection – Rare Japanese black pearls are the focus of this store's custom-made jewelry (phone: 822-7170).

Business Is Blooming – This small shop features leis and tropical flowers and ships to the mainland (phone: 742-1575).

Garden Isle Bake Shop – Find macadamia nut and cinnamon rolls, bran-mango muffins (in season), chocolate- and macadamia-filled croissants, and macadamia cream pies, all baked fresh daily (phone: 742-6070).

Jewels Kauai – At this shop, owned by Maui Divers, coral provides a centerpiece for many of the custom-designed pieces that are artfully displayed (phone: 742-1303).

Ship Shore Gallery – Here's everything from ships-in-a-bottle to antique guns, from paintings to shipboard brass (phone: 742-7123).

Tutu's Toy House – As the name implies, the focus is on kids, with *tutu* (auntie) supplying the requisite selection of stuffed animals and toys (phone: 742-7008).

NIGHTLIFE: The *Sheraton's Drum Lounge* starts the evening with Hawaiian music. Dancing to more contemporary sounds from 9 PM to midnight weekdays, 9 PM to 1 AM weekends. For "easy listening," a guitarist plays Tuesdays through Saturdays at the *Waiohai's Terrace Restaurant,* and a pianist performs at the hotel's *Tamarind Lounge;* weekends, there's dancing at the *Terrace Restaurant* (phone: 742-9511). And right next door, at the *Poipu Beach* hotel's *Poipu Beach Club* (phone: 742-1681), there's live guitar to accompany dinner. Hot spots for mingling are the bars at *Keoki's Paradise* (phone: 742-7534), *Mango's* (phone: 742-7377), or *Brennecke's* (phone: 742-7588). Looking for a luau? Try the one at the *Sheraton* Wednesdays and Sundays, or the luau on the grounds of the *Waiohai,* Mondays from 6 to 9 PM.

Otherwise, Poipu nights are best appreciated with a stroll along the beach under Kauai's usually star-filled skies, which explains why Poipu has become a popular destination with honeymooners.

 CHECKING IN: Beachfront hotels and condominiums are generally at a premium. Smaller, often less expensive off-beach condominiums are found at either end of its central beaches. It is advisable to ask about location and facilities as well as price when making reservations. Expect to pay $160 and up for two at accommodations listed as expensive; $75 to $155 at those places listed as moderate; and under $75 at an inexpensive place. These categories are based on a typical 1-bedroom condominium apartment or double hotel room. At press time, ground had been broken for the 605-room *Hyatt Regency Kauai,* a low-rise, pricey property set for completion in late 1990. An 18-hole golf course adjacent to the hotel is scheduled to open at the same time. All telephone numbers are in the 808 area code unless otherwise indicate.

Poipu Kapili – Neighbor to the *Sheraton Kauai,* this small (60-unit) condominium offers privacy and is beautifully maintained, with pool and tennis on-property. Poipu Beach (phone: 742-6449; 800-443-7714). Expensive.

Stouffer Waiohai – Quiet elegance, a prime beachfront setting, fully equipped spa, tennis, and excellent food are the hallmarks of this resort. Rooms have recently been redecorated in pastels, with wicker and rattan furnishings, creating a tropical atmosphere. Lanais, the majority of which offer partial sea views, face landscaped gardens that lead to swimming pools (there are three on the property) and the beach. In the tradition of great resorts, it also offers myriad guest activities, among them snorkeling lessons, botanical tours of the grounds, petroglyph drawing, aerobics, and hula lessons. Poipu Beach (phone: 742-9511; 800-426-4122). Expensive.

Aston Poipu at Makahuena – An oceanfront site provides these 1-, 2-, and 3-bedroom units with lovely views; the courtyard units that surround the pool afford less privacy. The place is well maintained and offers front desk and maid services. High-season rates drop substantially after Easter. Poipu (phone: 742-5500; 800-922-7866). Expensive to moderate.

Kiahuna Plantation – A first-rate beach, tennis, and golf resort, offering a prime beachfront location, expansive lawns, and landscaped grounds. Today's manicured look restored *Kiahuna's* appeal after the extensive damage done by Hurricane Iwa. White beachfront cottages and low-rise, plantation-style buildings with balconies blend comfortably with the setting. Inside, the 1- and 2-bedroom apartments follow a tropical scheme — high ceilings, louvered windows, redwood-trimmed walls, patterned pastel fabrics, and rattan furnishings. Be prepared to walk: It's a good distance to the pool. Poipu Beach (phone: 742-6411; 800-367-7052). Expensive to moderate.

Poipu Kai Resort – It consists of 4 separate condominiums — *Poipu Sands, Makanui, Kahala, Manualoha* — each different in style, but all having telephones, daily maid service, tennis courts, and swimming pools. There's a lot of attractive architecture here; many of the 1- and 2-bedroom apartments have cathedral ceilings, sleeping lofts, and 2-level living areas. And though a bit underdecorated, all the units are comfortably furnished. None of the buildings is on the beach, however — it's a few minutes' walk away. Construction of the adjacent *Hyatt Regency Kauai* may cause inconvenience at some *Poipu Kai* units. Poipu (phone: 742-6464; 800-367-6046). Expensive to moderate.

Sheraton Kauai – Fortunately for Sheraton, it had completed the garden wing of this hotel late in 1982, so when hurricane Iwa all but demolished the original beachfront structure, there was a new hotel building still intact across the street. Today, the totally rebuilt ocean wing and a 120-room addition re-create the same low-rise plantation style of the original; the garden wing, which was built around freshwater lagoons, is open and breezy, with spacious guest rooms and handsome common areas. A fitness center and 3 tennis courts have also been added. Poipu Beach (phone: 742-1661; 800-325-3535). Expensive to moderate.

Nihi Kai Villas – Near Brennecke's Beach (popular with body surfers) and Poipu's public beach, *Nihi Kai*'s fully equipped 2-bedroom apartments are also within walking distance of Poipu's hotels and restaurants. Poipu (phone: 742-6458; 800-331-8076). Moderate.

Stouffer Poipu Beach – Those seeking tranquillity as well as an attractive environment need look no further. Here are a lovely spacious courtyard facing the beach, a poolside grill where guests can cook their own lunches, and country western shindigs most every night. The large, newly renovated rooms all have ocean views, terraces, and kitchenettes. One of Poipu's best buys. Next door to the *Waiohai* at Poipu Beach (phone: 742-1681; 800-426-4122). Moderate.

Poipu Crater Resort – Within the curving basin of an extinct crater, *Poipu Crater Resort*'s 2-bedroom apartments offer quiet, privacy, and lower rates to compensate for the 10-minute walk to the beach. Rates vary with length of stay. Poipu (phone: 245-6600; 800-367-8020). Moderate.

Poipu Bed and Breakfast Inn – Set in Koloa, this 1933 inn offers a dose of plantation-scale charm and comfort. Rounding out the rentable options are 6 rooms, plus a large house and a condo apartment. Guests can use the pool and courts at the Kiahuna Tennis Club. Rates start at $65. 2720 Hoonani Rd. (phone: 742-1146; 800-688-8800). Moderate.

Waimea Plantation Cottages – One of Hawaii's most unique properties, it gives a sense of the plantation lifestyle that dominated on Kauai for nearly a century. Beautifully restored and modernized, these comfortable cottages (19 at press time, with dozens more to come) are set amid towering palms. The beachside pool is lovely. Advance reservations are required much of the year. At the edge of Waimea Town (phone: 338-1625; 800-992-4632). Moderate.

Kuhio Shores – The beach may be small, but the sunset ocean views from the apartments can be spectacular. The 1- and 2-bedroom units are comfortably furnished and well-priced. No daily maid service. Weekly rates available. Poipu (phone: 742-7555; 800-367-8022). Moderate to inexpensive.

Koloa Landing Cottages – A good buy, this small oceanfront property provides simple and comfortable accommodations, with cable TV, full kitchens, and in-unit telephones. 2740-B Hoonani Rd. (phone: 742-1470). Inexpensive.

 EATING OUT: For a meal for two, excluding wine, tips, and drinks, expect to pay $50 or more in a place listed as expensive; $20 to $45, moderate; under $20, inexpensive. Although it is popular, the *Koloa Fish House* deserves a caution sign for those who appreciate good food. All telephone numbers are in the 808 area code unless otherwise indicated.

Tamarind – A first class restaurant with continental and Asian-inspired dishes, such as Colonial Rice, a delicately flavored hot Thai curry of lobster, shrimp, scallops, and chicken. The decor of the *Tamarind* is equal to the food: subtly colored Thai silk and striking brass pillars add the flavor of the Orient to the banquette seating and very French table settings. Dinner only. Reservations advised. In the Waiohai, Poipu Beach (phone: 742-9511). Expensive.

Terrace – Not only does the restaurant at the *Waiohai* serve a fabulous brunch with over 100 selections, but it may be the best place for dinner in Poipu, if not on the whole island. At the Sheraton Waiohai (phone: 742-9511). Expensive.

The Beach House – After being swept off its foundation by Hurricane Iwa, it has been rebuilt to emerge, once again, as the South Shore's most popular (some say overrated) eatery. Fresh fish and seafood and prime ribs are dishes of choice, and the sunset is the entertainment. Open daily for dinner. Reservations advised. Poipu Beach (phone: 742-7575). Expensive to moderate.

House of Seafood – Many consider this the best of Kauai's seafood restaurants. Potted plants, lots of wicker, and pastel fabrics give it a breezy, fashionable look. The menu offers 8 to 12 varieties of fresh fish daily, from 5:30 to 9:30 PM. Reservations advised. Poipu Kai Resort, Poipu (phone: 742-6433). Expensive to moderate.

Keoki's Paradise – Keoki left little to the imagination in putting together a Garden of Eden setting, complete with waterfalls, streams, and lush plantings of orchids and ferns. The ambience belies its setting at the entrance to a shopping center. Seafood and taco bar open from 4:30 PM to midnight; dinner, nightly from 5:30 to 10 PM, includes steak, seafood, and fresh fish. Reservations advised. Kiahuna Shopping Village (phone: 742-7534). Expensive to moderate.

Plantation Gardens – This restaurant, housed in a charming plantation manager's house from the 1930s, withstood the wrath of Hurricane Iwa, which so ravaged the surrounding gardens. The culinary emphasis here is on seafood — appetizers of sashimi and poached oysters, entrées of crab, shrimp, lobster, and abalone as well as deliciously prepared fresh catch of the day. Open for dinner daily. Reservations advised. Kiahuna Plantation, Poipu Beach (phone: 742-1695). Expensive to moderate.

Mango's – Contemporary cuisine with a tropical tilt — crispy scallops in sweet and sour sauce, a tropical fruit boat, sandwiches and salads — are served in a casual atmosphere. Open daily from 7 AM to 10 PM. Reservations advised. In Koloa (phone: 742-7377). Moderate.

Brennecke's – Kiawe broiled steak, chicken and seafood, fresh fish, pasta, and a generous salad bar are the specialties. Good food and service and a friendly atmosphere attract a spirited mix of locals and visitors, making it worth a recommendation. Hamburgers are the popular lunch item. Open daily for lunch, dinner (until 10 PM) and bar (until midnight weekdays, 2 AM on weekends). Reservations advised. Poipu Beach (phone: 742-7588). Moderate to inexpensive.

Flamingo's Cantina – People rave about the fajitas and Mexican specialties served in this place decorated with pink flamingoes and huge tropical fish in *Sea World*-size tanks. Open for dinner daily. Reservations unnecessary. On Nalu Rd.: Take the first left past Brennecke's Beach (phone: 742-9505). Moderate to inexpensive.

Wrangler – An Old West mood pervades this place, and island-grown beef and Mexican fare, both well prepared, make up the menu. Open daily, except Sundays, for lunch and dinner. Reservations advised. In the renovated Ako Building, on Waimea's main drag (phone: 338-1218). Moderate to inexpensive.

Fez's Pizza – The pizza alone would be worth a recommendation, but the lasagna is even more noteworthy. The perfect place to head for a casual, inexpensive dinner. Open daily from 11:30 AM to 9:30 PM. No reservations. Koloa (phone: 742-9096). Inexpensive.

Koloa Ice House – A great place for lunch or a light dinner, serving an interesting selection of sandwiches, soups, salads, and hot specials, such as nachos, lasagna, and chili. Open daily. No reservations. Koloa (phone: 742-6063). Inexpensive.

Mustard's Last Stand – The specialty is the hot dog, with lots of styles from which to choose. This is a good place for a quick midday snack. Open daily from 8:30 AM to 6:30 PM. No reservations. On Lawai Rd., just before it joins the main highway, next to Lee Sand's eelskin shop (phone: 332-7245).

Waimea Canyon

Down the western third of the island runs a 10-mile-long gash known as Waimea Canyon. The sculptor of this monumental work is the modest Waimea River, which, viewed from the rim of the canyon, looks like nothing more than a slim silver ribbon curled on the canyon floor. The river rises in the Alakai swamp, which, in turn, is fed by Mt. Waialeale. But on its way to the sea it cuts through much drier terrain. Instead of the jungle greens of the mountains, Waimea's tones are of the desert — the pink of the iron-rich soil and the pale green of the vegetation.

There are two roads leading to Waimea Canyon (and Kokee State Park beyond). The Waimea Canyon Road, starting in Waimea, affords some lovely backward glances at Waimea Bay and the flatlands of sugarcane fields. The Kokee Road, starting at Kekaha, leads through dry, scrubby land with lots of dog-eared cactus. Since it's interesting to see the change that just a few miles makes in the landscape of the island, drive up one road and down the other. Both are full of curves and hairpin turns, but are wide, well marked, and well graded. Go early in the morning before the traffic gets heavy. It's cooler then, too; the drive up can get warm by midmorning, even though it's always cool at the top of the canyon. Some days the canyon is enveloped in mist, which makes it difficult, if not impossible, to view anything from the lookouts. To avoid this, call ahead to Kokee State Park for the day's weather conditions (phone: 335-5871). If there's no answer, try the *Kokee Lodge* (phone: 335-6061).

About 12 miles up, from either Waimea or Kekaha, is the first lookout, from which you can see smaller canyons link up with Waimea. Another 2 or 3 miles beyond is Puu Hinahina lookout. Because people tend to stop at the first lookout, this one is a little less crowded. There are two views from here: one of the canyon and another facing southwest toward the island of Niihau.

If you want a close look at Waimea, the Kukui Trail, just a few miles before the first lookout, leads to the canyon floor. The hike down and back (5 miles altogether) can be made in a day, but there is an overnight shelter, the Wiliwili Camp, at the end of the trail where you can spend the night.

 SHOPPING: The old plantation towns of Hanapepe and Waimea are beginning to attract artists and artisans who appreciate their authenticity and charm. In Hanapepe, *Tropical Tantrum* (phone: 335-5110) features an excellent selection of hand-painted clothing, and *Collectibles & Fine Junque* (phone: 338-9855), on Kaumualii Hwy., and *Yesterday's Things,* on Poole St. (phone:

338-9855), offer the kind of back room browsing and bargains that make for enjoyable — and affordable — antiques hunting. There is also lots of Hawaiiana to be found in both places. In Waimea, *Lele Aka Gallery,* 3876 Hanapepe Rd. (no phone), is the place to check out. In Hanapepe, drop by the *James Hoyle Gallery* (phone: 335-3582), and Dave and Cheryl Saunders' *Images in Wood* (phone: 335-3737). The *Station* (phone: 335-5731), on Hwy. 50 just outside Hanapepe, features an unusual selection of Hawaiian-designed needlepoint kits and supplies.

Kokee State Park

Another few miles along this road will bring you to Kokee State Park, a 4,345-acre nature reserve that's a magnet for picnickers, hikers, campers, and others who just appreciate the sights and smells of nature at its purest.

There are more than a dozen hiking trails — ranging from one-tenth of a mile to 3½ miles — that lead through fragrant forests of koa, pine, and redwood trees, and hibiscus, mokihana, and maile, the vine and berries used to make Kauai brides' wedding leis. Native forest birds flit in and out, and wild goats roam at will. At the end of most trails, you're rewarded with a scenic vista and a secluded picnicking spot. Since some trails are still closed as a result of hurricane damage, it's best to call the ranger station in advance (phone: 335-5871).

You can camp here, in tents or in trailers, or rent one of the park's cabins for $35 ($45 for a newer, cedar cabin); an additional $8 ($9 in the new cabins) gets you firewood. There are a dozen cabins and they're very popular, so make reservations in advance, although a call *may* find cabins available even at the last minute (Kokee Lodge, PO Box 819, Waimea, Kauai, HI 96796; phone: 335-6061). You can also, with permission of the park rangers (their headquarters is at the entrance to the park), pick up 10 pounds of the small, tart plums that grow wild on Kauai. The season usually starts in June or July and lasts from a few weeks to 2 months.

If you have less time to give to Kokee, follow the road to the end of the park to Kalalau Valley Lookout. At 4,000 feet, the air is sweet and cool, and the view of the broad green valley opening out to the sea is dramatic. The small slip of surf at the foot of the valley is Kalalau Beach, the end of the 11-mile trail that starts at Haena State Park on the northern side of the island. The only other way to reach it is by sea. There are picnic tables and fireplaces at the lookout. A second lookout a mile farther (at the end of the road) offers equally expansive views and serves as a trailhead for several hikes along the ridge.

Kokee has its own small restaurant, *Kokee Lodge* (phone: 335-6061), serving modestly priced breakfasts and lunches daily, and excellent dinners on Fridays and Saturdays (try the fine, light homemade cornbread). Next door is Kokee Natural History Museum (phone: 335-9975), a pocket-sized natural history museum with a large relief map of western Kauai and exhibits of native birds, animals, and shells. The museum bookstore focuses on natural history, but also carries Hawaiian literature and poetry books. Open daily from 10 AM to 4 PM. No admission charge.

NIIHAU

For over a century, this small, private island, 17 miles off the leeward coast of Kauai, has been closed to the world. Besides an occasional doctor or government official, only invited guests of Niihau's 225 inhabitants are allowed to visit, and then only at the discretion of the owners, the Robinson family of Kauai. The only regular transportation to Niihau is a World War II landing craft that makes weekly runs to Port Allen on Kauai's southern shore, and securing passage on it is more difficult than getting an audience with the Pope. Curious outsiders who try to land their own boats on Niihau are firmly turned away. Today that isolation has been modestly compromised by helicopter tours offered by *Niihau Helicopters* (PO Box 370, Makaweli, HI 96769; phone: 335-3500). The helicopter was purchased by the Robinson family for use in medical emergencies and the tours are their way of subsidizing the cost of purchase and maintenance. After a sightseeing flight over the island, the helicopter lands near the northern coast, far from the island's only village, thereby maintaining Niihau's isolation and its uniquely Hawaiian lifestyle.

Niihau wasn't always so reclusive. When Captain Cook's ships, the *Discovery* and *Resolution,* drifted from anchorage in Kauai's Waimea Bay to neighboring Niihau, the islanders welcomed the strange white men from the "floating islands," as the Hawaiians referred to Cook's massive ships, and traded local yams and salt for seeds of foods then unknown in Hawaii — onions, melons, and pumpkins. Niihau went on supplying whalers and trading ships with yams, which were thought to be of superior quality to those grown on Kauai or Oahu, well into the 19th century.

Its isolation began in 1864, when King Kamehameha V sold the entire island for $10,000 to Elizabeth Sinclair, the daughter of a wealthy Scottish merchant and the widow of a New Zealand rancher. Mrs. Sinclair and her grown children (including Helen Sinclair Robinson, whose descendants now own the estate) turned the 46,000-acre island into a cattle and sheep ranch, employing the Hawaiians — who until then had worked their own yam and taro patches — as ranch hands and building a grand manor house with wood shipped from Boston around Cape Horn. Although Niihau's flat grassy meadows and numerous freshwater lakes — a rarity in the Hawaiian islands — proved ideal for ranching, the Sinclair clan soon tired of the heat and humidity and after a few years moved to Kauai, where they continued to run the Niihau ranch from the green valleys of that more temperate island.

Somewhere along the way, Mrs. Sinclair decided that the traditional Hawaiian way of life on Niihau should be preserved, which to her meant the lifestyle of the white ranchers, not the easygoing existence of the pre-Cook Hawaiians who lived on fish and poi and happily abandoned fields and labors whenever the waves were good for surfing. Succeeding generations have

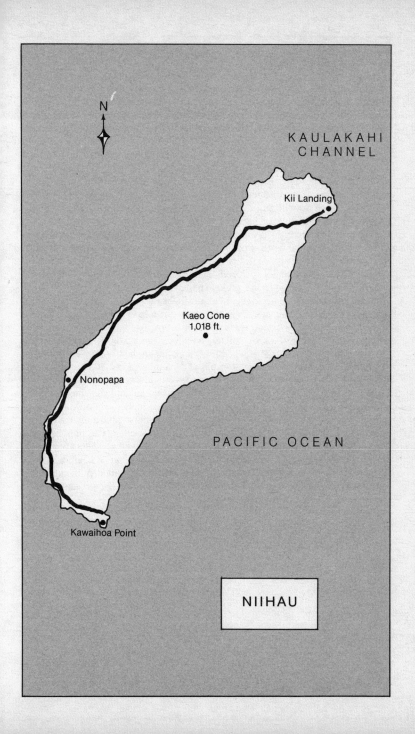

faithfully observed the old woman's wish, so that today Niihau still belongs to the 19th century.

The islanders, most of whom are full-blooded Hawaiians, all work for the ranch, living in small wooden houses more reminiscent of the Kansas frontier than Polynesia and sending their children to the ranch-run school. Life is simple and, by modern standards, backward. There's electricity at the school and the homestead kept by the Robinsons, but elsewhere oil lamps illuminate houses at night. There are no telephones or television sets, no shops, cinemas, or restaurants, and few motorized vehicles, with the medical helicopter a recent addition. The staples of life are provided by the ranch, although each family keeps a garden, fishes, and hunts wild pigs and turkeys to supplement the beef and mutton produced on the ranch. What Niihauans can't grow or hunt they often do without, even though they could catch the barge to Kauai to shop for commonplace luxuries.

The only private industry allowed is the making of Niihau shell leis, intricately worked garlands that often fetch thousands of dollars in galleries on the major islands. Every October the work stops and the islanders comb the beaches for the tiny, multicolored shells used to make the leis. The shells, which range from beige to hot pink, are then painstakingly sorted by size and quality and strung into necklaces of exquisite beauty. It takes weeks to fashion the more complex designs, such as the many-stranded kipona lei or the pikake lei, whose clusters resemble the pikake blossom. An intricate, multicolored strand can cost hundreds of dollars; however, there are enough Niihauans practicing this old art that it's possible to get a simple lei for as little as $15.

Because Niihau is a living example of Hawaii's recent past, it arouses a great deal of curiosity. But fearing a deluge of requests for access, the Robinsons resolutely refuse to allow any visits or interviews, and they have rebuffed attempts by the Hawaiian legislature to buy the island so it could be turned over to native Hawaiians for homesteading. There may come a time, however, when the family may have to reconsider the state's offer. The population of Niihau has been steadily dwindling over the years. No newcomers are allowed to settle, and youngsters, who attend high school on Kauai or at the Kamehameha School in Honolulu, seldom return permanently to the island once they've had a taste of the outside world. But for the present, Niihau remains an enigma, a mysterious outline on the horizon.

KAHOOLAWE

To an outsider, Kahoolawe seems a Hawaiian anomaly — an undesirable piece of real estate. Seven miles off the south coast of East Maui, Kahoolawe is a barren, windswept island whose only inhabitants are wild goats barely able to subsist on its sparse and scrubby vegetation and streams that dry up after the winter rains. Kahoolawe lies in the shadow of Maui's looming Haleakala, the dormant volcano that blocks most of the rain and cool breezes borne by the trade winds. Consequently, it's hot and humid during the day and cold at night. And to add to its natural disadvantages, for more than 40 years it's been pounded by naval artillery and bombers, using this bleak, unhappy island for target practice.

Yet Kahoolawe is one of the most hotly contested parcels of land in the state. Native Hawaiians want it back, partially because it's the most blatant example of *haole* disregard for their homeland and, more practically, because in an island state, land of any kind is valuable. Since 1976, when a group called Protect Kahoolawe Ohana ("family" in Hawaiian) occupied the island against the express orders of the navy, Kahoolawe has become the symbol of native Hawaiian consciousness. Although the navy has made some concessions, such as allowing limited fishing and visitation rights, it refuses to surrender what is a supremely convenient site for practice bombing. After all, Pearl Harbor, the headquarters for all US military operations in the Pacific, is just 110 miles away.

The Ohana wants the island to be set aside for cultural and educational purposes. Kahoolawe, named in ancient times after Kanaloa, one of the four major Hawaiian gods, is a sacred island, mentioned often in the chants and legends passed down through the ages. At one time, all travelers to Tahiti stopped here to perform rituals before continuing on their way. And as late as 1874, King David Kalakaua was sent here by his *kahuna* (priest) to purge himself before he ascended the throne. Thanks to the isolation imposed by the navy's bombing, many of the ancient temples and fishing shrines are in excellent repair, and the Ohana sees the island as an unprecedented opportunity to add to the knowledge of their past. While attention has shifted from the issue in recent years, the future will demand a resolution.

Although the bombing, which is occasionally audible and visible from Maui and Lanai, continues, the Ohana has scored some impressive successes in its efforts to regain civilian control of Kahoolawe. It forced the navy to make a comprehensive study of the environmental impact of the bombing and to conduct a survey of the archaeological sites. It also managed, in March 1981, to get the island named a National Historic Site — the only one, Ohana members like to point out, that is routinely bombed by the government that decided it was worthy of protection. The Ohana also won the right to visit the island 4 days a month for 10 months of the year. During these times, men,

KEALAIKAHIKI CHANNEL

ALALAKEIKI
CHANNEL

Lua Makika
1,477 ft.

● Kealaikahiki Point

N

PACIFIC OCEAN

KAHOOLAWE

women, and children gather on Kahoolawe's northeast shore to celebrate ancient festivals, reenacting as closely as possible the dress, chants, and rituals of their ancestors; to explore, with military guides, the old ruins; or to simply "talk story," the Hawaiians' traditional way of passing on their heritage.

Not even the Ohana foresees the return of a permanent population to Kahoolawe, although the island supported ranches before World War II and its soil has been judged to be particularly good for modern agriculture. Kahoolawe has been uninhabited for more years than it has been home to humans. The ancient Hawaiians lived here until the 13th century, when an apparent shift in climate forced them to move to the well-watered valleys of the other islands. Except for fishermen, who used Kahoolawe as a temporary base while they fished the rich waters around it, the island was uninhabited until the 1830s, when it became a penal colony for men. The inmates were so brazen about raiding East Maui settlements for food, however, that after a short time King Kamehameha III decided to abandon the practice of exiling criminals. Kahoolawe was then settled by cattle ranchers, who moved to the island in the 1870s and stayed until the US government confiscated it for bombing and landing practice after the attack on Pearl Harbor. With the navy's takeover, the island became progressively less habitable. The wild goat population grew uncontrollably, destroying the fragile ground cover and thus exacerbating soil erosion. And without man's management of the water resources, the island became ever more parched, until today much of it is a no-man's-land.

Maui County, which would also like control of the island, is considering several plans that would return it to human use by reforesting, decreasing the goat population, and, of course, halting the bombing. Who will ultimately win this tug of war is anybody's guess. But there's a chance, albeit a slim one, that the rich archaeological sites of the island won't be off-limits to visitors forever.

DIVERSIONS

For the Body

Dream Beaches

The best beaches of Hawaii? Even the ones considered only ordinary by *akamai* (in-the-know) residents are often exquisite by mainland standards, with their bright seascapes of blue skies and even bluer waters, strands of white or black sand ringed by sea palms, pandanus, and ironwood pines, and an ocean surf ranging from gentle baby swells to monster rollers up to 30 feet high.

The beachcombing possibilities in Hawaii are endless. More than 1,500 varieties of shells wash up on the islands' beaches, and in some areas the remnants of wrecked ships can also be found. Some coastlines have wave-washed rocky shores and lava ledges as well as exposed tidepools and shallow reef flats. Exploring these areas for marine invertebrates can be a fascinating alternative to sun worshiping. Protective gloves and shoes are recommended for wading in tidepools and walking on the reefs.

To avoid angering residents by trespassing on private property, look for Public Access to Beach signs. If you're searching for secluded beaches, check around; an unmarked road cut through a sugar plantation will often lead to an isolated, heavenly oceanside site.

Be mindful of sea conditions in Hawaii. Rip tides, dangerous undertows, sharp coral bottoms, and other such hazards are not always readily discernible to *malihinis* (newcomers). So check with lifeguards, surfers, or residents before entering the water.

OAHU

WAIKIKI: This 2-mile arc of sand lined with resort hotels is probably the single most famous beach in the world. Waikiki is relatively clean and free of litter but is often carpeted instead with large numbers of sunbathers. Replacement sand that's been trucked in to bolster "the Beach" is constantly washed out to sea and has altered the contour of the offshore ocean floor. Consequently, the shape and size of Waikiki's famous surfing waves are changing. Surfboard rentals, catamaran sails, and outrigger canoe rides are available at concession stands up and down the beach. The best sections of beach lie closer to Diamond Head, a 15-minute walk from central Waikiki. An acquired taste by day, Waikiki is a great place to go for a moonlight stroll, and the hours immediately after dawn make rising early worth the effort.

ALA MOANA PARK: Honolulu residents and Waikiki exiles flock to this 76-acre park to build sand castles, fly kites, or spread a picnic in a grassy area. Safe, reef-sheltered waters make it a popular place to bring kids. Those bored with sun and surf activities can walk across the street to the Ala Moana Shopping Center, a huge complex of more than 200 stores.

HANAUMA BAY BEACH PARK: An extinct volcanic crater shaped into a huge outdoor aquarium by sea erosion, Hanauma Bay is one of Oahu's top areas for underwater exploration. Now a designated marine preserve, it has sand pockets within the reef that provide good swimming, especially the Keyhole, and a small inlet with a natural rock-carved hole called the Toilet Bowl. Bring food: The fish will eat out of your hand on the reef. In addition, the tidepools contain many fascinating creatures.

Snorkelers should be wary of a turbulent area of the bay known as Witches Brew, as well as the Molokai Express, a strong current that sweeps across the outer edge of the bay. Movie buffs (especially Elvis Presley fans) will recognize Hanauma as the backdrop for the 1961 film *Blue Hawaii*.

GOAT ISLAND (MOKUAUIA BEACH): Simply wade across a narrow strait of water — on a calm day, at low tide — to reach this small island off the North Shore's Kalanai Point. (Wear sneakers to protect your feet from the coral, and don't attempt to cross if the surf is rough.) The island's sandy beach is protected by an offshore reef that makes swimming ideal, especially for children. Goat Island is a state bird refuge, with many bird species in its ironwood trees.

SUNSET: Along with other legendary North Shore surf sites such as Waimea Bay, Banzai Beach (home of the deadly Pipeline), and Ehukai Beach Park, Sunset is where towering mountains of water crash into shore during the winter. One of Oahu's largest tracts of sand, Sunset Beach stretches for 2 miles. Be aware that swimming in certain stretches can be dangerous, except for a few weeks in the summer. It may be wiser just to pack a picnic lunch and bring a pair of binoculars to watch the world's most daring surfers challenge the largest surfable waves on earth.

HAWAII

PUNALUU BEACH PARK: In the Kau district between Kona and Hilo, Punaluu is a black sand beach adjacent to a lagoon. Despite an occasional stop by tour buses, it attracts few swimmers or sunbathers. Check with the lifeguard or with residents before wading in; strong currents can make swimming dangerous here. A short distance away is Ninole Cove, a miniature (and secluded) version of its big brother that is ideal for private outings.

OLD AIRPORT: This is one of the few fine beaches Mother Nature deposited along the Big Island's Kona Coast. The skin diving in this area is unrivaled for underwater beauty. Protected from prevailing trade winds by the twin volcanic peaks of Mauna Loa and Mauna Kea, the water at Old Airport (and its neighboring beaches) is usually smooth. Near the *King Kamehameha* hotel and Kailua's former airport, this white sand beach is guarded by a rocky entrance. Skin divers who negotiate it successfully are rewarded by marine life and coral formations that are mesmerizing.

ANAEHOOMALU: A wide crescent of beach separates an iridescent bay from ancient coastal fish ponds. Full beach services are available, including snorkel gear and Hobie Cat rentals. A road provides public access to this central beach within the Waikoloa Resort.

MILOLII: On the southern Kona Coast near the fishing village of the same name is one of the state's most authentically Hawaiian villages. Fishermen still salt and dry their day's catch in the hot sun, usually in the front yards of their ramshackle homes. And though the rough-hewn beach does not have acres of sand, the coastal reef offers good snorkeling and the tidepools along the shoreline are worlds unto themselves. (To reach the nearby sandy beach, pick up the coastal trail at the end of the Milolii Beach road, a 10-minute walk.)

HAPUNA: About half an hour north of Kailua, this double-crescent beach has fine sunbathing and swimming, although the current is strong. Full picnic, shower, and barbecue facilities make it a popular family beach. Just south of the *Mauna Kea Beach* hotel.

MAUI

KAPALUA BAY: This small crescent of golden sand at the foot of the *Kapalua Bay* hotel on West Maui is lovely. Coconut palms surround the beach, an entrancing view of Molokai faces it, and rocky points reach out into the bay on either side, creating gentle, sparkling, and clear inshore waters that attract snorkelers and divers in addition to swimmers. Given its location in the midst of civilization, it's not a beach where sunbathers will ever be alone, but it's one worth sharing.

KAANAPALI: Hotels and condominiums line most of this beach, which edges the Kaanapali resort for 2 miles and then extends north for another mile. Hotels and condos notwithstanding, the strip of sand remains pretty as a picture, with the less crowded north beach providing a backdrop of lawns, golf courses, sugarcane fields, and the West Maui mountains. The offshore islands are visible across the azure water. Black Rock, an outcropping of lava on which the *Sheraton Maui* is built, divides the beach in two, and the skin diving in this vicinity rivals that of the Big Island's Kona Coast for undersea splendor. Most of the beach is good for swimming, as long as bathers heed the warning signs that hotels put up when the surf is rough.

KAMAOLE PARKS I, II, III: Conveniently set along South Kihei Road on East Maui are three fine, wide sandy beaches framed from afar by the blue-green mass of the West Maui mountains. The Kamaole beaches are especially popular with families and new swimmers and may be quite crowded on weekends. The stretch of beach at the Maalaea end of the coast is much less crowded, though the shallower waters are less appealing to swimmers. The parks have picnic areas, showers, and restrooms, and there's even a playground for kids at Kamaole III.

WAILEA RESORT: Besides its hotels and a host of plush condominiums, the Wailea resort has five lovely beaches — Keawakapu, Mokapu, Ulua, Wailea, and Polo — strung along 2 miles of coastline. Like the Kamaole beaches to the north, they have no protective reef. Swimming is possible, however, as long as the kona winds aren't blowing. All have clear water for snorkeling, which is especially good around the rocky points that separate them. Because of its position between the two hotels, Ulua Beach is the most heavily trafficked, but a backing of dunes and a certain amount of seclusion can be found by heading toward the beaches to the south. Limited public access parking is available.

MAKENA: It used to be known as Oneloa Beach, and since Oneloa is Hawaiian for "long sands," that was the perfect moniker for this very long, very wide swath of beachfront south of Wailea. Bounded by cliffs and a scrub forest of kiawe trees, Makena is possibly Maui's most beautiful beach. It's blessed with good underwater visibility for snorkelers, but it, too, has no protective reef and is, therefore, to be approached with care during heavy surf. Makena was a popular hippie hangout during the 1960s (it was even called Hippie Beach for a while), but the impromptu settlements built by the counterculture crowd are long gone, replaced in part by nearby resort development. Fortunately, the beach remains undeveloped — a result, no doubt, of continuing efforts to protect it by making it a state park. A rocky outcrop separates Oneloa from Little Makena, long a peaceful nudist hideaway. A recent court ruling has stopped unwarranted police raids against the nudists.

SEVEN POOLS: A few miles south of Hana, in the Kipahulu section of Haleakala National Park, are the well-known plunge pools that are often referred to as the Seven Sacred Pools. There are more than seven of them, and though there is no evidence that they were ever sacred, ancient Hawaiians certainly must have splashed around in them. The rocks bordering the pools are slippery when wet, but the water is refreshingly cool, however you manage to enter. The grove of kamani trees bordering the pools, the view down the Oheo Stream to the rough ocean (too rough for swimming), and the view upstream toward Haleakala make this an enchanting spot in one of Maui's most beautiful regions.

MOLOKAI

MOOMOMI: Moomomi Bay is a sizable indentation along Molokai's west coast, sheltering one of the finest beaches and congregations of sand dunes in the state.

Freshwater pools are nestled in some of the dunes, though most folks spend their time snorkeling along the reef or beachcombing for driftwood. Moomomi is rarely crowded because it is difficult to find: The right fork of Farrington Avenue (a dirt road near the beach) must be followed to the park.

PAPOHAKU: This is one of the largest and widest (and prettiest) sandy beaches in Hawaii. The vast expanse of sand is offset by undulating dunes covered by scrub growth. Near the *Kaluakoi* hotel on the west coast of the island, Papohaku is not always safe for swimming (rip currents are prevalent), but the beach is simply too beautiful to pass up.

LANAI

HULOPOE: Though by no means its least crowded park, Hulopoe is probably Lanai's finest beach. A long, wide arc of sand fringed by kiawe trees and marked by a pair of lava points, Hulopoe has a partially protected swimming area, as well as a large tidal pool blasted out of the lava shoreline that serves as a children's swimming pool. Colorful tropical fish are trapped in the shoreline's tidal pools each day by the outgoing tide. Good snorkeling and scuba diving can be found just offshore. There are also beachfront tables for picnics. Hotel and condominium development is underway on adjacent land, but the beach has been set aside as a park with public access.

SHIPWRECK: By driving along Keomuku Road until it forks near the shoreline, visitors can discover 8 miles of undisturbed berm and dunes stretching from Polihua Beach to Kahokunui. Powerful winds off Lanai's north coast have driven many boats up on the reef, from great wooden schooners to World War II tankers, and the flotsam from these wrecks eventually drifts in to shore. In addition to the free pickings on the beach, lobsters can be taken near the reef by snorkelers with quick hands.

KAUAI

MAHAULEPU: Once-isolated Mahaulepu now has the *Hyatt Regency Kauai* as a neighbor. Still, the setting remains somewhat wild, with dramatic coastal panoramas. Winds and currents deposit beach glass and driftwood on the shore, and who knows, you might even find a bottle with a message in it. Mahaulepu's reef-protected water offers ideal swimming conditions, too. The film *Islands in the Stream,* starring George C. Scott, was shot here.

POLIHALE STATE PARK: At the end of a long, winding (and bumpy) cane road on the west end of Kauai, Polihale is a great place to soak up the rays in relative peace. The beach is known for its extraordinary sunsets, a great variety of seashells, a distant view of the island of Niihau, and its unique geographical position as the westernmost park in America.

ANINI PARK: In the Hanalei area, with a protective reef 200 yards offshore that provides placid waters for safe swimming. That, and its picnic area, make Anini especially popular with families. Shell collectors also find it rewarding. Folks looking for a place to get away from it all should take the shore road, on either side of Anini, to one of the numerous unnamed, rarely visited, very secluded small beaches.

LUMAHAI: This is where Mitzi Gaynor tried to wash that man right out of her hair in the movie version of *South Pacific.* Lumahai is a jewel of a beach tucked into a small cove surrounded by lush green hills and hala trees. Beachgoers must descend a precipitous dirt trail that winds down the hillside to reach it, but it's worth the effort. Black lava rock formations at either end of the beach create fairly protected swimming waters, and, pity poor Mitzi, the setting is certainly not conducive to forgetting. If you had to pick the single most beautiful beach in Hawaii, Lumahai would be it. Two even more isolated beaches can be reached on foot from Lumahai.

Sensational Surfing

"Let's go surfing now, everybody's learning how, come on a safari with me." So the Beach Boys sang of surfing's heyday during the 1960s, when "woodies" (old wood-sided station wagons loaded with surfboards), "hanging ten" (putting all ten toes over the front edge of the board), and bleached-blond surfers were the rage. Interest in the sport may have peaked on the mainland, but in Hawaii surfing remains an endless summer of sandy beaches, open-air snack bars, and near-perfect surfing conditions.

The individual Hawaiian islands are actually the tops of volcanic mountains rising from the ocean floor, and without a continental shelf to slow them down or shrink them, the North Pacific's winter swells attain monstrous proportions by the time they reach Hawaii's coastline. The raw energy of these great rollers combines with the contour of the ocean bottom to create the biggest (and best-shaped) surfing waves in the world.

But the beginning surfer need not feel left out in Hawaii. Oahu's Waikiki Beach, as well as some ocean parks on neighbor islands, have relatively tame conditions where, in a short time, a novice can learn how to balance the board — and ultimately how to catch a wave. (It takes years to refine technique and develop a personal style.)

One-hour group instruction rates range from $10 to $15, including the use of a board. Private lessons are higher. Surfboard rentals start at $8 per hour and go to $20 per day. The Morey Doyle boards are recommended for "gremlins" (novice surfers). These boards are made from a soft fiber foam that is more buoyant and stable than the hard, fiberglass boards. (A hard stringer running from tip to tail makes these boards firm enough to stand on.) "Boogie boards," short body-surfing boards made of soft polyurethane that are ridden in a kneeling or prone position, are also popular in the islands. Rental fees range from $5 to $12 for a full day.

The appeal of surfing escapes definition. It is a spontaneous, creative activity that is never the same twice because each wave has its own characteristics. Surfboards have come a long way from the long flat wooden planks used by Hawaiian royalty, who surfed to prove the worthiness of their leadership, but the sensation hasn't changed in 200 years. Said Captain Cook of a surfer he observed in 1777: "I could not help concluding that this man felt the most supreme pleasure while he was driven so fast and so smoothly by the sea." So if the surf's up and you're so inclined, go catch a wave.

OAHU: Just the thought of this island is guaranteed to raise goose pimples on any serious surfer's surface. In part because of its fortuitous location, Oahu has some of the finest surfing breaks in the world. The North Shore, where giant 30-foot waves arrive in the winter, is still the ultimate proving ground for professionals and top amateurs.

Beginners confine themselves to the mellow swells at Waikiki Beach, where professional "beach boys" are available for surfing lessons at a number of concessions along the beach. The instructors at *Waikiki Beach Services,* for example, go through the motions of surfing on land with students before wading into the "soup" (foamy white water) to get the feel of the board underfoot. "We eliminate the fear aspect of the sport," said one teacher. Once gremlins learn to stand with their feet parallel and wide apart, their knees bent, and their weight forward, they are in position to ride a wave. Willing students with good balance can learn to surf in an hour. Catching a wave takes a bit more practice, but the sensation of being carried along on the board is indescribably exhilarating. Information: Waikiki Beach Services, c/o Outrigger Reef Hotel, 2169

Kalia Rd., Honolulu, HI 96815 (phone: 923-3111, ext. 4940), or Sheraton Waikiki, 2255 Kalakaua Ave., Honolulu, HI 96815 (phone: 922-4422).

In addition to Waikiki, Oahu's other top beginner and intermediate beaches include Ala Moana, Diamond Head, and Koko Head. Black Point near Diamond Head, with the great brown and green slopes of the eroded volcanic cone overlooking the surf, is one of the most beautiful settings for wave riding in the islands.

The *Haleiwa Surf Center* at the Alii Beach Park on Oahu's North Shore is a water sports center run by the island's Department of Parks and Recreation where surfing (including using the board) is taught *free of charge* on weekends. The beach park is well south of the more famous North Shore sites, where the waves are often higher than most of the homes in the area! The surf at Alii Beach averages 2 to 4 feet, ideal for beginners. Information: Haleiwa Surf Center, 66167 Haleiwa Rd., Haleiwa, HI 96712 (phone: 637-5051).

When the great North Pacific swells roll in from Alaska and Siberia in late fall and early winter, the cream of the sport gathers on the North Shore for pro tournaments and competitions. The three top sites, strictly for experts, are Sunset Beach, Waimea Bay, and the Banzai Pipeline. Waves break in a curl and envelop surfers in a tube at the famed Pipeline, but this is probably the most dangerous surfing site on earth, as surfers risk being thrown onto the sharp coral reef bottom. Mistakes here are costly — and painful.

HAWAII: The Big Island is rarely mentioned as a top place to surf, but kona winds and northern swells can produce exceptional conditions in the vicinity of Hilo Bay.

Orchid Land Surfboards is one of the few board rental outlets on the island. Private lessons (Sundays are best) are a summer possibility. Good surfing sites can also be found on the Big Island's South Shore beaches.

With few exceptions, the island's Kona coastline is not suitable for novices. There is lots of lava, but unfortunately very little sand for soft landings on the leeward side of the island. Top surfers gravitate to Banyans at Kailua Bay, where a Masters Tournament is held in the winter. Lyman's Cove also has excellent surf up to 10 feet.

"Boogie boarders" and body-surfers usually head to Magic Sands Beach Park, where wave riders can glide into a near fluorescent white sandy beach. Information: Orchid Land Surfboards, 832 Kilauea Ave., Hilo, HI 96720 (phone: 935-1533); Pacific Vibrations, 75-5755 Alii Dr., Kailua-Kona, HI 96740 (phone: 329-4140); Hobie Sports Kona, Kona Inn Shopping Village, Kailua-Kona, HI 96740 (phone: 329-1001).

MAUI: Though windsurfing has swept the island, stalwart wave riders still frequent a number of top surfsites on the Valley Isle, depending on the season. In the winter, capable surfers head north to Honolua Bay and Hookipa Beach Park near Paia. (*Hookipa* means "hospitality" in Hawaiian, but this surfsite is anything but gracious when the swells rise up in huge walls of rolling water.) Come summer, the action gravitates to Maui's more southerly shores, where Kaanapali Beach, Lahaina Harbor, and Maalaea Bay are the top gathering spots. Ambitious surfers fasten their boards to overhead car racks and travel the coast road between Kaanapali and Makena in search of uncrowded beaches with perfect waves. They are seldom disappointed. Little-known hot spots, with names like Shark Pit, Hot Sands, and Breakwall, are the places to check out.

Gremlins should head to Lahaina, Maui's surfing center, where *Lahaina Beach Center* rents Morey Doyle boards, which simplify the beginner's first encounter with surfing. Inquire at the shop about lessons. Information: Lahaina Beach Center, 505 Front St., Lahaina, HI 96761 (phone: 661-5762). For Kihei or Wailea, contact *Lightning Bolt,* 55 Kaahumanu Ave., Kahului, HI 96732 (phone: 877-3484).

KAUAI: The Garden Isle is only a step or two behind Oahu as the best surfing destination in the state. It is also the state's best-kept surfing secret, with few professional tournaments and little media exposure. Aging surfers retire to Kauai because of its lovely waves, ideal weather, and uncrowded beaches.

Surf shops (and good surf) are concentrated in two areas. On the south shore, Poipu Beach near Makahuena Point has several fine surfing sites that come to life in July and August, when summer swells of 6 to 8 feet attract advanced practitioners.

Kapaa, on Kauai's windward coast, also has fine surfing. The mouth of the Wailua River south of Anahola Bay has good waves in the summer for surfers who have mastered the basics. On Kauai's north shore, the ferocious winter surf challenges the best and most daring riders. The top surf site is Hanalei Bay, where the rollers scrape the sky from October through January. Tunnels, a site frequented by locals near Na Pali Coast State Park, has winter surf conditions similar to those at the famous Banzai Pipeline on Oahu's North Shore.

Pedal & Paddle in Hanalei (phone: 826-9069), *South Shore Activities* at the *Sheraton* in Poipu (phone: 742-6873), and *Progressive Expressions* in Koloa (phone: 742-6041) all rent surfboards and can probably arrange lessons.

Windsurfing

 The fastest growing sport in the world, windsurfing has found a special home in Hawaii. This is because the ideal learning conditions for beginners include a bay with a wide sandy beach, smooth warm water, and a light breeze; Hawaii has all of these elements in abundance. Most of the islands also have prevailing onshore, or sea, breezes that blow at an angle to shore and prevent a careless novice from being swept out to sea.

In addition to its ideal beginner conditions, Hawaii has some of the best expert and competition waters in the world. "Surf-sailing" and wave-jumping, advanced techniques using wind *and* waves to produce an exciting (and often airborne) ride, are among the windsurfing variations that have been pioneered in Hawaii.

Instructors say novices require a minimum of 2 hours of lessons to acquaint themselves with the rudiments of the sport; dancers, sailors, and skiers tend to pick it up most quickly. One Oahu instructor thinks that women often make rapid improvement because they "plug into the feel of the wind and its effect on the sail without trying to resort to sheer strength." Windsurfing lessons start at $30 for a 2-hour session. A half hour is usually spent on a ground simulator to learn wind theory. Windsurfer rentals start at $10 per hour with half- and full-day discounts available.

OAHU: The Kailua Beach Park area, on the windward side of the island, lays claim to some of the finest windsurfing grounds in the world. A mere 30 minutes by car from Honolulu, Kailua is a gathering place for hot shots, gurus, and top board and sail designers, all of whom congregate in much the same way that surfers did on the North Shore in the 1950s to test-ride new fiberglass boards. World Cup windsurfing competitions are held here each year.

Windsurfing Hawaii's *Kailua Beach School* runs 3-hour classes ($40) and provides equipment rentals for beginner and advanced sailors. Because there are no hotels on its beaches, the Kailua area is relatively uncrowded and, therefore, ideal for windsurfing. From the water, sailors see a white sand beach ringed by palm trees, with the vivid green and often cloud-encircled peaks of the Koolau Range in the distance. For those who want to purchase a sailboard, the *Windsurfing Hawaii* shop, 5 minutes from the beach, probably has the best selection of beginner and high-performance custom boards and accessories in the islands; Waikiki hotel pick-ups are provided. Information: Kailua Beach School, 156C Hamakua Dr., Kailua, HI 96734 (phone: 261-3539). Waikiki departures, with lessons over in Kailua, including 5 hours of board use, are offered by *Aloha Windsurfing*, 437 Launiu St., Honolulu, HI 96815 (phone: 926-1185).

HAWAII: *Captain Nemo's Ocean Sports,* which runs a windsurfing concession from the *Royal Waikoloan* on the Kona Coast, is on a large crescent beach that serves as an ideal launching point for novices. A reef across the entrance of tiny Anaehoomalu Bay protects the waters and keeps surf activity to a minimum. The mountains behind the bay shield it from strong winds. Sailors have views of Mauna Loa and Mauna Kea, the island's two large volcanic cones that are snow-capped in winter. The area typically receives a light breeze in the morning, a moderate wind at midday, and calmer winds again in late afternoon. Good onshore winds prevail most of the year, though conditions are best in the spring, summer, and fall. *Captain Nemo's* has equipment for children 10 to 12 years old who want to try the sport. Introductory lessons and certification courses are available. Information: Captain Nemo's Ocean Sports, PO Box 3291, Waikoloa, HI 96743 (phone: 885-5555).

MAUI: The *Maui Sailing Center* teaches windsurfing on Maalaea Bay, on the southern shore of Maui's central valley. Since this is on the leeward side of the island, windsurfers must contend with offshore, or land, breezes, which are more fitful and less constant than prevailing onshore breezes. For this reason, the school's 2-hour introductory course starts out with an hour spent on a land simulator and an hour spent in the bay on a sailboard tethered to an underground line.

The school claims a 100% success rate for novices. Within an hour, most students can pull up the boom and sail back and forth in a straight line. The sight of the tiny volcanic island of Molokini, as well as the feathery kiawe trees shading some of Maui's best sandy beaches, makes Maalaea Bay one of the loveliest places to sail. The season runs year-round, though there are periods when strong winds make it impossible to take beginners out. Information: Maui Sailing Center, 101 N. Kihei Rd., Kihei, HI 96753 (phone: 879-5935). *Magic Maui Windsurfing* has rentals and lessons available from Kanaha Beach on central Maui's north shore. Information: The Maui Windsurfing Co., 520 Keolani Pl., Kahului, HI 96732 (phone: 877-4816).

KAUAI: *Pedal and Paddle,* Ching Young Village, Hanalei, HI 96714 (phone: 826-9069); *Hanalei Sailboards,* 5-5016 Kuhio Hwy., Hanalei, HI 96714 (phone: 826-9732); and *Waiohai Beach Services,* Poipu, HI 96756 (phone: 742-9511) can each arrange for windsurfing rentals and lessons.

MOLOKAI: If you're proficient, give George Peabody a call for escorted runs and lessons, departing his Waialua lagoon-front home for windsurfing along Molokai's south coast. Information: George Peabody, Star Rte. 329, Kaunakakai, HI 96748 (phone: 558-8253).

Best Depths: Snorkeling and Scuba Diving

As beautiful as the Hawaiian landscape is, some of the islands' most ravishing scenery is found beneath the sea. A fascinating kaleidoscope of coral-lined caves, great lava tubes, and cathedral-sized archways, Hawaii's underwater terrain is also home to a varied and interesting marine life, with a cast of characters ranging from giant spiny puffers to barber pole shrimp. The overall effect of this sensate world on the visiting snorkeler or scuba diver is one of nonstop, wide-eyed wonder, for nowhere are nature's gifts of life, movement, and beauty more concentrated than around the islands' coral reefs.

Underwater visibility, especially in the outer islands, is usually 100 feet or more. Water temperature is 74 to 80F, ideal for extended explorations. A scuba diver can bring his or her own mask, fins, snorkel, wet suit, regulator with pressure gauge, and buoyancy compensator. Heavier equipment (tanks, weights, backpack, etc.) can be rented, though most dive shops make scuba equipment available only to certified divers. Certification courses, that is, those accredited by the National Association of Underwater Instructors (NAUI) or the Professional Association of Diving Instructors (PADI), are offered by most major dive concessions.

Scuba prices range from $45 for an introductory dive to $275 and up for a 5-day scuba certification class. One-, two- or three-tank dives can be arranged. Most excursions are run from 25- to 42-foot boats with open decks, from which diving is easy. Because a good portion of Hawaii's sea life is nocturnal, night dives are popular. Underwater camera rentals are available at most dive shops.

Snorkelers can bring their own masks, fins, and snorkels, or rent all necessary gear from local dive shops. Beach or boat snorkel tours start at $20.

Because of the fragility of the underwater environment, undersea explorers are strongly requested to "take only pictures, leave only bubbles."

OAHU: Oahu is the most dived island in the Hawaiian chain and is especially good for novices seeking instruction. (There is an abundance of reputable dive shops in Honolulu.) Hanauma Bay, on the island's southeast shore between Diamond Head and Koko Head, is probably Oahu's best snorkeling and scuba divesite. Though daily conditions on this side of the island are variable, Hanauma Bay is protected from water-disturbing winds and enjoys near-perfect dive conditions year-round. Most divers make a beach entry to the inner reef lagoon, though visibility and the variety of fish increase dramatically in the outer bay, where a maze of canyon-life surge channels can be explored. The fish here are quite tame and can be fed from your hand. Hanauma Bay is ideal for the beginning skin or scuba diver. *Snorkel Hanauma Bay* (phone: 955-5680) provides 4 round trips a day from Waikiki hotels; rental gear is available.

Another top site on the southeast shore is Fantasy Reef, off Kahala, where intermediate and advanced divers can ride the back of a turtle or watch manta rays glide effortlessly through the water.

Because of the great distance between beach and reef, diving on Oahu's windward shore is best accomplished from a boat. Manana (Rabbit) Island and Makapuu Point attract experienced divers to depths of 60 feet, where the basalt rock bottom is overgrown with coral. Sharks are sighted here occasionally, but seldom threaten divers.

Oahu's North Shore offers good diving opportunities from late spring to late summer, especially for beginners. (In the winter, the waves at Waimea Bay and other top surfing beaches reach gigantic proportions, creating unsafe conditions.) Large fish and brightly colored sponges can be identified at Pupukea (Shark's Cove), known for its many caves and steep drop-offs (but not its sharks; few are ever sighted here). Nearby Three Tables, accessible by beach entry, has several pockmarked caves and is inhabited by schools of small fish.

In addition to Waikiki Beach, Oahu's top snorkeling sites include Black Point near Diamond Head, where ancient lava flows protrude into the ocean and form the basis of a coral reef teeming with life, and Kahe Point on the Waianae (leeward) coast, where the large shallow-water coral reef gives skin divers enough underwater terrain to keep them happy all day.

Information: *Dan's Dive Shop,* 660 Ala Moana Blvd., Honolulu, HI 96813 (phone: 536-6181); *Waikiki Diving,* 420 Nahua St., Honolulu, HI 96815 (phone: 922-7188); *Waikiki Diving Center,* 1734 Kalakaua Ave., Honolulu, HI 96815 (phone: 955-5151); *Aloha Dive Shop,* Koko Marina, Hawaii Kai, Honolulu, HI 96825 (phone: 395-5922); *South Seas Aquatics,* Ward Warehouse, 1050 Ala Moana Blvd., Honolulu, HI 96814 (phone: 538-3854); *Steve's Diving Adventures,* 1860 Ala Moana Blvd., Honolulu, HI 96814 (phone: 947-8900); *Leeward Dive Center,* 87066 Farrington Hwy., Waianae, HI 96792 (phone: 696-3414).

HAWAII: The Big Island's Kona Coast offers visiting divers some of the most exciting underwater formations and marine life in the Pacific. Because the Kona Coast is protected from trade winds by three high volcanic peaks, surface conditions are usually placid — and, therefore, ideal for diving. The shallow reefs along the coastline are especially good for snorkeling, though most sites accommodate both snorkelers and scuba divers.

Working south from Kawaihae, Hawaii's top sites for skin diving include: Puako Boat Ramp (lovely coral formations); Keauhou Cliffs (large chunks of lava shaped like giant blocks of granite); Anaehoomalu Bay (a beautiful beach with clear, calm water; be sure to duck under the windsurfers); Kahaluu Beach Park (popular with families who like to feed cheese to the fish inside a natural breakwater); and Hookena Beach Park (worth the bumps and grinds caused by the tortuous access road).

Even though some of the Big Island's top scuba diving sites suffered damage from hurricane Iwa in 1982 and still bear the scars, they remain the stuff of legends: Kaumoo Bay, its lava arches and deep ravines inhabited by Hawaiian lobster and Kona crabs; Red Hills, once part of an ancient volcanic cinder cone, its bottom decorated with large flat lava mesas; the Tubes, an offshore area honeycombed with long lava tunnels, some of them as large as a two-car garage; the Arches, named for eight sculptured lava archways formed by the rapid cooling of molten lava poured into the sea long ago; and Old Airport Beach Park near Kailua, known for its coral archways, lava tubes, and excellent spearfishing.

Other top dive sites south of Kailua include: Magic Sands Beach Park, where the sand disappears in winter and miraculously returns in summer; Kealakekua Bay, the landing site of Captain Cook and the current home of a pair of tame moray eels (named Orville and Wilbur by locals) who love to pose for photographs (provided you feed them some squid); and City of Refuge, the former religious sanctuary for defeated warriors where diving is popular behind the visitors' center and off the boat ramp.

Night dives along the Kona Coast give adventurous scubaphiles equipped with hand-held lights a chance to visit caverns to see creatures that only emerge at night. There is something eerily exciting about scuba diving after dark. It is also a flash photographer's delight. Information: *Gold Coast Divers,* Kona Inn Shopping Village, Kailua-Kona, HI 96740 (phone: 329-1328); *Dive Makai Charters,* PO Box 2955, Kailua-Kona, HI 96745 (phone: 329-2025); *Jack's Diving Locker,* Kona Inn Shopping Village, Kailua-Kona, HI 96740 (phone: 329-7585); *Kona Activities Center,* PO Box 1035, Kailua-Kona, HI 96745 (phone: 329-3171); *Kohala Divers Ltd.,* PO Box 4935, Kawaihae, HI 96743 (phone: 882-7774); *Kona Coast Divers,* 75-5614 Palani Rd., Kailua-Kona, HI 96745 (phone: 329-8802); and *Nautilus Dive Center,* 382 Kamehameha Ave., Hilo, HI 96720 (phone: 935-6939).

MAUI: Because of its proximity to the surrounding islands of Molokai, Lanai, Kahoolawe, and Molokini, the Valley Isle offers some of the most varied and exciting dive sites in the state. Weather conditions usually determine which island is dived on any given day. The top dive sites likely to be visited on a guided two- or three-tank inter-island trip include: Mokuhooniki Rock off Molokai, where strong currents sweep in tremendous numbers of fish; the famous Lanai Cathedrals, a series of open-ended and well-lit lava caves and grottoes frequented by Japanese barracuda and small sharks; and Becks Cove off Kahoolawe, known for its black coral forest and large jacks.

On Maui, the top underwater spots for novice and intermediate divers are Kaanapali's Black Rock, where there is a small cave with many varieties of fish accessible to beginners; and La Perouse Bay, where huge lava caves shelter very large fish. Honolua Bay, a protected marine preserve, also offers excellent diving and snorkeling. Another popular locale is the island of Molokini, lying between Wailea, on Maui, and the neighboring island of Kahoolawe. Molokini is accessible via Maui dive shop excursions or aboard the *Wailea Kai* catamaran, with Maalaea Harbor departures. In addition, the west coast of Maui off Lahaina is known for the Outside Drift Drive, where whaling artifacts are littered across the ocean floor. Schools of goatfish numbering in the thousands can be seen here. Black Rock, at Kaanapali, and the promontories at Wailea are easily accessible and offer excellent snorkeling.

Snorkeling enthusiasts have a wide range of beach parks from which to choose. Honolua Bay, near D. T. Fleming Park, is a large, protected bay with good visibility to the right and left of the harbor mouth. The large shallow reef at Olowalu is ideal for snorkeling, with a great variety of fish found in the deeper waters surrounding it. Five Caves near Makena Beach demands a long surface swim to offshore rocks, but below them are five caves worth exploring.

A small caveat to divers visiting Maui in the winter: You may find yourself sharing space in the sea with humpback whales, which visit from November through April.

Information: *Central Pacific Divers,* 780 Front St., Lahaina, HI 96761 (phone: 661-8718); *Dive Maui,* Lahaina Marketplace, Lahainaluna Rd., Lahaina, HI 96761 (phone: 667-2080); *Lahaina Divers,* 710 Front St., Lahaina, HI 96761 (phone: 667-7496); *Aloha Activity Center,* Whalers Village, Kaanapali, HI 96761 (phone: 667-9564); *Maui Dive Shop,* PO Box 1018, Kihei, HI 96753 (phone: 879-3388), with shops in Lahaina, Kahului, and Kihei; *Scuba Schools of Maui,* 1000 Limahana Pl., Suite A, Lahaina, HI 96761 (phone: 661-8036; 800-445-2163).

KAUAI: The Garden Isle has some of the finest dive sites in Hawaii. As the oldest major island, Kauai has a great diversity of marine life and coral formations. A lack of good beach entry and exit points, however, make a boat dive imperative on Kauai.

Kauai divers usually frequent the south shore (Poipu Beach) in the fall, winter, and spring, moving up to the north shore (Hanalei Bay, where *South Pacific* was filmed) in the summer, when underwater visibility is at its best. Top north shore dive sites include the Shell Graveyard, a cave at Hanalei Bay where a great number of mollusks and crustaceans have abandoned their calcium homes; and King's Reef, a large underwater canyon lined with coral growth.

Divers on the south shore can explore Sheraton Caverns, the home of many graceful sea turtles, and Oasis Reef, an underwater playground where divers can arm-wrestle small octopi. Nearby, thousands of yellow butterfly fish feed on the plankton-covered reef. Perhaps the most entertaining dive site on Kauai is Koloa Landing, where tame fish will accompany divers on their trek across the reef. Here divers can meet tame moray eels who, for a morsel of squid, will pose for a photo coiled around your neck. *Fantasy Island Boat Tours* makes its way from Kukuiula harbor to the magnificent beach, bay, and valley at Kipukai. Still privately owned, Kipukai is Hawaii at its best. When waters are calm, there's good snorkeling and diving off the bay's western arm. Information: *Fathom Five Divers,* PO Box 907, Koloa, HI 96756 (phone: 742-6991); *Sea Sage Diving Center,* 4-1378 Kuhio Hwy., Kapaa, HI 96746 (phone: 822-3841); *Fantasy Island Boat Tours,* PO Box 10, Hanalei, HI 96714 (phone: 826-9033; 800-426-3293).

Gone Fishing

 Because of its serendipitous position at the crossroads of game fish migration paths, Hawaii enjoys some of the best deep-sea fishing in the world. And though the smooth, glassy waters off the Big Island's Kona Coast are revered as the finest Pacific blue marlin grounds on the planet, the Waianae coast of Oahu, the southwest coast of Maui, and the waters off Kauai's Na Pali cliffs are also very productive.

Visitors who want to try their hands at deep-sea fishing need not be old salts. As one

Kona captain noted, "If we had to depend on experienced anglers for all our business, we'd all be broke." The main thing for *malihinis* (newcomers) to remember is to follow the instructions of the captain and the mate when a fish is hooked.

Most of Hawaii's top game-fishing ports have both private and share charters. Obviously, a private charter is the way to go, especially if there are three or more people in your party. (Most boats accommodate up to six.) Private charters run from $400 to $450 for a full day (8 hours), $225 to $325 for three quarters of a day (6 hours), and $200 to $300 for a half day (4 hours). Rates vary according to the type of vessel.

On share charters, anglers pay an individual rate of from $70 to $120 and share time with up to five other cohorts. All boats have a democratic rotation system, where anglers draw lots for position and take turns minding the rods. On all charters, fishing tackle and equipment are supplied; anglers usually bring their own lunch and beverages (don't, however, take a banana on board, as they're considered bad luck for fishing). And don't forget your camera, sunscreen, and broad-brimmed hat.

Deep-sea fishing in Hawaii is good year-round, but for folks serious about hooking a marlin, chances of success are best from late June to November. No fishing license is required for saltwater fishing in Hawaii.

Though Pacific blue marlin is *the* premier game fish, the supporting cast of heavyweights is also impressive. Hawaiian waters are rich with *ahi* (yellowfin tuna), an extremely fast, torpedo-like fish ranging up to 300 pounds; *mahimahi* (dolphin fish), a beautiful phosphorescent fish known for its leaping, spirited battles; *ono* (wahoo), a fast swimmer averaging 30 pounds, with a mouthful of sharp teeth; and *aku* (skipjack tuna), a school fish highly prized by sashimi lovers. Black and striped marlin, as well as sailfish, are also taken in Hawaiian waters.

Unless previous arrangements are made, it is customary in Hawaii for the catch to be left with the crew, which usually fillets enough fish for the client's party and then sells the rest at the market. This arrangement permits charter captains to keep prices down. (Most of the larger marlin are ground up into fishcakes. Better-tasting dolphin and wahoo are sold to restaurants.)

A word of advice for the prospective deep-sea angler with time to spare: Go to the harbor in the area you plan to fish and talk to the captain and crews of each charter boat. You'll hear some tall stories, but you'll also get a good feel for who's hot — and who's not.

Because Hawaiian charters are among the least expensive and most accessible to top fishing grounds, deep-sea fishing excursions throughout the state are considered a bargain. If you've only tried freshwater stream or lake fishing for pan fish, the feeling of a large game fish tugging powerfully at the rod while it tail-dances across the surface of the water may render you speechless for the rest of your vacation.

OAHU: Honolulu's Kewalo Basin (Fisherman's Wharf), only 10 minutes by car from Waikiki hotels, is the base for a fleet of sportfishing boats ranging from 40 to 63 feet. These cruisers sail off Koko Head to the Penguin Banks southwest of Molokai or off the Waianae coast. (The world's largest Pacific blue marlin caught on rod and reel, a 1,805-pound monster now on display at the International Market Place in Waikiki, was taken off the Waianae coast by a Kewalo charter vessel in 1971.)

Boats on Oahu can be chartered for 1- or 2-day trips by reserving them in advance. Although the custom is for a group to book the entire boat for a day, single anglers are placed with private parties when space is available. Honolulu boats stalk a mixed bag of game fish — depending on the size and species of fish running, a variety of artificial plugs and live swimming baits are used to capture marlin, tuna, wahoo, and dolphin. For North Shore fishing, charters are available at Pokai Bay and Haleiwa at slightly lower rates than at Kewalo Basin. Information: *Island Charters,* Kewalo Basin, Honolulu, HI 96814 (phone: 536-1555); *Coreene C's,* Kewalo Basin, Honolulu, HI

96814 (phone: 536-7472); *Golden Eagle,* Kewalo Basin, Honolulu, HI 96814 (phone: 531-4966).

HAWAII: Sheltered from the northeast trade winds by the twin volcanoes of Mauna Kea and Mauna Loa, the Big Island's Kona Coast is world-renowned for its huge marlin. In recent years, no less than 20 *au* (marlin) weighing more than 1,000 pounds have been taken off the Kona Coast. Record weights top 1,400 pounds. In 1981, about half of Kona's 60-odd charter boats landed more than *100* marlin. The great fish is attracted by schools of smaller fish that breed rapidly in these plankton-rich waters.

Unlike in other deep-sea fishing ports, Kona marlin and other game fish are usually taken within 10 miles of the harbor mouth and along 20 miles of the Kona coastline marked by the Keahole Lighthouse. This means anglers get the most for their money and spend very little time getting to and from the fishing grounds.

The sleepy fishing town of Kailua hosts the Hawaiian International Billfish Tournament every summer, an angling extravaganza that is considered the world's premier marlin fishing event. Teams from around the world compete for world championship honors in an Olympics-style format. In addition, jackpot tournaments are held from March to November. Anglers put up a cash entry fee in a gamble to collect more than $35,000 for landing the largest fish.

Though a small, live skipjack tuna or bonito is occasionally harnessed with a heavy marlin hook and set free to swim at the end of a line, the choice method of fishing in Hawaii is with large, plastic, rubber-skirted lures. These Kona Head plugs are trolled at 8 to 10 knots for marlin and tuna. The lures are attached to specially designed heads that create trails of bubbles and give the mini–hula skirts a wiggling action. Experienced captains say the fish strike out of anger or curiosity, not hunger.

For a longer trip, take a 2-day run past extinct lava flows to South Point, the southernmost point in the US, where the right tide conditions can produce some of the fastest and most furious fishing action in the world. *Ahi* (yellowfin tuna, known for their blistering 60 mph "freight train" runs), *ulua* (jack crevalle, a large reef fish ranging up to 100 pounds), and *mahimahi* (dolphin fish) can be taken here in great numbers.

A visitor's chance of landing a trophy gamefish off the Kona Coast is probably just as good as his or her chance of winning money in Las Vegas. Kailua's expert charter captains, however, can slant the odds in your favor. Information: *Kona Coast Activities,* PO Box 5397, Kailua-Kona, HI 96745 (phone: 329-2971; 800-367-5105); *Kona Charter Skippers Association,* 75-5663 Palani Rd., Kailua-Kona, HI 96745 (phone: 329-3600; 800-367-8047, ext. 360); *Kona Marina Sport Fishing Charters,* 74-425 Kealakehe Pkwy., Kailua-Kona, HI 96740 (phone: 329-1115).

MAUI: The colorful missionary outpost and former whaling center of Lahaina, on Maui's west coast near Kaanapali Beach, is the game-fishing center of the Valley Isle. Maui charter boats head for waters in the triangle formed by Lanai, Kahoolawe, and Maui and troll near fish aggregation buoys placed by the state at strategic locations. Waters at the southeast tip of Lanai produce good marlin runs during the fall months, though the island's best all-around fishing is from May to August. *Mahimahi* (dolphin fish), pound for pound one of the toughest (and prettiest) fish in the ocean; *ono* (wahoo), a very good eating fish — *ono* is the Hawaiian word for "good" or "delicious"; and various species of small tuna are what anglers expect to catch in Maui's waters. Because the chances of landing a trophy fish are best in early morning, Maui captains prefer to leave port at 6:30 AM in the spring and summer, and at 7 AM in the fall and winter. Full-day charters are recommended for the serious angler, as marlin are usually found quite a distance from Maui, in deep waters off Lanai. Information: *Ocean Activities Center,* 1325 S. Kihei Rd., Suite 212, Kihei, HI 96753 (phone: 879-4485; 800-367-8047, ext. 448); *Aloha Activity Center,* Whalers Village, Kaanapali, HI 96761 (phone: 667-9564).

KAUAI: The Garden Isle probably has the greatest variety of fishing in the state. In addition to the great schools of tackle-smashing *ahi* (yellowfin tuna), weighing up to 250 pounds, that cruise into Kauai waters in late spring, the island's charter captains troll for *mahimahi* (dolphin fish) and smaller tuna year-round. There are also unusually large bonefish, a near translucent game fish prized for its fighting abilities, found on the flats off Hanalei on the north shore. (Kauai held the world record for bonefish — 19 pounds, 2 ounces — for many years.)

For the freshwater enthusiast, bass, catfish, and carp can be taken at Wailua reservoir. A 30-day license ($3.75) is available from the Department of Land and Natural Resources in Lihue or at fishing tackle shops. *Bass Guides of Kauai,* PO Box 3525, Lihue, HI 96766 (phone: 822-1405) provides half- and full-day lake fishing excursions (on private land; no permit required).

Information: *Bob Kutkowski, Seabreeze III,* Anini, HI 96746 (phone: 828-1285); *Sea Fever Sport Fishing,* PO Box 403, Hanalei, HI (phone: 826-6815); *Blue Odyssey Adventures,* PO Box 10, Hanalei, HI 96714 (phone: 826-9033); *Sports Fishing Kauai,* PO Box 1195, Koloa, HI 96756 (phone: 742-7013).

Sailing the South Seas

Experienced sailors, diehard adventurers, and even carefree day-trippers who delight mostly in watching fish wriggle in the water through the glass bottom of a Polynesian canoe may all find their respective pleasures in Hawaii. Bareboat charters are available to seamen worthy of the challenge of open ocean sailing, while raft rides along Kauai's Na Pali Coast usually attract the shoot-the-rapids crowd. Theme cruises aboard diesel-powered craft or catamarans are popular on Oahu, the Big Island, and Maui, with morning snorkeling tours and late afternoon sunset sails leading the list of favorites. In the end, boating opportunities in Hawaii are as diverse as the islands themselves.

OAHU: Outrigger Canoe Rides – An ideal way to get the feel of surfing, without mastering board-balancing skills, is to take an outrigger canoe ride on the modest breakers off Waikiki Beach. By paddling hard at the right moment, passengers can assist the two crewmen in putting the 30-foot surfing canoe on the crest of a wave. A pontoon jutting out from the side of these long banana-shaped boats gives them stability. Paddlers get a good workout, along with three thrilling rides during the 30- to 40-minute experience. The price is $6 to $8. (Several of the canoe concessions also have hour-long catamaran rides.) Information: *Waikiki Beach Services,* c/o Outrigger Reef Hotel, 2169 Kalia Rd., Honolulu, HI 96815 (phone: 923-3111); *Beach Services,* c/o Waikiki Outrigger Hotel, 2335 Kalakaua Ave., Honolulu, HI 96815 (phone: 923-0711); *Waikiki Beach Services,* c/o Sheraton-Waikiki, 2255 Kalakaua Ave., Honolulu, HI 96815 (phone: 922-4422).

Cruises – Several companies offer cruises off Waikiki beaches; others provide transportation from Waikiki, with departures set from Kewalo Basin. The following outfits include both free hotel pick-ups and drop-offs.

Hilton Hawaiian Village offers sails aboard the 72-foot catamaran *Hilton Rainbow I,* departing from the *Hilton* end of Waikiki Beach. The breakfast sail is from 8 to 10 AM, a Pearl Harbor Cruise from 1 to 4 PM, and a dinner sail, with open bar and entertainment, from 5:30 to 7:30 PM; the cost per person is $39. Information: *Hilton Catamaran,* 2005 Kalia Rd., Honolulu, HI 96815 (phone: 949-4321).

The *Hyatt Regency*'s 48-passenger catamaran *Manu Kai* heads out for hour-long sails and 1½-hour-long cocktail sails from a beachfront location. Information: Hyatt Regency Waikiki, 2424 Kalakaua Ave., Honolulu, HI 96815 (phone: 922-9292).

Windjammer offers a sunset dinner sail ($39) and a moonlight cruise ($39, including buffet; $24, cocktails only) aboard the 1,000-passenger *Rella Mae.* Those seeking quiet, romantic moments should look elsewhere: The sunset sail includes a Polynesian revue, and the moonlight sail comes complete with a Broadway-style musical. Information: Windjammer Cruises, PO Box 99, Honolulu, HI 96815 (phone: 521-0036).

Aikane Catamarans operates three 150-passenger cats on two nightly dinner sails, with 5:15 and 7:45 departures from Kewalo Basin. The sails, at $35 and $37 per person, respectively, both include table service dinner, an open bar, and Polynesian entertainment inviting audience participation. Those in a romantic mood may wish to make a getaway to the upper deck and enjoy the breezes, moonlight, and relative quiet. Information: Aikane Catamarans, 677 Ala Moana Blvd., Honolulu, HI 96813 (phone: 522-1533).

Yacht Charters – Skippered charters are available from *Hawaii C Charters,* which offers a Cal 27, a Hunter 37, and a Cal 46 as its fleet. Half-day, full-day, and overnight inter-island sails (a 7-day minimum is required for inter-island itineraries) are available, with half-day rentals starting at $195. Rates include hotel pickup and drop-off. Only licensed skippers with knowledge of Hawaiian waters can set sail unescorted. Licensed skippers unfamiliar with Hawaiian waters are provided with a guide at no additional cost. Information: Hawaii C Charters, 47-217A Hui Akikiki Pl., Kaneohe, HI 96744 (phone: 239-6493). *Silver Cloud Limousine* offers crewed charters aboard its custom-built 39-foot sloop. A 3-hour minimum, starting at $350, is required. A Wetsail 43 and a Hunter 54 round out the fleet. Information: Silver Cloud Limousine, PO Box 15773, Honolulu, HI 96815 (phone: 524-7999).

HAWAII: Captain Nemo's Ocean Sports – After several years of service on Maui, *Me A'u,* a 42-foot catamaran, is now owned by *Captain Nemo's* and moored in Anaehoomalu Bay near the *Royal Waikoloan. Me A'u* is used for morning snorkel/lunch sails as well as afternoon cocktail sails. The ship accommodates up to 36 passengers and has plenty of deck space.

The morning snorkel cruises are often run to Kiholo Bay, 5 miles south of Waikoloa at the edge of an 1859 lava flow. Underwater visibility at the site exceeds 100 feet. Excursions are also run to Makaiwa to the north, where skin diving offshore of the black sand beach is superb. A light lunch is served on board, and when the wind picks up in the afternoon, the boat sails back to port. The morning snorkel cruise costs $55 per person, which includes all equipment and instruction. A one-tank scuba sail is available at $85.

In the winter (the best time of year for sighting humpback whales), afternoon sails start at 3 PM; in summer, they start at 5 PM, when the *Me A'u* is used for cocktail trips that cruise by lava formations found along the rugged Kona coastline. Drinks and *pupus* (Hawaiian hors d'oeuvres) are included. The price is $29 per person. *Me A'u* can be chartered for sunset or evening cruises. Information: Captain Nemo's Ocean Sports, PO Box 5000, Kohala Coast, HI 96743 (phone: 885-5555).

Kona Coast Activities – A mixed bag of boating adventures is available through this all-purpose sports complex. *Captain Beans'* cruises, held aboard an 85-foot Polynesian canoe with a glass-bottom viewing area, are the perennial favorites. The craft departs from Kailua pier daily for cruises of the Kona Coast. The 4½-hour cruise to Kealakekua Bay is a highlight. Underwater divers feed fish at reef sites so that armchair frogmen can see marine activity without getting wet.

In the evening, *Captain Beans'* offers a dinner cruise. The 2-hour sail, for $38, departs at 5 PM and features an open bar, lots of good food, and a starlit Hawaiian dancing and music show.

The Captain Cook cruise, a narrated 3-hour history/water sports tour of Kealakekua Bay, is run daily from Kailua pier at 8:45 AM. The *Captain Cook VII,* a large craft with four decks that hold up to 240 passengers, moors near the Captain Cook Monument, where swimming and snorkeling are available off the boat. The tour price is $22 for adults, $10 for children under 12.

One of the center's more popular cruises is its 4-hour morning sail ($49, including lunch) from lovely Keauhou Bay (near the *Kona Surf* hotel) to Kealakekua Bay aboard the *Fairwind,* a 50-foot trimaran equipped with a water slide and bar. Snorkelers sit down to a barbecue lunch when they return to the boat. The *Fairwind* also offers a 3-hour afternoon cruise with snacks. The price is $30 for adults, $17 for children. *Kamanu Charters* offers two 3-hour-long catamaran sails for up to 24 passengers from Honokahau Harbor to Kaiwi Point for $30, $15 for children under 12. Sunset sails (no children) are also offered. Information: Kona Coast Activities, PO Box 5397, Kailua-Kona, HI 96745 (phone: 329-2971; 800-367-5105).

MAUI: Ocean Activities Center – A smorgasbord of sailing excursions is offered by this sports packager. The best trips are run on the 65-foot catamarans *Wailea Kai* and *Maka Kai.* The tours, which depart from Maalaea Harbor include a snorkeling cruise to the marine preserves of Molokini and La Perouse Bay, where sea life is varied and abundant. Visitors need bring only a towel — all equipment is provided. The buffet lunch (preceded by fresh Maui pineapple and papaya) is quite good. The price is $60 for adults, $40 for children. Day trips to Lanai (half-day, $55; full-day, $85) depart Lahaina Harbor daily, although landings are made Tuesdays, Thursdays, and Saturdays only.

From December to April, there are 2-hour whale watches aboard the *Wailea Kai* and the *Maka Kai,* with a marine biologist on hand to provide information about the magnificent humpbacks who visit Hawaii each year to mate. Drinks and *pupus* are available. The tour departs at 1:30 PM from Maalaea Harbor, and free transportation is provided from Wailea hotels and selected Kihei condominiums. The price is $20 for adults, $10 for children.

The center's 2-hour sunset dinner cruise (also known as the "champagne sail") features an open bar (try a mai-tai) and a buffet dinner. There is perhaps no more romantic way to take in a Maui sunset than from the deck of the *Wailea Kai.* The tour costs $40 for adults and children, who get soft drinks in lieu of champagne. The tour leaves Maalaea Harbor at 5:30 PM (5 PM in the winter). Information: Ocean Activities Center, 1325 S. Kihei Rd., Suite 212, Kihei 96753 (phone: 879-4485; 800-367-8047, ext. 448).

Seabern Yachts – Two 42-foot, 6-passenger sailboats are available for skippered charters out of Lahaina. Rates start at $160 for a 2-hour sail (sunset sails include pupus and champagne) and go as high as $3,500 to $4,200 per week, depending on the number of passengers aboard. Share-boat rates are also available. Half-day sails cruise along the Maui coast, while multiday charters usually set course for Manele Bay on Lanai and Kaunakakai on Molokai. The sailing season runs throughout the year. Information: Seabern Yachts, PO Box 1022, Lahaina, HI 96767 (phone: 661-8110).

KAUAI: Captain Zodiac Boat Expeditions – Aboard large inflatable rafts similar to those used by Jacques Cousteau, passengers explore portions of the rugged Na Pali Coast that are accessible only by air or water. From the craft, wild goats can be seen picking their way along the brown cliffs that rise 3,000 feet from the water's edge. Schools of dolphin and flying fish break the water, as do the humpback whales in the winter. When a fish hits, the rod is handed to a passenger. The rafts, powered by twin outboard engines, are anchored over a virgin reef, where razorback turtles (an endangered species) and other sea life can be seen by snorkelers. The tour also explores the many sea caves found along the coast.

The expedition boats hold up to 15 persons, and advance reservations are required. The 3½-hour tour from Hanalei is priced at $60; 5½-hour tours that include a 2-hour landing at Nualolokai and lunch cost $90. This is probably one of the most exciting boating adventures in the islands.

During the winter months, when Na Pali coast waters may be rough, raft trips leave from Nawiliwili Harbor for Kipukai, with its beautiful beach and excellent snorkeling. The 3½-hour trip departs daily and costs $60, which includes a chance to see the humpbacks that visit south shore waters.

For those interested in camping along the Na Pali coast, the expedition company runs a camper and backpacker drop-off service May through September. The cost is $60 one way, $120 round trip. Information: Captain Zodiac, PO Box 456, Hanalei, HI 96714 (phone: 826-9371; 800-422-7824.

Fantasy Island Tours – This Poipu adventure group uses a 20-passenger customized raft on 3- to 4-hour snorkel and pleasure cruises along the south shore, including visits to beautiful Kipukai. Other options include a nightly sunset cruise with champagne and pupus. Information: Fantasy Island Boat Cruises, PO Box 10, Hanalei, HI 96714 (phone: 826-9033; 800-426-3293).

The Islands' Top Tennis

 While Hawaii's warm sun, blue canopy of a sky, and prevailing trade winds create almost perfect year-round playing conditions, visiting tennis players — novice and advanced alike — can find themselves too easily distracted by court settings that range from simply beautiful to dramatically spectacular. Windbreaks, for example, are often bedecked with oleander and bougainvillea, and vistas of green cliffs, blue surf, and white sandy beaches are the rule, not the exception.

Tennis courts in the islands are generally very well kept and constructed with all-weather Laykold or Plexipave surfaces, though the Wailea Tennis Club in Maui features the state's only grass courts.

In addition to hotel and resort tennis complexes, where hourly rates range from $5 to $10 per hour or are free to guests, several of the islands have well-maintained county courts, where playing time is usually free of charge. Details on county courts are available from local parks and recreation departments. Information on tournaments can be supplied by the Hawaii Pacific Tennis Association, 3538 Waialae Ave., Honolulu, HI 96816 (phone: 735-3008).

Most hotels and resorts with tennis facilities will arrange a match for an unattached visiting player. Individual lessons for players of all abilities range from $20 to $25 per hour, while group lessons and clinics usually average about $6 per hour. Videotaping and playback are also available. Several of Hawaii's tennis resorts are staffed by members of Peter Burwash International (PBI), a consortium of teaching professionals that specializes in the management of racquet facilities at hotels. PBI, based in Honolulu, has an especially strong footing at resorts throughout the state.

A list of the best public and private tennis facilities around the state follows.

OAHU: The top three municipal facilities in the Honolulu/Waikiki area are the 10 Laykold courts at *Ala Moana Beach Park,* all of which are lighted for night play until 9 PM (phone: 521-7664), the unlighted, 9-court *Diamond Head Tennis Center* in Kapiolani Park (phone: 923-7927), and the 4 lighted *Kapiolani Park Courts,* also in Kapiolani Park, which are open until 2:30 AM (phone: 923-7927). Free classes are offered at the Ala Moana facility.

Also in the Honolulu area are the noteworthy *Honolulu Tennis Club* and the *Ilikai* hotel courts. The former is a good place to go to avoid the crowds of *malihinis* (newcomers) that mainland snowstorms have driven to the islands in search of sun. Its 4 Laykold courts have a third-floor rooftop location atop a department store, from which players have a view of the Waikiki skyline on the *makai* (ocean) side of the building and a panorama of the Manoa Valley on the *mauka* (mountain) side. The courts, which are at their busiest from the end of November through April, have a pro on hand for lessons. For the four-wall crowd, there are also 3 racquetball courts. A free pickup service is available to and from Waikiki hotels. Information: Honolulu Tennis Club, 2220 S. King St., Honolulu, HI 96826 (phone: 944-9696).

The *Ilikai* has 6 Plexipave tennis courts, including the lighted Yacht Harbor court (open until 10 PM) on top of the hotel's main ballroom, overlooking the Ala Wai Yacht Harbor. The hotel's other showcase court is the Diamond Head court, with the famous extinct volcano providing background distraction. The remaining courts, on the hotel's seventh floor, provide players with fine views of the ocean and marina below.

All reservations for court time and lessons at the *Ilikai,* which is staffed by two tennis pros, are made through the hotel's Sports Desk. A final note: The *Ilikai* has one of the best-stocked tennis shops on the island. Information: Ilikai Hotel, 1777 Ala Moana Blvd., Honolulu, HI 96815 (phone: 949-3811).

Outside Honolulu, two Oahu resorts are standout tennis destinations. On the North Shore, the *Turtle Bay Hilton* has 10 Plexipave courts (4 lighted at night) set in a grove of coconut palms near the golf course. The courts, cooled by ocean breezes, are within sight of stark volcanic peaks in the Koolau Range. In the interests of privacy, there are no adjoining courts. The resort's player matching service pairs off partners of equal ability based on its rating system. Clinics and social doubles events are also part of the program. The best times to visit are spring and summer — washouts are not uncommon in late fall and winter. Information: Turtle Bay Hilton and Country Club, Kahuku, HI 96731 (phone: 293-8811).

On Oahu's leeward coast, in the vast natural arena of Makaha Valley, is the *Sheraton Makaha* resort, a secluded hotel in a country club setting. Four Plexipave courts, 2 lighted, are set in this horseshoe-shaped development. Because there is little wind or rain on the leeward coast, *Sheraton Makaha* guests enjoy near-perfect playing conditions year round, and since the resort is 40 miles from the bustle of Honolulu, its tennis facilities are not pressed to the limit. The *Sheraton Makaha* is a great place to perfect your backhand without fear of discovery by rivals. "It's just you and the tennis here," commented the resident pro. "People come for the quiet." Information: Sheraton Makaha Resort, PO Box 896, Makaha, HI 96792 (phone: 695-9511).

HAWAII: Among the Big Island's excellent county tennis courts is Hilo's *Hoolulu Park.* A mile from Hilo Bay, the complex boasts 8 courts, 3 of them lighted. The peak of Mauna Kea, snow-covered in winter, smiles down on the serve-and-volley crowd, and those having trouble with their ground strokes can later seek comfort in the city's many luxuriant public and commercial gardens (Hilo is the orchid-growing capital of the world). For those who perform best in front of an audience, the covered tennis stadium at Hoolulu Park seats 2,000 fans and admirers. Hoolulu is one of the few county facilities that charges an hourly rate ($2 to $4 per court, depending on the time of day; phone: 961-9868).

The queen of the Big Island's resorts is the *Mauna Kea Beach,* a world class property first developed by Laurance Rockefeller on the Kona Coast at the base of the dormant volcano for which it is named. The resort is just down the road from a lava desert, yet plumeria and bougainvillea bloom in profusion on the property. The *Mauna Kea* has 13 Plexipave courts and, like the Wailea Tennis Center on Maui, it is listed among the top 50 US tennis complexes by *Tennis* magazine. In addition to magnificent ocean views, players at the tennis park will find such nice touches as an ice machine courtside, a juice bar, and lots of thick, thirsty towels. On the staff is a full-time tennis hostess whose sole purpose is to greet guests, show them around the facilities, and arrange for instruction and matches. Daily clinics and round-robin tournaments are also part of the *Mauna Kea* tennis program. Exhibitions and pro appearances are conspicuously absent from the resort's tennis schedule. "The guests aren't interested in names," a staffer comments. "They're here to play tennis." And they do: The 13 courts are reserved for the hotel's patrons and their guests. Note that this super-deluxe approach to the sport does not come inexpensively: The *Mauna Kea*'s tennis packages are some of the most expensive in the state. Information: Mauna Kea Beach Hotel, PO Box 218, Kamuela, HI 96743 (phone: 882-7222).

In Waikoloa, the *Royal Waikoloan* features 6 courts, open to guests and non-guests alike, and a pro shop. Lessons are also available. Information: Sheraton Royal Waikoloa, PO Box 5000, Waikoloa, HI 96743 (phone: 885-6789).

Unfortunately, enthusiasts will likely find the 8 courts at the 1,244-room *Hyatt* monopolized by guests.

In Kona, the *King Kamehameha* has 4 Laykold courts (2 lighted) set on Kailua Bay at the base of 8,271-foot Mt. Hualalai. Because of its top-flight staff and dependably fine weather — little rain and wind, lots of sun — the *King Kamehameha* offers a tennis experience as fine as that available anywhere in the islands. As an extra bonus, after a rigorous match, overheated players can cool off in the ocean at Kailua Bay. Information: Hotel King Kamehameha, Kailua-Kona, HI 96740 (phone: 329-2911).

The *Kona Hilton* and *Kona Surf* also offer commendable tennis facilities. Information: Kona Hilton, PO Box 1179, Kailua-Kona, HI 96745 (phone: 329-3111); Kona Surf, 78-128 Ehukai St., Kailua-Kona, HI 96740 (phone: 322-3411).

In Hilo, the *Naniloa*, 93 Banyan Dr., Hilo, HI 96720 (phone: 969-3333) has 4 newly built courts, all nightlit.

MAUI: The Valley Isle's top public courts are situated between the sea and the West Maui peak of Puu Kukui in Lahaina, a former whaling center and missionary outpost. The *Lahaina Civic Center's* 5 Laykold courts (all lighted), within walking distance of the beach, are free and operate on a first-come, first-served basis (phone: 661-4685).

Kaanapali's *Royal Lahaina Tennis Ranch* has 11 Plexipave tennis courts, plus one practice wall; 6 courts are lighted for night play. Available on request is the stadium court. The hotel's tennis director is Bernard Gusman, who heads a staff chosen and trained by the Peter Burwash tennis organization. *Royal Lahaina*'s courts are surrounded by the fairways of the *Royal Kaanapali* golf courses on a 500-acre planned resort that was once a sugar plantation. The hotel stresses that proper tennis attire is required at all times. No cutoffs, aloha shirts, or bikinis on the courts, please. Information: Royal Lahaina Tennis Ranch, Kaanapali Resort, Kaanapali, HI 96761 (phone: 661-3611).

Kapalua's 10-court *Tennis Garden* gives the *Royal Lahaina* a good run for its money. Information: Kapalua Tennis Garden, Kapalua, HI 96761 (phone: 669-5656).

On the lower slopes of Haleakala, where the sun shines 355 days a year, is Hawaii's largest tennis complex, the *Wailea Tennis Club*. On a typical crystal clear day, the islands of Lanai, Molokini, and Kahoolawe can be spotted from the court complex. During the winter, players run the very real risk of being distracted by humpback whales frolicking offshore.

In addition to *Wailea*'s 11 Plexipave courts (3 lighted) and an amphitheater-style tennis stadium with lava rock seats, the resort's 3 grass courts (the only ones in the state) afford players a surface that does not radiate heat (a definite plus in the tropics) and are easier on the joints, not to mention having more aesthetic appeal. Like the *Mauna Kea Beach* on the Big Island, Wailea is listed by *Tennis* magazine as one of the top 50 tennis resorts in the US. Information: Wailea Tennis Club, 131 Wailea Iki Pl., Wailea, HI 96753 (phone: 879-1958).

Of the 6 courts at the Makena resort, 3 are lighted for night play. There is also a pro shop and a restaurant. Information: Makena Tennis Club, 5415 Makena Ala Nui, Kihei, HI 96753 (phone: 879-8777).

KAUAI: Taken together, the Garden Isle's tennis facilities are some of the most beautiful in the state. The island's county courts, for the most part modest double-court facilities, include *New Park* in *Kapaa*, where the 2 lighted courts are bordered by coconut palms and favored by a cool breeze. Near Kokee State Park, within sight of the ocean, are 2 lighted courts at *Kekaha.* The courts are patronized by residents, but visitors are welcome on a first-come, first-served basis. A $10 deposit, payable at the Parks Permit Section, Finance Department, 4280A Rice St., Lihue, is required for night play (phone: 245-1881).

One of the shining stars of Hawaiian tennis is the *Hanalei Bay* resort on Kauai's north shore, which has 11 terraced Laykold courts (3 lighted) overlooking Hanalei Bay, of *South Pacific* film fame. The setting of the tennis courts, among bougainvillea flowers and coconut trees, is a Bali Hai all its own. When they're not hitting the ball, players see the velvety outlines of the Wainiha *palis* (cliffs) and long furrows of surf breaking against the old rice and taro piers in Hanalei Bay. There is perhaps no more breathtaking spot in which to smack a fuzzy yellow ball past an opponent. The teaching program includes videotape playback. Showers in the morning and evening feed the hundred or so waterfalls in the vicinity of the resort and keep everything lush, though heavy rain can frustrate play in midwinter. Residents claim, however, it is impossible to get rained out for an entire day. There is a $5 charge for non-guests. Information: Hanalei Bay Resort, PO Box 220, Hanalei, HI 96714 (phone: 826-6522).

Though hallowed ground for golfers (the 4 Princeville nines comprise one of the world's great golf courses), tennis players flock to the *Princeville* resort's 6 Plexipave courts for the stunning view of the Wainiha Mountains and general *bonhomie* of the place. Players convene at *Princeville*'s clubhouse, one of the classiest watering holes in the islands, to discuss the finer points of the game. Players looking for partners will be matched up by clubhouse personnel. The best time to visit is from April to December, when clear weather is more likely. Information: Princeville at Hanalei, Hanalei, HI 96714 (phone: 826-6561).

Kauai's other top tennis resort is the *Kiahuna Plantation,* a series of airy and handsome beachfront condominiums at Poipu Beach on the island's south shore. Kiahuna (Polynesian for "a special place") has 10 tennis courts set in splendid gardens and bordered by blue and white pavilions, as well as a courtside restaurant. There is a $5 per hour and $9 per day charge for non-guests. Information: Kiahuna Plantation, RR 1, Box 73, Koloa, HI 96756 (phone: 742-9533). Some *Kiahuna* guests have playing privileges at the *Stouffer Waiohai*'s 6 courts (4 nightlit). Information: Stouffer Waiohai, 2249 Poipu Rd., Koloa, HI 96756 (phone: 742-9511).

In addition to 8 Plexipave courts, the new *Westin Kauai* also includes a tennis stadium. Guests and non-guests pay $20 an hour, which includes use of the adjacent spa. Information: Westin Kauai, Kalapaki Beach, Lihue, HI 96766 (phone: 245-5050).

MOLOKAI: There are 4 nightlit Laykold courts for play at Colony Resorts' *Kaluakoi* hotel. Information: Kaluakoi Hotel and Golf Club, Maunaloa, HI 96770 (phone: 552-2555).

Great Golf

The problem with playing golf in Hawaii is that the scenery that surrounds golf holes in the 50th state is as dramatic as can be imagined, and keeping your head down requires a very determined act of will. In all candor, we're not sure it's worth the effort: The normal run of duffer may enjoy looking at the snowcapped peak behind the Mauna Kea golf course much more than watching his or her errant shot dive into the crashing surf.

But if you take your golf game seriously, there are now nearly five dozen layouts scattered around the islands, only about one dozen of which are private. Regrettably, the *Waialae Country Club* (4997 Kahala Ave., Honolulu; 734-2151), probably the most familiar Hawaiian course to visitors (it's the site of the televised Hawaiian Open each winter), is one of these private oases, as is the *Oahu Country Club* (150 Country Club

Rd., Honolulu; 595-6331). The *Mid-Pacific Country Club* (266 Kaelepulu Dr., Kailua; 262-8161) occasionally allows outsiders to play. There are, however, at least two (often successful) gambits for gaining access to these otherwise exclusive enclaves, the most productive of which is to ask the manager of your Honolulu hotel to try to intercede on your behalf. Alternatively, you might present a letter from your own club president and/or resident pro requesting course privileges — a good idea, incidentally, whenever you travel — and you may be pleasantly surprised at the result. In any event, there's no harm in asking.

TURTLE BAY HILTON AND COUNTRY CLUB, Kahuku, Oahu: George Fazio is a course architect who has never really received the sort of recognition he deserves, and after you've played a round or two here, you'll certainly wonder why: The course is rather flat, but it's cleverly designed to provide many challenges. Though golf dominates this remote resort complex, there are many other activities to enjoy: tennis, scuba diving, snorkeling, and horseback riding. And the setting, with the ocean in one direction and the peaks of the Koolau Range in the other, is nearly as memorable as the golf itself. Course: 18 holes, par 72, 6,366 yards; resident pro, Jody Shaw. At press time, work was soon to begin on a second 18-hole course. Information: Turtle Bay Hilton and Country Club, Kahuku, HI 96731 (phone: 293-8811).

MAKAHA VALLEY, Makaha, Oahu: The two William Bell–designed courses here — the West Course and the Makaha Valley Country Club — lie in a deep valley well within view of notorious Makaha Beach, where championship surfers regularly pit their tanned bodies against some of the planet's most violent waves. The golf courses are slightly safer, though the tougher West Course requires a combination of cool temperament and substantial power. The greens on both courses are undulating and difficult to read, and the fairness of the fairways (and their usually superb condition) will provide scant solace for soaring scores. Makaha Valley Country Club: 18 holes, par 72, 6,530 yards; managed by Nitto Kogyo, 84-627 Makaha Valley Rd., Waianae, HI 96792 (phone: 695-9578). West Course: 18 holes, par 72, 6,400 yards; resident pro, Ron Kiaaina; managed by the Sheraton Makaha Resort, PO Box 896, Makaha, HI 96792 (phone: 695-9511).

KEAUHOU-KONA COUNTRY CLUB, Kailua-Kona, the Big Island of Hawaii: The Big Island's black lava rock poses real challenges at this oceanside course designed by William Bell. After your ball lands in the deep crags of the mini-canyons here, you'll pray for rough that's just long grass. There are compensations, however: The surrounding Kona Coast scenery is breathtaking, and the weather the best in the islands. Course: 27 holes, par 36 nines, approximately 6,800 yards, depending on choice of nines. Information: Keauhou-Kona Country Club, 78-7000 Alii Dr., Kailua-Kona, HI 96740 (phone: 322-2595).

MAUNA KEA BEACH, Kohala Coast, the Big Island of Hawaii: It would be worth the 30-minute flight from Honolulu to Kona just to play a round on this magnificent Pacific gem built on solidified lava flows and designed by Robert Trent Jones, Sr. Cloudless skies and incredible vistas of the 13,800-foot dormant volcano for which the resort is named are the primary reasons why this golf course may be the most photographed anywhere. The course is also quite challenging, despite a recent "softening" to make it more compatible with the skills of resort visitors. Course: 18 holes, par 72, 6,781 yards; golf director, John Ebersberger. Information: Mauna Kea Beach Hotel, PO Box 218, Kamuela, HI 96743 (phone: 882-7222).

MAUNA LANI RESORT, Kohala Coast, the Big Island of Hawaii: Built atop jagged black lava flows, using thousands of tons of imported topsoil, this is one of the most beautiful courses in the islands. Although panoramic vistas can be seen from all the holes, oceanfront hole number 6 has perhaps the most dramatic setting, including a 150-yard clifftop carry over a small bay. Hazards range from the conventional complement of sand traps to huge lava boulders that evoke images of Japanese gardens. Beauty aside, the course provides a true test of golfing skill and has all but replaced

Mauna Kea as the best test on the Big Island. Pro shop and restaurant are at the clubhouse. Course: 18 holes, par 72, 6,259 yards. Work is underway on a second 18-hole course, scheduled to open in 1991. Information: Mauna Lani Resort, Box 4959, Kohala Coast, HI 96743 (phone: 885-6655).

WAIKOLOA BEACH GOLF CLUB, Waikoloa, the Big Island of Hawaii: Course designer Robert Trent Jones, Jr., describes this as "a unique golf course . . . a contrast of Eden-like green grass amidst black lava." Jones began as a landscape architect, and the way in which this seaside layout is sculpted reflects his past training. His marriage of landscape technique and golf course design craft — the latter doubtless inherited from his famous father, who is responsible for the Mauna Kea course just up the road — has produced dramatically beautiful results. The fairways adjacent to the *Sheraton Royal Waikoloa* are lush with palm trees, bougainvillea, wedelia, oleander, and plumeria, providing a sharp contrast to the moon-like black lava that serves as rough here. Shots hit toward the sea — such as the drive at number 17 — often have the added background of a whale cavorting out in the Pacific. Course: 18 holes, par 71, 6,003 yards. A new, even more challenging 18-hole course, currently in the works, is set to open early in the year. Information: Waikoloa Beach Golf Club, Box 5100, Waikoloa, HI 96743 (phone: 885-6060).

ROYAL KAANAPALI GOLF COURSES, Kaanapali, Maui: The golf courses here serve a resort strip that is among the most popular in the neighbor islands. Among the hazards in this less than pastoral place are resort guests who shouldn't, but do, cut through the fairways en route to the beach and the distraction of a tourist-filled sugarcane train, which chugs along tracks cut through the layout en route to and from Lahaina. Still, the long (7,179 championship yards) North Course, designed by Robert Trent Jones, Sr., is one of Hawaii's best; Arthur Jack Snyder's South Course is shorter and flatter and doesn't range as far from the sea. North Course: 18 holes, par 72, 6,305 yards. South Course: 18 holes, par 72, 6,250 yards. Golf director, Ray DeMello. Information: Royal Kaanapali Golf Courses, Kaanapali Resort, Kaanapali, HI 96761 (phone: 661-3691).

KAPALUA GOLF CLUB, Kapalua, Maui: Arnold Palmer and Francis Duane designed the Kapalua resort's original, spectacular Bay Course on hilly seaside acres formerly dedicated to the growing of pineapples. The newer Village Course, created by Palmer and Ed Seay, pushes up even farther into the mountains, and sidehill lies are a constant here. It is the Village track that knowledgeable players proclaim to be the best in the islands. After a round on either course, however, you'll welcome an escape to the lavish luncheon buffet put on daily by the adjacent *Kapalua Bay* hotel. *Kapalua Bay* is currently the equal of the better known *Mauna Kea Beach* hotel; certainly the buffet is the finest in the islands, and the Kapalua pro shop is also among golf's best. The Isuzu Kapalua International tournament is held here in November. Bay Course: 18 holes, par 72, 6,160 yards. Village Course: 18 holes, par 71, 6,194 yards. Golf director, Gary Planos. A third 18-hole course, designed by Ben Crenshaw, is scheduled to open in late 1990. Information: Kapalua Golf Club, 300 Kapalua Dr., Kapalua, HI 96761 (phone: 669-8044).

WAILEA GOLF CLUB, Wailea, Maui: Try to arrange to tee it up on the Orange Course at exactly two minutes before dawn, and if this seems a bit early to crank up your body, be aware that watching the sun come up over the Haleakala crater is one of the most spectacular sights in the Pacific. In winter, the Blue Course often offers its own views, in this case of the humpback whales that come to this area of the world to mate and calve. Arthur Jack Snyder is responsible for the design of both courses, and the golf's pretty darn good — as are the pro shop and the clubhouse restaurant. Blue Course: 18 holes, par 72, 6,152 yards. Orange Course: 18 holes, par 72, 6,304 yards. Information: Wailea Golf Club, 120 Kaukahi St., Kihei, HI 96753 (phone: 879-2966).

MAKENA GOLF COURSE, Makena, Maui: A beautifully maintained 18 holes (with

18 more set for play in late 1990), made challenging by narrow fairways, Makena skirts the sea and climbs uphill for panoramic views. Number 15, an oceanside par 3, and number 6, with views that range from Molokini Island to the West Maui mountains, are two of the more spectacular holes of the Robert Trent Jones, Jr. design. Course: 18 holes, par 72, 6,210 yards. Information: Makena Golf Course, 5415 Makena Alanui, Kihei, HI 96753 (phone: 879-3344).

KALUAKOI GOLF COURSE, Kaluakoi, Molokai: The western end of Molokai was first developed during the late 1970s, and its resort area thus far consists only of Colony Resorts' *Kaluakoi* hotel and two condominiums in various stages of completion. However, for the golfer who appreciates solitude, Kaluakoi offers a very special bonus — a first-rate golf course, designed by Ted Robinson, that curls along the sea and ranks among the best in the islands. Course: 18 holes, par 72, 6,618 yards. Golf director Ben Neely. Information: Kaluakoi Golf Course, PO Box 26, Maunaloa, HI 96770 (phone: 552-2739).

PRINCEVILLE MAKAI GOLF CLUB, Hanalei, Kauai: The risks of golfing on Kauai almost equal the allures, for this island includes the wettest spot on earth — and is also one of the most verdant. Still, the golf opportunities at Princeville, on the north shore, far outweigh most other considerations, and it has become normal to add the word "unbelievable" to any description of this extraordinary golf site. The original three nines were created by Robert Trent Jones, Jr., son of golf's best-known resort course creator, and each has a distinctive personality. There's an Ocean nine, a Woods nine, and a Lake nine the last complete with a Zen garden bunker, jungle caverns gaping between tee and green, and lots of pounding sea to complement the other hazards. The latest addition to Princeville's golf inventory are the 18 holes of the Prince Course. You owe yourself at least one crack at Princeville, if just to see what all the raving is about. Three original 9-hole, par-36 courses, 3,058, 3,098, and 3,018 yards, and the 18-hole Prince Course: par 72, 5,433 yards; resident pro, Neil Finch. Information: Princeville Makai Course, PO Box 3040, Princeville, HI 96722 (phone: 826-6561).

KIAHUNA GOLF CLUB, Poipu, Kauai: This nicely maintained course, built as part of the Kiahuna Resort, covers flat terrain and skirts several important historic Polynesian sites. The holes are relatively straightforward, and the pace on the course is relaxed. At press time, two additional 18-hole courses were in the planning stages. Course: 18 holes, par 70, 5,631 yards; resident pro, Charlie Ortega. A 9-hole addition is planned with opening set for 1990. Information: Kiahuna Golf Club, RR1, Box 73, Koloa, HI 96756 (phone: 742-9595).

WESTIN KAUAI, Nawiliwili, Kauai: Hawaii's newest resort courses are a pair of 18-holers designed by Jack Nicklaus, who also serves as the resort's director of golf. Manmade lagoons and the ocean provide plenty of overcarries. The 190-acre Kauai Lagoons course is a country club–style links, relatively straight and well-manicured. The sprawling, 262-acre Kiele Classic is intended to be tournament class, with substantial room for a gallery. The new courses are part of the resort's Golf & Racquet Club, which also includes a driving range, instruction, and a pro shop. Information: Westin Kauai, Kalapaki Beach, Lihue, HI (phone: 245-5050; 800-228-3000).

Hiking the Hawaiian Wilderness

The only way to experience Hawaii fully is to walk along its more remote trails. The paradise of picture postcards and mournful legends reveals itself to those willing to explore regions beyond the vision of resort-bound vacationers. However, visitors need not be able to leap tall cliffs in a single bound. The trails listed below include easy strolls and nature walks less than a mile long, some with swimming holes and picnic tables along the way.

The key to Hawaiian hiking is variety: Trekkers can sample humid rain forests and moon-like volcanic craters, as well as deserted beaches scattered with the flotsam and jetsam of shipwrecks. Sights along the way include groves of sweet mountain apples, slim waterfalls cascading into deep pools, and fertile valleys where nature has all but reclaimed the remnants of earlier civilizations.

Hikers should be aware of Hawaii's unique hiking conditions. For example, climbing should not be attempted on volcanic surfaces, which tend to crumble when pressure is applied by hand or foot. (Be sure to wear sturdy boots for hiking in volcanic areas.) In the tropics, night drops like a curtain after sunset; plan to be off the trail a few minutes before twilight unless you're going to spend the night. Carry a canteen — not all of Hawaii's water is potable. Bring insect repellent for all hikes on terrain below 3,000 feet — the mosquitoes in low-lying regions can be fierce. As a final note, it is wise to stick to marked trails, since taking shortcuts can disturb the delicate ecological balance of the environment.

Malihinis (newcomers) seeking guidance and companionship can contact the various organizations listed below that arrange group hiking trips. These provide an excellent introduction to the state's wilderness regions. To return home without discovering one or two of them is to miss seeing the real Hawaii.

OAHU

Though it offers few extended wilderness treks for an advanced hiker, Oahu has several fine day hikes, many of them just a few miles from Honolulu. To hike with a group, contact the Hawaiian Trail and Mountain Club, PO Box 2238, Honolulu, HI 96804 (phone: 247-3922); or the Sierra Club, 1100 Alakea St., Honolulu, HI 96813 (phone: 946-8494). For trail information and maps, contact the Department of Land and Natural Resources, Division of Forestry, 1151 Punchbowl St., Honolulu, HI 96813 (phone: 548-2861).

DIAMOND HEAD: Though most visitors know it only as the big green and brown landmark at the far end of Waikiki Beach, Diamond Head also is a fine place for a short hike. Inside this extinct volcano is a trail cut into the crater's interior walls (a flashlight is recommended) that climbs 760 feet to the top of the rim (Point Leahi), where hikers are treated to a panoramic view of Honolulu and the surrounding mountains. Military fortifications built inside the crater during World War II are still there. The crater is open from 6 AM to 6 PM daily, allowing sunrise and sunset climbs from late November through April. For groups of 25 or more, a permit is required to hike Diamond Head. For information: Department of Land and Natural Resources, Division of State Parks, 1151 Punchbowl St., Honolulu, HI 96813 (phone: 548-7455).

JUDD MEMORIAL: This 1.3-mile loop trail, in the Nuuanu Valley, may well be the most entertaining hike in the state. After passing through a stand of eucalyptus, Norfolk pine, and bamboo trees, the trail comes upon one of the best mud-sliding chutes on the island. In the rainy winter months, bring a sheet of heavy plastic for a slick ride down a muddy hill. A fork in the trail leads to Jackass Ginger Pool, a fine place to swim (or wash off the mud). There is a short waterfall slide at the pool for the clean fun crowd.

BLOWHOLE TO HANAUMA BAY: This seaside trail (2 miles, one way) follows a rock shelf past a variety of fascinating formations created by the erosive action of the sea, including caves and tidal pools. Wear a bathing suit and sneakers for this hike — waves wash over the shelf in some places. Start the hike at the Blowhole and walk back to Hanauma Bay, where a tidepool known as the Toilet Bowl can be seen filling and flushing with each wave. Caution is urged: Several people have been killed diving into its surging waters.

WAIMANO TRAIL: An all-day hike on this 7-mile trail affords enough spectacular views of Windward Oahu to convince anyone of the island's great beauty. On the climb up to 1,600 feet, hikers can cool off in one of the many swimming holes found in Waimano Stream. The *palis* (cliffs) of the Koolau Range rise up majestically along this trail. Hikers should be in good shape for this trek.

HAWAII

The Big Island has some of the most dramatic volcanic trails in the Pacific. Because of its size, hiking routes are longer and the variety of trails is greater on Hawaii than on other islands. Nowhere else in the state can trekkers walk the hot-bedded floor of an active volcano — and live to talk about it. For guided hikes, check with the Sierra Club, 1100 Alakea St., Room 330, Honolulu, HI 96813 (phone: 538-6616). For trail information and maps, contact the Department of Land and Natural Resources, Division of Forestry, 1643 Kilauea Ave., Hilo, HI 96720 (phone: 961-7221).

HAWAII VOLCANOES NATIONAL PARK: The state's most fascinating volcanic trails crisscross the area around the Kilauea Crater. The easiest of the lot is *Devastation Trail,* a short jaunt of less than a mile that passes through the skeletal remains of an ohia forest that was rained on by volcanic showers in 1959. There is a per-vehicle or -person charge for park entry.

The 4-mile *Kilauea Iki Trail* leaves from a large volcanic tunnel known as the Thurston Lava Tube and descends a few hundred feet onto the crater floor. To the uninitiated, walking on the thick lava crust that blankets a red-hot molten pool of liquid rock can be like walking on eggs. The soles of your shoes will really heat up from this hike.

Experienced hikers seeking a good overview of the park itself should take a full-day tour on *Crater Rim Trail,* encircling the Kilauea Crater. The 11.6-mile route starts at the park's *Volcano House* and passes through the barren Kau Desert, skirting several steam vents along the way (hold your breath; the sulfurous clouds of smoke smell like rotten eggs). Make a detour off the trail to see the Halemaumau "fire pit," a hellish lake of steam.Good views can also be had on a hike to the summit of Mauna Loa, which takes 2 to 3 days and requires overnighting at park-run cabins. At press time, ranger-escorted hikes departed the Wahaula Visitor Center to view the recently hardened lava fields by the coast.

WAIPIO/WAIMANU VALLEY TRAILS: On the Big Island's northern tip are a pair of green, green valleys at the base of the rugged Kohala Mountains, where time stands still. A rich and fertile land once planted with acres of taro and favored by Hawaiian royalty, the valleys today are virtually unpopulated. A 2-to-3-day trip is necessary to penetrate this verdant retreat, far removed from the island's volcanic regions. In addition to the twin 1,000-foot waterfalls of Hiilawe, the four-wheel-drive road of the Waipio Valley takes hikers past ancient ruins, as well as by homes flattened by two *tsunami* (tidal waves) in the 1940s. Ambitious trekkers can scale the Z-shaped trail leading from Waipio Valley to the smaller and more secluded Waimanu Valley, where magnificent waterfalls and numerous beachfront campsites greet the backpacker.

MAUI

From the luxuriant rain forests of Hana to the otherworldly moonscape of Haleakala Crater, the Valley Isle has a superb variety of trails. Resort and condominium development may have inundated several coastal areas, but Maui's interior regions and the Hana coastline remain as untamed as ever for those willing to forgo civilized comforts in favor of natural wonders, at least for an afternoon. Walks and hikes in Haleakala National Park are led by park rangers on a seasonal, weather-permitting schedule. Call park headquarters (phone: 572-9306) for information on any scheduled crater rim walks (in the past they've taken place only during the summer) and the Kipahulu District office (phone: 248-8260) for details of the Saturday hikes to Waimoku Falls. Non-members may join the guided hikes of the Sierra Club, usually held on Saturdays and Sundays. They're announced in the Datebook section of the *Maui News* or you can call the Sierra Club Hawaii Chapter on Oahu (phone: 946-8494) for the telephone numbers of the Maui group's officers. For trail information and maps, contact the Department of Land and Natural Resources, Division of Forestry, 54 High St., Wailuku, HI 96793 (phone: 244-4352).

HALEAKALA NATIONAL PARK: Thirty-two miles of trails crisscross the crater depths of the massive dormant volcano known as "the House of the Sun." Trails lead down the crater walls or stretch across the crater floor 3,000 feet below the rim. Multicolored cinder cones and rare silversword plants punctuate this infernal landscape. The three main trail systems within the volcano are *Sliding Sands Trail,* a steep path of ash and cinders that drops precipitously to the crater floor; *Kaupo Trail,* which leaves the crater through Kaupo Gap and continues several miles south to the sea; and *Halemauu Trail,* a lovely path bordered by red and green ferns that winds past volcanic vents, large cones, and ancient lava flows. In addition to wild goats, hikers may spot the nene, a variety of goose that's been designated as Hawaii's state bird. Park headquarters has a brochure with a map, and also can provide details on the best trails for individual hikers. (Most of Haleakala's trails have steep grades and are fairly strenuous.) The park charges a small entrance fee.

KEANAE ARBORETUM: This short hike (1.5 miles) above the Keanae Peninsula near Hana is a perfect spot for a relaxed family outing. The garden contains domestic Hawaiian plants, native trees, and non-native tropical species. Several varieties of taro are grown (poi, a traditional Hawaiian food, is made from the taro root) as well as papayas, bananas, and sweet potatoes. Picnics are popular along the Piinaau Stream, which makes a fine swimming hole.

WAIKAMOI RIDGE: This is the shortest, easiest, and one of the most pleasurable trails on the island. Leading up an evenly graded slope to a grassy area with picnic tables overlooking Kolea Reservoir, the ridge trail passes bamboo and eucalyptus trees as well as large ferns. Waikamoi Ridge Trail is off the Hana Highway near Kailua; the hiking trail is convenient to good swimming and picnic areas at Twin Falls and Puohokamoa Falls.

MOLOKAI

Though most of its land is restricted, the Friendly Isle has several fine trails cut through four north coast valleys. One of the best (and the only one accessible by car) is the *Halawa Valley Trail,* a half-day hike for intermediate trekkers that leads to a pair of lovely waterfalls at the valley's end. These are Moaula Falls, two successive cascades that drop 250 feet to a large clear pool ideal for swimming, and Hipupua Falls, a high ribbon of water that tumbles over a *pali* (cliff) into a pool in the shape of a dog bone. This second waterfall is reached by hopping rocks leading up the Halawa Stream, an approach that should not be attempted if rain has made the rocks slippery.

LANAI

In addition to three rather arduous trails that meander around the rim of its spectacular interior gorge, Lanai has one of the best beachcombing hikes in the state. *Polihua Beach,* a trackless expanse of sand on the island's northwest shore, invites hikers to travel as many miles as they please along an almost endless stretch of berm and dunes. Hikers can discover the remnants of shipwrecks, as well as myriad seashells along the way. The island of Molokai is plainly visible across the Kalohi Channel from the beach. Polihua is accessible by foot or Jeep only; four-wheel-drive vehicles are available from rental agencies in Lanai City.

KAUAI

Only 20 minutes by air from Honolulu, the Garden Isle's top hiking trails are nevertheless far removed from civilization. The Hawaii of most people's fantasies can be seen on treks into the spectacular Waimea Canyon, along the plunging seacliffs of the Na Pali Coast, or on the fringes of the primordial Alakai Swamp. For trail information and maps, contact the Department of Land and Natural Resources, Division of Forestry, 3060 Eiwa St., Lihue, HI 96766 (phone: 245-4444).

KALALAU TRAIL: One of the finest wilderness hiking trails on earth. A strenuous and incredibly scenic route that winds above the massive seacliffs of the Na Pali Coast, the trail follows an ancient Hawaiian path for 11 miles through dense rain forests and groves of wild fruit trees. Day-trippers can turn back along the *Hanakapiai Valley Loop Trail* after stopping for a breather at Hanakapiai Falls and the sandy beach nearby. Hardy backpackers can continue along the Kalalau Trail to Hanakoa Valley, where the grade steepens considerably and their efforts are rewarded by the lovely sight of Hanakoa Falls, as well as marvelous views of the coastline. Snacks of wild guava and mountain apple can be enjoyed before descending Kalalau Valley, where there are several fine campsites near the beach. For those up to the challenge, this may well be the most beautiful and exciting hike in the state.

KUKUI TRAIL: This rugged 2½-mile trail descends 2,000 feet to the Waimea River, along the western edge of the famed "Grand Canyon of the Pacific." Though ideal for intermediate day hikers, the Kukui Trail provides access to the network of trails found on the Waimea Canyon floor, where experienced backpackers can continue on to campsites. Multicolored rocks that change in hue throughout the day, lush tropical forests, and many rare and colorful birds are among the sights glimpsed along this trail.

PIHEA LOOKOUT TRAIL: Here's a short trail (1.7 miles) that can be traversed in 2 hours, and yet provides the novice hiker with an excellent view of Kalalau Valley from a series of high *palis*. The path also skirts Alakai Swamp, sparing hikers the necessity of sinking in mud. Try taking this trail in the early morning hours, when wild goats can be seen hopping along the cliffs. The trail begins at Puu O Kila Lookout, where the 3,000-foot-high Na Pali seacliffs reach down like brown fingers to the crashing surf. The views along this modest trail are as wondrous as the floral profusion alongside it.

Camping from Crater to Coastline

Better known for its extravagant resorts that pamper guests with every luxury, Hawaii also boasts a generous supply of campgrounds for visitors who prefer more primitive accommodations. The range of environments is remarkable: Only in Hawaii can a camper spend one night in the eerie netherworld of a volcanic crater and the next in a beachfront park where tents are pulled taut on a grassy lawn within a stone's throw of pounding surf.

Camping in Hawaii is permitted in 2 national parks, 11 state parks, and 37 county parks. There is more than one way to go: It's possible to hike to a secluded campsite and pitch a tent (or sleep out under the stars). Camping equipment can be brought from home or rented at a number of sporting goods stores around the islands. Lightweight tents with a sewn-in floor are best for Hawaiian camping. Pack warm clothing for mountain camping; the weather is anything but tropical at 10,000 feet.

With the exception of three cabins in Haleakala Crater on Maui and cabins at the Namakani Paio campsite in Hawaii Volcanoes National Park, camping at Hawaii's federal parks is free. State park permits are free and usually allow camping for up to 1 week. Cabins at state parks are free or range from $3 per person to $25 per cabin per night. County park permits cost $1 for adults per night and 50¢ for children. These permits are issued for stays of from 3 to 7 days.

A small caveat for Hawaiian campers: Don't leave valuables unprotected. Theft is not uncommon at campsites, especially on Oahu. On the bright side, there are no snakes, poisonous insects, or poison ivy in the islands. A review of the top camping sites in the state follows.

OAHU

KEAIWA HEIAU STATE PARK: In the foothills of the Koolau Range, a few miles from Pearl Harbor, this upcountry park has a decidedly non-tropical climate, as well as a fascinating history. Keaiwa Heiau (a *heiau* is an ancient temple) is where Hawaiian medicine men cultivated herbs and other plants used to heal the sick. The campground here is a few hundred yards from temple ruins and herb gardens, all of it surrounded by dense forests of pine and eucalyptus trees. Keaiwa Heiau is best for tent camping; RVs can stay overnight with a permit. Closed Wednesdays and Thursdays. Information: Department of Land and Natural Resources, Division of State Parks, 1151 Punchbowl St., Room 310, Honolulu, HI 96813 (phone: 548-7455).

BELLOWS FIELD BEACH PARK: Though limited to weekend and holiday use, this lovely park, 20 miles east of Waikiki, is actually the small oceanfront corner of a large military base. Its barbecue pits and picnic tables make it popular with day-trippers, and the white sandy beach and calm sea make it a favorite of campers who also like to swim and snorkel. Visitors pitch tents near the forest of ironwood trees that rings the beach. A wonderful pastime here is watching the Pacific mole crabs ("sand turtles") burrow into the sand between waves. Bellows is convenient to Hanauma Bay, a designated marine preserve much enjoyed by snorkelers, and to Sea Life Park, where leaping porpoises and trained whales are the main attractions. A permit is required and must be obtained in person. Open weekends only. Information: Department of Parks and Recreation, 650 S. King St., Honolulu, HI 96813 (phone: 523-4525).

The Division of State Parks operates the Waimanalo Bay State Recreational Area adjacent to Bellows Field. Camping is allowed daily, except Wednesdays and Thursdays, and permits are required. Information: Department of Land and Natural Resources, Division of State Parks, 1151 Punchbowl St., Room 310, Honolulu, HI 96813 (phone: 548-7455).

KAHANA BAY BEACH PARK: A beautiful grove of ironwood pines on a wide crescent beach, with sawtooth mountains as a backdrop, makes this park on windward Oahu particularly inviting. The beach is very popular and safe for swimming, with a sandy ocean bottom and a gentle slope. Kahana Bay also offers shoreline fishing, and the park provides shower and barbecue facilities. Other top campsites in this region include *Nanakuli Beach Park* (tent and trailer camping allowed) and *Lualualei Beach Park* (tent camping only). Permits required for all parks. No camping allowed on Wednesdays and Thursdays. Information: Department of Parks and Recreation, 650 S. King St., Honolulu, HI 96813 (phone: 523-4525).

The state offers beachfront camping (daily except Wednesdays and Thursdays; permit required) at Malaekahana Beach, several miles up the coast from Kahana. Information: Department of Land and Natural Resources, Division of State Parks, 1151 Punchbowl St., Room 310, Honolulu, HI 96813 (phone: 548-7455).

HAWAII

HAWAII VOLCANOES NATIONAL PARK: Even hardened scoutmasters have been known to react like tenderfeet at the sight of this ethereal volcanic parkland. Some 30 miles from Hilo, the park is centered around 13,680-foot Mauna Loa and the flat, sloping volcano of Kilauea, the legendary home of Pele, Hawaiian goddess of fire. From the rim of the Halemaumau Firepit, campers can watch as Kilauea Crater belches sulfurous clouds of steam — recently it has erupted often to offer a far more spectacular show. The contrasts here are nearly surreal: giant fern forests not far from hardened lava flows punctuated by scorched trees.

The park maintains three fine drive-in campsites. At *Namakani Paio,* large eucalyptus trees shade individual RV camping slots. The campsite also has 10 cabins, as well as room for several tents. Temperatures here can drop below freezing at night. Even during the summer, campers curl up in down sleeping bags and often spend the night around large fireplaces near the site's pavilions. Reservations for cabins ($24 per day for up to 4 people) can be made at the *Volcano House.* You may need to bring an extra blanket, as only one is provided.

Kipuka Nene, a secluded campsite favored by residents, is surrounded by a ghostly forest of dead trees, all overshadowed by the volcanic cone of Mauna Loa. At the upper rim of Kilauea, off Chain of Craters Road, the site has a flat grassy area for tent campers and a parking lot for RVs. Like all of the park campsites, *Kipuka Nene* can be windy and rainy, but there are few more dramatic camping sites in the state.

In the lower reaches of the park, near Kalapana, is *Kamoamoa,* an oceanfront campsite bordered by a stand of ohia lehua trees ablaze with red pompom blossoms. The ruins of an ancient Hawaiian village can be explored here, and petroglyphs (pictures and ideographs carved in rock) can be found along the rugged lava coastline. There is a pleasant stretch of grass within earshot of the pounding surf where campers like to spread their picnics. *Kamoamoa* is quiet, private, and hauntingly beautiful. The lava flows of late 1986 and 1987 entered the sea not far from here. Information for all three sites: Hawaii Volcanoes National Park, HI 96718 (phone: 967-7311).

MAUNA KEA STATE PARK: Mauna Loa's volcanic twin sister is the 13,796-foot peak of Mauna Kea. The 500-acre state park on the slopes of the mountain can be reached by negotiating the Saddle Road (rent a four-wheel-drive vehicle for this excursion) to an elevation of 6,500 feet, where the state maintains 15 cozy log cabins. Five of the cabins have fireplaces, and all have bedding and kitchen utensils. (Advance reservations are advised.) Though the sun is intense during the day, the weather turns sharply colder at night. (The cabins are popular with skiers during the winter.) The night sky at Mauna Kea is so dense with stars that it's worth rolling out of bed to see; the cabins are a great place to stay if you plan to make a night visit to the Onizuka Center or Mauna Kea's summit for a look through one of the telescopes set up for visitors. Information: Division of State Parks, 75 Aupuni St., Hilo, HI 96720 (phone: 961-7200).

HAPUNA BEACH STATE PARK: Though often a bit crowded, Hapuna has six screened A-frame cabins across the street from one of the finest white sand beaches in the state. Each cabin accommodates four people on rather spartan wooden platforms (bring your own bedding). Like most Kona Coast beaches, Hapuna has abundant and varied marine life and coral formations; it is especially popular with campers who like to snorkel. In addition, there are spacious picnic areas shaded by coconut palms and hala trees. Maui's volcano, Haleakala, is plainly visible from the park. Advance reservations are advised. Information: Division of State Parks, 75 Aupuni St., Hilo, HI 96720 (phone: 961-7200).

MAUI

HALEAKALA NATIONAL PARK: Though the opportunities are limited, the fortunate few who get to camp inside Haleakala Crater are said to be transformed by the experience. Whether from excitement or the cold, campers usually awaken early to see the crater's red cinder cones and spiny silversword plants bathed in the purplish light that appears just before dawn.

There are two campgrounds inside this vast dormant volcano: *Holua* and *Paliku* are both wilderness sites 3,000 feet below the crater rim, accessible by trail. Each campground is limited to 25 persons. Overnight stays are limited to 2 days at one site and 3 days' total at both, and a permit is required. There is also a 12-person cabin at each campsite, but these shelters are so popular that a monthly lottery is held to determine their use. If you're lucky enough to make it to "the House of the Sun," dress warmly; temperatures regularly drop below freezing inside the moonlike crater.

In addition to the crater campsites, a tent campground and picnic facilities are in a forested area near the park entrance at Hosmer Grove. In marked contrast to the arid crater landscape, Hosmer is lush, wooded, and serene. No permit is required, but camping is limited to 3 days. Information: Haleakala National Park, PO Box 369, Makawao, HI 96768 (phone: 572-9306).

POLIPOLI SPRINGS STATE PARK: On the slopes of Haleakala in central Maui, Polipoli has cabin and tent camping for those who manage to survive a hair-raising 10-mile drive on a bumpy dirt road leading to the campsite (a four-wheel-drive vehicle is suggested). This secluded upcountry retreat is nestled in a dense forest of redwood, pine, and cypress trees, and is usually blanketed by a morning fog that lifts in the afternoon to reveal a stunning view of several surrounding islands. The 3-bedroom cabin at the site sleeps 10 people. Dress warmly; the weather (by Hawaiian standards) can be very damp and cold. A permit is required, as is an advance deposit. Information: Division of State Parks, PO Box 1049, Wailuku, HI 96793 (phone: 244-4354).

WAIANAPANAPA STATE PARK: On a grassy bluff overlooking a black sand beach along the Hana coast, this 120-acre park has both tent sites and cabins. The ocean is too rough for swimming here, but the opportunities for hiking and exploring are unsurpassed. The list of natural attractions includes ancient lava flows, dramatic sea arches, shallow lava caves, a small blowhole, and a lovely footpath that winds along the coastline to Hana. With its exuberant vegetation and fine facilities, Waianapanapa is considered one of the state's top campsites. A permit is required, also an advance deposit. Information: Division of State Parks, PO Box 1049, Wailuku, HI 96793 (phone: 244-4354).

MOLOKAI

PALAAU STATE PARK: A 34-acre mountain wilderness of koa, paperbark, ironwood, and cypress trees, this north coast park is known for its spectacular view of Makanalua, the peninsula where Father Damien founded his famous leper colony. In addition to having a series of petroglyphs carved in rock near the campground, the site is just a few hundred yards from a 6-foot-high phallic symbol that was visited long ago by infertile women hoping to change their luck. There is tent camping only at Palaau. A permit is required. Information: Division of State Parks, PO Box 627, Kaunakakai, HI 96748 (phone: 567-6083).

KAUAI

KOKEE STATE PARK: Tent and trailer camping is available at this tropical mountain forest of silver oak and wild plum trees marked off by Waimea Canyon and Kalalau

Lookout. The views of Kauai and the blue ocean that surrounds it, as seen from Kokee's 45 miles of trails, are simply breathtaking. In addition to rustic campsites with minimal facilities along these hiking trails, the state maintains 12 cabins, each of which can accommodate 3 to 7 people. Reservations for the latter should be sent to Kokee Lodge, PO Box 819, Waimea, HI 96796 (phone: 335-6061). Kokee also accommodates trailer campers (a permit is required for RVs). Plan your trip during the summer; heavy rains can turn Kokee's trails to mud at other times of the year. Permits are required. Information: Division of State Parks, PO Box 1671, Lihue, HI 96766 (phone: 245-4444).

HAENA BEACH PARK: This county-run site on Kauai's north shore, sandwiched between the raging ocean (strong currents and rip tides make swimming dangerous here) and steep lava cliffs, is a good base from which to see a variety of attractions. Just across the street from the park is the Maniniholo Dry Cave, a lava tube worth exploring. Up the road a piece are the Waikapalae and Waikanaloa Wet Caves, both ideal for a bracing swim. Ocean bathers are advised to go to Kee Beach, at the head of the Kalalau trail. Adventurous beachgoers can hike a 2-mile trail to Hanakapiai Beach, or a more difficult 11-mile trail to Kalalau Beach, or follow the dirt roads leading off Route 56 to any number of unnamed (and uncrowded) beaches. Haena has tent and trailer camping, and a permit is required. Information: Parks Permit Section, 4280A Rice St., Lihue, HI 96766 (phone: 245-1881).

ANINI BEACH PARK: Take the turn-off 2 miles past Kilauea Village to this large beach park which is set amid ancient ironwood pines and grassy lawns, with two camping areas that can accommodate up to 200 people at a time. Facilities include cold showers, picnic and barbeque sites, and uncovered pavilions for eating. Safe swimming and a large, uncrowded beach are the lures. Camping is permitted for 7 consecutive nights. As with other Kauai County parks, mail-in reservations are accepted, but payment for out-of-staters ($3 per night, per adult) must be made at the park's permit section, or, if they are closed, at the Lihue police station, 3060 Umi St., which can accept payments from campers 24 hours a day. Information: Parks Permit Section, 4193 Hardy St., Lihue, HI 96766 (phone: 245-1881).

Hawaii on Horseback

 For those partial to four-legged means of transportation, Hawaii's riding facilities offer the adventurous equestrian all-day or overnight treks, as well as horses on an hourly basis. Even for rank beginners, there are few more delightful ways to explore dormant volcanoes, mountain rain forests, or hidden waterfalls than on horseback or mule.

MAUI: Overnight trail rides into the crater of Haleakala, the 10,023-foot "House of the Sun," where the legendary demigod Maui lassoed the sun and held it captive in a primitive form of daylight saving time, gives visiting cowpokes a firsthand look at the natural wonders that spawned island mythology. The vast crater (Manhattan would easily fit inside it) is creased with trails that descend to a moon-like surface littered with multicolored cinder cones. Within this volcanic netherworld are several more miles of marked trails that meander through exotic vegetation and grazing areas for the horses. Travelers stay at one of three cabins maintained by park rangers or take refuge in campsites or caverns, and since the air turns cool at night in the crater, sweaters or heavy sleepwear is recommended. The trek, limited to two to six riders, has rates with ($150) and without ($125) meals included ($200 with or without meals if the ride is limited to two or three riders), although it's said that the trail leader's wife packs a fried chicken and potato salad dinner that far surpasses freeze-dried trail food. The 8-hour trip from the ranch to Haleakala is a rather arduous ride, but the chance to chase the rising sun across the crater on horseback is not soon forgotten. Rides must be booked a month or two in advance. Information: Charley's Trail Rides and Pack Trips, c/o Kaupo Store, Hana, HI 96713 (phone: 248-8209).

Rainbow Ranch and *Kaanapali Kau Lio* make tame ascents to west Maui's panoramic upcountry. *Adventures on Horseback* meets riders at the Halawa Bridge on the Hana Highway for rides inland and to the sea. Information: Rainbow Ranch, PO Box 10066, Lahaina, HI 96761 (phone: 669-4991); Kaanapali Kau Lio, PO Box 10656, Lahaina, HI 96761 (phone: 667-7896); Adventures on Horseback, PO Box 1771, Makawao, Hi 96768 (phone: 242-7445).

MOLOKAI: On the isolated Makanalua Peninsula, accessible only by plane, boat, or mule, is Kalaupapa, the famed 19th-century leper colony founded by the Belgian priest Father Damien. After a brief stop at Kalaupapa Lookout, 1,600 feet above the peninsula, riders on sure-footed mules edge down a steep 3-mile trail cut from a rain forest. The lacy waterfalls and sheer *palis* (cliffs) seen during the descent make up some of Hawaii's most dramatic scenery. At trail's end, a 3-hour mini-bus tour of this historic settlement gives visitors an insight into the life of the unfortunate leper outcasts of 100 years ago. (The disease has since been largely arrested.) The group breaks for a picnic lunch at Kalawao Park before returning their mounts to the Kalae corral.

Mule rides to the Makanalua Peninsula are limited to visitors over 16 years and under 225 pounds. The price for the all-day trek is $75. Information: Molokai Mule Ride, PO Box 200, Kualapuu, HI 96757 (phone: 567-6088; 800-843-5978).

KAUAI: In addition to a 1-hour ride ($23) across ranchlands bordering the upper reaches of beautiful Hanalei Valley on Kauai's north shore, visitors can saddle up for a 2-hour shoreline ride ($45) that crisscrosses the famous Princeville Ranch and affords impressive views of the coast. One of the more popular trips on the island is a 3-hour Waterfall Picnic Ride ($75), which stops at the 70-foot Kalihiwai waterfall for a cool swim followed by a picnic lunch. Children or adults with mobility problems are excluded because the hike to the waterfall, though short, is strenuous. The first weekend in August, Pooku hosts the Hanalei Stampede rodeo, featuring the islands' top *paniolos* (cowboys). Information: Pooku Stables, PO Box 888, Hanalei, HI 96714 (phone: 826-6777).

In Poipu, *CJM Country Stables* offers three types of rides. In the morning, there is the 3-hour Breakfast Ride ($55 per person), which heads inland before stopping for breakfast on a secluded beach, and in the afternoons, there are 1- and 2-hour beach rides ($20 and $40, respectively). Information: CJM Country Stables, 5598 Tapa St., Koloa, HI 96756 (phone: 245-6666).

HAWAII: West Hawaii's ranchland provides beautiful upcountry pastures for horseback riding. *Ironwood Outfitters,* PO Box 832, Kamuela, HI 96743 (phone: 885-4941), offers the best rides in Hawaii, both for the scenic grandeur of the Kohala Mountains and the chance for riders to let loose and gallop. The first light ride (8 to 9:30 AM) catches the sunrise over Mauna Kea, while the 2½-hour morning ride (10 AM to 1 PM) reaches panoramic heights 5,000 feet above sea level. Riders are more tamely escorted at *Waikoloa Stables,* PO Box 3466, Waikoloa, HI 96743 (phone: 883-9335), and at the *Mauna Kea Stables,* PO Box 218, Kamuela, HI 96743 (phone: 885-4288), whose routes rove Parker Ranch land on the slopes of Hualalai.

Hunting

Hawaii, believe it or not, has some of the most productive hunting grounds in the world. In the cool mountain uplands roam wild boar descended from the pigs first brought to Hawaii by the original Polynesian settlers. Feral sheep and wild goats are found on the high slopes of the Big Island's dormant volcanoes, while axis deer are hunted on Molokai. In addition, game birds ranging from pheasant and quail to wild turkey and chukar partridge challenge the buckshot artist.

The state hunting license and permit for non-residents is $15, and there are usually trophy fees for game taken. Though there are nearly 20 public hunting areas in the state, the best hunting opportunities are found on private lands, for which guide services are available. Rates for these services range from $250 to $350 per hunter per day, and usually include a guide, transportation, and meals. Rifles and ammunition are available at $20 to $25 per day. A maximum of four hunters per party is the rule.

HAWAII: The finest hunting in the state is found on the slopes of Mauna Kea and Mt. Hualalai on the Kona Coast. Eugene Ramos, who *is Hawaii Hunting Tours* and to whom the *Mauna Kea Beach* hotel refers prospective hunters, has access to 20,000 acres of the Parker Ranch, on the slopes of Mauna Kea. Corsican sheep and wild goats are the main quarry. Wild boar, weighing up to 300 pounds, with short curling tusks, are found in wet areas. Hunters travel by Jeep to selected sites and then stalk game on foot. Ramos claims that nowhere else in the world can a big-game hunter be "successful" and return to his hotel the same day. He also notes that hunters can be stalking game in the snows of Mauna Kea in the morning and go swimming in the afternoon. Bird hunting on the Big Island is especially good for Nepal Kaliz pheasant, Erckel's francolin (a type of grouse), chukar partridge, and Japanese quail. The game bird season runs from the first Saturday in November through the third Sunday in January. Information: *Hawaii Hunting Tours,* PO Box 58, Paauilo, HI 96776 (phone: 776-1666).

MAUI: Maui's best hunting grounds are found in the forest reserves of East Maui, on the slopes of Haleakala. Here the feral goat and wild boar are the choice game mammals, though wild boar are also found in the forests below the Eke Crater on West Maui. Valley Isle hunters conduct their searches on fertile territory, where the air is often scented by pine and eucalyptus trees.

At press time there were no guided hunting tours on Maui. Individual hunters with state-issued permits can go after game, although this may be difficult and risky without a guide.

MOLOKAI: Modeled after the commercial hunting preserves in Texas, the *Molokai Ranch* offers year-round hunting for axis deer (bucks weigh up to 200 pounds) and barbary sheep on a fee basis. (It costs $600 for each animal taken, in addition to the $400 daily fee payable even by unsuccessful hunters.) Exclusivity is guaranteed: The number of hunters on the ranch is limited to five on any given day.

From November to January, weekends and holidays only, the ranch permits hunting for upland game birds. The fee is $300 for the season ($25 per day). A detailed map is provided in lieu of a guide. Hunters must bring their own equipment. Information: Molokai Ranch, PO Box 8, Maunaloa, HI 96770 (phone: 552-2767).

Gliding and Hang Gliding

HANG GLIDING: Thanks to recent aerodynamic improvements in flying equipment, hang gliding is no longer considered a "fringe" sport, suited only for potential kamikaze pilots. Hawaii, in fact, has some of the world's most beautiful sites for this highly individual pursuit. The *Tradewinds Hang Gliding Center* runs a beginner program for those interested in savoring the immediate and thrilling sense of flight unavailable to those inside an aircraft. According to the US Hang Gliding Association, the sport is "great physical and mental therapy for those frustrated by the daily constraints of modern living." (The USHGA also believes that hang gliding most closely realizes the flying imagined in dreams.)

Following USHGA guidelines, Lani Akiona and state champion Mike Benson of *Tradewinds* organizes small classes (no more than six pupils in a group) for introductory lessons, during which novices "tackle some pretty good-sized sand dunes." The 2- to 3-hour sessions cost $50. Akiona emphasizes that achieving great height is not necessary to experience the exhilaration of hang gliding. Whether you are 12 inches or 1,200 feet in the air, the excitement of lifting off the ground on a pair of wings is the same. Only the view is different.

Tradewinds' emphasis during the introductory lessons is on fun. The basic course is designed to show beginners how hang gliders fly, to familiarize them with the glider and its equipment, and to enable them to experience the thrill of launching themselves into the air safely. Novices can look forward to 10 mini-flights during the first session. Akiona only teaches when the weather is good, which is about 75% of the time. (In the same way that a surfer needs waves to surf, a hang glider needs wind to fly.) Safety is the overriding concern, but Akiona insists the only injury incurred during her classes was a blister someone received from holding on to the control bar too tightly.

In further support of the sport, Akiona says hang glider equipment at present is vastly improved over "wings" made less than 5 years ago, which are now considered unsafe. The flying characteristics of new certified gliders permit pilots to climb higher, go farther, and land more safely. Turning, handling, and performance are all greatly improved on new models. Accidents caused by design inadequacies are virtually nonexistent these days.

Tradewinds runs excursions for advanced flyers to the main ridge of Makapuu, among the velvety green *palis* (cliffs) of the Koolau Range. Waimanalo is also a favorite ridge-soaring site of accomplished hang glider pilots. Back to the beginners: Akiona says that many visitors who take the introductory lesson pursue the sport back home. No finer setting could be provided for a first taste of do-it-yourself flying, though the timid need not apply. Information: Tradewinds Hang Gliding Center (phone: 396-8557).

GLIDING: Those who feel more secure flying *inside* even a motorless aircraft can book a *Glider Rides* flight at Dillingham Airfield, near the Mokuleia polo grounds in northwest Oahu. The 15-to-20-minute flights, narrated and piloted by veterans who have logged more than a million miles in gliders, soar to mountain range heights of up to 3,000 feet, depending on lift conditions. Visibility extends more than 30 miles from Kahuku and the patchwork sugarcane plantations at Waialua to Kaena Point, at the western tip of the island. Sights include the famous North Shore surfing playgrounds, brilliant coral reefs, and various Oahu resort complexes as well as the US Air Force Satellite Tracking Station and leaping schools of dolphin and humpback whales. On a clear day, 80-mile-distant Kauai may be spotted.

The bubble-top gliders seat one or two passengers and leave Dillingham Airfield every 20 minutes from 10:30 AM to 5:30 PM. Rides are $40 for one person, $60 for two. Glider pilot instruction is available by appointment. The service operates year-round; pilots report no more than 30 unflyable days a year. Gliders provide a tranquil, safe, and almost noiseless high-altitude view of Oahu. Information: Glider Rides, PO Box 626, Waialua, HI 96791 (phone: 677-3404).

On Kauai, *Tradewinds Gliders* departs Burns Field for 20-minute ($75 for one person, $90 for two) and 40-minute ($125 for one person, $150 for two) flights over the south coast, from Waimea to Poipu. Weather permitting, gliders head inland for views of the waterfalls and canyons of Hanapepe. Information: Tradewinds Gliders, PO Box 2099, Lihue, HI 96766 (phone: 335-5086).

Flightseeing

 Perhaps the most interesting aspect of either helicopter or fixed-wing flight-seeing tours of the Hawaiian islands is each visitor's reaction to being borne aloft over sections of paradise inaccessible to all but the air traveler. "Too beautiful to describe," "Absolutely unreal," and "Purely and uniquely of the Lord" are among the entries found in the ledger of one Maui helicopter company.

There is no more glamorous tour in Hawaii than a flightseeing excursion. With their champagne picnics at secluded spots and drops on deserted beaches, the helicopter companies are the ultimate trailblazers. "We're not in the transportation business — we're in the 'experience-providing' business," says one company owner, who calls his trips "adventures set to music." Most helicopters and tour planes are equipped with headsets, through which passengers hear the pilot's narration or music appropriate to the natural wonder below.

Yes, flightseeing prices are high, but many travelers consider them a relative bargain for the quality of the experience delivered. Prices range from under $30 for a short hop along the Waikiki coast to $275 for a 2-hour all-island tour of Kauai that includes a drop in the middle of nowhere for a picnic lunch or a volcano tour departing West Hawaii's Keahole Airport. The helicopters, most of them flown by former air force fighter pilots, seat four to six passengers. By all means, bring your camera; you'll have rare opportunities to capture crater rims, deep gorges, sheer cliffs, and other sights to which only birds and other privileged sightseers are usually privy. Refer to *A Shutterbug's Hawaii,* in this section, for advice on how best to take photos aloft. In general, March through October is the best season for flightseeing, though it's possible year round.

Apart from the more publicized helicopter services whose tours are extensively described below, there are several smaller competing flightseeing services over Hawaii. Sometimes they offer significant discounts. Check local listings. Fixed-wing commuter aircraft are also used for aerial tours. For those uncomfortable with the thought of helicopter flying, this may be the answer. It also costs less, on the average.

OAHU: Though the dramatic scenery of Hawaii's outer islands draws most of the flightseeing raves, Oahu is also worth seeing. In addition to its famous surfing beaches on the North Shore and beautiful interior valleys, the island has points of historical interest that take on a new dimension from the air.

Hawaii Pacific Helicopters runs a series of six tours ranging from a few minutes to an hour. The Oahu Experience provides an excellent condensed tour of the island. Passengers fly over Waikiki Beach, the extinct volcano of Diamond Head, and the exclusive residential community of Kahala before hovering near Hanauma Bay, where the love scenes of *From Here to Eternity* were filmed. The helicopter follows the rugged coastline to Makapuu Beach before passing over Sea Life Park near the *palis* (cliffs) of the Koolau Range. Here the aircraft rises suddenly to climb over the twin peaks of 1,643-foot tall Olomana. The scenic highlight of the trip may well be the visit to Nuuanu Pali, where sheer 1,000-foot drop-offs, sawtooth mountains blanketed in green, and waterfalls whose cascades are blown upward by the wind are sprawled out in the Nuuanu Valley. It is a magnificent vista.

The Oahu Epic ($180) skips Nuuanu Pali but visits the North Shore. Sunset and the Banzai Pipeline, the famous surfing beaches where the waves reach a height of 30 feet in winter, and Waimea Bay, known for its beautiful valley and 45-foot waterfall, also are included. Large fields of pineapple and sugarcane, stretching to the fuzzy blue peaks of the Waianae Mountains, signal the approach to Pearl Harbor, where the elegant, white Arizona Memorial can be seen, marking the resting place of the sunken battleship. Another tour flies past Waikiki and Honauma Bay to Molokai, past the dramatic North Coast cliffs and valleys, with a stop for lunch at the *Kaluakoi* resort before returning to Waikiki via the windward coast ($275). Information: Papillon Hawaii Pacific, 421 Aowena Pl., Honolulu, HI 96819 (phone: 836-1556; 800-367-8047, ext. 142).

Cherry Helicopters offers three tour itineraries that depart from the helipad at the Turtle Bay Resort. There's a 15-minute look at the North Shore beaches ($40), a 30-minute visit to Sacred Falls ($80), and a Fly 'n' Shop visit to Honolulu that includes 30 minutes in the air and a 4- to 5-hour stopover in Honolulu for shopping ($80). Information: Cherry Helicopters, 410 Aowena Pl., Honolulu, HI 96819 (phone: 833-4339).

Royal Helicopters, with departures from a helipad just outside of Waikiki, offers among its tours a 6- to 8-minute introduction to Waikiki and downtown Honolulu ($25); a 20-minute tour of either downtown and Pearl Harbor or Waikiki and Hanauma Bay ($60); a ½-hour Pali Pass tour that follows the route of the Japanese Pearl Harbor bombers ($90), and the Oahu Adventure, which covers about two-thirds of the island in an hour-long tour ($150). Information: Royal Helicopters, PO Box 29531, Honolulu, HI 96820 (phone: 836-2868).

HAWAII: Departing from the Waikoloa Resort, on the Big Island's west coast, *Kenai Air*'s Volcano, Kohala Mountains, and Kona Coast helicopter tours fly over some of the most dramatic volcanic scenery in the world. On the Volcano tour, passengers soar above lava flows that stretch from the sea to the top of Kilauea, and the pilot guides the whirling craft over the eruption zone, passing by 13,680-foot Mauna Loa and its neighbor, 13,796-foot Mauna Kea, for a bird's eye view of this great volcano — the highest point in Hawaii. The vista from this mountaintop perspective is absolutely awesome. The observant sightseer may spot feral goats, sheep, and wild boar on the slopes of Mauna Loa. The Kona Coast tour includes Kailua-Kona and the coast down to Puuhonua O Honaunau (City of Refuge), a sanctuary set in a lush coconut grove. It was in this asylum that defeated warriors, and those excommunicated from their tribes for violating sacred *kapus* (taboos), sought refuge. While the pilot narrates the enclave's fascinating history, look for the tall stone tikis depicting Polynesian gods located inside the thick lava stone walls encircling the temple grounds.

The next stop is Kealakekua Bay. Here the Captain Cook Monument juts out into the water where the great British navigator, who discovered the Hawaiian islands, died. The helicopter then skims over the shiny green coffee plantations on the Kona Coast, pausing at lovely Keauhou Bay to see how lava flows created this sparkling body of water. The great size of the Big Island (comparable in land mass to Connecticut) is best appreciated from the air. Information: Kenai Air Hawaii, PO Box 4118, Kailua-Kona, HI 96745 (phone: 329-7424; 800-367-2603). Similar tour itineraries are offered by *Papillon Helicopters,* PO Box 55, Kamuela, HI 96743 (phone: 883-8808; 800-562-5641 from other islands), which departs from Waikoloa, and by *Kona Helicopters,* 75-6160 Alii Dr., Kailua-Kona, HI 96740 (phone: 329-0551), which departs from Keahole Airport, Mauna Lani Resort, Waikoloa Resort, Kona Village Resort, and the *Kona Surf.*

For tours that focus on Hawaii Volcanoes National Park, there is *Hilo Bay Air,* which departs from Hilo's General Lyman Field, and *Volcano Helitours,* which leaves from the helipad at the national park. Due to their proximity to the park, these volcano viewing tours are much less expensive than Kailua-Kona departures. Information: Hilo Bay Air, PO Box 4278, Hilo, HI 96720 (phone: 969-1545 or -1547); Volcano Helitours, PO Box 626, Volcano, HI 96785 (phone: 967-7578).

Big Island Air offers twin-prop aircraft departures from Keahole Airport. Its 2-hour Circle Island itinerary ($135) is about the most comprehensive aerial view of the Big Island offered by anyone. A full 6-hour Volcano-Combo Tour ($235) includes ground tours of Hilo and of Hawaii Volcanoes National Park, with lunch at the *Volcano House* restaurant. No flights on Sundays. Information: Big Island Air, PO Box 1476, Kailua-Kona, HI 96745 (phone: 329-4868).

MAUI: With the possible exception of those over Kauai, and over the Big Island when its volcanoes are active, helicopter tours of the Valley Isle are the most exciting in the state. *Maui Helicopters* operates five air tours of the island, plus custom charters, departing from the helicopter air terminal at Kahului. The company's most popular trip is its Panoramic Journey, which combines a number of Maui highlights.

After lifting off in Kahului and passing over the lava flows and coral reefs along the Kihei shoreline, the four-passenger helicopter swings over Makena Beach. From late November to April, passengers may catch sight of a humpback whale breaking the surface offshore. The pilot then steers the craft away from the sea, moving inland up the steep incline of Haleakala. The helicopter climbs to the rim of this 10,023-foot volcanic cone and then descends nearly 3,000 feet into the crater to explore an unearthly moonscape that stretches for 19 square miles. Passengers can see vividly colored cinder cones, cavernous pits, and winding footpaths cut through this desolate caldera.

Emerging from the interior of the crater, the pilot steers directly to Hana, the heavenly region on the eastern slope of Haleakala, where the great profusion of jungles, waterfalls, and cliffs is spellbinding. The tour also soars over the Seven Pools near Kipahulu and the burial site of aviator Charles A. Lindbergh. Creeping up the north shore, the helicopter flies over the double-spouted Wailua Falls and countless unnamed · valleys and rain forests before touching down on the Kahului's helipad. *Maui Helicopters* calls Panoramic Journey "lovely, exotic, memorable." Sometimes there *is* truth in advertising. Information: Maui Helicopters, Box 1002, Kihei, Maui, HI 96753 (phone: 879-1601; 800-367-8003).

"I'll never stop smiling again!" and "High point of my life" are among the comments made by passengers on returning from *Papillon Helicopters'* top-of-the-line Maui Odyssey flight. The 2-hour excursion, departing from Napalihau near Kapalua, is an air/land experience: In addition to extensive exploration of the West Maui mountains and other sites where green velvet walls soar to 5,000 feet, the helicopter sets down at the Hana Airport for a picnic lunch. The flight also includes Iao Needle and the pinwheel of valleys and cliffs that surrounds it, the tropical geometry of the taro fields of the Keanae Peninsula, and the lunar reality of Haleakala.

Papillon also runs a spectacular Haleakala Sunrise flight, which lasts 1½ hours and includes a stop in Hana. Information: Papillon Helicopters, PO Box 1690, Lahaina, HI 96767 (phone: 669-4884; 800-367-7095).

MOLOKAI: Formed thousands of years ago by the upsurge of two volcanic domes, Molokai is paradise preserved. It is a perfect flightseeing destination for those who prefer the quiet seclusion of an isolated beach between their airborne adventures. *Kenai Air* (see above) runs a Wailau Beach Picnic that deposits lovers and explorers on Molokai's north shore. A picnic lunch with wine is provided, as the pristine setting of plunging seacliffs and virgin beaches tends to work up an appetite. With its day-long opportunities for beachcombing and hiking into the lovely Wailau Valley, this beach picnic is probably Hawaii's top getaway tour.

Papillon Helicopters (see above) runs a 1-hour West Maui/Molokai trip departing from West Maui. It must be booked 48 hours in advance and for a minimum of four passengers. After crossing the Pailolo Channel (watch for humpback whales in the winter), the whirlybirds fly over southeast Molokai, where deep valleys stretch like so many fingers to a sea that seems bluer than anywhere else in Hawaii. On the northern coastline, the pilot flies close to Molokai's famous *palis,* the sheer 2,000-foot seacliffs creased with waterfalls that crash triumphantly into the surf. The photographic opportunities here are unsurpassed. The heli-tour continues on to the Makanalua Peninsula, the flat volcanic plateau where the Belgian priest Father Damien founded his leper colony in 1873. It includes a half-hour ground tour at Kalaupapa, on the peninsula's west coast, where the colony has resided since 1888. While it's interesting to explore Kalaupapa on foot, the settlement's geographic isolation from the rest of the island can be best appreciated from the air.

KAUAI: One airborne trip over Kauai is enough to convince anyone that the Garden Isle is one of Mother Nature's masterpieces. Seen from the air, Kauai is Hawaii at its best — lush, serene, and spectacularly beautiful.

Papillon Helicopters, which has transported entire wedding parties to remote coastline settings, runs five tours of the island. These range from 30 minutes to 3 hours in length and from $85 to $225 per person in price, taking in those twin splendors of Kauai — Waimea Canyon, the island's smaller version of Arizona's Grand Canyon, and the Na Pali Coast, where cliffs rise 3,000 feet from the sea. Looking down at this untamed coastline from the air is known to make people ecstatically giddy or unusually silent. Departures from Princeville Airport. Information: Papillon Helicopters, Princeville Airport, PO Box 339, Hanalei, HI 96714 (phone: 826-6591; 800-367-7095).

Kenai Air's most popular air tour of Kauai is its 1-hour Garden Island Deluxe trip ($129). The airborne theme is one of contrast: The helicopter flies over the 5,000-foot rim of Waialeale Crater to enter a world of thin streaming waterfalls and leafy green cliffs half-shrouded in mist. Passengers next view the vast barren insides of the 10-mile-long Waimea Canyon, where mountain goats leaping among the rocks and the ever-changing hues of the landscape are the main sources of wonder. The tour passes over Hanalei Valley, the "birthplace of rainbows," before traversing the sacred valleys of the ancient Hawaiians along the Na Pali Coast. Here, forbidding 3,000-foot mountain walls shelter a string of isolated beaches and hidden valleys. Departures from Lihue Airport. Information: Kenai Helicopters, PO Box 3270, Lihue, HI 96766 (phone: 245-8591; 800-622-3144).

South Sea Helicopter also offers a range of aerial tours of the garden isle. Information: South Sea Helicopter, PO Box 1445, Lihue, HI 96766 (phone: 245-7781; 800-367-2914).

Fly Kauai flies several Cessna aircraft on ½- and 1-hour tours for considerably less than their helicopter counterparts: $39 and $69, respectively. The 1-hour Circle Island itinerary includes a fly-by of Kipukai and Poipu, which are not included on helicopter tours. The ½-hour tour heads straight from Lihue Airport to Waimea Canyon and the Na Pali Coast. Information: Fly Kauai, PO Box 3778, Lihue, HI 96766 (phone: 828-1344).

For the Mind

Museums, Churches, and Mission Houses

The Hawaiian culture is an ancient one, reaching back more than 1,400 years to its South Seas roots, and several noteworthy museums stand as testimony to the state's cultural diversity. Like the islands themselves, they are small in size but full of delightful surprises. Our museum selection traces the islands' multiracial heritage and development, ranging from the early Polynesian settlers to European traders and American whalers, then on to the various Asian groups imported to till the soil. It includes several churches and mission houses, which so poignantly chronicle Hawaii's conversion to Christianity, as well as the homestead of a former sugarcane plantation, which provides a glimpse into the lives of those who shaped Hawaii's present.

BISHOP MUSEUM, Honolulu, Oahu: For a real whale of a time, enjoy all 55 feet, 22 tons, of one right here. A sperm whale is suspended from the ceiling in the Hawaiian Hall, recalling the days when whaling brought Hawaii much of its reputation and prosperity. Of the numerous exhibition halls in the museum, this one is easily the most interesting. On three separate levels plus a newly opened wing, the museum traces the story of the islands from prehistoric times. Among the exhibits: "Hawaii: The Royal Isles," tracing the islands' monarchy. This section of the museum has portraits of all the islands' kings and queens, together with thrones, crowns, and regalia, plus examples of their uniforms and clothes. Also on display is a fine collection of artifacts common to the islands before the arrival of Captain Cook. A shallow bowl supported by humanoid figurines, an ornate bone fishhook that would be commendable as a brooch, and feather cloaks, capes, and helmets in the royal colors of yellow, red, and black catch the eye here. The second level features a lovely collection of tapa cloth, as well as exhibits on 19th-century whaling. In the Polynesian Hall is a magnificent display of materials from other islands of the Pacific. Look particularly for an elaborate mourning costume from the Society Islands, an ornamental headdress from Samoa, and a highly decorated mask from Melanesia. A stunning array of exquisitely formed mollusks is displayed next to the Hall of Natural History. In the Science Center is an exhibit of rainbow-colored insects arranged like bracelets and necklaces in a jeweler's window. There is more besides: hula and Hawaiian crafts at the Atherton Halau, astronomy shows in the planetarium, and examples of indigenous trees and shrubs in the charming Garden Courtyard. Information: The Bishop Museum, 1525 Bernice St., Honolulu, HI 96817 (phone: 847-3511).

HONOLULU ACADEMY OF ARTS, Honolulu, Oahu: A special delight for connoisseurs of small art museums. But even for those who never give paintings or sculpture a second glance, a worthwhile hour or two can be spent here, particularly if you take in one of the excellent special exhibits. The academy's Spanish Court and Chinese

Courtyard, both cloistered patios, are the most civilized oases in Honolulu, the perfect escape from the hectic trading in the merchant houses of downtown and from the hedonistic throng on Waikiki. Handsome as the gallery's design and architecture are — and they are very handsome indeed — it is the collections that give the academy its nationwide reputation. Among the most celebrated of these are its Asian holdings, consisting of ceramics, paintings, furniture, bronzes, lacquerwork, and sculpture; the Kress Collection of Italian Renaissance paintings; and the Michener Collection of Japanese prints. Among items that remain vividly in one's memory are a bronze and silver mirror from the T'ang dynasty of China, between the 7th and 10th centuries; the 14th-century statue *Kuan Yin,* also from China; Segna de Bonaventura's painting *Madonna and Child,* from the early Italian Renaissance; Paul Gauguin's *Two Nudes on a Tahitian Beach;* and one of Monet's superb studies of *Water Lilies.* There's also an intriguing collection of Roman glass and an elegant English drawing room with a table set for tea. Closed Mondays. Information: Honolulu Academy of Arts, 900 S. Beretania St., Honolulu, HI 96814 (phone: 538-3693).

MISSION HOUSES MUSEUM, Honolulu, Oahu: "The clapboards are bare and admit quantities of dust which the trade winds bring in such fearful clouds as to suggest the fate of Pompeii. We have three chairs, a table, a bedstead, and a nice little secretary." So wrote Laura Fish Judd, wife of the evangelist Gerrit P. Judd, in August 1828 of the house they shared with the despotic Reverend Hiram Bingham, the first of the Protestant missionaries who were to leave an indelible imprint on Hawaiian life, both socially and architecturally. As if to underscore their uncompromising moral attitudes, the missionaries rejected the practical, relaxed, and airy grass shacks inhabited by the Hawaiians, including the King, in favor of the prim and proper (and stuffy and dusty) dwellings that replicated those they had known in Massachusetts. All over the islands, postage-stamp-size versions of New England hamlets sprung up, looking incongruous among the exotic tropical trees and shrubs that surrounded and overshadowed them. The *Mission Houses* are the most elaborate complex remaining that recalls this typical example of Yankee obstinacy. The Frame House, which Mrs. Judd described, was shipped to Hawaii in 1820 from Boston and is the oldest existing house in Hawaii. In the parlors, bedrooms, and kitchen is a collection of the original furniture and utensils. The Printing House next door, built from coral blocks in 1831, contains a replica of the old-fashioned Rampage handpress used by the printer, Elisha Loomis, to produce a Hawaiian translation of the Bible, schoolbooks, and hymnals. On the *makai* (ocean) side of the Chamberlain House, built in 1841 — the latest and largest in the complex — the block and tackle used to haul missionary supplies up to the second-floor storehouse is still visible. Also in the Chamberlain House is a model of the mission station in 1850, which graphically illustrates how Honolulu has changed. Information: Mission Houses Museum, 553 S. King St., Honolulu, HI 96813 (phone: 531-0481).

LYMAN MISSION HOUSE AND MUSEUM, Hilo, the Big Island of Hawaii: Like their mentors, the Binghams and the Judds, the Reverend David and Mrs. Lyman built themselves a New England–style homestead when they arrived in the rain-sodden town of Hilo in 1832. The house is currently arranged much as it was from 1840 to 1880, which suggests that missionary life must have had its compensations, for the sturdy, simple furnishings are quite lovely. The whole house has an atmosphere of merriment and comfort totally different from the feeling of austerity that one associates with strict religious households. "Puddled" glass is used in the windows, antique wallpaper covers the walls, and the bedrooms, with their four-posters, marble-topped washstands, and handmade quilts and throw rugs, are as cozy and quaint as in any New England inn. The floors throughout the house are made from unevenly cut planks of native koa and look unusually fine. As a gesture to the tropical environment, the stools and tables in the conservatory are made from ohia wood and stand on legs fashioned from crooked branches. The *Lyman Museum,* in a modern building adjacent to the Mission House, is stuffed with haphazardly arranged collections relating to ancient Hawaii, the missionaries, immigrants to the islands, volcanology, geology, and mineralogy. The collections need considerable pruning and rearranging to make the museum truly rewarding as an educational and aesthetic experience; too much is currently exhibited in too small a space. There are some quite remarkable artifacts, however, among which must be counted the more than 400 glass paperweights. Closed Sundays. Information: Lyman Mission House and Museum, 276 Haili St., Hilo, HI 96720 (phone: 935-5021).

HISTORIC PARKER RANCH HOMES, Kamuela, the Big Island of Hawaii: Both *Puuopelu,* the family home of Parker Ranch owner Richard Smart, and *Mana,* the 1847 home of Smart's ancestor John Palmer Parker, have recently been opened to the public. Surrounded by rich and beautiful upcountry pasture, the real surprise is found inside *Puuopelu,* where an art collection that includes works by Degas, Renoir, and Chagall is housed in six rooms. Tickets are available at the Parker Ranch Visitor Center; a visit to both homes will take at least an hour. Admission $3.50; closed Sundays. Parker Ranch tours also include the historic homes and a van tour of the surrounding ranchland. Information: Parker Ranch, PO Box 458, Kamuela, Hawaii, HI 96743 (phone: 885-7655).

GROVE FARM HOMESTEAD, Lihue, Kauai: Perhaps nothing so profoundly shaped modern Hawaii as sugarcane. From the 1840s on, ambitious settlers looked to cane to make their fortunes, turning vast tracts of forest and jungle into cultivated fields and bringing in thousands of foreign laborers — from Portugal, Japan, Korea, China, and the Philippines — who would make Hawaiians a minority in their own country. And until inexpensive and frequent air travel established Hawaii as a prime tourist destination after World War II, cane was the prime source of livelihood for the majority of islanders.

Grove Farm Homestead on Kauai offers a fascinating glimpse into Hawaii's plantation past. Founded in 1864 by 25-year-old George Wilcox, a Yale engineering graduate and the son of missionaries in Hawaii, Grove Farm was the center of a thriving cane plantation for nearly 75 years and, after the company headquarters moved, was a self-sufficient family estate for another 40 years. It was Mabel Wilcox, a niece of George and the last occupant of the house, who determined that the homestead should become a museum. Two years after her death, in 1978, Grove Farm opened to the public.

Everything within the low stone wall enclosing the main compound has been carefully restored: from a modest worker's cottage, furnished with belongings donated by the Wilcox family laundress, to the fernery, a small louver-sided building whose sole purpose is to house ferns too delicate to tolerate direct sunlight. The main house contains much of the furniture Wilcox commissioned local cabinetmakers to build out of koa wood. An interesting example of the planter's resourcefulness is the old wood stove that covers the entire back wall of the kitchen — which, incidentally, is still used to bake cookies for museum guests. By running the water pipes behind it, the family was able to heat its water supply without burning extra fuel. The homestead's spacious grounds, rich with pines, palms, ironwoods, and numerous fruit trees, as well as vegetable and flower gardens, also help illuminate a past that is all too quickly fading.

Grove Farm is open Mondays, Wednesdays, and Thursdays. Reservations for the 2-hour tour (scheduled at 10 AM and 1 PM), limited to two or three groups of six, are required. Information: Grove Farm Homestead, Nawiliwili Rd., Lihue, HI 96766 (phone: 245-3202).

WAIOLI MISSION HOUSE MUSEUM, Hanalei, Kauai: Missionary links to New England are evident in this trim white home set amid Hawaii's lush landscape. Built in 1841 by early Protestant missionaries, it has been a museum for more than 60 years. A short guided tour of the mission house is given on Tuesdays, Thursdays, and Saturdays, and it provides a glimpse of old Hawaii as well as of the founding family's history and that of Hanalei. Waioli Huiia Church, the still-active mission church that once was associated with the house, is nearby. No admission charge. Open from 9 AM to 3 PM. Information: Waioli Mission House Museum, Hanalei, Kauai, HI 96714 (phone: 245-3202).

CHURCHES, Islandwide: Along with their zeal and religious convictions, the missionaries who came to the islands in the 19th century brought with them a determination to see their beliefs made solidly manifest in the form of churches. Though architecturally unimpressive, their historical associations and/or decorative details make them noteworthy.

The Episcopal *St. Andrew's Cathedral* (at Beretania and Queen Emma Sts., Honolulu) was the inspiration of Kamehameha IV and his wife, Queen Emma, anglophiles both, who adopted the religion of English aristocracy. Although the cathedral's design, and some of its building materials, were imported from Britain, it was the *Kawaiahao Church* (957 Punchbowl St., Honolulu), built by New Englanders and dedicated by Kamehameha III, that became known as the "Westminster Abbey of Hawaii" for the number of royal baptisms, weddings, and funerals held there. In the church gallery is the Hoffstot Collection, 21 portraits of all of Hawaii's rulers and most of their consorts. Especially moving is the portrait of King Kamehameha III, who in the church sanctuary first used the words that were to become Hawaii's motto: *"Ua mau ke ea o ka aina i ka pono"* ("The life of the land is perpetuated in righteousness"). Today, *kahilis* (feather standards) adorn both sides of the sanctuary, and at most Sunday services at least one hymn is sung in Hawaiian. Also in Honolulu, at the Fort Street Mall, is *Our Lady of Peace Cathedral,* where Joseph de Veuster, Father Damien, was ordained in 1864. The *Queen Liliuokalani Church* (66-090 Kamehameha Hwy., Haleiwa) is special for its old clock with seven dials and seven hands showing the month, day of the week, week of the year, and phases of the moon, and a dial indicating the hours of the day that uses the 12 letters of the Queen's name instead of numbers. *St. John the Apostle and Evangelist Church* (95-370 Kuahelani Ave., Mililani Town) is as austere as an early Christian abbey, with its stark granite altar and concrete walls. Highlights are the sculptures depicting the 14 Stations of the Cross, the modernistic stained-glass windows, and the bronze statues of the Blessed Virgin Mary and St. John.

The most famous of the churches on the Big Island is *Mokuaikaua Church* (Alii Dr., Kailua), which stands across the road from Hulihee Palace. Built in 1837 using cornerstones that were reputedly hewn in the 16th century, Mokuaikaua is the oldest and most historic church in the state. Walls made from lava rock and cemented with coral, and beams and posts constructed from ohia wood brought down from the mountains, give this church its distinctly Hawaiian character. Standing on a small side road off Route 16, which branches from the main highway (Route 11) a few miles south of Captain Cook, is *St. Benedict's,* known as "the Painted Church," the most celebrated Catholic church in the islands. Although this small church has a humble frame exterior, its interior is brightly decorated with Hawaiian scenes and, behind the altar, a quite unexpected *trompe l'oeil* rendering of the nave of Burgos Cathedral in Spain. Another small Catholic house of worship in this painted tradition is *Star of the Sea Church,* close to the black sand beach at Kalapana on Route 13. Among the church's several ornamentations is a late Renaissance nativity scene above the front entrance. At Kapaau, on the north side of the island, is *Kalahikiola Church,* which was truly a labor of love. Stones were brought to the site on men's backs from nearby gulches. Others went out in canoes to dive for coral, and ohia wood was brought down from the mountains to make pillars and beams. Today, this white edifice stands amid trim lawns, witness to the faith of the parishioners who built it.

One of the most photographed churches on Maui is the *Church of the Holy Ghost,* set on a gentle, green hillside below the summit of Haleakala, just off the highway near Waiakoa. The interior of this octagonal church contains wooden, gold-leaf bas-reliefs and an altar that was brought around Cape Horn from Austria. At Wailuku is the equally photogenic *Kaahumanu Church,* named for Queen Kaahumanu, who asked that the first permanent church on this spot be named after her. The present structure, built in 1876, replaces a stone church that was erected in 1837. The svelte form of the present New England–style building is delightfully emphasized by its dark green trim. This is probably the most elegant of the many graceful wooden churches in the islands.

Among the most moving experiences in Hawaii is visiting the tiny, recently restored *St. Philomena Church* at Kalawao, Molokai, which was completed by Father Damien during the late 1870s. It was here, during a morning mass on the first Sunday in June 1885, that Damien began his sermon not with the customary "My brethren," but with the significant salutation "We lepers." Close by is the beautifully constructed Protestant *Siloama Church,* whose white, geometric simplicity and spare green spire contrast vividly with the surrounding soft tapestry of tropical foliage.

Ancient Ruins and Historic Sites

 Unlike the Celts and Romans in Europe, the Polynesians built no tombs or burial chambers, no forts or castles, no great walls or monuments. For the most part, nature, not man, still dominates the Hawaiian landscape, and many of the most critical events in Hawaiian history — the death of Captain Cook, the abandonment of the *kapus,* the arrival of the first missionaries and whalers, the overthrow of the monarchy — are marked in memory, not in stone. Listed below are a few of the important historical sites still extant, ranging from the ruins of two ancient *heiaus* (temples) to the modern memorial at Pearl Harbor.

IOLANI PALACE, Honolulu, Oahu: This neo-Florentine edifice, with its stone verandas and Corinthian columns, is the only former royal palace in the United States. It was completed for King David Kalakaua in 1882 and cost more than $350,000. Kalakaua had traveled around the world and had been received by a number of reigning monarchs. He was particularly attracted by the courts of Europe, and he set out to copy their customs, clothes, and houses in his Polynesian homeland. He instituted Royal Household Guards with formal uniforms, complete with epaulets and ribbons; he built a coronation stand, where today the smartly turned out Royal Hawaiian Band gives concerts; he had crowns made for himself and his Queen, Kapiolani; and on February 12, 1883, he began a coronation ceremony that continued for 2 weeks. Thereafter the palace, with its Victorian armoires and settees, became the scene of balls, receptions, dinners, and musical soirees. These displays of what they perceived as an effete way of life, as well as Kalakaua's high-handed style of government, disturbed and offended the American entrepreneurs in Hawaii. Kalakaua's successor, his sister Liliuokalani, reigned for only 2 years before she was deposed in 1893 by a provisional government headed by the pineapple magnate Samuel B. Dole. For the next 3 years, Iolani was periodically a prison for the ex-queen.

In 1898, sovereignty of the islands was transferred to the government of the United States, and the American flag flew above the former royal residence. The Territory of Hawaii was administered from here, and when the islands became the 50th state, the palace became the executive building. In 1969, the splendid new state capitol was opened, and a group called the Friends of Iolani Palace began looking for funds to restore it to its original opulence. Many of the furnishings and artifacts had been dispersed among Liliuokalani's family, as well as to collectors and museums. But little by little, donations and purchases have enabled a growing number of items to return to their original setting. The mirrored throne room, with its gilt trim and crystal chandeliers, once again evokes a sense of 19th-century court elegance. Negotiations are under way to restore the original thrones, now at the *Bishop Museum.* The main stairwell, made of highly polished koa wood and trimmed with ohia and cedar carvings, glows as it did when Robert Louis Stevenson stopped by to pay his respects and to note that Kalakaua could demolish five bottles of champagne in an afternoon. The walls of the King's bedroom still retain the silver-leaf decoration and eggshell blue paint of his day; and a portrait of Louis Philippe, King of the French, which he presented to Kamehameha III in 1848, still hangs on the first-floor landing. From time to time, people can be seen sipping champagne on the verandas. Usually these are visiting chieftains from other Polynesian islands being entertained by Edward Kawanankoa, the pretender to the Hawaiian throne. Although Mr. Kawanankoa receives no official recognition from the state, he is extended these minor courtesies in memory of the Kamehamehas, from whom he is descended. Although much remains to be done before the house regains its original palatial status, it nevertheless offers a glimpse of how a semi-Europeanized Polynesian court thought it ought to live. Tours last 45 minutes and are offered from 9 AM to 2:15 PM, Wednesdays through Saturdays; telephone for reservations. Admission is $4. Information: Iolani Palace, Box 2259, Honolulu, HI 96804 (phone: 538-1471; for reservations, 522-0822).

QUEEN EMMA'S SUMMER PALACE, Honolulu, Oahu: Unlike the ornate Iolani Palace, Queen Emma's summer retreat up in the Nuuanu Valley above Honolulu looks like the home of a well-to-do plantation owner. Built sometime between 1847 and 1850, it is a simple square building with Doric columns supporting the roof over the front lanai. Queen Emma, wife of Kamehameha IV, inherited the property in 1857, and in 1869 she added a large back room in the expectation of throwing a party for Queen Victoria's second son, Alfred, Duke of Edinburgh. The prince never showed up, but the room is still called the Edinburgh Room. After 1872, Emma no longer lived there. Following her death in 1885, the house fell into disrepair and was about to be torn down when the Daughters of Hawaii rescued it in 1913. Since 1915, they have operated it as a museum, displaying many of the artifacts that belonged to Emma and her family, as well as materials relating to that period in Hawaiian history. Some exotic pieces that visitors find especially appealing among the *kahilis* (feather standards) and Victorian furniture are an elaborate, three-tiered Gothic cabinet bordered with cruciform fretwork and finials, a gift from Queen Victoria's consort, Prince Albert; a stereopticon, presented to the Queen by Napoleon III; and a necklace hung with tiger claws decorated with seed pearls embedded in rolled gold. Queen Emma's only son, Albert, died when he was 4 years old. His christening robe, embroidered with the royal coat of arms, hangs in his mother's bedroom, not far from the simple red jacket and brass megaphone given to the infant prince when he was made an honorary member of the Honolulu Volunteer Fire Department. Many of the plants found here in Emma's day still flourish on the grounds, and a delightful view of the house is seen from the driveway, framed by kukui and koa trees and surrounded by roses, geraniums, spider lilies, and serpentine ferns. Admission is $4. Information: Queen Emma's Summer Palace, 2913 Pali Hwy., Honolulu, HI 96817 (phone: 595-3167).

ARIZONA MEMORIAL, Pearl Harbor, Oahu: The Arizona Memorial is a perfect example of what a material tribute to those who died in the service of their country should be: simple, graceful, and intensely moving. The white concrete structure, in the blue-green water off the tip of Ford Island in Pearl Harbor, spans the battleship USS *Arizona,* whose sunken hull lies beneath the memorial, entombing the 1,102 servicemen who were aboard on the morning of December 7, 1941, when Japanese planes attacked the base. The memorial is divided into three parts. There is a museum room, containing among other mementos the *Arizona*'s ship's bell; an open assembly area, from which visitors may look down at the battleship's rusted and barnacled hull; and the shrine, where a marble tablet is inscribed with the names of those who died on the *Arizona.* It reads like a cross section of the immigrant groups who traveled to America in search of freedom, prosperity, and peace: Aarons, Abercrombie, Blake, Blanchard, Blankenship, Jastremski, Le Gros, Lynch, McGuire, Tambolleo, Van Horn, Vosti, Zimmerman. The American flag that flies above the memorial is attached to a flagpole anchored in the ship's hull. Each morning and evening, the flag is raised and lowered by an honor guard. Alfred Preis, architect of the memorial, said of it: "The overall effect is one of serenity. Overtones of sadness have been omitted to permit the individual to contemplate . . . his own innermost feelings." The US navy operates the short boat trip to the memorial from the USS *Arizona* Visitor Center — which is run by National Park Rangers — from 8 AM to 3 PM daily; the Visitor Center itself is open from 7:30 AM to 5 PM. Commercial sea tours from Kewalo Basin sail along "battleship row," past memorial buoys that mark where other battleships were sunk during the raid, among them the USS *Missouri* and the USS *Utah*. Only passengers on US navy boats, however, are allowed to disembark at the Arizona Memorial. Information: Arizona Memorial Navy Boat Tours, Pearl Harbor, HI 96701 (phone: 422-0561).

PUUHONUA O HONAUNAU NATIONAL HISTORICAL PARK, Honaunau, the Big Island of Hawaii: There are many things that attract visitors to the Kona Coast: swaying palms, tidepools with live corals, and the ocean surging into rocky coves. But here is the most complete restoration in the islands of an ancient Hawaiian place of sanctuary for defeated warriors and for people who had broken a *kapu,* or taboo. Here the ground was sacred to both the pursued and the pursuer, and any miscreant who reached it and received absolution from a *kahuna* (temple priest) was considered a free man once more. There were, however, certain impediments involved in getting here. The only access in ancient days was by swimming across a bay known as the shark's den, and once on the temple grounds, a 10-foot-high wall had to be scaled. The wall, built during the 16th century, still stands, 1,000 feet long and 6 feet wide, like a monstrous three-dimensional abstract jigsaw puzzle. Around a splendidly reconstructed *heiau* (temple) at the ocean's edge stands a half circle of tall tikis, with countenances suggesting growls and grimaces. Even in the water, close to an old outrigger canoe carved from ohia wood, a smaller figure stands sentinel to warn the common folk that this part of the shoreline is for the *alii* (nobles) only. In the palace ruins on the non-sacred side of the wall are the skeletons of two A-frame buildings, one with just enough dried grass attached to indicate how thatching was performed. Local handicraft workers demonstrate how to make tapa cloth, fishnets, poi, and feather leis, helmets, and capes. For a change of pace, visitors can sit on smooth stone and play *konane,* the ancient Hawaiian game of checkers, which is set out on a rock on the beach. Here, as elsewhere in the US, the National Park Rangers prove that they are among our best informed and dedicated public servants. Information: Puuhonua O Honaunau National Historical Park, PO Box 129, Honaunau, HI 96726 (phone: 328-2326).

HULIHEE PALACE, Kailua-Kona, the Big Island of Hawaii: This is another gem of a house that owes its preservation to the Daughters of Hawaii, who rescued it from near ruin in 1925. Hulihee was built in 1838 by John Adams Kuakini, governor of the Big Island and a cousin of Kamehameha the Great, and was inherited in the 1850s by Princess Ruth Keelikolani. The palace stands by the ocean with landscaped lawns, palm trees, and a lovely garden of tropical plants. Apart from one mock-gothic window in the upstairs sitting room above the front entrance, the building is classically simple. Princess Ruth, known for her generosity, used the palace for entertaining and housing guests. Among these were Queen Emma, her husband, Kamehameha IV, and their son, Prince Albert, who used it frequently as a vacation retreat from Honolulu; King Lunalilo; and King David Kalakaua, who bought the palace after Ruth's death and filled it with rugs, china, glassware, sofas, satin cushions, prints, paintings, and family mementos similar to those he had seen in Europe. Today the house is more simply furnished, with some representative pieces from the royal era, and the floors are covered with handsome *lau hala* mats. In the north bedroom there is a beautifully made bed and a fine crib that belonged to the infant Prince Albert. In the Kuakini Room are several ancient artifacts, including a huge round stone used by Kamehameha the Great as an exercise ball. Everywhere there is the smooth, lustrous sheen of koa and other natural hardwoods. Many visitors come here again and again just to see the collection of koa bowls, although there is much else besides: Victorian marble busts of the Hawaiian royals; old prints of Hawaii; old *kahilis* (feather standards) that used to accompany the monarchs wherever they went; and David Kalakaua's helmet, medals, and guitar. Information: Hulihee Palace, 75-5718 Alii Dr., Kailua-Kona, HI 96740 (phone: 329-1877).

PUUKOHOLA HEIAU, Kawaihae, the Big Island of Hawaii: One of the goals of the 19th-century New England missionaries was to eradicate Hawaii's ancient *heiaus* (temples). Among the most famous and best preserved of these is the Puukohola Heiau, which stands impressively between the ocean and the highway at Kawaihae. It was built in 1791 on the remains of a 16th-century temple by Kamehameha the Great, following a prophecy that if he constructed a temple to his war god, Kukailimoku, he would become conqueror of all the islands. On the day of the *heiau*'s dedication, the King slew his chief enemy, who was at the ceremony, and offered him to the god as a sacrifice. The Reverend Hiram Bingham, the most famous of the Protestant missionaries, commented on the 224-foot-long, 100-foot-wide, and 15-foot-high *heiau* built of ominous black lava and set in a hill overlooking the sea:

> I visited Puukohola, the large heathen temple at that place, a monument of folly, superstition, and madness, which the idolatrous conqueror [Kamehameha] and his murderous priests had consecrated with human blood to the senseless deities of Pagan Hawaii . . . The frowning structure is so large and prominent, that it can be distinctly seen with the naked eye, from the top of Maunakea, a distance of about 32 miles. As a fortification of Satan's kingdom, its design was more for war against the human species than the worship of the Creator. [From *A Residence of Twenty-One Years in the Sandwich Islands* (New York: Converse, 1847).]

After a review like that, who could resist a visit? Open from 7:30 AM to 4 PM. Information: Puukohola Heiau National Historic Site, Kawaihae, HI 96743 (phone: 882-7218).

MOOKINI HEIAU, the Big Island of Hawaii: Still preserved by the family that was responsible for its upkeep in the days of Kamehameha the Great, this coastal *heiau*, or temple, is among the best-preserved in Hawaii, retaining more architectural detail than most others that survive. This is where Kamehameha was taken for the celebration of his birth rites, and the site of his birth is within walking distance of the *heiau*. Located off Rte. 227, between Upolu Point and Lapakahi.

LAPAKAHI STATE HISTORICAL PARK, Kawaihae, the Big Island of Hawaii: Though this archaeological site is comprised mostly of simple rock walls and walkways, these remains of a 14th-century Hawaiian fishing village supply a fascinating idea of how things were back when. Guided and self-guided tours traverse the fascinating sun-dried landscape that is relieved only by gnarled keawe trees and the bits of shade they provide. Information: Lapakahi State Historical Park, Kawaihae, Hawaii, HI 96744 (phone: 889-5566).

LAHAINA, Maui: Since its designation as a National Historic Landmark in 1962, this waterfront town of 10,000 people has become West Maui's main attraction. Before the European discovery of Hawaii, Lahaina was the haunt of Maui's ruling elite, and with the advent of Kamehameha the Great, the native village became an early political center of the united Hawaiian kingdom. Protestant missionaries arrived in the 1820s, just as Lahaina was about to lose its innocence: The whaling era, which was to have the greatest impact upon the town, was under way. From approximately 1820 to 1860, this tiny Hawaiian port turned into the most important provisioning stop for America's entire Pacific whaling fleet, becoming the whaling capital of the world, in fact. While the ships took on stores and their hard-bitten crews indulged themselves with women and grog, the missionaries tried to save souls, and these two sets of foreign intruders (ironically, both mainly New Englanders) fought — like the virtual forces of good and evil — for the hearts and minds of the Hawaiian people.

Today, Lahaina is no Williamsburg, but a good deal of restoration of its largely wood (and some coral stone) buildings has been carried out by concerned citizens and the Lahaina Restoration Foundation. Much of the reclaimed town consists of shopfronts along the main thoroughfare, Front Street, though there are more things to see than the average tourist on a shopping spree might imagine. The *Baldwin House Museum,* home of the medical missionary Dr. Dwight Baldwin during the mid-19th century, is furnished as it was when he lived there. Not far away, a huge banyan tree, planted in 1873 to commemorate 50 years of missionary work on the island, flourishes in the town's main square. Across the street is the *Pioneer Inn,* an old hotel that opened at the turn of the century and is still in use. It appeared on the scene after the whaling ships had gone, but around the harbor in front of it, there's the *Carthaginian,* a ship of relatively recent vintage, true-rigged like the brigs of whaling days. Other remains of the past are the Courthouse, some rubble of the Old Fort that Lahaina was forced to build to deal with rioting seamen, and the reconstructed Hale Paahoa, or Old Prison, which also became necessary as rowdiness increased. The Wo Hing Society Hall, also on Front St., provides a perspective on the lives led by the Chinese immigrants who came to work West Maui's cane fields. The grave of Queen Keopuolani, the wife of Kamehameha the Great and the first Hawaiian chief to be converted to Christianity, along with the graves of other members of the royal family, are in Waiola Cemetery, next to Waiola Church, which stands where the first stone church to be built in the islands once stood. On the grounds of historic Lahainaluna School is Hale Pai (printing house), where some of the first Hawaiian-language books were printed during the 1830s. Information: Lahaina Restoration Foundation, PO Box 338, Lahaina, HI 96761 (phone: 661-3262); or Maui Visitors Bureau, 380 Dairy Rd., Kahului, HI 96732 (phone: 871-8691).

KALAUPAPA NATIONAL HISTORIC MONUMENT, Kalaupapa, Molokai: Leprosy appeared in the Hawaiian islands during the middle of the 19th century and, by 1860, fear of the terrible new disease convinced Hawaii's rulers that something had to be done. As a result, the most remote and inaccessible place in the islands was found, Molokai's Makanalua Peninsula, then barren and deserted, and lepers were exiled there in a horrible "prison" from which no escape was possible — cliffs 1,600 feet high backed the 12-square-mile tongue of volcanic rock, and the raw power of the sea enclosed it on the three other sides. The first lepers were dumped overboard off the peninsula on January 6, 1866, and those who made it ashore commenced a life of lawless horror and hardship. The first settlement was at Kalawao, a harsh spot on the east coast, but one with drinking water; the colony did not move to Kalaupapa, on the more pleasant west coast of the peninsula, until 1888, when water was first piped in. It was into this corner of hell that Father Damien Joseph de Veuster, now known as "the Martyr of Molokai," came in 1873 to tend a flock of perhaps 1,000 damned souls. Father Damien brought not only religion — he carried with him order, organization, and justice. The Belgian priest himself eventually contracted leprosy and died of it at Kalaupapa in 1889, at the age of 49.

Today, leprosy (now renamed Hansen's disease) has been tamed by the sulfone drugs introduced during the 1940s, and Kalaupapa's residents, now fewer than 100, are free to leave. But they stay to live out their lives in the simple, state-supported settlement founded in such terror a century ago. Kalaupapa itself was named a National Historical Monument in 1976, and it became part of the National Park System in 1980.

It has been possible for some years to visit Kalaupapa and the peninsula, since the disease is no longer contagious (although children under 16 are not allowed). Still, visitors must obtain an entry permit issued by the State Department of Health in Honolulu. If you participate in a tour, the permit is included. There is a small airstrip to which several commuter lines fly small, twin-engined craft from Maui, the Hoolehua Airport on topside Molokai, and other points in the islands. Experienced trekkers may also climb down the 3-mile-plus trail from overlooking Palaau State Park, but it is a treacherous and difficult hike; a mandatory tour at the bottom must be arranged in advance with *Damien Tours* (phone: 567-6171). *Air Molokai* and *Aloha IslandAir* offer service to Kalaupapa. Connections can be made for Honolulu, Maui, and Lanai. When booking a flight, it is very important to indicate Kalaupapa, not Molokai. Most Molokai-bound flights head for the main airport at Hoolehua. *Damien Tours* offers trips both in conjunction with these airlines and independently.

The most popular method of visiting Kalaupapa, however, is on muleback. *Molokai Mule Ride* runs a mule train down a 3⅛-mile trail that takes more than two dozen hairpin switchbacks to descend the 1,600-foot cliffs. The full-day trips, which include a tour of the settlement, leave the stable site near the Kalaupapa lookout at 9 AM and return around 3:30 PM. Reservations are necessary; rides are limited to visitors over 16 years and under 225 pounds. Information: PO Box 200, Kualapuu, HI 96757 (phone: 567-6088; 800-843-5978).

A Shutterbug's Hawaii

The dramatic juxtaposition of land and sea, vibrant color, beautiful weather, and a diverse and exotic population are Hawaii's photographic stock in trade. Even a beginner can achieve remarkable results with a surprisingly basic set of lenses and filters. Equipment is, in fact, only as valuable as the imagination that puts it into use.

Don't be afraid to experiment. Use what knowledge you have to explore new possibilities. Don't limit yourself by preconceived ideas of what's hackneyed or corny. Because a hibiscus has been photographed hundreds of times before doesn't make it any less worthy of your attention.

In Hawaii, as elsewhere, spontaneity is one of the keys to good photography. Whether it's a sudden shaft of light bursting through the clouds or workers in a taro field in the midst of harvesting, don't hesitate to shoot if the moment is right. If photography is indeed capturing a moment and making it timeless, success lies in judging just when a moment worth capturing occurs.

A good picture reveals an eye for detail, whether it's a matter of lighting, of positioning your subject, or of taking time to crop a picture carefully. The better your grasp of the importance of details, the better your results will be photographically.

Patience is often necessary. Don't shoot a view of Diamond Head if a cloud suddenly covers it with shadows. A dead tree in a panorama of Hanalei Valley? Reframe your image to eliminate the obvious distraction. People walking toward a scene that would benefit from their presence? Wait until they're in position before you shoot. After the fact, many of the flaws will be self-evident. The trick is to be aware of the ideal and have the patience to allow it to happen. If you are part of a group, you may well have to trail behind a bit in order to shoot properly. Not only is group activity distracting, but bunches of people hovering nearby tend to stifle spontaneity and overwhelm potential subjects.

The camera provides an opportunity, not only to capture Hawaii's straightforward beauty, but to idealize it. What it takes is a sensitivity to the surroundings, a knowledge of the capabilities of your equipment, and a willingness to see things in new ways.

BASIC EQUIPMENT: Most single lens reflex (SLR) cameras come with a conventional 50mm lens, an all-purpose lens good for street scenes taken at a distance of 25 feet or more and full body portraits shot at usual distances. You can expand your options considerably by including wide-angle and telephoto lenses.

Any lens from 35mm on down offers wide-angle capabilities, which in effect pull portions of peripheral vision into the picture and are especially handy for panoramas and landscapes. A wide-angle lens in the 20–28mm range is made for Hawaii. Where the normal perspective of a 50mm lens provides an uninteresting view of Waikiki Beach or Diamond Head, a 20mm incorporates the two in one flowing scene. While a 50mm lens cuts the dimensions of the Big Island's Akaka Falls in half, a 20mm not only takes in its full height but accentuates the lush setting by framing the falls with translucent ferns. The wide-angle lens is also excellent for linking people with their surroundings because its great depth of field can focus pictures between 3½ feet and infinity. And it can also be valuable when there's very little space between you and your subject.

Keep in mind that wide-angle lenses have a tendency to distort when used very close to a subject or when dealing with vertical lines. Tall palms or a high-rise hotel may seem to converge toward the top of the frame, for example. Once you're aware of these effects, you can use them to creative advantage.

Where a wide-angle lens extends normal perspective, a telephoto lens focuses on a portion of the overview, providing perspective in detail. Telephotos range from 65mm to 1000mm and more, and permit dramatic silhouettes of sailboats against a setting sun, of surfers poised on the crest of a wave, of detailed portraits, floral design, and candids. A 105mm or 135mm telephoto lens offers the most versatility, with a 200mm a close second.

In addition to individual telephotos, a number of telephoto zoom lenses have become popular with travel photographers. Zooms incorporate a range of focal lengths. A typical telephoto zoom ranging from 80mm to 200mm, for example, allows you to frame a picture as you want it by choosing the most appropriate lens setting for the situation. That means carrying one lens with millimeter-to-millimeter variations from 80mm to 200mm. The drawbacks of a zoom are its weight and a potential loss of clarity when compared with individual telephotos. Both problems are being eliminated by technological advances.

A 2X Teleconverter is a simple addition to a Hawaii camera kit. Lightweight and easy to carry, the 2X doubles the focal length of various lenses, converting a 20mm into a 40mm, a 50mm into a 100mm, and so forth. Though there is again a potential loss of clarity, the 2X is a versatile accessory that's easy to use.

While it may seem excessive, a small lightweight tripod is a real asset in assuring picture quality. This is particularly true when the heavier telephoto lenses are used, or in situations where the available light is limited and shots will be made at speeds slower than 1/25 of a second. For sharp detail, closeups, night, or limited-light pictures while in the islands, a tripod is a must.

A battery-run flash unit, commonly called a strobe, is another worthwhile piece of equipment. Subjects as varied as the Thurston Lava Tube in Hawaii Volcanoes National Park, a missionary home, and a Polynesian revue all become photographable with a strobe. It can also provide frontal light for a backlit subject and additional light in a variety of dim situations, such as Hawaii's tropical rain forests.

Filters are a final addition to a Hawaii camera kit. Take a skylight filter (1A, 1B) for each lens. There's no need to remove it except to replace it with a different filter. Not only will it provide the filtration needed to combat atmospheric haze and ultraviolet light, it will also protect the lens surface.

A polarizer goes one step beyond the skylight, cutting out reflections from nonmetallic surfaces (water and glass, for instance) and penetrating haze for extra clarity and rich color saturation. It will add impact to all those greens and blues in the

Hawaiian landscape. While its effects are dramatic, it can be a difficult filter to use, cutting back on speed (it's a dark filter), creating deep shadows, and working well under only certain lighting conditions. In spite of these drawbacks, it remains an excellent filter to try.

Unless you plan to experiment with the increasingly diverse range of specialty filters now available (diffraction, multiple image, and closeup, for instance), skylights and a polarizer are just about all that's needed. Stick to the medium-priced glass filters (Hoya, Tiffen, or Vivitar, for example) to maintain picture quality.

FILM: Travel photographs work best in color. Good slide films are Kodachrome 64 and Fujichrome 50, both moderate- to slow-speed films that provide saturated colors and work well in most outdoor light. For very bright conditions, try slower film like Kodachrome 25. If the weather is cloudy, or you're indoors with only natural light, use a faster film, such as Kodachrome 200. It can be "pushed" to higher speeds. There are now even faster films on the market for low-light situations. The result may be pictures with whiter, colder tones and a grainier image, but high-speed films open up picture possibilities that slower films cannot.

Films tend to render color in slightly different ways. Kodachrome brings out reds and oranges. Fujichrome is noted for its yellows, greens, and whites. You might test films as you test your camera (see above) to determine your taste.

If you prefer film that develops into prints rather than slides, try Kodacolor 100 or 400 for most lighting situations. Vericolor is a professional film that gives excellent results, especially for skin tones, but suffers shifts in color when subjected to temperature extremes; bring it along for taking shots of people *if* you're sure you can protect it from heat and cold. All lens and filter information applies equally to print and slide films.

LANDSCAPES AND SEASCAPES: The Hawaiian landscape is of such compelling beauty that it is often the photographer's primary focus. Even Honolulu and Waikiki are best captured in the context of their setting, sandwiched between the lush, saw-toothed Koolaus and the variegated blues and greens of the Pacific.

Color and form are the obvious ingredients here, and how you frame your pictures can be as important as getting the proper exposure. Study the shapes, angles, and colors that make up the scene and create a composition that uses them to best advantage.

Lighting is a vital component in landscapes and seascapes. Take advantage of the richer colors of early morning and late afternoon whenever possible. The overhead light of midday is often harsh and without the shadowing that can add to the drama of a scene. This is when a polarizer is used to best effect. Most polarizers come with a mark on the rotating ring. If you can aim at your subject and point that marker at the sun, the sun's rays are likely to be right for the polarizer to work for you. If not, stick to your skylight filter, underexposing slightly if the scene is particularly bright. Most light meters respond to an overall light balance, with the result that bright areas may appear burned out.

Although a standard 50mm to 55mm lens may work well in some landscape situations, most will benefit from a 20mm to 28mm wide-angle. Waikiki, Hanauma Bay, Haleakala Crater, Kilauea, Waimea Canyon, and the Pali Lookout are just some of the panoramas that fit beautifully into a wide-angle format, allowing not only the overview, but the opportunity to include people or other points of interest in the foreground. A flower, for instance, may be used to set off a view of Diamond Head; or people can provide a sense of perspective in a shot of Haleakala.

To isolate specific elements of any scene, use your telephoto lens. Perhaps there's a particular segment of Kauai's Hanalei Valley that would make a lovely shot, or it might be the interplay of light and shadow on Oahu's Pali, or a distant waterfall cascading down the side of Waimea Canyon. The successful use of a telephoto means developing your eye for detail.

PEOPLE: As with taking pictures of people anywhere, there are going to be times in Hawaii when a camera is an intrusion. Your approach is the key: Consider your own reaction under similar circumstances, and you have an idea as to what would make others comfortable enough to be willing subjects. People are often sensitive to having a camera suddenly pointed at them, and a polite request, while getting you a share of refusals, will also provide a chance to shoot some wonderful portraits that capture the spirit of the islands as surely as the scenery does. For candids, use a telephoto in the 105–200mm range; at a distance of 50 feet or more, it allows you to remain unobtrusive while the telephoto lens draws the subject closer. And for portraits, a telephoto can be used effectively as close as 2 or 3 feet.

For authenticity and variety, select a place likely to produce interesting subjects. Waikiki is an obvious spot for visitors, but if it's local color you're after, visit Chinatown, wander into a pineapple field, or go to one of the North Shore beaches that are popular with surfers. Aim for shots that tell what's different about Hawaii. In portraiture, there are several factors to keep in mind. Morning or afternoon light will add richness to skin tones, emphasizing tans. To avoid the harsh facial shadows cast by direct sunlight, shoot in the shade or in an area where the light is diffused. The only filter to use is a skylight.

SUNSETS: Not every Hawaiian night is preceded by a brilliant sunset, but there are likely to be some that will seem to typify every magical impression ever dreamed of the tropics.

Since many of the major resort areas face the setting sun, it's not difficult to be in the right place at the right time. Waikiki, Kona, Kaanapali, Wailea, Kapalua, Kihei, Napili, Poipu, and Princeville all offer excellent opportunities to catch the sun as it slips below the horizon.

When shooting sunsets, keep in mind that the brightness will distort meter readings. When composing a shot directly into the sun, frame the picture in the viewfinder so that only half of the sun is included. Read the meter, set, and shoot. Whenever there is this kind of unusual lighting, shoot a few frames both overexposing and underexposing in relation to the meter reading. Bracketing, as this is called, can provide a range of images, the best of which may well be other than the one shot at the meter's recommended setting.

Use any lens for sunsets. A wide-angle is good when the sky is filled with color-streaked clouds, when the sun is partially hidden, or when you're close to an object that silhouettes dramatically against the sky.

Telephotos also produce wonderful silhouettes, either with the sun as a backdrop or against the palette of a brilliant sunset sky. Bracket again here. For the best silhouettes, wait 10 to 15 minutes after sunset. A tripod is recommended.

Red and orange filters are often used to accentuate a sunset's picture potential. Orange will help turn even a gray sky into something approaching a photogenic finale to the day and can provide particularly beautiful shots linking the sky with the sun reflected on the ocean. If the sunset is already bold in hue, the orange may overwhelm the natural colors. A red filter will produce dramatic, highly unrealistic results.

NIGHT: If you think that picture possibilities end at sunset, you're presuming that night photography is the exclusive domain of the professional. If you've got a tripod, all you'll need is a cable release to attach to your camera to assure a steady exposure (which is often timed in minutes rather than fractions of a second).

For situations such as luaus, Polynesian revues, and other nighttime entertainments, a strobe does the trick, but beware: Flash units used improperly. You can't take a view of Diamond Head with a flash. It may reach out 30 to 50 feet, but that's it. Strobes usually are programmed to fire at 1/60 or 1/125 of a second, so if you set the exposure properly and shoot within range, you should come up with pretty sharp results.

CLOSEUPS: Whether of people or of objects such as lava, closeups can add another dimension to your photography. There are a number of shooting options, one of which is to use a 105mm or a 200mm lens at its closest focusable distance. Unless you're working in bright sunlight, a tripod will be worthwhile. If you are very near your subject and there is a good deal of reflective light, it may pay to underexpose a bit in relation to the meter reading.

If you do not have a telephoto lens, you can still shoot closeups using a set of magnification filters. Filter packs of one-, two-, and three-time magnification are available, making a 50mm a closeup lens.

AERIAL VIEWS: An inter-island flight or a helicopter tour can inspire some great pictures, but you have to be prepared. Get your equipment ready as soon as you're seated, test the meter against the horizon's light, and set for the proper exposure. Have spare film unpackaged and handy so you can change it quickly, and try to start off with a full roll rather than waste time (and photo opportunities) while airborne.

You can use a wide-angle lens from the air, although it will flatten things out and may well include sections of the plane in the picture. A 50mm can be used, and a telephoto will pick out details. Don't shoot through glass that is curved or at too extreme an angle; it will cause distortion. If there's bright sunlight, it's possible to underexpose a bit, yet still have enough light to shoot at speeds of 1/500 or 1/1000: fast enough to get results. Below 1/250 the outcome is questionable.

VIDEO: Video equipment rentals are now available on all islands. On Kauai, try *Aloha Video Camera* (phone: 822-2920) in Kapaa; on Maui, try *Point and Shoot* (phone: 879-1811) or *Rainbow Video* (phone: 879-8905) in Kihei, and *Wave Video* (phone: 661-5885) in Lahaina. On the Big Island, there's *Ohana Video*, World Square (phone: 329-0531), and on Oahu it's *King Video Camera Rentals* on Royal Hawaiian Ave. (phone: 922-6510) and *Video Camera Rentals* on Ala Moana Blvd. near the *Hilton* (phone: 942-2866), which offers delivery service.

SOME FINAL TIPS: Get organized. A small, lightweight canvas camera bag with cushioning and Velcro dividers is perfect for carrying lenses, lens tissue, filters, rolls of film, and a strobe. It's amazing how compact camera equipment is when packed properly.

If you are concerned about airport security X-rays damaging undeveloped film (X-rays do not affect processed film), store it in one of the lead-lined bags, sold in camera shops. This possibility is not as much of a threat as it used to be, however. In the US, incidents of X-ray damage to unprocessed film (exposed or unexposed) are few because low-dosage X-ray equipment is used virtually everywhere. As a rule of thumb, photo industry sources say that film with speeds up to ASA 400 can go through security machinery in the US five times without any noticeable effect. Nevertheless, if you're traveling without a protective bag, you may want to ask to have your photo equipment inspected by hand. (Naturally, this is possible only if you're carrying your film and camera on board with you — a good idea, because it helps to preclude loss or theft or the possibility at some airports that checked baggage will be X-rayed more heavily than hand baggage.) One type of film that should never be subjected to X-rays is the new, very high speed ASA 1,000 film; there are lead-lined bags made especially for it. Finally, the walk-through metal detector devices at airports do not affect film, though the film cartridges will set them off.

How much film should you take? If you are serious about your photography, pack one roll of film (36 exposures) for each day of your trip. You'll have no trouble getting any standard film in Hawaii; it's sold everywhere. And processing, even on the neighbor islands, can often be done overnight. Kodak even has a processing lab in Honolulu.

Most Waikiki hotels and other resort areas charge a premium for film. If you want to buy a lot of film, try *City Art Works* (1133 Nuuanu Ave.; phone: 536-4066) or *Super Save Camera* (1334 Young St.; phone: 536-6431). *Long's,* a chain of drugstores with outlets on all the main islands, also sells discounted film and handles processing. For equipment, check the daily newspaper for increasingly common discount prices. Should your camera need repairs while in the islands, call *Photocine* (738 Kaheka St., Ste. 305; phone: 941-4133), which provides warranty and out-of-warranty service for almost all models. On Maui, *Nagamine Camera* (Whalers Village Shopping Complex; phone: 667-5494) offers a full range of film supplies and 1-hour processing; *Kihei Camera* (Azeka Pl., 1280 S. Kihei Rd.; phone: 879-6351) provides underwater camera rentals, along with film supplies and 1-hour processing. Shops offering 1-hour processing are now found on all the major islands.

A SHORT PHOTOGRAPHIC TOUR

OAHU: For people shots, you can't beat Chinatown, particularly the early morning market on King Street. A visit to any of Oahu's beaches will also provide lots of subjects: Try Waikiki for all sorts and shapes of sunbathers; Diamond Head and Kailua Beach for windsurfers; Sunset and the Banzai Pipeline for championship surfboarders; Hanauma Bay for snorkelers, marine life, and one of Hawaii's largest reefs. For the latter, you'll need an underwater casing. You might try an 81B (brown) filter to warm up beach shots or underexpose a bit if you're using a skylight to compensate for reflective glare.

A drive to the Tantalus Lookout offers spectacular cityscapes that include Diamond Head, Waikiki, and downtown Honolulu. The lookout at Punchbowl National Cemetery also features panoramas of the city. Early morning is the best time to shoot unless you're after sunsets, in which case the obvious time is late afternoon.

For the definitive shot of Diamond Head, wait until afternoon and head down the beach to the jetty in front of the *Reef.* The beach to the right of the *Hilton Hawaiian Village* and the Magic Island section of Ala Moana Beach Park also have clear, uncluttered views. So do the lounge and restaurant atop the *Sheraton-Waikiki.*

The view from the Pali Lookout is one of the most encompassing in Hawaii, offering picture possibilities anytime during the day before 4 PM, when the Windward Coast becomes covered in shadow. Even better is a morning's drive up the Windward Coast to the North Shore and beyond for its 2-hour sweep of rugged mountains, ribbon beaches, ever-changing seas, and thick green vegetation. Also noteworthy are the pineapple fields of the Schofield Plains — especially if a harvest is taking place — and the charming town of Haleiwa, which sees some beautiful sunsets.

THE BIG ISLAND OF HAWAII: For volcanoes and Hawaiiana, visit the Big Island. Hawaii Volcanoes National Park provides access to the active Halemaumau Crater, as well as to the smaller ones along the Chain of Craters Road. A wide-angle lens will capture the vastness of the setting, while a telephoto will help record the exciting detail. Don't expect jets of flaming lava; it could happen, but it's unlikely. There will, however, be powerful images of the living earth and the scars it leaves behind after moments of eruptive fury. The best lookouts are behind the *Volcano House* hotel, as well as those along the Rim Road, which encircles the crater, allowing a direct look into the central pit itself.

Several easy trails lead to portions of the crater floor, passing through thick fern forest before opening upon the barren crust of newly hardened lava. The rim-level Devastation Trail has an easy walk through the site of a major eruption in 1959. Stark shapes and colors are the major elements here.

The Big Island is at its scenic best along the Hamakua Coast — 40 miles of canefields, upcountry, and dusty old towns beginning in Hilo and ending at Waipio Valley Overlook. Hire a Jeep (and a driver) to go down into the valley to see its 1,500-foot waterfall, black sand beach, and marshy taro plots.

The area between Waimea and Hawi provides still another Hawaiian perspective, with volcanic craters now covered by lush grass cropped slowly by grazing cattle. Long views of the Kohala Coast all the way to Kona are part of the drive south; morning or afternoon light is best.

The City of Refuge, south of Kona, is a reconstruction of an important temple complex, with crafts and lifestyle exhibits. Try shooting the major temples and tikis silhouetted against the setting sun.

MAUI: Haleakala is not to be missed. One of the world's largest dormant volcanoes, its crater is 19 square miles of colorful cliffs, cinder cones, and slides of lava ash. From its 10,023-foot summit there are often views of the distant peaks of the Big Island, neighboring Molokai, Lanai, and Kahoolawe.

Sunrise and sunset are the best times for pictures because the midday light in the crater is often flat, and by late afternoon much of the crater is already in shadow. Wide-angles, telephotos, and standard lenses will all prove useful. The best vistas are from the Haleakala Visitor Center and from the summit overlook. Since weather may be a problem here (frequent rain and clouds), call park headquarters before making the long drive to the top.

The Hana Highway is Maui's other great photographic asset. This 50-mile road from Kahului to Hana ties together such disparate scenery as the "artsy" town of Paia, the taro fields of Keanae, the pastures of Hana, and the forests and streams of the Seven Pools. Morning and afternoon are equally good for picture-taking.

On West Maui is semi-restored Lahaina, with its old whaling town architecture. An afternoon's walk on the rock jetty that surrounds the yacht harbor will yield some good views of the town and the mountains, as well as of boats, surfers, and windsurfers.

Along the drive from Kapalua to Lahaina and Maalaea to Makena are impressive vistas of distant Molokai, Lanai, and Kahoolawe. Early morning and afternoon are best.

MOLOKAI: The Makanalua Peninsula, majestically situated beneath 2,000-foot cliffs, has been the home of Kalaupapa, the famous leper colony, for almost a century. At the eastern end of the island, reached via four-wheel-drive vehicle through the mountains and along the coast, are Halawa Valley's twin waterfalls and beach.

LANAI: This is Hawaii's Pineapple Island, and the sprawling plantation is the focus of interest, especially during harvest season. The mostly Filipino workers in their harvest attire make a very "foreign" and fascinating shot; early morning is the best time to visit the fields. Another possibility is the Lanai Hale Road. At 3,500 feet above sea level, it offers some breathtaking looks at neighboring Molokai and Maui that are easy to frame with the unusual silhouettes of Cook pines.

KAUAI: Thought by many to be the most photogenic of the Hawaiian islands, Kauai offers both variety and beauty. And with its range of blues and greens, Kauai reproduces especially well with a polarizer.

The Princeville and Na Pali Coast areas are perfect for those *South Pacific* shots. Some places to watch for are the taro fields in Hanalei Valley, the overlook for Hanalei Bay, the Lumahai Beach Lookout, and the towering cliffs of the Na Pali Coast. For the best view of the coast, walk around the rocks to the left of Haena Beach or, if you've got the energy and time, hike to the half-mile marker on the Kalalau Trail, which also begins at Haena.

The highway from Lihue to Waimea Canyon runs through some of Kauai's quaintest towns; Hanapepe and Waimea, for example. If you take the back road up to Waimea Canyon, the panoramas may include neighboring Niihau, Hawaii's "forbidden island." The best natural light for shots of the canyon itself occurs in the afternoon, when the sun hits the canyon's east wall directly, drawing out the rich mix of purples and reds. The view of Kalalau Valley and the sea can be wonderful if the weather is clear; however, mist and heavy clouds frequently roll in to block it.

For the Experience

Quintessential Hawaii

 You've sat on the beach at Waikiki until you're nut-brown and watched a succession of glorious sunsets from your private lanai. You've quaffed many a mai tai; donned a muumuu or aloha shirt; and sampled opakapaka, pupus, and three-finger poi. You've even decided that morning coffee will never again taste as good unless there's a tiny orchid floating in it. But while all of the foregoing are a pleasant part of any Hawaiian vacation, only after visiting the places described below — which allow a visitor to be a part of the real Hawaii — can a trip to these unique islands be considered a complete experience.

WAIMEA FALLS PARK, Haleiwa, Oahu: This is among the most beautiful spots on Oahu, with a gem of a cascade that tumbles into a rock-girt pool straight out of *Tarzan* or *The Blue Lagoon*. Even when the pathways through the gardens and around the natural, waterfall-fed pool are fairly crowded, which they often are on weekends and holidays, it's easy to escape the human traffic by climbing the lovely trails that wind through the hillsides and woods above the falls. Apart from its considerable scenic charm, Waimea Falls Park inspires both historical and botanical fascination. The land once belonged to the high priest who served Kamehameha the Great, a man said to be buried hereabouts, though no one is quite sure where. Just off the main path are remnants of an ancient Hawaiian village, terraces where fruit and vegetables were cultivated, and fishing shrines. Psychics tell of feeling distinct vibrations in this area, although whoever is trying to relay a message seems to be placated by the sight and sound of old Hawaiian games such as *ulu maika,* a form of lawn bowling, which is taught and played in a meadow close by. The Waimea Arboretum and Botanical Gardens, on the meadows and hillsides between the visitors' entrance and the falls, is a wonderland of tropical flora. Amid this paradise of trees, shrubs, and plants are plots devoted to heliconia and ginger, hibiscus, ferns, bamboo, and exotic vegetation from such distant places as Bermuda, the Canary Islands, Sri Lanka, and Madagascar. A favorite conversation piece among visitors is the world's only known specimen of a tree called *kokia cookei.* Another is the 35 varieties of banana plants. The park is also home to some species of Hawaiian wildlife, including nene geese, Kona nightingales — wild donkeys — from the Big Island, peacocks, and wild boar. The annual *Makahiki Festival,* held during the first weekend in October, is recommended Hawaiiana. Also worthy of note: The park opens on nights when the moon is full, and guided walks are conducted. Information: Waimea Falls Park, 59-864 Kamehameha Hwy., Haleiwa, HI 96712 (phone: 638-8511).

POLYNESIAN CULTURAL CENTER, Laie, Oahu: Like the Polynesian people themselves, their artifacts, dance, and music exemplify grace, beauty, and a highly refined artistic imagination. A dazzling array of all these qualities can be seen at the Polynesian Cultural Center on Brigham Young University's Hawaiian campus at Laie, on Oahu's windward coast. Students from many distinct Polynesian backgrounds, working in replicas of their native villages, explain the life, customs, rituals, ceremonies, habits, arts, crafts, and food of their homelands to visitors. The things to see, and sometimes participate in, include Tongan women making *ngatu*, or tapa cloth; Tahitian girls, lovely as moonlight, making shell leis and grass skirts; elaborate pint-size wooden tikis outside a small Marquesan village temple; Fijians playing music on pipe organs; Maoris from New Zealand throwing spears in their own unique manner; Samoan men walking unscathed through a curtain of flame; and Hawaiians making poi, something no one should leave the islands without seeing. The villages, authentic in every detail, have been built by students of the university, who are very friendly and carry a storehouse of detailed information in their heads. Fortunately, they also talk about up-to-date clothes, modern music, and baseball scores, which infuse a little real life into this museum village community. Don't miss the Tongan House and the Chief's House in the Fiji village. A film on the cultures of Polynesia is scheduled to begin showing on an oversize (IMAX) theater screen early in the year. The center also features a series of musical performances throughout the day, including *Pageant of the Long Canoes*, a canoe spectacle that is included in the $25 entry fee, and *This Is Polynesia*, an extravagant song and dance revue performed evenings and selected afternoons. The entry fee, dinner, and show package, at $37, is a good buy. For an additional $5, you can substitute the nightly luau for the dinner buffet. Information: Polynesian Cultural Center, 55-370 Kamehameha Hwy., Laie, HI 96762 (phone: 293-3333).

SEA LIFE PARK, Waimanalo, Oahu: "An educational experience" may sound like just the sort of thing you've come to Hawaii to escape, but the didactic side of Sea Life Park is riveting, far more appealing than the show-biz side. The outstanding feature of the park is the Hawaiian Reef Tank, a 300,000-gallon re-creation of an undersea Pacific reef. Spiraling around the tank's transparent sides from top to bottom is a ramp with illuminated panels above the windows. These displays help visitors to identify some of the more obscure marine species, such as hermit crabs, which normally exist at depths of 200 to 300 feet; saddleback fish; and vivid butterfly and banded-angel fish. The panels also give the scientific names of some specimens that may be vaguely familiar already, such as the hammerhead shark, reef shark, brown sting rays, eagle rays, and moray eels. In the Science Theater, dolphins and penguins perform, while the recently opened Rocky Shores Exhibit shows a cross section of tidal ecology. At Whaler's Cove, porpoises wearing leis and whales towing a rowboat also take part in a sub-Disneyish scenario, which is about as edifying as watching a poodle turn somersaults. A number of small pools hold sea turtles, whiskered harbor seals, and a variety of seabirds normally found in the chain of islets strung out for 1,000 miles northwest of Hawaii. The Pacific Whaling Museum displays the largest collection of whaling artifacts and scrimshaw in the Pacific, not to mention the skeleton of a 38-foot sperm whale. Walls full of brightly illustrated explanatory texts inspire a desire to go probing around full fathom five and deeper. Sea Life Park's location at the foot of a sheer Koolau cliff and beside the ocean at Makapuu Beach is exceptionally beautiful. On Thursdays, Fridays, and Sundays, the park is open until 10 PM. The last show is at 7 PM, and includes Hawaiian music and dance as well as marine shows. Admission is $8.25. Information: Sea Life Park, Makapuu Point, Waimanalo, HI 96795 (phone: 259-7933).

HAWAII VOLCANOES NATIONAL PARK, the Big Island of Hawaii: The Hawaiian islands are rich in myth and legend, and among the pantheon of gods frequently mentioned, none looms so large, so tangible, or so memorable as Pele. This capricious firebrand has dwelt on all the major islands, and now makes her uneasy home on the Big Island in the very active Kilauea Crater, 4,077 feet above sea level, which is the dramatic focal point of the park. Pele has been repeatedly displaying her irascible temper during the series of eruptions that have been more or less constant over the last several years, and with a succession of fiery events toward the end of 1986 she sent waves of sun-red lava pouring down the hillsides and into the ocean along the island's south coast. The lava Pele sent heading for the sea destroyed more than a dozen homes and covered Route 13, closing the Hilo–Chain of Craters Road circuit via Wahaula, and she repeated her performance soon after the road was restored to use. (At press time, the route was closed and there was little likelihood of its being restored for use in the near future.) Ranger-led tours depart daily from Wahuaula to the eruption zone at 1 PM, except Sundays. Even when the goddess is resting, hissing steam vents and evil-smelling sulfur vents in the crater and on the surrounding bluffs confirm her presence and her readiness to rumble at any moment. Evidence of her wrath is everywhere: in the Kau Desert, where shiny folds of lava look like burnished chrome; along the surrealistic Devastation Trail, where scarred, gray wrecks of trees lie abandoned like driftwood on an ocean of cinders; and in the ohia forests, where molten droplets of lava have frosted branches and leaves and crystallized into gossamer forms, a phenomenon known as "Pele's hair." In other parts of the park, the world seems to have turned topsy-turvy and dreamlike: The Thurston Lava Tube looks like a tunnel burrowed by a giant earthworm; giant ferns tower over Lilliputian visitors in the Fern Jungle; and all along the beaches, beneath familiar palm trees, are unfamiliar sands of jet black. For the botanist, ornithologist, paleontologist, geologist, and volcanologist, the park is a vast and bountiful laboratory. To laypeople it is almost always beautiful, frequently eerie, and invariably full of wonders. Because the park is so easily accessible by road, and Kilauea Crater and some smaller craters can frequently be seen by car, it has been dubbed "the Drive-in Volcano." Information: Hawaii Volcanoes National Park, HI 96785 (phone: 967-7311). For eruption reports, phone: 967-7977.

HAWAII TROPICAL BOTANICAL GARDEN, Hilo, the Big Island of Hawaii: This once private garden and nature preserve, located on scenic acreage along the Hamakua Coast just 4 miles north of Hilo, offers one of Hawaii's most successful blends of native rain forest and formal garden. Palm groves lead to waterfalls and coastal lookouts, with lush plantings of heliconia, bromeliads (the pineapple family), banana, hibiscus, and orchids en route. A visit starts at the old country church, restored to serve as Hawaii Tropical's headquarters. From here, a van transports visitors to the garden, where two trails provide both beauty and privacy. Information: Hawaii Tropical Botanical Garden, RR 143-A, Papaikou, HI 96781 (phone: 964-5233).

NANI MAU GARDENS, Hilo, the Big Island of Hawaii: Nani Maui's 20 acres contain an abundance of flowering orchids and exotic trees and shrubs planted so that blooms are showing off no matter what the season. Well-marked plants and a short brochure make a self-guided tour both pleasant and informative, and at the end of the visit a selection of tropical fruits from Nani Maui's trees and plants, including several likely to be first-time experiences, are served. Located just off the highway linking Hilo with Hawaii Volcanoes National Park. The turnoff is marked by a Visitor Bureau sign. Information: Nani Maui Gardens, 421 Makalika St., Hilo, HI 96720 (phone: 959-3541).

WAIPIO VALLEY, the Big Island of Hawaii: Secret gardens, desert islands, and shangri-las of various kinds have always had a fascination for the traveler. Unfortunately, they are becoming harder and harder to find. One such place still exists on the northeast coast of the Big Island of Hawaii, about 50 miles north of Hilo. Called Waipio Valley, it's a broad, deep cleft in the Kohala Mountains rampant with as much floral exuberance as can be gathered in one place. On its three landward sides, it is flanked by precipitous cliffs many hundreds of feet high. Its oceanfront is guarded by often pernicious surf. Although there are taro patches here and there and remnants of sugarcane plots and rice paddies, most of the valley is an entangled umbrage of banana, guava, passion fruit, noni apple, avocado, mango, papaya, and grapefruit trees, with ginger, hibiscus, and orchids adding to the tumult of color and tall ferns with arabesque fronds lending a touch of mystery. Clear, fast-flowing streams run through these luxuriant groves, fed by the narrow, lacy Hiilawe Falls, which plunge 1,300 feet down from the mountains. Legend has it that in the late 18th century, Kamehameha the Great was assigned his war god here before embarking on his conquest of the islands. In 1823, a traveler recorded that 1,325 people lived in the valley, and as scattered dwellings and multicolored outrigger canoes along the beach indicate, some still do. But their numbers have dwindled dramatically as tidal waves and other natural disasters have, albeit infrequently, made a hell of this paradise, driving many people to higher, safer ground. This lovely wilderness is penetrable on foot — allow a day to take full advantage — or with a four-wheel-drive vehicle, the only kind that can safely maneuver the steep grades and angles of the road. Perhaps the best way to explore the valley is in one of the Jeeps operated by the *Waipio Valley Shuttle,* whose colorful drivers know the local lore, history, flora and fauna, or with *Waipio Wagon Tours,* which makes 2-hour visits in mule-drawn wagons that follow the four-wheel-drive descent to the valley floor. For those who wish to spend the night, which is magnificently alive with fragrant tropical breezes and stars, there's the *Waipio* motel — not so much a motel as a retreat, where a room costs $10 a night per person. The few bedrooms are lit with kerosene lamps, and drinking water is hauled in from Hilo. Unless you're fasting or are prepared to search the valley for some of its abundant fruits, remember to bring your own food, which can be prepared on the propane burners in the kitchen. Information: Waipio Valley Shuttle, PO Box 5128, Kukuihaele, HI 96727 (phone: 775-7121); Waipio Wagon Tours, PO Box 1340, Honokaa, HI 96727 (phone: 775-9518); Waipio Motel, 25 Malama Pl., Hilo, HI 96720 (phone: 775-0368 or 935-7466; advance reservations necessary).

MAUNA KEA SUMMIT, the Big Island of Hawaii: At 13,796 feet, Mauna Kea is not only the tallest mountain in Hawaii but, measured from its base 18,000 feet under the surface of the Pacific, it is also the tallest, most massive mountain on Earth. The summit — usually well above the clouds — is home to one of the most important astronomical observatory complexes in the world. *Paradise Safaris* runs day trips in four-wheel-drive vehicles that make easy work of the long road of flattened cinders which climbs to the summit and includes an observatory tour and remarkable panoramas. (Those who prefer to make the trip on their own should rent a four-wheel-drive vehicle.) In winter, there's likely to be snow covering the cinder cones dotting the summit, making the road extra difficult to navigate. Information: Paradise Safaris, Box A-D, Kailua-Kona, HI 96745 (phone: 329-9282).

At 9,000 feet, adjacent to the Hale Pohaku dormitories and facilities for the summit observatories' staff and astronomers, the Onizuka Center for International Astronomy offers interesting displays on Mauna Kea and its state-of-the-art observatories, and invites visitors to stargaze through its small (11-inch) but effective telescope on Fridays from 7 to 9 PM. Tours of the summit depart from the site of the University of Hawaii's 88-inch telescope Saturdays and Sundays at 2:30 PM. On weekends there's stargazing from the university's 24-inch telescope for a limit of 30 participants; reservations are required. A four-wheel-drive vehicle is a necessity for the drive from Hale Pohaku to the summit, as are warm clothes, since weather at the summit is changeable. Those with respiratory or heart conditions are advised not to go higher than Hale Pohaku, and children under 16 are not permitted on tours. Information: Institute for Mauna Kea Support Services, 177 Makaala St., Hilo, HI 96720 (phone: 935-3371).

SUNRISE AT HALEAKALA NATIONAL PARK, Maui: Those folks seen staggering into your hotel at around 10 o'clock in the morning, looking tired but happy and weighed down by heavy sweaters, jackets, and blankets, have just returned from one of Maui's classic excursions — the trip to the top of Haleakala to see the sun rise. Haleakala, meaning "House of the Sun," is Maui's huge dormant volcano, and it has been known by that name at least since the Polynesian demigod Maui climbed to its 10,023-foot summit to lasso the rising sun and force it to move more slowly across the sky, thereby providing his mother with a few more hours of warm daylight in which to dry her tapa cloth. Latter-day visitors who retrace Maui's steps do it in a more reverent spirit. Mark Twain, in fact, wrote that it was the "sublimest spectacle" he ever saw, the memory of which would remain with him always.

The first requirement for the Haleakala pilgrimage is warm clothing. Temperatures at the summit can drop to as low as 35F in the summer and another 10 degrees lower in the winter, though the average is about 30 degrees lower than the temperature at sea level. A further requirement is the willpower to roll out of bed while the rest of the world is asleep. Sunrise occurs anywhere between about 5:45 AM in the summer and 7 AM in the winter, and it's necessary to be on the scene at least a half hour before dawn to witness the full spectacle. (Check the *Maui News* for the exact time of the next day's sunrise, call the park's recorded information number, 572-7749, or the Maui Recreational Forecast, 871-5054.) *Papillon Helicopters* (phone: 669-4884) offers a sunrise itinerary ($220). Sunrise ground tours are offered by *Akamai Tours* ($34; phone: 871-9551) and *Trans Maui* ($29; phone: 877-7308).

The road from Kahului to the top of the volcano is the only road on earth that rises from sea level to above 10,000 feet in a distance of only 40 miles. It will take about 1½ hours to drive and will deposit you above the cloud layer at the highest point on Maui, Puu Ulaula, a volcanic cone on which the glass-walled observation shelter that is the traditional spot for sunrise watching is perched. The shelter provides relative warmth and, poised as it is on the western rim of Haleakala's vast 19-square-mile crater, presents no obstruction of the view. Outside, as fellow pilgrims shiver and set their tripods pointing east, the sky brightens and the far edge of the sea of fluffy clouds takes on a border of spreading red and gold. When the sun finally appears, it comes up quickly (though portions of the crater do remain in shadow until late in the day), but in the meantime, the play of light at the top of the world will have left an indelible impression. Afterward, there's plenty of time to observe the crater's barren landscape of cinder cones and ash from several vantage points and still make it out of the park before the visitor center opens and the day's tourists arrive. Information: Haleakala National Park, PO Box 369, Makawao, HI 96768 (phone: 572-9306, 572-9177).

MOLOKAI RANCH WILDLIFE PARK, Molokai: A square mile resembling Africa's open game land was carved out of the Friendly Island's dry, rolling western hills in 1977 and stocked with such exotic and endangered species of animals native to India and Africa as axis deer, sable antelope, Indian black buck, barbary sheep, oryx, zebra, and ibex. Molokai Ranch Ltd.'s plan was to use an area similar to the animals' native habitat to breed them, thus serving as a transition supply point for the world's zoos and parks. But when guests at the nearby *Kaluakoi* hotel (which opened in 1977) heard of the park and expressed an interest in touring it, the company realized it had an automatic tourist attraction in what really is a working animal preserve. A very low-key van tour that lasts 1½ hours is now available; check with the *Kaluakoi*'s tour desk or with the park's representative in front of the hotel's entrance drive. The tour route runs over rough, rutted dirt roads (no pampering here) and affords good views of many of the 300 animals in the park. Tickets are $12 plus tax, $6 for children; under age 7 free. Molokai Ranch Wildlife Park, PO Box 8, Mauna Loa, HI 96770 (phone: 552-2555).

DAY SAILS TO LANAI: Several boats leave Maui daily for sails to the Pineapple Island of Lanai, where the attractions are a get-away-from-it-all setting and crystal clear waters that provide some of Hawaii's best snorkeling and scuba. Among those sailing are *Trilogy Excursions* and *Club Lanai* from Lahaina, and *Ocean Activities Center* out of Maalaea. The cost ranges from $60 to $95, with more expensive sails that include a land tour of Lanai. *Club Lanai* spends the day at an 8-acre beachfront retreat where a full lunch is served and the range of activities includes snorkeling, scuba, volleyball, boating, and private walks along a mile-long deserted beach. *Trilogy* and *Windjammer* head to Hulopoe Bay, where a crescent beach faces snorkeling-perfect waters. Lunch is served here. *Ocean Activities* includes lunch at the rustic *Lanai* hotel, complete with Hawaiian show as well as snorkeling and swimming time. Information: Trilogy Excursions, PO Box 1121, Lahaina, HI 96767 (phone: 661-4743; 800-874-2666); Club Lanai, 333 Dairy Rd., Suite 201A, Kahului, HI 96732 (phone: 871-1144); Ocean Activities Center, 1325 S. Kihei Rd., Suite 212, Kihei, HI 96753 (phone: 879-4485; 800-367-8047, ext. 448).

NA PALI COAST STATE PARK, Kauai: No roads run through Na Pali; the ridges and valleys etched into the northwest coast of Kauai are so steep and narrow that they've even confounded the master builders of the last few decades, who've strung challenging highways elsewhere over the world. To see Na Pali, therefore, the adventurous must take a boat, skirting massive cliffs occasionally broken by sparkling white beaches; hire a helicopter to fly deep into the densely forested valleys; or hike in on foot, using the trail left by the ancient Hawaiians. Despite this inconvenience, most people who spend any time on Kauai get to Na Pali, for not to experience the awesome beauty of these jagged cliffs and hanging valleys is like visiting Paris and missing the *Louvre*.

Most people choose to see Na Pali by boat or helicopter, but for those who have the time — and stamina — to see it on foot, it's by far the best choice. The Kalalau Trail, starting at Haena State Park on the north coast and ending at Kalalau Valley 11 miles away, plunges into an Eden rich with fruit trees, wild orchids, sweet-smelling ginger, and Hawaii's majestic monkeypod, kukui, and koa trees. It's possible to camp overnight in a mango grove, pick sweet guava, bananas, and mountain apples for your breakfast, and bathe in a pristine pool at the foot of a waterfall. Scattered up the valleys, some so narrow a trekker hardly reaches the bottom before beginning the ascent up the other side, are the remains of stone-walled taro fields built by the early Polynesians, who chose this rugged and isolated terrain for the protection it offered from warring neighbors. Indeed, Na Pali has always offered refuge to those threatened from outside. One entire tribe is said to have fled into a valley west of Kalalau, never to be seen or heard of again. In more recent times, Koolau, a cowboy condemned to the Molokai leper colony, escaped with his family to one of Na Pali's valleys, where he successfully fought off the troops sent to take him back.

The first 2 miles of the trail to Hanakapiai Beach can be done in less than 2 hours by a walker in reasonable shape. Beyond that, the trail becomes steeper and more slippery and requires a measure of hiking expertise and stamina. For those planning to cover the entire trail, camping equipment (and permission from the state parks department) is necessary, since the hike to Kalalau and back takes at least 2 to 3 days. Equipment for purchase or rent is available from *Hanalei Camping and Backpacking*, Ching Young Shopping Center, Hanalei, HI 96714 (phone: 826-6664). For information on boat and helicopter tours, see *Sightseeing Tours*, KAUAI. Hiking and camping information (and camping permits) can be obtained from the Division of State Parks, State Bldg., 3060 Eiwa St., Lihue, HI 96766 (phone: 245-4444). Permits are issued by mail when applicants send a photocopy of their driver's license as I.D.

PACIFIC TROPICAL BOTANICAL GARDEN, Lawai, Kauai: Gardens are a special pleasure in Hawaii, where *everything* grows quickly and profusely. This garden, which runs down sunny Lawai Valley on the south side of Kauai, offers more than most since it's the only tropical research garden in the US and cultivates plants as rare as the white Tahitian mountain apple alongside hundreds of variations of the ubiquitous palm. (At last count, the garden had 800 different palms, about one third of the known varieties.)

In addition to studying and preserving tropical plant life, the garden conducts regular tours to acquaint the public with its work. The 2-hour-plus tours, limited to about a dozen people, are led by knowledgeable volunteers who take the time to explain what's being seen and to answer visitors' questions. The result is an intimate and expert introduction for the layman to the staggering abundance of tropical flora.

For a young garden — only 20 years old — its collections are extensive. In a section devoted to plants used for clothing, housing, food, and building, there are some 20 varieties of the hau tree, a member of the hibiscus family, which was important to early Polynesians both as a source of cordage (from the bark) and lightweight lumber for their outriggers. Among the many edible plants and spices raised by the garden are bananas (in a mere 60 varieties), coconuts, breadfruit, jackfruit, taro, Java plums, ginger, clove, allspice, cardamom, cinnamon, tumeric, and peppercorns.

Much of the garden is devoted to ornamental plants — red, waxy-leaved bromeliads; anthuriums; coral erythrinas; bamboos; and flowering trees, bushes, and ground covers in a multitude of shades and shapes. But the biggest crowd-pleaser is the fantastically large (big enough to support the weight of a small child) Victoria Amazonica, a green and pink water lily that rightfully belongs on the other side of Alice's looking glass.

Adjoining the Pacific Garden is the Allerton estate. The work of Robert Allerton, a wealthy Chicago banker, and his son John Gregg Allerton, it is an enchanting combination of formal gardens and tropical jungle. The younger Allerton, an architect by training, created outdoor "rooms" using living nature as his building material. The walls of his Thanksgiving Room, for instance, are formed by panax trees, slim-trunked trees used by Tahitians to support vanilla bean vines, while two sheltering monkeypod trees, flanking a classical water fountain, serve as a leafy roof.

The Pacific and Allerton gardens are open to the public on weekdays, with tours departing at 9 AM and 1 PM. Weekend tours do not include beach portions of the estate. Groups are limited to about 12, and reservations are required. The tour costs $15. Membership in the Garden costs $35 for two and includes the tour charge for the holder and immediate family members. Membership also allows entry to Satellite Gardens at Limahuli (on the north shore of Kauai) and in Hana, Maui. Information: Pacific Tropical Botanical Garden, PO Box 340, Lawai, HI 96765 (phone: 332-7361).

Whale Watching

 Every year from November to May, Hawaii plays host to some unusually distinguished guests, the humpback whales, who leave their summer home in the Gulf of Alaska to winter in the warm waters off Hawaii. Between 500 to 800 whales congregate in the large shallow basin formed by the islands of Maui, Lanai, Molokai, and Kahoolawe, an area called, appropriately enough, the "bedroom of the whales," since it is here that they mate and give birth to their calves. Except for those glimpsed in Southern California waters, the humpbacks in Hawaii constitute the largest gathering of whales routinely visible to humans, and in recent years, watching the aquatic antics of these remarkable creatures has been delighting thousands of visitors to the islands.

Measuring from 40 to 50 feet long and weighing about 40 tons, the humpback has distinctive characteristics that make it easily identifiable: bumps on its snout, unusually long flippers, and a scalloped tail fin, called a fluke, that is often 18 feet across. For all its bulk, the humpback is an agile and even graceful swimmer. In one incredible display, known as "breaching," the whale will propel its entire body up out of the water and then land on its back or side, sending up a wall of spray. Whether it breaches to communicate its location, to dislodge the many barnacles and lice that cling to its ample body, or simply to express a natural exuberance, no one knows for certain. But the display is undeniably impressive.

What fascinates biologists and laymen alike about whales is their intelligence and their highly developed social structure. A mother and her calf are always accompanied by a third whale, usually male, perhaps the father, who helps teach the newborn the necessities of life — diving, breathing, breaching — and runs interference for the mother and calf should anything threaten them.

The most striking evidence of their sense of community is their singing — sonorous, otherworldly sounds thought to be mating calls or communications to whales hundreds of miles away. The songs are complicated sequences, lasting anywhere from 6 to 30 minutes, repeated over and over. Not only do all the whales in a given community sing the same song (North Pacific humpbacks sing a different song from humpbacks in the North Atlantic), but the song changes, subtly, from year to year, and everybody learns the new verses. Just how they do it is something that no doubt will baffle and challenge scientists for years to come.

Maui is by far the best island base for whale watching. They can easily be seen from several spots along the shore, and because Maui is a popular tourist destination, there are a number of whale watching cruises that leave from Lahaina and Maalaea harbors. The cruise sponsored by the *Pacific Whale Foundation* (101 N Kihei Rd., Kealia Beach Plaza, Kihei, HI 96753; phone: 879-8811), a research organization, is perhaps the most informative, but others run by residents well acquainted with the waters can be just as fruitful. (If you book your cruise through the *Pacific Whale Foundation,* a portion of your fare will go to its efforts on behalf of the whales.)

Don't, however, take a boat out on your own. There are strict federal regulations regarding the observation of whales, and fines of up to $20,000 for violating them. Although the humpback has been a protected animal since 1966, its numbers have continued to drop until today there are only an estimated 1,000 to 1,500 left in the Pacific. Some think that one of the reasons for the decline is due to human-generated activity, such as the buzz of a boat's motor around their breeding grounds, which interferes with mating. Since females give birth to a single calf only once every 2 years, it's not hard to appreciate how perilously close to extinction the humpback is.

Because of these concerns, naturalists are encouraging people to watch whales from the shore. Shore-spotting is excellent on Maui, from Kaanapali to Maalaea Bay on West Maui, and down the coast of East Maui to Makena. There are a number of high spots where observers can pull off the road to watch them, but the scenic lookout at McGregor Point, near the town of Maalaea, offers the best viewing.

Whales are also visible from Molokai and Lanai, but the best viewing spots are difficult for tourists to reach. (Kahoolawe is used for target practice by the US Navy and, therefore, is usually off limits.) A small group of whales spends time at Kawaihae Bay, on the northwest side of the Big Island, and, with a little patience, it's possible to spot them from one of several elevated places along the coast. There are some winter sightings from Kauai's south coast, but the better months are April and May, when great numbers pass offshore on their trek back north. Any high spot along Poipu, especially Makahuena and Nukumoi points, is likely to reward a patient observer with the sight of a group of two or three humpbacks swimming along the surface at a good clip. If they're not cavorting around, there's plenty of spray coming from their blowholes to track them by. *Fantasy Island Boat Tours* offers motorized raft whale watch tours during winter months from Poipu's Kukuiula Harbor (phone: 742-9303). On Oahu, whales are occasionally spotted from lookouts between Diamond Head and Makapuu.

There's no great trick to successful shore-spotting, but a few tips should help first-timers get started. To begin with, use elevated ground for your observation point. Then go early in the morning or late in the afternoon. By midday, the wind is stronger and churns up the water, making it more difficult to spot the whales, but a few hours before sunset, which comes promptly at 6 PM, the whales tend to come closer to shore, sometimes as near as 50 feet away. Finally, be patient. Scan the horizon till you see what looks like an explosion of smoke about 18 feet high. That's the blow of the humpback. If you have binoculars, by all means, take them along. They're especially good for spotting the light blow of a calf. When a humpback lifts its head out of the water, an activity dubbed "spy hopping" since its eyes are just above the surface, it's just playing around. But when it lifts its tail straight up out of the water (called a fluke-up dive), it's going under for a prolonged dive and won't surface again for another 20 minutes or so.

To bone up on humpbacks before setting off on a watch, the Pacific Whale Foundation gives a number of lectures at hotels and condominiums around Maui. (Call 879-8811 for a schedule of upcoming lectures.) It's also possible to catch two films on whales at the *Carthaginian,* a boat–cum–whaling museum anchored at Lahaina Harbor. And at the Whale Report Center, on the dock next to the *Carthaginian,* there's updated news on where whales have been sighted most recently. Also worth a visit is the *Whalers Village Whale Museum* at Kaanapali, the *Pacific Whale Museum* at Oahu's *Sea Life Park,* and the *Hawaii Maritime Center* adjacent to Aloha Tower in downtown Honolulu, all of which feature excellent displays on the great whales and artifacts of the hunt. If you come away as fascinated by these creatures as most people do, treat yourself to Richard Ellis's beautiful and comprehensive work, *The Book of Whales* (Knopf; $25); Bob Goodman's interesting book, *Whale Song;* or a Robert Lyn Nelson painting (very expensive) or lithograph (affordable).

Hawaii's Heavenly Hotels

 Contrary to popular conception, Hawaii does not have a long innkeeping tradition. In fact, most of its hotels, resorts, and condominiums have been constructed in the decades since World War II, when the islands experienced a tremendous boom in tourism. Many of these facilities were ill planned and hastily constructed, resulting in too many faceless concrete high-rises and such hodge-podge developments as Waikiki (on Oahu) and Kihei (on Maui). Still, the state has several very fine hostelries, notable for their history, architecture, ambience, setting, or luxury, and it is in this context that they are discussed below.

BED-AND-BREAKFAST: Just a few years ago, there were no bed-and-breakfast accommodations in Hawaii. Today, several hundred island families open their homes to visitors at per person rates that start at $25 and climb to just over $150, depending on location, amenities, and room size. Most bed-and-breakfast accommodations include a private bath, and many have a private entrance. In some cases, entire apartments are available. Four Hawaii-based agencies now handle bookings. Oldest and largest is *Bed & Breakfast Hawaii,* which includes properties on all the islands and sells a book listing bed-and-breakfast options. Information: Bed & Breakfast Hawaii, PO Box 449, Kapaa, HI 96746 (phone: 822-7771); Bed & Breakfast Honolulu, 3242 Kaohinani Dr., Honolulu, HI 96817 (phone: 595-7533; 800-288-4666); Bed and Breakfast Maui Style, Box 886, Kihei, HI 96753 (phone: 879-7865); and Pacific-Hawaii Bed and Breakfast, 19 Kai Nani Pl., Kailua, HI 96734 (phone: 262-4848). For individual bed-and-breakfast recommendations, see *Checking In* in each island chapter.

KAHALA HILTON INTERNATIONAL, Honolulu, Oahu: There is something about staying here that is reminiscent of spending a few days at a superbly run country house; considering that there are 370 rooms in the complex, this is no mean feat. It may be the hotel's comparative isolation, surrounded as it is by the Waialae Golf Course and the ocean, or it may be the subdued harmony that exists between the polite, friendly, Hawaiian staff and the rather more formal European management. Whatever the individual ingredients, they add up to an operation that manages to be scrupulously (but unobtrusively) attentive to detail. News of the *Kahala*'s singular reputation and the seductive beauty of its setting has been brought to ears influential enough to persuade the Queen of England and her consort and the King of Spain and his wife to spend a few days here, as well as a host of other celebrities. Besides the main building, with its bright and airy rooms, there are oceanside bungalows and a two-story wing overlooking the hotel lagoon. The public areas are worth a visit even if you are not spending the night. The 30-foot-high lobby is dominated by a copper sculpture surrounded by orchids and two huge chandeliers, both weighing more than a ton and made from more than 30,000 pieces of Italian glass. The lagoon and adjacent ponds hold penguins, sea turtles, more than 1,000 reef fish, and a pair of dolphins that are constantly on the lookout for mischief. Among the more than 50 varieties of flora are hau, fiddleleaf, and autograph trees; cycad, livistonia, phoenix, traveler's, and bottle palms; and heliconia, bird of paradise, hibiscus, torch and shell ginger, Tahitian gardenias, spider lilies, and silver gazania. The *Maile* restaurant, under the hotel lobby, is one of the best known, most elegant eating places in Honolulu. The *Hala Terrace,* where scrumptious lunch snacks are served, looks out onto a perfect South Seas idyll of ocean, palm trees, and a tiny "desert island" just offshore. Information: Kahala Hilton International Hotel, 5000 Kahala Ave., Honolulu, HI 96816 (phone: 734-2211; 800-367-2525).

HILTON HAWAIIAN VILLAGE, Honolulu, Oahu: With more than 2,500 rooms, Waikiki's largest hotel has been totally renovated and rebuilt (at a cost of nearly $100 million), with very appealing results, not least of which is the comfortable lounging area by the free-form, beachside pool, complete with waterfalls and grottoes. The remake of the hotel's original Ocean Tower, reborn as the Alii Tower, provides guests with a private pool and full concierge services. But the best rooms, in terms of spectacular views of Diamond Head and spaciousness, are those in the new Rainbow Tower. Fine dining (the *Golden Dragon* is a definite award winner), a full complement of shops and boutiques, and a less hectic location at the west end of Waikiki Beach are also among its many assets. Information: Hilton Hawaiian Village, 2005 Kalia Rd., Honolulu, HI 96815 (phone: 949-4321; 800-445-8667).

HYATT REGENCY WAIKIKI, Honolulu, Oahu: The builders set out to prove that all tall concrete hostelries on famous seaside avenues do not have to be totally devoid of character, and they have largely succeeded. The structure is easily recognized from a distance because of the two octagonal towers that have become a Honolulu landmark. In the atrium, it is possible to forget that Kalakaua Avenue is just steps away and to enjoy the cool spray from the 3-story-high waterfall that cascades dramatically into a garden pool. All the guestrooms have spacious lanais with panoramic views, but the most luxurious of rooms are in the Regency Club, on floors 37 through 40, for which a special elevator key is required. A penthouse suite in each tower provides Regency Club guests with a lounge where breakfast is served each morning and cocktails are served in the evening. A concierge is on duty daily. Culinary talent is exhibited at *Bagwell's,* the hotel's prize-winning restaurant, and at the elegant *Musashi,* which offers a serene Oriental atmosphere and Japanese cuisine. Action of a noisier sort can be found in *Spats,* a disco that looks like an upper-crust speakeasy designed for preppy gangsters. The late-evening jazz at *Trapper's* lounge draws night owls of all ages. Hyatt Regency Hotel, 2424 Kalakaua Ave., Honolulu, HI 96815 (phone: 923-1234; 800-228-9000).

SHERATON MOANA SURFRIDER, Honolulu, Oahu: When the *Moana* was built in 1901, it stood all alone on Waikiki Beach, surrounded by taro fields, rice paddies, ponds, and swamps. In spite of predictions that it was too far from downtown to attract customers, it quickly became *the* place to stay, and was preferred by the blue-blood set even when the *Royal Hawaiian* was attracting millionaires and silent-movie stars. In the era of flappers and Bright Young Things, the Prince of Wales (later Duke of Windsor) and his cousin Lord Louis Mountbatten (later Earl Mountbatten of Burma) stayed at the *Moana.* In keeping with its historic past the *Moana* has been completely restored, at a cost of more than $50 million. The original Greek Revival portico has been reconstructed and the rooms redesigned with a combination of turn-of-the-century elegance and contemporary chic. The clutter that nearly obscured the great beachfront banyan has been removed, re-creating the atmosphere of by-gone days that once inspired Robert Louis Stevenson, who used to sit and write here even before the *Moana* was imagined. The new *Moana* has been joined with the neighboring *Surfrider* into a single hotel, and although the *Surfrider* wing offers rooms with spectacular views of Diamond Head, the historic charm and elegance of the original hotel provides its guests with a more unique experience. Information: Sheraton Moana Surfrider, 2365 Kalakaua Ave., Honolulu, HI 96815 (phone: 922-3111; 800-325-3535).

ROYAL HAWAIIAN, Honolulu, Oahu: It is from Waikiki Beach that the Pink Lady, as she is affectionately known, is seen best. Most of the surrounding buildings tower over her rudely, but the *Royal Hawaiian*'s Spanish-Moorish hacienda lines and gaudy pink color still catch the eye immediately. When it was opened in 1927, amid much pomp and circumstance, the Pink Lady was only the second hotel of any note along Waikiki, a kind of flashy Hollywood rival to the *Moana,* the prim, New England–style, seaside hotel just down the street. But the years when steamer trunks were carried to the *Royal Hawaiian* by Chinese coolies riding on the backs of trucks, when *kamaaina* servants stood around the dining rooms waiting on *haole* ladies wearing vast brimmed hats and flowery frocks, have gone. The restaurants have efficient staffs now, and jogging shorts, jeans, and tennis togs are the current fashions for guests. But some nostalgic touches still linger, such as the afternoon tea dances, at which elderly swains whirl handsome matrons around the floor, and the romantic pink decor, which is so pervasive that one feels an obligation to blush in order not to appear conspicuous. And visitors sitting on the porch at sunset, listening to the palms rustling in the breeze and the faint music wafting up from the bars along the beach, can't help but imagine that they belong — however fleetingly — to an earlier and much different time. Information: Royal Hawaiian Hotel, 2259 Kalakaua Ave., Honolulu, HI 96815 (phone: 923-7311; 800-325-3535).

HALEKULANI, Honolulu, Oahu: Considered by many (including us) to be Waikiki's finest, most luxurious hostelry. Once a bungalow-style hotel, this property has reopened as a 456-room luxury high-rise at a reconstruction cost of $125 million. Incorporating several of the hotel's original buildings, the Halekulani features 2 restaurants and beautifully landscaped grounds consisting of 5 acres of prime Waikiki beachfront. Facing the beach is the hotel's *House Without A Key* open-air lounge — a perfect place to sip cocktails at day's end, listen to Hawaiian music, and admire the fine views of Diamond Head. The oceanfront *La Mer* is one of Waikiki's finest restaurants, and service throughout the hotel provides a personal touch. Altogether, *Halekulani* seems to provide the essence of Polynesian romance. Information: The Halekulani, 2199 Kalia Rd., Honolulu, HI 96815 (phone: 923-2311; 800-367-2343).

SHERATON-MAKAHA RESORT, Makaha Valley, Oahu: The precipitous valley walls soaring up to jagged peaks suggest a fortress. Along these mysterious ramparts, mists linger in the early mornings, then later tumble in rivulets down the steep mountainsides, along which there is also a daily display of ever-changing light and shadow. In the middle of this diorama is the *Makaha Resort,* a complex of attractively furnished bungalows and low Polynesian-style buildings set amid green lawns, palm trees, and a striking jumble of bougainvillea, plumeria, and hibiscus. Sports are a major attraction here. There are jogging and hiking trails, tennis courts, and horses to ride up into the remoter parts of the valley, where peacocks screech and wild turkeys gobble. The main pastime, however, is golf: The challenging 7,200-yard West Course is one of the best in Hawaii. Watching the sunset beside the pool is a favorite evening entertainment, for the setting sun sinks slowly over the Pacific horizon and casts a haunting, roseate glow over Makaha Beach, a mile or so away at the foot of the valley. Afterward, there is dinner in the elegant *Kaala Room,* and the next day more limbs to be stretched and lungs to be expanded in this serene, rural retreat, 40 miles from the hustle and bustle of Waikiki. Information: Sheraton-Makaha Resort, PO Box 896, Makaha, HI 96792 (phone: 695-9511; 800-325-3535).

TURTLE BAY HILTON AND COUNTRY CLUB, the North Shore, Oahu: Five miles of beach, stables for horseback riding, tennis, golf, helicopter tours, snorkeling, and scuba add up to a self-contained, neighbor island–style resort an hour's drive from Waikiki. Hub of a much larger resort now in the planning stages, the *Hilton* features accommodations in a mid-rise tower and in lovely low-rise, seafront bungalows that are spacious and private. The location provides easy access to the famous North Shore surfing beaches (some of Hawaii's most beautiful), the Polynesian Cultural Center, and Waimea Falls Park. The only drawback is an occasional high wind that sends sand flying and makes the surf dangerous. The Towers Concept of concierge services, preferential reservations, and special amenities is available to guests staying in rooms on the west wing of the sixth floor. Information: Turtle Bay Hilton and Country Club, PO Box 187, Kahuku, HI 96831 (phone: 293-8811; 800-445-8667).

VOLCANO HOUSE, Hawaii Volcanoes National Park, the Big Island of Hawaii: *Volcano House* is a small mountain lodge (37 units) and adjacent bungalow with compact but comfortable rooms, an unpretentious restaurant serving satisfactory food, a bar where guests can listen to relaxing music in the evenings, and a flagstone sitting room–lobby, where a fire burns to lessen the summer humidity and remove the winter chill. But by far its main allure is its site above the Halemaumau Crater. Usually all there is to see are vapors rising from steam and sulfur vents. But sometimes there are the more dramatic pyrotechnic demonstrations of the goddess Pele, when she begins spouting molten lava into the sky from the nearby Kilauea firepit. When this happens, guests and sightseers by the hundreds watch the show from the restaurant, the bar, or, if you're on the crater side, your own room. In recent years, the hotel has gotten a bit worn, but it still retains its easy access to the marvelous view. Information: Volcano House, Hawaii Volcanoes National Park, HI 96718 (phone: 967-7321).

MAUNA LANI BAY, Kawaihae, the Big Island of Hawaii: Long before this 351-room, arrow-shaped property opened on Valentine's Day 1983, rumor had it that the hotel was targeted to become one of the most luxurious in Hawaii. The predictions, it turned out, were right on the mark. Guests are greeted with leis in a lobby complete with waterfalls, palm trees, garden, and pool. The guestrooms, with their ivory and burgundy color schemes, are no less striking, though a tad more sedate. Downstairs, there are 4 restaurants, including the elegant *Third Floor*, which serves mullet from the hotel's ancient fish ponds, which once belonged to Kamehameha I. Much of the *Mauna Lani*'s appeal lies in the way the architects preserved rather than transformed the landscape. Amateur archaeologists will enjoy exploring the 15th-century rock shelters that were left standing under orders from Ken Brown, the hotel's president and a direct descendant of Hawaiian royalty. Those of a less studious bend may opt for swimming at the pool or beach, outrigger canoe rides, helicopter tours, or, most often, golf. The 18-hole course is a natural wonder, with green fairways that snake through black lava fields broken by coastal inlets. Though the course isn't quite as formidable as it first appears, players often find themselves distracted by the occasional cavorting of migrating whales, jumping out of the ocean less than half a mile from the sixth tee. Information: Mauna Lani Bay Hotel, Box 4000, Kohala Coast, HI 96743 (phone: 885-6622; 800-367-2323).

HYATT REGENCY WAIKOLOA, Waikoloa, the Big Island of Hawaii: With 1,244 rooms and 62 oceanfront acres, this $365-million resort is Hawaii's newest, most extravagant, and the most costly to construct. Perfectly manicured grounds provide the background for a tapestry of manmade canals, waterfalls, and lagoons. Millions of dollars in artwork grace the hotel's 3 separate wings and the mile-long walkway that meanders through corridors and landscaped grounds. The majority of the guestrooms have ocean views. Facilities include tennis and raquetball courts, health spa, several swimming pools (the largest of which covers ¾ of an acre), and 7 restaurants. A third 18-hole golf course is scheduled for construction on adjacent property. Information: Hyatt Regency Waikoloa, Waikoloa, Kamuela, HI 96743 (phone: 885-1234; 800-228-9000).

MAUNA KEA BEACH, Kamuela, the Big Island of Hawaii: There is little doubt that the Hawaiian gods smiled on *Mauna Kea.* This monument to extraordinary luxury and good taste, built above the Big Island's most beautiful white sand beach, has been so pleasing to them that they have rewarded management and visitors with a quite unexpected attraction. For several hours each evening, drawn by a large searchlight placed for some now forgotten reason on a rocky outcrop not far from the hotel, huge manta rays, sometimes as many as six, come and play around a reef barely submerged close to the shore. Their mesmerizing performance includes graceful pirouettes and turns, underwater somersaults, and some generally fancy aquabatics that are as much a topic of conversation among the well-heeled clientele as the hundreds of Oriental and South Pacific antiques — relics of the original Rockefeller (Rockresorts) stewardship — that grace the cool and elegant lobbies and landings and line the corridor walls. Although the current Westin management lacks some of the flair of the nonpareil Rockresort folks, life at Mauna Kea is still almost as perfect as it can be. Rooms are prepared by not one but a team of maids, who make sure that even the darkest corners are scrupulously clean. They have brightly polished tile floors with handsome carpets, bleached wicker bedsteads and armchairs, bedspreads of the sunniest colors, and no television sets. Lanais are generous enough to accommodate a dining table for two, an armchair, and a chaise longue. Breakfasting out here, on eggs Benedict and Kona coffee, or sipping a cocktail as the sun sets, is enough to inspire genuine feelings of despair at the thought of leaving. If there is a beach in heaven, it probably looks like this one. Mostly it consists of gently sloping white sands with just enough reef to make snorkeling a joy. The spectacular golf course is one of Hawaii's most scenic, and keeping your head down around here requires an act of will that may not be worth the strain. Other sports facilities are similarly first rate. Information: Mauna Kea Beach Hotel, PO Box 218, Kamuela, HI 96743 (phone: 882-7222; 800-228-3000).

KONA VILLAGE RESORT, Kaupulehu, the Big Island of Hawaii: If you've ever dreamed of living in a Polynesian grass shack, this is the place. *Kona Village Resort* is marvelously situated in a 62-acre enclave surrounded by thousands of acres of semibarren lava fields. The beach, however, is fringed with palm trees and tropical vegetation and interspersed with 125 rustic *hales* (houses) in Hawaiian, Tahitian, Samoan, Fijian, and Tongan designs. Guests staying a week or more can select accommodations in the island style of their choice, otherwise you accept what's available. Rustic they may be without, but within they are as swanky as they can be short of being plush, with grass mats, louvered doors, wicker furniture, crisp, colorful coverings on the beds, plants, and paintings. There are no in-room telephones or television sets, or newspapers. If you are hyperactive, there are tennis courts, sailboats, volleyball, shuffleboard, outrigger canoes, and a helipad for tours. For the more sedate, there are lessons in lei-making and flower-arranging, and for those blessed with true slothfulness, hammocks are slung between palm trees on the beach. The food here (it's all included in the American plan price) is good, if a connoisseur's standard. There are 12 rotating dinner menus, featuring beef Wellington, roast pork au whiskey, *escalope de veau* with mountain mushrooms, and roast rack of venison with pear and currant jelly. Weekly specials include a *paniolo* steak panfry and a Friday night luau. A favorite conversation corner at the resort is the *Shipwreck Bar,* which is named with wry precision. It was constructed from the remains of a 42-foot sloop that sank in a storm before the resort was developed. Information: Kona Village Resort, PO Box 1299, Kaupulehu-Kona, HI 96745 (phone: 325-5555; 800-367-5290).

HANA-MAUI, Hana, Maui: Most hotels have brochures, and this one does, too. But it also has a newsletter, *Mana O Hana (The Spirit of Hana),* which goes out regularly to former guests, announcing such things as the birth of a foal in the stable, the birth of a baby to a staff member, the addition of new drapes to the White Garden rooms, or of new carp to the fishpond. Dull reading, perhaps, but to the *Hana-Maui*'s loyal clientele it has the same significance as a subscription to the hometown newspaper long after you've moved away. The hotel is on the eastern coast of East Maui in the isolated ranching village of Hana, a settlement with a worldwide reputation for peace, quiet, and the simple spirit of old-time Hawaii. The *Hana-Maui* embraces this ideal and elaborates on it with a definitively understated interpretation of luxury. The hotel has just completed an extensive upgrading and facelift under the aegis of Rosewood hotels. This is the same group that has turned the *Remington* (Houston), the *Mansion at Turtle Creek* (Dallas), and the *Bel-Air* (Beverly Hills), among others, into the leading bastions of transient luxury in this country. This level of luxury does not come inexpensively, though tariffs include breakfast, lunch, and dinner, since there really is only one other place to eat in Hana. Public areas are handsome, particularly the large dining room, lobby, and poolside lounge, and the lawns are rife with the sort of vegetative prodigality for which Hana is famous. The *Hana-Maui* is *the* place for horse lovers; it has its own stables and offers an assortment of breakfast rides, cookout rides, sunrise rides, and moonlight rides, as well as English and Western riding lessons. A heated outdoor pool is on the grounds and there are private facilities at Hamoa Beach, 3 miles away and the prettiest beach in the district — albeit with seasonally rough surf. The rebuilt 1929 Packard that takes guests there is another *Hana-Maui* touch, as is the umbrella — a tip of the hat to Hana's showery weather. This is not the place for folks who crave action and excitement; it is Eden for the self-sufficient who truly wish to get away from it all. Information: Hotel Hana-Maui, Hana, HI 96713 (phone: 248-8211; 800-321-4262).

HYATT REGENCY MAUI, Kaanapali Resort, Maui: From afar, this seems like just another clump of ultramodern high-rises sprung full blown from the architect's drawing board and deposited randomly on the sand of the *Kaanapali* resort. More informed word of mouth sends most visitors to West Maui snooping, however, and closer inspection reveals where the $80 million it cost to build it went. The grounds, for instance, are as lavishly landscaped and waterscaped as a theme park whose purpose is to recreate a world of tropical exuberance, tempered only by fairy-tale touches and some slight Oriental restraint. A mile-long network of streams and waterfalls splish-splashes through a formal Japanese garden, laps at the edges of a lagoon, dribbles and drops over natural boulders and mock lava, slickens a 130-foot water slide, and fills up the largest swimming pool on Maui, a free-form fantasy divided in two by a mound of rock over which the water cascades onto swimmers below in a final display of aquatic artistry. The hotel's central Atrium Tower, open to the sky, is one of 3 towers containing the 815 guestrooms, but before guests even see their quarters, their eyes will have scanned a multi-million-dollar collection of Asian and Pacific art distributed throughout the lobbies and promenades with seeming disregard for security. A few steps over handwoven Chinese carpets, the way lit by German chandeliers of shell-shaped glass, a trip in a teak elevator furnished with settees, and guests arrive at last in rooms finished in soft shades of peach, beige, and mauve, and the ashtray-snatchers among them may fall asleep to grandiose dreams of smuggling home a giant buddha or one of the pair of 7-foot cloisonné vases displayed downstairs. The *Hyatt* has a slick *Swan Court* restaurant with a front-row-center view of swans gliding on the lagoon, a gleaming (but more casual) restaurant called the *Lahaina Provision Company,* the most popular disco on the island (*Spats II*), and its showiest Polynesian revue ("Drums of the Pacific"), plus several other spots to wine, dine, or be entertained. Throw in the beachfront location, the 55-foot catamaran for snorkel sails and cocktail cruises, the Regency

Health Club with exercise room and sauna, tennis courts, volleyball in the swimming pool, proximity to the *Kaanapali Beach Resort*'s 2 golf courses, all the hula lessons and lei-making demonstrations typical of a Hawaiian hotel, an arcade of shops, extensive convention facilities, and you'll have a picture of a hotel that occasionally lapses into giddiness but is never stodgy. Tops among the Kaanapali hotels, and the perfect place for those who like lots of glitz in their getaway. Information: Hyatt Regency Maui, 200 Nohea Kai Dr., Lahaina, HI 96761 (phone: 661-1234; 800-228-9000).

WESTIN MAUI, Kaanapali Resort, Maui: More than $165 million was spent to create the 762-room *Westin Maui* from the old *Maui Surf,* one of Kaanapali's first hotels. After redesign and more than a year of reconstruction, a hotel in the style of the neighboring *Hyatt Regency* has emerged. Maui's newest resort is a showpiece, with millions of dollars in art and magnificently landscaped grounds surrounding an exceptional 5-level pool, with grottoes, waterslides, and waterfalls connecting its five levels, each of which has plenty of space for lounging. Although somewhat on the small side, the rooms make up for their lack of spaciousness with very stylish decor. Three restaurants, a grotto bar, 700 feet of prime beachfront, and a fully equipped spa are other facilities offered in conjunction with Kaanapali's golf, tennis, and water activities. Information: Westin Maui, 2365 Kaanapali Pkwy., Lahaina, HI 96761 (phone: 667-2525; 800-228-3000).

KAPALUA BAY, Kapalua, Maui: The 750-acre *Kapalua* resort, on the northwestern corner of West Maui, is as magnificent a plot of land as exists anywhere in Hawaii. Pineapple fields bordered by rows of neat Cook pines stretch behind the development, velvety fairways and clipped lawns roll through it to the edge of the water, and across the Pailolo Channel, the island of Molokai looms like a large mirage. The *Kapalua Bay,* the focal point of the resort, is not the same sort of overpowering (often gaudy) showplace as the *Hyatt Regency,* several miles down the coast, but it was probably the glorious setting that suggested restraint to its creators. It is quieter in its approach to· luxury, it doesn't strive for flashy effects, but it is eye-catching nonetheless. The hotel has fewer than 200 rooms, all alike in size and rust or blue decor, in two main wings, one of which reaches out from the lobby toward the beach at Kapalua Bay, a picturesque, palm-lined crescent. Other beaches surround the *Kapalua* property, so there is no shortage of opportunities for water sports such as scuba diving, snorkeling, or surfing, and the resort also has a 10-court Tennis Garden, as well as two of the most distractingly scenic island golf courses in existence, with a third set to open late in 1990. In addition, the hotel has two of Maui's most respected restaurants: the *Bay Club,* at the far end of Kapalua Beach and the *Plantation Veranda,* the site of a spectacular Sunday luncheon buffet — its groaning tables are an invitation to excess eagerly accepted by visitors from all over the island. And for some of the most tempting merchandise on the island, *Kapalua* guests have to go no farther than the *Kapalua Shops,* the resort's fine, small shopping center, which adjoins the hotel. Information: Kapalua Bay Hotel, One Bay Dr., Kapalua, HI 96761 (phone: 669-5656; 800-367-8000).

KAPALUA VILLAS, Kapalua, Maui: Nearly half the accommodations available on Maui are condominiums. Most often these units are a solid, multi-story block of apartments or a low line of attached apartments shaped in a U or V, facing the sea. The *Kapalua Villas* fit neither description, but cluster in various spots around the *Kapalua* resort property — the *Bay Villas* close to the water, the *Ridge Villas* above and behind them, and the *Golf Villas* still farther up behind one of 2 golf courses — and the overall effect is that of an exclusive residential community in a supremely fortunate setting. For anywhere from several hundred thousand dollars to more than $1 million, it's possible to buy a 1- or 2-bedroom loft unit with a fully equipped tiled kitchen, an enormous bathroom fit for a sybarite, a living room with fresh wicker and rattan furniture, and a wraparound lanai facing the islands of Lanai and Molokai. For a sum more within the grasp of a mortal traveler, these exact same opulent apartments can be rented for a day, a week, or longer. The various condominium clusters have their own recreation facilities — pools, tennis courts, Jacuzzis, barbecue pits — in addition to their proximity to the resort's Tennis Garden, the 2 courses of the Kapalua Golf Club, and 3 beaches. Villa residents may also take part in the activities offered by the *Kapalua Bay*. Villa residents do not, however, enjoy the full range of hotel services: There's no room service, so those anxious to sip champagne while sitting in the sunken marble bathtub will have to go out and get it. Information: Kapalua Villas, 500 Bay Dr., Kapalua, HI 96761 (phone: 669-5656; 800-367-8000).

MAUI INTER-CONTINENTAL WAILEA, Wailea, Maui: Not too long ago, the Wailea coast of East Maui was a dry scrub forest of kiawe trees with a scalloped edge of wonderful beaches. Then developers turned on the sprinklers, made the land green, and began to build. The *Wailea* resort that emerged has the advantage of being within striking distance of all Maui's major tourist attractions, while remaining somewhat apart from the bustle — although that may change somewhat when three new luxury hotels, now under construction, finally open. Now Wailea has a selection of first-rate hotels to recommend it further. The *Inter-Continental* has an open-air lobby furnished with wicker and rattan sofas and easy chairs in handsome groups among the stuccoed pillars. The initial impression of clean white surfaces and simple lines continues through the rest of the hotel. Its stylish rooms are in a tower and a series of low structures scattered across the grounds that seem much more extensive than they could possibly be. A detailed map of the property is provided at check-in to help guests find their way around the sprawling landscape. Also provided is a *Flowers and Plants* guide, which is very useful while touring the grounds. The 14 tennis courts, 2 championship golf courses, and shopping village are just a short sprint away, and the nearest of the resort's 5 fine beaches is only a short walk to the north or south edge of the property. The *Ocean Activities Center* takes care of guests' snorkeling, scuba diving, deep-sea fishing, surfing, and sailing needs, while the hotel provides the volleyball net, the shape-up and yoga exercises, the hula lessons, and the weekly luau. The *Inter-Continental* has a variety of places to eat, ranging in casualness from the *Sun Spot*, a health food snack bar next to one of the 3 swimming pools, through the poolside *Kiawe Broiler* and the *Lanai Terrace* dining room, to the intimate, elegant *La Perouse*, one of the island's best restaurants. On Sundays, the Makani Room serves up an excellent champagne brunch. And to round out an active day, there is the *Inu Inu Lounge*, a cocktail lounge with a dance floor that features the area's only sushi bar. Information: Maui Inter-Continental Wailea, PO Box 779, Wailea, HI 96753 (phone: 879-1922; 800-367-2960).

STOUFFER WAILEA BEACH RESORT, Wailea, Maui: The *Inter-Continental*'s neighbor to the north in the *Wailea* resort is also a place where the most active sports enthusiast will find enough to do to fill up an exhausting day (it, too, provides a jogging map). The 350-room *Wailea Beach* works hard at cultivating an air of refinement to go with the sportsmanly posture, with the result that it is a bit more formal and more elegant. Its 350 rooms are in 3 wings of 7 stories projecting from a central lobby; the entrance is flanked by reflecting pools and two concrete walls with sculptures that depict events in the life of the demigod Maui. This is only the first of the hotel's contemporary, island-inspired works of art, however. Inside, the lobby is dominated by a huge yarn and sisal wall hanging of bold reds, yellows, and oranges running into blues and greens — a volcanic eruption sending lava to the sea. Other fabric murals grace the public areas, which are furnished with rattan and spread with generous expanses of striking, custom-made carpet. Similarly, the walls of the *Palm Court*, one of the hotel's 3 restaurants, are hung with giant quilts of tropical birds and flowers, and smaller quilted banners — parrots, anthuriums, heliconia — hang from the ceiling. Out back, a waterfall drops from the lobby level and splits into streams that flow under bridges and form more cascades on the sloping, landscaped, and flower-filled grounds. A wing of low suites operated as the deluxe Mokapu Club, a swimming pool, and an arbor-shaded poolside café (the *Maui Onion*), plus a statue of Maui in the act of fishing the Hawaiian islands from the sea, are all that come between the bulk of the hotel and Mokapu Beach, a lovely pocket of sand that is the smallest of the five *Wailea* beaches. The *Ocean Activities Center* here is charged with supplying guests with the equipment and instruction necessary for a variety of water sports (including windsurfing at this location), and the resort's tennis courts and golf courses are just across the road. Demonstrations of Hawaiian arts and crafts take place regularly; there is wake-up and shape-up music in the exercise room on weekdays, in addition to many other scheduled activities. The *Wailea Beach,* finally, can boast the *Lost Horizon* nightspot and the first class *Raffles',* one of Maui's best restaurants. Information: Stouffer Wailea Beach Resort, Wailea, HI 96753 (phone: 879-4900; 800-9-WAILEA).

MAKENA SURF, Wailea, Maui: These spacious, nicely furnished, 2-bedroom condominium apartments offer oceanfront privacy, adjacent beaches, beautifully landscaped grounds alive with birds of paradise and hibiscus, and amenities that include a large pool and tennis courts. Nearby are the golf courses of the Wailea and Makena resorts. Daily maid service, 24-hour front desk. Information: Makena Surf, 96 Makena Alanui Rd., Makena, HI 96753 (phone: 879-1331; 800-367-8047, ext. 510).

MAUI PRINCE, Makena Resort, Maui: This 300-room hotel is often overlooked by Maui-bound visitors, but behind the low profile are tastefully decorated rooms, a beachfront setting, and adjacent golf and tennis facilities that are among Maui's best. The pervading away-from-the-crowd feeling is a prime asset at a time when even resorts in "low-density" destinations are becoming a bit overdeveloped. Information: Maui Prince, 5400 Makena Alanui Rd., Kihei, HI 86753 (phone: 874-1111; 800-321-6284).

WAILEA CONDOMINIUMS, Wailea, Maui: Condominiums are as integral a part of the *Wailea* resort as they are of the *Kapalua* resort. Here there are three low-rise condominium villages. *Wailea Elua,* right on Ulua Beach between the resort's two hotels, is the most exclusive, but the others, *Wailea Ekolu* and *Wailea Ekahi,* are hardly less luxurious. *Wailea Ekolu,* for instance, on a sloping site above a plush golf course, consists of 1- and 2-bedroom apartments and 2-bedroom, 2½-bath townhouses in redwood-faced buildings set along driveways lined with orchid trees and oleanders. The upstairs units have grand vaulted ceilings, and all the units have wonderful views down to the sea and out to the islands of Kahoolawe, Molokini, and Lanai. Closer to the shoreline, the sand-colored stucco buildings of *Wailea Ekahi* lie amid a variety of palm trees on ground that tilts gently toward Keawakapu Beach. Its units, which include some economical studios, have tiled kitchens behind swinging doors, high, high, second-story ceilings, and ocean and garden views from lanais lavish with bougainvillea. Whereas *Wailea Ekolu* has two swimming pools, *Wailea Ekahi* has three, plus a beautifully tiled beach pavilion with a full kitchen for those who don't want to budge from the beachfront to fix lunch. *Wailea Elua* has its own beach pavilion and pool. Residents of all of the villages make heavy use of the 14-court Wailea Tennis Club, both of the resort's golf courses, and all five of *Wailea*'s first-rate beaches. Information: Wailea Condominiums, Wailea Villas, 3750 Wailea Alanui Blvd., Kihei, HI 96753 (phone: 879-1595; 800-367-5246).

LANAI, Lanai City, Lanai: At this upland country inn nestled amid a forest of tall pines, the climate is often bracing and cool, so folks with bare feet and swimsuits are seldom spotted. Yet this is undeniably Hawaii, with thousands of acres of pineapple fields stretched out below and lovely Hulopoe Beach 7 miles away. The *Lanai,* built by the Dole Pineapple Company in 1923 for its employees and official visitors, became a public hotel in the early 1940s. It has but 10 rooms for rent, all with private bath and some with private entry, and these are basic and clean. Guests seldom come to this inn for its physical facilities, but rather for its unique atmosphere. A comfortable dining room serves generous homemade meals, highlighted by salads, fresh fish, and daily specialties, and the lanai bar is relaxing — as well as the only such establishment on the entire island. Beach towels are provided for trips to Hulopoe Beach, and arrangements can be made to pick guests up at the airport. Information: Lanai Hotel, PO Box A-119, Lanai City, HI 96763 (phone: 565-6605; 800-367-8047).

KIAHUNA PLANTATION, Poipu Beach, Kauai: One of Hawaii's most complete condominium resorts, on Kauai's fashionable, sunny South Shore. Distinctive by any standard, its handsome 1- and 2-bedroom apartments, excellent tennis and golf facilities, superb beachfront, and first-rate restaurant are reasons enough for the loyal clientele it has won in the years since it opened. But what really sets *Kiahuna* apart from similarly well-appointed condominiums are the grounds, 50 acres of natural splendor, where flowering shrubs screen terraces, line walks, and cascade down slopes in a profusion of tropical reds and purples and sunstruck yellows. The gardens are a little less showy these days, since they're still recovering from damage inflicted by a hurricane a few years back, but they still provide an unparalleled setting.

Among this luxuriant growth are low white buildings with steep roofs hanging over the balconies. High ceilings and long louvered windows keep the apartments comfortably cool without air conditioning, so guests can smell the heady fragrance of the gardens inside, too. The apartments are big (a 1-bedroom can easily accommodate four people) and have fully equipped kitchens, including dishwashers. They're smartly decorated, too, in pastel prints and rattan furniture that nicely complement the redwood-trimmed white walls.

Besides the beauty and comfort of the place — *Kiahuna* has daily maid service and other hotel amenities — beach sports (including surfing lessons from champion Margo Oberg) and tennis are the main draws. *Kiahuna* has a very attractive tennis complex: 10 courts, a good pro shop, and a courtside café. Best of all, guests play for free. The new golf course across the road will add golf enthusiasts to *Kiahuna*'s long list of regulars. Information: Kiahuna Plantation, 2253 Poipu Rd., Koloa, HI 96756 (phone: 742-6411; 800-367-7052).

WESTIN KAUAI, Nawiliwili, Kauai: "Extravagant" is the only word to describe this remake of the modest *Kauai Surf,* now a showplace that combines grand scale, millions of dollars in artwork, a made-to-order beachfront setting, and facilities that rival those of any resort anywhere. Whether all this is necessary in a place as naturally beautiful as Kauai is the question. Those seeking a quiet retreat had best head elsewhere, as just a glimpse of the 800 lounge chairs surrounding the oversize pool will quickly tell them. On-site facilities include 36 holes of Jack Nicklaus-designed golf (Nicklaus is also the resort's director of golf), fully equipped men's and women's spas, restaurants, shops and lounges galore, and hundreds of landscaped acres that sport lagoons, gardens, and seemingly endless lawns. The lagoons are traversed by canolas (outrigger canoe/gondola hybrids), and the grounds, by miles of carriage trails served by a fleet of elegant horsedrawn carriages. Last, but by no means least, guests can also enjoy a full range of watersports activities. Information: Westin Kauai, Kalapaki Beach, Lihue, HI 96766 (phone: 245-5050; 800-228-3000).

STOUFFER WAIOHAI, Poipu Beach, Kauai: From the stone-paved porte-cochère, where guests' cars are whisked away to the parking lot by ever-present bellhops, to the stack of thick towels in the sybaritic bathrooms, it's clear the *Waiohai* knows a thing or two about pampering.

Don't look for island quaintness here, though. The *Waiohai* is sleek and unabashedly modern in design and decor. Italian travertine stone, brass, and polished teak mix pleasingly to give the open-air public areas an unfussy but rich look, while the guest-rooms, which have spacious sitting areas discreetly set off from the beds by slim bamboo panels, are done in cool, contemporary pastels. Each room is also equipped with a small wet bar and a well-stocked, no-host refrigerator.

The *Waiohai* has also made an impressive show in the culinary field. *The Tamarind,* a restaurant strikingly decorated in salmon banquettes, a brass ceiling, and Thai silks, features various continental and Asian dishes, including a sublime Thai curry.

Like all resort hotels, the *Waiohai* offers a host of activities. There are 3 swimming pools (one with a bar built into it and one on a terrace over the hotel's lovely beach), poolside Jacuzzis, tennis courts, a full health club, and snorkeling and scuba lessons. For those who prefer diversions of a less rigorous nature, hotel hostesses give lessons in Hawaiian crafts and conduct botanical tours of the 2 courtyard gardens. For all the activity and despite its size — there are 434 rooms and 21 sumptuous suites — the *Waiohai*'s chief pleasure is its atmosphere of unruffled calm, and there's no shortage of friendly staff to help guests enjoy it. Information: The Waiohai, 2249 Poipu Rd., Koloa, HI 96756 (phone: 426-4122; 800-468-3571).

PRINCEVILLE RESORT, Princeville, Kauai: There are several attractive places to stay at the golfer's paradise known as Princeville, the resort on the 11,000-acre ranch overlooking Kauai's Hanalei Bay. Three condominiums are worthy of note, as is the newly opened *Sheraton Princeville.*

The *Makai Club Cottages, Pali Ke Kua,* and *Puu Poa* are each very special condominium complexes, each distinguished by spaciousness, appealing decor, and excellent location. *Puu Poa,* the smaller of the two, is the best priced, thanks to a sense of privacy, quality (the bathrooms are truly luxurious), oversized lanais, and clifftop views of the ocean. Ocean and mountain views can be had at *Pali Ke Kua,* though the apartments are a bit older and less airy, and a walkway connects *Pali Ke Kua* to a small private beach frequented by surfers who approach it from a precipitous cliffside trail. Spaciousness is the greatest luxury at the *Makai Club* cottages, which provide a pleasant garden setting facing the golf course. The best views at Princeville are undoubtedly those offered at the newly opened *Sheraton Mirage Princeville.* Recently upgraded and newly chic, the real asset are rooms that face Hanalei Bay from a clifftop perspective that is perhaps Hawaii's most dramatically beautiful. *Noble's* offers some of Kauai's finest food. Aside from golf, Princeville guests enjoy tennis, a wide range of water sports, and a chance to explore the magnificent coast from Princeville to the end of the road at Kee Beach. Information: Pali Ke Kua and Puu Poa, Hawaiian Island Resorts, PO Box 212, Honolulu, HI 96810 (phone: 826-9066; 800-367-7042); Sheraton Mirage Princeville, Princeville, HI 96722 (phone: 826-9644; 800-325-3535).

Delightful Island Dining

Although the islands are better known for volcanoes and black sand beaches, today's Hawaii offers a wide variety of first class restaurants and a broad spectrum of ethnic cuisines.. Reflecting its history, Hawaii's culinary repertoire embraces traditional Polynesian, American, and continental dishes, as well as those from other nations around the world, including China, Japan, Korea, the Philippines, Thailand, and Vietnam. Thus menus will often feature a variety of dishes, including lomilomi salmon, sashimi, Portuguese bean soup, egg rolls, veal Oscar, teriyaki steak, *coquilles St.-Jacques,* Korean kal bi ribs, macadamia nut ice cream, and lots of fresh fruit. The following selection of restaurants represents the very best of island eateries.

BAGWELL'S, Honolulu, Oahu: Sculpture, etched glass, and soothing pastels have been stylishly combined to create a tropical environment of unusual harmony. The main room is large, with semi-circular, high-backed banquettes and raised dining platforms that offer the kind of privacy that diners don't often get to enjoy these days.

Like the wonderful decor, the menu features dishes that harmonize traditional as well as island elements, with entrées such as whole breast of roast duck with puréed bananas and broiled lamb chops in a sauce of red bell peppers with caramelized garlic cloves. To make decisions easier, guests can preview sample portions of just about everything on the menu as well as taste by the glass in the adjacent Wine Bar. As expected of an establishment of this caliber, service is conscientious yet unobtrusive. Information: Bagwell's Restaurant, Hyatt Regency, 2424 Kalakaua Ave., Honolulu, HI 96815 (phone: 922-9292).

JOHN DOMINIS, Honolulu, Oahu: Every town has one restaurant that attracts local power brokers and politicos, and this is Honolulu's. Approaching this restaurant can make a first-timer want to turn back: It is surrounded by small factories and warehouses on a street of zero charm. But once inside, there's the pleasure of dining on a promontory overlooking the Kewalo Boat Basin, with a view clear down to Diamond Head, and the restaurant's tiered structure gives nearly everyone at least a glimpse of the ocean. And even if you don't have one, you are probably sitting next to a saltwater pool brimming with tropical fish and Hawaiian spiny lobsters that eventually end up on one of the restaurant's stout tables. Another eye-catching feature of the dining room is a central island packed with ice, where much of the day's seafood catch lies arranged for inspection in a vast, scaly brocade of silver, blue, and pink. At the same counter, a chef shucks oysters and steams clams in baskets.

The cooking is first rate. While there are steaks, Chinese dishes, and the odd Italian specialty on the menu, to come here and not eat seafood is a sacrilege. Island specialties such as *opelu* (mackerel), *hapuu* (grouper), and *ono* (wahoo) are all available in season. When decision making becomes too difficult, diners often compromise with a cioppino (stew) of soft-shell crabs, seafood, and fresh island fish cooked in tomatoes, herbs, and spices. The bar is another bonus, one of the few in Honolulu restaurants where the drinks are good and the atmosphere inviting enough to make a cocktail or after-dinner drink a pleasure. Information: John Dominis Restaurant, 43 Ahui St., Honolulu, HI 96813 (phone: 523-0955).

MAILE, Honolulu, Oahu: The *Kahala Hilton International* occupies one of the most beautiful settings on Oahu. What does this do for its *Maile* restaurant? Not much, for the dining room is under the hotel's lobby. To compensate for the lack of view, however, the *Maile* has a sumptuous decor of pools, heliconia, anthuriums, orchids, and a variety of tropical plants. The maile is a leaf often made into leis and always worn by a Hawaiian bridegroom on his wedding day. Here the maile motif is seen on the gold-rimmed china, a patrician touch that is further underlined by tablecloths of Belgian lace. Among the items on the menu are some native specialties that receive opulent treatment: *mahimahi* glazed with bananas served on creamed mushrooms; filet of *opakapaka* (pink snapper) with *beurre blanc* sauce; and luscious dessert soufflés. Petits fours and chocolate are served with coffee, and unobtrusive background music is provided by a classical guitarist or pianist. Meals are deftly served by ladies in kimonos who seem to sum up all that is traditionally feminine and graceful about the East. There is a touch of enchantment about dining in the *Maile* restaurant. Information: The Maile Restaurant, Kahala Hilton, 5000 Kahala Ave., Kahala, HI 96816 (phone: 734-2211).

MICHEL'S, Honolulu, Oahu: Scattered across the south of France are scores of medium-sized restaurants that scornfully eschew the "folksy-rustic" look in favor of an ambience that suggests upper-middle class prosperity. The cooking in these places is usually impeccable. So it is with *Michel's*. There is no hint of rattan or bamboo here, even though the restaurant is right on a palm-fringed beach. Diners sit under crystal chandeliers on banquettes or chairs upholstered in Belgian velvet with Regency stripes, at tables elegantly set with fine china, brilliantly polished glass, and crisp, snow-white napery. Ordering Pernod before dinner seems almost de rigueur. The senior waiters at *Michel's* are French, gray-haired, quiet, and skillful; service is civilized, without fuss or pressure, and whatever tempers may be flaring in the kitchen, the dining room is cautiously relaxed. Most of the dishes on the menu are classics, such as lobster bisque with brandy and roast rack of veal. When local produce is used, it is treated in a classic fashion. Fresh *opakapaka,* for instance, is poached in champagne and served with hollandaise sauce and grapes to become *Opakapaka poche au champagne Véronique* — triumphantly. Everything considered, *Michel's* ranks as the most elegant restaurant in Hawaii. Information: Michel's, 2895 Kalakaua Ave., Honolulu, HI 96815 (phone: 923-6552).

THE WILLOWS, Honolulu, Oahu: Ah, *The Willows!* Outdoors, indoors, in a grass shack–like longhouse, under thatched umbrella roofs, by a carp pond, or surrounded by palms and hibiscus, wherever you sit you experience the graceful flavor of a bygone era — not the one that existed before the missionaries arrived, but something akin to that found by the early passengers on the Pacific liners that used to call at Honolulu en route from San Francisco to the Far East. While dining, listen to old Hawaiian songs performed without the dubious benefits of electronic enhancement, accompanied only by the bass and the ukulele and the intense hush of a tropical night. It represents the distillation of island music, and you'll feel you've never heard the familiar songs before.

To really appreciate *The Willows,* it is probably necessary to eat here more than once. A specialty of the house is the Poi Supper, which includes most of the ingredients of a real luau on a smaller scale, such as laulau, a mixture of fish and pork wrapped in ti leaves and steamed; chicken luau, simmered with ti leaves and coconut milk; lomilomi salmon, chopped salt salmon mixed with onions and tomatoes; sweet potatoes; and poi itself, the bland, smooth paste made from the taro root that is a Hawaiian staple. Desserts are a specialty, so indulge yourself with the coconut soufflé or chocolate gâteau. Information: The Willows, 901 Hausten St., Honolulu, HI 96826 (phone: 946-4808).

FUJI, Hilo, the Big Island of Hawaii: Unfancy and largely unsung, it is housed in a hotel that has seen better days, in a not very glamorous town. Diners not seated facing the undistinguished prints on the walls or the few plants that straggle out of pots suspended from the ceiling may have to gaze at the quite ordinary swimming pool area. What, then, does the *Fuji* have? Atmosphere, that's what, the kind that no amount of trendy design or other artifice can produce, the kind that just happens. Tourists are irrelevant here. They are welcome, but the *Fuji* exists mostly for islanders. There are *kamaaina* ladies enjoying a weekday lunch together and Japanese families celebrating a birthday or anniversary. Residents with business in the area — the sort who always have favorite obscure eating places — are seen here. Eating utensils are arranged on the tables in a rigid pattern that seems to belie the restaurant's general run-down look. The food is served with the same attention to aesthetic detail, each platter looking like a delicate arrangement of flower petals. It is also excellently prepared. The sashimi seems to melt on contact with the palate, and the tempura dishes boast a batter that is ephemerally thin. This, and the Graham Greene ambience, brings people back again and again. Information: Restaurant Fuji, 142 Kinoole St., Hilo, HI 96720 (phone: 961-3733).

ROUSSELS, Hilo, the Big Island of Hawaii: Even more surprising than the Cajun style of the cooking is the high quality of the food, which — from breads and appetizers to entrées and desserts — is unfailingly first rate. The brothers who own *Roussels* are Louisiana born and bred, bringing recipes from home like oysters Bienville (baked in a creamy shrimp and mushroom sauce), seafood gumbo, shrimp Créole (in a rich, piquant tomato sauce), chicken Pontalba (boned, sautéed, and served with bernaise sauce), soft shell crab, and a mouthwatering selection of duck and vegetarian dishes. From light lunches to full dinners, this is not only one of Hawaii's finest restaurants, but it is also reasonably priced. A real find. Information: Roussels, 60 Keawe St., Hilo, HI 96720 (phone: 935-5111).

DONATELLO's, Hyatt Regency Waikoloa, the Big Island: One of Hawaii's best

Italian restaurants, it does justice to an extensive menu that ranges from appetizers such as tender *calamari fritti* to pasta such as the *linguine al pescatore,* with its perfect combination of mussels, scallops, and clams; from entrées like *osso buco alla milanese* (veal shanks with vegetables, white wine, and tomatoes) to exotic, delicious pizza. Service is impeccable, the decor elegantly Mediterranean. Reservations necessary. In the Hyatt Regency Waikoloa, Kohala Coast, HI 96743 (phone: 885-1234).

IMARI, Hyatt Regency Waikoloa, Kohala Coast, the Big Island: Everything Japanese, from the cuisine to the decor. Selections range from shabu shabu chicken to sukiyaki beef, from teppanyaki to *kaiseki* dinners. Shoji screens open to take in the setting: free-running streams and meticulous gardens. Reservations necessary. In the Hyatt Regency Waikoloa, Kohala Coast, HI 96743 (phone: 885-1234).

EDELWEISS, Waimea, the Big Island of Hawaii: The perfect place to make a midday or end-of-day stop when passing through upcountry Waimea. It's even worth the drive from the Kohala Coast resorts for flavorful German and continental specialties with a tasteful focus on veal. Try the Edelweiss Papaya — an imaginative dish consisting of scallops and stroganoff sauce, baked in a half-papaya. Closed Mondays and September. Information: Edelweiss, Route 19, Waimea, HI 96743 (phone: 885-6800).

BAY CLUB AND PLANTATION VERANDA, Kapalua, Maui: More than one visit is necessary to sample the products of the famed kitchens of the *Kapalua Bay,* the centerpiece of West Maui's *Kapalua* resort. More than one visit could be devoted just to the *Bay Club,* which, though part of the hotel, is at the other end of the crescent-shaped beach on a point of lava rock jutting out into the water. This is an open-air restaurant decorated with rattan furniture and the handsomest of batik prints, completed at lunch by a color scheme of nature's own sea and sky blue; of the hotel's three eating spots, this is the one with the view. At the *Bay Club,* lunch can be as exotic as a papaya boat stuffed with shrimp and crabmeat in a sauce of Rémy Martin, or as simple as a good wiener. Dinner, however, is soft lights and sophistication all the way, with three rotating fixed-price menus — featuring châteaubriand, lamb, and veal chops — and a varied selection of continental and nouvelle cuisine entrées available à la carte.

Equally distinguished (but more intimate) is the *Plantation Veranda,* a charmingly enclosed restaurant facing a courtyard in the hotel itself, open for dinner only. Here the decor — hooked rugs in peach, gray, and blue, blond wood chairs, peach tablecloths, and pewter serving plates — recalls the interior of an old plantation house, except that its white walls are covered by large, lovely murals of Hawaiian women by the contemporary artist Pegge Hopper. At the *Veranda,* diners can begin with a selection of homemade pâtés, then choose filet mignon, a South Seas version of bouillabaisse, or medallions of veal in white wine and cream, with a simple salad (one of the most popular on the menu) of Maui onions, tomatoes, and Stilton cheese on the side. The restaurant specializes in California wines, the desserts are delicious, and as they leave, women diners are presented with a sprig of orchids or some other flower. Information: Kapalua Bay Hotel, One Bay Dr., Kapalua, HI 96761 (phone: 669-5656).

HAKONE, Maui Prince Hotel, Kihei, Maui: The decor is a bit spartan and cold, but the food is beautifully presented and delicious. The menu starts with delicately flavored specialties like *chawan mushi* (steamed egg custard with chicken, shrimp, shiitake mushrooms, and ginko nuts), egg flower soup (Japanese broth with egg beaten in), and elegant sushi, then continues with sukiyaki, teriyaki, and *kaiseki* dinners. There's a sushi bar as well as table seating. Maui Prince Hotel, 5400 Makena Alanui, Kihei, Maui 96753 (phone: 874-1111).

LA PEROUSE, Wailea, Maui: There's many a restaurant on Maui where guests in their best bib and tucker are greeted by a waiter in a safari jacket. Here, at the *Inter-Continental*'s fine dining room, your waiter wears black tie and perhaps studies prestidigitation on the side. Classical piano music wafts across a space muffled in carpets, layers of tablecloth, and padded banquettes, and the warm glow of candlelight dances on the wineglasses, the ice buckets, and the cutlery. *La Perouse* is an elegant indoor spot, only faintly Polynesian in atmosphere, with an eclectic menu. For instance, for starters there are Hawaiian shrimp in red wine, traditional Japanese sashimi, and poached oyster glazed in lobster cream sauce among the cold and hot appetizers; soups include a clear broth of venison with noki mushrooms and the restaurant's exquisite (and very popular) callaloo soup of crabmeat, coconut milk, and taro leaves. Catch of the day, prepared meunière, steamed, or in a creamy wine sauce, appears among the entrées, along with such things as lobster tail filled with ambrosia mousse wrapped in crisp pastry, as well as venison, lamb, and smoked duckling. When it's time for dessert, the waiter will wheel out the pastry cart or set fire to something scrumptious, and rest assured that he'll do it with perfect aplomb. Information: *Maui Inter-Continental Wailea,* Wailea, HI 96753 (phone: 879-1922).

RAFFLES', Wailea, Maui: Another outstanding restaurant in the *Wailea* resort, *Raffles',* in the *Stouffer Wailea Beach,* aspires to re-create the late-19th-century style and historic standards of excellence exhibited by that outpost of the British Empire in the Far East, *Raffles* hotel in Singapore. Just inside the etched-glass doors is a foyer filled with the sort of Orientalia an old colonial administrator might have collected — Chinese Fu dogs, Oriental vases, teak cabinets — and from there, Oriental carpets on teak floors lead back to the dining area, where part of the seating is provided by upholstered easy chairs such as the same colonial governor might have imported from home. This, too, is an indoor room, but a window wall draped in swag curtains allows diners to peer past brass pots of fishtail wine palms out to the setting sun. Bronze chandeliers light the scene, and the sound of a tinkling piano animates as waiters go capably about their tasks. The restaurant aims for a mix of East and West in its menu, with consistently fine entrées ranging from island fish — *mahimahi* and *opakapaka* — to noisette of lamb Sir Stamford Raffles and suprême of duck breast cassis. The lobster with watercress sauce and nasturtiums is a delicious cold appetizer; other appetizers, hot and cold, include oyster cassoulette with fresh sea urchin and Riesling, fresh sautéed goose liver in sherry vinegar and honey, and gravlax (salmon marinated in dill and anise with mustard sauce). After a dessert of chocolate mousse, a confection from the pastry cart, or some flamboyant flambéed fruit, there are petits fours to nibble and an after-dinner liqueur to sip slowly. Information: Stouffer Wailea Beach Resort, Wailea, HI 96753 (phone: 879-4900).

NOBLE'S, Sheraton Mirage Princeville, Kauai: The small dining room provides both dining intimacy and a menu that lives up to high expectatiohns. Specialties on the fixed-price menu include French goose liver pâté, venison, buffalo, abalone, as well as more traditional fare: shrimp, beef, poultry, and fish. This is very likely Kauai's best restaurant, with service that matches the quality of the food. Reservations advised. Jacket required and available at the door. The Sheraton Mirage Princeville, Princeville Resort, Princeville, HI 96722 (phone: 826-9644).

GAYLORD'S, Lihue, Kauai: The elegant 1930s ambience is enhanced by the setting in the old Wilcox mansion. Tables are turned out with fine linen, crystal, and silver and, although indoor seating is certainly lovely here, al fresco dining is a special treat, with tables hugging the central courtyard afforded welcome proximity to the green lawns that lead to panoramic views of Kauai's central massif. The excellent service is matched by the menu, which features fresh lamb, venison, and veal in a variety of styles. The chicken stuffed with prawns and cream cheese is delicious. Information: Gaylord's, 3-2087 Kaumuali Hwy., Lihue, HI 96753 (phone: 245-9593).

Shopping Spree

Most of what Hawaii's merchants have to offer falls into the souvenir and gift category — T-shirts, shell leis, woven hats, Polynesian bric-a-brac — or alohawear, a designation that includes any clothes with the casual island look, from elegant evening skirts of handpainted silk to inexpensive muumuus. These items are in alarming abundance virtually everywhere. As expected, hotel boutiques and shops near popular tourist attractions tend to be more expensive than stores catering to a resident clientele. But if you're only buying a $4.95 T-shirt or carved keychain, it's probably not worth wasting precious vacation time looking for the very best prices.

Beyond the mountains of trinkets and flowered shirts, however, are some goods of a distinctly higher caliber, and chances are there will come a time to contemplate a more serious purchase. Thanks to heightened native Hawaiian consciousness, there has been a revival of interest in traditional crafts. Niihau shell leis, intricately worked garlands of the tiny, lustrous shells found on the leeward beaches of the island of Niihau, and elaborate feather leis are highly prized collector's items found in galleries on all the major islands. There has also been a flowering of contemporary art: Painters, sculptors, ceramists, jewelers, woodturners, and glassblowers are producing a prodigious amount of island-inspired work. Much of it is amateurish, to be sure, but some is attracting the attention of the serious art world.

Because of its whaling past, Hawaii also does a lively trade in scrimshaw, the art of etching on whale bone practiced by 19th-century sailors to relieve the tedium of long voyages. Most of what is in the shops is contemporary and is done on the fossilized mammoth and walrus bone unearthed by the ton during the digging of the Alaska pipeline. (Trading in whale ivory has been illegal since whales came under the protection of the Endangered Species Act of 1973.) Very few of the pieces created when Hawaii was the center of the Pacific whaling industry still exist. The work of licentious sailors, much of the early scrimshaw depicted bawdy scenes and was destroyed by priggish missionaries. However, there are some 40 scrimshanders working in Hawaii today, turning out pieces that range from quickly etched pendants the size of a postage stamp to exquisitely worked pieces that fetch thousands of dollars. Some very good work also comes from scrimshanders living in Washington State.

Since Hawaii has always been a trading center between East and West, it is also the place to pick up such treasures as jade from Burma and Taiwan, Japanese porcelain, Cambodian and Tibetan antiques, Thai silks, or hand-embroidered linens from China. Though not easily found, shops selling Oriental antiques do exist on all the main islands. Ivory carvings are also found in abundance, though visitors are advised against buying them because of the damage trafficking in ivory has caused to remaining wild elephant herds.

BEST BUYS

Following is an item-by-item guide to the best shopping in the islands. More comprehensive discussions of shopping appear in the chapter on each island.

Alohawear – Any loose-fitting, casual garment made in a bright floral print qualifies as alohawear. *Liberty House,* the Macy's of Hawaii, and *Andrade* are both well known for good-quality island attire, and both have a number of stores on all the major islands. *W. H. Smith's* is another big name. Its larger outlets on Oahu, the Big Island of Hawaii, and Maui are factory and store combined; so eager are they to dress you up in Polynesian patterns that they operate a bus to take you there. The *Goodwill Thrift Shop* at 580 N Nimitz Hwy., Honolulu, is a good place to pick up nearly new shirts and muumuus at very low prices. For alohawear a cut above average, try *Apparels of Pauline,* Lahaina Marketplace, Lahaina, Maui, and *Royal Hawaiian* hotel and *Hilton Hawaiian Village,* both in Waikiki, Oahu; and *Alfred Shaheen,* King's Village, Ala Moana Center, and the *Ilikai,* all three locations in Honolulu, Oahu. For vintage aloha shirts, drop in at the *Clothes Addict* in Paia, Maui, and *Bailey's Antique Clothing,* Kapahulu St., Honolulu, Oahu, where prices range from $20 to $500.

Arts and Crafts – Paintings, watercolors, prints, sculpture, ceramics, handblown glasswork, jewelry, and carved wood, much of it by local artists and inspired by island themes, can be found at a number of galleries. Among them: *Artists Guild,* Ward Warehouse, Honolulu, Oahu; *Jafar,* King Kamehameha Mall, Kona, Hawaii; *Volcano Art Center,* Hawaii Volcanoes National Park, Hawaii; *Nikko,* Waimea, Hawaii; *The Gallery of Fine Things,* Waimea Village Green, Waimea, Hawaii; *Elephant Walk:* Hyatt Regency, Kaanapali, Maui; Westin, Nawiliwili, Kauai; Wailea Shopping Village, Wailea, Maui, and Ala Moana Center, Honolulu, Oahu; *Maui Artists Guild,* Paia, Maui; *Distant Drums,* The Shops, Kapalua, Maui; *Village Gallery,* 120 Dickenson St., Lahaina, Maui; *Stones Printsellers and Gallery,* Kukui Grove Center, Lihue, Kauai; *Kahn Gallery,* Coconut Plantation, Wailua, Kauai, and Sheraton Mirage Princeville, Princeville, Kauai; *The Gallery,* Waiohai Hotel, Poipu, Kauai; *Kauai Crafts in Progress,* 1384 Kuhio Hwy., Kapaa, Kauai; *Artisans Guild,* Hanalei, Kauai; *Plum Tuckered,* Coconut Plantation and Kilohana, Kauai; *Ola's,* Hanalei, Kauai; *Ship's Store Gallery* (for marine arts) in the Kiahuna Shopping Village, Kauai; and *Hawaiian Handcraft,* 760 Kilauea Ave., Hilo, Hawaii.

Coral – All those necklaces of pinkish orange bunched twigs are white coral from Japan and Taiwan, dyed to give the coral effect; they are not precious coral. The pink precious coral in island shops comes from the Kaiwi Channel between Molokai and Oahu, and so does the gold coral, which is found only in the Hawaiian Islands. (There is some in Alaska, but it is not quite the same color.) Black coral is harvested off the coast of Maui, while the dark, oxblood red coral, considerably more expensive, is a Mediterranean import. *Coral Grotto,* Hemmeter Center, 2424 Kalakaua Ave., Honolulu, Oahu, and also at the Ala Moana Shopping Center in Honolulu and at The Wharf, Lahaina, Maui; *Golden Reef,* Wailea Shopping Village, Wailea, Maui; *The Necklace Gallery,* Market Place at Coconut Plantation, Wailua, Kauai; outdoor vendors at the Spouting Horn, Poipu, Kauai; *Maui Divers,* Lahaina, Maui, and Kona Inn Shopping Center, Kailua-Kona, Hawaii.

Eastern Art and Artifacts – Exquisite jade and ivory carvings, Japanese ceramics, and Chinese cloisonné are some of the Eastern arts that have found their way to Polynesian America. *T. Fujii,* Manoa Market, Honolulu, Oahu; *Bushido Antiques,* Eaton Square and Mauna Kea St., Honolulu, Oahu; *Friendship Store,* Andrade, Royal Hawaiian Shopping Center, Honolulu, Oahu; *Nikko* and *Yugen,* Waimea (Kamuela), Hawaii; *Garakuta-do* and *Sweet By-Gones,* Mauna Kea St., Honolulu, Oahu; *Robyn Buntin,* Eaton Square and Mauna Kea St., Honolulu, Oaho; *Bernard Hertig's Oriental Treasures,* Kahala Hilton, Oahu; *Future Heirlooms,* Ward Warehouse, Honolulu, Oahu; *Iida's,* Ala Moana Shopping Center, Honolulu, Oahu; *Orientations,* Honolulu, Oahu; *Herman Miller Antiques,* Mauna Lani Bay Hotel, Kawaihae, Hawaii; *Gallery,* Mauna Kea Beach Hotel, Kawaihae, Hawaii; *The Gallery,* 716 Front St., Lahaina, Maui; *Kong Lung,* Kilauea, Kauai.

Edibles – Papayas, avocados, and bananas must be treated before they can be taken to the mainland; coconuts and pineapples may go as they are. Even so, it's best to buy all fruit from airport shops on your way home (so you won't have to lug your lovely bunch of coconuts around the islands) or from "take home" stores elsewhere, many of which will deliver to your flight. Macadamia nuts, Kona coffee, Maui potato chips, taro chips, and crack seed — preserved fruits, nuts, and seeds — can be found in many shops catering to tourists, as can the Hawaiian Plantations line of products, including tropical fruit jams and mango chutney. *Hawaiian Holidays Macadamia Nut Company,* Kalakaua Ave., Waikiki, Oahu, and Front St., Lahaina, Maui; *Maui Potato Chip Factory,* 295 Lalo St., Kahului, Maui; *Woolworth's,* 2222 Kalakaua Ave., Waikiki, Oahu; *Duty Free Shops,* Honolulu International Airport, Oahu; *Maaloa Sunrise,* Kilauea, Kauai; *Kauai Crafts in Progress,* 1384 Kuhio Hwy., Kapaa, Kauai; *Mapulehu Mango Grove,* South Shore, Molokai.

Enameled Jewelry – During the 19th century, Hawaii's royal ladies developed a liking for this jewelry, black enamel on gold inscribed with their names. Modern examples of the art can cost between $100 and $400 for a ring and between $300 and $1,200 for a bracelet. *Precious Metals Hawaii,* Pan Am Building, 1600 Kapiolani Blvd., Suite 616, Honolulu, Oahu; *Rainbow Bazaar,* Hilton Hawaiian Village, Honolulu, Oahu.

Fabrics – Silks from Europe and the Far East, handpainted Hawaiian panels, and untold yards of tropical prints fill boutiques and department stores across the islands. *Plantation Stitchery,* Market Place at Coconut Plantation, Wailua, Kauai; *Singer,* Kukui Grove Shopping Center, Lihue, Kauai; *Kahului Fairgrounds Swap Meet,* Kahului, Maui; *Singer's,* Kahului, Maui; *Sew Special,* Kaahumanu Center, Kahului, Maui; *Fare Tahiti,* Kona Inn Shopping Village, Kailua-Kona, Hawaii; *Kapaia Stitchery,* Lihue, Kauai; *Tahiti Imports,* Market Place at Coconut Plantation, Kauai.

Feather Leis – This ancient Hawaiian art has been revived and updated, using the feathers of peacocks and pheasants to create beautiful and fanciful hatbands. A feather leï can cost from $50 to $1,000. *Maui Mad Hatter,* The Wharf, Lahaina, Maui; *The Gallery,* Waiohai Hotel, Poipu Beach, Kauai; *Stone's Gallery,* Kukui Grove Shopping Center, Lihue, Kauai.

Flower Leis – The symbol of Hawaiian hospitality and a joy to indulge in as often as possible during your stay, flower leis are sold at airports, by street vendors, and at hotels and shops all over the islands. There's a fine selection at *Marvie's Floral Boutique,* King Kamehameha Hotel, Kailua, Hawaii. Also try the lineup of lei stands at Honolulu International Airport in Oahu, a short walk from the main terminal. Honolulu's Chinatown also features small lei shops on Mauna Kea, Nuuanu, and King streets, where prices are generally less than at the airport or Waikiki lei stands. For special *haku* leis (dried flowers), try *Ah Lan's* at the Hilo Airport, Hawaii; *Lotus Blossom,* Koloa, Kauai; *Joe Rossi's,* Kihei, Maui; *Exotica,* Wailuku, Maui.

Hawaiiana – Guides, maps, books on Hawaiian flora, fauna, history, culture, legends, language, food, crafts — any printed material to feed the curiosity of the new Hawaiiphile comes under this heading. *Upstart Crow and Company,* The Wharf, Lahaina, Maui; *Artful Dodger's,* Kahului, Maui; *Waldenbooks,* Waikiki Shopping Plaza and Ward Warehouse, Honolulu, Oahu; *Honolulu Book Shop,* Ala Moana Shopping Center and 1001 Bishop St., Honolulu, Oahu; *Shop Pacifica,* 1525 Bernice St., Honolulu, Oahu; *The Vestibule Shop* at the Bishop Museum, 1355 Kalihi St., Honolulu, Oahu; *Huki Like,* Banyan Dr., Hilo, Hawaii; *Kilauea Visitors Center,* Hawaii Volcanoes National Park, Hawaii; *Middle Earth Book Shop,* 75-5719 Alii Dr., Kailua-Kona, Hawaii; *Artisans Guild,* Hanalei, Kauai; *Kauai Museum Gift and Book Shop,* at 4428 Rice St. and also at Kilohana, Lihue, Kauai; *Hawaiian Arts and Museum,* Kilauea, Kauai.

Hawaiian Music – At first hearing, the falsetto singing of traditional Hawaiian music may sound peculiar to Western ears, but before long most people are seduced by its sweet and strange melodiousness. Musicians and groups for which to look include the Brothers Cazimero, Eddie Kamae, Palani Vaughn, the Beamer Brothers, the Sons of Hawaii, and the Makaha Sons of Niihau. *Jack Wada's,* Lihue, Kauai; *Larry's Music,* Kapaa, Kauai; *House of Music,* Kaahumanu Center, Kahului, Maui and Ala Moana

Center, Honolulu, Oahu; *J.R.'s Music Shop,* Maui Mall, Kahului, Maui; *Tower Records,* Keaumoku St., Honolulu, Oahu.

Hawaiian Quilts – Introduced by New England missionaries, local quilt-making quickly developed a unique Hawaiian style by introducing designs of native flora and motifs from the royal era. It's almost impossible to buy an authentic antique example, but quilt kits and patterns are widely available. *Volcano Art Center,* Volcanoes National Park, Hawaii; *Crewel World Stitchery,* Wailea Shopping Village, Wailea, Maui; *Pineapple Patch,* Holualoa, Hawaii; *Kapaia Stitchery,* Lihue, Kauai; Hawaii Quilts, King St., Honolulu, Oahu.

Jade – Much of the jade jewelry and objets d'art in the islands is from Burma or Taiwan. Burmese jade, which comes in a rainbow of greens, reds, and lavenders, is the connoisseur's choice. *Alberta's Gazebo,* The Wharf, Lahaina, Maui; *Monarch Jade,* Honolulu, Oahu; *Goldsmith's Gallery,* Kinipopo Shopping Village, Kapaa, Kauai; *Security Diamond,* Ala Moana Center, Honolulu, Oahu.

Kukui Nut Jewelry – Called the candlenut because its oil was used in lamps, the nut of the ubiquitous kukui tree is polished to a high sheen and made into necklaces, bracelets, and other jewelry. Black is the least expensive ($8 for a plain choker); brown, slightly higher; and jewelry made of the rare white nut, the most expensive. *Kukui Nuts of Hawaii,* 66-935 Kaukonohua Rd., Waialua, Oahu (phone: 637-5620), Hawaii's only manufacturer of kukui nut jewelry, also offers the widest selection. Also available at *Vestibule Shop,* Bishop Museum, 1355 Kalihi St., Honolulu, Oahu; *The Grass Shack,* Rt. 11, Kealakekua, Hawaii.

Lau Hala – Products woven from the leaves of the pandanus tree range from big-weave place mats, napkin rings, baskets, and boxes to finely textured hats of distinction. *The Little Grass Shack,* Rte. 11, Captain Cook (Kona Coast), Hawaii; *Sugawara Lauhala & Gift Shop,* 59 Kalakaua Ave., Hilo, Hawaii; *Hale Manucraft,* on Highway 11 between Hilo and Volcano, Hawaii; *Products of Hawaii,* Ala Moana Shopping Center, Honolulu, Oahu; *Maui Mad Hatter,* The Wharf, Lahaina, Maui; *Rehabilitation Unlimited,* across from the Coco Palms Hotel, Wailua, Kauai.

Leather Goods – Like any ranching country, Hawaii has its share of shops that cater to the needs of cowboys and would-be cowboys who simply appreciate fine leatherwork. *Makawao Leather,* 3647 Baldwin Ave., Makawao, Maui; *Rare Discovery* and *The Artists Guild,* Ward Warehouse, Honolulu, Oahu; *Paddock Shop,* Parker Ranch Shopping Center, Kamuela, Hawaii; *Lee Sands Eel Skin,* Lawai, Kauai; *Yokahama-Okadaya,* Royal Hawaiian Shopping Center, Waikiki, Oahu; *Bebe's,* Waikiki Trade Center, Waikiki, Oahu; *Raku Leather,* 2201 Kalakaua Ave., Waikiki, Oahu.

Niihau Leis – The most prized of permanent leis, Niihau leis are made from hundreds of tiny shells that wash up on the shore of Niihau, the small private island off Kauai. A simple choker can cost as little as $15, but more complicated designs, such as the pikake lei — so called because its clusters resemble the pikake flower — can cost several thousand dollars. *The Gallery,* Waiohai Hotel, Poipu Beach, Kauai; *Koloa Gallery,* Sheraton Kauai, Poipu Beach, Kauai; the outdoor vendors at the Spouting Horn Lookout, Poipu, Kauai; *Kahn Gallery,* Coconut Plantation, Kapaa, Kauai; *Kong Lung,* Kilauea, Kauai; *Pendragon,* Old Town Koloa, Kauai; *Ka Honu Gift Gallery,* Whalers Village, Kaanapali, Maui; *Hawaiian Traders,* King Kamehameha Hotel and Kona Surf Hotel, Kailua, Hawaii.

Pacific Art and Artifacts – Balinese paintings, antiques from Borneo and the Marshall Islands, and Malaysian kites are among the many imports from Hawaii's Pacific neighbors. *South Seas Trading Post,* 851 Front St., Lahaina, Maui; *Nikko,* Waimea (Kamuela), Hawaii; *The Lady Jane Company,* Hanamaulu, Kauai; *Distant Drums,* Kapalua Shops, Kapalua, Maui; *Traders of the Lost Art,* Wailuku, Maui; *Distant Drums,* The Shops, Kapalua, Maui; *Waipio Woodworks* and *Kamaaina Woods,* Kukuihaele, Hawaii.

Plants – Seeds, cuttings, and potted specimens of Hawaii's abundant and exotic plant life — plumeria, ginger, orchids, birds of paradise, protea, anthuriums, hibiscus, ti, bamboo — inspected by the Department of Agriculture and packed to travel, are available at several airport shops, as well as at other places around the islands. Some of the larger stores will mail plants. *The Center for Performing Plants,* Kaahumanu Center, Kahului, Maui; *Hana Gardenland,* Hana Hwy. (4 miles from the town of Hana), Maui; *Hawaii Protea Co-operative,* Hwy. 37, Kula, Maui; *Maui Sunburst,* Kula, Maui; *Nani Mau Gardens,* 421 Makalika St., Hilo, Hawaii; *Orchids of Hawaii,* 2801 Kilauea Ave., Hilo, Hawaii; *Shimunishi Nursery,* Hanapepe, Kauai.

Scrimshaw – The 19th-century whalers' art of carving ivory is alive and well in Hawaii these days. It's possible to spend as little as $10 for a small pendant or ring, or as much as $10,000 for an elaborately etched display piece. Lahaina is the center of Hawaiian scrimshaw, with the largest selection and most competitive prices. *Lahaina Scrimshaw Factory–Pier 49,* 845 Front St., Lahaina, Maui, and the Marriott Hotel and Whalers Village, Kaanapali, Maui; *Alihi Creations,* Parker Ranch Shopping Center, Kamuela, Hawaii; *Kahn Gallery,* Market Place, Coconut Plantation, Wailua, Kauai.

Swimwear – As expected, there's a dizzying selection. *Liberty House,* on all islands; *Downunder Honolulu,* Kuhio Ave., Waikiki, Oahu; *Reyn's,* Kapalua Shops, Kapalua, Maui; *Wow of Hawaii,* Kaahumanu Center, Kahului, Maui, and *Azeka Place Shopping Center,* Kihei, Maui; *Surf Sports,* Front St., Lahaina, Maui; *Bikini Company,* Front St., Lahaina, Maui; *Butterfly Boutique,* Seaside Mall, Kailua, Hawaii; *Shops of the Marketplace,* Coconut Plantation, Wailua, Kauai; *Suits Me,* Waiohai Hotel, Poipu, Kauai.

Tapa Cloth – Also called kapa, tapa is the bark fabric worn by Hawaiians before Westerners introduced them to cotton. Most of the tapa found in Hawaii today, in the form of wall hangings, table linen, placemats, boxes, and purses, comes from Samoa and Tonga, although it's possible to get an old piece of Hawaiian tapa for $100 and up. *Vestibule Shop,* Bishop Museum, 1355 Kalihi St., Honolulu, Oahu; *The Lady Jane Company,* Hanamaulu, Kauai.

T-Shirts – Even the most out-of-the-way places have them, emblazoned with an endless variety of designs and messages. Among the dozens of shops throughout the islands are *Novelty World,* Ward Warehouse, Honolulu, Oahu; *Tropical Dreams,* Kapaa, Kauai; and *Crazy Shirts,* with outlets at 865 Front St. and The Wharf, Lahaina, Maui; Koloa and the Kiahuna Shopping Village, Kauai; and Kailua-Kona, Hawaii; *Tropical Shirts,* Kiahuna Shopping Village and Coconut Plantation, Kauai.

Wood Items – Out of the islands' native woods, woodturners make beautiful art of everyday objects, such as bowls, trays, and boxes. The best known wood, koa, is often called Hawaiian mahogany because of its rich, reddish tone and lustrous finish. Mango wood, whitish to tan in color, is shot through with streaks of pink, yellow, and sometimes green, producing what one artisan calls rainbow wood. Monkeypod ranges from light to dark brown, while milo wood is reddish with patches of beige. A very rare and lovely wood is kaimani, which is light to reddish pink in tone and is finely grained. *Martin & MacArthur Koa Wood Furnishings,* Honolulu, Oahu; *The Artists Guild,* Ward Warehouse, Honolulu, Oahu; *Koa Ohana,* 54 Waianuenue Ave., Hilo, Hawaii; *Waimea General Store,* across from the Hawaii Prep Academy Campus, Rt. 19, Kamuela, Hawaii; *Hawaiian Traders,* King Kamehameha Hotel, Kailua, Hawaii; *Kamaaina Woods, Inc.,* Rt. 19, Honokaa, Hawaii; *Waipio Woodworks,* Kukuihaele, Hawaii; *Kahn Gallery,* Market Place, Coconut Plantation, Wailua, Kauai; *Kong Lung Center,* Kilauea, Kauai; *Stone's Gallery at Kiohana,* Lihue, Kauai, *Ola's,* Hanalei, Kauai; *The Lady Jane Company,* Hanamaulu, Kauai; *Artisans Guild,* Hanalei, Kauai; *Ka Honu Gift Gallery,* Whalers Village, Kaanapali, Maui.

INDEX

Index